D1725259

Handbook of Research on Fuzzy and Rough Set Theory in Organizational Decision Making

Arun Kumar Sangaiah
VIT University, India

Xiao-Zhi Gao
Aalto University, Finland

Ajith Abraham
Machine Intelligence Research Labs, USA

A volume in the Advances in Business Strategy and Competitive Advantage (ABSCA) Book Series

www.igi-global.com

Published in the United States of America by
    IGI Global
    Business Science Reference (an imprint of IGI Global)
    701 E. Chocolate Avenue
    Hershey PA, USA 17033
    Tel: 717-533-8845
    Fax: 717-533-8661
    E-mail: cust@igi-global.com
    Web site: http://www.igi-global.com

Library of Congress Cataloging-in-Publication Data

Names: Sangaiah, Arun Kumar, 1981- editor. | Gao, Xiao-Zhi, 1972- editor. |
  Abraham, Ajith, 1968- editor.
Title: Handbook of research on fuzzy and rough set theory in organizational
  decision making / Arun Kumar Sangaiah, Xiao-Zhi Gao, and Ajith Abraham,
  editors.
Description: Hershey, PA : Business Science Reference, [2017] | Series:
  Advances in business strategy and competitive advantage | Includes
  bibliographical references and index.
Identifiers: LCCN 2016028984| ISBN 9781522510086 (hardcover) | ISBN
  9781522510093 (ebook)
Subjects: LCSH: Decision making--Mathematical models. | Fuzzy sets.
Classification: LCC T57.95 .H355 2017 | DDC 511.3/223--dc23 LC record available at https://lccn.loc.gov/2016028984

This book is published in the IGI Global book series Advances in Business Strategy and Competitive Advantage (ABSCA) (ISSN: 2327-3429; eISSN: 2327-3437)

British Cataloguing in Publication Data
A Cataloguing in Publication record for this book is available from the British Library.

All work contributed to this book is new, previously-unpublished material. The views expressed in this book are those of the authors, but not necessarily of the publisher.

For electronic access to this publication, please contact: eresources@igi-global.com.

Advances in Business Strategy and Competitive Advantage (ABSCA) Book Series

Patricia Ordóñez de Pablos
Universidad de Oviedo, Spain

ISSN: 2327-3429
EISSN: 2327-3437

MISSION

Business entities are constantly seeking new ways through which to gain advantage over their competitors and strengthen their position within the business environment. With competition at an all-time high due to technological advancements allowing for competition on a global scale, firms continue to seek new ways through which to improve and strengthen their business processes, procedures, and profitability.

The **Advances in Business Strategy and Competitive Advantage (ABSCA) Book Series** is a timely series responding to the high demand for state-of-the-art research on how business strategies are created, implemented and re-designed to meet the demands of globalized competitive markets. With a focus on local and global challenges, business opportunities and the needs of society, the **ABSCA** encourages scientific discourse on doing business and managing information technologies for the creation of sustainable competitive advantage.

COVERAGE

- Core Competencies
- International Business Strategy
- Strategic management
- Strategy Performance Management
- Economies of Scale
- Value Chain
- Entrepreneurship & Innovation
- Business Models
- Cost Leadership Strategy
- Globalization

IGI Global is currently accepting manuscripts for publication within this series. To submit a proposal for a volume in this series, please contact our Acquisition Editors at Acquisitions@igi-global.com or visit: http://www.igi-global.com/publish/.

Titles in this Series

For a list of additional titles in this series, please visit: www.igi-global.com

Case Studies as a Teaching Tool in Management Education
Dominika Latusek (Kozminski University, Poland)
Business Science Reference • copyright 2017 • 326pp • H/C (ISBN: 9781522507703) • US $190.00 (our price)

Analyzing the Relationship between Corporate Social Responsibility and Foreign Direct Investment
Marianne Ojo (North West University, South Africa)
Business Science Reference • copyright 2016 • 322pp • H/C (ISBN: 9781522503057) • US $185.00 (our price)

Comparative Perspectives on Global Corporate Social Responsibility
Dima Jamali (American University of Beirut, Lebanon)
Business Science Reference • copyright 2017 • 367pp • H/C (ISBN: 9781522507208) • US $215.00 (our price)

Crowdfunding for Sustainable Entrepreneurship and Innovation
Walter Vassallo (MC Shareable, Monaco)
Business Science Reference • copyright 2017 • 336pp • H/C (ISBN: 9781522505686) • US $205.00 (our price)

Handbook of Research on Driving Competitive Advantage through Sustainable, Lean, and Disruptive Innovation
Latif Al-Hakim (University of Southern Queensland, Australia) Xiaobo Wu (Zhejiang University, China) Andy
Koronios (University of South Australia, Australia) and Yongyi Shou (Zhejiang University, China)
Business Science Reference • copyright 2016 • 743pp • H/C (ISBN: 9781522501350) • US $365.00 (our price)

Ethical and Social Perspectives on Global Business Interaction in Emerging Markets
Minwir Al-Shammari (University of Bahrain, Bahrain) and Hatem Masri (University of Bahrain, Bahrain)
Business Science Reference • copyright 2016 • 372pp • H/C (ISBN: 9781466698642) • US $185.00 (our price)

Strategic Approaches to Successful Crowdfunding
Djamchid Assadi (Burgundy School of Business, France)
Business Science Reference • copyright 2016 • 378pp • H/C (ISBN: 9781466696044) • US $205.00 (our price)

Handbook of Research on Entrepreneurship in the Contemporary Knowledge-Based Global Economy
Neeta Baporikar (University of Pune, India)
Business Science Reference • copyright 2016 • 607pp • H/C (ISBN: 9781466687981) • US $345.00 (our price)

Competitive Strategies for Academic Entrepreneurship Commercialization of Research-Based Products
Anna Szopa (Jagiellonian University, Poland) Waldemar Karwowski (University of Central Florida, USA) and
David Barbe (University of Maryland, College Park, USA)
Business Science Reference • copyright 2015 • 317pp • H/C (ISBN: 9781466684874) • US $195.00 (our price)

www.igi-global.com

701 E. Chocolate Ave., Hershey, PA 17033
Order online at www.igi-global.com or call 717-533-8845 x100
To place a standing order for titles released in this series, contact: cust@igi-global.com
Mon-Fri 8:00 am - 5:00 pm (est) or fax 24 hours a day 717-533-8661

List of Contributors

Table of Contents

Detailed Table of Contents

Chapter 1

Pradheep Kumar K., BITS Pilani, India
Venkata Subramanian D., Hindustan Institute of Technology & Science, India

This paper is intended to design a fuzzy based approach to assess standards and quality of big data. It also serves as a platform to organizations that intend to migrate their existing database environment to big data environment. Data is assessed using a multidimensional approach based on quality factors like accuracy, completeness, reliability, usability, etc. These factors are analysed by constructing decision trees to identify the quality aspects which need to be improved. In this work fuzzy queries have been designed. The queries are grouped as sets namely Excellent, Optimal, Fair and Hybrid. Based on the fuzzy data sets formed and the query compatibility index, a query set is chosen. A data set that has a very high degree of membership is assigned a fair query set. A data set with a medium degree of membership is assigned a optimal query set. A data set that has a lesser degree of membership is assigned a Excellent query set. A data set which needs a combination of queries of all the above is assigned a hybrid query set. The fuzzy query based approach reduces the query compatibility index by 36%, compared to a normal query set approach.

Chapter 2

Selvakumar Kamalanathan, Anna University, India
Sai Ramesh Lakshmanan, Anna University, India
Kannan Arputharaj, Anna University, India

In many applications such as disaster management, temperature control, weather forecasting, industrial control system and forest fire detection, it is very difficult for a human to monitor and control each and every event in real time. Even with advancement in technology, this issue has remained a challenging task. The existing Wireless Network may not be suitable for data communication with human network. Hence, to monitor and control the physical parameters of the environment, a special device with needed functionalities is required. The network which is formed with these devices is known as sensor network. This is used to monitor, control and send the collected information to the end user. These networks are formed with a large number of sensor nodes with limitation such as self-energized, low computation power, infra-structure less, multi-hop communication and without central administrator control. Due to the ad hoc nature, the nodes are deployed unevenly over a geographical region, it is necessary to provide some mechanism to manage and control the topology of the sensor nodes to prolong their life time. Clustering algorithms are useful for data mining, compression, probability density estimation and many other important tasks like IDS. Clustering algorithm utilize a distance metric in order to partition network traffic patterns so that patterns within a single group have same network characteristics than in a different group. The proposed system builds a Fuzzy logic clustering model that can perform three different types of clusters in order to achieve the secure and energy aware routing of packets.

Chapter 3

The prediction and estimation software risks ahead have been key predictor for evaluating project performance. Discriminating risk is vital in software project management phase, where risk and performance has been closely inter-related to each other. This chapter aims at hybridization of fuzzy multi-criteria decision making approaches for building an assessment framework that can be used to evaluate risk in the context of software project performance in following dimensions: 1) user, 2) requirements, 3) project complexity, 4) planning and control, 5) team, and 6) organizational environment. For measuring the risk for effectiveness of project performance, we have integrated Fuzzy Multi-Criteria Decision Making (FMCDM) and Fuzzy Technique for Order of Preference by Similarity to Ideal Solution (TOPSIS) approaches. Moreover the fusion of FMCDM and TOPSIS has not been adequately investigated in the exiting studies.

Chapter 4

In this present paper a basic inventory model is solved in different imprecise environments. Four different cases are discussed: 1) Crisp inventory model, that is, the quantity at present and demand is crisp number; 2) Inventory model in fuzzy environment, that is, the quantity and demand both are fuzzy number; 3) Inventory model in interval environment, that is, the quantity and demand both are interval number and lastly; 4) Inventory model in time dependent fuzzy environment, that is, quantity and demand are both time dependent fuzzy number. Different numerical examples are used to illustrate the model as well as to compute the efficiency of imprecise differential equation approach to solve the model.

Chapter 5

Gamification can be viewed as a process design which encapsulates competition, achievements, status and self-expression. Gamification is used as a tool for improving physical fitness. In this chapter the physical activity using treadmill walking is considered. Calorie burn calculation plays a vital role in the gamification design. In treadmill calorie burn calculation, traditional and fuzzy based methods are compared for effective gamification. In the traditional calorie burn calculation method different equations are used for different incline levels. In the fuzzy logic method fuzzy reasoning technique is applied to calculate the calorie burn for different incline levels. It is identified that fuzzy based calorie calculation enhances physical activity and supports Gamification. Fuzzy based calorie burn calculation methods produces approximate values and supports the players to choose higher incline levels instead of lower incline levels and thereby burning more calories.

Chapter 6

Data clustering has been an integral and important part of data mining. It has wide applications in database anonymization, decision making, image processing and pattern recognition, medical diagnosis and geographical information systems, only to name a few. Data in real life scenario are having imprecision inherent in them. So, early crisp clustering techniques are very less efficient. Several imprecision based models have been proposed over the years like the fuzzy sets, rough sets, intuitionistic fuzzy sets and many of their generalized versions. Of late, it has been established that the hybrid models obtained as combination of these imprecise models are far more efficient than the individual ones. So, many clustering algorithms have been put forth using these hybrid models. The focus of this chapter is to discuss on some of the data clustering algorithms developed so far and their applications mainly in the area of decision making.

Chapter 7

An attempt in implementing on-demand, QoS supported Vehicular Ad hoc Network (VANET) routing algorithms has taken new dimensions. Delivering information in time to achieve reliability across vehicles (nodes) is still being a challenge among the VANET research groups. An effort to develop a QoS adaptive routing schemes using soft computing techniques is made in this research work. SADVA – An adaptive fuzzy based QoS service oriented approach for VANET is presented in this paper. The performance of SADVA is compared with AODV, GV-GRID, DSR, FSR, DYMO, REDEM, and QARS. SADVA employs fuzzy logic system to determine the vehicle's speed over an effective time period for different types of service in use between multiple VANET nodes to engage or cooperate in communication. This chapter focuses on designing and developing QoS aware routing protocol for multi-hop VANET. Metrics such as number of packets received per second, percentage of packet loss and time for route establishment are used to analyse the network situation. Simulation test runs are carried out using Two Ray Ground propagation model where vehicular traffic is generated according to a Poisson process.

Chapter 8

Dynamic Programming Problem (DPP) is a multivariable optimization problem is decomposed into a series of stages, optimization being done at each stage with respect to one variable only. DP stands a suitable quantitative study procedure that can be used to explain various optimization problems. It deals through reasonably large as well as complex problems; in addition, it involves creating a sequence of interconnected decisions. The technique offers an efficient procedure for defining optimal arrangement of decisions. Throughout this chapter, solving procedure completely deliberate about as Fuzzy Dynamic Programming Problem for single additive constraint with additively separable return with the support of trapezoidal membership functions and its arithmetic operations. Solving procedure has been applied from the approach of Fuzzy Dynamic Programming Problem (FDPP). The fuzzified version of the problem has been stated with the support of a numerical example for both linear and nonlinear fuzzy optimal solutions and it is associated to showing that the proposed procedure offers an efficient tool for handling the dynamic programming problem instead of classical procedures. As a final point the optimal solution with in the form of fuzzy numbers and justified its solution with in the description of trapezoidal fuzzy membership functions.

The proposed chapter aims at explaining theoretical frameworks of the Fuzzy AHP and Fuzzy TOPSIS extension approaches and also summarizes the recent research around these two concepts. To help reader understand the practical usage of the two approaches, it also demonstrates their applications on the significant problem of ERP Selection. The techniques are further illustrated with the help of an organization case study located in NCR, Delhi (India). Further, a comparative analysis will be made between the two techniques by taking into account their time complexities.

Chapter 10

In industrial applications, approximately, 60% of world's consumption of electrical energy passes through the windings of squirrel-cage induction motors. Hence it is necessary to select an efficient drive circuit for induction motor to save energy. The MC are preferred to replace VSC in industrial applications. To control the performance of the MC, fuzzy logic technique is proposed and simulated using Matlab/Simulink. In this chapter, the basic concepts of MCs are discussed. The implementation of fuzzy logic technique to improve the performance of MC in driving induction motor is discussed in detail. The design of fuzzy controllers and the closed loop control of induction motor is shown. It seen that the introduction of fuzzy controllers in the closed loop helped to reduce the overshoot at starting and maintain the reference speed when running with load torque. Also the input and output voltage of the MC is maintained sinusoidal.

Nilamadhab Dash, C. V. Raman College of Engineering, India
Rojalina Priyadarshini, C. V. Raman College of Engineering, India
Brojo Kishore Mishra, C. V. Raman College of Engineering, India
Rachita Misra, C. V. Raman College of Engineering, India

Developing suitable mathematical or algorithmic model to solve real life complex problems is one of the major challenges faced by the researchers especially those involved in the computer science field. To a large extent Computational intelligence has been found to be effective in designing such models. Bio inspired computing is the technique which makes the machines intelligent by adapting the behavior and methods exhibited by the human beings and other living organisms while forming intelligent systems. These intelligent models include the intelligent techniques such as Artificial Neural Network (ANN), evolutionary computation, swarm intelligence, fuzzy system, artificial immune system accompanied by fuzzy logic, expert system, deductive reasoning. All these together form the area of Bio inspired computing. The chapter deals with various bio inspired technique, giving emphasis on issues, development, advances and practical implementations of ANN.

Suresh Kumar Nagarajan, VIT University, India

The utilization of relative shading size of a picture to extricate the vegetation of a study range Vellore, Tamilnadu, India was proposed. This novel hereditary based calculation utilizes the pixel guide of every picture and tries to figure out the ranges using so as to fit the right determination for vegetation Biomass the hereditary based methodology. The simplicity of execution permits any further changes to the calculation in future. Capable picture handling component permitted improved control of picture A Google Programming interface was utilized to concentrate and yield picture. It permitted simple augmentation of the work to any demographic range. The proposed calculation is superior to anything some present day devices as it is taking into account singular pixel values as opposed to layers. All the more vitally, no pre-meaning of the picture or layer is needed. Pixel control permits blending the effectively utilized procedures with other more up to date picture handling strategies that would prompt a more far reaching and multi-useful calculation. The advances utilized are between operable and can be kept as a steady stage for further up degree. The calculation does endure in computational speed and can be upgraded by utilizing better equipment offices. Parallel registering may be another choice to accelerate the handling of free pixels. Certain area methodologies can be utilized to upgrade honing of picture and better limits.

Sankar Ganesh S., VIT University, India
Mohanaprasad K., VIT University, India
Arunprakash Jayaprakash, VIT University, India
Sivanantham Sathasivam, VIT University, India

Next generation wireless communication systems promise the subscribers with Giga-bit-data-rate experience at low Bit Error Rate (BER) under adverse channel conditions. In order to maximize the overall system throughput of Orthogonal Frequency Division Multiplexing (OFDM), adaptive modulation is one of the key solutions. In adaptive modulated OFDM, the subcarriers are allocated with data bits and energy in accordance with the Signal to Interference Ratio (SIR) of the multipath channel, which is referred to as adaptive bit loading and adaptive power allocation respectively. The number of iterations required allocating the target bits and energy to a sub channel is optimized. The key choice of the paper is to allocate the bits with minimum number of iterations after clustering the sub channels using fuzzy logic. The proposed method exhibits a faster convergence in obtaining the optimal solution.

Reliability is a major concern in qualitative research. Most of the current research deals with finding the reliability of the data, but not much work is reported on how to improve the reliability of the unreliable data. This paper discusses three important aspects of the data pre-processing: how to detect the outliers, dealing with the missing values and finally increasing the reliability of the dataset. Here authors have suggested a framework for pre-processing of the inter-judged data which is incomplete and also contains erroneous values. The suggested framework integrates three approaches, Krippendorff's alpha for reliability computation, frequency based outlier detection method and a hybrid fuzzy c-means and multilayer perceptron based imputation technique. The proposed integrated approach results in an increase of reliability for the dataset which can be used to make strong conclusions.

Chapter 15

Soft sets were introduced by Molodtsov to handle uncertainty based problems. In 2003, Maji et al. extended the soft set approach to decision making. Decision making plays an integral role in daily life. In this chapter we describe soft sets and its impact in decision making problems. In this chapter, we discuss some of the basic notions of fuzzy soft sets and interval valued fuzzy soft sets. We also discuss application of fuzzy soft sets and interval valued fuzzy soft sets in decision making. In this chapter, we are going to see how parameter reduction is used in soft set theory.

The environmental pressure from various stakeholders, particularly in the selection of green suppliers in the industrial sector, is alarming. The companies are realizing the significance of incorporating green practices in their daily operations. This chapter proposes a framework on the criteria of GSCM practices using MCDM analysis to select green suppliers for an Indian electronics company. The authors have collected the data from a set of 10 available suppliers. The authors use fuzzy AHP and fuzzy TOPSIS approach to rank the suppliers based on the decision makers' preferences on the selection of green suppliers using GSCM practices. The three dominating criteria concluded by the results are the commitment of senior management towards GSCM; product design that incorporates three R's policy for component, materials, and energy; abidance with environmental laws and auditing programs. This chapter carries out a comparison between Fuzzy Analytical Hierarchy Process (FAHP) and Fuzzy TOPSIS method to enhance the quality of decision making and validate the rankings.

Chapter 17

With the increased interest of online users in E-commerce, the web has become an excellent source for buying and selling of products online. Customer reviews on the web help potential customers to make purchase decisions, and for manufacturers to incorporate improvements in their product or develop new marketing strategies. The increase in customer reviews of a product influence the popularity and the sale rate of the product. This lead to a very important question about the analysis of the sentiments (opinions) expressed in the reviews. As such internet does not have any quality control over customer reviews and it could vary in terms of its quality. Also the trustworthiness of the online reviews is debatable. Sentiment Analysis (SA) or Opinion Mining is the computational analysis of opinions, sentiments, emotions and subjectivity of text. In this chapter, we take a look at the various research challenges and a new dimension involved in sentiment analysis using fuzzy sets and rough sets.

Software engineering is an engineering approach for software development. It is a discipline whose aim is the production of fault-free, delivered on-time and within budget software that satisfies the user's needs. Software engineering principles need to be followed to ensure a successful software development project. Within organizations that are involved in software development, the challenge is to select the appropriate process model for the software project. The objective of this chapter is to determine the factors which influence the process model selection. This chapter presents an automated framework for selection of process model using fuzzy-based rule engine and to bring more accuracy for choice of process model, J-48 decision tree was used considering factors as inputs. The user has to give characteristic value of the prioritized factor as input and on the basis of the rules, model is anticipated. The developed framework will be profitable for project managers, experts and venture pioneers in software companies.

Chapter 19

    Farhana Ferdousi, East West University, Bangladesh
    Arun Kumar Sangaiah, VIT University, India

A productive investment climate is key to the growth of any developing country. Given the limited literature and importance of economic zone in attracting FDI, this paper conducts a study on the Export Processing Zone to provide an insight into the investment climate factors and its association with firms' performance. A total of 30 firms were chosen from the garment industry, in particular from the EPZ of Bangladesh. Findings reveal that all six factors were considered as important indicators affecting investment climate of EPZ firms. Moreover, five factors were found to be significantly associated with the firm performance. An important implication of the findings is that government and garment associations can get an important insights into the factors that are critical to the investment climate and accordingly take necessary steps to arrange better utilities provide sound governance, improve credit facilities, ensure a favorable trade union together with other infrastructural facilities that require for creating better investment climate for both the EPZ and non-EPZ firms.

Foreword

When I was invited to write a foreword for this book *Handbook of Research on Fuzzy and Rough Set Theory in Organizational Decision Making,* I was very happy to note the variety of applications in computational intelligence techniques. This book is a significant collection of 19 chapters covering fuzzy sets and rough sets, as well as their applications in organizational decision making that have emerged in the recent decades. This book provides an excellent platform to review various areas of computational intelligence in depth, and caters for the needs of both novices to the field and seasoned researchers and practitioners. The rapid growth and advances in a wide variety of applications of fuzzy sets and rough sets paradigms are documented in this book, such as neuro-fuzzy, genetic algorithms, and optimization techniques, which are focused at real-world decision making analysis, modeling and control problems.

To my knowledge, this is the first attempt of its kind, providing an intensive and in-depth coverage of the key subjects in the fields of fuzzy sets and rough sets on organizational decision making and analytics. This book is an invaluable, topical, and timely source of knowledge in the field, which serves nicely as a major text book for several courses at both undergraduate and post graduate levels. It is also a key reference for scientists, professionals, researchers, and academicians, who are interested in new challenges, theories, practice and advanced applications of the specific areas mentioned above.

I am happy to commend the editors and authors on their accomplishment, and to inform the readers that they are looking at a major piece in the development of computational intelligence on organizational decision making. This book is a main step in this field's maturation and will serve to unify, advance, and challenge the scientific community in many important ways.

Michael Sheng
The University of Adelaide, Australia

Preface

During the past decades, the use of fuzzy and rough sets approaches has been extended to various applications. Besides, there is evidence that fuzzy set theory and rough set approaches have become a key research area in the context of organizational decision making and have received more attention as indicated by recent research. Furthermore, the concept of applying computational intelligence approaches (fuzzy sets and rough sets) into decision making analysis is realistic and sound. Thus, fuzzy sets and rough sets have demonstrated their ability to handle uncertain information and subjective vagueness (human intervention) in the real-world decision making problems. Moreover, the essence of computational intelligence approaches likely to play a significant role in theoretical and practical domains has been explored in depth for conception and design of hybrid intelligent decision making systems. This book provides a comprehensive overview of constituent paradigms underlying fuzzy, rough sets, evolutionary computational intelligence methods, which are illustrating more attention as they evolve. Hence, the main objective of the book is to facilitate a forum to a large variety of researchers, where decision making approaches under fuzzy sets and rough sets are adapted to demonstrate how the proposed procedures as well as empirical observations can be applied in practice.

NEED FOR A BOOK ON THE PROPOSED TOPICS

Fuzzy and rough set theory has fostered a broad research area, and their significance has also been clearly justified at many applications. This book addresses a wide spectrum of fuzzy and rough set theory research, making decisions of an industry or organization happens at all the levels. Fuzzy and rough set theory approaches has been significant research topic in fuzzy set theory and rough set theory. Over recent decades, many of useful methods have been observed to solve organizational decision making problems.

This book will aim to provide relevant theoretical frameworks and the latest empirical research findings in the area. While computational approaches such as fuzzy and rough set applied to organizational decision making systems usually has received more attention in recently published volumes. Based on this context, there is need envisioning for a key perspective into current state of practice of computational techniques to address the predicative analysis of various domains such as business intelligence, e-governance, and software engineering methodologies. Some the key needs of this book as follows:

1. CI techniques (fuzzy sets and rough sets) are more suitable for handling uncertainty and the complexity of enterprise business process compared to traditional statistical approaches and tools presently being utilized.

2. Research in the fields of fuzzy sets and rough sets related to organization decision making and analytics as part of design, analysis, and development modeling have gained rapid momentum among industry members, but a book with an in-depth coverage of all the functional components still remains to be published. Hence, this book and its topics may command a broad audience, due to its practical value and variety of application domains.

3. Recently, fuzzy sets and rough sets theory approaches have been applied to a wide variety of complex problems, including engineering, science, and business. However, due to complexity and uncertainty in these problems, it becomes indeed difficult to find the optimal solution. Therefore, there is a great need to explore in depth the various CI techniques in conjunction with organization decision support and adaptive computational models for solving real world problems.

4. The main objective is to explore novel contributions that bridge the gap between applying fuzzy sets and rough sets to business intelligence, data analytics processes, and the overall business success of the organization.

5. The major outcome of this book, i.e., hybridization of CI techniques, advances in the design of computational models, algorithms, and case studies, may help in proposing novel solutions to contemporary engineering problems.

ORGANIZATION OF THE BOOK

The book is organized into 19 chapters. A brief description of each chapter is given as follows:

Chapter 1 gives an overview of fuzzy based approach to assess standards and quality of big data. The authors have designed fuzzy based SQL queries for assessing the quality of data. The overall aim of the chapter is to compare the fuzzy based query approach and a normal query based approach.

Chapter 2 covers an energy aware and intelligent secured routing algorithm that uses fuzzy clustering approach. The authors argue that proposed fuzzy clustering approach produces the optimal routes for communication. It also identifies the importance of reduction in energy usage and increase in the amount of packets delivered using fuzzy clustering approach.

Chapter 3 presents the hybridization of fuzzy multi-criteria decision making approaches for building up an assessment framework that can be used to evaluate risk in the context of software project performance. The authors of this chapter integrated the Fuzzy Multi-Criteria Decision Making (FMCDM) and Fuzzy Technique for Order of Preference by Similarity to Ideal Solution (TOPSIS) approaches. This chapter also reveals that the fusion of FMCDM and TOPSIS has not been adequately investigated in the exiting study.

Chapter 4 analyses the classical inventory model in different imprecise environments, such as fuzzy, interval and time dependent fuzzy environment. The author also examines the fuzzy differential equation approach and interval differential equation approach. This chapter state that fuzzy and interval differential equation approach is a very promising method for solving fuzzy or interval inventory problem.

Chapter 5 makes an effort to explore the means of increasing physical activity through effective gamification. The authors address the traditional method of calorie calculation for a treadmill, which is compared with the fuzzy based calorie calculation for different incline levels.

Chapter 6 discusses the overview of data clustering algorithms and their applications in the context of decision making process. The authors further suggest that importance should be paid to developing hybrid clustering algorithms for handling voluminous data.

Chapter 7 presents the Quality of Service (QoS) adaptive routing schemes using soft computing techniques. The chapter authors have designed and made an attempt in implementing on demand adaptive fuzzy based QoS service oriented approach for Vehicular Ad hoc Network (VANET).

Chapter 8 discusses the solving procedure of a Fuzzy Dynamic Programming Problem for single additive constraint with additively separable return with the support of trapezoidal membership functions and its arithmetic operations. Moreover, this chapter states that the proposed procedure offers an efficient tool for handling the dynamic programming problem instead of classical procedures.

Chapter 9 introduces two popular approaches, namely Fuzzy-AHP and Fuzzy TOPSIS for ERP selection problem. The author contends that how Fuzzy TOPSIS behaves better than the technique of Fuzzy AHP on agility, rank consistency and time complexity computational efficiency.

Chapter 10 addresses the fuzzy based matrix converter drive for induction motor. The chapter author argues that introduction of fuzzy controllers in the closed loop help to reduce the overshoot at starting and maintain the reference speed when running with load torque.

Chapter 11 reviews various bio inspired techniques, giving emphasis on issues, development, advances and practical implementations of Artificial Neural Networks (ANN). This chapter provides a detailed practical approach towards the data classification problem with both conventional and advanced ANN.

Chapter 12 investigates the genetic based estimation of biomass using geographical information system. The chapter author proposed the novel hereditary based calculation utilizes the pixel guide of every picture and tries to figure out the ranges using so as to fit the right determination for vegetation Biomass the hereditary based methodology.

Chapter 13 presents a fuzzy theory based solution to the adaptive bit loading problem formulated as a constrained optimization problem. In this chapter, an adaptive loading and modulation scheme is proposed, in which all the parameters are adapted using a fuzzy logic base system.

Chapter 14 describes the efficient methodology to perform pre-processing in content analysis research. The chapter authors have used fuzzy c-means and MLP based imputation, which can increase the overall reliability of the dataset.

Chapter 15 reviews the parameter reduction in soft set models with applications in decision making. In this chapter, the authors have discussed some of the basic notions of fuzzy soft sets (FSS) and interval valued fuzzy soft sets (IVFSS).

Chapter 16 proposes a framework on the criteria of Green Supply Chain Management (GSCM) practices using a Multi Criteria Decision Making (MCDM) analysis to select green suppliers for an Indian electronics company. The chapter authors have compared Fuzzy Analytical Hierarchy Process (FAHP) and Fuzzy TOPSIS method for enhancing the quality of decision making and validating the rankings.

Chapter 17 reviews various research challenges and a new dimension involved in sentiment analysis using fuzzy sets and rough sets. The chapter authors have applied rough sets based dimension reduction method for sentiment analysis.

Chapter 18 designs the automated framework for software process model selection based on soft computing approach. The overall objective of this chapter is to provide a guide to choose process model for each particular project. The chapter authors have introduced fuzzy interface system for prediction of process model on the basis of certain rules.

Chapter 19 presents the investment climate factors with reference to firm performance in Bangladesh. The authors identify the key factors, such as human resource, access to finance, infrastructure, power and energy, governance, trade union) that are found as critical indicators affecting investment climate of firms.

AUDIENCE

The intended audiences of this book are scientists, professionals, researchers, and academicians, who deal with the new challenges and advances in the specific areas mentioned above. Designers and developers of applications in these fields can learn from other experts and colleagues through studying this book. Many universities have started to offer courses on computational intelligence (CI), knowledge representation and reasoning on the graduate/post graduate level in information technology and management disciplines. This book starts with an introduction to fuzzy sets and rough sets and CI paradigms, hence suitable for university level courses as well as research scholars. Major contributions of chapters are expected from leading researchers, industry practitioners, and implementers. Their insightful discussions and knowledge, based on references and research work, will lead to an excellent book and a great knowledge source.

ACKNOWLEDGMENT

We would like to express our sincere gratitude to all the contributors, who have submitted their high-quality chapters, and to the experts for their supports in providing insightful review comments and suggestions on time.

Arun Kumar Sangaiah
VIT University, India

Xiao Zhi Gao
Aalto University, Finland

Ajith Abraham
Machine Intelligence Research Labs, USA

Chapter 1
Fuzzy-Based Querying Approach for Multidimensional Big Data Quality Assessment

Pradheep Kumar K.
BITS Pilani, India

Venkata Subramanian D.
Hindustan Institute of Technology & Science, India

ABSTRACT

This paper is intended to design a fuzzy based approach to assess standards and quality of big data. It also serves as a platform to organizations that intend to migrate their existing database environment to big data environment. Data is assessed using a multidimensional approach based on quality factors like accuracy, completeness, reliability, usability, etc. These factors are analysed by constructing decision trees to identify the quality aspects which need to be improved. In this work fuzzy queries have been designed. The queries are grouped as sets namely Excellent, Optimal, Fair and Hybrid. Based on the fuzzy data sets formed and the query compatibility index, a query set is chosen. A data set that has a very high degree of membership is assigned a fair query set. A data set with a medium degree of membership is assigned a optimal query set. A data set that has a lesser degree of membership is assigned a Excellent query set. A data set which needs a combination of queries of all the above is assigned a hybrid query set. The fuzzy query based approach reduces the query compatibility index by 36%, compared to a normal query set approach.

INTRODUCTION

In today's world with an increase in the amount of data processing and information requirement it is essential to develop strategies to effectively manage and assess the data for essential quality checks. The database forms the basis of day to day decisions taken by the organization. Data obtained from employees need to be periodically updated for effective utilization. In this work, an attempt has been made to assess data quality based on certain measures or parameters like Accuracy, Completeness, Reliability, Usability, etc as discussed by Pradheep et al in (2014). Based on these parameters the data set is queried to assess

DOI: 10.4018/978-1-5225-1008-6.ch001

the effectiveness of attributes like accuracy, usability, reliability, timeliness, etc. The parameters or quality factors such as Accuracy, completeness, etc are further subdivided into minor factors. Accuracy is sub divided into Syntactic and Semantic accuracy as explained by Pradheep et al (2014). The sub factors in turn have a parameter which is a measure and this parameter has an acceptable set of values.

To assess the effectiveness of the big data, a model is constructed for a Knowledge Management System which is a Multi-Dimensional Framework for quality checks. The different attributes are each modeled as a decision tree. The combination of all these form a Decision forest tree. A model for the decision forest tree was proposed by Criminisi et al in (2011). The decision forest tree model was a probabilistic model based on classification and regression analysis. The data under consideration could be textual, video, photographs to form a random forest of decision trees. To analyse this data effectively for information several data mining techniques were proposed. Berendt and Preibusch (2014) have proposed several techniques to extract data from databases based on the choice of attributes. Another technique which is map and reduce technique for large data sets had been proposed by Doulkeridis and Norvag in (2014). A large number of data visualizing techniques have been explained in this regard by Doulkeridis and Norvag (2014), Venkat et al (2011), Gorodov et al (2013), Serban et al (2013), Shamsi et al (2013), Jennex and Olfman (2003), Evans et al (2013) and Banerjee et al (2014).

A data dictionary needs to be available which acts as a repository for storing the data. The data dictionary would contain metadata of the data related to the nature, type, volume, etc. Data integrity is another feature which decides on the reliability of data. Data access should be provided according to the role based privileges. This is done based on access privileges and functional aspects. The access privileges may vary from time to time based on the effectiveness of the queries which are also assessed to ensure minimal processing time and memory. Based on this approach the queries are classified into sets. Based on the decision tree analysis carried out the entire data is partitioned into smaller datasets. The size of the dataset may vary arbitrarily based on data volume and processing speed of the database.

The datasets are discretised based on the degree of membership. The queries are classified based on the query processing time and memory. A data set that has a very high degree of membership would have data points very closely spaced. This type of data set has a scattering distance which is negligible. The distance is measured by Euclidean method. In other words the data points would be clustered and would belong to only a single fuzzy set. Hence it would be ideal to use a query set which has a low query compatible index. This would not have a very high impact on the query cost, thereby optimizing the same. When the degree of membership is partial, we would need a slightly more efficient query set to work on this type of data set. Here the data set is spaced a bit and may belong to two different fuzzy sets. To accomplish this, the query would need to work on both fuzzy sets to return precise information. In such cases the data points are separated by a finite scattering distance. Here there is no clustering. For these data sets the query set should have an average or optimal query compatibility index.

When the degree of membership of the data is very low, the data points are widely scattered with a very large scattering distance. Here there is no question of clustering and the data points are distributed among multiple fuzzy sets. This would imply a very large scattering distance. To extract precise information, it is essential to assign highly efficient query set with a very high query compatibility index. A Mamdani's fuzzy inference engine is used as the inputs are non-linear and are provided as fuzzy sets. In this work a triangular membership function has been used to determine the degree of membership. The entire approach aims at ensuring no compromise in performance and optimal assignment of datasets with query sets.

This chapter has been organized in the following manner: Section 2 reports a literature on the work carried out in this context and also analyses the pros and cons of existing techniques. Section 3 explains the proposed work, the fuzzy rule set classification. It also explains the salient points of the algorithm used. Section 4 explains the simulation results based on performance in detail. Section 5 gives a conclusion to the chapter highlighting the different features discussed. Section 6 explains the directions for future research.

MOTIVATION AND BACKGROUND

Decision tree analysis is a powerful tool to analyse the effectiveness of quality of data. A Knowledge Management System using a multidimensional model has been explained by Venkat et al (2011, 2012). A decision forest model proposed by Criminisi et al in (2011) describes a probabilistic approach. A large number of constraints were indicated by Jennex and Olfman (2003) which defines features such as system quality, knowledge and information quality. Models formulated by Ma Calls, Boehms assess software quality to a greater content. Several data visualizing techniques were discussed and illustrated by Venkat et al (2011), Yurevich and Vasilevich (2013), Serban et al (2013), Shamsi et al (2013), Jennex and Olfman (2003), Evans et al (2013), Banerjee et al (2014), Marcio et al (2014), Jennex (2011), Kwon and Mun (2013), Strhomeier and Piazza (2013) and Basili and Weiss (1984). Venkata and Geetha (2011 & 2012) proposed a system based on knowledge management. Pradheep et al (2014) proposed a multidimensional model for a quality assessment as shown in Figure 1.

To assess precisely the effectiveness of the data, the query set needs to be efficient. The SQL queries used cannot always be designed to operate on single column attributes and return values. The efficiency of the query could be adjudged only if precise information is obtained. To obtain precise information, fuzzy based queries are designed as discussed by Pawar et al in (2011) to effectively extract information. The efficiency of the query is ascertained based on a Query Compatible Index (QCI) as explained by Hudec (2012) and Poonam (2014) using Gefred Query Builder model.

Proposed Work

In this work fuzzy based SQL queries are designed to assess the quality of the data. The fuzzy based queries are categorised based on the query processing time and memory consumed. The queries are broadly classified as Excellent, Optimal and Fair. The data set is discretised as fuzzy sets. Each fuzzy set is mapped on to a triangular membership function.

A normal SQL query would be of the form

SELECT Age AND Year FROM Athletes WHERE ((Age > =P and Age<=Q) AND (Year >=R and Year<=S))

The values P, Q, R and S are crisp values.

This query would list out data matching the criteria. In addition if we need to specify a range for the attributes a normal SQL would not yield precise information and also the query designed would be complex resulting in large query cost. The query cost is a parameter based on processing time and memory consumed by the query. The next section explains the different fuzzy membership functions and values for the linguistic variables.

Figure 1. Model to assess the different quality attributes of big data

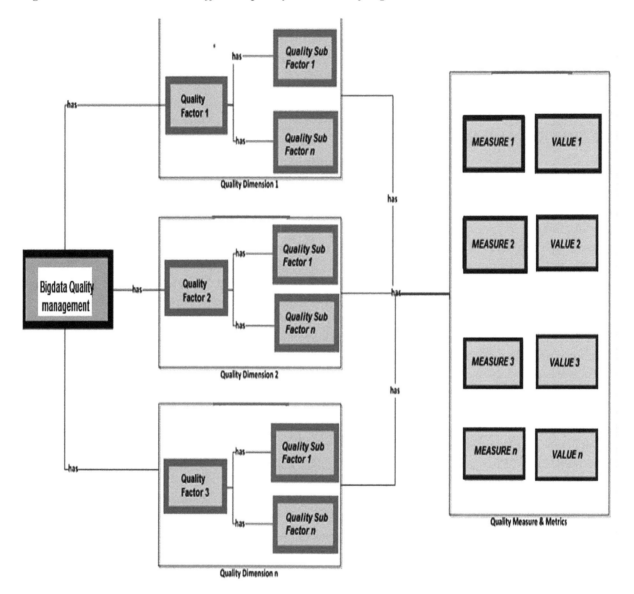

Fuzzy Membership Functions

In this work two fuzzy linguistic variables, Age and Year have been used. There are 4 values for Age namely AMATEUR, INTERMEDIATE, EXPERT and MASTER. The range of values for AMATEUR, INTERMEDIATE, EXPERT and MASTER are (16-19), (20-23), (24-27) and (28-31) respectively. The values for Age are VERY OLD, OLD, NEW and RECENT. The corresponding range of values for VERY

Figure 2. Membership function for the age attribute

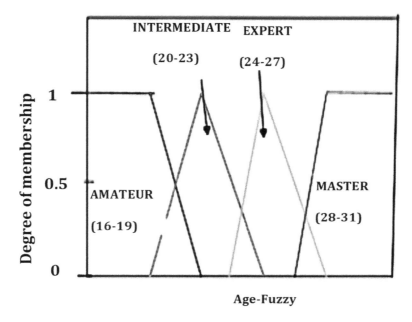

Figure 3. Membership function for the year attribute

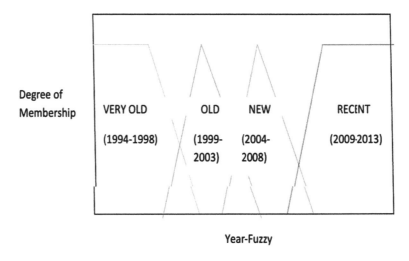

OLD, OLD, NEW and RECENT are (1994-1998), (1999-2003), (2004-2008) and (2009-2012) respectively. The membership functions for Age and Year are shown in Figure 2 and Figure 3, respectively.

The next section explains the fuzzy rule base and all possible rules used. It also classifies the fuzzy rule set into Excellent, Optimal and Fair queries based on the data discretisation and membership of a fuzzy set.

Fuzzy Rule Base

This work attempts to assign the right query set to a particular data set thereby reducing the query cost and optimizing the same. A typical fuzzy based query would be of the form:

SELECT AgeFuzzy AND YearFuzzy FROM SPORTS WHERE ((AgeFuzzy is AMATEUR) AND ((YearFuzzy is NEW)).

The entire fuzzy rule base (Excellent, Optimal and Fair query sets) comprising of 66 rules are listed below:

1. SELECT AgeFuzzy AND YearFuzzy FROM SPORTS WHERE ((AgeFuzzy is AMATEUR) AND (YearFuzzy is VERY OLD));
2. SELECT AgeFuzzy AND YearFuzzy FROM SPORTS WHERE ((AgeFuzzy is AMATEUR) AND (YearFuzzy is OLD));
3. SELECT AgeFuzzy AND YearFuzzy FROM SPORTS WHERE ((AgeFuzzy is AMATEUR) AND (YearFuzzy is NEW));
4. SELECT AgeFuzzy AND YearFuzzy FROM SPORTS WHERE ((AgeFuzzy is AMATEUR) AND (YearFuzzy is RECENT));
5. SELECT AgeFuzzy AND YearFuzzy FROM SPORTS WHERE ((AgeFuzzy is INTERMEDIATE) AND (YearFuzzy is VERY OLD));
6. SELECT AgeFuzzy AND YearFuzzy FROM SPORTS WHERE ((AgeFuzzy is INTERMEDIATE) AND (YearFuzzy is OLD));
7. SELECT AgeFuzzy AND YearFuzzy FROM SPORTS WHERE ((AgeFuzzy is INTERMEDIATE) AND (YearFuzzy is NEW));
8. SELECT AgeFuzzy AND YearFuzzy FROM SPORTS WHERE ((AgeFuzzy is INTERMEDIATE) AND (YearFuzzy is RECENT));
9. SELECT AgeFuzzy AND YearFuzzy FROM SPORTS WHERE ((AgeFuzzy is EXPERT) AND (YearFuzzy is VERY OLD));
10. SELECT AgeFuzzy AND YearFuzzy FROM SPORTS WHERE ((AgeFuzzy is EXPERT) AND (YearFuzzy is OLD));
11. SELECT AgeFuzzy AND YearFuzzy FROM SPORTS WHERE ((AgeFuzzy is EXPERT) AND (YearFuzzy is NEW));
12. SELECT AgeFuzzy AND YearFuzzy FROM SPORTS WHERE ((AgeFuzzy is EXPERT) AND (YearFuzzy is RECENT));
13. SELECT AgeFuzzy AND YearFuzzy FROM SPORTS WHERE ((AgeFuzzy is MASTER) AND (YearFuzzy is VERY OLD));
14. SELECT AgeFuzzy AND YearFuzzy FROM SPORTS WHERE ((AgeFuzzy is MASTER) AND (YearFuzzy is OLD));
15. SELECT AgeFuzzy AND YearFuzzy FROM SPORTS WHERE ((AgeFuzzy is MASTER) AND (YearFuzzy is NEW));
16. SELECT AgeFuzzy AND YearFuzzy FROM SPORTS WHERE ((AgeFuzzy is MASTER) AND (YearFuzzy is RECENT));

17. SELECT AgeFuzzy AND YearFuzzy FROM SPORTS WHERE (((AgeFuzzy is AMATEUR) OR (AgeFuzzy is INTERMEDIATE)) AND (YearFuzzy is VERY OLD));
18. SELECT AgeFuzzy AND YearFuzzy FROM SPORTS WHERE (((AgeFuzzy is AMATEUR) OR (AgeFuzzy is INTERMEDIATE)) AND (YearFuzzy is OLD));
19. SELECT AgeFuzzy AND YearFuzzy FROM SPORTS WHERE (((AgeFuzzy is AMATEUR) OR (AgeFuzzy is INTERMEDIATE)) AND (YearFuzzy is NEW));
20. SELECT AgeFuzzy AND YearFuzzy FROM SPORTS WHERE (((AgeFuzzy is AMATEUR) OR (AgeFuzzy is INTERMEDIATE)) AND (YearFuzzy is RECENT));
21. SELECT AgeFuzzy AND YearFuzzy FROM SPORTS WHERE (((AgeFuzzy is EXPERT) OR (AgeFuzzy is MASTER)) AND (YearFuzzy is VERY OLD));
22. SELECT AgeFuzzy AND YearFuzzy FROM SPORTS WHERE (((AgeFuzzy is EXPERT) OR (AgeFuzzy is MASTER)) AND (YearFuzzy is OLD));
23. SELECT AgeFuzzy AND YearFuzzy FROM SPORTS WHERE (((AgeFuzzy is EXPERT) OR (AgeFuzzy is MASTER)) AND (YearFuzzy is NEW));
24. SELECT AgeFuzzy AND YearFuzzy FROM SPORTS WHERE (((AgeFuzzy is EXPERT) OR (AgeFuzzy is MASTER)) AND (YearFuzzy is RECENT));
25. SELECT AgeFuzzy AND YearFuzzy FROM SPORTS WHERE (((AgeFuzzy is AMATEUR)) AND (YearFuzzy is VERY OLD) OR ((YearFuzzy is OLD));
26. SELECT AgeFuzzy AND YearFuzzy FROM SPORTS WHERE (((AgeFuzzy is INTERMEDIATE)) AND (YearFuzzy is VERY OLD) OR ((YearFuzzy is OLD));
27. SELECT AgeFuzzy AND YearFuzzy FROM SPORTS WHERE (((AgeFuzzy is EXPERT)) AND (YearFuzzy is VERY OLD) OR ((YearFuzzy is OLD));
28. SELECT AgeFuzzy AND YearFuzzy FROM SPORTS WHERE (((AgeFuzzy is MASTER)) AND ((YearFuzzy is VERY OLD) OR (YearFuzzy is OLD)));
29. SELECT AgeFuzzy AND YearFuzzy FROM SPORTS WHERE (((AgeFuzzy is AMATEUR)) AND ((YearFuzzy is OLD) OR (YearFuzzy is NEW)));
30. SELECT AgeFuzzy AND YearFuzzy FROM SPORTS WHERE (((AgeFuzzy is INTERMEDIATE)) AND ((YearFuzzy is OLD) OR (YearFuzzy is NEW)));
31. SELECT AgeFuzzy AND YearFuzzy FROM SPORTS WHERE (((AgeFuzzy is EXPERT)) AND ((YearFuzzy is OLD) OR (YearFuzzy is NEW)));
32. SELECT AgeFuzzy AND YearFuzzy FROM SPORTS WHERE (((AgeFuzzy is MASTER)) AND ((YearFuzzy is OLD) OR (YearFuzzy is NEW)));
33. SELECT AgeFuzzy AND YearFuzzy FROM SPORTS WHERE (((AgeFuzzy is AMATEUR)) AND ((YearFuzzy is NEW) OR (YearFuzzy is RECENT)));
34. SELECT AgeFuzzy AND YearFuzzy FROM SPORTS WHERE (((AgeFuzzy is INTERMEDIATE)) AND ((YearFuzzy is NEW) OR (YearFuzzy is RECENT)));
35. SELECT AgeFuzzy AND YearFuzzy FROM SPORTS WHERE (((AgeFuzzy is EXPERT)) AND (YearFuzzy is NEW) OR (YearFuzzy is RECENT)));
36. SELECT AgeFuzzy AND YearFuzzy FROM SPORTS WHERE (((AgeFuzzy is MASTER)) AND (YearFuzzy is NEW) OR ((YearFuzzy is RECENT)));
37. SELECT AgeFuzzy AND YearFuzzy FROM SPORTS WHERE (((AgeFuzzy is AMATEUR) OR (AgeFuzzy is INTERMEDIATE)) AND ((YearFuzzy is VERY OLD) OR ((YearFuzzy is OLD)));
38. SELECT AgeFuzzy AND YearFuzzy FROM SPORTS WHERE (((AgeFuzzy is AMATEUR) OR (AgeFuzzy is INTERMEDIATE)) AND ((YearFuzzy is OLD) OR (YearFuzzy is NEW));

39. SELECT AgeFuzzy AND YearFuzzy FROM SPORTS WHERE (((AgeFuzzy is AMATEUR) OR (AgeFuzzy is INTERMEDIATE)) AND ((YearFuzzy is NEW) OR (YearFuzzy is RECENT)));
40. SELECT AgeFuzzy AND YearFuzzy FROM SPORTS WHERE (((AgeFuzzy is EXPERT)) AND ((YearFuzzy is VERY OLD) OR (YearFuzzy is OLD)));
41. SELECT AgeFuzzy AND YearFuzzy FROM SPORTS WHERE ((AgeFuzzy is EXPERT)) AND ((YearFuzzy is OLD) OR (YearFuzzy is NEW)));
42. SELECT AgeFuzzy AND YearFuzzy FROM SPORTS WHERE ((AgeFuzzy is EXPERT) AND ((YearFuzzy is NEW) OR (YearFuzzy is RECENT)));
43. SELECT AgeFuzzy AND YearFuzzy FROM SPORTS WHERE ((AgeFuzzy is MASTER)) AND ((YearFuzzy is VERY OLD) OR (YearFuzzy is OLD)));
44. SELECT AgeFuzzy AND YearFuzzy FROM SPORTS WHERE ((AgeFuzzy is MASTER)) AND ((YearFuzzy is OLD) OR (YearFuzzy is NEW)));
45. SELECT AgeFuzzy AND YearFuzzy FROM SPORTS WHERE ((AgeFuzzy is MASTER) AND ((YearFuzzy is NEW) OR ((YearFuzzy is RECENT)));
46. SELECT AgeFuzzy AND YearFuzzy FROM SPORTS WHERE ((AgeFuzzy is EXPERT) OR (AgeFuzzy is MASTER) AND ((YearFuzzy is VERY OLD) OR (YearFuzzy is OLD)));
47. SELECT AgeFuzzy AND YearFuzzy FROM SPORTS WHERE ((AgeFuzzy is EXPERT) OR (AgeFuzzy is MASTER)) AND ((YearFuzzy is OLD) OR ((YearFuzzy is NEW)));
48. SELECT AgeFuzzy AND YearFuzzy FROM SPORTS WHERE ((AgeFuzzy is EXPERT) OR (AgeFuzzy is MASTER)) AND (YearFuzzy is NEW) OR ((YearFuzzy is RECENT)));
49. SELECT AgeFuzzy AND YearFuzzy FROM SPORTS WHERE ((AgeFuzzy is AMATEUR) OR (AgeFuzzy is INTERMEDIATE) OR (AgeFuzzy is EXPERT)) AND (YearFuzzy is VERY OLD)));
50. SELECT AgeFuzzy AND YearFuzzy FROM SPORTS WHERE ((AgeFuzzy is AMATEUR) OR (AgeFuzzy is INTERMEDIATE) OR (AgeFuzzy is EXPERT)) AND (YearFuzzy is OLD)));
51. SELECT AgeFuzzy AND YearFuzzy FROM SPORTS WHERE ((AgeFuzzy is AMATEUR) OR (AgeFuzzy is INTERMEDIATE) OR (AgeFuzzy is EXPERT)) AND (YearFuzzy is NEW));
52. SELECT AgeFuzzy AND YearFuzzy FROM SPORTS WHERE (((AgeFuzzy is AMATEUR) OR (AgeFuzzy is INTERMEDIATE) OR (AgeFuzzy is EXPERT) AND (YearFuzzy is RECENT));
53. SELECT AgeFuzzy AND YearFuzzy FROM SPORTS WHERE ((AgeFuzzy is AMATEUR) AND ((YearFuzzy is VERY OLD) OR (YearFuzzy is OLD) OR (YearFuzzy is NEW)));
54. SELECT AgeFuzzy AND YearFuzzy FROM SPORTS WHERE ((AgeFuzzy is INTERMEDIATE) AND ((YearFuzzy is VERY OLD) OR (YearFuzzy is OLD) OR (YearFuzzy is NEW)));
55. SELECT AgeFuzzy AND YearFuzzy FROM SPORTS WHERE ((AgeFuzzy is EXPERT) AND ((YearFuzzy is VERY OLD) OR (YearFuzzy is OLD) OR (YearFuzzy is NEW)));
56. SELECT AgeFuzzy AND YearFuzzy FROM SPORTS WHERE ((AgeFuzzy is MASTER) AND ((YearFuzzy is VERY OLD) OR (YearFuzzy is OLD) OR (YearFuzzy is NEW)));
57. SELECT AgeFuzzy AND YearFuzzy FROM SPORTS WHERE ((AgeFuzzy is AMATEUR) OR (AgeFuzzy is INTERMEDIATE) OR (AgeFuzzy is EXPERT)) AND ((YearFuzzy is VERY OLD) OR (YearFuzzy is OLD) OR (YearFuzzy is NEW)));
58. SELECT AgeFuzzy AND YearFuzzy FROM SPORTS WHERE ((AgeFuzzy is AMATEUR) OR (AgeFuzzy is INTERMEDIATE) OR (AgeFuzzy is EXPERT) OR (AgeFuzzy is MASTER)) AND (YearFuzzy is VERY OLD));

59. SELECT AgeFuzzy AND YearFuzzy FROM SPORTS WHERE ((AgeFuzzy is AMATEUR) OR (AgeFuzzy is INTERMEDIATE) OR (AgeFuzzy is EXPERT) OR (AgeFuzzy is MASTER)) AND (YearFuzzy is OLD)));

60. SELECT AgeFuzzy AND YearFuzzy FROM SPORTS WHERE ((AgeFuzzy is AMATEUR) OR (AgeFuzzy is INTERMEDIATE) OR (AgeFuzzy is EXPERT) OR (AgeFuzzy is MASTER) AND (YearFuzzy is NEW)));

61. SELECT AgeFuzzy AND YearFuzzy FROM SPORTS WHERE ((AgeFuzzy is AMATEUR) OR (AgeFuzzy is INTERMEDIATE) OR (AgeFuzzy is EXPERT) OR (AgeFuzzy is MASTER) AND (YearFuzzy is RECENT)));

62. SELECT AgeFuzzy AND YearFuzzy FROM SPORTS WHERE ((AgeFuzzy is AMATEUR) AND ((YearFuzzy is VERY OLD) OR (YearFuzzy is OLD) OR (YearFuzzy is NEW) OR (YearFuzzy is RECENT)));

63. SELECT AgeFuzzy AND YearFuzzy FROM SPORTS WHERE ((AgeFuzzy is INTERMEDIATE)) AND ((YearFuzzy is VERY OLD) OR (YearFuzzy is OLD) OR (YearFuzzy is NEW) OR (YearFuzzy is RECENT)));

64. SELECT AgeFuzzy AND YearFuzzy FROM SPORTS WHERE ((AgeFuzzy is EXPERT) AND ((YearFuzzy is VERY OLD) OR (YearFuzzy is OLD) OR (YearFuzzy is NEW) OR (YearFuzzy is RECENT)));

65. SELECT AgeFuzzy AND YearFuzzy FROM SPORTS WHERE ((AgeFuzzy is MASTER)) AND ((YearFuzzy is VERY OLD) OR ((YearFuzzy is OLD) OR (YearFuzzy is NEW) OR (YearFuzzy is RECENT)));

66. SELECT AgeFuzzy AND YearFuzzy FROM SPORTS WHERE ((AgeFuzzy is AMATEUR) OR (AgeFuzzy is INTERMEDIATE) OR (AgeFuzzy is EXPERT) OR (AgeFuzzy is MASTER)) AND ((YearFuzzy is VERY OLD) OR (YearFuzzy is VERY OLD) OR (YearFuzzy is NEW) OR (YearFuzzy is RECENT)));

The fuzzy inference engine to process the queries is an engine designed by Mamdani and Assilan (1975). The Mamdani's fuzzy inference engine accepts inputs as fuzzy sets give more flexibility as compared to Sugeno's inference engine that uses inputs which are linear as discussed by Sugeno in (1984). The Fuzzy Inference engine is shown in Figure 4.

Figure 4. Fuzzy inference engine

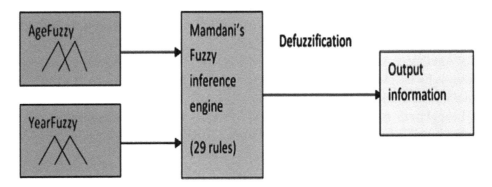

For these queries we compute a Query Compatible Index (QCI) which is the weighted average of query processing time and memory consumed. A threshold is computed which is the average of QCI for all such designed fuzzy based queries. The next section explains how to classify the queries based on the QCI.

$$QCI = \frac{\left(W1 * queryprocessingtime\right) + (W2 * memoryconsumed)}{(W1 + W2)} \tag{1}$$

Query Classification

The queries are grouped into 4 query sets as follows based on the QCI:

1. Excellent,
2. Optimal,
3. Fair,
4. Hybrid (Combination of Excellent, Optimal and Fair).

Excellent Query Set

Excellent query set is a set of queries that have a query processing time lesser than 50% of the threshold set from the QCI. This query set is used on a data set that has a lower degree of membership as the query processing would be consuming large time. Thus, the query cost (QC) of this query set is given by:

$$QC = \left(\min(QCI)\right) \tag{2}$$

where QCI is the query compatibility index.

Such a query set is used on data sets which have a very low degree of membership as the data points would be widely scattered with a very large scattering distance. Such data are not clustered or grouped. The data belongs to more than 2 fuzzy sets. Hence an excellent query set would enable a reduction in query processing time.

The fuzzy SQL rules which are used for an Excellent query set (9 queries) are listed below:

1. SELECT AgeFuzzy AND YearFuzzy FROM SPORTS WHERE ((AgeFuzzy is AMATEUR) OR (AgeFuzzy is INTERMEDIATE) OR (AgeFuzzy is EXPERT) OR (AgeFuzzy is MASTER)) AND (YearFuzzy is VERY OLD));
2. SELECT AgeFuzzy AND YearFuzzy FROM SPORTS WHERE ((AgeFuzzy is AMATEUR) OR (AgeFuzzy is INTERMEDIATE) OR (AgeFuzzy is EXPERT) OR (AgeFuzzy is MASTER)) AND (YearFuzzy is OLD)));
3. SELECT AgeFuzzy AND YearFuzzy FROM SPORTS WHERE ((AgeFuzzy is AMATEUR) OR (AgeFuzzy is INTERMEDIATE) OR (AgeFuzzy is EXPERT) OR (AgeFuzzy is MASTER) AND (YearFuzzy is NEW)));

4. SELECT AgeFuzzy AND YearFuzzy FROM SPORTS WHERE ((AgeFuzzy is AMATEUR) OR (AgeFuzzy is INTERMEDIATE) OR (AgeFuzzy is EXPERT) OR (AgeFuzzy is MASTER) AND (YearFuzzy is RECENT)));

5. SELECT AgeFuzzy AND YearFuzzy FROM SPORTS WHERE ((AgeFuzzy is AMATEUR) AND ((YearFuzzy is VERY OLD) OR (YearFuzzy is OLD) OR (YearFuzzy is NEW) OR (YearFuzzy is RECENT)));

6. SELECT AgeFuzzy AND YearFuzzy FROM SPORTS WHERE ((AgeFuzzy is INTERMEDIATE)) AND ((YearFuzzy is VERY OLD) OR (YearFuzzy is OLD) OR (YearFuzzy is NEW) OR (YearFuzzy is RECENT)));

7. SELECT AgeFuzzy AND YearFuzzy FROM SPORTS WHERE ((AgeFuzzy is EXPERT) AND ((YearFuzzy is VERY OLD) OR (YearFuzzy is OLD) OR (YearFuzzy is NEW) OR (YearFuzzy is RECENT)));

8. SELECT AgeFuzzy AND YearFuzzy FROM SPORTS WHERE ((AgeFuzzy is MASTER)) AND ((YearFuzzy is VERY OLD) OR ((YearFuzzy is OLD) OR (YearFuzzy is NEW) OR (YearFuzzy is RECENT)));

9. SELECT AgeFuzzy AND YearFuzzy FROM SPORTS WHERE ((AgeFuzzy is AMATEUR) OR (AgeFuzzy is INTERMEDIATE) OR (AgeFuzzy is EXPERT) OR (AgeFuzzy is MASTER)) AND ((YearFuzzy is VERY OLD) OR (YearFuzzy is VERY OLD) OR (YearFuzzy is NEW) OR (YearFuzzy is RECENT)));

Optimal Query Set

Optimal query set is a set of queries that have a query processing time equal to 50% of the threshold set from the QCI. This query set is used on a data set where the query processing time equal to the threshold. Thus, the query cost (QC) of this query set is given by:

$$QC = \left(average(QCI) \right) \tag{3}$$

where, QCI is the query compatibility index.

Such query sets are used on data sets that have a medium degree of membership as the data points are neither widely scattered nor clustered or grouped. The scattering distance between data points would be lesser compared to the scattering distance of data points in a single fuzzy set. Hence using an optimal query set reduces the query processing time. The data belongs to 2 distinct fuzzy sets.

The fuzzy SQL rules which are used for an optimal query set (33 queries) are listed below:

1. SELECT AgeFuzzy AND YearFuzzy FROM SPORTS WHERE (((AgeFuzzy is AMATEUR) OR (AgeFuzzy is INTERMEDIATE)) AND (YearFuzzy is VERY OLD));

2. SELECT AgeFuzzy AND YearFuzzy FROM SPORTS WHERE (((AgeFuzzy is AMATEUR) OR (AgeFuzzy is INTERMEDIATE)) AND (YearFuzzy is OLD));

3. SELECT AgeFuzzy AND YearFuzzy FROM SPORTS WHERE (((AgeFuzzy is AMATEUR) OR (AgeFuzzy is INTERMEDIATE)) AND (YearFuzzy is NEW));

4. SELECT AgeFuzzy AND YearFuzzy FROM SPORTS WHERE (((AgeFuzzy is AMATEUR) OR (AgeFuzzy is INTERMEDIATE)) AND (YearFuzzy is RECENT));

5. SELECT AgeFuzzy AND YearFuzzy FROM SPORTS WHERE (((AgeFuzzy is EXPERT) OR (AgeFuzzy is MASTER)) AND (YearFuzzy is VERY OLD));
6. SELECT AgeFuzzy AND YearFuzzy FROM SPORTS WHERE (((AgeFuzzy is EXPERT) OR (AgeFuzzy is MASTER)) AND (YearFuzzy is OLD));
7. SELECT AgeFuzzy AND YearFuzzy FROM SPORTS WHERE (((AgeFuzzy is EXPERT) OR (AgeFuzzy is MASTER)) AND (YearFuzzy is NEW));
8. SELECT AgeFuzzy AND YearFuzzy FROM SPORTS WHERE (((AgeFuzzy is EXPERT) OR (AgeFuzzy is MASTER)) AND (YearFuzzy is RECENT));
9. SELECT AgeFuzzy AND YearFuzzy FROM SPORTS WHERE (((AgeFuzzy is AMATEUR)) AND (YearFuzzy is VERY OLD) OR ((YearFuzzy is OLD));
10. SELECT AgeFuzzy AND YearFuzzy FROM SPORTS WHERE (((AgeFuzzy is INTERMEDIATE)) AND (YearFuzzy is VERY OLD) OR ((YearFuzzy is OLD));
11. SELECT AgeFuzzy AND YearFuzzy FROM SPORTS WHERE (((AgeFuzzy is EXPERT)) AND (YearFuzzy is VERY OLD) OR ((YearFuzzy is OLD));
12. SELECT AgeFuzzy AND YearFuzzy FROM SPORTS WHERE (((AgeFuzzy is MASTER)) AND ((YearFuzzy is VERY OLD) OR (YearFuzzy is OLD)));
13. SELECT AgeFuzzy AND YearFuzzy FROM SPORTS WHERE (((AgeFuzzy is AMATEUR)) AND ((YearFuzzy is OLD) OR (YearFuzzy is NEW)));
14. SELECT AgeFuzzy AND YearFuzzy FROM SPORTS WHERE (((AgeFuzzy is INTERMEDIATE)) AND ((YearFuzzy is OLD) OR (YearFuzzy is NEW)));
15. SELECT AgeFuzzy AND YearFuzzy FROM SPORTS WHERE (((AgeFuzzy is EXPERT)) AND ((YearFuzzy is OLD) OR (YearFuzzy is NEW)));
16. SELECT AgeFuzzy AND YearFuzzy FROM SPORTS WHERE (((AgeFuzzy is MASTER)) AND ((YearFuzzy is OLD) OR (YearFuzzy is NEW)));
17. SELECT AgeFuzzy AND YearFuzzy FROM SPORTS WHERE (((AgeFuzzy is AMATEUR)) AND ((YearFuzzy is NEW) OR (YearFuzzy is RECENT)));
18. SELECT AgeFuzzy AND YearFuzzy FROM SPORTS WHERE (((AgeFuzzy is INTERMEDIATE)) AND ((YearFuzzy is NEW) OR (YearFuzzy is RECENT)));
19. SELECT AgeFuzzy AND YearFuzzy FROM SPORTS WHERE (((AgeFuzzy is EXPERT)) AND (YearFuzzy is NEW) OR (YearFuzzy is RECENT)));
20. SELECT AgeFuzzy AND YearFuzzy FROM SPORTS WHERE (((AgeFuzzy is MASTER)) AND (YearFuzzy is NEW) OR ((YearFuzzy is RECENT)));
21. SELECT AgeFuzzy AND YearFuzzy FROM SPORTS WHERE (((AgeFuzzy is AMATEUR) OR (AgeFuzzy is INTERMEDIATE)) AND ((YearFuzzy is VERY OLD) OR ((YearFuzzy is OLD)));
22. SELECT AgeFuzzy AND YearFuzzy FROM SPORTS WHERE (((AgeFuzzy is AMATEUR) OR (AgeFuzzy is INTERMEDIATE)) AND ((YearFuzzy is OLD) OR (YearFuzzy is NEW));
23. SELECT AgeFuzzy AND YearFuzzy FROM SPORTS WHERE (((AgeFuzzy is AMATEUR) OR (AgeFuzzy is INTERMEDIATE)) AND ((YearFuzzy is NEW) OR (YearFuzzy is RECENT)));
24. SELECT AgeFuzzy AND YearFuzzy FROM SPORTS WHERE (((AgeFuzzy is EXPERT)) AND ((YearFuzzy is VERY OLD) OR (YearFuzzy is OLD)));
25. SELECT AgeFuzzy AND YearFuzzy FROM SPORTS WHERE ((AgeFuzzy is EXPERT)) AND ((YearFuzzy is OLD) OR (YearFuzzy is NEW)));
26. SELECT AgeFuzzy AND YearFuzzy FROM SPORTS WHERE ((AgeFuzzy is EXPERT) AND ((YearFuzzy is NEW) OR (YearFuzzy is RECENT)));

27. SELECT AgeFuzzy AND YearFuzzy FROM SPORTS WHERE ((AgeFuzzy is MASTER)) AND ((YearFuzzy is VERY OLD) OR (YearFuzzy is OLD)));

28. SELECT AgeFuzzy AND YearFuzzy FROM SPORTS WHERE ((AgeFuzzy is MASTER)) AND ((YearFuzzy is OLD) OR (YearFuzzy is NEW)));

29. SELECT AgeFuzzy AND YearFuzzy FROM SPORTS WHERE ((AgeFuzzy is MASTER) AND ((YearFuzzy is NEW) OR ((YearFuzzy is RECENT)));

30. SELECT AgeFuzzy AND YearFuzzy FROM SPORTS WHERE ((AgeFuzzy is EXPERT) OR (AgeFuzzy is MASTER) AND ((YearFuzzy is VERY OLD) OR (YearFuzzy is OLD)));

31. SELECT AgeFuzzy AND YearFuzzy FROM SPORTS WHERE ((AgeFuzzy is EXPERT) OR (AgeFuzzy is MASTER)) AND ((YearFuzzy is OLD) OR ((YearFuzzy is NEW)));

32. SELECT AgeFuzzy AND YearFuzzy FROM SPORTS WHERE ((AgeFuzzy is EXPERT) OR (AgeFuzzy is MASTER)) AND (YearFuzzy is NEW) OR ((YearFuzzy is RECENT)));

33. SELECT AgeFuzzy AND YearFuzzy FROM SPORTS WHERE ((AgeFuzzy is AMATEUR) OR (AgeFuzzy is INTERMEDIATE) OR (AgeFuzzy is EXPERT)) AND (YearFuzzy is VERY OLD)));

Fair Query Set

Fair query set is a set of queries that have a query processing time greater than 50% of the threshold set from the QCI. This query set is used on a data set that has a higher degree of membership as query processing would consume lesser time. Thus, the query cost (QC) of this query set is given by:

$$QC = \left(\max(QCI) \right) \tag{4}$$

where, QCI is the query compatibility index.

Such query sets are used on data sets that have a very high degree of membership where data points are clustered or grouped. The scattering distance between the data points are insignificant or negligible. Hence using a fair query set would reduce the query processing time.

The fuzzy SQL rules which are used for Fair query set (16 queries) are listed below:

1. SELECT AgeFuzzy AND YearFuzzy FROM SPORTS WHERE ((AgeFuzzy is AMATEUR) AND (YearFuzzy is VERY OLD));

2. SELECT AgeFuzzy AND YearFuzzy FROM SPORTS WHERE ((AgeFuzzy is AMATEUR) AND (YearFuzzy is OLD));

3. SELECT AgeFuzzy AND YearFuzzy FROM SPORTS WHERE ((AgeFuzzy is AMATEUR) AND (YearFuzzy is NEW));

4. SELECT AgeFuzzy AND YearFuzzy FROM SPORTS WHERE ((AgeFuzzy is AMATEUR) AND (YearFuzzy is RECENT));

5. SELECT AgeFuzzy AND YearFuzzy FROM SPORTS WHERE ((AgeFuzzy is INTERMEDIATE) AND (YearFuzzy is VERY OLD));

6. SELECT AgeFuzzy AND YearFuzzy FROM SPORTS WHERE ((AgeFuzzy is INTERMEDIATE) AND (YearFuzzy is OLD));

7. SELECT AgeFuzzy AND YearFuzzy FROM SPORTS WHERE ((AgeFuzzy is INTERMEDIATE) AND (YearFuzzy is NEW));

8. SELECT AgeFuzzy AND YearFuzzy FROM SPORTS WHERE ((AgeFuzzy is INTERMEDIATE) AND (YearFuzzy is RECENT));
9. SELECT AgeFuzzy AND YearFuzzy FROM SPORTS WHERE ((AgeFuzzy is EXPERT) AND (YearFuzzy is VERY OLD));
10. SELECT AgeFuzzy AND YearFuzzy FROM SPORTS WHERE ((AgeFuzzy is EXPERT) AND (YearFuzzy is OLD));
11. SELECT AgeFuzzy AND YearFuzzy FROM SPORTS WHERE ((AgeFuzzy is EXPERT) AND (YearFuzzy is NEW));
12. SELECT AgeFuzzy AND YearFuzzy FROM SPORTS WHERE ((AgeFuzzy is EXPERT) AND (YearFuzzy is RECENT));
13. SELECT AgeFuzzy AND YearFuzzy FROM SPORTS WHERE ((AgeFuzzy is MASTER) AND (YearFuzzy is VERY OLD));
14. SELECT AgeFuzzy AND YearFuzzy FROM SPORTS WHERE ((AgeFuzzy is MASTER) AND (YearFuzzy is OLD));
15. SELECT AgeFuzzy AND YearFuzzy FROM SPORTS WHERE ((AgeFuzzy is MASTER) AND (YearFuzzy is NEW));
16. SELECT AgeFuzzy AND YearFuzzy FROM SPORTS WHERE ((AgeFuzzy is MASTER) AND (YearFuzzy is RECENT));

Hybrid Query Set

There is one more query set which is a combination of the earlier 3 query sets namely Excellent, Optimal and Fair query set. The query cost is computed using the equation

$$QC = average\left(\left(\min(QCI) + \left(0.5 \times average(QCI)\right)\right), \left(\max(QCI) - \left(0.5 \times average(QCI)\right)\right)\right) \qquad (5)$$

This query set can be used in a restricted manner based on the need for extracting information. If the data is available as an intersection of 3 fuzzy sets, we need not directly use the excellent query set. Instead we could use the hybrid query set to get the required information.

The fuzzy SQL rules which are used for Hybrid query set (8 queries) are listed below:

1. SELECT AgeFuzzy AND YearFuzzy FROM SPORTS WHERE ((AgeFuzzy is AMATEUR) OR (AgeFuzzy is INTERMEDIATE) OR (AgeFuzzy is EXPERT)) AND (YearFuzzy is OLD)));
2. SELECT AgeFuzzy AND YearFuzzy FROM SPORTS WHERE ((AgeFuzzy is AMATEUR) OR (AgeFuzzy is INTERMEDIATE) OR (AgeFuzzy is EXPERT)) AND (YearFuzzy is NEW));
3. SELECT AgeFuzzy AND YearFuzzy FROM SPORTS WHERE (((AgeFuzzy is AMATEUR) OR (AgeFuzzy is INTERMEDIATE) OR (AgeFuzzy is EXPERT) AND (YearFuzzy is RECENT));
4. SELECT AgeFuzzy AND YearFuzzy FROM SPORTS WHERE ((AgeFuzzy is AMATEUR) AND ((YearFuzzy is VERY OLD) OR (YearFuzzy is OLD) OR (YearFuzzy is NEW)));
5. SELECT AgeFuzzy AND YearFuzzy FROM SPORTS WHERE ((AgeFuzzy is INTERMEDIATE) AND ((YearFuzzy is VERY OLD) OR (YearFuzzy is OLD) OR (YearFuzzy is NEW)));

6. SELECT AgeFuzzy AND YearFuzzy FROM SPORTS WHERE ((AgeFuzzy is EXPERT) AND ((YearFuzzy is VERY OLD) OR (YearFuzzy is OLD) OR (YearFuzzy is NEW)));

7. SELECT AgeFuzzy AND YearFuzzy FROM SPORTS WHERE ((AgeFuzzy is MASTER) AND ((YearFuzzy is VERY OLD) OR (YearFuzzy is OLD) OR (YearFuzzy is NEW)));

8. SELECT AgeFuzzy AND YearFuzzy FROM SPORTS WHERE ((AgeFuzzy is AMATEUR) OR (AgeFuzzy is INTERMEDIATE) OR (AgeFuzzy is EXPERT)) AND ((YearFuzzy is VERY OLD) OR (YearFuzzy is OLD) OR (YearFuzzy is NEW)));

Data Classification

The data is classified and grouped into fuzzy sets. The choice of query set for the data is decided based on degree of membership. Five broad categories of membership degrees are used for the data analysis:

- Very High,
- High,
- Medium,
- Low,
- Very Low.

Very High

The data with very high degree of membership uses a Fair query set. This is because we know for sure the information could be extracted from a single fuzzy set.

High

The data with High degree of membership uses a Hybrid query set. Here we use a combination of 3 types of queries excellent, optimal and fair to extract the information. Typically such queries encompass 3 fuzzy sets.

Medium

The data with Medium degree of membership uses a Optimal query set. The information here is predicted to come from 2 fuzzy sets. Such queries optimally check only 2 fuzzy sets to extract the desired information.

Low

The data with Low degree of membership uses a Hybrid query set. Here again the desired information is predicted to come from 3 fuzzy sets for which we use a combination of the 3 types of queries (Excellent, Optimal and Fair).

Very Low

The data with Very Low degree of membership uses an excellent query set. This type of data relies on maximum efficiency of the query to extract information as the data is expected to come from 4 fuzzy sets and is widely scattered.

The next section discusses the salient points of the algorithm proposed in this technique.

Algorithm

- Define fuzzy based rules on SQL.
- Compute the QCI for fuzzy based SQL statement as (QCI= ((w1 * Query execution time)+(w2* Query memory utilized))/ (w1+w2).
- Set Threshold (T1) for query set as average of query processing times.
- If (query processing time < (0.5 *T1)):
  ◦ Group query set as Excellent.
- If (query processing time =(0.5 * T1)):
  ◦ Group query set as Optimal.
- If (query processing time > (0.5 * T1)):
  ◦ Group query set as Fair.
- Based on QCI split the fuzzy rule sets into 4 categories:
  ◦ Quick processing rule set (Excellent query set),
  ◦ Average processing rule set (Optimal query set),
  ◦ Slow processing rule set (Fair query set),
  ◦ Combination of Excellent, Optimal and Fair (Hybrid query set).
- Classify the data based on degree of membership VERY HIGH, HIGH, MEDIUM, VERY LOW and LOW.
- When the degree of membership is VERY HIGH:
  ◦ Use Fair query set,
  ◦ QC = max(QCI).
- When degree of membership is HIGH or LOW:
  ◦ Use Hybrid query set,
  ◦ QC=average (((min (QCI) +(0.5 * average (QCI)))& (max(QCI) – (0.5 * average (QCI)))).
- When degree of membership is MEDIUM
  ◦ Use Optimal query set
  ◦ QC=average (QCI)
- When degree of membership is VERY LOW:
  ◦ Use Excellent query set,
  ◦ QC=min(QCI).
- End the procedure.

SIMULATION RESULTS

The algorithm has been simulated using SQL Fiddle on Oracle 11 database using a data set comprising of 120 records using fuzzy variables of Age and Year. The output on executing the Fuzzy SQL queries on Oracle 11 database has been illustrated in Figure 5.

The simulation results based on the performance attributes has been analysed in the next section.

Performance Attributes

The datasets were examined with fuzzy queries comparing the query cost and memory. The simulations were carried out using normal SQL queries which uses crisp values and the same was compared against fuzzy SQL queries where fuzzy values were also used.

The performance has been evaluated based on 3 parameters:

1. Query processing time,
2. Query Memory consumed,
3. Query Compatibility Index (QCI).

Query Processing Time

The query processing time tends to reduce when a fuzzy query is being used based on data set after discretisation. It could be observed from the experimental simulation that the processing time for a query

Figure 5. Output on executing the fuzzy SQL query

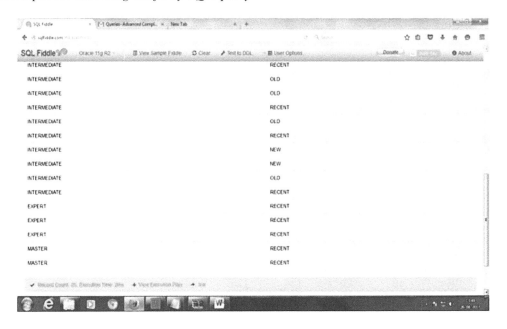

tends to increase with increase in number of data records as shown in Figure 6. When 40 records are being processed, a normal SQL query consumes 30 units as compared to a fuzzy query which consumes only 8 units. When 140 records are being processed, a normal query consumes 51 units whereas a fuzzy query consumes 47 units. On average for 40 records, the normal query consumes 40 units whereas a fuzzy query would take 29 units of time as shown in Figure 7. The reduction in time on using a fuzzy SQL query would be 21%, compared to a normal query as indicated in Figure 8.

Figure 6. Table on query effectiveness

Table on Query Effectiveness

No. of data records	Normal query			Fuzzy Query			Reduction query time Rqt = ((Nqt-Fqt)/Nqt))*100	Reduction query memory Rqm = ((Nqm-Fqm)/NQm))*100	Query effectiveness (QE) = (QCI(NQ)-QCI(FQ)) / QCI(NQ))
	Normal Query processing time (Nqt)	Normal Query memory (Nqm)	QCI(NQ) = ((2*Nqt) + (3*Nqm)) / 5	Fuzzy Query processing time (Fqt)	Fuzzy Query memory (Fqm)	QCI(FQ)=((2*Fqt) + (3*Fqm))/5			
40	30	45	39	8	18	14	40	60	64.1
60	34	47	41.8	22	21	21.4	38.24	55.32	48.8
80	35	48	42.8	29	28	28.4	20	41.67	33.64
100	43	55	50.2	34	39	37	9.3	29.09	26.29
120	47	56	52.4	37	43	40.6	8.51	23.21	22.52
140	51	58	55.2	43	47	45.4	7.84	18.97	17.75
Average	40	51.5	46.9	28.83	32.67	31.13	20.65	38.04	35.52

Figure 7. Comparison of query processing times

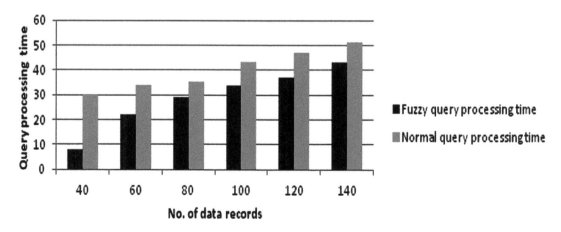

Figure 8. Reduction in query processing times

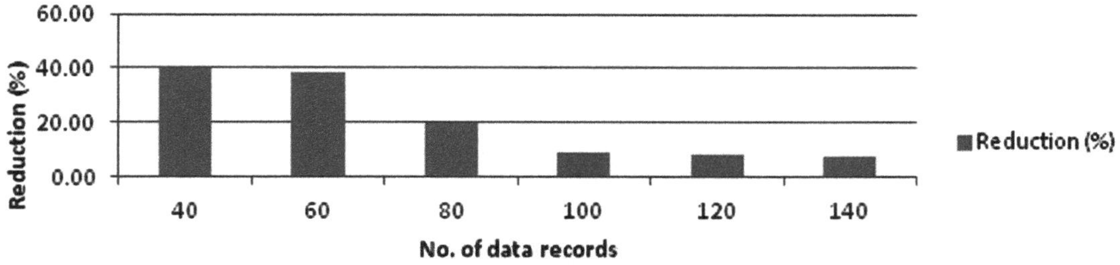

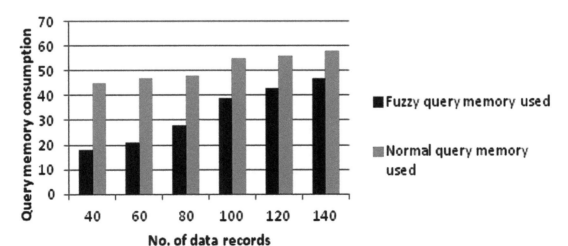

Query Memory Consumed

The query memory consumed also tends to increase when the number of records increases. When 40 records are queried with a normal SQL query, the memory consumed would be 45 units, compared to a fuzzy query which consumes only 18 units (see Figure 6). For 140 records, a normal query consumes 58 units whereas a fuzzy query consumes 47 units (see Figure 9 and Figure 10). On average 40 records would consume 51.5 units when a normal query is used and 32.67 units when a fuzzy query is used (see Figure 6 and Figure 9). The reduction in query memory consumed on using a fuzzy query is 38%, compared to a normal SQL query (see Figure 10).

Query Compatibility Index (QCI)

The normal SQL query is compared with a fuzzy SQL using a query compatibility index which is a weighted average of the query processing time and query memory consumed. It could be observed that the QCI increases with increase in number of data records. When 40 records are accessed, the normal

Figure 9. Comparison of memory consumed by queries

Figure 10. Reduction in consumption of memory

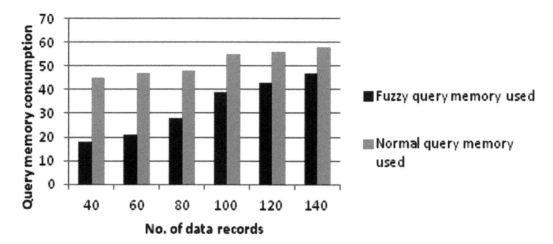

SQL has a QCI of 39 whereas a fuzzy SQL query has a QCI of 14 (Figure 6). When 140 records are accessed, a normal SQL query has a QCI of 55.2 whereas a fuzzy SQL query has a QCI of 45.4 (Figure 6 and Figure 11). On average for 40 records, the normal SQL query has a QCI of 46.90, compared to a fuzzy SQL query which has a QCI of 31.13. The reduction in QCI on using a fuzzy SQL query is 36%, compared to a normal SQL query (Figure 12). The average query effectiveness lies between 26% to 33%.

CONCLUSION

A fuzzy query based approach for a single database with many data sets has been presented to assess the big data quality aspects. This work has made a comparison of a fuzzy based query approach and a

Figure 11. Comparison of Query Compatibility Index (QCI)

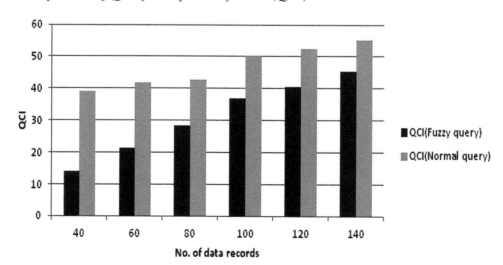

Figure 12. Reduction in QCI (%)

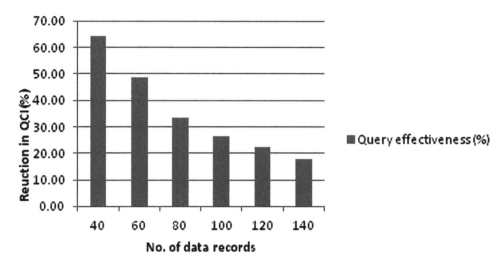

normal query based approach. A fuzzy rule base has been constructed and the rules have been categorized as EXCELLENT, OPTIMAL, FAIR and HYBRID based on the Query Compatibility Index. This work attempts to ensure that information is obtained with an optimal query processing time and memory based on the data set examined. The work also highlights the complexity level that could be added to the query for an optimal query compatibility index. The fuzzy rules have been formulated using Mamdani's Inference engine where the inputs and outputs are chosen as fuzzy sets. The query rule set is chosen based on the scattering of data points in a data set.

FUTURE RESEARCH DIRECTIONS

The work can be extended to a Big data platform like Hadoop. The query set categorization could also be analysed by using Hive queries by integrating multiple databases. Instead of analyzing only the scattering of data points within a data set from a single database, the complexity of the data set may be increased. The data set could be an intersection of multiple databases and the data sets could be grouped as a cluster.

Using these data sets in a Hadoop database the fuzzy based query model could be extended to such a scenario.

REFERENCES

Banerjee, M., Chen, Z., & Gangopadhyay, A. (2014). A generic and distributed privacy preserving classification method with a worst-case privacy guarantee.Journal Distributed and Parallel Database, 32(1), 5-35.

Basgalupp, M. P., Barros, R. C., De Carvilo, & Freitas. (2014). Evolving Decision Trees with beam search based initialization and lexicography multiobjective evaluation. Journal Information Sciences, 258, 160-181.

Basili, V. R., & Weiss, D. M. (1984). A Methodology for Collecting Valid Software Engineering Data. *IEEE Transactions on Software Engineering*, *10*(3), 728–738. doi:10.1109/TSE.1984.5010301

Berendt, B., & Preibusch, S. (2014). Better decision support through exploratory discrimination-aware data mining: Foundations and empirical evidence. Journal Artificial Intelligence and Law, 22(2), 175-209.

Criminisi, A., Shotton, J., & Konukoglu, E. (2011). Decision Forests: A unified Framework for Classification, Regression, Density Estimation, Manifold learning and Semi Supervised Learning. *Journal Foundation and Trends in Computer Graphics and Vision*, *7*(2-3), 1–150.

Doulkeridis & Norvag. (2014). A survey of large-scale analytical query processing in MapReduce. *The VLDB Journal, 23*(3), 1-27.

Evans, L., Lohse, N., & Summers, M. (2013). A fuzzy-decision-tree approach for Manufacturing technology selection exploiting experience-based information.Journal Expert Systems with Applications, 40(16), 6412-6426.

Gorodov & Gubarev. (2013). Analytical review of data visualization methods in application to Big Data. *Journal of Electrical and Computer Engineering*, (22), 1-7.

Hudec, M. (2011). Fuzzy Improvement of the SQL. *Yugoslav Journal of Operations Research*, *21*(2), 239–251. doi:10.2298/YJOR1102239H

Jennex, M. E. (2011). *Knowledge Management System Success Factors* (2nd ed.). doi:10.4018/978-1-60566-709-6

Jennex, M. E., & Olfman, L. (2003). A Knowledge Management Success Model (2003). An Extension of DeLone and McLean's IS Success Model.*Ninth Americas Conference on Information Systems*.

Kumar, P. K., Venkata Subramanian, D., Chokkalingam, S.P., & Manoharan. R. (2014).*Multidimesnsional and Decision Tree Based Frameworks for Big Data Quality Assessment*. 2014 International Conference on Business Intelligence and Analytics.

Kwon, O., & Sim, J. M. (2013). Effects of data set features on the performances of classification algorithms. *Journal Expert Systems with Applications: An International Journal*, *40*(5), 1847–1857. doi:10.1016/j.eswa.2012.09.017

Mamdani, E. H., & Assilan, S. (1975). An Experiment in Linguistic Synthesis with a Fuzzy Logic Controller. *International Journal of Man-Machine Studies*, *7*(1), 1–13. doi:10.1016/S0020-7373(75)80002-2

Pawar, Y.S., Sapre, R.G. & Sayali, R. S. (2011). On Effective Data Retrieval from SQL by use of Fuzzy logic. *International Journal of Fuzzy Mathematics and Systems, 1*(2), 173-180.

Poonam. (2014). Fuzzy to SQL Conversion using Gefred Model with the help of MATLAB. *International Journal of Computer Applications, 104*(17).

Serban, Vanschoren, Kietz & Bernstein. (2013). A survey of intelligent assistants for Data Analysis. *Journal ACM Computing Surveys, 45*(3).

Shamsi, Khojaye, & Qasmi. (2013). Data Intensive Cloud Computing: Requirements, Expectations, Challenges and Solutions. *Journal of Grid Computing, 11*(2), 281-310.

Strohmeier, S., & Piazza, F. (2013). Domain Driven Data mining in Human Resource Management: A review of current research.Journal Expert Systems with Applications, 40(7), 2410-2420.

Subramanian, V. D., Geetha, & Hussain. (2011). Measurement Process and Multi-dimensional Model For Evaluating Knowledge Management Systems. *International Conference on Research and Innovation in Information Systems*. International Islamic University, Malaysia (IIUM) and Universiti Teknologi Malaysia(UTM).

Subramanian, V., & Geetha, A. (2012). Application of Multi-dimensional Metric Model, Database and WAM for KM System Evaluation. *International Journal of Knowledge Management*, 8(4), 1–21. doi:10.4018/jkm.2012100101

Suegno, M. (1985). *Industrial Applications of Fuzzy Control*. New York, NY: Elsevier Science Inc.

Venkat & Geetha. (2012). Application of Multidimensional metric model, database and WAM for KM system evaluation. *International Journal of Knowledge Management*, 1–21.

Venkata, S. D., Geetha, A., & Hussain, M. (2011). Measurement Process and Multi-dimensional Model For Evaluating Knowledge Management Systems.*IEEE International Conference on Research and Innovation in Information Systems*.

Chapter 2
Fuzzy–Clustering–Based Intelligent and Secured Energy–Aware Routing

Selvakumar Kamalanathan
Anna University, India

Sai Ramesh Lakshmanan
Anna University, India

Kannan Arputharaj
Anna University, India

ABSTRACT

In many applications such as disaster management, temperature control, weather forecasting, industrial control system and forest fire detection, it is very difficult for a human to monitor and control each and every event in real time. Even with advancement in technology, this issue has remained a challenging task. The existing Wireless Network may not be suitable for data communication with human network. Hence, to monitor and control the physical parameters of the environment, a special device with needed functionalities is required. The network which is formed with these devices is known as sensor network. This is used to monitor, control and send the collected information to the end user. These networks are formed with a large number of sensor nodes with limitation such as self-energized, low computation power, infra-structure less, multi-hop communication and without central administrator control. Due to the ad hoc nature, the nodes are deployed unevenly over a geographical region, it is necessary to provide some mechanism to manage and control the topology of the sensor nodes to prolong their life time. Clustering algorithms are useful for data mining, compression, probability density estimation and many other important tasks like IDS. Clustering algorithm utilize a distance metric in order to partition network traffic patterns so that patterns within a single group have same network characteristics than in a different group. The proposed system builds a Fuzzy logic clustering model that can perform three different types of clusters in order to achieve the secure and energy aware routing of packets.

DOI: 10.4018/978-1-5225-1008-6.ch002

INTRODUCTION

The heavy control overhead of high-density WSNs requires a cluster structure for achieving better performance since cluster structure reduces the routing overhead. Clustering helps to form small groups of nodes by dividing a large network into sub groups based on certain rules (Hsi-Lu Chao & Chen-Lung Chang 2008). Any node in each cluster is dynamically elected to the role of cluster head based on some criterion (e.g., Energy, Distance from the Base Station, lowest ID). Nodes within minimum hop within the transmission range of a cluster head will become the cluster member. A Gateway is a non-cluster head node with inter-cluster links, so it can access neighbouring clusters and forward information between clusters. Various distributed computation techniques can be applied to create clusters dynamically in WSNs.

A cluster topology provides a way to effectively manage the resources to improve the computation power, reduce overhead during data transmission, minimize end to end delay and maximize throughput. Hence, a new and efficient secure routing protocol called "Fuzzy Clustering based Intelligent and Secured Energy Aware Routing (FCISEAR) Protocol" has been proposed in this paper for providing effective and energy aware routing. The main usage of this newly developed protocol is that this protocol is secure as well as energy efficient and is independent of the application areas. Since it use fuzzy logic clustering is proposed for routing decisions, it is more efficient than the existing protocols.

In this work, the clustering process is conducted in three phases namely, Cluster Head Election, Cluster formation, Cluster based Routing and Maintenance. The cluster head election phase will be conducted under different conditions as initial condition, cluster head failure and critical energy level. The cluster heads are elected based on the cost metric computed using the node's remaining energy and the distance from the base station. It is assumed that the node will know its position using some localization technique. In addition to this, it is assumed that the consumption of energy is only due to transmission of the data. One among the nodes will be elected as a cluster head based on the metrics.

After the election, the CH will use the Modified-K Hop Clustering algorithm to form the cluster. Then, all the nodes within the K-hop distance will become the member of the cluster head and participate in the routing process. Traditionally, in the sensor network every node will send the information using multi-hop communication and flooding to reach the destination. Though, the multi-hop communication reduces the transmission energy but the flooding causes more energy loss due to duplication of the same information in all the directions through every node in the network. This degrades the performance and drastically reduces the network lifetime. In order to address these issues, in this research work a self-optimization technique using a modified Minimum Spanning Tree algorithm has been proposed and implemented. In this algorithm, nodes in the cluster can be grouped and operated in any one of the following three cluster groups such as Low packet transmission node group, Medium packet transmission cluster group and High packet transmission cluster group. Due to this, the participation of the number nodes can be reduced at a time of routing. So, the overall network energy consumption is minimized and performance can be improved. In addition to this, the routing concepts can be incorporated along with optimization to improve the routing process by avoiding floods and routing loops in the networks.

BACKGROUND

The main goal of developing secured routing protocols is to ensure that transmission of messages that takes place between the nodes of the wireless networks and thereby the forwarding of data through the intermediate nodes is consistent and protected. Provision of Quality of Service (QoS) is an important issue in the design of wireless sensor networks. In the past Logambigai and Kannan (2014) proposed an efficient routing technique called Quality of Service aware Energy Efficient Routing protocol for WSNs. Two QoS metrics namely hop count and energy are used in their work. Zhou and Haas (1999) have used threshold cryptography to provide secure routing and to establish secure key management service. However, a dealer should be present to issue the global secret key. This increases the complexity and vulnerability. Guerrero et al (2000) have used a different approach wherein extra facilities are installed in the network to detect and mitigate routing misbehaviour with the help of watchdogs and path raters. This consumes more memory and increases the computation demands at the intermediate node. Moreover, this protocol is able to work only with source routing protocols like DSR and unable to work with distance vector routing protocol like AODV. Many researchers have worked in the area of secure routing protocols and these protocols have their own advantages and limitations (Hu et al 2002, Papadimitrators & Haas 2002).

Many of the secure routing protocols are in requirements of a companion key management algorithm to encrypt the routing messages. These key management algorithms suffer from excessive overhead due to the self-organizing nature of wireless and mobile ad hoc networks (Guerrero & Asokan 2002). Kong et al (2001) proposed a distributed mechanism for issuing and renewing the tokens. In this token mechanism, each node has to renew the token from its neighbours once its token expires to continue to take part in the network. Moreover, in this scheme, only a group of nodes can collaboratively sign the token and individual nodes can not to do so. Most of the existing protocols concentrate in the encryption of routing messages and thereby to make the routing table reliable. However, they did not focus on the authenticity of nodes that are forwarding routing messages and data. Therefore, new research works have been carried out to provide effective security for routing in wireless sensor networks.

A packet forwarding ratio based evaluation of node trust and a continued product of node trusts to estimate a path trust (Feng Li et al 2010) combined with the simple model, a novel multipath reactive routing protocol, ad hoc on demand trusted-path distance vector is proposed to discover trustworthy forward paths and alleviate the attacks from malicious nodes. In this protocol, a source establishes multiple trustworthy paths as candidates to a destination in a single route discovery. A route discovery is initiated only when all paths break or fail to meet the trust requirements of data packets. This protocol provides a flexible and feasible approach to choose a shortest path in all path candidates. Performance comparison of the existing routing protocols shows that this protocol is able to achieve a remarkable improvement in the packet delivery ratio and detect most malicious attacks.

An autonomic trust management solution for the component-based software system is proposed (Zheng Yan et al 2011). This solution is based on the adaptive trust control model that facilitates specification, evaluation, establishment, and ensuring the trust relationships among system entities. They introduced the influence of control mechanisms into the trust model, which supports adaptive trust control and management according to trust assessment based on runtime performance observation and perform the routing in on-demand based approach (Hui Xia et al 2013).

A highly scalable cluster-based hierarchical trust management protocol (Fenye et al 2012) for Wireless Sensor Networks (WSNs) to effectively deal with selfish or malicious nodes. Their protocol designed by comparing subjective trust generated as a result of protocol execution at runtime against objective trust obtained from actual node status. To demonstrate the utility of their hierarchical trust management protocol, they apply it to trust-based geographic routing and trust-based intrusion detection. For trust-based intrusion detection, they discover that there exists an optimal trust threshold for minimizing false positives and false negatives. Furthermore, trust-based intrusion detection outperforms traditional anomaly-based intrusion detection approaches in both the detection probability and the false positive probability.

A multipath extension of a hierarchical routing (Jemili et al 2012), which constructs link-disjoint paths and selects less congested and correlated paths for an efficient data transfer and resources use. The performance of the multipath algorithm is witnessed by simulation results. The proposed multipath extension is more effective under various traffic loads in terms of packet delivery ratio and control overhead.

A novel trust computation model called Secured Trust for evaluating agents in multi agent environments (Anupam Das et al 2012). Secured Trust can ensure secured communication among agents by effectively detecting strategic behaviours of malicious agents. Serique et al (2012) proposed an evaluation mechanism that aims to mitigate routing misbehaviour and other network failures. Four attributes of the routes are considered: level of activity, trust, mobility and number of hops. They performed simulations using the DSR protocol in scenarios with selfish nodes and dynamic topology in order to cause anomalies in the network. The routing information obtained containing the paths taken, the success rates and the attributes of the routes. To learn the best routes, they trained the decision tree by induction using the C 4.5 algorithm.

Comparing with all these works available in the literature, the work proposed in this thesis is different in many aspects. First, hybrid routing is proposed in this work so that the benefits of both proactive and reactive routing protocols are provided here. This work uses a proactive algorithm for route discovery and route maintenance where the nodes of the network maintain topological information of the network. Second, in route discovery, we make use of a novel modified minimum spanning tree algorithm to optimize distance and energy of nodes. Third, in route maintenance, the 1-hop neighbours of active nodes are maintained as passive nodes. These passive nodes will become active whenever a node or link failure occurs and hence provides an automatic recovery from failures. As a result of all these features, we are able to reduce the energy consumption and routing overhead using fuzzy K-means clustering approach.

Moreover, the existing reactive routing protocols use flooding of route requests throughout the network for route discovery and hence consume more power at the nodes and also network bandwidth. In this research work, the bandwidth consumption is reduced by restricting the propagation of route request packets during route discovery by using fuzzy clustering. In such systems, path failures are notified to the source and when the source node knows the path failures, it reinitiates the finding the route. In this thesis, a new reactive route maintenance scheme has been proposed which can repair the broken links locally by maintaining some additional details in the nodes on the path with negligible overhead. Finally, security is considered in addition to the handling of link and node failures in this research works.

FUZZY CLUSTERING BASED INTELLIGENT AND SECURED ENERGY AWARE ROUTING (FCISEAR) PROTOCOL

This research work considers three parameters such as node trust value, path trust value and packet transmission range of node's that are sent to the Fuzzy clustering module to cluster the nodes. Cluster based routing algorithms are energy-efficient in wireless sensor networks due to the use of CHs for routing. This work focuses on Clustering based routing using Fuzzy C-means (FCM) mechanism and a random node will be selected as cluster head since initially all nodes have the same amount of power and the node having the highest residual energy elects itself cluster head. Figure 1 shows the algorithm representation of FCISEAR protocol.

Figure 1. Algorithm representation of FCISEAR approach and modified minimum spanning tree based shortest path estimation

Algorithm : Fuzzy Clustering based Intelligent and Secured Energy Aware Routing (FCISEAR)

Input : Let Z be the set of 25 sensor nodes from WSN

Output: c number of clusters C_c

Given the dataset Z, N, TV, P_r, PTR the number of nodes, $\varepsilon > 0$ -the tolerance value and matrix A.

repeat for j=1 to N do

    Step 1: Initialize the partition matrix randomly, such that $U^{(0)} \in M_{fc}$

    Step 2: Computed the weighted means:

$$Z_j = \frac{\sum_{i=1}^{N} \mu_{ij}^m O_i}{\sum_{i=1}^{N} \mu_{ij}^m}, \quad 1 \le i \le c$$

    Step 3: Use the distance formula given below to obtain the distance:

$$dij = \sqrt{\left(o_i - z_i\right)^2 + \left(o_j - z_j\right)^2}, \quad 1 \le i \le c, \quad 1 \le j \le N$$

    Step 4: Modify the obtained through partition:

        for $1 \le j \le N$

            if $d_{ij} > 0$ *for all* $i = 1, 2, ..., c$

$$u_{ij} = \frac{1}{\sum_{k=1}^{c} \left(\dfrac{d_{ij}}{d_{kj}}\right)^{2/m-1}},$$

    otherwise

$$u_{ij} = 0, \text{if } d_{ij} > 0, \text{and } u_{ij} \in [0,1] \text{ with } \sum_{i=1}^{c} \mu_{ij} = 1$$

for j=1 to n do

Step 5: Compute the Threshold value (Th_o):

$$R_i = \left[\frac{d_i}{E_i}\right]_{i=0}^{n}, (excluding CH \text{ and } BCH)$$

Identify the node n_i (choose a node randomly from the network.)

Step 6: if (energy of all nodes is equal) **then**
    if (metric (n_i) > Th_o)
        elect the node n_i as the new cluster head as CH
        new metric = metric (CH)
    else goto **Step 7**

Step 7: if (metric (n_i) < new metric) **then**
    elect the node as Backup CH.
    else goto **Step 5**

Step 8: If energy-level > Min-energy and dist (Base station) < CH:

$$Th_1 = \frac{E_n - \max\{K_i * E_c * t\} * n}{n}$$

if (metric (n_i) > Th_1)
    elect n_i as new cluster head as CH and call FCM algorithm
    new metric = metric (CH)

Step 9:   **if** (metric (n_i) < new metric) then
    elect the node as Backup CH.
    else goto **Step 5**

until $\left\| U^j - U^{j-1} \right\| < \in$ **(the algorithm is converged)**

Step 10: Call the Modified MST algorithm to find the optimal path

Step 11: Maintain the routing Table with Energy and Security Extensions

Step 12: Find the route whose path cost is minimum and construct the spanning tree.

Update the necessary details into the topology table.

Step 13: Compute the Metric value

$$Th_0 = \min\{d_i\}_{i=1 \text{ to } n}$$

if Metric of the neighbour is high

Update the information in the routing table

The node along the minimal cost path will be in the active mode.

The non-participating neighbour nodes of the active node will be in the passive mode.

The Packets are routed the cluster Head from the Source to the destination.

Step 14: if CH failed during routing **then**

goto **Step 15**

else

The Cluster Sub Head will take the control.
Advertised to the entire node within the cluster.
end if

Step 15: Call the Cluster Head Election Process

Step 16: Route the Packet to
end for

Cluster head election is one of the key processes in the cluster formation (Khalid Hussain et al 2013). This is due to fact that the remaining phases of the clustering process mainly depended on the election process. The CH election process is conducted under two different conditions namely initial deployment of the nodes and while the system is active after initiation. During the initial condition, every node is assumed to have the same energy level. The election process proposed in this work considers the energy level of as well as its distance as the metrics for each sensor node. Cluster head election is performed based on trust values and behaviour analysis of the nodes existing in the networks. In this work, the trace data are analyzed for intrusions in order to avoid malicious behaviour of the node as well as the trust of nodes. Algorithm Representation of this process is shown Figure 2.

In this work, routing of packets performed only through cluster heads. Since the FCM cluster protocol is a centralized cluster algorithm, the base station is responsible for measuring energy consumption and selecting the trust in paths for routing. This work tends to contemplate let N be a set of sensor nodes and let C_1, C_2, ..., Cc be the clusters formed from the N nodes. The main advantage of this type of routing is to reduce the distance between communication nodes.

In this novel approach model, initially it computes the basic trust using direct discussion with the neighbours. In each node, intelligent agent are deployed in order to compute the basic trust and to maintain history about the neighbours using the Equations 1 to 5. This basic trust is updated dynamically based on the communication using the metrics namely energy consumed, delay values, number of packets dropped by the node, capacity of the node and cooperation of the node with its neighbours. The updated trust values are known as current trust. There are two types of trusts namely basic and current trust are represented by BT_{ij} and current trust denoted by CT_{ij}. The past trust is computed by using basic trust and current trust and is denoted by PTV_{ij}.

$$PTV\left(t\right)_{ij} = \alpha BT\left(t\right)_{ij} + \beta CT\left(t\right)_{ij}, t_1 \leq t \leq t_2 \tag{1}$$

The weights α and β (α, β >=0, α > β, and α + β = 1) are assigned to BT_{ij} and CT_{ij}. Now the basic trust is computed using the relation represented by $SE_m(i,j)$.

Figure 2. Algorithm representation of cluster head election process

Step 1: Find the neighbors of each node **n**.

Step 2 : Calculate the trust score and the distance d of nodes.

Step 3: For every node, compute the sum of the distance **s** and the trust score **TS_i**, with all its neighbors.

Step 4: Apply rules to analyze the past behavior of the nodes.

Step 5: Select the node with maximum trust score, higher behavior value and minimum total distance as the cluster head.

Step 6: Repeat **steps 1** to **5** for all clusters.

$$BT\left(t\right)_{ij}^{t_k} = \frac{\sum\limits_{m=1}^{N_{t_k}} SE_m\left(i,j\right)}{N_{t_k}} \qquad (2)$$

Creditability is another factor established from trust using a threshold. If a node has trust value greater than the threshold, then its creditability is high else if it is near the threshold and goes up and down dynamically, it is called medium. Otherwise, it is called as low.

$$CT\left(t\right)_{irj} = CC\left(t\right)_{ir} \times BT\left(t\right)_{rj}, t_1 \leq t \leq NOW \qquad (3)$$

In this work, current trust is computed using the following mathematical representation is

$$CC\left(t\right)_{ir} = BT\left(t\right)_{i1} \times BT\left(t\right)_{12} \times BT\left(t\right)_{23} \times ... \times BT_{(r-1)r}, t_1 \leq t \leq NOW$$

If *n* nodes are present in the communication, we have current trust values:

$$CT\left(t\right)_{rP1j}, CT\left(t\right)_{rP2j}, ..., CT\left(t\right)_{iPnj}$$

Using these *n* values, *CT(t)* is computed using the form

$$CT\left(t\right)_{ij} = \sum\limits_{k=1}^{n} W_{P_k} \times CT\left(t\right)_{iP_{kj}} \qquad (5)$$

Table 1 shows the basic trust value, current trust vale and path trust value of the each node existing in this experimental setup of this research work. This table existing node based trust vales and its path trust values are provided as input trust value for the clustering phase of this proposed algorithm to perform effective clustering for group communication.

In this research work, the proposed model incorporates Gaussian fuzzifiers for estimating membership values of the number of packets transmitted by each node using the Equation 6. Based on the knowledge of domain experts, input parameters Low, Medium and High are selected. The range of fuzzy value for each linguistic variables of number of packets transmitted is 0.0 to 0.5, 0.4 to 0.8 and 0.7 to 1.0 respectively. Based on this fuzzy membership value the nodes are clustered into three clusters namely; low packet communication, medium packet transmission and high packet transmission nodes. Table 1 depicts the nodes membership value as well as their corresponding linguistic representation.

Packet transmission is performed through the corresponding cluster heads (CH) hence the unwanted packet flooding is completely controlled and energy is preserved. In this proposed model continually monitor and cluster based on their number of packet transmitted per unit time from current cluster to specific cluster. Figure 2 shows the pictorial representation of the three cluster form of the entire nodes describes in Table 1 as well as the number of iteration is taken to form a cluster.

Table 1. Basic trust (BT), Current trust (CT), Path trust (PT) and number of packets sent by node's, fuzzy membership values of packets sent and its linguistic labels

Node	BT	CT	TV	P_T	No. of Packet Sent (PTR)	Mem_Value for No. Packet	Mem_Value Equivalent Ling_variable
N_1	0.98	0.804	0.892	0.791136	5	0.679047	MEDIUM
N_2	0.984	0.84	0.912	0.81144	7	0.845905	HIGH
N_3	0.966	0.891	0.9285	0.708345	3	0.497791	MEDIUM
N_4	0.795	0.907	0.851	0.871627	2	0.411941	LOW
N_5	0.961	0.873	0.917	0.795303	15	0.821682	MEDIUM
N_6	0.911	0.852	0.8815	0.642408	9	0.962306	HIGH
N_7	0.754	0.975	0.8645	0.3627	17	0.650089	MEDIUM
N_8	0.372	0.433	0.4025	0.423041	3	0.497791	LOW
N_9	0.977	0.773	0.875	0.715025	1	0.333246	LOW
N_{10}	0.925	0.852	0.8885	0.283716	14	0.892859	HIGH
N_{11}	0.333	0.277	0.305	0.226863	10	0.992024	HIGH
N_{12}	0.819	0.73	0.7745	0.67379	7	0.845905	HIGH
N_{13}	0.923	0.846	0.8845	0.792702	8	0.912528	HIGH
N_{14}	0.937	0.715	0.826	0.312455	19	0.46969	LOW
N_{15}	0.437	0.361	0.399	0.235372	23	0.186723	LOW
N_{16}	0.652	0.497	0.5745	0.478611	9	0.962306	HIGH
N_{17}	0.963	0.885	0.924	0.57702	17	0.650089	MEDIUM
N_{18}	0.652	0.634	0.643	0.398152	12	0.984845	HIGH
N_{19}	0.628	0.702	0.665	0.65637	15	0.821682	MEDIUM
N_{20}	0.935	0.839	0.887	0.731608	5	0.679047	MEDIUM
N_{21}	0.872	0.919	0.8955	0.309703	22	0.243297	LOW
N_{22}	0.337	0.244	0.2905	0.229116	21	0.309899	LOW
N_{23}	0.939	0.885	0.912	0.885	3	0.497791	LOW
N_{24}	1	0.967	0.9835	0.556025	15	0.821682	MEDIUM
N_{25}	0.575	0.528	0.5515	0.556025	9	0.962306	HIGH

IMPLEMENTATION SCENARIO

The simulation of Fuzzy Clustering based Intelligent and Secured Energy Aware Routing (FCISEAR) has been carried out using NS2 simulator version 2.3.5. In the simulation model, there are 25 (N_1 to N_{25}) WSNs are put in a 1000x1000 square meter area. All nodes have equal energy of 1 Joule at the start of the simulation. The height of the antenna used was 1.5 Metres above the ground and gain of both receiving and transmitting antenna was of value 1. The radio speed was 1 Mega Bytes per Second and the radio electronics energy was 50 Nano joules per bit. Mac Layer type was 802.11. There was a processing delay of 50 micro seconds. The packet transmission power was 0.2 Watt with TwoRay Ground Propagation.

Table 2. NS 2.3.5 simulation parameter

Parameters	Value
Number of nodes	25
Simulation area	1000m x 1000m
Base station location	(75,150)
Mac Layer Type	802.11
Radio propagation speed	3×10^8 m/s
Processing delay	50 us
Radio speed	1 Mbps
Radio electronics energy	50 nJ/bit
Gain of transmitting antenna	1
Gain of receiving antenna	1
Height of the antenna above the ground	1.5 m
Routing Protocol	FCISEAR
Propagation	Two RayGround
Packet Transmission Power	0.2 Watt

The simulation times were set to 1 hour to 1 hour 30 minutes. The simulation parameters are shown in Table 2. Here, the cluster heads are represented in * symbol to differentiate from the other cluster nodes shown in Figure 3.

RESULT AND DISCUSSION

The results obtained from this work are compared with existing works in this section. The packet delivery ratio of the cluster based routing in comparison with the LEACH and other Protocols. It can be observed that the proposed FCISEAR based secured cluster based packet routing approach provides with respect to end-to-delivery rate when it is compared with LEACH, MTE, K-Means and SOC protocols.

Figure 3. Fuzzy cluster representations of sensor nodes

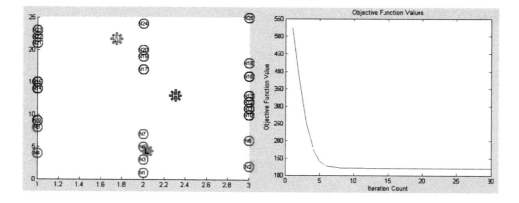

This is because of the CHs does not fail frequently due the non-availability of energy. In direct communication, nodes are quickly losing their energy due to high amount of data transmission. So broadcasting approach also consumes huge volume of energy to forwarding the packets which may not necessary or it may reach the destination already.

Figure 4. Packet delivery ratio

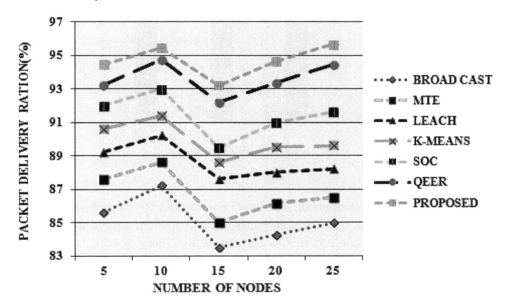

Figure 5. Energy consumption in broad casting

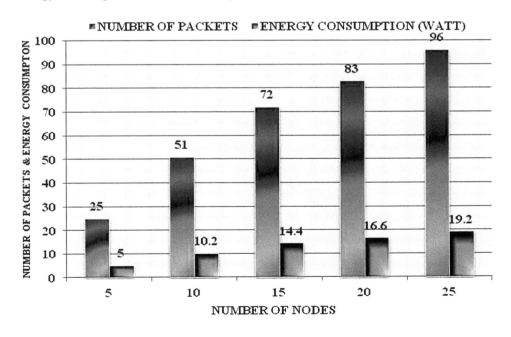

Figure 6. Energy consumption in proposed model

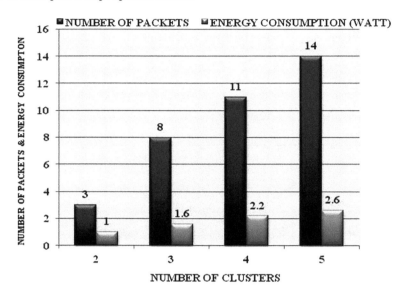

Here, the experiments show that the amount of energy consumed by this approach is drastically reduced when compared with broadcasting approach (10-15 percent of energy is saved). Instead of simply flooding the packets, here packets are routed to corresponding cluster head (CH). Hence, the cluster head is going to identify its routing table to verify whether destination node belongs to it or not. Also compared with existing approaches, the FCISEAR based clustering process takes less amount of energy for transmitting packets. This is due to the fact that the clustering reduces the number of transmissions needed for routing.

Figure 7. Energy consumption comparison

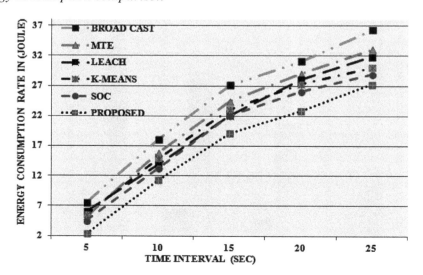

Figure 8. Network life time analysis

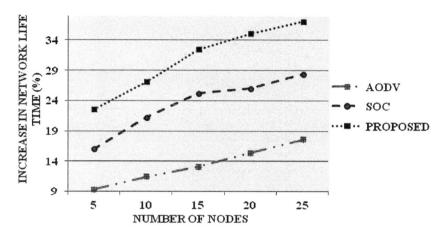

Figure 9. Routing overhead comparison

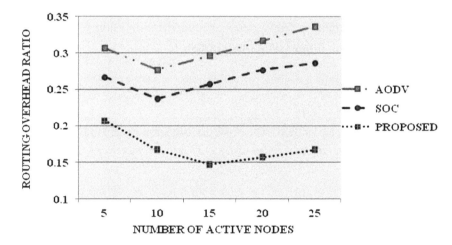

It is observed that the proposed FCISEAR based clustering process increases the network lifetime in comparison with the existing AODV and SOC protocol. Since clustering reduces the amount of required nodes needed for routing and therefore, it compensates the additional time and energy which were required to perform clustering when compared with the existing SOC and AODV protocol. This proves that the proposed protocol is superior to other routing protocols in routing overhead when mobility is considered as well as is more efficient in terms of energy which are shown in Figures 4-10.

CONCLUSION

In this proposed model, an energy aware and intelligent secured routing algorithm that uses Fuzzy clustering approach has been proposed. This proposed fuzzy clustering based approach produces optimal routes for communication. Moreover, with the assistance of cluster head rotation and modified Minimum

Figure 10. Mobility speed vs level comparison

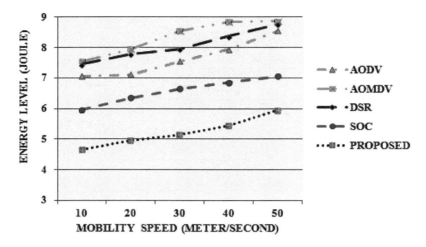

spanning tree approach, primarily based packet routing methods provide optimal performance based on three major clusters from. The major achievements are reduction in energy usage and increase in the amount of packets delivered using fuzzy clustering approach.

REFERENCES

Atakan, , & Taflan Imre, . (2014). M-FDBSCAN: A Multicore Density-Based Uncertain Data Clustering Algorithm. *Turkish Journal of Electrical Engineering & Computer Sciences*, *22*, 143–154. doi:10.3906/elk-1202-83

Bezdek, J. C. (1981). *Pattern Recognition with Fuzzy Objective Function Algorithms. Plenum Press.* New York: Kluwer Academic Publishers. doi:10.1007/978-1-4757-0450-1

Elhawary & Haas. (2011). Energy-Efficient Protocol for Cooperative Networks. *IEEE/ACM Transactions on Networking, 19*(2), 561-574.

Haider & Yusuf. (2009). A Fuzzy Approach to Energy Optimized Routing for Wireless Sensor Networks. *The International Arab Journal of Information Technology, 6*(2), 179-188.

Hussain, K., Abdullah, A. H., Awan, K. M., Ahsan, F., & Hussain, A. (2013). Cluster Head Election Schemes for WSN and MANET: A Survey. *World Applied Sciences Journal*, *23-5*, 611–620.

Jerusha, S. K. (2012). Location Aware Cluster Based Routing In Wireless Sensor Networks. *International Journal of Computer & Communication Technology*, *3-5*, 1–6.

Li, X., Jia, Zhang, Zhang, & Wang. (2010). Trust-Based on-Demand Multipath Routing in Mobile Ad Hoc Networks. *IET-Information Security, 4*(4), 212–223.

Liu, Zheng, Zhang, Chen, & Shen. (2012). Secure and Energy-Efficient Disjoint Multipath Routing for WSNs. *IEEE Transactions on Vehicular Technology, 61*(7), 3255-3265.

Logambigai, R., & Kannan, A. (2014). QEER: QoS aware Energy Efficient Routing Protocol for Wireless Sensor Networks. *Sixth IEEE International Conference on Advanced Computing (ICoAC)*. doi:10.1109/ICoAC.2014.7229745

Maham, Hjørungnes, & Narasimhan. (2011). Energy-Efficient Space-Time Coded Cooperation in Outage-Restricted Multihop Wireless Networks. *IEEE Transactions on Communications, 59*(11), 3111-3121.

Nikhil, R. (2005). Possibilistic Fuzzy c-Means Clustering Algorithm. *IEEE Transactions on Fuzzy Systems, 13-4*, 517–530.

Shu, Krunz, & Liu. (2010). Secure Data Collection in Wireless Sensor Networks Using Randomized Dispersive Routes. *IEEE Transactions on Mobile Computing, 9*(7), 941-954.

Sun, Y.L., Yu, Han, & Ray Liu. (2006). Information Theoretic Framework of Trust Modeling Evaluation for Ad Hoc Networks. *IEEE Journal on Selected Areas in Communications, 24*(2), 305–319.

Vijayakumar, P., Bose, S., & Kannan, A. (2013). Centralized Key Distribution Protocol using the Greatest Common Divisor Method. *Computers & Mathematics with Applications (Oxford, England), 65*(9), 1360–1368. doi:10.1016/j.camwa.2012.01.038

Xia, H., Jia, Z., Ju, L., Li, X., & Sha, E. H.-M. (2013). Impact of Trust Model on On-Demand Multi-Path Routing in Mobile Ad Hoc Networks. *Computer Communications, 36*(9), 1078–1093. doi:10.1016/j.comcom.2012.09.002

Xia, H., Jia, Z., Ju, L., & Zhu, Y. (2011). Trust Management Model for Mobile Ad Hoc Network based on Analytic Hierarchy Process and Fuzzy Theory, IET Wireless. *Sensory Systems, 1-4*, 248–266.

Zhu, J., & Wang, X. (2011). Model and Protocol for Energy-Efficient Routing over Mobile Ad Hoc Networks. *IEEE Transactions on Mobile Computing, 10-11*(11), 1546–1557. doi:10.1109/TMC.2010.259

Chapter 3
Fusion of Fuzzy Multi-Criteria Decision Making Approaches for Discriminating Risk with Relate to Software Project Performance:
A Prospective Cohort Study

Arun Kumar Sangaiah
VIT University, India

Vipul Jain
Victoria University of Wellington, New Zealand

ABSTRACT

The prediction and estimation software risks ahead have been key predictor for evaluating project performance. Discriminating risk is vital in software project management phase, where risk and performance has been closely inter-related to each other. This chapter aims at hybridization of fuzzy multi-criteria decision making approaches for building an assessment framework that can be used to evaluate risk in the context of software project performance in following dimensions: 1) user, 2) requirements, 3) project complexity, 4) planning and control, 5) team, and 6) organizational environment. For measuring the risk for effectiveness of project performance, we have integrated Fuzzy Multi-Criteria Decision Making (FMCDM) and Fuzzy Technique for Order of Preference by Similarity to Ideal Solution (TOPSIS) approaches. Moreover the fusion of FMCDM and TOPSIS has not been adequately investigated in the exiting studies.

DOI: 10.4018/978-1-5225-1008-6.ch003

INTRODUCTION

Software industries realize the importance in the prioritization of project risks for the success of project in the context of performance characteristics. Earlier studies (Chen, 2015; Han, 2015; Na et al., 2007; Takagi et al., 2005) have revealed and identified a wide variety of project management, project failure measures due to cost-schedule overrun, requirements misinterpretations and client dissatisfaction. There are a certain risks (project, technical, and business) involved for any worthwhile software project. Software risk management is vital and has become one of the key factor to obtaining good project outcome and performance. This fact highlights the need for early prediction of software risk and risky projects to enable the planning of essential risk management activities and resources during their implementation, where the risk and performance are closely integrated each other. Suitable planning of resources and actions can effectively increase the success rates of such software projects. Subsequently, previous researchers (Liu & Wang, 2014; Keil et al., 2013; Na et al., 2007; Han & Huang, 2007) have investigated the correlation between risk factors and project outcome. Consistent with earlier literatures, this chapter focuses at proposing an assessment methodology that can be utilized to measure risk in the context of software project performance via five dimensions:

1. Requirements;
2. Estimations;
3. Planning and control;
4. Team organization; and
5. Project management.

Numerous binary prediction approaches have been constructed by statistical techniques for classifying risk-prone projects in the literature. Examples include logistic regression, Bayesian classification, and the association rule. Although the overall classification accuracy of these approaches is at an acceptable level, correctly identifying a risky project at a true-positive rate is still a challenge. Effort investment without the premise that a risky project is correctly identified at the initial stage is ineffective. For project managers, misjudging a risky project diminishes their alertness during implementation. Consequently, the failure rates of the project would increase without prior warning and thus, a great cost would be expended in controlling the crisis. In other words, the incorrect classification of not risky projects at the initial stage does not increase failure rates, even if extra effort and resources are invested. In this context, the classification and prioritization of software risks measured through fuzzy set theory has been presented in this chapter.

THEORETICAL FOUNDATIONS

In this chapter, the FMCDM approach is integrated with TOPSIS the assessment of software risk factors in the context of software project performance using Triangular Fuzzy Numbers (TFNs). The proposed framework for measuring the risk factors on software project performance evaluation methodology covers of two main stages: Firstly, we measure weights of the risk criteria, incorporating FMCDM approach. Secondly, FMCDM weights have been applied in TOPSIS approach to identify the rank and significance that is overall prospect value (risk performance index) of each risk factor.

Fuzzy Multi-Criteria Decision Making (FMCDM) and Fuzzy TOPSIS

The FMCDM approach helps the decision makers to select, evaluate and rank problems according to their weights of a finite set of criteria (Sangaiah & Thangavelu, 2013). Earlier works (Sangaiah et al., 2015; Gopal et al., 2015; Sangaiah et al., 2014) have addressed FMCDM for the assessment of multiple criteria and especially to deal uncertainty and subjective vagueness during the decision-making process for a wide variety of applications through the fuzzy set theory. Therefore, this chapter extends FMCDM approach to determine the risk in the context of software project performance; this is consistent with earlier studies.

TOPSIS, one of the conventional MCDM methods has been widely used to compute the relative importance of alternatives and solving practical decision making problems with its high computational efficiency and comprehensibility (Sangaiah et al., 2014). In addition, recent researches (Sangaiah et al., 2015; Gopal et al., 2015; Sangaiah et al., 2014; Kannan et al., 2014) have explored TOPSIS to handle MCDM problems. Similarly, the basic principle of using TOPSIS in this research is to compute ideal solution (best values realistic of criteria) and negative ideal solution (worst values realistic of criteria) for ranking the software risk factors with relate project outcome/performance.

Previous studies have investigated the impact of FMCDM and TOPSIS for a wide variety of applications. Similarly, earlier studies have investigated hybridization of various approaches such as FMCDM-DEMATEL (Gopal et al., 2015; Patil & Kant, 2014), DEMATEL-TOPSIS (Sangaiah et al., 2014; Baykasoğlu et al., 2013), DEMATEL-FMCDM-TODIM (Sangaiah et al., 2015). However, only limited studies have adopted the hybridization of FMCDM-TOPSIS methods from the perspective of risk analysis in the related literatures. Thus, to address the research gap this chapter study explores the FMCDM-TOPSIS approach while outlining the hybrid methodology for the real data set obtained from the OMRON organization. The computational procedures of FMCDM and TOPSIS approach have been illustrated in the following sections.

FMCDM Approach

The following steps elucidate the FMCDM operational procedure and its data analysis has been summarized as follows:

Step 1: *Determining fuzzy possible rating for the effectiveness of software risk factors.* The decision matrix has been created $\tilde{Y}$ for the possible ratings of software risk factors $\left(c_j, j = 1, 2, 3, \dots n \right)$. The respondents $\left(R^i, i = 1, 2, 3, \dots m \right)$ provided their subjective assessments about the possible ratings of each risk factor with reference to project performance using linguistic scales, as listed in Table 1.

Table 1. Fuzzy membership with Triangular Fuzzy Numbers

Ordinal Scale	Fuzzy Linguistic Variable	Corresponding TFN
3	Strongly agree	(0.9,1.0, 1.0)
2	Agree	(0.7,0.9,1.0)
1	Neither disagree nor agree	(0.3,0.5,0.7)
0	Disagree	(0.0,0.1,0.3)

The decision matrix $\tilde{Y}$ is as follows:

$$
\begin{array}{c}
\\
C_1 \\
C_2 \\
C_3 \\
\vdots \\
C_n
\end{array}
\begin{array}{ccccc}
R^1 & R^2 & R^3 & \cdots & R^m \\
\tilde{a}_1^{1} & \tilde{a}_1^{2} & \tilde{a}_1^{3} & \cdots & \tilde{a}_1^{m} \\
\tilde{a}_2^{1} & \tilde{a}_2^{2} & \tilde{a}_2^{3} & \cdots & \tilde{a}_2^{m} \\
\tilde{a}_3^{1} & \tilde{a}_3^{2} & \tilde{a}_3^{3} & \cdots & \tilde{a}_3^{m} \\
\vdots & \vdots & \vdots & \ddots & \vdots \\
\tilde{a}_n^{1} & \tilde{a}_n^{2} & \tilde{a}_n^{3} & \cdots & \tilde{a}_n^{m}
\end{array}
, i = 1,2,...,m; j = 1,2,...,n
\tag{1}
$$

In this decision matrix, recall that m denotes the number of respondents and n the number of risk factors. Elements $\tilde{y}_i^j = \left(La_i^j, Ma_i^j, Ua_i^j \right)$ represents the fuzzy degree of impact as assessed by i^{th} respondents for j^{th} influential factor.

Step 2: *Aggregating fuzzy possible rating for the effectiveness of software risk factors.* The subjective assessments of each expert may vary according to their experience and knowledge. This study employs the average score method as shown in Eqn. (10), to incorporate the fuzzy performance values of m respondents.

$$
\varpi_j = \frac{1}{m} \left[\sum_{i=1}^{m} \tilde{a}_j^{i} \right]
\tag{2}
$$

where $\varpi_j = \left(L\omega_j, M\omega_j, U\omega_j \right)$ denotes the synthesized fuzzy importance weight of jth influential factor.

Step 3: *Defuzzifying of possible rating for the effectiveness of software risk factors.* Subsequent to the defuzzification process, the triangular fuzzy numbers are aggregated into Best Non-fuzzy Performance (BNP) values; BNP_{w_j} is taken to denote the BNP values for the triangular fuzzy number ϖ_j and this can be produced through Eqn. (11).

$$BNP_{w_j} = \frac{\left[(U\omega_j - L\omega_j) + (M\omega_j - L\omega_j)\right]}{3} + L\omega_j \tag{3}$$

where w_j denotes the important weights of jth influential factor in crisp numbers format.

Step 4: *Apply rank order weight method to calculate the weight of each attribute for effectiveness of software project* performance. First, possible ratings of risk factors on software project performance are determined. Then the important weights of software risk factors are applied in Fuzzy TOPIS method in order to obtain a software risk aspects with reference to software project performance.

$$w(i) = n - \frac{(i+1)}{Sum\ of\ Ranks} \tag{4}$$

where W_i denotes the normalized priority weight of jth software risk criteria obtained through the FMCDM method.

TOPSIS Approach

Step 1: Construct normalized decision matrix.

To transform the various attribute dimensions into non-dimensional attributes, which allows comparisons across the criteria. The normalize scores or data are as follows:

$$R_{ij} = \left. x_{ij} \middle/ \left(\sum_{i=1}^{m} x_{ij}^2\right) \right. \quad for\ i = 1,...,m; j = 1,...,m \tag{5}$$

Step 2: Construct the weighted normalized decision matrix.

Assume we have a set of weights for each criterion is w_j, $for\ i = 1,...,n$. Multiply each column of the normalized decision matrix by its associated weight. Weights used in this step have been derived from FMCDM approach given in Eqn.(4). These weights will be applied on normalized decision matrix R.

An element of the new matrix is:

$$T = \left(t_{ij}\right)_{m \times n_{ij}} = \left(w_j \times r_{ij}\right)_{m \times n}, i = 1,2,...,m \tag{6}$$

Here, weighted normalized decision matrix is represented as t_{ij} is calculated by multiplying weights $\left(w_j\right)$ of the constructs with the normalized fuzzy decision matrix $\left(r_{ij}\right)$.

Step 3: Compute the fuzzy positive ideal solution (FPIS) and fuzzy negative ideal solution (FNIS).

The FPIS and FNIS of the alternatives are computed as follows:
Ideal solution:

$$d_{ib} = \sqrt{\sum_{j=1}^{n}\left(t_{ij} - t_{bj}\right)^2}, i = 1, 2, ..., m \tag{7}$$

Negative ideal solution:

$$d_{iw} = \sqrt{\sum_{j=1}^{n}\left(t_{ij} - t_{wj}\right)^2}, i = 1, 2, ..., m \tag{8}$$

where d_{ib} represents the fuzzy positive ideal solution and d_{iw} represents the fuzzy negative ideal solution. It can be derived with the help of the t_{ij} and t_{wj} fuzzy decision matrices.

Step 5: Compute the closeness coefficient $\left(s_{iw}\right)$ each alternative.

The closeness coefficient c_i represents the distances to the fuzzy positive ideal solution $\left(d_{ib}\right)$ and the fuzzy negative ideal solution $\left(d_{iw}\right)$ simultaneously. The closeness coefficient of each alternative is calculated as:

$$s_{iw} = d_{iw} \Big/ \left(d_{iw} + d_{ib}\right), 0 \le s_{iw} \le 1, i = 1, 2, ..., m \tag{9}$$

Step 6: Rank the alternatives.

In this step, the different alternatives are ranked according to the closeness coefficient $\left(s_{iw}\right)$ in decreasing order. The best alternative is closest to the FPIS and farthest from the FNIS

ASSESSMENT FRAMEWORK FOR SOFTWARE RISK VIA FUZZY SET THEORY

The earlier studies on prioritization of software project risk for the success of project performance have not been adequately available in the existing studies.

Similarly, integrating risk dimensions as shown in Table 2 (requirements, estimations, planning and control, team organization and project management) for the analysis of software project performance is very limited. Furthermore, hybridization of FMCDM-TOPSIS has not been addressed in depth. To address this gap, this chapter has presented the integration of FMCDM-TOPSIS approach for validating project risk from the perspective of software project performance is addressed in this chapter.

The schematic diagram of proposed framework and its computation procedure of hybridization of FMCDM and TOPSIS approaches under a fuzzy environment has shown in Figure 1.

Table 2. Summary of source of measurements obtained from OMRON datasets on evaluation criteria of software risk analysis

Criteria and Sources of Measurement	Code	Evaluation Criteria of Software Risks
Requirements (*R*)	R1	Ambiguous requirements
	R2	Insufficient explanation of the requirements
	R3	Misunderstanding the requirements
	R4	Lack of commitment regarding requirements between the customer and project members
	R5	Frequent requirement changes
Estimations (*E*)	E1	Insufficient awareness of the importance of the estimation
	E2	Insufficient skills or knowledge of the estimation method
	E3	Insufficient estimation for the implicit requirement
	E4	Insufficient estimation for the technical issues
	E5	Lack of stakeholder's commitment for the estimation
Planning (*P*)	P1	Lack of management review for the project plan
	P2	Lack of assignment of responsibility
	P3	Lack of breakdown of the work products
	P4	Unspecified project review milestones
	P5	Insufficient planning of project monitoring and controlling
	P6	Lack of project member's commitment for the project plan
Team Organization (*T*)	T1	Lack of skills and experience
	T2	Insufficient allocation of resources
	T3	Low morale
Project Management (*M*)	M1	Project manager's lack of resource management throughout the project
	M2	Inadequate project monitoring and controlling
	M3	Lack of data needed to keep objective track of a project

Figure 1. The proposed framework of hybrid Fuzzy DEMATEL-TODIM-FMCDM approach for evaluating software risk factors

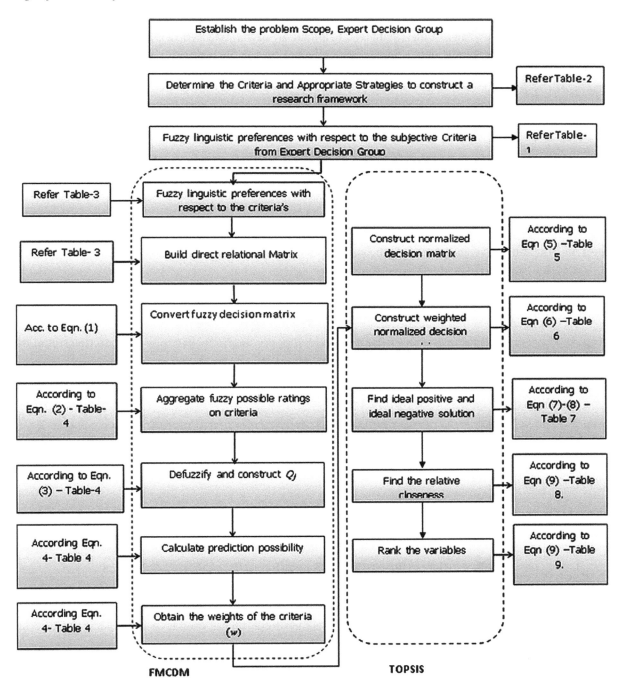

MATERIALS AND METHODS FOR EVALUATING THE SOFTWARE RISK

Consistent with earlier researches (Han, 2015; Takagi et al., 2005) on software risk evaluation, OMRON data set has been used in this chapter to evaluate the effectiveness and efficiency of the proposed methodology. Originally, the data set has been collected for the purpose of predicting risky projects by the Software Engineering Process Group (SEPG) of the Social Systems Business Company (SSBC), OMRON Corporation [15]. The data set covers 40 projects and 22 project risk-related attributes in 5 dimensions, as shown in Table 2. It is noteworthy to point out that the OMRON data set has been collectively identified in (Han, 2015; Takagi et al., 2005).

Calculate the Possible Weights of Software Risk Criteria with Reference to Project Outcome/Performance by FMCDM

The basic steps of FMCDM approach adopted in this chapter are as follows:

Step 1: The subjective judgment of 40 project data used the linguistic assessments for the possible weights of each software risk criteria.

Step 2: The linguistic assessment is assigned into a triangular scale fuzzy numbers in order to form the fuzzy decision matrix and compute the fuzzy possible weights of each criterion by using Eqn. (1), as shown in Table 3.

Step 3: The weighted performance of interval-valued fuzzy decision matrix is build to determine the average fuzzy value of each risk criterion by using Eqn. (2), as shown in Table 4.

Step 4: The BNP value BNP_{w_j} of all constructs are determined (possible weights in crisp number format) by using Eqn. (3), as shown in Table 4.

Step 5 *:* The values of w_j (priority weight across the criteria) of each project is determined by using Eqn. (4). Then w_j values can be used in the fuzzy TOPSIS as shown in Eq.(6) to obtain the possible ratings of risk factors.

Table 3. Corresponding TFNs of software risk factors

Project	R1	R2	R3	R4	R5	E1	E2	E3
1	(0.0,0.1,0.3)	(0.0,0.1,0.3)	(0.0,0.1,0.3)	(0.0,0.1,0.3)	(0.0,0.1,0.3)	(0.7,0.9,1.0)	(0.9,1.0,1.0)	(0.9,1.0,1.0)
2	(0.0,0.1,0.3)	(0.0,0.1,0.3)	(0.0,0.1,0.3)	(0.0,0.1,0.3)	(0.0,0.1,0.3)	(0.0,0.1,0.3)	(0.0,0.1,0.3)	(0.0,0.1,0.3)
3	(0.0,0.1,0.3)	(0.0,0.1,0.3)	(0.0,0.1,0.3)	(0.0,0.1,0.3)	(0.9,1.0,1.0)	(0.0,0.1,0.3)	(0.0,0.1,0.3)	(0.7,0.9,1.0)
4	(0.9,1.0,1.0)	(0.9,1.0,1.0)	(0.7,0.9,1.0)	(0.7,0.9,1.0)	(0.9,1.0,1.0)	(0.0,0.1,0.3)	(0.0,0.1,0.3)	(0.7,0.9,1.0)
5	(0.0,0.1,0.3)	(0.0,0.1,0.3)	(0.0,0.1,0.3)	(0.0,0.1,0.3)	(0.7,0.9,1.0)	(0.0,0.1,0.3)	(0.0,0.1,0.3)	(0.0,0.1,0.3)
6	(0.0,0.1,0.3)	(0.9,1.0,1.0)	(0.7,0.9,1.0)	(0.0,0.1,0.3)	(0.0,0.1,0.3)	(0.7,0.9,1.0)	(0.7,0.9,1.0)	(0.7,0.9,1.0)
7	(0.0,0.1,0.3)	(0.0,0.1,0.3)	(0.7,0.9,1.0)	(0.9,1.0,1.0)	(0.7,0.9,1.0)	(0.0,0.1,0.3)	(0.0,0.1,0.3)	(0.0,0.1,0.3)
8	(0.0,0.1,0.3)	(0.7,0.9,1.0)	(0.9,1.0,1.0)	(0.9,1.0,1.0)	(0.0,0.1,0.3)	(0.3,0.5,0.7)	(0.0,0.1,0.3)	(0.7,0.9,1.0)
9	(0.0,0.1,0.3)	(0.7,0.9,1.0)	(0.0,0.1,0.3)	(0.7,0.9,1.0)	(0.9,1.0,1.0)	(0.0,0.1,0.3)	(0.0,0.1,0.3)	(0.0,0.1,0.3)
10	(0.0,0.1,0.3)	(0.0,0.1,0.3)	(0.0,0.1,0.3)	(0.0,0.1,0.3)	(0.7,0.9,1.0)	(0.0,0.1,0.3)	(0.7,0.9,1.0)	(0.7,0.9,1.0)

Table 4. Corresponding TFNs of software risk factors

Project	E4	E5	P1	P2	P3	P4	P5	P6
1	(0.7,0.9,1.0)	(0.0,0.1,0.3)	(0.7,0.9,1.0)	(0.0,0.1,0.3)	(0.0,0.1,0.3)	(0.0,0.1,0.3)	(0.0,0.1,0.3)	(0.0,0.1,0.3)
2	(0.0,0.1,0.3)	(0.0,0.1,0.3)	(0.0,0.1,0.3)	(0.0,0.1,0.3)	(0.0,0.1,0.3)	(0.7,0.9,1.0)	(0.0,0.1,0.3)	(0.0,0.1,0.3)
3	(0.9,1.0,1.0)	(0.0,0.1,0.3)	(0.0,0.1,0.3)	(0.0,0.1,0.3)	(0.0,0.1,0.3)	(0.0,0.1,0.3)	(0.7,0.9,1.0)	(0.0,0.1,0.3)
4	(0.7,0.9,1.0)	(0.0,0.1,0.3)	(0.7,0.9,1.0)	(0.7,0.9,1.0)	(0.0,0.1,0.3)	(0.0,0.1,0.3)	(0.0,0.1,0.3)	(0.3,0.5,0.7)
5	(0.0,0.1,0.3)	(0.0,0.1,0.3)	(0.0,0.1,0.3)	(0.7,0.9,1.0)	(0.0,0.1,0.3)	(0.7,0.9,1.0)	(0.7,0.9,1.0)	(0.0,0.1,0.3)
6	(0.0,0.1,0.3)	(0.7,0.9,1.0)	(0.0,0.1,0.3)	(0.7,0.9,1.0)	(0.0,0.1,0.3)	(0.0,0.1,0.3)	(0.0,0.1,0.3)	(0.0,0.1,0.3)
7	(0.0,0.1,0.3)	(0.0,0.1,0.3)	(0.0,0.1,0.3)	(0.7,0.9,1.0)	(0.0,0.1,0.3)	(0.9,1.0,1.0)	(0.0,0.1,0.3)	(0.0,0.1,0.3)
8	(0.0,0.1,0.3)	(0.0,0.1,0.3)	(0.7,0.9,1.0)	(0.7,0.9,1.0)	(0.0,0.1,0.3)	(0.0,0.1,0.3)	(0.7,0.9,1.0)	(0.7,0.9,1.0)
9	(0.0,0.1,0.3)	(0.0,0.1,0.3)	(0.7,0.9,1.0)	(0.7,0.9,1.0)	(0.0,0.1,0.3)	(0.7,0.9,1.0)	(0.7,0.9,1.0)	(0.0,0.1,0.3)
10	(0.0,0.1,0.3)	(0.0,0.1,0.3)	(0.0,0.1,0.3)	(0.7,0.9,1.0)	(0.0,0.1,0.3)	(0.0,0.1,0.3)	(0.7,0.9,1.0)	(0.0,0.1,0.3)

Table 5. Corresponding TFNs of software risk factors

Project	O1	O2	O3	M1	M3	M3
1	(0.7,0.9,1.0)	(0.3,0.5,0.7)	(0.0,0.1,0.3)	(0.0,0.1,0.3)	(0.0,0.1,0.3)	(0.0,0.1,0.3)
2	(0.0,0.1,0.3)	(0.0,0.1,0.3)	(0.0,0.1,0.3)	(0.0,0.1,0.3)	(0.0,0.1,0.3)	(0.0,0.1,0.3)
3	(0.0,0.1,0.3)	(0.0,0.1,0.3)	(0.0,0.1,0.3)	(0.0,0.1,0.3)	(0.0,0.1,0.3)	(0.0,0.1,0.3)
4	(0.7,0.9,1.0)	(0.0,0.1,0.3)	(0.0,0.1,0.3)	(0.0,0.1,0.3)	(0.0,0.1,0.3)	(0.0,0.1,0.3)
5	(0.0,0.1,0.3)	(0.0,0.1,0.3)	(0.0,0.1,0.3)	(0.0,0.1,0.3)	(0.7,0.9,1.0)	(0.0,0.1,0.3)
6	(0.0,0.1,0.3)	(0.0,0.1,0.3)	(0.0,0.1,0.3)	(0.0,0.1,0.3)	(0.0,0.1,0.3)	(0.7,0.9,1.0)
7	(0.0,0.1,0.3)	(0.0,0.1,0.3)	(0.0,0.1,0.3)	(0.0,0.1,0.3)	(0.0,0.1,0.3)	(0.0,0.1,0.3)
8	(0.0,0.1,0.3)	(0.0,0.1,0.3)	(0.3,0.5,0.7)	(0.9,1.0,1.0)	(0.0,0.1,0.3)	(0.0,0.1,0.3)
9	(0.0,0.1,0.3)	(0.0,0.1,0.3)	(0.0,0.1,0.3)	(0.0,0.1,0.3)	(0.0,0.1,0.3)	(0.7,0.9,1.0)
10	(0.0,0.1,0.3)	(0.0,0.1,0.3)	(0.0,0.1,0.3)	(0.7,0.9,1.0)	(0.0,0.1,0.3)	(0.0,0.1,0.3)

Applying TOPSIS

The basic steps of Fuzzy-TOPSIS approach used in this study are as follows:

Step 1: Create fuzzy assessment decision matrix, compute possible ratings of alternatives, and normalize the scores in order to find the best criteria as shown in Tables 7-10.

Step 2: Apply the weights which is determined from the FMCDM approach to compute the weighted normalized decision matrix as shown Tables 10-12.

Step 3: The best evaluation and worst evaluation value with respect to each criterion is determined through FPIS and FNIS as shown in Tables 13-15 and Tables 16-18.

Step 4: Obtain relative closeness coefficient to the ideal solution and ranking the risk criteria as given in Table 19.

Table 6. FMCDM: calculation of weights in software risk criteria

Risk Criteria	$\tilde{\omega}_j$	Q_j	Weights	FMCDM Rank
R1	(0.09,0.19,0.37)	0.217	0.024	17
R2	(0.32,0.44,0.58)	0.447	0.069	5
R3	(0.30,0.43,0.58)	0.437	0.063	7
R4	(0.32,0.44,0.58)	0.447	0.069	6
R5	(0.48,0.61,0.72)	0.603	0.083	2
E1	(0.17,0.30,0.48)	0.317	0.043	12
E2	(0.23,0.35,0.51)	0.363	0.049	10
E3	(0.44,0.59,0.72)	0.583	0.079	3
E4	(0.23,0.35,0.51)	0.363	0.049	11
E5	(0.07,0.18,0.37)	0.207	0.018	18
P1	(0.28,0.42,0.58)	0.427	0.055	9
P2	(0.49,0.66,0.79)	0.647	0.087	1
P3	(0.0,0.1,0.3)	0.133	0.004	22
P4	(0.30,0.43,0.58)	0.436	0.059	8
P5	(0.35,0.50,0.65)	0.500	0.075	4
P6	(0.10,0.22,0.41)	0.243	0.028	16
O1	(0.14,0.26,0.44)	0.280	0.034	14
O2	(0.03,0.14,0.34)	0.170	0.010	21
O3	(0.03,0.14,0.34)	0.171	0.010	20
M1	(0.16,0.27,0.44)	0.290	0.040	13
M2	(0.07,0.18,0.37)	0.207	0.018	19
M3	(0.14,0.26,0.44)	0.28	0.034	15

RESULTS AND DISCUSSION

This chapter addresses the key criteria for determining the software risk. The 5 risk dimensions and 22 evaluation criteria have been used to investigate the possible ratings of software risk factors in the context of software project performance. Recall the risk factors have been listed in Table 2. The proposed FMCDM-TOPIS methodology reveals that the DM's have more than one optimum preference in methods for computing the risk factors, while judging the human thoughts in decision making process via hybrid MCDM problem. Subsequently, this chapter justify on two valuable inputs: a cohesive assessment methodology of the risk factors, thus addressing software project performance and a hybrid

Table 7. Normalized decision matrix R1-E3

Project	R1	R2	R3	R4	R5	E1	E2	E3
FMCDM Weights	0.0237	0.0692	0.0632	0.0692	0.083	0.0435	0.0494	0.0791
1	0.0000	0.0000	0.0000	0.0000	0.0000	0.3015	0.3511	0.2739
2	0.0000	0.0000	0.0000	0.0000	0.0000	0.0000	0.0000	0.0000
3	0.0000	0.0000	0.0000	0.0000	0.2394	0.0000	0.0000	0.1826
4	0.3333	0.2716	0.1721	0.1803	0.2394	0.0000	0.0000	0.1826
5	0.0000	0.0000	0.0000	0.0000	0.1596	0.0000	0.0000	0.0000
6	0.0000	0.2716	0.1721	0.0000	0.0000	0.3015	0.2341	0.1826
7	0.0000	0.0000	0.1721	0.2705	0.1596	0.0000	0.0000	0.0000
8	0.0000	0.1811	0.2582	0.2705	0.0000	0.1508	0.0000	0.1826
9	0.0000	0.1811	0.0000	0.1803	0.2394	0.0000	0.0000	0.0000
10	0.0000	0.0000	0.0000	0.0000	0.1596	0.0000	0.2341	0.1826
11	0.0000	0.2716	0.2582	0.1803	0.0000	0.0000	0.0000	0.2739
12	0.0000	0.1811	0.1721	0.1803	0.0000	0.0000	0.2341	0.0000
13	0.0000	0.1811	0.0000	0.1803	0.0000	0.0000	0.0000	0.0000
14	0.0000	0.0000	0.0000	0.0000	0.2394	0.0000	0.0000	0.0000
15	0.0000	0.1811	0.1721	0.1803	0.1596	0.0000	0.2341	0.1826
16	0.0000	0.0000	0.0000	0.0000	0.1596	0.0000	0.2341	0.0000
17	0.0000	0.0000	0.0000	0.0000	0.0000	0.0000	0.2341	0.0000
18	0.0000	0.0000	0.0000	0.0000	0.0798	0.0000	0.0000	0.0000
19	0.0000	0.0000	0.0000	0.0000	0.2394	0.0000	0.0000	0.0000
20	0.0000	0.1811	0.2582	0.1803	0.2394	0.0000	0.0000	0.0000
21	0.0000	0.1811	0.1721	0.0000	0.0000	0.0000	0.0000	0.0000
22	0.3333	0.1811	0.2582	0.2705	0.1596	0.3015	0.1170	0.2739
23	0.2222	0.1811	0.0000	0.1803	0.2394	0.0000	0.0000	0.1826
24	0.2222	0.1811	0.2582	0.2705	0.2394	0.3015	0.2341	0.2739
25	0.3333	0.1811	0.0000	0.0000	0.2394	0.0000	0.0000	0.0000
26	0.0000	0.1811	0.2582	0.1803	0.1596	0.4523	0.0000	0.1826
27	0.0000	0.1811	0.1721	0.1803	0.1596	0.0000	0.3511	0.1826
28	0.2222	0.2716	0.2582	0.1803	0.1596	0.0000	0.0000	0.2739
29	0.3333	0.1811	0.2582	0.1803	0.0000	0.4523	0.2341	0.1826
30	0.2222	0.1811	0.2582	0.2705	0.1596	0.0000	0.0000	0.1826
31	0.0000	0.0000	0.0000	0.0000	0.0000	0.0000	0.0000	0.0000
32	0.2222	0.2716	0.2582	0.2705	0.1596	0.3015	0.3511	0.2739
33	0.2222	0.0000	0.0000	0.0000	0.0000	0.0000	0.2341	0.0000
34	0.0000	0.0000	0.0000	0.0000	0.0000	0.0000	0.0000	0.0000
35	0.2222	0.1811	0.1721	0.1803	0.2394	0.0000	0.2341	0.0000
36	0.0000	0.0000	0.0000	0.0000	0.1596	0.0000	0.0000	0.0000
37	0.0000	0.0000	0.0000	0.0000	0.0798	0.0000	0.0000	0.0000
38	0.3333	0.0000	0.0000	0.1803	0.1596	0.0000	0.2341	0.1826
39	0.2222	0.2716	0.2582	0.2705	0.1596	0.1508	0.1170	0.2739
40	0.2222	0.1811	0.1721	0.1803	0.2394	0.3015	0.0000	0.2739

Table 8. Normalized decision matrix E4-P6

Project	E4	E5	P1	P2	P3	P4	P5	P6
FMCDM Weights	0.0494	0.0178	0.0553	0.087	0.004	0.0593	0.0751	0.0277
1	0.2000	0.0000	0.1916	0.0000	0.0000	0.0000	0.0000	0.0000
2	0.0000	0.0000	0.0000	0.0000	0.0000	0.2020	0.0000	0.0000
3	0.3000	0.0000	0.0000	0.0000	0.0000	0.0000	0.1818	0.0000
4	0.2000	0.0000	0.1916	0.1650	0.0000	0.0000	0.0000	0.1132
5	0.0000	0.0000	0.0000	0.1650	0.0000	0.2020	0.1818	0.0000
6	0.0000	0.2500	0.0000	0.1650	0.0000	0.0000	0.0000	0.0000
7	0.0000	0.0000	0.0000	0.1650	0.0000	0.3030	0.0000	0.0000
8	0.0000	0.0000	0.1916	0.1650	0.0000	0.0000	0.1818	0.2265
9	0.0000	0.0000	0.1916	0.1650	0.0000	0.2020	0.1818	0.0000
10	0.0000	0.0000	0.0000	0.1650	0.0000	0.0000	0.1818	0.0000
11	0.3000	0.0000	0.0000	0.0000	0.0000	0.0000	0.0000	0.0000
12	0.0000	0.0000	0.0000	0.1650	0.0000	0.2020	0.0000	0.0000
13	0.0000	0.0000	0.1916	0.2474	0.2956	0.0000	0.1818	0.2265
14	0.0000	0.0000	0.0000	0.0000	0.0000	0.0000	0.0000	0.0000
15	0.0000	0.0000	0.0000	0.0000	0.0000	0.0000	0.0000	0.0000
16	0.2000	0.3750	0.2873	0.1650	0.0000	0.2020	0.2727	0.2265
17	0.0000	0.0000	0.1916	0.1650	0.1971	0.3030	0.1818	0.2265
18	0.0000	0.0000	0.0000	0.1650	0.1971	0.0000	0.0000	0.0000
19	0.0000	0.0000	0.0000	0.0000	0.0000	0.0000	0.0000	0.0000
20	0.0000	0.0000	0.2873	0.0000	0.0000	0.0000	0.2727	0.0000
21	0.0000	0.0000	0.0000	0.0000	0.0000	0.0000	0.0000	0.0000
22	0.2000	0.1250	0.0000	0.1650	0.1971	0.2020	0.0000	0.1132
23	0.3000	0.0000	0.1916	0.0000	0.1971	0.2020	0.2727	0.2265
24	0.2000	0.3750	0.2873	0.2474	0.2956	0.2020	0.2727	0.2265
25	0.0000	0.0000	0.2873	0.0000	0.0000	0.3030	0.2727	0.0000
26	0.2000	0.1250	0.0000	0.1650	0.0000	0.0000	0.1818	0.2265
27	0.3000	0.3750	0.0000	0.1650	0.1971	0.0000	0.0000	0.2265
28	0.3000	0.2500	0.2873	0.0000	0.2956	0.0000	0.1818	0.3397
29	0.2000	0.0000	0.0000	0.1650	0.1971	0.2020	0.2727	0.0000
30	0.0000	0.2500	0.1916	0.1650	0.1971	0.2020	0.1818	0.0000
31	0.0000	0.0000	0.2873	0.2474	0.2956	0.3030	0.2727	0.3397
32	0.3000	0.3750	0.2873	0.2474	0.2956	0.2020	0.2727	0.3397
33	0.2000	0.0000	0.0000	0.2474	0.1971	0.0000	0.0000	0.2265
34	0.0000	0.0000	0.0000	0.1650	0.0000	0.0000	0.0000	0.0000
35	0.0000	0.0000	0.0000	0.1650	0.1971	0.0000	0.0000	0.0000
36	0.2000	0.2500	0.1916	0.1650	0.0000	0.0000	0.0000	0.0000
37	0.0000	0.0000	0.0000	0.1650	0.0000	0.0000	0.0000	0.0000
38	0.3000	0.3750	0.0000	0.1650	0.1971	0.0000	0.0000	0.0000
39	0.1000	0.1250	0.0958	0.2474	0.2956	0.3030	0.0000	0.2265
40	0.0000	0.0000	0.2873	0.2474	0.2956	0.3030	0.2727	0.3397

Table 9. Normalized decision matrix O1-M3

Project	O1	O2	O3	M1	M2	M3
FMCDM Weights	0.0336	0.0099	0.0099	0.0395	0.0178	0.0336
1	0.1925	0.1302	0.0000	0.0000	0.0000	0.0000
2	0.0000	0.0000	0.0000	0.0000	0.0000	0.0000
3	0.0000	0.0000	0.0000	0.0000	0.0000	0.0000
4	0.1925	0.0000	0.0000	0.0000	0.0000	0.0000
5	0.0000	0.0000	0.0000	0.0000	0.2169	0.0000
6	0.0000	0.0000	0.0000	0.0000	0.0000	0.2341
7	0.0000	0.0000	0.0000	0.0000	0.0000	0.0000
8	0.0000	0.0000	0.1622	0.3638	0.0000	0.0000
9	0.0000	0.0000	0.0000	0.0000	0.0000	0.2341
10	0.0000	0.0000	0.0000	0.2425	0.0000	0.0000
11	0.0000	0.0000	0.3244	0.0000	0.0000	0.0000
12	0.0000	0.0000	0.0000	0.0000	0.0000	0.2341
13	0.1925	0.2604	0.0000	0.2425	0.2169	0.1170
14	0.0000	0.0000	0.0000	0.0000	0.0000	0.0000
15	0.2887	0.2604	0.0000	0.3638	0.0000	0.0000
16	0.2887	0.2604	0.0000	0.2425	0.2169	0.2341
17	0.0000	0.0000	0.0000	0.2425	0.2169	0.0000
18	0.0000	0.0000	0.0000	0.0000	0.0000	0.0000
19	0.0000	0.0000	0.0000	0.0000	0.0000	0.0000
20	0.1925	0.0000	0.0000	0.0000	0.3254	0.3511
21	0.0000	0.0000	0.0000	0.0000	0.0000	0.0000
22	0.2887	0.1302	0.3244	0.2425	0.2169	0.0000
23	0.0000	0.0000	0.0000	0.0000	0.2169	0.3511
24	0.2887	0.3906	0.0000	0.2425	0.2169	0.2341
25	0.0000	0.0000	0.0000	0.0000	0.0000	0.0000
26	0.0000	0.2604	0.3244	0.2425	0.0000	0.2341
27	0.1925	0.2604	0.0000	0.0000	0.0000	0.0000
28	0.1925	0.0000	0.3244	0.0000	0.2169	0.2341
29	0.1925	0.0000	0.3244	0.0000	0.3254	0.3511
30	0.2887	0.0000	0.3244	0.0000	0.2169	0.0000
31	0.2887	0.3906	0.0000	0.0000	0.3254	0.3511
32	0.2887	0.3906	0.3244	0.3638	0.3254	0.0000
33	0.2887	0.0000	0.0000	0.2425	0.0000	0.0000
34	0.0000	0.0000	0.0000	0.0000	0.0000	0.2341
35	0.0000	0.0000	0.0000	0.0000	0.0000	0.0000
36	0.0000	0.0000	0.0000	0.0000	0.0000	0.0000
37	0.0000	0.0000	0.0000	0.0000	0.0000	0.0000
38	0.1925	0.3906	0.0000	0.3638	0.3254	0.0000
39	0.1925	0.1302	0.4867	0.0000	0.0000	0.0000
40	0.0000	0.0000	0.0000	0.0000	0.2169	0.2341

Table 10. Weighted normalized decision matrix R1-E3

Project	R1	R2	R3	R4	R5	E1	E2	E3
FMCDM Weights	0.0237	0.0692	0.0632	0.0692	0.083	0.0435	0.0494	0.0791
1	0.0000	0.0000	0.0000	0.0000	0.0000	0.0131	0.0173	0.0217
2	0.0000	0.0000	0.0000	0.0000	0.0000	0.0000	0.0000	0.0000
3	0.0000	0.0000	0.0000	0.0000	0.0199	0.0000	0.0000	0.0144
4	0.0079	0.0188	0.0109	0.0125	0.0199	0.0000	0.0000	0.0144
5	0.0000	0.0000	0.0000	0.0000	0.0132	0.0000	0.0000	0.0000
6	0.0000	0.0188	0.0109	0.0000	0.0000	0.0131	0.0116	0.0144
7	0.0000	0.0000	0.0109	0.0187	0.0132	0.0000	0.0000	0.0000
8	0.0000	0.0125	0.0163	0.0187	0.0000	0.0066	0.0000	0.0144
9	0.0000	0.0125	0.0000	0.0125	0.0199	0.0000	0.0000	0.0000
10	0.0000	0.0000	0.0000	0.0000	0.0132	0.0000	0.0116	0.0144
11	0.0000	0.0188	0.0163	0.0125	0.0000	0.0000	0.0000	0.0217
12	0.0000	0.0125	0.0109	0.0125	0.0000	0.0000	0.0116	0.0000
13	0.0000	0.0125	0.0000	0.0125	0.0000	0.0000	0.0000	0.0000
14	0.0000	0.0000	0.0000	0.0000	0.0199	0.0000	0.0000	0.0000
15	0.0000	0.0125	0.0109	0.0125	0.0132	0.0000	0.0116	0.0144
16	0.0000	0.0000	0.0000	0.0000	0.0132	0.0000	0.0116	0.0000
17	0.0000	0.0000	0.0000	0.0000	0.0000	0.0000	0.0116	0.0000
18	0.0000	0.0000	0.0000	0.0000	0.0066	0.0000	0.0000	0.0000
19	0.0000	0.0000	0.0000	0.0000	0.0199	0.0000	0.0000	0.0000
20	0.0000	0.0125	0.0163	0.0125	0.0199	0.0000	0.0000	0.0000
21	0.0000	0.0125	0.0109	0.0000	0.0000	0.0000	0.0000	0.0000
22	0.0079	0.0125	0.0163	0.0187	0.0132	0.0131	0.0058	0.0217
23	0.0053	0.0125	0.0000	0.0125	0.0199	0.0000	0.0000	0.0144
24	0.0053	0.0125	0.0163	0.0187	0.0199	0.0131	0.0116	0.0217
25	0.0079	0.0125	0.0000	0.0000	0.0199	0.0000	0.0000	0.0000
26	0.0000	0.0125	0.0163	0.0125	0.0132	0.0197	0.0000	0.0144
27	0.0000	0.0125	0.0109	0.0125	0.0132	0.0000	0.0173	0.0144
28	0.0053	0.0188	0.0163	0.0125	0.0132	0.0000	0.0000	0.0217
29	0.0079	0.0125	0.0163	0.0125	0.0000	0.0197	0.0116	0.0144
30	0.0053	0.0125	0.0163	0.0187	0.0132	0.0000	0.0000	0.0144
31	0.0000	0.0000	0.0000	0.0000	0.0000	0.0000	0.0000	0.0000
32	0.0053	0.0188	0.0163	0.0187	0.0132	0.0131	0.0173	0.0217
33	0.0053	0.0000	0.0000	0.0000	0.0000	0.0000	0.0116	0.0000
34	0.0000	0.0000	0.0000	0.0000	0.0000	0.0000	0.0000	0.0000
35	0.0053	0.0125	0.0109	0.0125	0.0199	0.0000	0.0116	0.0000
36	0.0000	0.0000	0.0000	0.0000	0.0132	0.0000	0.0000	0.0000
37	0.0000	0.0000	0.0000	0.0000	0.0066	0.0000	0.0000	0.0000
38	0.0079	0.0000	0.0000	0.0125	0.0132	0.0000	0.0116	0.0144
39	0.0053	0.0188	0.0163	0.0187	0.0132	0.0066	0.0058	0.0217
40	0.0053	0.0125	0.0109	0.0125	0.0199	0.0131	0.0000	0.0217

Table 11. Weighted normalized decision matrix E4-P6

Project	E4	E5	P1	P2	P3	P4	P5	P6
FMCDM Weights	0.0494	0.0178	0.0553	0.087	0.004	0.0593	0.0751	0.0277
1	0.0099	0.0000	0.0106	0.0000	0.0000	0.0000	0.0000	0.0000
2	0.0000	0.0000	0.0000	0.0000	0.0000	0.0120	0.0000	0.0000
3	0.0148	0.0000	0.0000	0.0000	0.0000	0.0000	0.0137	0.0000
4	0.0099	0.0000	0.0106	0.0144	0.0000	0.0000	0.0000	0.0031
5	0.0000	0.0000	0.0000	0.0144	0.0000	0.0120	0.0137	0.0000
6	0.0000	0.0045	0.0000	0.0144	0.0000	0.0000	0.0000	0.0000
7	0.0000	0.0000	0.0000	0.0144	0.0000	0.0180	0.0000	0.0000
8	0.0000	0.0000	0.0106	0.0144	0.0000	0.0000	0.0137	0.0063
9	0.0000	0.0000	0.0106	0.0144	0.0000	0.0120	0.0137	0.0000
10	0.0000	0.0000	0.0000	0.0144	0.0000	0.0000	0.0137	0.0000
11	0.0148	0.0000	0.0000	0.0000	0.0000	0.0000	0.0000	0.0000
12	0.0000	0.0000	0.0000	0.0144	0.0000	0.0120	0.0000	0.0000
13	0.0000	0.0000	0.0106	0.0215	0.0012	0.0000	0.0137	0.0063
14	0.0000	0.0000	0.0000	0.0000	0.0000	0.0000	0.0000	0.0000
15	0.0000	0.0000	0.0000	0.0000	0.0000	0.0000	0.0000	0.0000
16	0.0099	0.0067	0.0159	0.0144	0.0000	0.0120	0.0205	0.0063
17	0.0000	0.0000	0.0106	0.0144	0.0008	0.0180	0.0137	0.0063
18	0.0000	0.0000	0.0000	0.0144	0.0008	0.0000	0.0000	0.0000
19	0.0000	0.0000	0.0000	0.0000	0.0000	0.0000	0.0000	0.0000
20	0.0000	0.0000	0.0159	0.0000	0.0000	0.0000	0.0205	0.0000
21	0.0000	0.0000	0.0000	0.0000	0.0000	0.0000	0.0000	0.0000
22	0.0099	0.0022	0.0000	0.0144	0.0008	0.0120	0.0000	0.0031
23	0.0148	0.0000	0.0106	0.0000	0.0008	0.0120	0.0205	0.0063
24	0.0099	0.0067	0.0159	0.0215	0.0012	0.0120	0.0205	0.0063
25	0.0000	0.0000	0.0159	0.0000	0.0000	0.0180	0.0205	0.0000
26	0.0099	0.0022	0.0000	0.0144	0.0000	0.0000	0.0137	0.0063
27	0.0148	0.0067	0.0000	0.0144	0.0008	0.0000	0.0000	0.0063
28	0.0148	0.0045	0.0159	0.0000	0.0012	0.0000	0.0137	0.0094
29	0.0099	0.0000	0.0000	0.0144	0.0008	0.0120	0.0205	0.0000
30	0.0000	0.0045	0.0106	0.0144	0.0008	0.0120	0.0137	0.0000
31	0.0000	0.0000	0.0159	0.0215	0.0012	0.0180	0.0205	0.0094
32	0.0148	0.0067	0.0159	0.0215	0.0012	0.0120	0.0205	0.0094
33	0.0099	0.0000	0.0000	0.0215	0.0008	0.0000	0.0000	0.0063
34	0.0000	0.0000	0.0000	0.0144	0.0000	0.0000	0.0000	0.0000
35	0.0000	0.0000	0.0000	0.0144	0.0008	0.0000	0.0000	0.0000
36	0.0099	0.0045	0.0106	0.0144	0.0000	0.0000	0.0000	0.0000
37	0.0000	0.0000	0.0000	0.0144	0.0000	0.0000	0.0000	0.0000
38	0.0148	0.0067	0.0000	0.0144	0.0008	0.0000	0.0000	0.0000
39	0.0049	0.0022	0.0053	0.0215	0.0012	0.0180	0.0000	0.0063
40	0.0000	0.0000	0.0159	0.0215	0.0012	0.0180	0.0205	0.0094

Table 12. Weighted normalized decision matrix O1-M3

Project	O1	O2	O3	M1	M2	M3
FMCDM Weights	0.0336	0.0099	0.0099	0.0395	0.0178	0.0336
1	0.0065	0.0013	0.0000	0.0000	0.0000	0.0000
2	0.0000	0.0000	0.0000	0.0000	0.0000	0.0000
3	0.0000	0.0000	0.0000	0.0000	0.0000	0.0000
4	0.0065	0.0000	0.0000	0.0000	0.0000	0.0000
5	0.0000	0.0000	0.0000	0.0000	0.0039	0.0000
6	0.0000	0.0000	0.0000	0.0000	0.0000	0.0079
7	0.0000	0.0000	0.0000	0.0000	0.0000	0.0000
8	0.0000	0.0000	0.0016	0.0144	0.0000	0.0000
9	0.0000	0.0000	0.0000	0.0000	0.0000	0.0079
10	0.0000	0.0000	0.0000	0.0096	0.0000	0.0000
11	0.0000	0.0000	0.0032	0.0000	0.0000	0.0000
12	0.0000	0.0000	0.0000	0.0000	0.0000	0.0079
13	0.0065	0.0026	0.0000	0.0096	0.0039	0.0039
14	0.0000	0.0000	0.0000	0.0000	0.0000	0.0000
15	0.0097	0.0026	0.0000	0.0144	0.0000	0.0000
16	0.0097	0.0026	0.0000	0.0096	0.0039	0.0079
17	0.0000	0.0000	0.0000	0.0096	0.0039	0.0000
18	0.0000	0.0000	0.0000	0.0000	0.0000	0.0000
19	0.0000	0.0000	0.0000	0.0000	0.0000	0.0000
20	0.0065	0.0000	0.0000	0.0000	0.0058	0.0118
21	0.0000	0.0000	0.0000	0.0000	0.0000	0.0000
22	0.0097	0.0013	0.0032	0.0096	0.0039	0.0000
23	0.0000	0.0000	0.0000	0.0000	0.0039	0.0118
24	0.0097	0.0039	0.0000	0.0096	0.0039	0.0079
25	0.0000	0.0000	0.0000	0.0000	0.0000	0.0000
26	0.0000	0.0026	0.0032	0.0096	0.0000	0.0079
27	0.0065	0.0026	0.0000	0.0000	0.0000	0.0000
28	0.0065	0.0000	0.0032	0.0000	0.0039	0.0079
29	0.0065	0.0000	0.0032	0.0000	0.0058	0.0118
30	0.0097	0.0000	0.0032	0.0000	0.0039	0.0000
31	0.0097	0.0039	0.0000	0.0000	0.0058	0.0118
32	0.0097	0.0039	0.0032	0.0144	0.0058	0.0000
33	0.0097	0.0000	0.0000	0.0096	0.0000	0.0000
34	0.0000	0.0000	0.0000	0.0000	0.0000	0.0079
35	0.0000	0.0000	0.0000	0.0000	0.0000	0.0000
36	0.0000	0.0000	0.0000	0.0000	0.0000	0.0000
37	0.0000	0.0000	0.0000	0.0000	0.0000	0.0000
38	0.0065	0.0039	0.0000	0.0144	0.0058	0.0000
39	0.0065	0.0013	0.0048	0.0000	0.0000	0.0000
40	0.0000	0.0000	0.0000	0.0000	0.0039	0.0079

Table 13. Positive deviation matrix R1-E3

Project	R1	R2	R3	R4	R5	E1	E2	E3
FPIS	0.0079	0.0188	0.0163	0.0187	0.0199	0.0197	0.0173	0.0217
1	0.00006	0.00035	0.00027	0.00035	0.00039	0.00004	0.00000	0.00000
2	0.00006	0.00035	0.00027	0.00035	0.00039	0.00039	0.00030	0.00047
3	0.00006	0.00035	0.00027	0.00035	0.00000	0.00039	0.00030	0.00005
4	0.00000	0.00000	0.00003	0.00004	0.00000	0.00039	0.00030	0.00005
5	0.00006	0.00035	0.00027	0.00035	0.00004	0.00039	0.00030	0.00047
6	0.00006	0.00000	0.00003	0.00035	0.00039	0.00004	0.00003	0.00005
7	0.00006	0.00035	0.00003	0.00000	0.00004	0.00039	0.00030	0.00047
8	0.00006	0.00004	0.00000	0.00000	0.00039	0.00017	0.00030	0.00005
9	0.00006	0.00004	0.00027	0.00004	0.00000	0.00039	0.00030	0.00047
10	0.00006	0.00035	0.00027	0.00035	0.00004	0.00039	0.00003	0.00005
11	0.00006	0.00000	0.00000	0.00004	0.00039	0.00039	0.00030	0.00000
12	0.00006	0.00004	0.00003	0.00004	0.00039	0.00039	0.00003	0.00047
13	0.00006	0.00004	0.00027	0.00004	0.00039	0.00039	0.00030	0.00047
14	0.00006	0.00035	0.00027	0.00035	0.00000	0.00039	0.00030	0.00047
15	0.00006	0.00004	0.00003	0.00004	0.00004	0.00039	0.00003	0.00005
16	0.00006	0.00035	0.00027	0.00035	0.00004	0.00039	0.00003	0.00047
17	0.00006	0.00035	0.00027	0.00035	0.00039	0.00039	0.00003	0.00047
18	0.00006	0.00035	0.00027	0.00035	0.00018	0.00039	0.00030	0.00047
19	0.00006	0.00035	0.00027	0.00035	0.00000	0.00039	0.00030	0.00047
20	0.00006	0.00004	0.00000	0.00004	0.00000	0.00039	0.00030	0.00047
21	0.00006	0.00004	0.00003	0.00035	0.00039	0.00039	0.00030	0.00047
22	0.00000	0.00004	0.00000	0.00000	0.00004	0.00004	0.00013	0.00000
23	0.00001	0.00004	0.00027	0.00004	0.00000	0.00039	0.00030	0.00005
24	0.00001	0.00004	0.00000	0.00000	0.00000	0.00004	0.00003	0.00000
25	0.00000	0.00004	0.00027	0.00035	0.00000	0.00039	0.00030	0.00047
26	0.00006	0.00004	0.00000	0.00004	0.00004	0.00000	0.00030	0.00005
27	0.00006	0.00004	0.00003	0.00004	0.00004	0.00039	0.00000	0.00005
28	0.00001	0.00000	0.00000	0.00004	0.00004	0.00039	0.00030	0.00000
29	0.00000	0.00004	0.00000	0.00004	0.00039	0.00000	0.00003	0.00005
30	0.00001	0.00004	0.00000	0.00000	0.00004	0.00039	0.00030	0.00005
31	0.00006	0.00035	0.00027	0.00035	0.00039	0.00039	0.00030	0.00047
32	0.00001	0.00000	0.00000	0.00000	0.00004	0.00004	0.00000	0.00000
33	0.00001	0.00035	0.00027	0.00035	0.00039	0.00039	0.00003	0.00047
34	0.00006	0.00035	0.00027	0.00035	0.00039	0.00039	0.00030	0.00047
35	0.00001	0.00004	0.00003	0.00004	0.00000	0.00039	0.00003	0.00047
36	0.00006	0.00035	0.00027	0.00035	0.00004	0.00039	0.00030	0.00047
37	0.00006	0.00035	0.00027	0.00035	0.00018	0.00039	0.00030	0.00047
38	0.00000	0.00035	0.00027	0.00004	0.00004	0.00039	0.00003	0.00005
39	0.00001	0.00000	0.00000	0.00000	0.00004	0.00017	0.00013	0.00000
40	0.00001	0.00004	0.00003	0.00004	0.00000	0.00004	0.00030	0.00000

Table 14. Positive deviation matrix E4-P6

Project	E4	E5	P1	P2	P3	P4	P5	P6
FPIS	0.0148	0.0067	0.0159	0.0215	0.0012	0.0180	0.0205	0.0094
1	0.00002	0.00004	0.00003	0.00000	0.00000	0.00032	0.00042	0.00009
2	0.00022	0.00004	0.00025	0.00046	0.00000	0.00004	0.00042	0.00009
3	0.00000	0.00004	0.00025	0.00046	0.00000	0.00032	0.00005	0.00009
4	0.00002	0.00004	0.00003	0.00005	0.00000	0.00032	0.00042	0.00004
5	0.00022	0.00004	0.00025	0.00005	0.00000	0.00004	0.00005	0.00009
6	0.00022	0.00000	0.00025	0.00005	0.00000	0.00032	0.00042	0.00009
7	0.00022	0.00004	0.00025	0.00005	0.00000	0.00000	0.00042	0.00009
8	0.00022	0.00004	0.00003	0.00005	0.00000	0.00032	0.00005	0.00001
9	0.00022	0.00004	0.00003	0.00005	0.00000	0.00004	0.00005	0.00009
10	0.00022	0.00004	0.00025	0.00005	0.00000	0.00032	0.00005	0.00009
11	0.00000	0.00004	0.00025	0.00046	0.00000	0.00032	0.00042	0.00009
12	0.00022	0.00004	0.00025	0.00005	0.00000	0.00004	0.00042	0.00009
13	0.00022	0.00004	0.00003	0.00000	0.00000	0.00032	0.00005	0.00001
14	0.00022	0.00004	0.00025	0.00046	0.00000	0.00032	0.00042	0.00009
15	0.00022	0.00004	0.00025	0.00046	0.00000	0.00032	0.00042	0.00009
16	0.00002	0.00000	0.00000	0.00005	0.00000	0.00004	0.00000	0.00001
17	0.00022	0.00004	0.00003	0.00005	0.00000	0.00000	0.00005	0.00001
18	0.00022	0.00004	0.00025	0.00005	0.00000	0.00032	0.00042	0.00009
19	0.00022	0.00004	0.00025	0.00046	0.00000	0.00032	0.00042	0.00009
20	0.00022	0.00004	0.00000	0.00046	0.00000	0.00032	0.00000	0.00009
21	0.00022	0.00004	0.00025	0.00046	0.00000	0.00032	0.00042	0.00009
22	0.00002	0.00002	0.00025	0.00005	0.00000	0.00004	0.00042	0.00004
23	0.00000	0.00004	0.00003	0.00046	0.00000	0.00004	0.00000	0.00001
24	0.00002	0.00000	0.00000	0.00000	0.00000	0.00004	0.00000	0.00001
25	0.00022	0.00004	0.00000	0.00046	0.00000	0.00000	0.00000	0.00009
26	0.00002	0.00002	0.00025	0.00005	0.00000	0.00032	0.00005	0.00001
27	0.00000	0.00000	0.00025	0.00005	0.00000	0.00032	0.00042	0.00001
28	0.00000	0.00000	0.00000	0.00046	0.00000	0.00032	0.00005	0.00000
29	0.00002	0.00004	0.00025	0.00005	0.00000	0.00004	0.00000	0.00009
30	0.00022	0.00000	0.00003	0.00005	0.00000	0.00004	0.00005	0.00009
31	0.00022	0.00004	0.00000	0.00000	0.00000	0.00000	0.00000	0.00000
32	0.00000	0.00000	0.00000	0.00000	0.00000	0.00004	0.00000	0.00000
33	0.00002	0.00004	0.00025	0.00000	0.00000	0.00032	0.00042	0.00001
34	0.00022	0.00004	0.00025	0.00005	0.00000	0.00032	0.00042	0.00009
35	0.00022	0.00004	0.00025	0.00005	0.00000	0.00032	0.00042	0.00009
36	0.00002	0.00000	0.00003	0.00005	0.00000	0.00032	0.00042	0.00009
37	0.00022	0.00004	0.00025	0.00005	0.00000	0.00032	0.00042	0.00009
38	0.00000	0.00000	0.00025	0.00005	0.00000	0.00032	0.00042	0.00009
39	0.00010	0.00002	0.00011	0.00000	0.00000	0.00000	0.00042	0.00001
40	0.00022	0.00004	0.00000	0.00000	0.00000	0.00000	0.00000	0.00000

Table 15. Positive deviation matrix O1-M3

Project	O1	O2	O3	M1	M2	M3
FPIS	0.0097	0.0039	0.0048	0.0144	0.0058	0.0118
1	0.00001	0.00001	0.00002	0.00021	0.00003	0.00014
2	0.00009	0.00001	0.00002	0.00021	0.00003	0.00014
3	0.00009	0.00001	0.00002	0.00021	0.00003	0.00014
4	0.00001	0.00001	0.00002	0.00021	0.00003	0.00014
5	0.00009	0.00001	0.00002	0.00021	0.00000	0.00014
6	0.00009	0.00001	0.00002	0.00021	0.00003	0.00002
7	0.00009	0.00001	0.00002	0.00021	0.00003	0.00014
8	0.00009	0.00001	0.00001	0.00000	0.00003	0.00014
9	0.00009	0.00001	0.00002	0.00021	0.00003	0.00002
10	0.00009	0.00001	0.00002	0.00002	0.00003	0.00014
11	0.00009	0.00001	0.00000	0.00021	0.00003	0.00014
12	0.00009	0.00001	0.00002	0.00021	0.00003	0.00002
13	0.00001	0.00000	0.00002	0.00002	0.00000	0.00006
14	0.00009	0.00001	0.00002	0.00021	0.00003	0.00014
15	0.00000	0.00000	0.00002	0.00000	0.00003	0.00014
16	0.00000	0.00000	0.00002	0.00002	0.00000	0.00002
17	0.00009	0.00001	0.00002	0.00002	0.00000	0.00014
18	0.00009	0.00001	0.00002	0.00021	0.00003	0.00014
19	0.00009	0.00001	0.00002	0.00021	0.00003	0.00014
20	0.00001	0.00001	0.00002	0.00021	0.00000	0.00000
21	0.00009	0.00001	0.00002	0.00021	0.00003	0.00014
22	0.00000	0.00001	0.00000	0.00002	0.00000	0.00014
23	0.00009	0.00001	0.00002	0.00021	0.00000	0.00000
24	0.00000	0.00000	0.00002	0.00002	0.00000	0.00002
25	0.00009	0.00001	0.00002	0.00021	0.00003	0.00014
26	0.00009	0.00000	0.00000	0.00002	0.00003	0.00002
27	0.00001	0.00000	0.00002	0.00021	0.00003	0.00014
28	0.00001	0.00001	0.00000	0.00021	0.00000	0.00002
29	0.00001	0.00001	0.00000	0.00021	0.00000	0.00000
30	0.00000	0.00001	0.00000	0.00021	0.00000	0.00014
31	0.00000	0.00000	0.00002	0.00021	0.00000	0.00000
32	0.00000	0.00000	0.00000	0.00000	0.00000	0.00014
33	0.00000	0.00001	0.00002	0.00002	0.00003	0.00014
34	0.00009	0.00001	0.00002	0.00021	0.00003	0.00002
35	0.00009	0.00001	0.00002	0.00021	0.00003	0.00014
36	0.00009	0.00001	0.00002	0.00021	0.00003	0.00014
37	0.00009	0.00001	0.00002	0.00021	0.00003	0.00014
38	0.00001	0.00000	0.00002	0.00000	0.00000	0.00014
39	0.00001	0.00001	0.00000	0.00021	0.00003	0.00014
40	0.00009	0.00001	0.00002	0.00021	0.00000	0.00002

Table 16. Negative deviation matrix R1-E3

Project	R1	R2	R3	R4	R5	E1	E2	E3
FNIS	0	0	0	0	0	0	0	0
1	0.00000	0.00000	0.00000	0.00000	0.00000	0.00017	0.00030	0.00047
2	0.00000	0.00000	0.00000	0.00000	0.00000	0.00000	0.00000	0.00000
3	0.00000	0.00000	0.00000	0.00000	0.00039	0.00000	0.00000	0.00021
4	0.00006	0.00035	0.00012	0.00016	0.00039	0.00000	0.00000	0.00021
5	0.00000	0.00000	0.00000	0.00000	0.00018	0.00000	0.00000	0.00000
6	0.00000	0.00035	0.00012	0.00000	0.00000	0.00017	0.00013	0.00021
7	0.00000	0.00000	0.00012	0.00035	0.00018	0.00000	0.00000	0.00000
8	0.00000	0.00016	0.00027	0.00035	0.00000	0.00004	0.00000	0.00021
9	0.00000	0.00016	0.00000	0.00016	0.00039	0.00000	0.00000	0.00000
10	0.00000	0.00000	0.00000	0.00000	0.00018	0.00000	0.00013	0.00021
11	0.00000	0.00035	0.00027	0.00016	0.00000	0.00000	0.00000	0.00047
12	0.00000	0.00016	0.00012	0.00016	0.00000	0.00000	0.00013	0.00000
13	0.00000	0.00016	0.00000	0.00016	0.00000	0.00000	0.00000	0.00000
14	0.00000	0.00000	0.00000	0.00000	0.00039	0.00000	0.00000	0.00000
15	0.00000	0.00016	0.00012	0.00016	0.00018	0.00000	0.00013	0.00021
16	0.00000	0.00000	0.00000	0.00000	0.00018	0.00000	0.00013	0.00000
17	0.00000	0.00000	0.00000	0.00000	0.00000	0.00000	0.00013	0.00000
18	0.00000	0.00000	0.00000	0.00000	0.00004	0.00000	0.00000	0.00000
19	0.00000	0.00000	0.00000	0.00000	0.00039	0.00000	0.00000	0.00000
20	0.00000	0.00016	0.00027	0.00016	0.00039	0.00000	0.00000	0.00000
21	0.00000	0.00016	0.00012	0.00000	0.00000	0.00000	0.00000	0.00000
22	0.00006	0.00016	0.00027	0.00035	0.00018	0.00017	0.00003	0.00047
23	0.00003	0.00016	0.00000	0.00016	0.00039	0.00000	0.00000	0.00021
24	0.00003	0.00016	0.00027	0.00035	0.00039	0.00017	0.00013	0.00047
25	0.00006	0.00016	0.00000	0.00000	0.00039	0.00000	0.00000	0.00000
26	0.00000	0.00016	0.00027	0.00016	0.00018	0.00039	0.00000	0.00021
27	0.00000	0.00016	0.00012	0.00016	0.00018	0.00000	0.00030	0.00021
28	0.00003	0.00035	0.00027	0.00016	0.00018	0.00000	0.00000	0.00047
29	0.00006	0.00016	0.00027	0.00016	0.00000	0.00039	0.00013	0.00021
30	0.00003	0.00016	0.00027	0.00035	0.00018	0.00000	0.00000	0.00021
31	0.00000	0.00000	0.00000	0.00000	0.00000	0.00000	0.00000	0.00000
32	0.00003	0.00035	0.00027	0.00035	0.00018	0.00017	0.00030	0.00047
33	0.00003	0.00000	0.00000	0.00000	0.00000	0.00000	0.00013	0.00000
34	0.00000	0.00000	0.00000	0.00000	0.00000	0.00000	0.00000	0.00000
35	0.00003	0.00016	0.00012	0.00016	0.00039	0.00000	0.00013	0.00000
36	0.00000	0.00000	0.00000	0.00000	0.00018	0.00000	0.00000	0.00000
37	0.00000	0.00000	0.00000	0.00000	0.00004	0.00000	0.00000	0.00000
38	0.00006	0.00000	0.00000	0.00016	0.00018	0.00000	0.00013	0.00021
39	0.00003	0.00035	0.00027	0.00035	0.00018	0.00004	0.00003	0.00047
40	0.00003	0.00016	0.00012	0.00016	0.00039	0.00017	0.00000	0.00047

Table 17. Negative deviation matrix E4-P6

Project	E4	E5	P1	P2	P3	P4	P5	P6
FPIS	0.00000	0.00000	0.00000	0.00000	0.00000	0.00000	0.00000	0.00000
1	0.00014	0.00000	0.00000	0.00000	0.00000	0.00014	0.00000	0.00000
2	0.00000	0.00000	0.00000	0.00000	0.00000	0.00000	0.00019	0.00000
3	0.00000	0.00001	0.00021	0.00021	0.00000	0.00000	0.00000	0.00001
4	0.00014	0.00000	0.00021	0.00021	0.00000	0.00014	0.00019	0.00000
5	0.00000	0.00000	0.00021	0.00021	0.00000	0.00000	0.00000	0.00000
6	0.00032	0.00000	0.00021	0.00021	0.00000	0.00032	0.00000	0.00000
7	0.00000	0.00004	0.00021	0.00021	0.00000	0.00000	0.00019	0.00004
8	0.00014	0.00000	0.00021	0.00021	0.00000	0.00014	0.00019	0.00000
9	0.00000	0.00000	0.00021	0.00021	0.00000	0.00000	0.00019	0.00000
10	0.00000	0.00000	0.00000	0.00000	0.00000	0.00000	0.00000	0.00000
11	0.00014	0.00000	0.00021	0.00021	0.00000	0.00014	0.00000	0.00000
12	0.00000	0.00004	0.00046	0.00046	0.00000	0.00000	0.00019	0.00004
13	0.00000	0.00000	0.00000	0.00000	0.00000	0.00000	0.00000	0.00000
14	0.00000	0.00000	0.00000	0.00000	0.00000	0.00000	0.00000	0.00000
15	0.00014	0.00004	0.00021	0.00021	0.00000	0.00014	0.00042	0.00004
16	0.00032	0.00004	0.00021	0.00021	0.00000	0.00032	0.00019	0.00004
17	0.00000	0.00000	0.00021	0.00021	0.00000	0.00000	0.00000	0.00000
18	0.000	0.000	0.000	0.00000	0.00000	0.00000	0.00000	0.00000
19	0.000	0.000	0.000	0.00000	0.00000	0.00000	0.00042	0.00000
20	0.000	0.000	0.000	0.00000	0.00000	0.00000	0.00000	0.00000
21	0.000	0.000	0.000	0.00021	0.00000	0.00014	0.00000	0.00001
22	0.000	0.000	0.000	0.00000	0.00000	0.00014	0.00042	0.00004
23	0.000	0.000	0.000	0.00046	0.00000	0.00014	0.00042	0.00004
24	0.000	0.000	0.000	0.00000	0.00000	0.00032	0.00042	0.00000
25	0.000	0.000	0.000	0.00021	0.00000	0.00000	0.00019	0.00004
26	0.000	0.000	0.000	0.00021	0.00000	0.00000	0.00000	0.00004
27	0.000	0.000	0.000	0.00000	0.00000	0.00000	0.00019	0.00009
28	0.00000	0.00014	0.00021	0.00021	0.00000	0.00014	0.00042	0.00000
29	0.00000	0.00014	0.00021	0.00021	0.00000	0.00014	0.00019	0.00000
30	0.00000	0.00032	0.00046	0.00046	0.00000	0.00032	0.00042	0.00000
31	0.00021	0.00014	0.00046	0.00046	0.00000	0.00014	0.00042	0.00021
32	0.00021	0.00000	0.00046	0.00046	0.00000	0.00000	0.00000	0.00021
33	0.00021	0.00000	0.00021	0.00021	0.00000	0.00000	0.00000	0.00021
34	0.00021	0.00000	0.00021	0.00021	0.00000	0.00000	0.00000	0.00021
35	0.00021	0.00000	0.00021	0.00021	0.00000	0.00000	0.00000	0.00021
36	0.00021	0.00000	0.00021	0.00021	0.00000	0.00000	0.00000	0.00021
37	0.00021	0.00000	0.00021	0.00021	0.00000	0.00000	0.00000	0.00021
38	0.00000	0.00032	0.00046	0.00046	0.00000	0.00032	0.00000	0.00000
39	0.00021	0.00032	0.00046	0.00046	0.00000	0.00032	0.00042	0.00021
40	0.00046	0.00000	0.00000	0.00000	0.00000	0.00000	0.00000	0.00046

Table 18. Negative deviation matrix O1-M3

Project	O1	O2	O3	M1	M2	M3
FPIS	0	0	0	0	0	0
1	0.0097	0.0039	0.0048	0.0144	0.0058	0.0118
2	0.00004	0.00000	0.00000	0.00000	0.00000	0.00000
3	0.00000	0.00000	0.00000	0.00000	0.00000	0.00000
4	0.00000	0.00000	0.00000	0.00000	0.00000	0.00000
5	0.00004	0.00000	0.00000	0.00000	0.00000	0.00000
6	0.00000	0.00000	0.00000	0.00000	0.00001	0.00000
7	0.00000	0.00000	0.00000	0.00000	0.00000	0.00006
8	0.00000	0.00000	0.00000	0.00000	0.00000	0.00000
9	0.00000	0.00000	0.00000	0.00021	0.00000	0.00000
10	0.00000	0.00000	0.00000	0.00000	0.00000	0.00006
11	0.00000	0.00000	0.00000	0.00009	0.00000	0.00000
12	0.00000	0.00000	0.00001	0.00000	0.00000	0.00000
13	0.00000	0.00000	0.00000	0.00000	0.00000	0.00006
14	0.00004	0.00001	0.00000	0.00009	0.00001	0.00002
15	0.00000	0.00000	0.00000	0.00000	0.00000	0.00000
16	0.00009	0.00001	0.00000	0.00021	0.00000	0.00000
17	0.00009	0.00001	0.00000	0.00009	0.00001	0.00006
18	0.00000	0.00000	0.00000	0.00009	0.00001	0.00000
19	0.00000	0.00000	0.00000	0.00000	0.00000	0.00000
20	0.00000	0.00000	0.00000	0.00000	0.00000	0.00000
21	0.00004	0.00000	0.00000	0.00000	0.00003	0.00014
22	0.00000	0.00000	0.00000	0.00000	0.00000	0.00000
23	0.00009	0.00000	0.00001	0.00009	0.00001	0.00000
24	0.00000	0.00000	0.00000	0.00000	0.00001	0.00014
25	0.00009	0.00001	0.00000	0.00009	0.00001	0.00006
26	0.00000	0.00000	0.00000	0.00000	0.00000	0.00000
27	0.00000	0.00001	0.00001	0.00009	0.00000	0.00006
28	0.00004	0.00001	0.00000	0.00000	0.00000	0.00000
29	0.00004	0.00000	0.00001	0.00000	0.00001	0.00006
30	0.00004	0.00000	0.00001	0.00000	0.00003	0.00014
31	0.00009	0.00000	0.00001	0.00000	0.00001	0.00000
32	0.00009	0.00001	0.00000	0.00000	0.00003	0.00014
33	0.00009	0.00001	0.00001	0.00021	0.00003	0.00000
34	0.00009	0.00000	0.00000	0.00009	0.00000	0.00000
35	0.00000	0.00000	0.00000	0.00000	0.00000	0.00006
36	0.00000	0.00000	0.00000	0.00000	0.00000	0.00000
37	0.00000	0.00000	0.00000	0.00000	0.00000	0.00000
38	0.00000	0.00000	0.00000	0.00000	0.00000	0.00000
39	0.00004	0.00001	0.00000	0.00021	0.00003	0.00000
40	0.00004	0.00000	0.00002	0.00000	0.00000	0.00000

Table 19. Find the similarity of the projects

Project	s_{iw}	Predicted Value by Neural Network [2]	Predicted Value by Proposed Approach	Actual Status
1	0.3944	Not Risky	Not Risky	not confused
2	0.1498	Not Risky	Not Risky	not confused
3	0.3493	Not Risky	Not Risky	not confused
4	0.4740	Not Risky	Risky	Confused
5	0.3144	Not Risky	Not Risky	not confused
6	0.4065	Not Risky	Not Risky	not confused
7	0.3758	Not Risky	Not Risky	not confused
8	0.4830	Not Risky	Risky	Confused
9	0.4311	Not Risky	Risky	Confused
10	0.3700	Not Risky	Not Risky	not confused
11	0.4018	Not Risky	Not Risky	not confused
12	0.3649	Not Risky	Not Risky	not confused
13	0.4059	Not Risky	Not Risky	not confused
14	0.2283	Not Risky	Not Risky	not confused
15	0.4056	Not Risky	Not Risky	not confused
16	0.4762	Risky	Risky	not confused
17	0.3774	Not Risky	Not Risky	not confused
18	0.1949	Not Risky	Not Risky	not confused
19	0.2283	Not Risky	Not Risky	not confused
20	0.4539	Not Risky	Risky	Confused
21	0.2009	Not Risky	Not Risky	not confused
22	0.5762	Risky	Risky	not confused
23	0.5011	Risky	Risky	not confused
24	0.7913	Risky	Risky	not confused
25	0.4171	Risky	Risky	not confused
26	0.5446	Risky	Risky	not confused
27	0.4703	Risky	Risky	not confused
28	0.5283	Risky	Risky	not confused
29	0.5801	Risky	Risky	not confused
30	0.5207	Risky	Risky	not confused

continued on following page

Table 19. Continued

Project	s_{iw}	Predicted Value by Neural Network [2]	Predicted Value by Proposed Approach	Actual Status
31	0.4354	Risky	Risky	not confused
32	0.7955	Risky	Risky	not confused
33	0.3401	Not Risky	Not Risky	not confused
34	0.1984	Not Risky	Not Risky	not confused
35	0.3902	Not Risky	Not Risky	not confused
36	0.2894	Not Risky	Not Risky	not confused
37	0.1946	Not Risky	Not Risky	not confused
38	0.4376	Risky	Risky	not confused
39	0.5790	Risky	Risky	not confused
40	0.6295	Risky	Risky	not confused
Average	**0.4172**			

FMCDM-TOPSIS approach to determine the relative weights of the risk factors and the ranking the criteria via TFNs. Similarly, there are no existing researches on MCDM approach for solving this type of problem (*i.e.* risk assessment framework).

The 22 risk factors were summarized and explored in the context of software project performance, according to the weights W_j as shown in Table 4. The results reveal that weights of risk factors $P_2 > R_5 > E_3 > P_5 > R_2$ these factors (Lack of assignment of responsibility (P_2), Frequent requirement changes (R_5), Insufficient estimation for the implicit requirement (E_3), Insufficient planning of project monitoring and controlling (P_5) and Insufficient explanation of the requirements (R_2)) are highest weights of risk factors and more impact on software project performance among 22 factors.

Similarly, the hybrid FMCDM and TOPSIS risk performance index (s_{iw}) determined for the compare the software risk among 40 projects on the basis of OMRON datasets as shown in Table 9. The average risk performance index (s_{iw}) obtained through FMCDM and TOPSIS is 0.4172. Risk performance index value above or equal to the value, thus consider it risky/confused projects highlighted as blue are the predicted risky projects. This research, comparing with the results of the OMRON dataset obtained from earlier study, we got 4 wrongly identified projects (highlighted as yellow) from the proposed method. Subsequently, we have identified 36 project performance index values are same as the value of earlier study (Wen-Ming, 2015). While comparing the classification performance as shown in Table 19. So we have obtained the 92.5% prediction accuracy which is higher compare the statistical (linear regression) and neural network approaches as investigated in the earlier studies (Wen-Ming, 2015; Takagi, Mizuno & Kikuno, 2005). The results reveal that the efficiency classification of risky/not risky project has been achieved through our assessment framework. By emphasizing software risk criteria, the industries can attain the goals of effective risk management, thereby improving the software performance.

CONCLUSION

In recent years, the effective management of software risk in the context of project performance/outcome plays major impact. Thus, the aim of this chapter is to investigate a solution for this problem. The proposed assessment framework (FMCDM-TOPSIS) under fuzzy environment more capable and effectively accurate the risky projects on OMRON Corporation. This chapter presents an empirical predictive approach to determine risky software projects using FMCDM-TOPSIS, and compares its prediction accuracy with a previous study using Neural Network (Wen-Ming, 2015). This study results indicate that five important predictor variables (P2,R5,E3,P5,R2) can predict risky projects which is consistent with earlier studies.

Compared with existing methodologies, our proposed fuzzy framework presents a strong discrimination and effectively helps the DM during the assessment of software risk factors. Moreover, this chapter also addressed the comparative study of some existing measured risk factors investigated through regression analysis and neural network respectively. In addition, human uncertainty and subjective judgment within the decision making (DM) process effectively illustrated through TFNs. in addition, the case study of this chapter gives a precise measurement of the importance of risk factors in software project performance.

REFERENCES

Baykasoğlu, A., Kaplanoğlu, V., Durmuşoğlu, Z. D., & Şahin, C. (2013). Integrating fuzzy DEMATEL and fuzzy hierarchical TOPSIS methods for truck selection. *Expert Systems with Applications*, *40*(3), 899–907. doi:10.1016/j.eswa.2012.05.046

Chen, H. L. (2015). Performance measurement and the prediction of capital project failure. *International Journal of Project Management*, *33*(6), 1393–1404. doi:10.1016/j.ijproman.2015.02.009

Gopal, J., Sangaiah, A.K., Basu, A., Gao, X.Z. (2015). Integration of fuzzy DEMATEL and FMCDM approach for evaluating knowledge transfer effectiveness with reference to GSD project outcome. Article in Press. *International Journal of Machine Learning and Cybernetics*. Doi:10.1007/s13042-015-0370-5

Han, W.-M. (2015). Discriminating risky software project using neural networks. *Computer Standards & Interfaces*, *40*, 15–22. doi:10.1016/j.csi.2015.01.001

Han, W. M., & Huang, S. J. (2007). An empirical analysis of risk components and performance on software projects. *Journal of Systems and Software*, *80*(1), 42–50. doi:10.1016/j.jss.2006.04.030

Kannan, D., Jabbour, A. B. L. D. S., & Jabbour, C. J. C. (2014). Selecting green suppliers based on GSCM practices: Using fuzzy TOPSIS applied to a Brazilian electronics company. *European Journal of Operational Research*, *233*(2), 432–447. doi:10.1016/j.ejor.2013.07.023

Keil, M., Rai, A., & Liu, S. (2013). How user risk and requirements risk moderate the effects of formal and informal control on the process performance of IT projects. *European Journal of Information Systems*, *22*(6), 650–672. doi:10.1057/ejis.2012.42

Liu, S., & Wang, L. (2014). Understanding the impact of risks on performance in internal and outsourced information technology projects: The role of strategic importance. *International Journal of Project Management*, *32*(8), 1494–1510. doi:10.1016/j.ijproman.2014.01.012

Na, K. S., Simpson, J. T., Li, X., Singh, T., & Kim, K. Y. (2007). Software development risk and project performance measurement: Evidence in Korea. *Journal of Systems and Software*, *80*(4), 596–605. doi:10.1016/j.jss.2006.06.018

Omron. (n.d.). Retrieved from https://www.omron.com/

Patil, S. K., & Kant, R. (2014). A hybrid approach based on fuzzy DEMATEL and FMCDM to predict success of knowledge management adoption in supply chain. *Applied Soft Computing*, *18*, 126–135. doi:10.1016/j.asoc.2014.01.027

Sangaiah, A. K., Gopal, J., Basu, A., & Subramaniam, P. R. (2015). (Article in Press). An integrated fuzzy DEMATEL, TOPSIS, and ELECTRE approach for evaluating knowledge transfer effectiveness with reference to GSD project outcome. *Neural Computing and Applications, Springer Publishers*. doi:10.1007/s00521-015-2040-7

Sangaiah, A. K., Subramaniam, P. R., & Zheng, X. A. (2014). combined fuzzy DEMATEL and fuzzy TOPSIS approach for evaluating GSD project outcome factors. *Neural Computing & Applications*, *26*(5), 1025–1040. doi:10.1007/s00521-014-1771-1

Sangaiah, A. K., & Thangavelu, A. K. (2013). An exploration of FMCDM approach for evaluating the outcome/success of GSD projects. *Central European Journal of Engineering*, *3*(3), 419–435.

Takagi, Y., Mizuno, O., & Kikuno, T. (2005). An empirical approach to characterizing risky software projects based on logistic regression analysis. *Empirical Software Engineering*, *10*(4), 495–515. doi:10.1007/s10664-005-3864-z

Chapter 4
Solution of Basic Inventory Model in Fuzzy and Interval Environments:
Fuzzy and Interval Differential Equation Approach

Sankar Prasad Mondal
National Institute of Technology, Agartala, India

ABSTRACT

In this present paper a basic inventory model is solved in different imprecise environments. Four different cases are discussed: 1) Crisp inventory model, that is, the quantity at present and demand is crisp number; 2) Inventory model in fuzzy environment, that is, the quantity and demand both are fuzzy number; 3) Inventory model in interval environment, that is, the quantity and demand both are interval number and lastly; 4) Inventory model in time dependent fuzzy environment, that is, quantity and demand are both time dependent fuzzy number. Different numerical examples are used to illustrate the model as well as to compute the efficiency of imprecise differential equation approach to solve the model.

INTRODUCTION

The classical economic order quantity (EOQ) model was first developed by Harris (1915). Lots of researcher works on inventory control system and gives valuable contribution (e.g., Chang & Dye, 1999; Donaldson, 1977). A real-life inventory control model cannot be modeled without uncertainty or impreciseness in the parameters and/or variables. This uncertainty or impreciseness may be defined in stochastic and non-stochastic (fuzzy) sense and attempts to formulate and analyze such models (e.g., Chiang et al., 2005; Lee et al., 1999).

Though the demand and initial quantity of an item depends on several factors (such as selling rice, marketing cost, display of goods in showroom etc.), thus in reality it was estimated as random parameters with a probability distribution if sufficient past data available. These uncertain quantities can also be

DOI: 10.4018/978-1-5225-1008-6.ch004

estimated as fuzzy or interval parameter if past data is insufficient. We can assume that the sufficient past data are not available. Thus it is better to estimate parameters of quantity and demand as fuzzy or interval number rather than crisp or random number.

In this chapter, we look at the inventory problem with first order fuzzy differential equation (FDE) and interval differential equation (IDE). We solve the inventory model using FDE and IDE concepts. Presence of fuzzy and interval demand and quantity the model leads to FDE and IDE. Now the question arise in the readers mind that, "what is new approach for solving fuzzy and interval inventory model?". In the last few decay's many researcher consider the inventory models in fuzzy environment. But there is a problem. They first solve the inventory model with crisp number and at the solution then they substitute the concerned parameter by fuzzy number. Here the concept of fuzzy differential equation is missing. Moreover the application of fuzzy concept is violated (e.g., Guchhait et al. () etc). We consider two cases where the inventory model is considered with fuzzy differential equation. The solution procedure is used here namely generalized Hukuhara derivative approach, which is more recent general concept for solving fuzzy differential equation.

The uses of the interval number on this inventory model is also illustrates in a case. The interval number is taken as a new orientation. In interval environment the differential equation in present model converted to a interval differential equation. And by using the concepts of interval differential equation we solve the problem.

The concept of the fuzzy derivative was first initiated by Chang and Zadeh (1972). It was followed up by Dubois and Prade (1982). Other methods have been smeared by Puri and Ralescu (1983) and Goetschel and Voxman (1986). The concept of differential equations in a fuzzy environment was first formulated by Kaleva (1987). In fuzzy differential equation all derivative is deliberated as either Hukuhara or generalized derivatives. The Hukuhara differentiability has a deficiency (see Bede & Gal, 2005). The solution turns fuzzier as time goes by. Bede (2006) exhibited that a large class of BVPs has no solution if the Hukuhara derivative is applied. To exceeds this difficulty, the concept of a generalized derivative was developed and fuzzy differential equations were smeared using this concept (see Bencsik et al. (2007)). Khastan and Nieto (2010) set up the solutions for a large enough class of boundary value problems using the generalized derivative. Obviously the disadvantage of strongly generalized differentiability of a function in comparison H-differentiability is that, a fuzzy differential equation has no unique solution (see Bede and Gal (2005)). Recently, Stefanini (2008) by the concept of generalization of the Hukuhara difference for compact convex set, introduced generalized Hukuhara differentiability (see Stefanini and Bede (2009)) for fuzzy valued function and they displayed that, this concept of differentiability have relationships with weakly generalized differentiability and strongly generalized differentiability.

There are many approaches for solving FDE. Some researchers transform the FDE into equivalent fuzzy integral equation and then solve this (see Allahviranloo et al. (2011)). Another one is Zadeh extension (1975) principle method. In this method first solve the associated ODE and lastly fuzzify the solution and check whether it is satisfied or not. For details see Buckley and Feuring (2000, 2001). In the third approach, the fuzzy problem is converted to a crisp problem. Hüllermeier (1997), uses the concept of differential inclusion. In this way, by taking an α-cut of the initial value and the solution, the given differential equation is converted to a differential inclusion and the solution is accepted as the α-cut of the fuzzy solution. Laplace transform method is use many where in linear FDE (see Allahviranloo and Ahmadi, 2010). Recently, Mondal and Roy (2013) solve the first order Linear FDE by Lagrange multiplier method. Using generalized Hukuhara differentiability concept we transform the given FDE into two ODEs. And this ODEs also a differential equation involving the parametric form of a fuzzy number.

In spite of above mentioned developments, following lacunas are still exists in the formulation and solution of inventory models. Which are summarized below:

1. Though there are some articles of fuzzy inventory models which was solved by fuzzy differential equation approach (Das at al., 2008; Mondal et al., 2013; Guchhait at al., 2013), till now none has solve inventory problem with fuzzy differential equation approach by generalized Hukuhara derivative concepts.
2. In real-life inventory system sometimes the demand and quantity are time dependent. Here time dependent demand and quantity are considered and the model is solved using fuzzy differential equation concepts.
3. At the best of our knowledge in inventory model none has using the demand and quantity as interval valued function and solve using interval differential equation concepts.

The chapter is organized as follows: First section goes to introduction. In second section preliminaries and basic concepts on fuzzy number, fuzzy derivative, interval number and interval derivative are given. In third section assumption and notations of the proposed inventory model are listed. In fourth section contain four part. In first part basic inventory models are solved in crisp sense. Second part contains the same model with fuzzy data whereas third part is described in interval data and fourth part contain the solution of the model with time dependent fuzzy data. Fifth section goes to numerical example. Finally brief conclusions are drawn in sixth section.

PRELIMINARIES

Definition 1: Fuzzy Set

A fuzzy set $\tilde{A}$ is defined by $\tilde{A} = \left\{ \left(x, \mu_{\tilde{A}}\left(x\right) \right) : x \in A, \mu_{A}\left(x\right) \in \left[0,1\right] \right\}$. In the pair $\left(x, \mu_{\tilde{A}}\left(x\right) \right)$ the first element x belong to the classical set A, the second element $\mu_{\tilde{A}}\left(x\right)$, belong to the interval $\left[0,1\right]$, called Membership function.

Definition 2: α-Cut of a Fuzzy Set

The α-level set (or interval of confidence at level α or α-cut) of the fuzzy set $\tilde{A}$ of X is a crisp set A_{α} that contains all the elements of X that have membership values in $\tilde{A}$ greater than or equal to α i.e., $\tilde{A} = \left\{ x : \mu_{\tilde{A}}\left(x\right) \geq \alpha, x \in X, \alpha \in \left[0,1\right] \right\}$.

Definition 3: Fuzzy Number

A fuzzy number is fuzzy set like $u : R \to I = \left[0,1\right]$ which satisfies:

1. u is upper semi-continuous.
2. $u\left(x\right) = 0$ outside the interval $\left[c,d\right]$.

3. There are real numbers a, b such $c \leq a \leq b \leq d$, and:
    a. $u(x)$ is monotonic increasing on $[c, a]$,
    b. $u(x)$ is monotonic decreasing on $[b, d]$,
    c. $u(x) = 1$, $a \leq x \leq b$.

Let E^1 be the set of all real fuzzy numbers which are normal, upper semi-continuous, convex and compactly supported fuzzy sets (Zadeh, 2005).

Definition 4: Fuzzy Number (Parametric Form)

A fuzzy number u in a parametric form is a pair (u_1, u_2) of function $u_1(r), u_2(r), 0 \leq r \leq 1$, which satisfies the following requirments:

1. $u_1(r)$ is a bounded monotonic increasing left continuous function,
2. $u_2(r)$ is a bounded monotonic decreasing left continuous function,
3. $u_1(r) \leq u_2(r), 0 \leq r \leq 1$.

A crisp number x is simply represented by $(u_1(r), u_2(r)) = (x, x), 0 \leq r \leq 1$. By appropriate definitions, the fuzzy number space $\{(u_1(r), u_2(r))\}$ becomes a convex cone E^1 which could be embedded isomorphically and isometrically into a Banach space (Chang & Zadeh, 1972).

Definition 5

Let $x = (x_1(r), x_2(r))$, $y = (y_1(r), y_2(r)) \in E^1$, $0 \leq r \leq 1$ and arbitrary $k \in R$ (Goetschel & Voxman, 1986).

Then

1. $x = y$ iff $x_1(r) = y_1(r)$ and $x_2(r) = y_2(r)$,
2. $x + y = (x_1(r) + y_1(r), x_2(r) + y_2(r))$,
3. $x - y = (x_1(r) - y_2(r), x_2(r) - y_1(r))$,
4. $kx = \begin{cases} (kx_1(r), kx_2(r)), k \geq 0 \\ (kx_2(r), kx_1(r)), k < 0 \end{cases}$

Definition 6

For arbitrary $u = (u_1, u_2)$, $v = (v_1, v_2) \in E^1$, the quantity

$$D\left(u,v\right) = \left[\int\limits_{0}^{1}\left(u_1 - v_1\right)^2 + \int\limits_{0}^{1}\left(u_2 - v_2\right)^2\right]^{\frac{1}{2}}$$

is the distance between fuzzy numbers u and v (Kaleva, 1987).

Definition 7: Triangular Fuzzy Number

A Triangular fuzzy number (TFN) denoted by $\tilde{A}$ is defined as (a,b,c) where the membership function

$$\mu_{\tilde{A}}\left(x\right) = \begin{cases} 0, x \le a \\ \dfrac{x-a}{b-a}, a \le x \le b \\ 1, x = b \\ \dfrac{c-x}{c-b}, b \le x \le c \\ 0, x \ge c \end{cases}$$

Definition 8: α-Cut of a Fuzzy Set $\tilde{A}$

The α-cut of $\tilde{A} = (a,b,c)$ is given by

$$A_{\alpha} = \left[a + \alpha\left(b-a\right), c - \alpha\left(c-b\right)\right], \forall \alpha \in \left[0,1\right]$$

Definition 9: Generalized Fuzzy Number (GFN)

Generalized Fuzzy number $\tilde{A}$ as $\tilde{A} = \left(a_1, a_2, a_3, a_4; \omega\right)$, where $0 < \omega \le 1$, and a_1, a_2, a_3, a_4 $\left(a_1 < a_2 < a_3 < a_4\right)$ are real numbers. The generalized fuzzy number $\tilde{A}$ is a fuzzy subset of real line R, whose membership function $\mu_{\tilde{A}}\left(x\right)$ satisfies the following conditions:

1. $\mu_{\tilde{A}}\left(x\right) = R \rightarrow \left[0,1\right]$.
2. $\mu_{\tilde{A}}\left(x\right) = 0$ for $x \le a_1$.
3. $\mu_{\tilde{A}}\left(x\right)$ is strictly increasing function for $a_1 \le x \le a_2$.
4. $\mu_{\tilde{A}}\left(x\right) = w$ for $a_2 \le x \le a_3$.
5. $\mu_{\tilde{A}}\left(x\right)$ is strictly decreasing function for $a_3 \le x \le a_4$.
6. $\mu_{\tilde{A}}\left(x\right) = 0$ for $a_4 \le x$.

Definition 10: Generalized TFN

If $a_2 = a_3$ then $\tilde{A}$ is called a GTFN as $\tilde{A} = \left(a_1, a_2, a_4; \omega\right)$ or $(a_1, a_3, a_4; \omega)$ with membership function

$$\mu_{\tilde{A}}\left(x\right) = \begin{cases} \omega \dfrac{x - a_1}{a_2 - a_1} & if\ a_1 \leq x \leq a_2 \\ \omega \dfrac{a_4 - x}{a_4 - a_2} & if\ a_2 \leq x \leq a_4 \\ 0 & Otherwise \end{cases}$$

Definition 11: Time Dependent Triangular Fuzzy Number

A time dependent triangular fuzzy number (TFN) denoted by $A(t)$ is defined as $(a(t), b(t), c(t))$ where the membership function

$$\mu_{\tilde{A}}\left(x\right) = \begin{cases} 0, & x \leq a(t) \\ \dfrac{x - a(t)}{b(t) - a(t)}, & a(t) \leq x \leq b(t) \\ 1, & x = b(t) \\ \dfrac{c(t) - x}{c(t) - b(t)}, & b(t) \leq x \leq c(t) \\ 0, & x \geq c(t) \end{cases}$$

where $a(t) \leq b(t) \leq c(t)$.

Definition 12

Let $x, y \in E^1$. If there exists $z \in E^1$ such that $x = y + z$, then z is called the Hukuhara-difference of fuzzy numbers x and y, and it denoted by $z = x \ominus y$. Remark that $x \ominus y \neq x + \left(-1\right)y$ (Bede, 2006).

Definition 13

Let $f : \left[a, b\right] \to E^1$ and $t_0 \in \left[a, b\right]$ (Bede and Gal, 2005). We say that f is Hukuhara differential at t_0, if there exist an element $f'\left(t_0\right) \in E^1$ such that for all $h > 0$ sufficiently small, there exists $f\left(t_0 + h\right) \ominus f\left(t_0\right)$, $f\left(t_0\right) \ominus f\left(t_0 - h\right)$ and the limits exists in metric D.

$$\lim_{h \to 0} \frac{f\left(t_0 + h\right) \ominus f\left(t_0\right)}{h} = \lim_{h \to 0} \frac{f\left(t_0\right) \ominus f\left(t_0 - h\right)}{h} = f'\left(t_0\right)$$

Definition 14

Let $f : (a,b) \times E \to E$ and $x_0 \in (a,b)$ (Cano and Flores, 2008). We say that f is strongly generalized differential at x_0 (Bede-Gal differential) if there exists an element $f'(x_0) \in E$, such that

1. For all $h > 0$ sufficiently small, there exist $f(x_0 + h) -^h f(x_0)$ and $f(x_0) -^h f(x_0 - h)$ and the limits exist in the metric D

$$\lim_{h \searrow 0} \frac{f(x_0 + h) -^h f(x_0)}{h} = \lim_{h \searrow 0} \frac{f(x_0) -^h f(x_0 - h)}{h} = f'(x_0)$$

or,

2. For all $h > 0$ sufficiently small, there exist $f(x_0) -^h f(x_0 + h)$ and $f(x_0 - h) -^h f(x_0)$ and the limits exist in the metric D

$$\lim_{h \searrow 0} \frac{f(x_0) -^h f(x_0 + h)}{-h} = \lim_{h \searrow 0} \frac{f(x_0 - h) -^h f(x_0)}{-h} = f'(x_0)$$

or,

3. For all $h > 0$ sufficiently small, there exist $f(x_0 + h) -^h f(x_0)$, and $f(x_0 - h) -^h f(x_0)$ and the limits exist in the metric D

$$\lim_{h \searrow 0} \frac{f(x_0 + h) -^h f(x_0)}{h} = \lim_{h \searrow 0} \frac{f(x_0 - h) -^h f(x_0)}{-h} = f'(x_0)$$

or,

4. For all $h > 0$ sufficiently small, there exist $f(x_0) -^h f(x_0 + h)$ and $f(x_0) -^h f(x_0 - h)$ and the limits exists in the metric D

$$\lim_{h \searrow 0} \frac{f(x_0) -^h f(x_0 + h)}{-h} = \lim_{h \searrow 0} \frac{f(x_0) -^h f(x_0 - h)}{h} = f'(x_0)$$

(h and $-h$ at denominators mean $\frac{1}{h}$ and $-\frac{1}{h}$, respectively).

Definition 15

Let $f : R \to E$ be a function and denote $f(t) = \left(f_1(t,r), f_2(t,r) \right)$, for each $r \in [0,1]$ (Bede et al., 2007). Then

1. If f is (i)-differentiable, then $f_1(t,r)$ and $f_2(t,r)$ are also differentiable function and
    $$f'(t) = \left(f_1'(t,r), f_2'(t,r) \right).$$

2. If f is (ii)-differentiable, then $f_1(t,r)$ and $f_2(t,r)$ are also differentiable function and
    $$f'(t) = \left(f_2'(t,r), f_1'(t,r) \right).$$

Definition 16

Let $f : (a,b) \times E \to E$ and $x_0 \in (a,b)$ (Cano et al. (2007, 2008)). We define the nth-order derivative of f as follows: we say f is strongly generalized differentiable of the nth-order at x_0. If there exists an element $f^{(s)}(x_0) \in E$, $\forall s = 1, \ldots, n$, such that

For all $h > 0$ sufficiently small, there exist

$$f^{(s-1)}(x_0 + h) \ominus f^{(s-1)}(x_0) \text{ and } f^{(s-1)}(x_0) \ominus f^{(s-1)}(x_0 - h)$$

and the limits exist in the metric D

$$\lim_{h \searrow 0} \frac{f^{(s-1)}(x_0 + h) \ominus f^{(s-1)}(x_0)}{h} = \lim_{h \searrow 0} \frac{f^{(s-1)}(x_0) \ominus f^{(s-1)}(x_0 - h)}{h} = f^{(s)}(x_0)$$

or,

For all $h > 0$ sufficiently small, there exist

$$f^{(s-1)}(x_0) \ominus f^{(s-1)}(x_0 + h) \text{ and } f^{(s-1)}(x_0 - h) \ominus f^{(s-1)}(x_0)$$

and the limits exist in the metric D

$$\lim_{h \searrow 0} \frac{f^{(s-1)}(x_0) \ominus f^{(s-1)}(x_0 + h)}{-h} = \lim_{h \searrow 0} \frac{f^{(s-1)}(x_0 - h) \ominus f^{(s-1)}(x_0)}{-h} = f^{(s)}(x_0)$$

or,

For all $h > 0$ sufficiently small, there exist

$$f^{(s-1)}\left(x_0 + h\right) \ominus f^{(s-1)}\left(x_0\right) \text{ and } f^{(s-1)}\left(x_0 - h\right) \ominus f^{(s-1)}\left(x_0\right)$$

and the limits exist in the metric D.

$$\lim_{h \searrow 0} \frac{f^{(s-1)}\left(x_0 + h\right) \ominus f^{(s-1)}\left(x_0\right)}{h} = \lim_{h \searrow 0} \frac{f^{(s-1)}\left(x_0 - h\right) \ominus f^{(s-1)}\left(x_0\right)}{-h} = f^{(s)}\left(x_0\right)$$

or,

For all $h > 0$ sufficiently small, there exist

$$f^{(s-1)}\left(x_0\right) \ominus f^{(s-1)}\left(x_0 + h\right) \text{ and } f^{(s-1)}\left(x_0\right) \ominus f^{(s-1)}\left(x_0 - h\right)$$

and the limits exist in the metric D

$$\lim_{h \searrow 0} \frac{f^{(s-1)}\left(x_0\right) \ominus f^{(s-1)}\left(x_0 + h\right)}{-h} = \lim_{h \searrow 0} \frac{f^{(s-1)}\left(x_0\right) \ominus f^{(s-1)}\left(x_0 - h\right)}{h} = f^{(s)}\left(x_0\right)$$

(h and $-h$ at denominators mean $\frac{1}{h}$ and $-\frac{1}{h}$, respectively $\forall s = 1, \ldots, n$).

Definition 17: Generalized Hukuhara Difference

The generalized Hukuhara difference of two fuzzy numbers $u, v \in \mathcal{R}_\mathcal{F}$ is defined as follows

$$u -_g v = w \Leftrightarrow \begin{cases} (i)\, u = v \oplus w, or \\ (ii)\, v = u \oplus (-1)\, w \end{cases}$$

Consider $\left[w\right]_\alpha = \left[w_1\left(\alpha\right), w_1\left(\alpha\right)\right]$, then

$$w_1\left(\alpha\right) = \min\left\{u_1\left(\alpha\right) - v_1\left(\alpha\right), u_2\left(\alpha\right) - v_2\left(\alpha\right)\right\}$$

and

$$w_2(\alpha) = \max\left\{u_1(\alpha) - v_1(\alpha), u_2(\alpha) - v_2(\alpha)\right\}$$

Here the parametric representation of a fuzzy valued function $f : (a,b) \to \mathcal{R}_{\mathcal{F}}$ is expressed by

$$\left[f(t)\right]_\alpha = \left[f_1(t,\alpha), f_2(t,\alpha)\right], t \in [a,b], \alpha \in [0,1].$$

Definition 18: Generalized Hukuhara Derivative

The generalized Hukuhara derivative of a fuzzy valued function $f : (a,b) \to \mathcal{R}_{\mathcal{F}}$ at t_0 is defined as

$$f'(t_0) = \lim_{h \to 0} \frac{f(t_0 + h) -_g f(t_0)}{h}$$

In parametric form we say that

$f(t)$ is (i)-gH differentiable at t_0 if $\left[f'(t_0)\right]_\alpha = \left[f_1'(t_0,\alpha), f_2'(t_0,\alpha)\right]$

and

$f(t)$ is (ii)-gH differentiable at t_0 if $\left[f'(t_0)\right]_\alpha = \left[f_2'(t_0,\alpha), f_1'(t_0,\alpha)\right].$

Definition 19: Generalized Hukuhara Derivative for Second Order

The second order generalized Hukuhara derivative of a fuzzy valued function $f : (a,b) \to \mathcal{R}_{\mathcal{F}}$ at t_0 is defined as

$$f''(t_0) = \lim_{h \to 0} \frac{f'(t_0 + h) -_g f'(t_0)}{h}$$

If $f''(t_0) \in \mathcal{R}_{\mathcal{F}}$, we say that $f'(t_0)$ is generalized Hukuhara at t_0.

Also we say that $f'(t_0)$ is (i)-gH differentiable at t_0 if

$$f''(t_0;\alpha) = \begin{cases} \left[f_1''(t_0,\alpha), f_2''(t_0,\alpha)\right] if \ f \ be\,(i) - gH \ differentiable \ on\,(a,b) \\ \left[f_2''(t_0,\alpha), f_1''(t_0,\alpha)\right] if \ f \ be\,(ii) - gH \ differentiable \ on\,(a,b) \end{cases}$$

for all $\alpha \in [0,1]$, and that $f'(t_0)$ is (ii)-gH differentiable at t_0 if

$$f''\left(t_0;\alpha\right) = \begin{cases} \left[f_2''\left(t_0,\alpha\right), f_1''\left(t_0,\alpha\right)\right] if \ f \ be\left(i\right)-gH \ differentiable \ on\left(a,b\right) \\ \left[f_1''\left(t_0,\alpha\right), f_2''\left(t_0,\alpha\right)\right] if \ f \ be\left(ii\right)-gH \ differentiable \ on\left(a,b\right) \end{cases}$$

for all $\alpha \in \left[0,1\right]$.

Definition 20: Interval Number

An interval number I is represented by closed interval $[I_l, I_u]$ and defined by $I = [I_l, I_u] = \{x : I_l \leq x \leq I_u, x \in R\}$, where R is the set of real numbers, I_l and I_u are the left and right limit of the interval number respectively.

Lemma 1

The interval $[I_l, I_u]$ can also be represented as $h(p) = (I_l)^{1-p}(I_u)^p$ for $p \in [0,1]$.

Properties 1

If $I = [I_l, I_u]$ and $J = [J_l, J_u]$ be two interval can be written as interval-valued function as $h(p) = (I_l)^{1-p}(I_u)^p$ and $k(p) = (J_l)^{1-p}(J_u)^p$ for $p \in [0,1]$ then

1. $m(p) = (I_l + J_l)^{1-p}(I_u + J_u)^p$
2. $n(p) = (I_l - J_u)^{1-p}(I_u - J_l)^p$
3. $d(p) = (\min\{I_l J_l, I_l J_u, I_u J_l, I_u J_u\})^{1-p}(\max\{I_l J_l, I_l J_u, I_u J_l, I_u J_u\})^p$
4. $e(p) = \begin{cases} k(I_l)^{1-p}(I_u)^p if k > 0 \\ k(I_u)^{1-p}(I_l)^p if k < 0 \end{cases}$
5. $q(p) = \left(\min\left\{\dfrac{I_l}{J_l}, \dfrac{I_l}{J_u}, \dfrac{I_u}{J_l}, \dfrac{I_u}{J_u}\right\}\right)^{1-p}\left(\max\left\{\dfrac{I_l}{J_l}, \dfrac{I_l}{J_u}, \dfrac{I_u}{J_l}, \dfrac{I_u}{J_u}\right\}\right)^p$

where, $m(p), n(p), d(p), e(p), q(p)$ are interval valued function for $I+J, I-J, IJ, kI, I/J$ where k is constant and $p \in [0,1]$.

Theorem 1

The differential equation with interval valued coefficient and initial condition

$$x'(t) = f(t, k, x(t)), x(t_0) = x_0$$

where $x_0 \in [x_{0l}, x_{0u}]$ and $k \in [k_l, k_u]$ (coefficients)(are all > 0) are also written as interval-valued functional form as

$$x'(t; p) = f(t, (k_l)^{1-p}(k_u)^p, x(t; p))$$

with initial condition $x(t_0; p) = (x_{0l})^{1-p}(x_{0u})^p$ for $p \in [0,1]$.

Lemma 2

The condition for existence of the solution of the interval differential equation is

$$x(t; p = 0) \geq x(t; p = 1)$$

where, $x(t, p)$ be the solution of interval-valued differential equation.

PROBLEM DEFINITION AND MODEL FORMULATION

For the inventory model we take the notation:

$C_1 \equiv$ Holding cost/Unit quantity/Unit time.
$D \equiv$ Uniform Demand rate/Units/Unit time.
$C_3 \equiv$ Setup costs per order.
$U \equiv$ Purchasing cost per unit.
$Q \equiv$ Order quality.

Let $q(t)$ be the inventory at time t.

Let Q be the on hand stock at time $t = 0$ and due to demand the maximum inventory Q reduces to zero at time $t = T$ at the rate D units per unit time i.e., the rate of changes of inventory at any time t is equal to the negative effect of demand.

Therefore the governing differential equation is

$$\frac{dq(t)}{dt} = -D \text{ for } 0 \leq t \leq T$$

with initial condition $q(0) = Q$ and boundary condition $q(T) = 0$.

DEVELOPMENTS OF THE MODEL IN DIFFERENT IMPRECISE ENVIRONMENT

Model Developments in Crisp Environment

A basic inventory model in crisp environment is

Figure 1. Basic inventory model

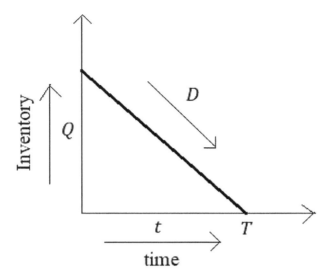

$$\frac{dq(t)}{dt} = -D \text{ for } 0 \le t \le T \tag{1}$$

with initial condition $q(0) = Q$ and boundary condition $q(T) = 0$.

Solution

Solution of the differential equation (1) is given by

$$q(t) = Q - Dt$$

Holding cost (HC) $= c_1 \int_0^T q(t)dt = c_1 \left[QT - \frac{DT^2}{2} \right]$

Total cost (TC) $= c_1 \left[QT - \frac{DT^2}{2} \right] + c_3$

Total average cost (TAC) $= c_1 \left[QT - \frac{DT^2}{2} \right] + \frac{c_3}{T}$

Now using initial condition we have $T = \frac{Q}{D}$. Therefore, TAC $= \frac{c_1 Q}{2} + \frac{c_3 D}{Q}$. The problem converted to

$$\text{Min TAC} = \frac{c_1 Q}{2} + \frac{c_3 D}{Q}$$

s.t., $Q > 0$.

Inventory Model with Fuzzy Number via Fuzzy Differential Equation Approach

If we take the demand and quantity are fuzzy number then the inventory model becomes

$$\frac{dq(t)}{dt} = -D \text{ for } 0 \leq t \leq T \tag{2}$$

with initial condition $q(0) = (Q_1, Q_2, Q_3)$ and boundary condition $q(T) = 0$ and $D = (D_1, D_2, D_3)$

Solution

There arise two cases for solving the problem (2).

Case 1: When $q(t)$ Is (i)-gH Differentiable

Then from (2) we get

$$\frac{dq_L(t,\alpha)}{dt} = -D_R(\alpha) \text{ and } \frac{dq_R(t,\alpha)}{dt} = -D_L(\alpha)$$

where

$$D_L(\alpha) = D_1 + \alpha(D_2 - D_1)$$

and

$$D_R(\alpha) = D_3 - \alpha(D_3 - D_2)$$

with boundary condition

$$q_L(0,\alpha) = Q_L(\alpha) = Q_1 + \alpha(Q_2 - Q_1),$$

$$q_R(0,\alpha) = Q_R(\alpha) = Q_3 - \alpha(Q_3 - Q_2),$$

$$q_L(T,\alpha) = 0$$

and

$$q_R(T, \alpha) = 0 \,.$$

The general solution is

$$q_L(t, \alpha) = -D_R(\alpha) + d_1 \text{ and } q_R(t, \alpha) = -D_L(\alpha) + d_2 \,.$$

Using initial condition we have

$$q_L(t, \alpha) = -D_R(\alpha) + Q_L \text{ and } q_R(t, \alpha) = -D_L(\alpha) + Q_R$$

[Note: Justification of FDE's solutions:

$$\frac{\partial q_L(t, \alpha)}{\partial \alpha} = (D_3 - D_2)t + (Q_2 - Q_1) \geq 0$$

$$\frac{\partial q_R(t, \alpha)}{\partial \alpha} = -(D_2 - D_1)t - (Q_3 - Q_2) \leq 0$$

and

$$q_L(t, 1) = -D_2 t + Q_2 = q_R(t, 1)$$

Hence all the conditions for existence of fuzzy differential equation are verified].
The holding cost:

$$HC_L(T, \alpha) = c_1 \int_{t=0}^{T} q_L(t, \alpha)dt = c_1 \left(-D_R(\alpha)\frac{T^2}{2} + Q_L(\alpha)T \right)$$

$$HC_R(T, \alpha) = c_1 \int_{t=0}^{T} q_R(t, \alpha)dt = c_1 \left(-D_L(\alpha)\frac{T^2}{2} + Q_R(\alpha)T \right)$$

The total cost:

$$TC_L(t, \alpha) = c_1 \left(-D_R(\alpha)\frac{T^2}{2} + Q_L(\alpha)T \right) + c_3$$

and

$$TC_R(T,\alpha) = c_1\left(-D_L(\alpha)\frac{T^2}{2} + Q_R(\alpha)T\right) + c_3$$

Now if $[TAC_L(T,\alpha), TAC_R(T,\alpha)]$ be the total average cost then

$$[TAC_L(T,\alpha), TAC_R(T,\alpha)]$$

$$= \left[\min\left\{\frac{c_3}{T} + c_1\left(-D_R(\alpha)\frac{T}{2} + Q_L(\alpha)\right), \frac{c_3}{T} + c_1\left(-D_L(\alpha)\frac{T}{2} + Q_R(\alpha)\right)\right\}\right],$$

$$\left[\max\left\{\frac{c_3}{T} + c_1\left(-D_R(\alpha)\frac{T}{2} + Q_L(\alpha)\right), \frac{c_3}{T} + c_1\left(-D_L(\alpha)\frac{T}{2} + Q_R(\alpha)\right)\right\}\right]$$

Using the above boundary conditions we get

$$TAC_L(T,\alpha) = \frac{c_1 Q_L(\alpha)}{2} + \frac{c_3 D_R(\alpha)}{Q_L(\alpha)}$$

$$TAC_R(T,\alpha) = \frac{c_1 Q_R(\alpha)}{2} + \frac{c_3 D_L(\alpha)}{Q_R(\alpha)}$$

Therefore the problem is converted to

$$\text{Min } TAC_L(T,\alpha) = \frac{c_1 Q_L(\alpha)}{2} + \frac{c_3 D_R(\alpha)}{Q_L(\alpha)}$$

$$\text{Min } TAC_R(T,\alpha) = \frac{c_1 Q_R(\alpha)}{2} + \frac{c_3 D_L(\alpha)}{Q_R(\alpha)}$$

s.t., $Q_L(\alpha), Q_R(\alpha) > 0$.

Case 2: When $q(t)$ Is (ii)-gH Differentiable

Then from (2) we have

$$\frac{dq_L(t,\alpha)}{dt} = -D_L(\alpha) \text{ and } \frac{dq_R(t,\alpha)}{dt} = -D_R(\alpha)$$

with same initial condition.

In this case the solution is written as

$$q_L(t,\alpha) = -D_L(\alpha)t + Q_L(\alpha)$$

and

$$q_R(t,\alpha) = -D_R(\alpha)t + Q_R(\alpha)$$

[Note: Justification of FDE's solutions:

$$\frac{\partial q_L(t,\alpha)}{\partial \alpha} = -(D_2 - D_1)t + (Q_2 - Q_1)$$

$$\frac{\partial q_R(t,\alpha)}{\partial \alpha} = (D_3 - D_2)t - (Q_3 - Q_2)$$

and

$$q_L(t,1) = -D_2 t + Q_2 = q_R(t,1)$$

The solution exists when:

$$\frac{\partial q_L(t,\alpha)}{\partial \alpha} \geq 0 \text{ i.e., } t \leq \frac{D_2(\alpha) - D_1(\alpha)}{Q_2(\alpha) - Q_1(\alpha)}$$

and

$$\frac{\partial q_R(t,\alpha)}{\partial \alpha} \leq 0 \text{ i.e., } t \geq \frac{D_3(\alpha) - D_2(\alpha)}{Q_3(\alpha) - Q_2(\alpha)}$$

i.e., when

$$\frac{D_3(\alpha) - D_2(\alpha)}{Q_3(\alpha) - Q_2(\alpha)} \leq t \leq \frac{D_2(\alpha) - D_1(\alpha)}{Q_2(\alpha) - Q_1(\alpha)},$$

hence all the conditions are verified. The solution is exist and it's a strong solution].

Let this condition is holds

$$HC_L(T,\alpha) = c_1 \int_{t=0}^{T} q_L(t,\alpha)dt = c_1\left(-D_L(\alpha)\frac{T^2}{2} + Q_L(\alpha)T\right)$$

$$HC_R(T,\alpha) = c_1 \int_{t=0}^{T} q_R(t,\alpha)dt = c_1\left(-D_R(\alpha)\frac{T^2}{2} + Q_R(\alpha)T\right)$$

Now if $[TAC_L(T,\alpha), TAC_R(T,\alpha)]$ be the total average cost then

$$[TAC_L(T,\alpha), TAC_R(T,\alpha)]$$

$$= \left[\min\left\{\frac{c_3}{T} + c_1\left(-D_R(\alpha)\frac{T}{2} + Q_L(\alpha)\right), \frac{c_3}{T} + c_1\left(-D_L(\alpha)\frac{T}{2} + Q_R(\alpha)\right)\right\}\right],$$

$$\left[\max\left\{\frac{c_3}{T} + c_1\left(-D_L(\alpha)\frac{T}{2} + Q_L(\alpha)\right), \frac{c_3}{T} + c_1\left(-D_R(\alpha)\frac{T}{2} + Q_R(\alpha)\right)\right\}\right]$$

Now,

$$TAC_L(T,\alpha) = \frac{c_1 Q_L(\alpha)}{2} + \frac{c_3 D_L(\alpha)}{Q_L(\alpha)}$$

$$TAC_R(T,\alpha) = \frac{c_1 Q_R(\alpha)}{2} + \frac{c_3 D_R(\alpha)}{Q_R(\alpha)}$$

Therefore the problem is converted to

$$\text{Min } TAC_L(T,\alpha) = \frac{c_1 Q_L(\alpha)}{2} + \frac{c_3 D_L(\alpha)}{Q_L(\alpha)}$$

$$\text{Min } TAC_R(T,\alpha) = \frac{c_1 Q_R(\alpha)}{2} + \frac{c_3 D_R(\alpha)}{Q_R(\alpha)}$$

s.t., $Q_L(\alpha), Q_R(\alpha) > 0$.

Inventory Model with Interval Number via Interval Differential Equation Approach

If we take the demand and quantity are interval number then the inventory model becomes

$$\frac{dq(t)}{dt} = -D \text{ for } 0 \le t \le T \qquad (3)$$

with initial condition $q(0) = (Q_l)^{1-p}(Q_u)^p$ boundary condition $q(T) = 0$ and $D = (D_l)^{1-p}(D_u)^p$

Solution

Therefore the above differential equation (3) can written in form of interval differential equation as follows

$$\frac{dq(t;p)}{dt} = -(D_u)^{1-p}(D_l)^p, \ p \in [0,1]$$

Therefore,

$$q(t,p) = -(D_u)^{1-p}(D_l)^p t + C$$

Using initial condition we get

$$q(t,p) = (Q_l)^{1-p}(Q_u)^p - (D_u)^{1-p}(D_l)^p t$$

Now,

$$HC(T;p) = c_1 \int_{t=0}^{T} q(t;p)dt = c_1 \int_{0}^{T} \{(Q_l)^{1-p}(Q_u)^p - (D_u)^{1-p}(D_l)^p t\}dt$$

$$= c_1(Q_l)^{1-p}(Q_u)^p T - (D_u)^{1-p}(D_l)^p \frac{T^2}{2}$$

$$TC(T;p) = c_1(Q_l)^{1-p}(Q_u)^p T - (D_u)^{1-p}(D_l)^p \frac{T^2}{2} + c_3$$

$$TAC(T;p) = c_1(Q_l)^{1-p}(Q_u)^p - (D_u)^{1-p}(D_l)^p \frac{T}{2} + \frac{c_3}{T}$$

Therefore the problem is converted to

$$\text{Min } TAC(T;p) = c_1 (Q_l)^{1-p} (Q_u)^p - (D_u)^{1-p} (D_l)^p \frac{T}{2} + \frac{c_3}{T}$$

s.t., $Q > 0$, i.e.,

$$\text{Min } TAC(T;p) = c_1 \frac{(Q_l)^{1-p} (Q_u)^p}{2} + \frac{c_3 (D_u)^{1-p} (D_l)^p}{(Q_l)^{1-p} (Q_u)^p}$$

s.t., $Q > 0$.

Inventory Model with Time Dependent Fuzzy Number via Fuzzy Differential Equation Approach

If we take the demand and quantity are time dependent fuzzy number then the inventory model becomes

$$\frac{dq(t)}{dt} = -D \text{ for } 0 \le t \le T \tag{4}$$

with initial condition $q(0) = (Q_l(t), Q_c(t), Q_r(t))$ and boundary condition $q(T) = 0$ and $D(t) = (D_l(t), D_c(t), D_r(t))$.

Solution

Case 1: When $q(t)$ Is (i)-gH Differentiable

Then we get from (4)

$$\frac{dq_L(t,\alpha)}{dt} = -D_R(t,\alpha) \text{ and } \frac{dq_R(t,\alpha)}{dt} = -D_L(t,\alpha)$$

where

$$D_L(t,\alpha) = D_l(t) + \alpha(D_c(t) - D_l(t))$$

and

$$D_R(t,\alpha) = D_r(t) - \alpha(D_r(t) - D_c(t))$$

with boundary condition $q_L(0,\alpha) = Q_L(t,\alpha)$, $q_R(0,\alpha) = Q_R(t,\alpha)$, $q_L(T,\alpha) = 0$, $q_R(T,\alpha) = 0$. The general solution is

$$q_L(t,\alpha) = -\int D_R(t,\alpha)dt + e_1$$

and

$$q_R(t,\alpha) = -\int D_L(t,\alpha)dt + e_2$$

Using initial condition we have

$$q_L(t,\alpha) = q_L(t,\alpha;T)$$

and

$$q_R(t,\alpha) = q_R(t,\alpha;T).$$

Case 2: When $q(t)$ Is (ii)-gH Differentiable

Then we get from (4)

$$\frac{dq_L(t,\alpha)}{dt} = -D_L(t,\alpha)$$

and

$$\frac{dq_R(t,\alpha)}{dt} = -D_R(t,\alpha)$$

where

$$D_L(t,\alpha) = D_l(t) + \alpha(D_c(t) - D_l(t))$$

and

$$D_R(t,\alpha) = D_r(t) - \alpha(D_r(t) - D_c(t))$$

with boundary condition $q_L(0,\alpha) = Q_L(t,\alpha)$, $q_R(0,\alpha) = Q_R(t,\alpha)$, $q_L(T,\alpha) = 0$, $q_R(T,\alpha) = 0$. The general solution is

$$q_L(t,\alpha) = -\int D_L(t,\alpha)dt + e_1$$

and

$$q_R(t,\alpha) = -\int D_R(t,\alpha)dt + e_2 \ .$$

Remarks: The solution procedure is same as before for suitable choice of $Q(t)$ and $D(t)$ we find $q_L(t,\alpha)$ and $q_R(t,\alpha)$ and optimize this.

NUMERICAL EXAMPLES

- **Problem 1:** Consider the basic fuzzy inventory model written in Equation (1) $c_1 = 1$, $D = 200$, $c_3 = 25$, $Q(0) = 100$.
  - **Solution:** In this case the solution is Min $TAC = 100$.
- **Problem 2:** Consider the basic fuzzy inventory model written in Equation (2) with given fuzzy data $c_1 = 1$, $D = (180, 200, 210)$, $c_3 = 25$, $Q(0) = (80, 100, 120)$.
  - **Solution:** The solution of this problem is:

Case 1: When *q*(*t*) Is (i)-gH Differentiable

The problem reduces to

Min $TAC_L(\alpha) = (40 + 10\alpha) + \dfrac{25(21 - \alpha)}{(8 + 2\alpha)}$

Min $TAC_R(\alpha) = (60 - 10\alpha) + \dfrac{25(9 + \alpha)}{(6 - \alpha)}$

s.t $80 + 20\alpha \geq 0$

$120 - 20\alpha \geq 0$

$\alpha \in [0,1]$

After solving this above problem we get the solution as shown in Table 1 and Figure 2.

Remarks

From this table and graph we conclude that

1. $TAC_L(\alpha)$ is decreasing and $TAC_R(\alpha)$ is increasing as α goes 0 to 1.
2. If the initial vale of a differential equation is taken as triangular fuzzy environments then it need not that the solution is triangular fuzzy number also.

Table 1. Optimal result for the fuzzy model in case 1 for different α

Figure 2. Graphical representation of optimal result for the fuzzy model in case 1 for different α

α	$TAC_L(\alpha)$	$TAC_R(\alpha)$
0	105.6250	97.5000
0.1	104.7195	97.5593
0.2	103.9048	97.6552
0.3	103.1744	97.7895
0.4	102.5227	97.9643
0.5	101.9444	98.1818
0.6	101.4348	98.4444
0.7	100.9894	98.7547
0.8	100.6042	99.1154
0.9	100.2755	99.5294
1	100.0000	100.0000

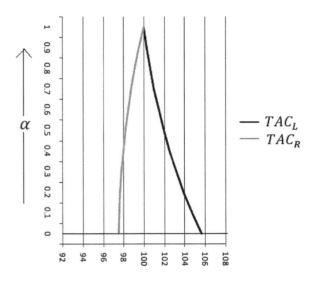

From conclusion 1 we can say that the solution is weak solution.

The solution can be written correctly as

$$[TAC_L^{*}(\alpha), TAC_R^{*}(\alpha)] = [\min\{TAC_L(\alpha), TAC_R(\alpha)\}, \max\{TAC_L(\alpha), TAC_R(\alpha)\}]$$

Hence the corrected solution is shown in Table 2 and Figure 3.

Case 2: When $q(t)$ Is (ii)-gH Differentiable

The problem reduces to

$$\text{Min } TAC_L(\alpha) = (40 + 10\alpha) + \frac{25(9 + \alpha)}{(4 + \alpha)}$$

$$\text{Min } TAC_R(\alpha) = (60 - 10\alpha) + \frac{25(21 - \alpha)}{(12 - 2\alpha)}$$

s.t $80 + 20\alpha \geq 0$

$120 - 20\alpha \geq 0$

Table 2. Optimal corrected result for the fuzzy model in case 1 for different α

α	$TAC^*_L(\alpha)$	$TAC^*_R(\alpha)$
0	97.5000	105.6250
0.1	97.5593	104.7195
0.2	97.6552	103.9048
0.3	97.7895	103.1744
0.4	97.9643	102.5227
0.5	98.1818	101.9444
0.6	98.4444	101.4348
0.7	98.7547	100.9894
0.8	99.1154	100.6042
0.9	99.5294	100.2755
1	100.0000	100.0000

Figure 3. Graphical representation of optimal corrected result for the fuzzy model in case 1 for different α

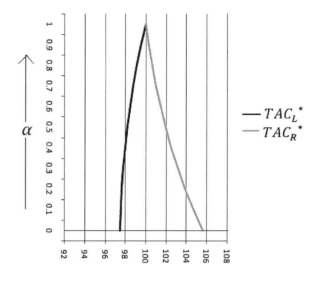

$$\alpha \in [0,1], t > 0$$

After solving this above problem we get the solution as shown in Table 3 and Figure 4.

Remarks

From this table we conclude that

1. $TAC_L(\alpha)$ is increasing and $TAC_R(\alpha)$ is decreasing as α goes 0 to 1.
2. If the initial vale of a differential equation is taken as triangular fuzzy environments then it need not that the solution is triangular fuzzy number also.

From conclusion 1 we say that the solution is strong solution. Acceptance of the solution in this case is strongly recommended.

Problem 3: Consider the basic interval inventory model written in Equation (3) with given interval data
$$c_1 = 1, \ D = (180)^{1-p}(210)^p, \ c_3 = 25, \ Q = (80)^{1-p}(120)^p, \ p \in [0,1].$$
Solution: The solution of this problem are comes from

$$\text{Min } TAC = \frac{(180)^{1-p}(210)^p}{2} + \frac{25(80)^{1-p}(120)^p}{(180)^{1-p}(210)^p}$$

Table 3. Optimal result for the fuzzy model in case 2 for different α

α	$TAC_L(\alpha)$	$TAC_R(\alpha)$
0	96.2500	103.7500
0.1	96.4878	103.2797
0.2	96.7619	102.8276
0.3	97.0698	102.3947
0.4	97.4091	101.9821
0.5	97.7778	101.5909
0.6	98.1739	101.2222
0.7	98.5957	100.8774
0.8	99.0417	100.5577
0.9	99.5102	100.2647
1	100.0000	100.0000

Figure 4. Graphical representation of optimal corrected result for the fuzzy model in case 2 for different α

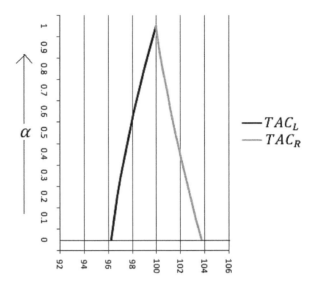

s.t. $(80)^{1-p}(120)^p \geq 0$

$p \in [0,1]$

and solving this above problem the results are written as shown in Table 4.

Note: we find the solution for some $p \in [0,1]$. Moreover the optimum result comes in interval also. At $p = 0, TAC = 90.4444$ and $p = 1, TAC = 105.5714$, i.e., the optimal result is also written in the form $[90.4444, 105.5714]$.

Problem 4: Consider the basic fuzzy inventory model written in Equation 2 with given fuzzy data $c_1 = 1, D = (170t, 200t, 220t), c_3 = 25, Q(0) = (80t, 100t, 110t)$.

Solution: The solution of this problem is:

Case 1: When $q(t)$ Is (i)-gH Differentiable

The solution comes from

$$\text{Min } TAC_L(\alpha) = c_1\left[\left(40T^* - \frac{110T^{*2}}{3}\right) + \left(10T^* - \frac{10T^{*2}}{3}\right)\alpha\right] + \frac{c_3}{T^*}$$

Table 4. Optimal result for the interval model for different p

p	TAC(Q; p)
0	90.4444
0.1	91.8539
0.2	93.2853
0.3	94.7391
0.4	96.2155
0.5	97.7151
0.6	99.2380
0.7	100.7848
0.8	102.3556
0.9	103.9511
1	105.5714

$$\text{Min } TAC_R(\alpha) = c_1\left[\left(55T^{**} - \frac{85T^{**^2}}{3}\right) - \left(5T^{**} + 5T^{**^2}\right)\alpha\right] + \frac{c_3}{T^*}$$

s.t $80t + 20t\alpha \geq 0$

$110t - 10t\alpha \geq 0$

$\alpha \in [0,1], t > 0$

where $T^* = \dfrac{8 + 2\alpha}{11 + \alpha}$ and $T^{**} = \dfrac{22 - 2\alpha}{17 + 3\alpha}$.

After solving the above problem we get the solution as shown in Table 5 and Figure 5.

Remarks

From Table 5 we see that $TAC_L(\alpha)$ is decreasing and $TAC_R(\alpha)$ is increasing as α goes 0 to 1. But the existence of solution is that $TAC_L(\alpha) \leq TAC_R(\alpha)$ for every α. But it does not holds here. So, the solution does not exists.

Table 5. Optimal result for the fuzzy model in case 1 for different α

α	$TAC_L(\alpha)$	$TAC_R(\alpha)$
0	45.8335	43.0443
0.1	45.7588	42.7321
0.2	45.7083	42.4603
0.3	45.6861	42.2326
0.4	45.6958	42.0423
0.5	45.7256	41.8900
0.6	45.7795	41.7728
0.7	45.8564	41.6958
0.8	45.9504	41.6526
0.9	46.0702	41.6410
1	46.2053	41.6667

Figure 5. Graphical representation of optimal result for the fuzzy model in case 1 for different α

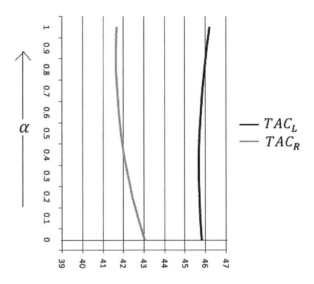

Case 2: When $q(t)$ Is (ii)-gH Differentiable

The solution are comes from

$$\text{Min } TAC_L(\alpha) = c_1\left[\left(40T^* - \frac{85T^{*2}}{3}\right) + \left(10T^* - 5T^{*2}\right)\alpha\right] + \frac{c_3}{T^*}$$

$$\text{Min } TAC_R(\alpha) = c_1\left[\left(55T^{**} - \frac{110T^{**2}}{3}\right) + \left(\frac{10T^{**2}}{3} - 5T^{**}\right)\alpha\right] + \frac{c_3}{T^{**}}$$

s.t $80t + 20t\alpha \geq 0$

$110t - 10t\alpha \geq 0$

$\alpha \in [0,1], t > 0$

where $T^* = \dfrac{16 + 4\alpha}{17 + 3\alpha}$ and $T^{**} = 1$.

After solving we get the results shown in Table 6 and Figure 6.

Remarks

From Table 6 we see that $TAC_L(\alpha)$ is increasing and $TAC_R(\alpha)$ is decreasing as α goes 0 to 1. Hence the solution is strong solution. Hence in this case the solution is highly recommended. Now the point is that, for different problem the results are varied. So, where the strong solution can found, then researcher should accept this results first.

CONCLUSION AND FUTURE RESEARCH SCOPE

In this chapter, a classical inventory model is solved in different imprecise environments such as fuzzy, interval and time dependent fuzzy environment. The solution procedures are used namely fuzzy differential equation approach and interval differential equation approach. In fuzzy inventory cases the use of generalize Hukuhara derivative of a function is taken and solve them (which is a most generalization of all fuzzy derivative). In interval inventory cases the interval number is taken as a interval-valued function and solve this by the concept of interval differential equation. The fuzzy and interval differential equation approach is a very promising method for solving fuzzy or interval inventory problem. In future any one can repeat this in different models involving fuzzy delay differential equation, system of fuzzy differential equation, fuzzy fractional differential equation and problems with inventory etc and solve them.

Table 6. Optimal result for the fuzzy model in case 2 for different α

α	$TAC_L(\alpha)$	$TAC_R(\alpha)$
0	39.1105	43.3333
0.1	39.3267	43.1667
0.2	39.5560	43.0000
0.3	39.7900	42.8333
0.4	40.0368	42.6667
0.5	40.2879	42.5000
0.6	40.5515	42.3333
0.7	40.8192	42.1667
0.8	41.0951	42.0000
0.9	41.3790	41.8333
1	41.6667	41.6667

Figure 6. Graphical representation of optimal result for the fuzzy model in case 2 for different α

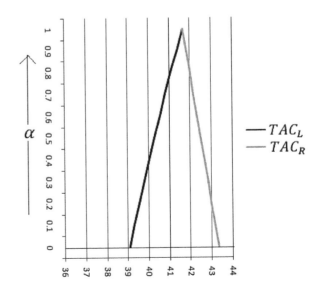

REFERENCES

Allahviranloo, T., Abbasbandy, S., Salahshour, S., & Hakimzadeh, A. (2011). A., A new method for solving fuzzy linear differential equations. *Computing*, *92*(2), 181–197. doi:10.1007/s00607-010-0136-6

Allahviranloo, T., & Ahmadi, M. B. (2010). Fuzzy Laplace transforms. *Soft Computing*, *14*(3), 235–243. doi:10.1007/s00500-008-0397-6

Bede, B. (2006). A note on "two-point boundary value problems associated with non-linear fuzzy differential equations". *Fuzzy Sets and Systems*, *157*(7), 986–989. doi:10.1016/j.fss.2005.09.006

Bede, B. (2008). Note on "Numerical solutions of fuzzy differential equations by predictor-corrector method". *Information Sciences*, *178*(7), 1917–1922. doi:10.1016/j.ins.2007.11.016

Bede, B., & Gal, S. G. (2004). Almost periodic fuzzy-number-value functions. *Fuzzy Sets and Systems*, *147*(3), 385–403. doi:10.1016/j.fss.2003.08.004

Bede, B., & Gal, S. G. (2005). Generalizations of the differentiability of fuzzy-number-valued functions with applications to fuzzy differential equations. *Fuzzy Sets and Systems*, 151581–151599.

Bede, B., Rudas, I. J., & Bencsik, A. L. (2007). First order linear fuzzy differential equations under generalized differentiability. *Inf.Sci.*, 1771648–1771662.

Buckley, J. J., & Feuring, T. (2000). Fuzzy differential equations. *Fuzzy Sets and Systems*, *110*(1), 43–54. doi:10.1016/S0165-0114(98)00141-9

Buckley, J. J., & Feuring, T. (2001). Fuzzy initial value problem for Nth-order linear differential equations. *Fuzzy Sets and Systems*, *121*(2), 247–255. doi:10.1016/S0165-0114(00)00028-2

Cano, Y. C., & Flores, H. R. (2008). On the new solution of fuzzy differential equations. *Chaos, Solitons, and Fractals*, *38*(1), 112–119. doi:10.1016/j.chaos.2006.10.043

Chang, H. J., & Dye, C. Y. (1999). An EOQ model for deteriorating items with timevarying demand and partial backlogging. *Journal of Operational Research*, *50*(S11), 1176–1182. doi:10.1057/palgrave.jors.2600801

Chang, S. L., & Zadeh, L. A. (1972). On fuzzy mapping and control. *IEEE Transactions on Systems, Man, and Cybernetics*, *2*(1), 30–34. doi:10.1109/TSMC.1972.5408553

Chiang, J., Yao, J. S., & Lee, H. M. (2005). Fuzzy inventory with backorder defuzzification by signed distance method. *Journal of Information Science and Engineering*, *21*, 671–694.

Das, B., Mahapatra, N. K., & Maity, M. (2008). Initial-valued first order fuzzy differential equation in Bi-level inventory model with fuzzy demand. *Mathematical Modeling and Analysis*, *13*(4), 493–512. doi:10.3846/1392-6292.2008.13.493-512

Donaldson, W. A. (1977). Inventory replenishment policy for a linear trend in demand-an analytical solution. *Operational Research Quarterly*, *28*(3), 663–670. doi:10.2307/3008916

Dubois, D., & Prade, H. (1982). Towards fuzzy differential calculus: Part 3, Differentiation. *Fuzzy Sets and Systems*, *8*(3), 225–233. doi:10.1016/S0165-0114(82)80001-8

Dubois, D., & Prade, H. (1982). Towards fuzzy differential calculus: Part 3, Differentiation. *Fuzzy Sets and Systems, 8*(3), 225–233. doi:10.1016/S0165-0114(82)80001-8

Goetschel, R. Jr, & Voxman, W. (1986). Elementary fuzzy calculus. *Fuzzy Sets and Systems, 18*(1), 31–43. doi:10.1016/0165-0114(86)90026-6

Guchhait, P., Maiti, M. K., & Maiti, M. (2013). A production inventory model with fuzzy production and demand using fuzzy differential equation: An interval compared genetic algorithm approach. *Engineering Applications of Artificial Intelligence, 26*(2), 766–778. doi:10.1016/j.engappai.2012.10.017

Guchhait, P., Maity, M. K., & Maity, M. (2014). Inventory model of a deteriorating item with price and credit linked fuzzy demand: A fuzzy differential equation approach. *OPSEARCH, 51*(3), 321–353. doi:10.1007/s12597-013-0153-2

Harris, F. (1915). *Operations and Cost-Factory management series*. Chicago, IL: A.W. Shaw Co.

Hullermeier, E. (1997). An approach to modeling and simulation of uncertain dynamical systems. *International Journal of Uncertainty, Fuzziness and Knowledge-based Systems, 5*(02), 117–137. doi:10.1142/S0218488597000117

Kaleva, O. (1987). Fuzzy differential equations. *Fuzzy Sets and Systems, 24*(3), 301–317. doi:10.1016/0165-0114(87)90029-7

Khastan, A., & Nieto, J. J. (2010). A boundary value problem for second-order fuzzy differential equations. *Nonlinear Analysis, 72*(9-10), 3583–3593. doi:10.1016/j.na.2009.12.038

Lee, H. M., & Yao, J. S. (1999). Economic order quantity in fuzzy sense for inventory without backorder model. *Fuzzy Sets and Systems, 105*(1), 13–31. doi:10.1016/S0165-0114(97)00227-3

Mondal, M., Maiti, M. K., & Maiti, M. (2013). A production-recycling model with variable demand, demand-dependent fuzzy return rate: A fuzzy differential equation approach. *Computers & Industrial Engineering, 64*(1), 318–332. doi:10.1016/j.cie.2012.10.014

Mondal, S.P., & Roy, T.K. (2013). First Order Linear Homogeneous Fuzzy Ordinary Differential Equation Based on Lagrange Multiplier Method. *Journal of Soft Computing and Applications*, 1-17.

Puri, M. L., & Ralescu, D. A. (1983). Differentials of fuzzy functions. *Journal of Mathematical Analysis and Applications, 91*(2), 552–558. doi:10.1016/0022-247X(83)90169-5

Puri, M. L., & Ralescu, D. A. (1983). Differentials of fuzzy functions. *Journal of Mathematical Analysis and Applications, 91*(2), 552–558. doi:10.1016/0022-247X(83)90169-5

Stefanini, L. (2008). A generalization of Hukuhara difference for interval and fuzzy arithmetic. In D. Dubois, M. A. Lubiano, H. Prade, M. A. Gil, P. Grzegorzewski, & O. Hryniewicz (Eds.), *Soft Methods for Handling Variability and Imprecision*. doi:10.1007/978-3-540-85027-4_25

Stefanini, L., & Bede, B. (2009). Generalized Hukuhara differentiability of interval-valued functions and interval differential equations. *Nonlinear Analysis, 71*(3-4), 1311–1328. doi:10.1016/j.na.2008.12.005

Zadeh, L. A. (1975). The concept of a linguistic variable and its application to approximate reasoning. *Information Sciences, 8*(3), 199–249. doi:10.1016/0020-0255(75)90036-5

KEY TERMS AND DEFINITIONS

Fuzzy Derivative: Since fuzzy difference are different than crisp difference so fuzzy derivative are different.

Fuzzy Difference: The fuzzy number is not like crisp number. So the fuzzy difference is not same as crisp difference.

Fuzzy Differential Equation: The differential equation associated with fuzzy number.

Fuzzy Number: The element of fuzzy sets is called fuzzy number.

Fuzzy Sets: A set which is a collection of object with graded membership function.

Impreciseness: When uncertainties with some problem then it is also called impreciseness.

Interval Differential Equation: The differential equation associated with interval number.

Chapter 5
A Fuzzy-Based Calorie Burn Calculator for a Gamified Walking Activity Using Treadmill

Prabhakar Rontala Subramaniam
University of KwaZulu-Natal, South Africa

Chitra Venugopal
University of KwaZulu-Natal, South Africa

Arun Kumar Sangaiah
VIT University, India

ABSTRACT

Gamification can be viewed as a process design which encapsulates competition, achievements, status and self-expression. Gamification is used as a tool for improving physical fitness. In this chapter the physical activity using treadmill walking is considered. Calorie burn calculation plays a vital role in the gamification design. In treadmill calorie burn calculation, traditional and fuzzy based methods are compared for effective gamification. In the traditional calorie burn calculation method different equations are used for different incline levels. In the fuzzy logic method fuzzy reasoning technique is applied to calculate the calorie burn for different incline levels. It is identified that fuzzy based calorie calculation enhances physical activity and supports Gamification. Fuzzy based calorie burn calculation methods produces approximate values and supports the players to choose higher incline levels instead of lower incline levels and thereby burning more calories.

INTRODUCTION

Overweight and obese is a growing threat for kids and adults. This is the main cause for many health risks such as heart disease, diabetes, blood pressure, cholesterol and cardio-vascular diseases (Strong, Malina, & Blimkie, 2005). There are many research reviews and published scientific articles examine the need for physical activity and fitness to enhance healthy life style in the present stressful environment (Castelli, Centeio, Hwang,Barcelona, Glowacki, Calvert, & Nicksic, 2014). The number of published articles that examined the relationships between physical activity and fitness is shown in Figure 1.

DOI: 10.4018/978-1-5225-1008-6.ch005

Figure 1. Number of articles examining physical activity and fitness published yearwise

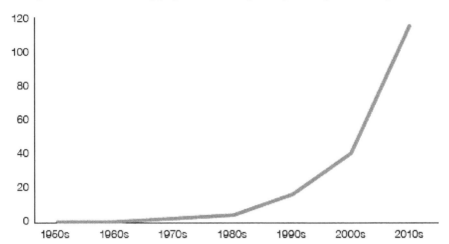

Physical activity can be defined as any bodily movement produced by skeletal muscles that results in energy expenditure (Carl, Kenneth, & Gregory, 1985). A planned, structured and repetitive physical activity is called an exercise (Carl, et al. 1985). There are many physical activities such as house hold work, occupational, sports, etc. that can be performed in daily life for energy expenditure.

The technology development and consistently growing stress in work environment that reflects in personal life reduces the ability of the people to spend energy through physical activities. A regular exercise is required to maintain physical fitness, reduced stress and good health. The low, moderate and high intensity exercise determines the amount of energy spent. The amount of energy spent is measured in kilojoules (kJ) or kilocalories (kcal). The intensity, duration and frequency of muscular contractions determines total amount of calorie burnt (Taylor, 1978).

There are many indoor and outdoor exercises available. The best outdoor exercises are walking, jogging, biking, swimming, and hiking. In spite of recommendations made by several researchers to exercise outdoor to burn more calories, several factors like time, personal safety, allergies and/or weather conditions limits outdoor activities (Atif, Oumair,Daciana, & Evor, 2013). So there is a need for people to make use of equipment to exercise outdoor activities at indoor. The commonly used indoor equipments are treadmill, elliptical, and bike. Among these treadmill is the most common equipment used by wide range of people. Treadmill can be used for various purposes like exercise, training, treatment of stress disorder, etc. which enables the user to set up an indoor exercise that can be carried out irrespective of outdoor conditions. Treadmill is a common piece of equipment that offers variety of benefits such as walk, jog and run. It helps to burn calories, build speed and endurance to improve the health condition. Many treadmills feature calorie counter that estimates the number of calories burnt during the workout.

Gamification is a technology based tool integrated into non-game applications. It increases involvement through participation to achieve pre-defined goals. Though exercising using treadmill is a preferred method for burning calories, there is a lack of motivation to achieve activity goals. Gamification can motivate exercise faster, longer, frequent and enjoyable physical activity. Gamification is defined as "the use of game design elements in non-game contexts" (Deterding, Dixon, Khaled, & Nacke, 2011).

The research conducted by (Fredrick, & Ryan, 1993), says that higher the internal motivation higher is the achievement during exercise. Gamification is extremely helpful in motivating the player and monitoring the activity to achieve higher goals.

Fuzzy logic is a technique that deals with concepts that cannot be expressed as completely "TRUE" or "FALSE" but rather as "Partially True" or "Partially False". In fuzzy logic the solution to the problem can be easily understood by the human operators which makes it easier to automate tasks that are already successfully performed by traditional methods.

This research targets to achieve player involvement by motivating player's participation to burn maximum calories while walking in a treadmill. This is achieved by designing a fuzzy based calorie burn calculator for treadmill walking exercise.

This chapter is organized by discussing gamification, various calorie burn calculation techniques, and fuzzy parameter and design of fuzzy rules for calorie burn calculation in comparison of fuzzy results with the traditional calorie burn calculation method in the following sections.

BACKGROUND

The term gamification was first coined in 2003 by Nick Pelling but it gained popularity after 2010 (Zac, 2015). Gamification is a concept that applies game mechanics to motivate people to achieve their goals. The success of gamfication depends on the game design technique that can enable WIN-WIN situation for the user and also the provider. The game mechanics plays an important role in deciding the WIN-WIN situation. There are few metrices which determine the success of the gamification are: Engagement, Influence, Loyality, User Generated Counts, Time spent and invite a friend activities (Ritterfeld, Cody, & Vorderer, 2009).

Zichermann and Cunningham, (2011) has identified four different types of players in gamification – explorer, achievers, socialisers and killers. Explorers are more concerned about their experience and proclaiming their discovery to the society. Achievers are concerned about achieving high results. Social-izers give priority to socialize rather than winning. Killers are small population of player type who are keen on winning at the same time keen on others failure.

The recently booming area in which multiple forms of gameplay techniques are used is health sector particularly in calorie burn and body building programs such as gym activities. Gamification not only motivates the user irrespective of their age but also helps those with chronic diseases to manage their eating and exercising schedules. The success of gameplay involves understanding of the user behaviour from the data, analysing the data to find out reasons for user behaviour and developing creative ideas to keep up the user in the game.

In gamification, internal and external motivation plays a major role in achieving the goal. The important aspect is that the internal motivation can be improved by external motivation. The calorie burn calculation plays a vital role in the gym activities and success of gameplay used. In this chapter, calorie burn is considered as internal motivation whereas, weight loss and looking beautiful/handsome is considered as external motivation.

In many calorie calculation methods, the calorie burn is based on the body measurements (such as height, weight, age, gender), type of sport (running, walking or jogging), distance covered, time, speed and heart rate (Katch, 2010). The more data is provided, the more accurate is the calorie burned calculated. The formulae for calculating the calorie burnt are not well defined. Different parameters are analysed to calculate the calorie burned.

The most common analysis is that the human body uses about 60% of calories just to carry on the natural processes at rest (Jonathan, Paul, Paul, & Steven, 2013). The general concept of burning high calorie depends on the lean muscle mass of the body. The more muscular physique built increases the ability of building more calories (Kelly, 2015).

The Basal Metabolic Rate (BMR) gives the amount of calories the body requires to carry on the vital functions to keep it alive or the calories burnt at rest. In Harris Benedict method (Harris, & Benedict, 1918), the BMR calculation is based on Weight, Height, Age and Gender of the person.

The formula for men and women (Amirkalati 2008) are,

$$BMR \text{ for Men} = 66.7 + (13.75 \times W) + (5.0 \times H) - (6.75 \times A)$$

$$BMR \text{ for Women} = 665.09 + (9.56 \times W) + (1.84 \times H) - (4.67 \times A)$$

where,

H = Height in cms,
W = Weight in kgs,
A = Age in years.

This BMR calculation is given in kCal per day and is not accurate. On an average, for men the body needs 2500 kcal for men and 2000kCal for women to perform the vital activities (Roza, Shizgal, Harry, 1984).

The BMR, body fat percentage, diet and exercise habits are interlinked in a weight loss or calorie need to be burnt to lose weight program (Muller, Meuk, Burgi, & Diem, 2001).

The weight loss programs needs the average BMR of a person to calculate how much calories need to be burnt to achieve the required weight in a given time. So the exercise habits are taken into consideration to calculate the calorie intake or diet.

The calculated BMR value is multiplied by activity multiplier to get the total daily energy expenditure (TDEE) which estimates the total energy expended in a day. The activity multiplier for different levels of activity people (Katch, 2010; Harris, & Benedict, 1918) are

- Sedantry people – 1.2.
- Lightly active (light exercise 1 to 3 times in a week) – 1.375.
- Moderately active people (exercise between 3 to 5 times in a week) – 1.55.
- Very active people (exercise between 6 to 7 times in a week) – 1.725.
- Extremely active people (exercise very hard) – 1.9.

In a weight loss program if the calorie intake of a person is equal to the BMR value then the rate of decrease of weight is reduced. The high activity shows that the body consumes more calories to do the vital function and hence the rate of decrease of weight is increased.

In Harris Benedict method (Harris, & Benedict, 1918), the body composition is not considered. The individuals with more muscle tend to be more metabolically active and burn more calories. The Harris

Benedict method overestimates calorie burn for individuals with a high body fat percentage and under-estimates calorie burn for those with low body fat which is not perfect (Roza,et al. 1984).

In Katch and McArdle (KA) method (Katch, 2010), the body composition is taken into consideration to calculate the BMR. It also uses activity multiplier as in Harris Benedict method. The disadvantage of KA method is the way of measuring the body fat measurement because it usually vary from person to person.

The other common method of calorie calculation is based on the heart rate. This heart rate is often measured by wearing a heart rate monitor or sport watch which can transmit the heart rate to the calculation unit to calculate the calorie burnt. The calorie calculation formula based on the heart rate (Swain, Abernathy, Smith, Lee, & Bunn, 1994) is given by

Calorie Burn for Women:

$$\left[\left(Age \times 0.074\right) - \left(Weight \times 0.05741\right) + \left(HeartRate \times 0.04472\right) - 20.4022\right] \times Time / 4.184$$

Calorie Burn for Men:

$$\left[\left(Age \times 0.2017\right) - \left(Weight \times 0.0936\right) + \left(HeartRate \times 0.6309\right) - 55.0969\right] \times Time / 4.184$$

The calorie calculation method provided by Keytle, (2005) uses delivery of oxygen level called VO2Max.

Calorie Burn for Women:

$$\left[\begin{array}{l}\left(Age \times 0.274\right) - \left(Weight \times 0.103\right) + \left(HeartRate \times 0.45\right) \\ + \left(V02Max \times 0.380 - 59.3954\right)\end{array}\right] \times Time / 4.184$$

Calorie Burn for Men:

$$\left[\begin{array}{l}\left(Age \times 0.271\right) - \left(Weight \times 0.394\right) + \left(Heart Rate \times 0.634\right) \\ + \left(VO2Max \times 0.404\right) - 95.7735\end{array}\right] \times Time / 4.184$$

The disadvantage of this calculation method is that the heart rate monitor should be in contact with the body and transmit the VO2max data for calculation. If the contact is lost, then the calculation would become in accurate.

The calorie burn calculation used in treadmill, elliptical and other cardio machines are just general estimates because they are not equipped to factor in the age, weight, heart rate, height and body fat percentage accurately (Keytel, Goedecke,Noakes, Hilloskorp, Laukkanen, Vander, Lambert,2005). These calorie burn calculations does not facilitate effective gamification. Hence it is required to have a standardised calorie estimation method to calculate the calorie burn using treadmill to facilitate effective gamification.

Fuzzy logic is a computational paradigm that is based on how human think. Fuzzy logic is a combination of human brain reasoning with uncertainties and computer computation of precise valuation technique (Hayward, & Davidson, 2003). Hence the fuzzy reasoning is implemented in the calorie calculation method. It estimates the calorie burn effectively compared to the other existing calculation methods. In this chapter, the treadmill equipment with incline and speed is considered as input for fuzzy based calorie burn calculation.

The advantage of fuzzy based calorie burn calculation is that it increases the motivation of the players to use treadmill with better targets leading to burn more calories and keep themselves physically fit.

TRADITIONAL VS. FUZZY BASED CALORIE BURN CALCULATION

The objective of implementing gamification for treadmill is to motivate the player to burn more calories by increasing participation and setting up higher goals. Calorie burn calculation plays an important role in motivating the player. A player is motivated to set up a higher target when a previous target is achieved. Player's motivation to set up higher goals depends upon the amount of calories burnt indicated during the physical activity. It is observed that less the calorie burn indication the goal setting is comparatively low to a calorie burn indication that is slightly higher. The calorie burn calculation using traditional method and fuzzy based method is explained below.

Traditional Calorie Burn Calculation

In its website, the famous Trojan fitness network advertises exercising using treadmill as an efficient and straight forward aerobic workout which has less impact on lower body joints than walking on the pavement or running on the road. Walking on the treadmill is a great cardio-vascular exercise and effective for burning calories.

The walking calorie burn calculator estimates the amount of calories burnt while walking for a given distance. The total calorie burn while walking depends on both the distance walked and the speed of walking. There is a difference in calorie burn while walking compared to running because the latter depends on the distance not the speed.

The calorie burn calculator takes into consideration the grade or incline level of the walking surface, weight, total walking distance and walking time. In the treadmill, it is required to input the incline and walking speed. The calculator will use the average weight and estimate the time to calculate the calorie burn. Equations 1 to 7 shows the walking calorie burn calculation equations for different incline levels used in treadmill (Margaria, Cerrefolli, Agnemo, & Sassi, 1963).

Incline = -1:

$$CB = \left[\left(0.022 \times Speed^3\right) - \left(0.1844 \times Speed^2\right) + \left(0.8546 \times Speed\right) + 1.4253\right] \times Weight \times Time \qquad (1)$$

Incline = 0:

$$CB = \left[\left(0.0215 \times Speed^3\right) - \left(0.1765 \times Speed^2\right) + \left(0.8710 \times Speed\right) + 1.4577\right] \times Weight \times Time \qquad (2)$$

Incline = 1:

$$CB = \left[\left(0.0171 \times Speed^3\right) - \left(0.1062 \times Speed^2\right) + \left(0.6080 \times Speed\right) + 1.8600\right] \times Weight \times Time \qquad (3)$$

Incline = 2:

$$CB = \left[\left(0.0184 \times Speed^3\right) - \left(0.1134 \times Speed^2\right) + \left(0.6566 \times Speed\right) + 1.9200\right] \times Weight \times Time \quad (4)$$

Incline = 3:

$$CB = \left[\left(0.0196 \times Speed^3\right) - \left(0.1205 \times Speed^2\right) + \left(0.7053 \times Speed\right) + 1.9800\right] \times Weight \times Time \quad (5)$$

Incline = 4:

$$CB = \left[\left(0.0208 \times Speed^3\right) - \left(0.1277 \times Speed^2\right) + \left(0.7539 \times Speed\right) + 2.0400\right] \times Weight \times Time \quad (6)$$

Incline = 5:

$$CB = \left[\left(0.0221 \times Speed^3\right) - \left(0.1349 \times Speed^2\right) + \left(0.8025 \times Speed\right) + 2.1000\right] \times Weight \times Time \quad (7)$$

where,

CB = Calorie Burn in calories,
Speed = Walking speed in kilometres per hour,
Weight = Body weight in kilograms.
Time is measured in hours.

It can be seen from the equations that there exists a non-linear relationship between walking speed and rate of calorie burn as opposed to running where a linear relationship exists between speed and rate of calorie burn. The incline level of the walking surface also adds effect to the calorie burn because more calories are burnt as the incline level increases for the same walking speed.

For incline levels between 6 and 15 the calorie burn discussed by Margaria, R. et al. (1963) is given by

$$CB = \left[\left(0.1 \times Speed\right) + \left(1.8 \times Speed \times Incline\right) + 3.5\right] \times Weight \times Time \times 60 \times 5 \,/\, 1000 \quad (8)$$

where,

Speed is given as meters per minute.

The major drawback of the equations from 1 to 7 is that it uses whole numbers for incline levels and requires independent calculation method for each incline levels from -1 to 5. The calorie burn calculation uses an average weight, incline and speed.

Calorie Calculation Using Fuzzy Approach

The fuzzy logic approach is about finding the degree of truth rather than finding true or false (0 or 1) where 0 and 1 are treated as extreme states of true and false. In finding the degree of truth it includes various intermediate states. It works on the user supplied rules called fuzzy rules. The fuzzy rules are converted into their mathematical equivalents for more accuracy (Zadeh, 1994). The benefits of fuzzy logic system are its simplicity and flexibility. It is proved to be an efficient method of handling imprecise and incomplete data and can produce a better solution for models with nonlinear functions of arbitrary complexity (Daniel, Paul, 1994).

The fuzzy inference system is a process of formulating the mapping from the given input to the output from which various decisions can be derived. The fuzzy inference system consists of membership functions, logical operations and if-then rules. The membership function of a fuzzy set represents the degree of truth as an extension of valuation (Timothy, 1995). There are two types of fuzzy inference system called Mamdani and Sugeno. In Mamdani Fuzzy Inference system, the output membership functions are fuzzy sets and each fuzzy sets are required for each output variable. The output membership function is clipped at the rule strength (Zadeh, 1994). It is then defuzzified using the selected defuzzification method. There are many defuzzification methods available. Centroid and weighted average methods are commonly used (Van, & Kerre, 1999).

The Sugeno Fuzzy Inference system is similar to that of Mamdani fuzzy inference system in fuzzification and applying fuzzy operator sections. The only difference between the Sugeno and Mamdani fuzzy inference system is that in sugeno, the output membership functions are either linear or constant (Guney, & Sarikaya, 2009). In sugeno, the output membership function is not clipped at the rule strength whereas it is a crisp value calculated by multiplying each input by a constant and then adding up the results (Guney, & Sarikaya, 2009). There is no output distribution available as in Mamdani whereas only a result which is mathematical combination of rule strength and output. The major disadvantage of sugeno method is that it can produce only crisp output (Guney, & Sarikaya, 2009).

In our design Mamdani Fuzzy inference system is used. The input variables considered are Speed and Incline. The output variable is the calorie burn. The following steps describes the design of Mamdani fuzzy inference system. The nine output membership functions chosen for the output variable calorie burn (CB) are N4, N3, N2, N1, ZE, P1, P2, P3 and P4. The fuzzy design for calorie burn calculation is explained in the following 6 steps.

Step 1: Design the fuzzy rules.

There are 49 fuzzy rules are designed for various input and output conditions. For eg.,

If Incline is zero and speed is high then CB is medium.

The incline zero is defined by the membership function NM of input1. The speed high is defined by the membership function PL of input 2. The output Medium is defined by the output membership function P2. The fuzzy rules are shown in Table 1.

The surface view of the fuzzy rules is shown in Figure 2. It can be seen from the surface view that the calorie burn increases linearly at higher incline (between 2 to 5) with lower speeds (1 to 4) and lower incline (-1 to 1.5) with higher speeds (4.5 to 7). This shows that more calorie can be burnt at high incline

Table 1. Fuzzy rule table

Speed Incline	NL	NM	NS	ZE	PS	PM	PL
NL	N4	N3	N3	N2	N2	N1	P1
NM	N4	N3	N3	N2	N1	ZE	P1
NS	N3	N3	N2	N1	N1	ZE	P2
ZE	N3	N3	N2	N1	N1	P1	P2
PS	N3	N2	N2	N1	ZE	P1	P3
PM	N2	N2	N1	N1	ZE	P2	P4
PL	N2	N2	N1	ZE	P1	P2	P4

or at high speed. At high incline and speed the calorie burn increases rapidly. Also it can be seen that the calorie burn converges at incline between 1.5 and 4 and speeds between 5 and 7. This indicates at medium incline and medium speed the calorie burn is not much appreciable.

Step 2: Fuzzify the inputs using membership functions.

The purpose of fuzzification is to map the incline and speed input values to values from 0 to 1 using a set of input membership functions. There are seven membership functions chosen for incline and speed inputs. The seven input membership functions are named as Negative Large (NL), Negative Medium (NM), Negative Small (NS), Zero (ZE), Positive Small (PS), Positive Medium (PM) and Positive Large (PL). The triangular shape of membership functions are chosen for both the inputs. The input member-

Figure 2. Surface view of the fuzzy rules

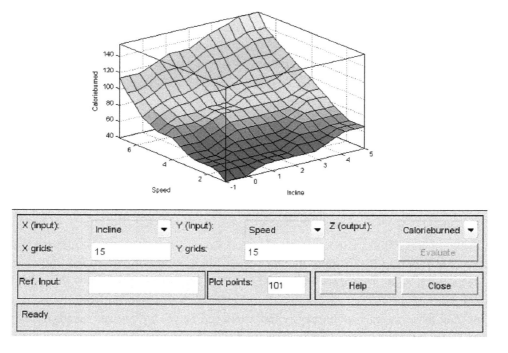

ship function could represent various incline levels such as incline 1, incline 1.5 etc. When choosing the input membership functions the incline level 1 or 1.5 could be different for each input. The membership functions of incline and speed are shown in Figure 3 and Figure 4 respectively.

Step 3: Combine the fuzzified inputs with the rules to determine the rule strength.

The fuzzy rules can be formed using either "AND" or "OR" fuzzy operators. The "AND" operator takes the minimum of two membership functions. The "OR" operator takes the maximum of two membership functions. In this design the "AND" fuzzy operator is used. This operator computes the fuzzy "AND" by multiplying the two membership functions.

Step 4: Combine the rule strength and output membership function to find the consequence of the rule.

The output membership function for calorie burn is shown in Figure 5. There are 9 membership functions in triangular shape are chosen for different calorie burn ranges.
The consequence of the fuzzy rule is computed in two steps

Step 4a: Compute the rule strength by combining the fuzzified inputs. The input membership functions are combined by fuzzy "AND" operator to determine the rule strength.
Step 4b: Clipping the output membership function at the rule strength.

For e.g.,

If incline is NM and speed is PL then CB is P1.

Figure 3. Membership functions for incline

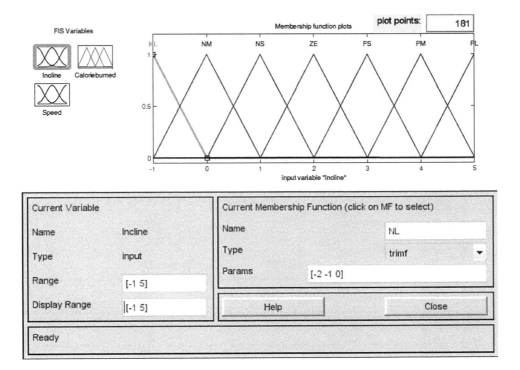

Figure 4. Membership functions for speed

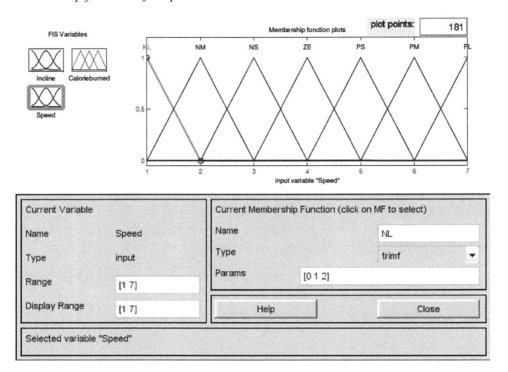

Figure 5. Membership functions for calorie burn

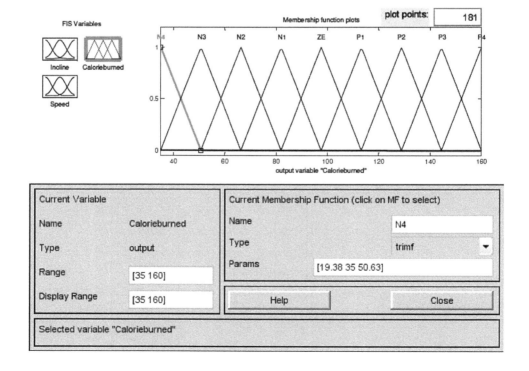

Step 5: Combine the consequences to get the output distribution

The selected output membership functions are combined using fuzzy "OR" operator to get the output distribution. This step is required for conditions when more than one rule is applied. For e.g., if the incline is set to 2.5 and speed is set to 6.5, then to calculate the calorie burn, two rules will be used

If incline is ZE and speed is PM then CB is P1.

If incline is PS and speed is PL then CB is P3.

Step 6: Apply defuzzification to get the crisp value of the output distribution.

It is required to get the single crisp value from the Fuzzy Inference system. The crisp number can be obtained by the process called defuzzification. Here centre of mass defuzzification method is used to get the crisp value of calorie burn. The chosen input membership function for incline, speed and the calorie burn is shown in Figures 6 to 11. The calculation of crisp value of calorie burn using centre of mass defuzzification is shown in Equation 9.

$$CalorieBurn = \frac{\left(97.5 + 113.1 + 128.8\right) \times 1 + \left(128.8 + 144.4 + 160\right) \times 1}{\left(1 + 1 + 1 + 1 + 1 + 1\right)} = 128.8 \tag{9}$$

Figure 6. Membership function ZE for incline at 2

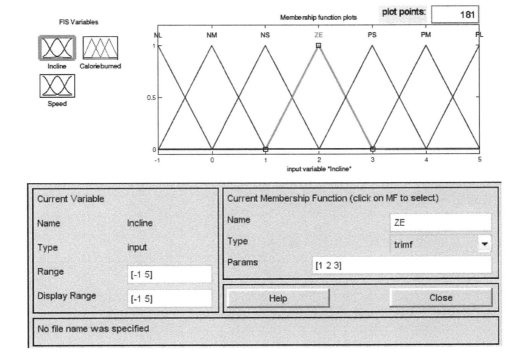

Figure 7. Membership function PS for incline at 3

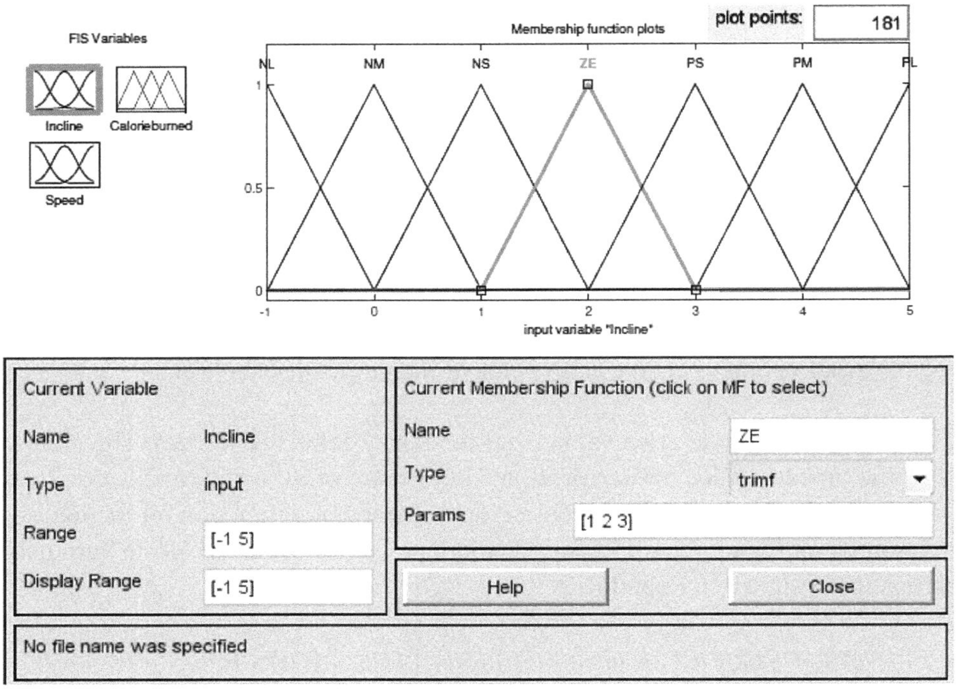

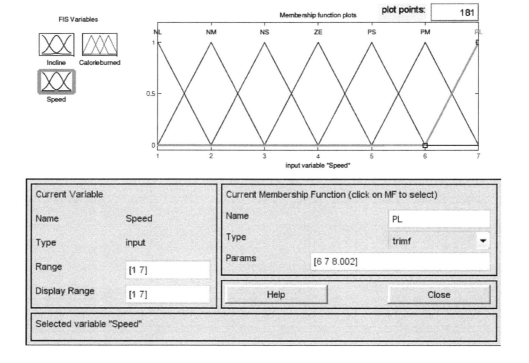

Figure 8. Membership function PL for speed at 6

Figure 9. Membership function PM for speed at 7

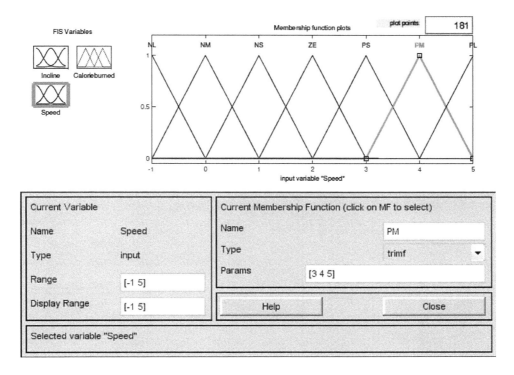

Figure 10. Membership function P1 for calorie burn

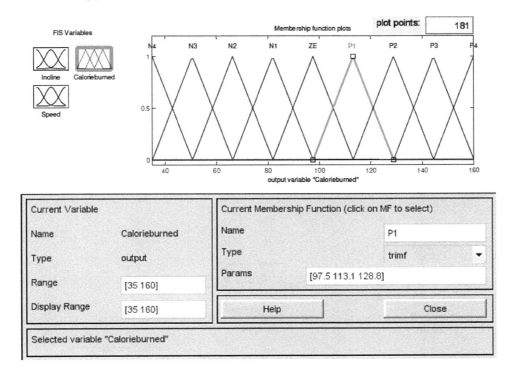

Figure 11. Membership function P3 for calorie burn

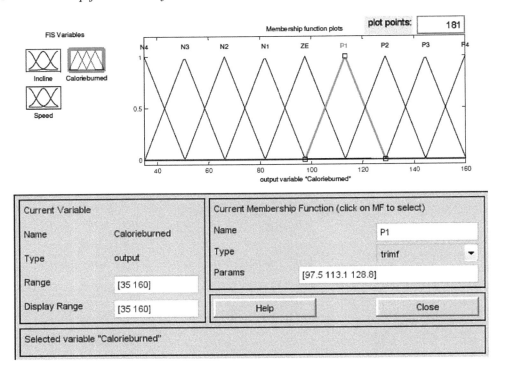

The crisp value of Calorie Burnt for an incline of 2.5 and speed of 6.5 is 128.8. The fuzzy calorie calculation model for the selected incline and speed levels is tested using matlab/Simulink toolbox and is shown in Figure 12.

DISCUSSION

Treadmill is one among the widely used exercise machines for physical fitness and walking is one of the best cardio vascular exercise. It is important to implement a calorie calculation method for treadmill which motivates the player to burn more calories.

Figure 12. Simulated model of fuzzy calorie burn calculation

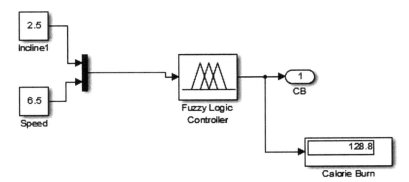

The traditional method used for treadmill is discussed in the previous section. It shows that the calculation method is laborious and the calculated value of calorie burn is distinct and accurate because it uses different equations for different incline levels. On the contrary, fuzzified calorie burn results indicates an approximate value. A calorie burn value obtained as a result of fuzzy based calculation, fall within a range of incline levels for a given speed. Table 2 shows a comparison of traditional and fuzzy based calorie burn results for different incline and speed levels. The results are discussed for the selected weight of 54Kgs and workout time of 1/3 Hrs.

The limitation of the traditional calculation method is that the calorie burn calculation can be performed for an incline value in whole number only. A negative incline value is used to set up a downward slope, a zero incline value is used to setup a ground level and a positive incline value is used to set up an upward slope on the treadmill during a workout. For testing, an incline value of -1 to 5 is used for analysis as shown in Table 2.

The advantage of fuzzy based method is that fractional incline values can also be selected. Table 3 shows the results of fuzzy based calculation for different speeds and fractional incline levels.

The calorie burn results presented in Table 3 also indicates, the computed results are also approximate values that fall within a range of incline levels for a given speed.

Table 2. Comparison of traditional and fuzzy calorie burn calculation

Incline	Speed													
	1		2		3		4		5		6		7	
	T	F	T	F	T	F	T	F	T	F	T	F	T	F
-1	38.1	39.8	46.3	50.6	52.7	50.6	59.7	66.3	69.5	66.3	84.8	81.9	107.8	113.1
0	39.1	39.8	48	50.6	55	50.6	62.9	66.3	73.6	81.9	89.5	97.5	113.1	113.1
1	42.8	50.6	50.2	50.6	57.4	66.3	66.4	81.9	78.9	81.9	96.8	97.5	122	128.8
2	44.7	50.6	52.7	50.6	60.6	66.3	70.4	81.9	84	81.9	103.5	113.1	130.9	128.8
3	46.5	50.6	55.2	66.2	63.7	66.3	74.3	81.9	89	97.5	110	113.1	139.2	144.4
4	48.4	66.2	57.7	66.2	66.9	81.9	78.2	81.9	93.9	97.5	116.3	128.8	148	155.2
5	50.2	66.2	60.2	66.2	70.1	81.9	82.2	97.5	99	113.1	123	128.8	156.4	155.2

T refers to traditional method, and F refers to fuzzy logic method.

Table 3. Fuzzy based calorie burn for fraction incline values

Incline	Speed						
	1	2	3	4	5	6	7
0.5	48.4	50.6	58.4	74.1	81.9	97.5	121
1.5	50.6	50.6	66.3	81.9	81.9	105.3	128.8
2.5	50.6	58.5	66.3	81.9	89.7	113.1	136.5
3.5	58.5	66.3	74.5	81.9	97.5	121	146.7
4.5	66.3	66.3	81.9	89.7	105.3	128.8	154.2

Comparing the accurate and approximate calorie burn results computed using traditional and fuzzy based methods respectively, it is observed that fuzzy based results motivates the player in setting up higher goals to enhance physical activity. This plays a major role in gamified system.

CONCLUSION

In health sector to improve the physical activity gamification plays a major role. Gamification not only motivates a player to achieve higher goals but also benefits the service provider. This chapter makes an effort to explore the means of increasing physical activity through effective gamification. Calorie burn calculation decides the success of gamification for physical activity. Amount of calories burnt are calculated using traditional methods. An effort to calculate calorie burn using fuzzy logic is made in this chapter. Incline and speed are the two important parameters in calculating the calorie burn. Increasing the incline level can increase the calorie burn to a greater extent. In this research, the traditional method of calorie calculation for a treadmill is compared with the fuzzy based calorie calculation for different incline levels. It is identified that fuzzy based calorie calculation enhances physical activity and support gamification in two ways.

Firstly, it can be seen that the traditional method of calculation is suitable only for the incline levels with whole numbers. Whereas the fuzzy based calorie burn calculation supports fractional incline levels. This limitation of traditional method restricts players in setting up higher targets. In traditional methods, players restricts themselves to a low incline value instead of higher intermediate value and thereby burning less calories. On the contrary, fuzzy based approach motivates the player to choose higher incline levels.

Secondly, traditional method of calculation generates distinct and accurate calorie burn value whereas, fuzzy based calorie burn calculation results in approximate value. A calorie burn value obtained as a result of fuzzy based calculation, fall within a range of incline levels for a given speed. This motivates the player in the low incline value to increase the incline value to incline value at the next higher range to burn more calories.

In treadmill application, fuzzy based results motivates and increases participation of explorers and achievers.

FUTURE WORK

The walking calorie calculation implemented using fuzzy inference system uses incline levels between -1 to 5 and speed levels from 1 to 7. The calorie calculation for running speeds from 8 to 20 Km/hr at any incline level can be estimated using fuzzy reasoning techniques. The running calories burn calculation is different from walking calorie burn calculation. The cardiorespiratory fitness level factor which is measured through VO2max estimation can be considered for running calorie burn calculation. Also other soft computing techniques such as neural network training methods can be implemented for better accuracy and personalized gamification results.

REFERENCES

Amirkalati. (2008). Comparison of Harris Benedict and Mifflin-St Jeor equations with indirect calorimetry in evaluating resting energy expenditure. *Indian Journal of Medical Sciences, 62*(7), 283-290.

Atif, A.K., Oumair, N., Daciana, I., & Evor, H. (2013). Fuzzy controller design for assisted omni-directional treadmill therapy. *The International Journal of Soft Computing and Software Engineering, 3*(8), 32-37.

Carl, J. C., Kenneth, E. P., & Gregory, M. C. (1985). Physical Activity, Exercise, and Physical Fitness: Definitions and Distinctions for Health-related research. *Public Health Reports, 100*(2), 126–131. PMID:3920711

Castelli, D. M., Centeio, E. E., Hwang, J., Barcelona, J. M., Glowacki, E. M., Calvert, H. G., & Nicksic, H. M. (2014). VII. The history of physical activity and academic performance research: Informing the future. *Monographs of the Society for Research in Child Development, 79*(4), 119–148. doi:10.1111/mono.12133 PMID:25387418

Daniel, M., & Paul, F. (1994). *Fuzzy logic*. Simon and Schuster.

Deterding, S., Dixon, D., Khaled, R., & Nacke, L. (2011). From game design elements to gamefulness: defining "Gamification".Proceedings MindTrek. ACM. doi:10.1145/2181037.2181040

Fredrick, C. M., & Ryan, R. M. (1993). Differences in motivation for sport and exercise and their relationship with participation and mental health. *Journal of Sport Behavior, 16*, 125–145.

Guney, K., & Sarikaya, N. (2009). Comparison of Mamdani and Sugeno fuzzy inference system models for resonant frequency calculation of rectangular microstrip antennas. *Progression in Electromagnetic Research, B*(12), 81 – 104.

Harris, J. A., & Benedict, F. G. (1918). A biometric study of human basal metabolism. *Proceedings of the National Academy of Sciences of the United States of America, 4*(12), 370–373. doi:10.1073/pnas.4.12.370 PMID:16576330

Hayward, G., & Davidson, V. (2003). Fuzzy logic application. *Analyst (London), 128*(11), 1304–1306. doi:10.1039/b312701j PMID:14700220

Jonathan, K.E., Paul, M.G., Paul, S.V., & Steven, J.K. (2013). *Clinical exercise physiology*. Academic Press.

Katch, V. L. (2010). *Essentials of exercise Physiology* (4th ed.). Wolters Kluwer Lippincot Williams and Wilkings.

Kelly, G. (2015). *Calorie Know-How: Get the equation right to get results*. Retrieved on 15 November 2015 from http://www.bodybuilding.com/fun/calorie-know-how-get-equation-right-to-get-results.htm

Keytel, L. R., Goedecke, J. H., Noakes, T. D., Hilloskorp, H., Laukkanen, R., Vander, M. L., & Lambert, E. V. (2005). Prediction of energy expenditiure from heart rate monitoring during sub maximal exercise. *Journal of Sports Sciences, 23*(3), 289–297. doi:10.1080/02640410470001730089 PMID:15966347

Margaria, R., Cerrefolli, P., Agnemo, P., & Sassi, G. (1963). Energy cost of running. *Journal of Applied Physiology, 18*, 367–370. PMID:13932993

Muller, B., Meuk, S., Burgi, U., & Diem, P. (2001). Calculating the basal metabolic rate and severe and morbid obesity. *Praxis (Bern 1994), 90*(45), 1955-63.

Ritterfeld, U., Cody, M., & Vorderer, P. (2009). *Serious Games: Mechanisms and effects.* London: Routledge.

Roza, A., Shizgal, H., & Harry, M. (1984). The Harris Benedict equation reevaluated: Resting energy requirements and the body cell Mass. *The American Journal of Clinical Nutrition, 40*, 168–182. PMID:6741850

Strong, W. B., Malina, R. M., Blimkie, C. J., Daniels, S. R., Dishman, R. K., Gutin, B., & Trudeau, F. et al. (2005). Evidence based physical activity for school-age youth. *The Journal of Pediatrics, 146*(6), 732–737. doi:10.1016/j.jpeds.2005.01.055 PMID:15973308

Swain, K.S., Abernathy, Smith, C.S., Lee, S.J., & Bunn, S.A. (1994). Target heart rates for the development of cardio respiratory fitness. *Sports Exercise, 26*(11), 112-116.

Taylor, H. L., Jacobs, D. R. Jr, Schucker, B., Knudsen, J., Leon, A. S., & Debacker, G. (1978). A questionnaire for the assessment of leisure time physical activity. *Journal of Chronic Diseases, 31*(12), 741–755. doi:10.1016/0021-9681(78)90058-9 PMID:748370

Timothy, J. R. (1995). Fuzzy logic with engineering applications (3rd ed.). John Wiley and Sons Ltd.

Van, L., & Kerre, E. E. (1999). Defuzzification: Criteria and classification. *Fuzzy Sets and Systems, 108*(2), 159–178. doi:10.1016/S0165-0114(97)00337-0

Zac, F. W. (2015). *A brief history of gamification.* Retrieved on 01 December 2015 from http://zefcan.com/2013/01/a-brief-history-of-gamification

Zadeh, L.A. (1994). The role of fuzzy logic in modeling, identification and control. *Model Identification and Control, 15*, 191-203.

Zichermann, G., & Cunningham, C. (2011). *Gamification by design: Implementing game mechanics in web and mobile apps* (1st ed.). Sebastopol, CA: O'Reilly Media.

KEY TERMS AND DEFINITIONS

Calorie: A unit of measuring energy released by food as it is digested by the human body which is equal to the amount of heat required to raise one gram of water by one degree celcius.

Fuzzy Inference System: A method of mapping the input to an output using set of fuzzy rules. Mamdani and Sugeno are the two fuzzy inference systems.

Fuzzy Logic: A computing paradigm which computes the degree of truth rather than "true" or "false" in contrast to the Boolean logic in which the true or false values of variables can be only 1 or 0.

Game Mechanics: The tools used as building blocks for gamifying an application. Using the right game mechanics leads to highly motivational user experience.

Gamification: The application of game mechanics and game design techniques in non-game context to motivate players to achieve higher goals.

Physical Activity: Defined as body workout that involves contraction of muscles to burn more calories than that required for normal body functioning. Examples of physical activities are walking, running, swimming, biking and hiking.

Physical Fitness: Achieved through physical activity to maintain good health and well-being of the human body.

Chapter 6
Clustering Approaches in Decision Making Using Fuzzy and Rough Sets

Deepthi P. Hudedagaddi
VIT University, India

B. K. Tripathy
VIT University, India

ABSTRACT

Data clustering has been an integral and important part of data mining. It has wide applications in database anonymization, decision making, image processing and pattern recognition, medical diagnosis and geographical information systems, only to name a few. Data in real life scenario are having imprecision inherent in them. So, early crisp clustering techniques are very less efficient. Several imprecision based models have been proposed over the years like the fuzzy sets, rough sets, intuitionistic fuzzy sets and many of their generalized versions. Of late, it has been established that the hybrid models obtained as combination of these imprecise models are far more efficient than the individual ones. So, many clustering algorithms have been put forth using these hybrid models. The focus of this chapter is to discuss on some of the data clustering algorithms developed so far and their applications mainly in the area of decision making.

On an important decision one rarely has 100% of the information needed for a good decision no matter how much one spends or how long one waits. And, if one waits too long, he has a different problem and has to start all over. This is the terrible dilemma of the hesitant decision maker. -Robert K. Greenleaf

DOI: 10.4018/978-1-5225-1008-6.ch006

INTRODUCTION

A cluster is a collection of data elements that are similar to each other but dissimilar to elements in other clusters. A vast amount of data is generated and made available across multiple sources. It is practically impossible to manually analyze the myriad of data and select the data that is required to perform a particular task. Hence, a mechanism that can classify the data according to some criteria in which only the classes of interest are selected and rests are rejected is essential. Clustering techniques are applied in the analysis of statistical data used in fields such as machine learning, pattern recognition, image analysis, information retrieval, and bioinformatics and is a major task in exploratory data mining (Bezdek & Pal, 1998; Tou & Gonzalez, 1974). A wide number of clustering algorithms have been proposed to suit the requirements in each field of its application.

SETS

The notion of a set is not only basic for the whole mathematics but it also plays an important role in natural language. Sets include collections of various objects of interest, e.g., collection of books, paintings, people etc. The notion of set was proposed by G. Cantor in 1983. It was not free from controversies like that of B. Russel which questioned the definition of a set proposed by Cantor as a collection of distinct and distinguishable elements. Intuitively a set can be defined as a well- defined collection of objects called elements.

Rough Sets

A rough set, first described by a Polish computer scientist Z. Pawlak (1982), is a formal approximation of a crisp set (i.e., conventional set) in terms of a pair of sets which give the lower and the upper approximation of the original set. In the standard version of rough set theory, the lower- and upper-approximation sets are crisp sets, but in other variations, the approximating sets may be fuzzy sets.

Definition of a Rough Set

A set X in a universal set U is considered to be rough or not with respect to an equivalence relation P defined over U. Since P is an equivalence relation, it decomposes U into nonempty disjoint equivalence classes. These equivalence classes are called the categories and are the granules of knowledge induced by P over U. The equivalence class of an element x with respect to P is denoted by $[x]_P$. By U/P, the set of equivalence classes generated by P over U is represented.

Pair of crisp sets is associated with any set X in U with respect to P and are called the P-lower approximation of X and P-upper approximation of X. They are denoted by $\underline{P}X$ and $\overline{P}X$ respectively, and defined as

$$\underline{P}X = \{x \mid [x]_P \subseteq X\} \tag{1}$$

$$\overline{P}X = \{x \mid [x]_P \cap X \neq \phi\} \tag{2}$$

Accuracy Measure

The tuple $< \underline{P}X, \overline{P}X >$ composed of the lower and upper approximation is called a rough set; thus, a rough set is composed of two crisp sets, one representing a lower boundary of the target set X, and the other representing an upper boundary of the target set X.

The accuracy of the rough-set representation of the set X can be given by the following:

$$\alpha_p(X) = \frac{|\underline{P}X|}{|\overline{P}X|} \tag{3}$$

That is, the accuracy of the rough set representation of X, $\alpha_p(X)$, $0 \le \alpha_p(X) \le 1$, is the ratio of the number of objects which can be positively placed in X to the number of objects that can possibly be placed in X – this provides a measure of how closely the rough set is approximating the target set. Clearly, when the upper and lower approximations are equal (i.e., boundary region empty), then $\alpha_p(X) = 1$, and the approximation is perfect; at the other extreme, whenever the lower approximation is empty, the accuracy is zero (regardless of the size of the upper approximation).

Let X, a subset of U, be a target set that we wish to represent using attribute subset P; that is, we are told that an arbitrary set of objects X comprises a single class, and we wish to express this class (i.e., this subset) using the equivalence classes induced by attribute subset P. It is worth noting that each attribute on a dataset induces an equivalence relation over it and hence generates equivalence classes. In general, X cannot be expressed exactly, because the set may include and exclude objects which are indistinguishable on the basis of attributes P.

For example, let us take $U = \{x_1, x_2, \ldots x_8\}$ and the equivalence classes generated by an equivalence relation P be

$$\left\{ \{x_1, x_3, x_5\}, \{x_2, x_4\}, \{x_6, x_7, x_8\} \right\}.$$

Then

$$[x_1]_P = \{x_1, x_3, x_5\}, [x_2]_P = \{x_2, x_4\}$$

and

$$[x_6]_P = \{x_6, x_7, x_8\}.$$

The set $X = \{x_1, x_2, x_3, x_4, x_5\}$ is exactly defined by P whereas $Y = \{x_1, x_2, x_4, x_5\}$ cannot be exactly defined through P.

Lower Approximation and Positive Region

The P-lower approximation, or positive region, is the union of all equivalence classes in $[x]_P$ which are contained by (i.e., are subsets of) the target set – in the example, $\underline{P}Y = \{x_2, x_4\}$, the union of the two equivalence classes in $[x]_P$ which are contained in the target set Y. The lower approximation is the complete set of objects in U/P that can be positively (i.e., unambiguously) classified as belonging to target set Y.

Upper Approximation and Negative Region

The P-upper approximation is the union of all equivalence classes in $[x]_P$ which have non-empty intersection with the target set – in the example, $\overline{P}Y = \{x_1, x_2, x_3, x_4, x_5\}$, the union of the three equivalence classes in $[x]_P$ that have non-empty intersection with the target set. The upper approximation is the complete set of objects that in U/P that cannot be positively (i.e., unambiguously) classified as belonging to the complement of the target set Y. In other words, the upper approximation is the complete set of objects that are possibly members of the target set Y.

The set $U - \overline{P}Y$ therefore represents the negative region, containing the set of objects that can be definitely ruled out as members of the target set.

Boundary Region

The boundary region, given by set difference $\overline{P}Y - \underline{P}Y$, consists of those objects that can neither be ruled in nor ruled out as members of the target set Y.

In summary, the lower approximation of a target set is a conservative approximation consisting of only those objects which can positively be identified as members of the set. (These objects have no indiscernible "clones" which are excluded by the target set.) The upper approximation is a liberal approximation which includes all objects that might be members of target set. (Some objects in the upper approximation may not be members of the target set.) From the perspective of U/P, the lower approximation contains objects that are members of the target set with certainty (probability = 1), while the upper approximation contains objects that are members of the target set with non-zero probability (probability > 0).

Rough Membership

Rough sets can be also defined employing, instead of approximation, rough membership function.

Let U be a universal set. B be an equivalence relation on U and $X \subseteq U$. We define

$$\mu_X^B : U \rightarrow [0,1],$$

defined by

$$\mu_X^B(x) = \frac{card([x]_B \cap X)}{card(X)}, \tag{4}$$

where $x \in X \subseteq U$.

The value of $\mu_X^B(x)$ can be interpreted as the degree that x belongs to X in view of knowledge about x expressed by B or the degree to which the elementary granule $[x]_B$ is included in the set X. The rough membership function satisfies the following properties.

$$\mu_X^B(x) = 1, iff \ x \in \underline{B}X \tag{5}$$

$$\mu_X^B(x) = 0, iff \ x \in U - \overline{B}X \tag{6}$$

$$0 < \mu_X^B(x) < 1, iff \ x \in BN_B(X) \tag{7}$$

$$\mu_U^B - (x) = 1 - \mu_X^B(x), for \ any \ x \in U \tag{8}$$

$$\mu_{X \cup Y}^B(x) \geq \max\left(\mu_X^B(x), \mu_Y^B(x)\right), for \ any \ x \in U \tag{9}$$

$$\mu_{X \cap Y}^B(x) \leq \min\left(\mu_X^B(x), \mu_Y^B(x)\right), for \ any \ x \in U \tag{10}$$

The rough membership function expresses conditional probability that x belongs to X given R and can be interpreted as a degree that x belongs to X in view of information about x expressed by R. Rough membership differs essentially from the fuzzy membership, for that the membership for union and intersection of sets, in general, cannot be computed, as in the case of fuzzy sets, from their constituents membership. Thus formally the rough membership is a generalization of fuzzy membership. Besides, the rough membership function, in contrast to fuzzy membership function, has a probabilistic flavor (Pawlak & Skowron 2007).

Applications of Rough Sets

Rough set methods can be applied as a component of hybrid solutions in machine learning and data mining. They have been found to be particularly useful for rule induction and feature selection (semantics-preserving dimensionality reduction). Rough set-based data analysis methods have been successfully applied in bioinformatics, economics and finance, medicine, multimedia, web and text mining, signal and image processing, software engineering, robotics, and engineering (e.g. power systems and control engineering).

Fuzzy Sets

Fuzzy sets are sets whose elements have degrees of membership. Fuzzy sets were introduced by Lotfi A. Zadeh (Zadeh, 1965; Zadeh et al. 2011) as an extension of the classical notion of set. At the same time, a more general kind of structures called L-relations were defined, which were studied in an abstract algebraic context. Fuzzy relations, which are used now in different areas, such as linguistics, decision-making and clustering are special cases of L-relations when L is the unit interval [0, 1].

In classical set theory, the membership of elements in a set is assessed in binary terms according to a bivalent condition — an element either belongs or does not belong to the set. By contrast, fuzzy set theory permits the gradual assessment of the membership of elements in a set; this is described with the aid of a membership function valued in the real unit interval [0, 1]. Fuzzy sets generalize classical sets, since the indicator functions of classical sets are special cases of the membership functions of fuzzy sets, if the latter only take values 0 or 1. In fuzzy set theory, classical bivalent sets are usually called crisp sets. The fuzzy set theory can be used in a wide range of domains in which information is incomplete or imprecise, such as bioinformatics (Sugeno, 1977).

Definition of a Fuzzy Set

A fuzzy set 'A' over a universal set U is characterised by its membership function μ_A such that $\mu_A : U \to [0,1]$. That is the function μ_A associate with every element x in U by its membership value $\mu_A(x)$, which is a real number lying in the interval [0, 1].

A fuzzy set reduces to a crisp set when the membership values of all the elements in U in it are 0 or 1. An element x for which $\mu_A(x) = 0$ is said to be not there in A and for an element x for which $\mu_A(x) = 1$ is said to be a certain element in A.

The set $\{x \in U \mid \mu_A(x) > 0\}$ is called the support of A and the set $\{x \in U \mid \mu_A(x) = 1\}$ is called its kernel.

Sometimes, more general variants of the notion of fuzzy set are used, with membership functions taking values in a (fixed or variable) algebraic structure L of a given kind; usually it is required that L be at least a poset or a lattice. These are usually called L-fuzzy sets, to distinguish them from those valued over the unit interval. The usual membership functions with values in [0, 1] are then called [0, 1]-valued membership functions.

Intuitionistic Fuzzy Set (IFS)

In the fuzzy set context the non-membership value of an element is defined as the 1's complement of its membership value. However, in real life situations this is not always true. There may be some hesitation component involved in it. Using this idea, a notion called intuitionistic fuzzy set was proposed by Atanassov (1986) where the sum of the membership value and the non-membership value lies in the interval [0, 1]. An IFS A in X is given as $\{x, \mu_A(x), \nu_A(x) \mid x \in X\}$, where $\mu_A(x) \to [0, 1]$ and $\nu_A(x) \to [0, 1]$ such that $0 \leq \mu_A(x) + \nu_A(x) \leq 1$. $\mu_A(x)$ and $\nu_A(x)$ are membership and non-membership values of an element x in A in X. When $\nu_A(x) = 1 - \mu_A(x)$ for every x in set A, then set A becomes a fuzzy set. For all IFSs, Atanassov also indicated a hesitation degree denoted by $\pi_A(x)$, which arises due to lack of knowledge in defining membership degree, for each element x in A and is given as

$$\pi_A(x) = 1 - \mu_A(x) - \nu_A(x), 0 \le \pi_A(x) \le 1 \tag{11}$$

The non-membership values of elements can be computed from their membership values in IFS using several methods. One of these methods is due to Sugeno (1977), using which the hesitation degree of an element can be computed as

$$\pi_A(x) = 1 - \mu_A(x) - \frac{1 - \mu_A(x)}{1 + \lambda\mu_A(x)} \tag{12}$$

Hybrid Approaches

In the beginning when rough set was introduced, it was considered as a rival theory to the established theory of Fuzzy sets. However, it was shown by Dubois and Prade in 1990 that far from this fear they complement each other. Proceeding further they proposed the hybrid models of rough fuzzy sets and fuzzy rough sets (Mitra et al. 2006). This was perhaps the beginning of a series of hybrid models using several of the uncertainty based models existing in literature. Every model has strong points as well as weak points. If the strong points of the individual components in a hybrid model can be retained then it provides better models. Combining rough set with intuitionistic fuzzy sets, the notion of Rough intuitionistic fuzzy set theory was proposed in (Saleha et al. 2002).

FUZZY AND ROUGH SET BASED DATA CLUSTERING ALGORITHMS

The first and most common clustering algorithm is Hard C-Means (HCM). However, uncertainty has become an integral part of modern day databases. There are many uncertainty based models in literature like the fuzzy sets introduced by Zadeh (1965), the rough sets introduced by Pawlak and Skowron (2007), the intuitionistic fuzzy sets introduced by Atanassov (1986) and their hybrid models like the rough fuzzy sets introduced by Dubois and Prade (1990) and the rough intuitionistic fuzzy sets introduced by Saleha et al. (2002). Several modifications to HCM framework led to the development of various uncertainty based C-Means algorithms such as Rough C-Means (RCM) (Maji et al. 2007), Fuzzy C-Means (FCM) (Maji et al. 2007), Rough-Fuzzy C-Means (RFCM) (Maji & Pal, 2007; Michalopoulos, 2001; Pawlak, 1982) and Intuitionistic Fuzzy C-Means (IFCM) (Davis, 1979), Rough Intuitionistic Fuzzy C Means (Tripathy et al. 2013). It has been established that IFCM works better than FCM. Also, it has been established by various authors that the hybrid algorithms work better than the individual algorithms. The combination of fuzzy or intuitionistic fuzzy techniques with the rough set techniques take care of graded membership or also graded non-membership of objects in clusters and the uncertainty through the boundary regions. The use of rough-fuzzy sets helps in controlling the uncertainty of data lying between the upper and lower approximations whereas the intuitionistic fuzzy set helps improve the accuracy in detection (Tripathy et al. 2002, 2013a, 2013b).

Fuzzy C-Means Algorithm (FCM)

Fuzzy c-mean is an algorithm proposed by James C. Bezdek (1981). In fuzzy clustering (also referred to as soft clustering), data elements can belong to more than one cluster, and associated with each element is a set of membership levels. These indicate the strength of the association between that data element and a particular cluster. Fuzzy clustering is a process of assigning these membership levels, and then using them to assign data elements to one or more clusters (Zadeh 1965).

1. Assign initial cluster centres or means for c clusters.
2. Calculate the distance d_{ik} between data objects x_k and centroids v_i using Euclidean formula

$$d(x,y) = \sqrt{\left(x_1 - y_1\right)^2 + \left(x_2 - y_2\right)^2 + \ldots + \left(x_n - y_n\right)^2} \tag{13}$$

3. Generate the fuzzy partition matrix or membership matrix U:

If $d_{ij} > 0$ then

$$\mu_{ik} = \frac{1}{\sum_{j=1}^{C} \left(\frac{d_{ik}}{d_{jk}}\right)^{\frac{2}{m-1}}} \tag{14}$$

Else

$$\mu_{ik} = 1$$

4. The cluster centroids are calculated using the formula

$$V_i = \frac{\sum_{j=1}^{N} \left(\mu_{ij}\right)^m x_j}{\sum_{j=1}^{N} \left(\mu_{ij}\right)^m} \tag{15}$$

5. Calculate new partition matrix by using step 2 and 3
6. If $\left\| U^{(r)} - U^{(r+1)} \right\| < \varepsilon$ then stop else repeat from step 4.

Rough-Fuzzy C-Means Algorithm (RFCM)

Rough Fuzzy C-Means is an algorithm proposed by S. Mitra and P. Maji; it combines the concepts of rough set theory and fuzzy set theory. The concepts of lower and upper approximations in rough set deals with uncertainty, vagueness and incompleteness whereas the concept of membership function in fuzzy set helps in enhancing and evaluating overlapping clusters.

1. Assign initial means v_i for c clusters.
2. Compute μ_{ik} using (14).
3. Let μ_{ik} and μ_{jk} be the maximum and next to maximum membership values of object x_k to cluster centroids v_i and v_j.

   If $\mu_{ik} - \mu_{jk} < \varepsilon$ then

   $x_k \varepsilon \underline{BU}_i$ and $x_k \varepsilon \overline{BU}_j$ and x_k cannot be a member of any lower approximation.

   Else

   $x_k \varepsilon \underline{BU}_i$

4. Calculate new cluster means by using

$$
v_i = \begin{cases} w_{low} \dfrac{\sum_{x_k \varepsilon \underline{BU}_i} x_k}{\left|\underline{BU}_i\right|} + w_{up} \dfrac{\sum_{x_k \varepsilon \overline{BU}_i - \underline{BU}_i} \mu_{ik}^m x_k}{\sum_{x_k \varepsilon \overline{BU}_i - \underline{BU}_i} \mu_{ik}^m}, if \left|\overline{BU}_i\right| \neq \phi \ and \left|\overline{BU}_i - \underline{BU}_i\right| \neq \phi \\[4mm] \dfrac{\sum_{x_k \varepsilon \overline{BU}_i - \underline{BU}_i} \mu_{ik}^m x_k}{\sum_{x_k \varepsilon \overline{BU}_i - \underline{BU}_i} \mu_{ik}^m}, if \left|\overline{BU}_i\right| \neq \phi \ and \left|\overline{BU}_i - \underline{BU}_i\right| \neq \phi \\[4mm] \dfrac{\sum_{x_k \varepsilon \underline{BU}_i} x_k}{\left|\underline{BU}_i\right|}, ELSE \end{cases} \tag{16}
$$

5. Repeat from step 2 until termination condition is met or until there are no more assignment of objects.
   Note: The range for values of m is [1.5, 2.5]. However, for all practical purposes, it is taken to be 2.

Intuitionistic Fuzzy C-Means Algorithm (IFCM)

The Intuitionistic fuzzy c-means proposed by T. Chaira brings in to account a new parameter that helps in increasing the accuracy of clustering. This parameter is known as the hesitation value and denoted by π.

1. Assign initial cluster centres or means for c clusters.
2. Calculate the distance d_{ik} between data objects x_k and centroids v_i using Euclidean formula (13).
3. Generate the fuzzy partition matrix or membership matrix U:

If $d_{ij} > 0$ then compute μ_{ik} using (14)

Else

$$\mu_{ik} = 1.$$

4. Compute the hesitation matrix π using (12)
5. Compute the modified membership matrix U' using

$$\mu'_{ik} = \mu_{ik} + \pi_{ik} \qquad (17)$$

6. The cluster centroids are calculated using the formula

$$V_i = \frac{\sum_{j=1}^{N}\left(\mu_{ij}\right)^m x_j}{\sum_{j=1}^{N}\left(\mu_{ij}\right)^m} \qquad (18)$$

7. Calculate new partition matrix by using step 2 to 5
8. If $\left\| U'^{(r)} - U'^{(r+1)} \right\| < \varepsilon$ then stop else repeat from step 4.

Rough Intuitionistic Fuzzy C Means Algorithm (RIFCM)

1. Assign initial means v_i for c clusters by choosing any random c objects as cluster.
2. Calculate d_{ik} using Euclidean distance formula (13).
3. Compute U matrix:

If $d_{ik} = 0$ or $x_j \varepsilon \underline{B}U_i$ then

$$\mu_{ik} = 1$$

Else compute μ_{ik} using (14).

4. Compute π_{ik} using (12)
5. Compute μ'_{ik} and normalize

$$\mu'_{ik} = \mu_{ik} + \pi_{ik}$$

6. Let μ'_{ik} and μ'_{jk} be the maximum and next to maximum membership values of object x_k to cluster centroids v_i and v_j.

If

$$\mu'_{ik} - \mu'_{jk} < \varepsilon$$

then

$x_k \varepsilon \underline{B}U_i$ and $x_k \varepsilon \overline{B}U_j$ and x_k cannot be a member of any lower approximation.

Else

$$x_k \in \underline{B}U_i.$$

7. Calculate new cluster means by using

$$v_i = \begin{cases} w_{low} \dfrac{\sum_{x_k \varepsilon \underline{B}U_i} x_k}{\left|\underline{B}U_i\right|} + w_{up} \dfrac{\sum_{x_k \varepsilon \overline{B}U_i - \underline{B}U_i} \mu_{ik}^m x_k}{\sum_{x_k \varepsilon \overline{B}U_i - \underline{B}U_i} \mu_{ik}^m}, if \left|\overline{B}U_i\right| \neq \phi \ and \left|\overline{B}U_i - \underline{B}U_i\right| \neq \phi \\[3em] \dfrac{\sum_{x_k \varepsilon \overline{B}U_i - \underline{B}U_i} \mu_{ik}^m x_k}{\sum_{x_k \varepsilon \overline{B}U_i - \underline{B}U_i} \mu_{ik}^m}, if \left|\overline{B}U_i\right| \neq \phi \ and \left|\overline{B}U_i - \underline{B}U_i\right| \neq \phi \\[3em] \dfrac{\sum_{x_k \varepsilon \underline{B}U_i} x_k}{\left|\underline{B}U_i\right|}, ELSE \end{cases} \qquad (19)$$

8. Repeat from step 2 until termination condition is met or until there are no more assignment of objects.

DATA CLUSTERING ALGORITHMS IN DECISION MAKING

Clustering analysis is an important research project in knowledge discovery and data mining (KDDM) (Chen et.al 2006). The process of grouping a set of physical or abstract objects into classes of similar objects is called clustering. A cluster is a collection of data objects that are similar to one another within the same cluster and are dissimilar to the objects in other clusters. A cluster of data objects can be treated collectively as one group and so may be considered as a form of data compression (Priyadarishini et.al 2011). In practical application, the data sets contain numerical and categorical (nominal) data in general.

Accordingly, clustering algorithm is required to able to deal with both numerical data and categorical data (Chen et.al 2006). Although classification is an effective means for distinguishing groups or classes of objects, it requires the often costly collection and labeling of a large set of training tuples or patterns, which the classifier uses to model each group (Priyadarishini et.al 2011). A number of algorithms for clustering categorical data have been proposed such as K-Means, Expectation-Maximization (EM) Algorithm, Association Rule, K-Modes, K-Prototypes, CACTUS (Clustering Categorical Data Using

Summaries), ROCK (Robust Clustering using Links), STIRR (Sieving Through Iterated Relational Reinforcement), LCBCDC (Link Clustering Based Categorical Data Clustering), fuzzy K-modes algorithm, fuzzy centroids algorithm etc.. These algorithms require multiple runs to establish the stability needed to obtain a satisfactory value for one parameter. While these methods make important contributions to the issue of clustering categorical data, they are not designed to handle uncertainty in the clustering process. This is an important issue in many real world applications where there is often no sharp boundary between clusters (Parmar et.al 2007).

There is a need for a robust clustering algorithm that can handle uncertainty in the process of clustering categorical data. This leads to another clustering algorithm named as Rough Set Theory (RST), which has received considerable attention in the computational intelligence literature (Parmar et.al 2007). Rough sets theory is a new mathematical tool to handle uncertainty and incomplete information. Polish mathematician Pawlak Z initially proposed it (Yang et.al 2006, Ho and Nguyen 2002). The theory consists of finite sets, equivalence relations and cardinality concepts (Hung et.al 2009). A principal goal of rough set theoretic analysis is to synthesize or construct approximations (upper and lower) offsets concepts from the acquired data (Mitra et.al 2003). Rough set theory clarifies set-theoretic characteristics of the classes over combinatorial patterns of the attributes. This theory can be used to acquire some sets of attributes for classification and can also evaluate the degree of the attributes of database that are able to classify data (Lee & Huang, 2002). Basically, when using rough set, the data itself is used to come up with the approximation in order to deal with the imprecision within. It can therefore be considered a self-sufficient discipline (Hung et.al 2009). Unlike fuzzy set based approaches, rough sets have no requirement on domain expertise to assign the fuzzy membership. Still, it may provide satisfactory results for rough clustering (Parmar et.al 2007).

Fuzzy classification offers an alternative to crisp logic by evaluating data set based on their membership into each category (Anushya & Pethalakshmi, 2012). Recently, fuzzy rule-based systems have often been applied to classification problems where non-fuzzy input vectors are to be assigned to one of a given set of classes. Many approaches have been proposed for generating and learning fuzzy IF–THEN rules from numerical data for classification problems. For example, fuzzy rule-based classification systems are created by simple heuristic procedures, neuro-fuzzy techniques, clustering methods, fuzzy nearest neighbor methods, and genetic algorithms (Ishibuchi & Nakashima, 2001). Some heuristic criteria's are used for extraction of pre-specified number of fuzzy rule. Genetic algorithm (GA) based rule selection criteria improves classification ability of extracted fuzzy rule (Pitambare & Kamde, 2013). One of the interesting applications of GA‟s is in pattern classification problems in which the goal is to develop a classifier capable of dealing with different classes of a specific problem. Genetic algorithms have been used as rule generation and optimization tools in the design of fuzzy rule based systems. Genetic algorithms are search algorithms that use operations found in natural genetic to guide the journey through a search space (Saniee at.al 2008). The special term "Genetic Fuzzy System" (GFS) was coined by the community to refer to fuzzy systems that use a genetic algorithm to create or adjust one or more of their components. Specifically, the classifications of GFSs are (1) the genetic tuning of an existing knowledge base; (22) the genetic learning of components of the knowledge base (Cintra et.al 2011).

Rough Set Based Data Clustering

This is a soft clustering method employing Rough Set Theory. It groups the given dataset into a set of overlapping clusters. Here, each cluster is represented by a lower approximation and an upper approximation. The lower approximation contains all the patterns that definitely belong to the cluster and the upper approximation permits overlap. This approach does not attempt to distinguish between the patterns that fall in the lower approximation of a cluster and hence are said to be indiscernible. Since the upper approximation permits overlaps, each set of data points that are shared by a group of clusters define indiscernible set. Thus, ambiguity in assigning a pattern to a cluster is captured using the upper approximation and it is achieved by restricting the discernibility at the level of the sets of data points shared by each group of clusters. Due to this ability to handle the inherent uncertainty involved in cluster analysis, rough set based approaches pose themselves as promising candidates for soft clustering. Some of the rough set based algorithms proposed in the literature for clustering datasets are Rough k-Means algorithm by Lingras and West (2004) and ARFL algorithm by Asharaf and Murty (2003).

Application of RST in Data Mining

RST has found a lot of interesting applications (http://arxiv.org/ftp/arxiv/papers/1311/1311.4121.pdf). Particularly, it appears of particular importance to decision support systems and data mining. The propriety of the absence of any preliminary or additional information about data is the main advantage of RST. The application of rough set theory is successful in many real-life problems like engineering, banking, medicine, pharmacology, financial and market analysis and others. A number of applications are listed.

- **Rough Set Approach to Materials Science:** this approach provides a new algorithmic method for predicting and understanding material properties and behavior, which can be very useful in creating new materials. Rough sets to material sciences are firstly applied in, which presents a great interest to this community (Jackson et.al 1996).
- **Rough Set Applications Requiring Suitable Software:** A lot of software systems for computers based on RST have been developed. The most known include Rough DAS and Rough Class (Sowiñski, 1992), LERS (Tsumoto 1996), and DATALOGIC (Woolery & Grzymala-Busse, 1994). Some of that software is commercial.
- **LERS Software:** The first version of LERS was developed in 1988 at the University of Kansas. Currently, LERS version is essentially a family of data mining systems. The LERS main objective is to compute decision rules from data. The classification of new cases or the interpretation of knowledge is based on the computed rule sets. The rule computation of LERS system starts from imperfect data (Tsumoto, 1996) (e.g., data characterized by missing attribute values or inconsistent cases). To deal with numerical attribute, LERS also uses a set of discretization schemas. In addition, LERS includes a variety of methods helping to handle missing attribute values. LERS computes lower and upper approximations of all set involved, for inconsistent data (that belongs to two different target sets and characterized by the same values of all attributes). LERS system was used in other areas (e.g., in the medical field by the comparison of the effects of warming devices for postoperative patients, assessing preterm birth) (Sowiñski, 1992) and used to diagnoses the melanoma (Woolery & Grzymala-Busse, 1994).
- **Other Applications:** Some different applications of rough set theory can be found in Tsumoto (1996), Sowiñski (1992), Woolery and Grzymala-Busse (1994), Lin and Cercone (1997), Lin and Wildberger (1994). Particularly, some sources realized experiments based on RST for pattern recognition, including speech recognition, music fragment classification, and handwriting

recognition, medical diagnosis and control. These technologies indicate that the trend to develop applications based on extensions of RST will continue.

Michalopoulos et al (2001) used fuzzy c-means clustering algorithm in decision making and demonstrated it with a real world application (for managing bank branches performance). Specifically, it is shown how the top-management team of a domestic bank network should decide, about granting the annual productivity bonus among the branches of its network. Likewise, Zadeh et al. (2011) use fuzzy c-means along with artificial neural network normalization algorithm for performance assessment of decision making units.

Michalopoulos suggest the use of fuzzy C-means for clustering, data. Initially, a classifier is generated by using a specific fuzzy C-means algorithm, contained in Data Engine to partition the data. Once the clusters have been identified through training, they are labelled. Labelling means to attach a corresponding linguistic description (e.g. 'group of high performance bank branches', 'group of bank branches with high level of cash transaction' etc.) to each cluster. Clusters can be labelled either by an expert or by the algorithm itself. As the ideal number of clusters is unknown, several runs of the algorithm are carried out, in order to establish the optimum number of clusters with the highest discriminant ability (in their approach the meaningful attempts were ranging between 2 and 14 classes). This methodology is a classic approach when one has to deal with a problem using FCM algorithm

CASE STUDY: BANK NETWORK

Decision Making Methodology

Now that the basic principles of cluster analysis and rule induction with machine learning have been delineated, the proposed decision making methodology is described. Specifically, a co-operative scheme of fuzzy cluster analysis and inductive learning algorithms is considered.:

1. A database is filled, which -in fact- is a collection of attribute value matrices, one for each evaluation period (year, month and week) and for every branch of the firm. Every attribute value vector, i.e. every line of the database matrix, represents the scoring of each branch in every decision variable, for the studied time period.
2. A fuzzy C-means clustering methodology is applied to the data set in order to group the contained attribute value vectors in uniform clusters. Taking into account priorities among the decision variables' scoring according to properly specified criteria set by the top management team, we should form the clusters in an hierarchical order (from more to less important overall scoring). The proposed clustering process does not exclusively depend on this information.
3. Once the fuzzy clusters are identified they are used as class names for the attribute vectors. Then a classification and-rule-induction process takes place, by applying inductive machine learning algorithms. The output is a decision tree representing as IF-THEN rules the discrimination properties of each cluster of the branches.
4. At last, the variation of each branches' position in the produced ordered list across time (i.e. annually) could be observed, resulting in useful mid-term and/or long-term strategic planning information for the administrative group of the firm.

This architecture accepts all kind of attribute values and involves human experts' intervention only in the initial stage of designing the database matrices and specifying the decision criteria. Practical difficulties in data collection for long time periods restrict the demonstration of the application results to one and only certain time period.

Considering a complex financial application domain such as a domestic bank network constituting of decades of branches and decision variables (cash transactions, Cheques, foreign currency, etc.), we seek for ways to define and utilize criteria for the evaluation of the overall performance of each branch compared to the others of the network. The form of the produced decision rules could be a handy strategic decision plan for the administration staff based on discriminant descriptions among the different clusters stated.

The application of C4.5 to the resulting cluster analysis data produced a set of 9 simple and comprehensible rules (Figure 2).

Evaluation of the Bank Network

In order to make more clear the steps of the proposed methodology, as well as the effects of the results for making strategic decisions, we considered a specific real bank network of a Greek firm, constituting of 27 branches for each of which the annual data for 28 selected financial characteristics, called decision variables, were summarized in an initial data matrix. Table 1 shows the selected decision variables as well as their encoding by which from now on we will refer to them for abstraction.

Table 2 summarizes the results of the final classification of the bank branches to one of the five alternative classes: the "elbow" criterion pointed out that the optimal number classes should be five (Figure 1).

Observing the decision tree, note that square shapes denote classes (and thus final decisions) while circle shapes denote decision nodes performing alternative tests represented on the left of the branches of the tree. The higher an attribute stands in the tree, the highest amount of information includes, and thus the most discriminative is considered. Beside each class indication in Figure 2, is denoted in brackets the number of examples covering the specific rule, showing how robust is this rule for the examined data set. The overall accuracy of the tree in covering the data set is 100%, i.e. these 9 rules discriminate accurately and perfectly all the given data in a somewhat abstracted manner.

Below are stated in detail some conclusions deriving directly from Figure 1, Figure 2, Table 1 and Table 2:

In total, 8 decision variables (C1, C2, C4, C5, C11, C13, C20, C28) prove sufficient for the rule induction part of our methodology, to discriminate perfectly the 27 branches. According to the number of branches described by each rule and those discriminated by a specific attribute value, criteria no. 4, 20 and 28 (checks issued on the basis of payment orders from banks, foreign exchange orders transmitted, bonds and interest coupons redeemed) are considered the most powerful in the extraction of the final decision. This result is in accordance with the expert's point of view on the examined decision making query.

The most informative and thus the most discriminative attribute (decision variable) is the personnel number of each branch. The calculated split point (527 employees) discriminates the branches in two categories, those belonging to the top two classes plus the top case of CLASS_3, and the rest of them which perform fairly poor in many decision criteria.

In CLASS_1 and CLASS_2 are included the branches that show a remarkable and balanced performance in the majority of the considered decision variables. CLASS_3 consists of 8 branches having a specific level of discrimination in cash transactions, checks issued and paid on the basis of payment

Table 1. Specified criteria for decision making in a bank network

C1	Personnel
C2	Cash Transactions Receipts
C3	Cash Transactions Payment Orders
C4	Cheques Issued on the Basis of Payment Orders from Banks
C5	Cheques Paid on the Basis of Payment Orders from Banks
C6	Foreign Currency Shipments Abroad
C7	Foreign Currency Shipments Abroad through the Head Office of the Bank of Greece
C8	Foreign Currency Shipments to the Head Office of the Bank of Greece
C9	Purchase of Foreign Currency
C10	Sale of Foreign Currency to Customers
C11	Sale of Foreign Currency to Customers & Shipments to the Head Office of the Bank of Greece
C12	Purchase of Cheques
C13	Issue of Cheques
C14	Entry of Payment Orders
C15	Issue of Payment Orders
C16	Foreign Exchange to Meet Other Requirements
C17	Entry of Items for Collection: Foreign – Domestic
C18	Items for Collection Pending with Third Parties
C19	Payment Orders – Clearing
C20	Foreign Exchange Orders Transmitted
C21	Import Approvals Issued
C22	Customs Clearance Licenses Issued
C23	Customs Clearance Licenses Pending Banks
C24	Customs Clearance Licenses without "Forex" Formalities
C25	Export Declarations Received
C26	Export Licenses Issued
C27	Export Declarations and Licenses Pending
C28	Bonds and Interest Coupons Redeemed

orders from banks, and bonds and interest coupons redeemed. CLASS_5 consists of branches with a small number of personnel, low cash transactions and also low checks issued on the basis of payment orders from banks and bonds redeemed. CLASS_4 differentiates from CLASS_5 in the (higher) number of checks issued. All the above observations sound reasonable and yet they consist a familiar and easy to learn decision guide for the decision maker.

Table 2. Class identification results

	CLASS_1	CLASS_2	CLASS_3	CLASS_4	CLASS_5
Branch	26,27	4,6,13,16,19	1,7,8,10,14,21,25	2,9,12,17,18	3,5,11,15,20,22,23,24

Figure 1. Lower and Upper Approximations of Rough set

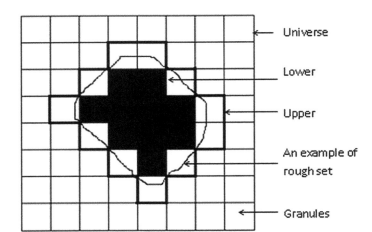

Figure 2. Decision tree representation of rules

If C1 ≤ 527

    If C2 ≤ 8415

        If C5 > 1750

            then CLASS_3 [0 0 1 0 0]

        Else

            If C4 ≤ 1930

                Then CLASS_5 [0 0 0 0 6]

            Else

                CLASS_4 [0 0 0 5]

    Else

        If C28 ≤ 4713

            Then CLASS_5 [0 0 0 0 8]

        Else

            If C11 ≤ 48

                Then CLASS_4 [0 0 0 1 0]

            Else

                CLASS_3 [0 0 5 0 0]

Else

    If C13 ≤ 240

        Then CLASS_3 [0 0 1 0 0]

    Else

        If C20 ≤ 66

            Then CLASS_2 [0 5 0 0 0]

        Else

            CLASS_1 [2 0 0 0 0]

DISCUSSION OF THE RESULTS

As mentioned above, the proposed decision making methodology proved a handy, accurate and meaningful tool for the administrative staff of the examined bank network. If we observe the produced decision rules from a general point of view, we can formulate numerous useful conclusions, verified by the corresponding bank experts which often use similar empirical rules when taking decisions. Some of these conclusions are stated below:

Branches with a low level of cash transactions are classified highly when having a large number of checks paid on the basis of payment orders from banks (e.g. branch 21, class_3).

Branches with a small number of personnel but satisfactory cash transactions, bonds redeemed and sale of foreign currency to customers are also rated in high order.

On the contrary, branches with a large number of personnel are classified in low position when having low performance in other important criteria (e.g. number of checks issued, like branch 8 placed in class_3).

Those branches consisting of a large number of personnel and having also a big amount of checks issued, are placed in very high order (class_2), while in class_1 are classified the top performance branches scoring high rates in all the examined decision criteria (Michalopoulos, 2001).

FUTURE SCOPE

IFCM, RCM, RFCM, RIFCM can be applied in the area of decision making like FCM being used in the case study. These hybrid algorithms have not yet been practically implemented in the field of decision making. However, application on FCM has shown the way.

CONCLUSION

Data clustering is an efficient way to handle the voluminous data. The uncertain based data clustering algorithms have found their applications in several domains. But a little work has been done in the field of decision making. These uncertain based hybrid data clustering algorithms promise a new arena of research in the field of decision making.

REFERENCES

Anushya, A., & Pethalakshmi, A. (2012). A Comparative Study of Fuzzy Classifiers with Genetic On Heart Data. *International Conference on Advancement in Engineering Studies and Technology*.

Asharaf, S., & Murty, M. N. (2003). An adaptive rough fuzzy single pass algorithm for clustering large data sets. *Pattern Recognition*, *36*(2), 3015–3018. doi:10.1016/S0031-3203(03)00081-5

Atanassov, K. T. (1986). Intuitionistic Fuzzy Sets. *Fuzzy Sets and Systems*, *20*(1), 87–96. doi:10.1016/S0165-0114(86)80034-3

Bezdek, J. C. (1981). *Pattern Recognition with Fuzzy Objective Function Algorithms*. New York: Plenum Press. doi:10.1007/978-1-4757-0450-1

Bezdek, J. C., & Pal, N. R. (1998). Some new indexes for cluster validity. *IEEE Transactions on Systems, Man, and Cybernetics. Part B, Cybernetics*, *28*(3), 301–315. doi:10.1109/3477.678624 PMID:18255949

Chen, D., Cui, D. W., Wang, C. X., & Wang, Z. R. (2006). A Rough Set-Based Hierarchical Clustering Algorithm for Categorical Data. *International Journal of Information Technology*, *12*(3), 149–159.

Cintra, M. E., Monard, M. C., Martin, T. P., & Camargo, H. A. (2011). *An Approach for the Extraction of Classification Rules from Fuzzy Formal Contexts*. Computer Science and Mathematics Institute Technical Reports.

Davis, D. L., & Bouldin, D. W. (1979). A cluster separation measure. *IEEE Transactions on Pattern Analysis and Machine Intelligence*, *PAMI-1*(2), 224–227. doi:10.1109/TPAMI.1979.4766909 PMID:21868852

Dubois, D., & Prade, H. (1990). Rough fuzzy sets model. *International Journal of General Systems*, *46*(1), 191–208. doi:10.1080/03081079008935107

Grzymala-Busse, J. P., Grzymala-Busse, J. W., & Hippe, Z. S. (2001). Melanoma prediction using data mining system LERS. *Proceedings of the 25th Anniversary AnnualInternational Computer Software and Applications Conference COMPSAC*. doi:10.1109/CMPSAC.2001.960676

Ho, T. B., & Nguyen, N. B. (2002). Nonhierarchical Document Clustering Based on a Tolerance Rough Set Model. *International Journal of Intelligent Systems*, *17*(2), 199–212. doi:10.1002/int.10016

Huang, Z. (1997). Clustering Large Data Sets With Mixed Numeric And Categorical Values. In *Proceedings of the First Pacific-Asia Conference on Knowledge Discovery and Data Mining*.

Hung, C. C., Purnawan, H., Kuo, B. C., & Letkeman, S. (2009). *Multispectal Image Classification Using Rough Set Theory and Particle Swarm Optimization*. Advances in Geoscience and Remote Sensing.

Ishibuchi, H., & Nakashima, T. (2001). Effect of Rule Weights in Fuzzy Rule-Based Classification Systems. *IEEE Transactions on Fuzzy Systems*, *9*(4), 506–515. doi:10.1109/91.940964

Jackson, A. G., LeClair, V., Ohmer, M. C., Ziarko, W., & Al-Kamhwi, H. (1996). *Acta Metallurgica et Materialia*. Academic Press.

Lee, S.C., & Huang, M.J. (n.d.). Applying AI technology and rough set theory for mining association rules to support crime management and fire-fighting resources allocation, Journal of Information. Technology and Society, 2, 65–78.

Lin, T. Y., & Cercone, N. (1997). Rough Sets and Data Mining - Analysis of Imperfect Data. Kluwer Academic Publishers.

Lin, T. Y., & Wildberger, A. M. (1994). *The Third International Workshop on Rough Sets and Soft Computing Proceedings RSSC'94*. San Jose State University.

Lingras, P., & West, C. (2004). Interval set clustering of web users with rough k-mean. *Journal of Intelligent Information Systems*, *23*(1), 5–16. doi:10.1023/B:JIIS.0000029668.88665.1a

Maji, P., & Pal, S. K. (2007). Rough Set Based Generalized Fuzzy C-Means Algorithm and Quantitative Indices. *IEEE Transactions on Systems, Man, and Cybernetics. Part B, Cybernetics*, *37*(6), 1529–1540. doi:10.1109/TSMCB.2007.906578 PMID:18179071

Maji, P., & Pal, S. K. (2007). RFCM: A Hybrid Clustering Algorithm using rough and fuzzy set. *Fundamenta Informaticae*, *80*(4), 475–496.

Michalopoulos, M., Dounias, G. D., Thomaidis, N., & Tselentis, G. (2001). *Decision Making Using Fuzzy C Means and Inductive Machine Learning For Managing Bank Branches Performance*. Academic Press.

Mitra, P., Pal, S. K., & Siddiqi, M. A. (2003). Non-convex clustering using expectation maximization algorithm with rough set initialization. *Pattern Recognition Letters*, *24*(6), 863–873. doi:10.1016/S0167-8655(02)00198-8

Mitra, S., Banka, H. & Pedrycz, W. (n.d.). Rough-Fuzzy Collaborative Clustering. System, Man, and Cybernetics, *Part B: Cybernetics*. IEEE Transactions on, 36(4), 795–805.

Mohammad, S.A., Jafar, H., & Emad, S. (2008). Induction of Fuzzy Classification Systems Via Evolutionary Aco-Based Algorithms. *International Journal of Simulation Systems, Science and Technology*, *9*(3).

Parmar, D., Wu, T., & Blackhurst, J. (2007). MMR: An algorithm for clustering categorical data using Rough Set Theory. *Data and Knowledge Engineering*, *63*(3), 879–893. doi:10.1016/j.datak.2007.05.005

Pawlak, Z. (1982). Rough sets. *Int. Jour. of Computer and Information Sciences*, *11*, 341-356.

Pawlak, Z., & Skowron, A. (2007). Rudiments of rough sets. *Information Sciences - An International Journal*, *177*(1), 3 – 27.

Pitambare, D. P., & Kamde, P. M. (2013). Literature Survey on Genetic Algorithm Approach for Fuzzy Rule-Based System. *International Journal of Engine Research*, *2*(2), 29–32.

Prather, J. C., Lobach, D. F., Goodwin, L. K., Hales, J. W., Hage, M. L., & Hammond, W. E. (1997). Medical Data Mining: Knowledge Discovery in a Clinical Data Warehouse.[). AMIA.]. *Proceedings of the AMIA Annual Fall Symposium*, *101*(5)

Priyadarishini, A., Karthik, S., Anuradha, J., & Tripathy, B. K. (2011). Diagnosis of Psychopathology using Clustering and Rule Extraction using Rough Set. *Advances in Applied Science Research*, *2*(3), 346–362.

Saleha, R., Haider, J. N., & Danish, N. (2002). Rough Intuitionistic Fuzzy Set. *Proc. of 8th Int. conf. on Fuzzy Theory and Technology* (FT & T).

Sowiñski, R. (1992). Intelligent Decision Support. Handbook of Applications and Advances of the Rough Set Theory. Kluwer Academic Publishers. doi:10.1007/978-94-015-7975-9

Sugeno, M. (1977). Fuzzy Measures and Fuzzy integrals-A survey. In M. Gupta, G. N. Sardis, & B. R. Gaines (Eds.), Fuzzy Automata and Decision Processes (pp. 89–102). Academic Press.

Tou, J. T., & Gonzalez, R. C. (1974). *Pattern Recognition Principles*. Addison-Wesley.

Tripathy, B. K., & Bhargav, R. (2013). Kernel Based Rough-Fuzzy C-Means, *PReMI*, ISI Calcutta. *December, LNCS, 8251*, 148–157.

Tripathy, B. K., & Ghosh, A. (2013). *Data Clustering Algorithms using Rough sets. Handbook of Research on Computational Intelligence for Engineering, Science and Business* (pp. 297–327). IGI Global Publications. doi:10.4018/978-1-4666-2518-1.ch012

Tripathy, B. K., Ghosh, S. K., & Jena, S. P. (2002). Intuitionistic Fuzzy Rough Sets[Bulgaria]. *Notes on Intuitionistic Fuzzy Sets, 8*(1), 1–18.

Tripathy, B. K., Tripathy, A., Dhull, R., Verma, E., & Swarnalatha, P. (2013). *Rough Intuitionistic Fuzzy C-Means Algorithm and a Comparative Analysis. In Proceedings of ACM Compute-2013* (pp. 21–22). VIT University.

Tsumoto, S., Kobayashi, S., Yokomori, T., Tanaka, H., & Nakamura, H. (1996). The Fourth Internal Workshop on Rough Sets. In *Proceedings of Fuzzy Sets and Machine Discovery*. The University of Tokyo.

Woolery, L.K., & Grzymala-Busse, J. (1994). Machine learning for an expert system to predict preterm birth risk. *J Am Med Inform Assoc., 1*(6), 439–446.

Yang, L., & Yang, L. (2006). Study of a Cluster Algorithm Based on Rough Sets Theory. In *Proceedings of the Sixth International Conference on Intelligent Systems Design and Applications*.

Zadeh, A., Saberi, M., & Anvari, M. (2011). Fuzzy Sets. *Computers and Industrial Engineering, 60*(2), 328-340.

Zadeh, L. A. (1965). Fuzzy Sets. *Information and Control, 8*(11), 338–353. doi:10.1016/S0019-9958(65)90241-X

Chapter 7
An Adaptive Fuzzy-Based Service-Oriented Approach with QoS Support for Vehicular Ad Hoc Networks

Prabhakar Rontala Subramaniam
University of KwaZulu-Natal, South Africa

ABSTRACT

An attempt in implementing on-demand, QoS supported Vehicular Ad hoc Network (VANET) routing algorithms has taken new dimensions. Delivering information in time to achieve reliability across vehicles (nodes) is still being a challenge among the VANET research groups. An effort to develop a QoS adaptive routing schemes using soft computing techniques is made in this research work. SADVA – An adaptive fuzzy based QoS service oriented approach for VANET is presented in this paper. The performance of SADVA is compared with AODV (Perkins, Royer, & Das, 2003), GV-GRID (Li, & Yu, 2007), DSR (Johnson, Maltz, & Hu, 2004), FSR (Gerla, 2002), DYMO (Chakeres, & Perkins, 2006), REDEM (Prabhakar, Sivanandham, & Arunkumar, 2011b), and QARS (Prabhakar et al, 2011a). SADVA employs fuzzy logic system to determine the vehicle's speed over an effective time period for different types of service in use between multiple VANET nodes to engage or cooperate in communication. This chapter focuses on designing and developing QoS aware routing protocol for multi-hop VANET. Metrics such as number of packets received per second, percentage of packet loss and time for route establishment are used to analyse the network situation. Simulation test runs are carried out using Two Ray Ground propagation model where vehicular traffic is generated according to a Poisson process.

DOI: 10.4018/978-1-5225-1008-6.ch007

INTRODUCTION

Vehicular ad hoc networks (VANETs) are self-organizing networks and self-manageable, where the data or information can be organized in a distributed fashion without any centralized authority (a predefined infrastructure) using 802.11-based WLAN technology. A VANET can be assumed as an integration of multiple wireless/mobile networking technologies such as WiFi IEEE 802.11, WiMAX 802.16, Bluetooth, IRA, ZigBee for providing an effective communication between vehicles on dynamic mobility.

VANET helps to incorporate safety measures in vehicles, and also supports streaming communication between vehicles, infotainment and telematics. Road Side Units (RSU) are gateways either fixed or minimal in mobility on the road sides, to provide interim connectivity to vehicles. Hence the vehicles and road side units form a vehicular ad hoc network. VANET has recently received considerable attention in the automotive sector, VIC'S (Chen, Lin, & Lee, 2010), CarTALK 2000 (Cartalk, 2011), NOW (NoW, 2010), (Torrent, 2008) and different industry groups (C2C-CC, 2011).

Reliability and timely information delivery are key objectives in VANETs, which bring QoS into the picture. Extensive research has been carried out to implement QoS support for on-demand multi-service routing algorithms for VANETs. Providing optimal QoS for a specific period of time with varying number of nodes (vehicles) is the biggest challenge for the VANET research groups. This research work addresses the importance of providing optimal QoS for multimedia applications in VANET as well as, in assessing the validity of the vehicle-to-vehicle and vehicle-to-interface communication scheme for effective QoS.

It has been understood that, in VANET communications, the key component is the movement pattern of vehicles, also called the mobility model. Mobility models determine the location and speed of nodes in the topology at any given instant, which in-turn strongly affect network connectivity and throughput.

Few of the mobility models being used from ns-2 simulator (NS2, 2010) are Manhattan Grid model (Baghavan, & Barghavan, 1997), and Random Waypoint Model (Bianchi, 2000). An accurate analysis outcome requires a good mobility model that has captured all the aspects of mobility as explained in (Bechler, Storz, & Franz, 2003; Briesmeister & Hommel, 2000a). Another challenging issue in VANETs is congestion control (Blum, Eskandarian & Hoffmann, 2004). In case of congestion, normally the end-points detect overload conditions at intermediate nodes and reduce its data rate.

In VANETs, the topology changes within seconds and a congested node used for forwarding just a few seconds ago, might not be used at all at the point in time when the source reacts to the congestion. Broadcasting in a wireless network suffers from a number of drawbacks (Namboodiri & Gao, 2007). If multiple nodes transmit at the same time, they cause destructive interference. This is known as a collision of the two messages at the given receiver. In order to avoid collision, each node needs to retransmit/broadcast information with a random delay. In spite of this random delay, collisions still occur, and this may result in a portion of the network not receiving a certain broadcast message.

Communication in VANETs can be either done directly between vehicles as one-hop communication, or vehicles can retransmit messages, thereby enabling the so called multi-hop communication. In order to increase coverage or robustness of communication, relays at the roadside can be deployed (Yousefi, Mousavi & Fathy, 2006). Since the nodes are highly mobile, data transmission is less reliable and sub optimal:

1. VANET's hybrid architecture consists of both infrastructure networks and ad hoc networks together. Hence, in any generic network phenomena, the concept of routing and its characteristics are highly linked with QoS to satisfy the throughput and delay requirements of such media streaming applications.
2. An analysis of MANET routing protocols shows that its performance is not acceptable in VANETs (Bernsen & Manivannan, 2008) due to MANET's feature of limited mobility. High mobility in VANETs lead to broken links, with high packet drop and overhead due to missing route repairs or route failure. This phenomenon leads to low throughput ratio and high delay in transmission.

In this proposed mobility model, fuzzy control system is applied as such systems are capable of solving imprecise problems efficiently. The proposed fuzzy mobility model has been designed based on the motion rules of different kinds of nodes, based on the type of the activity and environment. Fuzzy control system includes fuzzy rules that describe the nodes' mobility in an adaptable way with the environment. This model has a knowledge base, which can be changed based on node conditions, types of nodes and environment. By using such knowledge base, the mobility rules of every environment can be imposed upon a mobility model as inputs, until the mobility is created in that specific environment.

The proposed routing scheme is designed and implemented as per the DSRC specifications (ASTM, 2003) and IEEE 802.11p MAC (Bilstrup et al, 2008) standards. This chapter proposes a QoS-aware fuzzy based adaptive routing algorithm, which focuses on identifying optimal paths for effective routing in a highly dynamic mobile ad hoc network such as VANET, based on vehicle driver's behavior. The process of selection and utilizing the optimal QoS route gets updated on transmission.

The primary objective of research work carried out:

1. To study, identify and analyze the required optimal QoS for media streaming service over VANET. To provide optimal QoS in cases when the node density is less, or when nodes are out of the communication range.
2. To design an adaptive routing protocol to support QoS for vehicular safety services. Priority vehicles such as ambulances, and patrol vehicles require safe transit even on a congested road. This is also considered in this research.
3. Major challenge in protocol design of VANET is to improve the reliability of routing data, as well as to reduce delivery delay time and minimize packet retransmission. Vehicles which require high quality for service specific applications is a challenge in VANET, which had to be considered as 'priority' during routing.
4. To simulate and implement optimized QoS aware routing scheme for media streaming services. Abstract vehicular mobility is one of the major issues that lead to delay, making it necessary to design delay-bounded routing protocols. The designing of delay-bounded routing protocols is a challenge, since multicast carry and forward is an approach to deliver packets.
5. To support dynamic "high mobility" controllable QoS for VANET, using fuzzy architectural setup. High and dynamic mobility is always a major issue in Vehicular ad hoc networks due to changeable topology and locality updates.

BACKGROUND

In this section a discussion on system background is provided focusing light on the growth of VANETs and the standards required to implement the proposed routing scheme. This section also focus on a review of existing protocols thus establishing the need for a fuzzy based QoS routing scheme.

System Background

Ad Hoc Network

An ad hoc network (Borgonovo, Capone, Cesana, & Fratta, 2004) is a collection of wireless mobile hosts or terminals forming a distributed reconfigurable network topology. They can operate without the aid of any fixed infrastructure or centralized control and can be rapidly deployed and reconfigured. Ad Hoc networking (Alisson et al, 2011) is a networking paradigm for mobile, self-organizing networks. In these networks, every node functions as a router as well as an application node and forwards packets on behalf of other nodes. Ad hoc networks have the ability to form "on the fly" and dynamically handle the joining or leaving of nodes in the network.

General characteristics:

1. Dynamic network topology,
2. Limited Bandwidth,
3. Energy constrained nodes,
4. Limited physical security.

Mobile Ad Hoc Network

Mobile Ad hoc Networks (MANET) (Pravin, Girish, & Pradip, 2010) are formed dynamically by an autonomous system of mobile nodes that are connected via wireless links without using an existing infrastructure or centralized administration as shown in Figure 1. The nodes are free to move randomly and organize themselves arbitrarily; thus the network's wireless topology may change rapidly and unpredictably.

MANETs are infrastructureless networks i.e. they do not require any fixed infrastructure such as a base station for their operation. In general, routes between nodes in an ad hoc network may include multiple hops, making it appropriate to call such networks, as "multi-hop wireless ad hoc networks".

General Characteristics:

1. Dynamic topology,
2. Bandwidth and energy constraint,
3. Infrastructureless,
4. Uncontrolled moving patterns (or uncontrolled mobility),
5. Limited processing and storage capability.

Figure 1. MANET

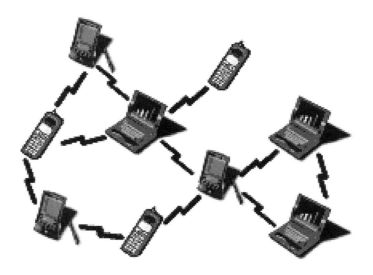

Vehicular Ad Hoc Network

Vehicular Ad Hoc Networks (VANETs) (Ghassan, Mosa, & Sidi, 2007), an outgrowth of traditional Mobile Ad Hoc Networks (MANETs), provides the basic network communication framework for application to an Intelligent Transportation System (ITS). A vehicular ad hoc network (Arunkumar & Sivanandham, 2007) is a phenomenon of mobile ad hoc networks, where vehicles and road infrastructures are equipped with wireless devices. Accordingly, the vehicles are able to communicate with each other, as well as interact with the road infrastructure as shown in Figure 2. One straightforward application of VANETs is safety, where communication is exchanged in order to improve the driver's responsiveness and enhance safety in road incidents.

Figure 2. VANET

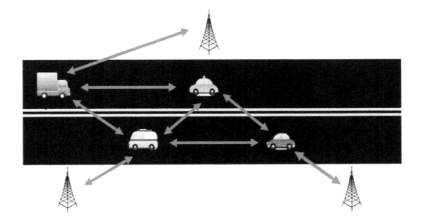

General Characteristics:

1. Highly dynamic mobility,
2. Vehicle density,
3. Driver behavior,
4. Mobility on controlled paths.

VANET Standard: Dedicated Short Range Communication (DSRC)

5.9 GHz DSRC (DSRC, 2012; FCC, 2011) is a short-to-medium range communication service that supports both public safety and private operations in roadside-to-vehicle and vehicle-to-vehicle communication environment. DSRC complements cellular communication, by providing very high data transfer rates in circumstances, where minimizing latency in the communication link and isolating relatively small communication zones are important. The 5.9 GHz DSRC link uses digital radio techniques to transfer data over short distances between roadside and vehicles, between vehicles themselves and between portable devices and vehicles. This link enables operations related to the improvement of traffic flow, highway safety, and other ITS applications in an application environment called DSRC/WAVE (Wireless Access in a Vehicular Environment).

The aim of this standard is to provide wireless communication capabilities for transportation applications within a 1000m range at typical highway speeds. It provides seven channels at the 5.9 GHz licensed band for ITS applications, with different channels designated for different applications, including one specifically reserved for vehicle-to-vehicle communication. Examples of such applications include en-route driver information propagation, collision warning & avoidance systems, and adaptive cruise control systems. By the year 2003, ASTM and IEEE adopted the DSRC and it was further standardized by the IEEE 802.11p task group (TGp). Figure 3 shows the composition of IEEE802.11p.

A few issues affecting VANET are:

1. High mobility,
2. Partitioned networks,
3. Quality of Service in VANET.

RELATED ROUTING PROTOCOLS

A routing protocol governs the way that two communicating entities exchange information. The protocol includes the procedure for establishing a route, decision in data forwarding, and action in maintaining the route or recovering from routing failure (Arunkumar & Gnanamurthy, 2006). The high mobility of nodes and the rapidly changing topology in VANETs make it hard to maintain or even establish an end-to-end connection as intermediate nodes are not always present between the source and destination. In the past few years, this has prompted researchers to find and investigate scalable routing [42] protocols that are robust enough for implementation in VANETs (Bernsen & Manivannan, 2008; Blazevic et al, 2005; Blum et al, 2004; Broch et al, 1998; Li & Yu, 2007). To cater to the unique characteristics and applications of VANETs, traditional MANET routing protocols have been modified (Briesemeister &

Figure 3. IEEE 802.11 MAC

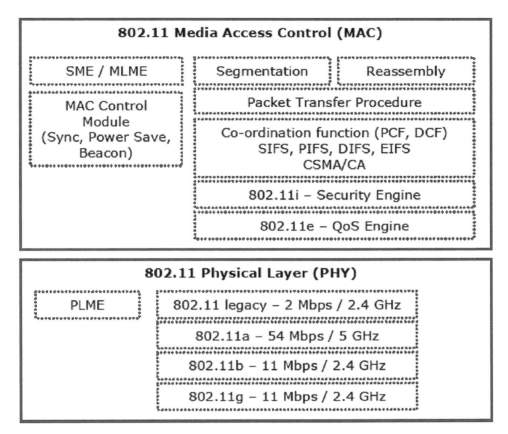

Hommel, 2000). These protocols have been designed and classified to deal with the mobility of nodes: by discovering new routes (reactive routing), updating routing tables (proactive routing), using geographical location information (position-based routing), identifying and detecting stable vehicle configurations (cluster-based routing), using vehicle's movements to support message transportation (geocast routing) and using broadcasting to support message forwarding (broadcast routing). In VANET, the routing protocols are classified into five categories based on Topology, Position, Cluster, Geocast, and Broadcast.

The proactive routing defines the routing information through the next forwarding node, which is maintained in the background irrespective of communication requests. The packets are constantly broadcasted and flooded among nodes to maintain the path. A table is constructed within each node, which indicates the next hop node towards a destination.

Reactive routing protocols are bandwidth efficient, on-demand routing protocols with lower overheads. Routing tables are constantly updated by flooding packets. The two main functions of the protocol are route discovery and route maintenance. Position based routing (Gokhan, 2006; Hartenstein et al, 2001) consists of a class of routing algorithm. They share the property of using geographic positioning information, in order to select the next forwarding hops. The packet is sent without any map knowledge to the one hop neighbor, which is closest to the destination. Position-based routing is beneficial, since no global route from the source node to the destination node needs to be created and maintained.

Geocast routing (Bachir & Benslimane, 2003; Harshavardhan & Joshi, 2006) is described as location-based multicast routing (Mauve et al, 2003) protocol. Its objective is to deliver the packet from source node to all other nodes within a specified geographical region (ZOR). In Geocast routing, vehicles outside the ZOR are not alerted to avoid unnecessary hasty reaction. Geocast is considered as a multicast service within a specific geographic region. It normally defines a forwarding zone, where it directs the flooding of packets in order to reduce message overhead and network congestion caused by simply flooding packets everywhere. In the destination zone, unicast routing can be used to forward the packet.

Broadcast routing (Fukuhara et al, 2005) is frequently used in VANET for sharing traffic, weather and emergency road conditions among vehicles and delivering advertisements and announcements. Broadcasting (Nathan & Jinhua, 2006) is used when the message needs to be disseminated to the vehicle beyond the transmission range i.e. multi hops are used. Broadcast sends a packet to all nodes in the network, typically using flooding. This ensures the delivery of the packet, but bandwidth is wasted and nodes receive duplicates. In VANET, it performs better for a small number of nodes.

Design of an adaptive routing protocol for wireless communication in VANETs presents specific challenges. Jing, Lu, & Kurt (2003) devised a model for discovery of spatio-temporal resources in an infrastructure-less environment, in which the database is distributed among the moving objects. In this model, two vehicles exchange their local databases when their distance is smaller than the wireless transmission range. Also Arunkumar & Ramesh (2010) proposes 2 new flooding strategies based on an adaptive algorithm VON. 1-hop, which enhances traditional source routing for low mobility nodes, reacting to VON efficiency decay and answer path routing failure. On the other hand, 2.5-hop also reacts to VON efficiency decay and answers path routing failure, but presents lower success rates and is less redundant.

Artimy et al (2005), consider density as an important parameter in their work. The rapid change in topology, due to traffic jams, is shown to disturb the homogenous distribution of vehicles on the road. Dynamic transmission of power has been proposed as a manner to maintain network connectivity and minimise the adverse effects of unregulated power. Alisson et al (2011) proposes a system to prioritise messages based on the context and content. On this basis, a function of relevance is calculated for each message, and each message will have different CWs (Contention Windows).

This chapter capitalizes on quorum based approaches to achieve efficient and self-organising location service management. Since it is important to have up-to-date information about destinations' locations, mobile nodes should be able to route the updating and querying messages to the location servers in a timely manner. Nevertheless, routing updating and querying messages in VANETs is challenging for three reasons.

1. Nodes in a VANET change their location frequently; as such they need to send location updating messages to the neighbouring servers with minimum delay. This process allows the location based neighbouring nodes to have an update of correct and up-to-date location information when replying to the location queries. Thus, it is important to select routes between nodes and neighbour servers that guarantee minimum delay.

2. Vehicles move with high velocity and they often change their speed and direction. Node random mobility affects route stability. When a route is established between two nodes, mobility of the source, destination, or intermediate nodes may cause the route to break. If two nodes on the route move out of transmission range, the link between these two nodes vanishes, and then the route fails. Figure 4 shows a route from the source node S to the destination node D through N1, N2 and

N3. Node D moves out of the transmission range of node N3 (as shown in Figure 5), and hence D cannot receive massages. In this case, the route from S to D breaks, because of mobility of node D, affecting the connectivity probability of the established route. Thus, it is critical to select routes that have a high connectivity probability.

3.   The route length measured in terms of number of hops affects quality of the route. To save bandwidth, which is precious in VANETs, it is important to select a route with a minimum number of nodes. One of the challenging tasks in the deployment of VANETs, therefore, is to design a routing protocol that minimizes the end to end delay while satisfying quality of service (QoS) constraints with respect to the probability of connectivity and hop count. In other words, it should be capable of handling frequent path disruptions caused by high mobility of vehicles and, at the same time, makes efficient use of the network bandwidth. Traditional routing protocols used in MANETs need to be modified so as to accommodate such unique characteristics of VANETs.

A brief overview of the protocols considered to analyze the efficiency of the proposed routing scheme is presented below. Figure 6 provides an insight of different classes of VANET routing protocols with the research outcome.

The Ad Hoc On-Demand Distance Vector (AODV) routing protocol (Perkins et al, 2003) develops on the DSDV algorithm previously. Basically, it minimizes the number of required broadcasts by creating routes on a demand basis, as opposed to maintaining a complete list of routes as in the DSDV algorithm (Yihai & Aaron, 2005). AODV broadcasts a route request (RREQ) packet from the initiator and then the requests are forwarded until the destination is found. AODV (Perkins & Royer, 2004) utilizes destination

Figure 4. Route from source 'S' to destination 'D'

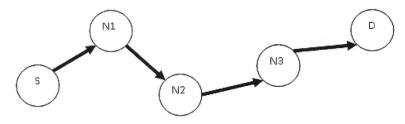

Figure 5. Broken route from source 'S' to destination 'D'

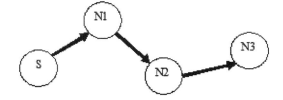

Figure 6. Overview of routing protocol strategies with research outcome

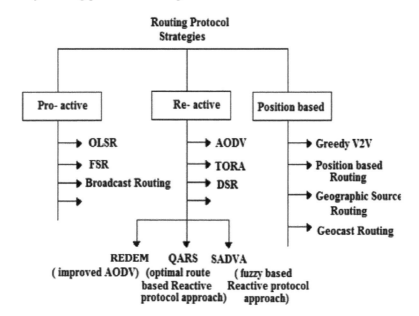

sequence numbers to ensure all routes are loop-free and contain the most recent route information. The Dynamic Source Routing (DSR) (Johnson et al, 2004) protocol provides a mechanism to make each node maintain route caches that contain newly updated information.

Earlier, GSR (Maihfer, 2004) was used in MANET. Then it was improved for use in VANET by incorporating greedy forwarding of messages toward the destination. If at any hop there are no nodes in the direction of the destination, then GPSR utilizes a recovery strategy known as perimeter mode. The perimeter mode has two components, one being distributed planarization algorithm that makes local conversion of connectivity graph into planar graph by removing the redundant edges. Second component is online routing algorithm that operates on planer graphs. So, in VANET perimeter mode of GPSR is used. In GPSR, if any obstruction or void occurs then algorithm enters perimeter mode and planner graph routing algorithm starts operations. This involves sending the message to an intermediate neighbour, instead of sending to farthest node. However, this method introduces long delays due to greater number of hop counts. Due to rapid movement of vehicles, routing loops are introduced which causes dissemination of messages to a long path (Lochert et al, 2005). GPSR uses a static street map and location information about each node. As GPSR does not consider vehicle density of streets, it is not an efficient method for VANET.

Position based routing protocols such as LAR (Ko & Vaidhya, 1998), DYMO (Chakeres & Perkins, 2006), GPSR (Baswant & Kung, 2000) require prior knowledge of geographic location information of vehicles (from a GPS service) that could be applied in VANETs for faster route information and performance. It has been noticed that position-based routing protocols also suffer from severe geographic routing failures due to the presence of "topology holes" (Lochert et al, 2003). Naumov & Gross (2007) propose spatially aware routing to overcome such drawbacks. But, the effectiveness in optimality of spatially aware routing could not be judged, due to spatial non-awareness. Hence, it could be proved and it could be further enhanced in order to improve performance. Task 3 (2005) final report follows an epidemic routing approach for VANET with tolerance support for delay. In sparse vehicular traffic (Wu et al, 2005), opportunistic forwarding mechanisms would be helpful for vehicle–to–vehicle ad hoc communications. AQVA (Arunkumar & Ramesh, 2010) routing protocol is dynamic in identifying route based on driver behavioural parameters. This scheme had been simulated using VanetMobiSim over ns2, with support for real time road scenario. The major drawback of this AQVA is that it lags in maintaining route delay, which is one of the major requirements of media streaming services in support of QoS.

Heuristics methods in Geographical Routing Protocol (Luis et al, 2015) improves the performance of geographical routing protocols using different local-search heuristics. Reducing duplicate packets in Unicast VANET communications (Luis et al, 2015) increases the available bandwidth by providing duplicate packet filtering in the routing layer thereby preventing the propagation of additional packet copies. REDEM (Prabhakar et al, 2011b) is modeled as a set of high speed vehicles on a straight highway, in which any vehicle can establish connectivity with any other vehicle(s) travelling in the same or opposite direction. REDEM proposes a distributed, receiver-based next-hop selection routing protocol to minimize the overhead. REDEM metrics are primary to identify the optimal QoS on-demand for various types of services between different nodes in communication. REDEM uses bandwidth, delay and packet loss as the QoS metrics.

QARS (Prabhakar et al, 2011a) works on route identification, route binding, update and deletion process, based on the validation of adaptive QoS metrics, before the optimal route selection process between the source and destination. The simulated results show that QAR protocol's performance is better than protocols discussed in this section. Performance of metrics such as successful data delivery and average delay, have been studied. QARS proposes two schemes of route connection between source and destination, based on radio propagation, (a) Connectivity between RSU and Vehicles (V2I), and (b) Vehicle to vehicle (V2V). Since, the intensity of nodes at cross-roads is higher; a RSU can help in maintaining the route between VANET nodes. The bandwidth of RSU can be shared between nodes at an instant; hence demand on QoS is controlled. While VANET nodes on a high way road or lane may be high mobility, the challenge lies in catering to demand on the QoS.

FUZZY LOGIC: AN INTRODUCTION

The probability theory can be used to formally represent information in stochastic decision environments. It represents the uncertainty associated with the randomness of events. The theory of fuzzy sets, in turn, seeks to represent the uncertainty associated with vague, inaccurate or independently unrelated information (Zadeh, 1965).

The present day complex networks are dynamic, involving a great degree of uncertainty associated with input traffic and other environmental parameters. This uncertainty leads to unexpected overloads, failures and disturbances, thereby defying accurate analytical modelling. In this scenario, fuzzy logic appears to be a promising approach to address key aspects of networks. The ability to model networks in the continuum mathematics of fuzzy sets rather than with traditional discrete values, coupled with extensive simulation, offers a reasonable compromise between rigorous analytical modeling and purely qualitative simulation (Meier et al, 2005).

SADVA: An Adaptive Fuzzy Based QoS Service Oriented Approach

Fuzzy logic approaches have been applied in multiple resource assignment and control related problems. Hence, it can play a major role in identifying and controlling the QoS on demand, based on differentiable services over a Vehicular Ad Hoc Network.

SADVA employs fuzzy logic systems to determine the vehicle's speed over an effective time period for any type of service in use between multiple VANET nodes that engage or co-operate in communication. Figure 7 and 8 shows the architecture and the f_A process of fuzzy QoS prediction module, respectively. The basic functions of the components in the module are described as follows. f_A can be gathered and determined based on fuzzification process, which consists of four modules:

1. **Fuzzifier:** The fuzzifier performs the fuzzification function that converts three inputs into suitable linguistic values which are needed in the inference engine.
2. **Fuzzy Rule Base:** The fuzzy rule base is composed of a set of linguistic control rules and the attendant control goals.
3. **Inference Engine:** The inference engine simulates human decision making based on the fuzzy control rules and the related input linguistic parameters.
4. **Defuzzifier:** The defuzzifier acquires the aggregated linguistic values from the inferred fuzzy control action and generates a non-fuzzy control output, which represents the predicted speed.

To establish adaptive QoS using Fuzzy sets theory (Bianchi, 2000), the notion of a membership function, $\gamma(A)$ and its relation has to be understood. If $V_i = \{m1, m2, \ldots mn\}$ be a set of well defined mobile nodes in a VANET network. Here any xi where i=\{1,2,..n\} is a subject of problem domain and its mapping relation $f_A = \{f, h, a, v, r, p\}$. If $\sigma(x)$ be the degree to which a fuzzy variable *x* is a member of a set. A complete membership is represented by 1, and no membership by 0, while all other intermediate values fall into the problem domain between 0 and 1. The membership function $\sigma(x)$, maps x into the interval [0, 1]. f_A (Xi) defines the fuzzy QoS value for set of mobile nodes being authenticated based on its membership function $\sigma(x)$.

Figure 7. Architecture of fuzzy QoS predication module

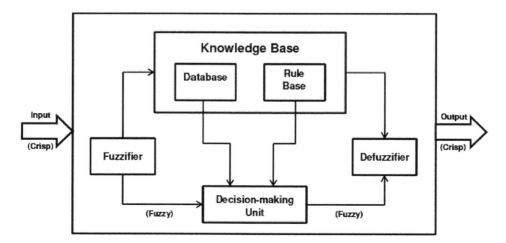

Figure 8. f_A process of identifying the QoS

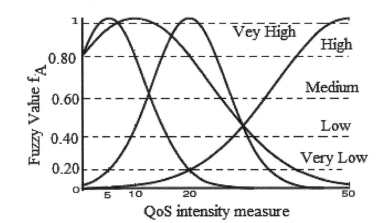

Definition 1

For ∃ mobile node Vi, should possess a defined fuzzy based QoS value f_A, such that f_A ∈ {f,h,a,g,r,p} when it needs to communicate with another node within a Cluster Ci or other Cluster Cj.

Proof

For all mobile nodes Vi in Cluster Ci, where i= 1,2,...n can follow a fuzzy based QoS value f_A. For any mobile node Vi ∈ Ci there extends a relation as Vi X f_A (Xi). This same rule stands true also for all Vj ∈ Cj.

f_A is a set of well defined QoS values ranging anywhere between 0 to 1, such that each f_A value possess f = Full QoS(1.0), h = High QoS (0.8,0.9), a = Acceptable QoS(0.6,0.7), g = Average QoS(0.4,0.5), r = Recommend QoS(0.2,0.3) and p=Poor QoS (0.0,0.1).

Figure 9 defines the f_A values based on varying node intensity, where node a, b, o and p possess Poor QoS value. Nodes c, d, e, f and l possess High QoS Values, g has Acceptable QoS, nodes h, i, j and k possess Average QoS, nodes m and n has Recommended QoS Value.

The input to the fuzzifier represents set of QoS 'f_A' parameters related to identifying an effective QoS measure for routing between a source vehicle and its front vehicle (forwarding vehicle) such that the destination node is reachable. The reachability of the destination node depends on the following fuzzy metrics:

1. Hopping distance between source and destination (information based on an earlier session),
2. Type of forward – servicing nodes between source and destination,
3. Type of service in use,
4. Demand on bandwidth,
5. Mobility factor (current speed of vehicle).

    As an example, IF the distance measure between the vehicle and its front vehicle is "intermediate", AND the current speed of the vehicle is "slow", THEN the estimated speed of the vehicle during the next time period is "slow". The non-fuzzy output of the defuzzifier can then be expressed as the weighted average of each rule's output.

Figure 9. QoS based fuzzy metrics adopted in f_A

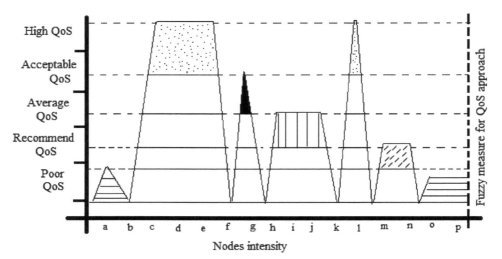

SADVA: Fuzzy Based Qos Evaluation

Adaptive QoS Based Fuzzy Approach

To measure the global or local QoS fuzziness, a suitable membership function f_A should be defined. Different functions are already used in the literature, such as the standard S-function (Briesmeister et al, 2000; Broch et al, 1998) and the Huang and Wang function (Yu & Fan, 2012). Tonguz (2007) defined the suitable threshold as fuzzy number $\mu(g)$ using LR function, which can be defined as Equation (1) is as follows:

$$\mu\big(g\big) = \begin{cases} o, g \leq g_{\min}\,(or)g \geq g_{\max} \\ L\big(g\big) = \left(\dfrac{g - g_{\min}}{T - g_{\min}}\right)^{\alpha}, g_{\min} \leq g \leq T \\ R\big(g\big) = \left(\dfrac{g_{\max} - g}{g_{\min} - T}\right)^{\beta}, T \leq g \leq g_{\max} \end{cases} \tag{1}$$

where

g is the intermediate QoS level,
gmin and *gmax* are the minimum and maximum QoS levels
$T \in [0, L - 1]$ is a suitable constant.
α and $\beta \in (0,\infty)$ can be determined with respect to the service based edge properties of the defined QoS.

However, the proper selection of parameters is not easy and can add more complexity to the algorithm on hand. Using a fuzzy number for calculation seems to be more natural, since the usual approach of

QoS classes (Briesmeister & Hommel, 2000) adopts only a preferable single number (a unique threshold for the entire service). If this approach fails, then advanced techniques for adaptive thresholding are employed. A single threshold, globally determined for an entire applied service function or locally calculated for an entire service applied hence remains uncertain. Therefore, removing the uncertainty around a crisp number by considering / representing it as a fuzzy number seems to be beneficial. To identify the fuzzy value Equation (2) is defined as:

$$\gamma_l(A) = \frac{2}{MN} \sum_{i=1}^{M-1} \sum_{j=1}^{N-1} \min\left[f_A(g_{ij}), 1 - f_A(g_{ij})\right] \tag{2}$$

The general algorithm for thresholding based on measures of fuzziness can be formulated as follows:

1. Select the type of membership function based on service in use.
2. Select a suitable measure of fuzziness (Equation (1)).
3. Calculate the QoS mapping value.
4. Initialize the position of the membership function.
5. Shift the membership function along the QoS -level range (Figure 9) and calculate in each position the amount of fuzziness, for instance using Equation(1).
6. Locate the position *gopt* with minimum/maximum fuzziness.
7. Threshold the assigned service with $T = gopt$.

The notion of fuzzy QoS evaluation (Arunkumar & Gnanamurthy, 2006) is being defined as the degree of "quality" metric about the consistent behaviour of system and entities in use. The QoS evaluation is based on the previous behavioural experience of the system in service with other entities and observation of its related actions (Bachir & Benslimane, 2003). The system has been incorporated as a unique mechanism for providing QoS, which can be interpreted as a relation of f_A among multiple nodes (Figure 10) that are willing to participate in various sharable services and handle resource management (Arunkumar & Ramesh, 2010). If $f_A = 0$ the uncertainty prevails among mobile nodes when each node requires one or more communication member to establish trusted communication among peer nodes.

Figure 10. Message communication between mobile nodes to initiate f_A

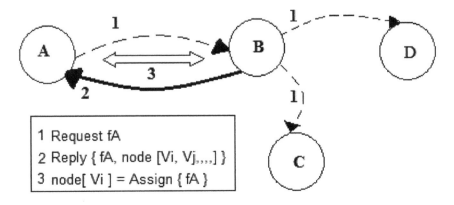

Figure 11. Establishment of SADVAv for node 'A' and 'B'

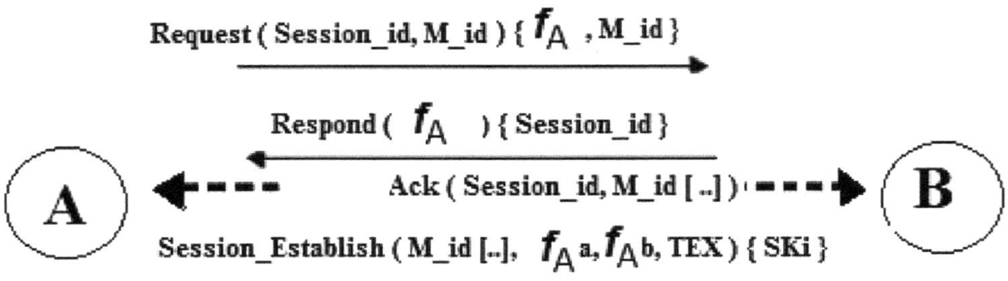

For providing effective QoS value of f_A among nodes, fuzzy set Vi plays its major role in simplifying the process of assigning f_A value among group of nodes based on node equality function. f_A needs to be checked and re-assigned when node A is in communication with node B. SADVA has to adopt the following procedures when node 'A' is engaged in trust communication with node 'B' (Figure 11).

1.   Node maintains a SADVAv for any defined event or activity between nodes.
2.   SADVAv for a node update while leaving or joining a cluster Ci.
3.   For any mobile node, its SADVAv is independent of its cluster.
4.   SADVAv for node 'n' may change in each cluster C.
5.   SADVAv update for node 'n' is dependent on its neighbor update and vote.

The trustworthiness of the potential interaction among mobile nodes depends upon the SADVAv, which works along with inference rules for each of the trust dimensions. SADVA defines the set of rules (based on node property in Table 1) for mobile nodes to establish communication or file transfer.
SADVA adopts the following rules for its update:

1.   Any mobile node 'Mi' can participate in f_A assignment among other nodes within cluster, in order to receive a SADVA value.
2.   A node can maintain its SADVA value until its Time in Cluster (TCL) or Time Expiry (TEX) or when a new mobile node joins the cluster or when a existing mobile node leaves the cluster.
3.   TEX (Time Expiry) of SADVAv for a mobile node is generated using random time scale, but limited to 100 ms.
4.   A node Mi can reside in a Cluster Ci, which does not adopt any defined time limits.

Table 1. Property/rules to be adopted for trust establishment

f_A	p	r	v	a	h	Metric
p	p	P	P	p	0	p
r	p	R	R	v	a	r
v	p	R	R	v	v	v
a	p	V	A	a	a	a
h	0	A	V	a	h	h

The Fuzzy Trust Value SADVAv at any instance depends on TEX for its update. The process of issuing or updating a SADVA f_A value for a node follows the steps given below. Figure 10 represents the process of initiation and updation of SADVA pictorially.

Step 1: Mobile node 'Mi' requests its identification through Cluster coordinator.
Step 2: Each Mobile node issues its existing SADVA value to SADVA Coordinator.
Step3: SADVA coordinator requests each mobile host within cluster to vote for mobile node 'Mi'.
Step 4: Based on Eq (2), coordinator identifies the f_A value for node 'Mi'.
Step 5: Coordinator assigns the value to node 'a'. The coordinator node is determined based on Eq(4).
Step 6: New mobile node 'k' joins the cluster, Cluster coordinator requests its Identity.
Step 7: Step 1 to Step 5 need to be followed, to renew SADVA for all nodes in the cluster.
Step 8: Node 'l' moves from cluster, hence repeat Step 7.

Nodes that cooperate rarely have low service reputation rate (SRR) and hence considered to be less trustworthy (assigned low trust value). To maintain the credibility of recommendation that SADVA f_A obtained from neighboring nodes, it would be best to update the information reputation of nodes. SRR denotes the service reputation rate which is obtained based on the Recommended Metric (RV) obtained by monitoring the node at any time 'k' and weighted average of votes (AV) from other neighbouring nodes.

Experimental Test Bed

The performance analysis of SADVA QoS adaptive routing scheme is tested on experimental test bed (Table 2) with varying types of services, since SADVA is designed for differing service architectures. The test-bed scenario uses a stretch of highway 6km long. All vehicles have OBUs (On Board Units)

Figure 12. Process of initiate and update of SADVA f_A

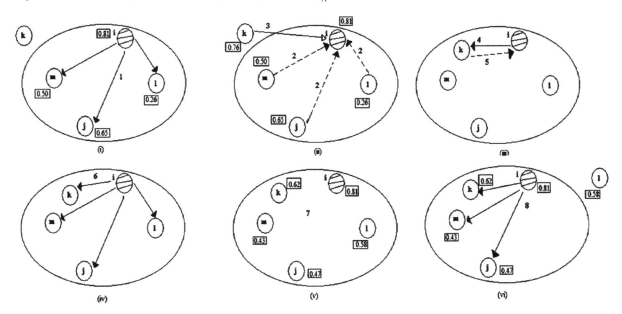

with static RSU (Road Side Unit) designed between every 2 kms. The propagation model used was the Two Ray Ground, where Vehicular traffic was generated according to a Poisson process. Three environments were tested using this scenario: a sparse density environment with 15 vehicles, an average density environment with 25 vehicles, and a highly dense environment with 50 vehicles.

The density of the network is 125 vehicles per kilometer square, the simulation time is 1200 seconds, the number of nodal clients is 100 and the number of requests range between 100 and 1000. In the course of experiment run time, the request number is defined along with the number of gateway queries sent by gateway clients. A gateway client can generate many gateway requests, which can be chosen to evaluate the performance of the proposed schemes using the following metrics:

1.	**Success Rate:** Indicates the average fraction of successful transactions;
2.	**Response Time:** Determines the average time of successful transactions.

It measures the elapsed time for getting a valid node reply in response to a gateway request sent by a vehicle. This metric takes into account several factors such as transmission and message processing delay, along with

Table 2. Simulation parameters

Parameter	Description
Frequency of operation	2.4GHz - 5.5GHz
Number of nodes	15, 25, 50
Node Speed	50ms, 70ms, 100ms
Node placement	Random / Uniform
Node pause time	0 – 10ms, 0 – 50ms
Mobility model	Random Way Point
Propagation model	Free space
Received power threshold	-81dBm
Transmitted power	7.89dBm
Transport layer	UDP,TCP
Network-layer protocols	ODMRP, AODV
MAC	IEEE 802.11p
Transmission range (mts)	1000
Type of service	Video/Audio/Text
Simulation time (secs)	1200
Adaptation period (secs)	150
Total number of requests	1000
Rate of service requests	1 unit of time
Average network range	100

1. **Bandwidth Usage:** Measures the overhead of proposed schemes in terms of the number of messages needed to satisfy the node requests;
2. **Average Bandwidth Usage per Request:** Calculates the average bandwidth used per every successful gateway request.

The vehicles have a maximum speed of 130km/h, maximum acceleration of 3m=s² and maximum deceleration of 5m=s². All vehicles have 1:5 meter omnidirectional antennas. The aim of the experiment is to compare the adaptive SADVA approach with fuzzy based GV-GRID approach, i.e., to compare the dynamic approach with the 802.11p standard. According to Bai et al. (2006), IEEE 802.11p uses backoff algorithm to identify any inter-lobular mobile objects, but has no support for QoS. To analyze the network situation, three metrics were used - number of packets received per second, which is similar to Packet Delivery Ratio (PDR), percentage of packet loss (PPL) and time for route establishment (TRE). The amount of packets lost is the sum of errors caused by collisions and discards. The success rate (SUC) is related to the number of packets received and the number of packets that should have been successfully received, if no losses occurred. Thus, SUC = (PDR - PPL).

In the f_A comparative chart (Figure 16), the adaptive QoS metric for SADVA is found to be optimal for varying types of services. The reliability measure of SADVA is higher when compared to AODV and QARS (Figure 15). This happens, because the densities calculated for each vehicle are very low in the first and the last moments. The vehicles enter and exit by the Poisson process, which is exponentially increasing with respect to time. These metrics will be highest when all vehicles are present on the track, when it has the highest density. The route discovery ratio is the most fundamental benchmark in evaluating the performance of route discovery ratio. In Figure 13, 14 and 15 with the adaptive approach, there is an improvement in the percentage of success and reliability because SADVA approach received more packets per second with less loss. This means that, considering the total number of packets that should be received, the adaptive approach was more successful than the standard approach.

Figure 15 explains the performance of SADVA (a fuzzy based adaptive protocol) in comparison with QARS and AODV. The QoS metric maintained in SADVA is a higher value compared to other QoS schemes.

Figure 13. Performance of SADVA with GV-GRID

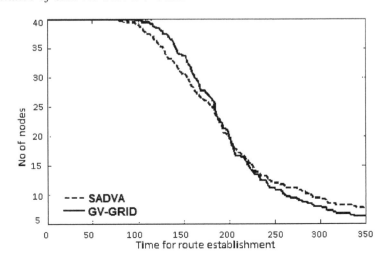

Figure 14. Percentage of packet loss with SADVA

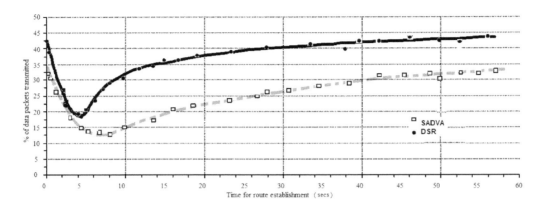

Figure 15. Performance of SADVA with QARS and AODV

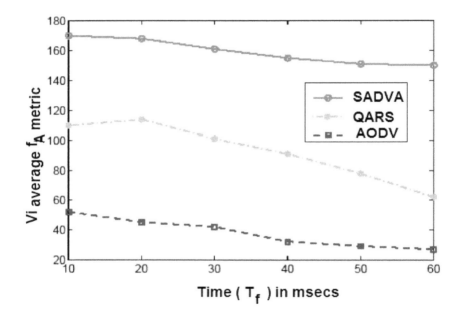

Performance Analysis

In order to be fair in comparison among the three proposed schemes, the existing proactive, reactive and hybrid existing discovery approaches (Blum et al, 2003), which are network layer-based and use the service based route discovery approach. To evaluate the QAR's performance using mobility traces that correspond to a Manhattan traffic pattern the ns2 simulator has been used. In simulation experiments carried out in this research work, the primary work is to understand and compare adaptive SADVA approach to existing approaches AODV (Perkins & Royer, 2004), DYMO (Chakeres & Perkins, 2006)

Figure 16. Comparative reliability of required QoS over evaluated QoS

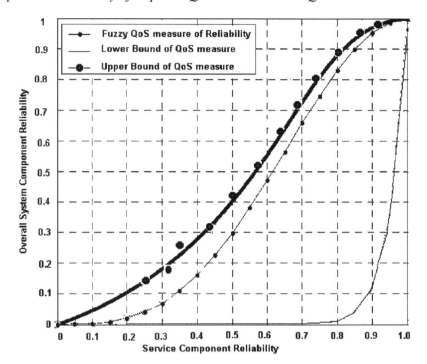

and FSR (Gerla, 2002), as well as with QARS (Prabhakar et al, 2011a), and REDEM (Prabhakar et al, 2011b) approach with different fixed radius (1, 2, and 3 hops) that can cater to large scale networks.

The idea of drawing a comparison among these approaches in a large-scale vehicular network, insists on proving that:

1. The proposed routing schemes outperform the existing reactive and the proactive approaches in some performance metrics.
2. Adaptive QoS scalable RSU aided discovery approach outperforms the standard hybrid gateway discovery approach in other performance metrics.
3. For a variable traffic density and five vehicles/km, the delivery ratio of REDEM routing schemes session establishment time (Figure 17) ranges between 93.56% and 98.35%. The curve progression of DYMO scheme shows a sharp decline at this juncture.
4. At traffic intensities, which are higher than 25 vehicles at 50km per hr, on average, the packet delivery ratio (Figure 19) of REDEM and FSR decreases by 12% compared to QARS, while DYMO's performance improves compared to FSR. Assuming a traffic density of 25 vehicles/km, SADVA's delivery ratio is 95.08%, while QARS achieves an average value of 83.12%, FSR transfers only 78.70% of the packets successfully.
5. The routing overload adopted compared to the intensity of user data that has been exchanged between the sender and receiver is discussed in Figure 18. Large variation between the throughput and packet loss have been identified in the routing schemes.

6. The overall analysis shows the behavior of SADVA to be comparatively better than DYMO and FSR. The framework also achieves fault tolerance, whereby a vehicular node on mobility can fail during transit; and

7. QARS approach scales well with the increase in the number of gateway requests.

    a. QARS (Prabhakar et al, 2011a) has been focused as an architectural framework for VANETs for supporting inter-vehicular communication in large-scale urban scenarios, where large numbers of vehicles moving with high velocity are formulated. To achieve a stable structure for the VANETs' framework, a novel QoS adaptive service management protocol is developed to achieve location querying and location updating using the concept of geographical clustering. Further, the framework employs message aggregation in both querying and updating, where location information is aggregated in an attempt to improve capacity utilisation of VANETs. In addition, since the communication pattern in VANETs is considered to a great extent, (i.e., vehicles inside one geographical cluster are more likely to communicate with each other), the framework also incorporates cluster awareness as a building block in the design process.

    b. The effectiveness of the QARS architecture is investigated by deriving analytical expressions for both location updating and querying cost. Furthermore, the total control overhead problem is formulated as an optimization problem of minimizing the communication overhead, allowing VANETs' designers the ability to consider alternative values for the network design parameters. Also, the performance of location information updating and querying is investigated based on simulation experiments using both Random Walk mobility model and real mobility traces. Analytical and simulation results show that the QARS framework can significantly reduce location updating cost and provide low querying overhead under various scenarios.

    c. Based on the number of RSUs as multi-hop servers to maintain current node information about the vehicular nodes in their vicinity SADVA is designed to be highly updatable. Since, it is important to have up-to-date information about destinations' locations, mobile nodes should be able to route the updating and querying messages to the local RSU in a timely manner. Therefore, this thesis proposes a new approach for routing delay-sensitive location updating and querying messages in vehicular ad hoc networks. QARS approach to this problem uses paths that minimize the end-to-end delay while maintaining a threshold on the probability of connectivity (connectivity degree) and maintaining a threshold on the hop count along the selected path. To achieve this, analytical expressions for the delay, hop count, and connectivity probability for a two-way road scenario are derived. The QoS routing problem is formulated as a constrained optimization problem for which, a genetic algorithm is proposed. Using both analytical and simulation studies, it is concluded that the proposed protocols QARS and SADVA achieve substantial end-to-end delay reduction, especially in sparse networks. SADVA therefore, stand out as promising candidates for large scale ad hoc networks such as VANETs.

In this research work the QoS requirements for VANET applications have been proposed. The requirements should be composed of not only priority-based variable QoS parameters, but also a more detailed variable service definition for expected QoS properties. It can be found that VANET applications exhibit high variation in requirements, depending on the service in use.

Figure 17. Session establishment time: performance of SADVA with DYMO, REDEM, and qars

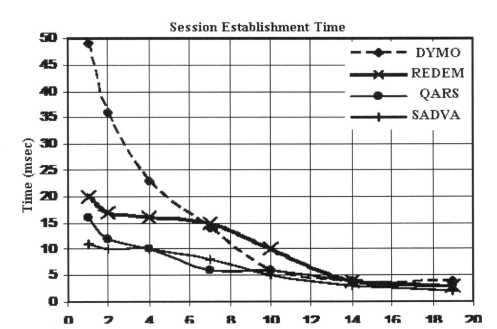

Figure 18. Load balancing capacity: performance of SADVA with DYMO, REDEM, and QARS

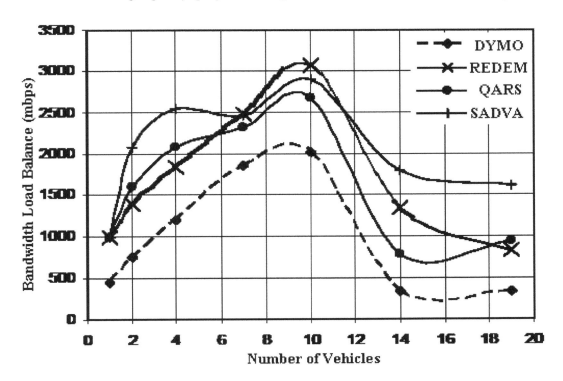

Figure 19. Packet delivery ratio: performance of SADVA with FSR, REDEM, and QARS

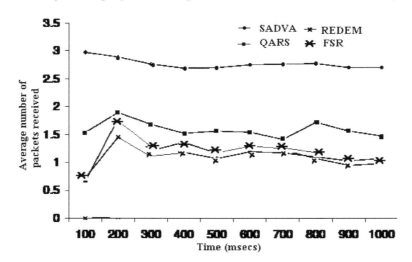

To evaluate the average response time of the proposed approaches, graphs have been used for analysis. These graphs (in Figure 17, Figure 18, Figure 19) show that the proactive approach has the lowest average response time of 15 milliseconds for 1000 requests, and that the reactive approach has the highest average latency of 80 milliseconds for 1000 requests. REDEM approach has an average latency, where the values are between that of the proactive and the reactive approaches for a number of requests ranging from 100 to 1000. Thus, we can conclude that our adaptation mechanism finds a good trade-off between SADVA and FSR / DYMO approaches.

CONCLUSION

Research work focuses on design development of QoS aware routing protocol for multi-hop vehicular ad hoc networks (VANETs). The routing protocol constructs a route on demand from a source (a fixed node or a station) to vehicles that exist in a destination region. The primary goal is to maintain a stable route, which provides better quality of communication and data transmission. For this purpose, we have designed three stable QoS schemes where the neighbour selection algorithm and the route selection algorithm are used to select a route by vehicles, which are likely to move at similar speeds and toward similar directions. The experimental results have shown that SADVA could provide routes with longer lifetime, compared with an existing method. Variable services such as vehicular safety and multi session establishment depend on the prediction of the behavior of both the traffic and the other road users. This prediction is of utmost importance, as it contributes to overall road safety and control effective traffic flow.

This chapter demonstrates the efficiency of fuzzy based adaptive QoS VANET routing protocol SADVA, based on their respective underlying protocols DYMO, REDEM, QARS, FSR, DSR and AODV. The performance analysis of these protocols is evaluated using the ns2 simulation environment and real-time test bed approach. The common VANET routing protocols DYMO, FSR, AODV, GV-GRID, which exploit the QoS weakness have been established in the earlier section. It can be noticed that the mobility model of nodes affects the number of data packets to the destinations.

The studies of these models incorporate substantial inputs for creating and incorporating QoS over wireless VANET nodes. The performance of SADVA in comparison with other protocols like, REDEM, QARS and AODV are evaluated using similar QoS metrics. The proposed scheme is evaluated with nodes varying from five to fifty incrementally, and 5 different scenarios are created. The ultimate goal of a routing protocol is to efficiently deliver the network data to the destinations; therefore, two metrics, Packet Delivery Fraction (PDF) and Normalized Routing Load (NRL), are used to evaluate the protocols. In order to get the accurate experimental results, each scenario is run for different iterations to calculate the average value of adaptive QoS evaluation metrics.

The procedure is summarized as below:

1. Protocols such as AODV, DYMO, FSR are used in a benign environment, in which there is no effective QoS model established to collect baseline values for the metrics. The differences amongst baseline values of the protocols are also discussed to get better understanding of each protocol's operation.
2. Each protocol is evaluated using different simulated environments and simulators. The measurements gathered are compared with the respective baseline values; in order to assess the impact of a specific service based QoS on protocol operation. Based on results collected, it can be concluded that, in the entire simulated scenario based environments, normal routing protocols (DSR, FSR and AODV) cannot guarantee the delivery of required QoS to the destinations, compared to the benign environments. In other words, the data is redirected or discarded due to the collisions or unequipped with MAC (IEEE 802.11p) on the routing protocol. When the number of VANET nodes increases, the number of received data packets decreases. Hence to ensure the "on demand" serviced based QoS for proposed routing protocol SADVA, specific design perspectives have been incorporated to detect changes in routing packets. However, under high complex scenarios such as route failure or node failure, SADVA protocol requires a "tolerance" mechanism, to maintain normal operation.

FUTURE WORK

As future work, investigation in more detail to the other parts of our VANET QoS architecture, the QoS monitor and the fault handler can be carried out. Our initial hypothesis is that by using the VANET as a sensor network, QoS measurements can be made and aggregated to form a knowledge-base for the QoS monitor.

The future perspectives for VANET routing protocols can include following:

1. **Improving Node Reliability:** A major challenge in protocol design in VANET is to improve node reliability, which is of prime importance.
2. **Considering Driver Behaviour:** Driver behaviour should be considered for designing of delay bounded routing protocols since carry and forward is the main approach to deliver packets.

3. **Considering Routing Methods for Comfort Applications:** Routing methods for comfort applications should also be considered. Comfort messages are usually tolerant of delay, as network bandwidth is generally reserved for emergency messages.

4. **Tuning QoS Parameter Optimisation and Selection Methods for High Mobility:** QoS Parameter optimization and selection methods tuned to services such as highway scenario would be beneficial for fast moving VANET nodes, since protocol should be highly independent of the specific network's topology and mobility.

REFERENCES

Alisson, B., Ana, L., Antonio, S., Filipe, M., & Joaquim, C. (2011). An Adaptive Mechanism for Access Control in VANETs.*ICN 2011: The Tenth International Conference on Networks*.

Arunkumar, T., & Gnanamurthy, R. K. (2006). Delivering Quality of Services for Media Streaming in Group Communication over Mobile Ad Hoc Networks. *ICIIS 2006 International Conference on Industrial and Information Systems*.

Arunkumar, T., & Ramesh, B. (2010). A simulated modeling approach towards providing adaptive QoS for vehicular safety services over VANET. *International Journal of Research and Reviews in Computer Science*, *1*(4), 110–116.

Arunkumar, T., & Sivanandam, S. N. (2007). Location Identification and Vehicular Tracking for Vehicular Ad Hoc Wireless Networks. *IEEE Explorer*, *1*(2), 112–116.

ASTM. E2213-03. (2003). Standard specification for telecommunications and information exchange between roadside vehicle systems – 5 GHz band Dedicated Short Range Communications (DSRC) Medium Access Control (MAC) and Physical Layer (PHY) Specifications.*Proceedings of ASTM*.

Bachir, A., & Benslimane, A. (2003). A multicast protocol in ad hoc networks: Inter-vehicles geocast. *Proceedings of the 57th IEEE Vehicular Technology Conference*. doi:10.1109/VETECS.2003.1208832

Baghavan, D., & Bharghavan, V. (1997). Routing in Ad Hoc Networks Using Minimum Connected Dominating Sets.*IEEE International Conference on Communications (ICC'97)*.

Bai, K. H., Sadekar, V., Holland, G., & Elbatt, T. (2006). Towards characterizing and classifying communication-based automotive applications from a wireless networking perspective. *Proceedings of the IEEE Workshop on Automotive Networking and Applications* (AutoNet).

Bai, & Krishnan, H. (2006). Reliability analysis of DSRC wireless communication for vehicle safety applications. *Proceedings of the IEEE Intelligent Transportation Systems Conference* (ITSC '06).

Baswant, K., & Kung, H. T. (2000). GPSR: Greedy Perimeter Stateless Routing for Wireless Networks. *Proceedings of the ACM/IEEE International Conference on Mobile Computing and Networking (MobiCom)*.

Bechler, L., Storz, O., & Franz, W. (2003). Efficient Discovery of Internet Gateways in Future Vehicular Communication Systems. *The 57th IEEE Semiannual Vehicular Technology Conference*. doi:10.1109/VETECS.2003.1207769

Bernsen, & Manivannan, D. (2008). Unicast routing protocols for vehicular ad hoc networks: A critical comparison and classification. *Pervasive and Mobile Computing*, 1-18.

Bianchi, G. (2000). Performance analysis of the IEEE 802.11 distributed coordination function. *IEEE Journal on Selected Areas in Communications*, *18*(3), 535–547. doi:10.1109/49.840210

Bilstrup, K., Uhlemann, E., & Strom, E. G. (2008). Medium Access Control in Vehicular Networks Based on the Upcoming IEEE 802.11p Standard. *Proceedings of World Congress on ITS*.

Blazevic, B., Le Boudec, J.-Y., & Giordano, S. (2005). A Location-Based Routing Method for Mobile Ad Hoc Networks. *IEEE Transactions on Mobile Computing*, *4*(1), 97–110. doi:10.1109/TMC.2005.16

Blum, J., Eskandarian, A., & Hoffmann, L. (2003). Mobility Management in IVC Networks.*IEEE Intelligent Vehicles Symposium*. doi:10.1109/IVS.2003.1212900

Blum, J., Eskandarian, A., & Hoffmann, L. (2004). Challenges of Intervehicle AdHoc Networks. *IEEE Transactions on Intelligent Transportation Systems*, *5*(4), 347–351. doi:10.1109/TITS.2004.838218

Borgonovo, Capone, A., Cesana, M., & Fratta, L. (2004). ADHOC MAC: a new MAC architecture for ad hoc networks providing efficient and reliable point-to-point and broadcast service. *ACM Wireless Network, 10*(4), 359–366.

Briesemeister, S. L., & Hommel, G. (2000). Disseminating messages among highly mobile hosts based on inter-vehicle communication. *IEEE Intelligent Vehicles Symposium*. doi:10.1109/IVS.2000.898398

Briesemeister, & Hommel, G. (2000). Overcoming fragmentation in mobile ad hoc net-works. *Journal of Communications and Networks, 2*, 182-187.

Broch, J., Maltz, D. A., Johnson, D. B., Hu, Y. C., & Jetcheva, J. (1998). A Performance Comparison of Multi-Hop Wireless Ad Hoc Network Routing Protocols. *Proceedings of ACM/IEEE MOBICOM*. doi:10.1145/288235.288256

C2C-CC. (2011). Retrieved November 15, 2011 from http://www.car-to-car.org/

Cartalk. (2011). Retrieved February 3, 2011 from http://www.cartalk.com

Chakeres, & Perkins, C. (2006). *Dynamic MANET On-Demand (DYMO) Routing*. Internet-Draft, draft-ietf-manet-dymo-06.txt.

Chen, Y., Lin, Y., & Lee, S. (2010). A Mobicast Routing Protocol for Vehicular Ad Hoc Networks. *ACM/Springer Mobile Networks and Applications (MONET), 15*(1), 20-35.

DSRC. (2012). *Dedicated Short Range Communications*. Retrieved September 18, 2012 from http://www.leearmstrong.com/dsrc/dsrchomeset.htm

FCC DSRC (Dedicated Short Range Communications). (2011). Retrieved December 03, 2011 from http://wireless.fcc.gov/services/its/dsrc/

Fukuhara, T., Warabino, T., Ohseki, T., Saito, K., Sugiyama, K., Nishida, T., & Eguchi, K. (2005). Broadcast methods for inter-vehicle communications system.*Proceedings of IEEE Wireless Communications and Networking Conference*.

Gaokhan, K. (2006). *GPS Based Wireless Communication Protocols for Vehicular AD-HOC Networks*. (Unpublished doctoral dissertation). The Ohio State University, Columbus, OH.

Gerla. (2002). *Fisheye State Routing Protocol (FSR)*. IETF Internet Draft, draft-ietf-manet-fsr-03.txt.

Ghassan, A., Mosa, A., & Sidi, M. (2007). Current Trends in Vehicular Ad Hoc Networks.*IEEE Global Information Infrastructure Symposium*.

Ghosh, & Celmins. (2008). A survey of recent advances in fuzzy logic in telecommunications networks and new challenges. *IEEE Transactions on Fuzzy Systems, 6*(3), 443–447.

Hakim, B., Anelise, M., Khaldoun, A., & Guy, P. (2003). QoS for Adhoc networking based on multiple Metrics: *Bandwidth and Delay. International Workshop on Mobile and Wireless Communications Networks*.

Harshvardhan, & Joshi, P. (2006). *Distributed Robust Geocast: A Multicast Protocol for Inter-Vehicle Communication*. (Unpublished Masters Dissertation). North Carolina State University.

Hartenstein, H., Bochow, B., & Ebner, A. (2001). Position-Aware Ad Hoc Wireless Networks for Inter-Vehicle Communications: The FleetNet Project.*MobiHoc'01: Proceedings of 2nd ACM International Symposium on Mobile Ad Hoc Networking & Computing*. New York: ACM Press. doi:10.1145/501416.501454

Ho, A., Ho, H., & Kien, A. (2008). Routing Protocols for Inter-Vehicular Networks: A Comparative Study in High-Mobility and Large Obstacles Environments. *Computer Communications Journal*, 2767-2780.

Jing, T., Lu, H., & Kurt, R. (2003). *Spatially Aware Packet Routing for Mobile Ad Hoc Inter-Vehicle Radio Networks*. Shangai, China: IEEE ITSC. doi:10.1109/ITSC.2003.1252743

Johnson, B., Maltz, D.A. & Hu, Y.C. (2004). *The Dynamic Source Routing Protocol for Mobile Ad Hoc Networks (DSR)*. draft-ietf-manet-dsr-10.txt.

Karp, B., & Kung, H. T. (2000). GPSR: Greedy Perimeter Stateless Routing for Wireless Networks. *MobiCom, 2000*, 29–36.

Ko, Y. B., & Vaidhya, N. H. (1998). Location-Aided Routing (LAR) in Mobile Ad Hoc Network. *Proceedings of ACM/IEEE MOBICOM'98*.

Kosch, T., Alder, C. J., Eichler, S., Schroth, C., & Strassberger, M. (2006). The scalability problem of vehicular ad hoc networks and how to solve it. *IEEE Wireless Communications, 13*(5), 22–28. doi:10.1109/WC-M.2006.250354

Li, & Yu, W. (2007). Routing in Vehicular Ad Hoc Networks: A Survey. *IEEE Vehicular Technology Magazine, 2*(2), 12-22.

Lochert, C., Hartenstein, H., Tian, J., Fubler, H., Hermann, D., & Mauve, M. (2003). A Routing Strategy for Vehicular Ad Hoc Networks in City Environments.*Proceedings of IEEE Intelligent Vehicles Symposium (IV2003)*. doi:10.1109/IVS.2003.1212901

Lochert, C., Mauve, M., Fubler, H., & Hartenstein, H. (2005). Geographic Routing in City Scenarios. *ACM SIGMOBILE Mobile Computing and Communications Review (MC2R), 9*(1), 69–72.

Luis, U., Almeida, D., Tripp-Barba, C., & Igartua, M. A. (2015). Heuristics Methods in Geographical Routing Protocols for VANETs. PE-WASUN '15, Cancun, Mexico.

Luis, U., Tripp-Barba, C., & Angel, R. (2015). Reducing Duplicate Packets in Unicast VANET Communications. PE-WASUN '15, Cancun, Mexico.

Maen, M., William, R., & William, J. (2005). Assignment of dynamic transmission range based on estimation of vehicle density.*Proceedings of the 2nd ACM International Workshop on Vehicular ad hoc Networks.*ACM.

Maihfer. (2004). A survey on geocast routing protocols. *IEEE Communications Surveys and Tutorials, 6*(2), 32-42.

Mauve, M., Fubler, H., Hartenstein, H., Kasemann, M., Vollmer, D. (2003). Location based Routing for Vehicular Ad Hoc Networks. *ACM SIGMOBILE Mobile Computing and Communications Review (MC2R), 7*(1), 47–49.

Meier, H. B., Cunningham, R., & Cahill, V. (2005). Towards realtime middleware for applications of vehicular ad hoc networks. *Proceedings of IFIP International Conference on Distributed applications and interoperable systems* (DAIS '05). doi:10.1007/11498094_1

NS2. (2010). *Network Simulator – 2*. Retrieved April 16, 2010 from http://www.isi.edu/nsnam/ns/

Namboodiri, & Gao, L. (2007). Prediction based routing for vehicular ad hoc networks. *IEEE Transactions on Vehicular Technology, 56*(4), 1-29.

Nathan, B., & Jinhua, G. (2006). Increasing broadcast reliability in vehicular ad hoc networks.*Proceedings of the 3rd international workshop on Vehicular ad hoc networks.*

Naumov, & Gross, T. (2007). Connectivity-aware routing (car) in vehicular ad hoc networks. *Proceedings of the IEEE International Conference on Computer Communications.*

Niranjan, P., & Atulya, M. (2006). Mobility Models for Vehicular Ad Hoc Network Simulations. *ACM SE, 06*, 746–747.

NoW. (2010).*Network on wheels.*Retrieved September 15, 2010 from http://www.network-on-wheels.de/

Perkins, C., Royer, E.B., & Das, S. (2003). *Ad Hoc On-Demand Distance Vector (AODV) Routing*. RFC 3561 Network Working Group.

Perkins, C., & Royer, E. M. (2004). *Quality of Service for Adhoc on-demand distance vector routing*. Retrieved September 18, 2010 from http://people.nokia.net/charliep/txt/aodvid/qos.txt

Prabhakar, R. S., Arunkumar, T., & Sivanandam, S. N. (2011a). A QoS Adaptive Routing Scheme (QARS) for highly dynamic Vehicular Networks with support to service and priority. *World Applied Sciences Journal, 13*(5), 1259–1268.

Prabhakar, R. S., Sivanandam, S. N., & Arunkumar, T. (2011b). Simulation study on service based adaptive QoS framework for Vehicular AdHoc Network – REDEM. *International Journal of Research and Reviews in Information Technology, 1*(3), 58–62.

Prabhakar, R. S., Sivanandam, S. N., & Arunkumar, T. (2011c). A Modeling Approach to achieve optimal Quality of Service for streaming media services over MANET. *International Journal of Research and Reviews in Information Technology*, *1*(1), 14–19.

Pravin, G., Girish, K., & Pradip, G. (2010). Mobile ad hoc networking: imperatives and challenges. *IJCA*, 153-158.

Qing, X., Raja, S., Tony, M., & Jeff, K. (2004). Vehicle-to-vehicle safety messaging in DSRC. *Proceedings of 1st ACM International Workshop on Vehicular Ad Hoc Networks* (VANET '04).

Sheng, H. M., Wang, J. C., Huang, H. H., & Yen, D. C. (2006). Fuzzy measure on vehicle routing problem of hospital materials (FBAC). *Expert Systems with Applications*, *30*(2), 367–377. doi:10.1016/j.eswa.2005.07.028

Task 3, Final Report. (2005). *Identify intelligent vehicle safety applications enabled by DSRC*. Retrieved July 12, 2008 from http://www.nrd.nhtsa.dot.gov/pdf/nrd-12/1665CAMP3web/index.html

Tonguz. (2007). Broadcasting in VANET. *Proceedings of IEEE Mobile Networking for Vehicular*.

Torrent, M., Festag, A., Strassberger, M., Lubke, A., Bochow, B., Schnaufer, S., & Kunisch, J. et al. (2008). NoW – Network on Wheels: Project Objectives, Technology and Achievements.*5th International Workshop on Intelligent Transportation (WIT)*.

Wu, H., Palekar, M., Fujimoto, R., Lee, J., Ko, J., Guensler, R., & Hunter, M. (2005). Vehicular networks in urban transportation systems.*Proceedings of the 2005 Conference on Digital Government Research*.

Yihai, Z., & Aaron, G. (2005). Quality of Service for Adhoc On-demand Distance Vector Routing. *Proceedings of IEEE WIMOB*, *05*(3), 192–196.

Yousefi, M., & Fathy, M. (2006). Vehicular ad hoc networks (VANETs) challenges and perspectives.*Proceedings of 6th IEEE International Conference on ITS Telecommunications*. doi:10.1109/ITST.2006.289012

Yu, W., & Fan, L. (2012). Vehicular Ad Hoc Networks. *Guide to Wireless Ad Hoc Networks, Computer communication and Networks*. doi: .10.1007/978-1-84800-328-6_20

Zadeh, L. A. (1965). Fuzzy sets. *Information and Control*, *8*(3), 338–353. doi:10.1016/S0019-9958(65)90241-X

KEY TERMS AND DEFINITIONS

Adaptive Routing: Also called as Dynamic Routing. Adaptive routing is the capability of the system to dynamically alter and adapt a path that is characterized by the destination due to the change in conditions that may rise in the established route.

Load Balancing: Number of requests served by a node. The number of requests received by a node cannot be predicted at any point of time. Load balancing is very crucial in Vehicular Ad hoc Networks.

Mobility Model: The mobility pattern of a mobile node. Location, velocity and acceleration change over time is taken into consideration while designing mobility models.

Packet Delivery Ratio: Proportion of number of packets delivered against the number of packets sent.

Quality of Service: The United Nations Consultative Committee for International Telephony and Telegraphy (CCITT) Recommendation E.800, has defined QoS as: "The collective effect of service performance which determines the degree of satisfaction of a user of the service". This is a widely accepted definition. But in the VANET context, QoS refers to different notions at different networking layers. At the physical layer, QoS refers to the data rate and packet loss on the wireless links, which is a function of the channel quality. At the MAC layer, QoS is related to the fraction of time, a node is able to successfully access and transmit a packet. At the routing layer, end-to-end QoS metrics would depend on the metrics at each hop of a multi-hop route. The routing layer must try to compute and maintain routes that satisfy the QoS requirement for the lifetime of a connection.

Route Establishment Time: The life time of a route is generally very short in VANETs due to the high mobility speed of the nodes. Shorter the time for establishing a high life time route makes the communication effective between the VANET nodes.

Session Establishment Time: A session refers to an interaction between two or more nodes in exchange of information. Session establishment time can also be viewed as establishing life time of route to communicate information between nodes in VANET. Refer to the definition of Route Establishment Time.

Chapter 8

Fuzzy Dynamic Programming Problem for Single Additive Constraint with Additively Separable Return by Means of Trapezoidal Membership Functions

Palanivel Kaliyaperumal
School of Advanced Sciences, VIT University, India

ABSTRACT

Dynamic Programming Problem (DPP) is a multivariable optimization problem is decomposed into a series of stages, optimization being done at each stage with respect to one variable only. DP stands a suitable quantitative study procedure that can be used to explain various optimization problems. It deals through reasonably large as well as complex problems; in addition, it involves creating a sequence of interconnected decisions. The technique offers an efficient procedure for defining optimal arrangement of decisions. Throughout this chapter, solving procedure completely deliberate about as Fuzzy Dynamic Programming Problem for single additive constraint with additively separable return with the support of trapezoidal membership functions and its arithmetic operations. Solving procedure has been applied from the approach of Fuzzy Dynamic Programming Problem (FDPP). The fuzzified version of the problem has been stated with the support of a numerical example for both linear and nonlinear fuzzy optimal solutions and it is associated to showing that the proposed procedure offers an efficient tool for handling the dynamic programming problem instead of classical procedures. As a final point the optimal solution with in the form of fuzzy numbers and justified its solution with in the description of trapezoidal fuzzy membership functions.

DOI: 10.4018/978-1-5225-1008-6.ch008

1. INTRODUCTION

Dynamic programming is different from linear programming on two counts. First, there does not be present a typical mathematical formulation of DPP. Accordingly, there is no procedure, similar to the simplex algorithm, that they can be preset to solve all the problems. DP is, proposed, a procedure that permits us to separate difficult into a sequence of sub problems, which are then evaluated by stages. This offers a generalized methodology to problem solving. Moreover, while linear programming problem is a method which gives single stage, that is one time – period solutions, DP has the power to determine the optimal solutions over, say, a one year time horizon by breaking the problem into twelve smaller one month time horizon problems and to solve each of these optimally. Thus, it uses a multistage approach to problem solving. There is a wide variety of problems which can be handled using dynamic programming. Dynamic programming problem was first developed in 1950, through the effect of Richard Bellman and his principle of optimality states that an optimality policy has the property that whatever the initial stages and decisions are, the remaining decisions must constitute an optimal policy with regards to the state resulting from the first decision. This implies that a wrong decision taken at one stage does not prevent from taking optimum decisions for the remaining stages. In dynamic programming problem, there do not exist any mathematical formulation. Particular equations must be developed to adequate for each distinct situation (Lushu, Li & Lai, 2001). DPP can be classifying different types such as single additive constraint with additively separable return or multiplicatively separable return and single multiplicative constraint with additively separable return. The problem of fuzzy dynamic problem has been dealt with many researcher (Baldwin & Pilsworth, 1982; Esogbue, 1983; Schweickardt & Miranda, 2007) in recent days with crisp state transformation function in terms of fuzzified dynamic programming (Zimmerman, 1991). Bellman and Zadeh (1970) suggested for the first time a fuzzy approach to the dynamic programming problem. Here also make an effort to fuzzifiy a dynamic programming problem and solve it to find a fuzzy optimal solution for single additive constraint with additively separable return with the support of trapezoidal membership functions and its arithmetic operations (Dinagar & Palanivel, 2009, 2016). The fuzzified version of the problem has been stated with the support of a numerical example for both linear and nonlinear fuzzy optimal solutions.

2. PRELIMINARIES

L.A. Zadeh advanced the fuzzy theory in 1965. The theory proposes a mathematical technique for dealing with imprecise concepts and issues that have several potential solutions. The conception of fuzzy mathematical programming on a general level was initially projected by (Tanaka et al., 1974) within the frame work of fuzzy decision of Bellmann and Zadeh (1970). Now it tends to present some necessary definitions are:

2.1 Basic Definitions

Definition

A real fuzzy number A is a fuzzy subset of the real number R with membership function μ_A satisfying the subsequent conditions.

1. μ_A is continuous from R to the closed interval [0, 1].
2. μ_A is strictly increasing and continuous on $[a_1, a_2]$.
3. μ_A is strictly decreasing and continuous on $[a_3, a_4]$ wherever $a_1, a_2, a_3 \ \& \ a_4$ are real numbers, and the fuzzy number denoted by $A = [a_1, a_2, a_3, a_4]$ is named as a trapezoidal fuzzy number.

Definition

A trapezoidal fuzzy number A can be expressed as $A = [a_1, a_2, a_3, a_4]$ and its membership function is outlined as:

$$\mu_A(x) = \begin{cases} \dfrac{x - a_1}{a_2 - a_1}, a_1 \leq x \leq a_2 \\ 1 \qquad , a_2 \leq x \leq a_3 \\ \dfrac{x - a_4}{a_3 - a_4}, a_3 \leq x \leq a_4 \end{cases}$$

The Pictorial representation of trapezoidal membership function μ_A is given in Figure 1.

Arithmetic Operations

Let $A = [a_1, a_2, a_3, a_4]$ and $B = [b_1, b_2, b_3, b_4]$ two trapezoidal fuzzy numbers then the arithmetic operations on A and B as follows:

Figure 1. Trapezoidal membership function $\mu_A(x)$

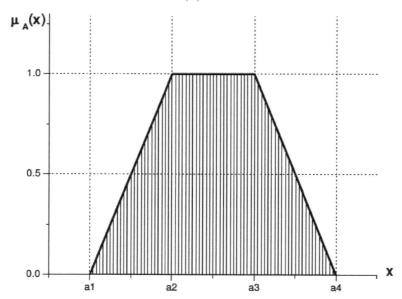

Addition:

$$A + B = \left(a_1 + b_1, a_2 + b_2, a_3 + b_3, a_4 + b_4 \right)$$

Subtraction:

$$A - B = \left(a_1 - b_4, a_2 - b_3, a_3 - b_2, a_4 - b_1 \right)$$

Multiplication:

$(i) \; if \; R(B) > 0$

$$A \bullet B = \left(\frac{a_1}{4}(b_1 + b_2 + b_3 + b_4), \frac{a_2}{4}(b_1 + b_2 + b_3 + b_4), \frac{a_3}{4}(b_1 + b_2 + b_3 + b_4), \frac{a_4}{4}(b_1 + b_2 + b_3 + b_4) \right)$$

$(ii) \; if \; \; R(B) < 0$

$$A \bullet B = \left(\frac{a_4}{4}(b_1 + b_2 + b_3 + b_4), \frac{a_3}{4}(b_1 + b_2 + b_3 + b_4), \frac{a_2}{4}(b_1 + b_2 + b_3 + b_4), \frac{a_1}{4}(b_1 + b_2 + b_3 + b_4) \right)$$

Since R(B) is the ranking index of the fuzzy number $B = \left[b_1, b_2, b_3, b_4 \right]$ and the ranking index of a mentioned fuzzy number is defined as follows:

$$R\left(B \right) = \frac{\left[b_1 + b_2 + b_3 + b_4 \right]}{4}$$

2.2 Recursive Relationship for Dynamic Programming Problem

Formulation of a dynamic programming problem requires the creation of recursive relationship. It needs us to define an optimal return function for every stage and state. The recursive relationship establishes the relationship between the optimal return functions at successive stages. In dynamic programming, it is possible to write a recursive relationship for every problem. Once it is written, it becomes much easier to solve the given problem. In other words, the recursive relationship expresses the notion that optimal return at any given stage, for any given state, is given as the value of the best alternative, when each alternative includes the total of the immediate return and the optimal return obtained in the previous stage. Accordingly, a recursive relationship identifies the optimal policy for stage n, given optimal policy for stage n+1 is available.

In general terms, the recursive relationship may be formulated and stated as follows.

Let:

j = Number of stages;

n = Index for current stage (i.e., $j = 1,2,3,\ldots n$);

$n + 1$ = Previous stage;

S_n = State of the system in the current stage for which the recursive relationship holds

S_{n+1} = State in the previous stage;

$f_n(S_n)$ = Total return for each alternative, starting from state S_n in stage n, to the end of the process;

$F_n(S_n)$ = Optimal total return (i.e., the best $f_n(S_n)$) from state S_n in stage n;

$F_{n+1}(S_{n+1})$ = Optimal total return obtained in the previous stage;

$C_n(S_n, x_n)$ = Immediate return in stage n when decision x_n is made for a specific value S_n of the stat variable;

x_n = Decision among alternatives made at stage n in the state under consideration.

The recursive relationship (for minimization) for state S_n at stage n may be stated as under:

$$F_n\left(S_n\right) = \min\left(x_n\right)\left\{C_n\left(S_n, x_n\right) + F_{n+1}\left(S_{n+1}\right)\right\}$$

Here $C_n(S_n, x_n)$ is attained by the values of c_{ij} when i is the current state and j is the current destination. For problems in which the variable of return is sought to be maximized, the recursive relationship would be:

$$F_n\left(S_n\right) = \max\left(x_n\right)\left\{C_n\left(S_n, x_n\right) + F_{n+1}\left(S_{n+1}\right)\right\}$$

3. THE FUZZIFIED FORM OF DYNAMIC PROGRAMMING PROBLEM

3.1 Single Additive Constraint with Additively Separable Return

Fuzzy dynamic programming problem is defined as the problem of determining a fuzzy vector

$$\left(\left[u_1^{(1)}, u_1^{(2)}, u_1^{(3)}, u_1^{(4)}\right], \left[u_2^{(1)}, u_2^{(2)}, u_2^{(3)}, u_2^{(4)}\right], \ldots, \left[u_n^{(1)}, u_n^{(2)}, u_n^{(3)}, u_n^{(4)}\right]\right)$$

where $\left[u_j^{(1)}, u_j^{(2)}, u_j^{(3)}, u_j^{(4)}\right]$ is a trapezoidal fuzzy number and $j = 1, 2, 3, \ldots, n$ which optimizes the fuzzy objective function $\left[z^{(1)}, z^{(2)}, z^{(3)}, z^{(4)}\right]$ which is a separable fuzzy additive function of 'n' fuzzy variables $\left[u_j^{(1)}, u_j^{(2)}, u_j^{(3)}, u_j^{(4)}\right]$ and it is gives as

$$\left[z^{(1)}, z^{(2)}, z^{(3)}, z^{(4)}\right] = \sum_{j=1}^{n}\left(\left[f_j\left(u_j\right)^{(1)}, f_j\left(u_j\right)^{(2)}, f_j\left(u_j\right)^{(3)}, f_j\left(u_j\right)^{(4)}\right]\right)$$

Subject to the fuzzy constraints,

$$\sum_{j=1}^{n} \left(\left[a_j \left(u_j \right)^{(1)}, a_j \left(u_j \right)^{(2)}, a_j \left(u_j \right)^{(3)}, a_j \left(u_j \right)^{(4)} \right] \right) \geq \left[b^{(1)}, b^{(2)}, b^{(3)}, b^{(4)} \right]$$

where

$$\left[a_j^{(1)}, a_j^{(2)}, a_j^{(3)}, a_j^{(4)} \right] \geq 0, \ \left[b^{(1)}, b^{(2)}, b^{(3)}, b^{(4)} \right] \geq 0$$

$$\left[u_j^{(1)}, u_j^{(2)}, u_j^{(3)}, u_j^{(4)} \right] \geq 0, j = 1, 2, 3, \ldots, n$$

The problem as an n stage problem, the suffix j is indicating the stage. Now to decide the value of which minimizes the fuzzy objective function under the given fuzzy additive constraints. Here each $\left[u_j^{(1)}, u_j^{(2)}, u_j^{(3)}, u_j^{(4)} \right]$ will be called fuzzy decision variables; a fuzzy return function

$$\left[f_j \left(u_j \right)^{(1)}, f_j \left(u_j \right)^{(2)}, f_j \left(u_j \right)^{(3)}, f_j \left(u_j \right)^{(4)} \right]$$

is associated which is the return at the jth stage. It is a case of single additive constraint with additively separable return.

3.2 Computational Procedure

Let us introduce the fuzzy state variables

$$\left(\left[x_1^{(1)}, x_1^{(2)}, x_1^{(3)}, x_1^{(4)} \right], \left[x_2^{(1)}, x_2^{(2)}, x_2^{(3)}, x_2^{(4)} \right], \ldots, \left[x_n^{(1)}, x_n^{(2)}, x_n^{(3)}, x_n^{(4)} \right] \right)$$

defined as follows:

$$\left[x_n^{(1)}, x_n^{(2)}, x_n^{(3)}, x_n^{(4)} \right] = \sum_{j=1}^{n} \left(\left[a_j \left(u_j \right)^{(1)}, a_j \left(u_j \right)^{(2)}, a_j \left(u_j \right)^{(3)}, a_j \left(u_j \right)^{(4)} \right] \right) \geq \left[b^{(1)}, b^{(2)}, b^{(3)}, b^{(4)} \right]$$

$$\left[x_{n-1}^{(1)}, x_{n-1}^{(2)}, x_{n-1}^{(3)}, x_{n-1}^{(4)} \right] = \sum_{j=1}^{n-1} \left[a_j \left(u_j \right)^{(1)}, a_j \left(u_j \right)^{(2)}, a_j \left(u_j \right)^{(3)}, a_j \left(u_j \right)^{(4)} \right]$$

$$= \left[x_n^{(1)}, x_n^{(2)}, x_n^{(3)}, x_n^{(4)} \right] - \left[a_n \left(u_n \right)^{(1)}, a_n \left(u_n \right)^{(2)}, a_n \left(u_n \right)^{(3)}, a_n \left(u_n \right)^{(4)} \right]$$

$$\left[x_{n-2}^{(1)}, x_{n-2}^{(2)}, x_{n-2}^{(3)}, x_{n-2}^{(4)}\right] = \sum_{j=1}^{n-2}\left[\left[a_j\left(u_j\right)^{(1)}, a_j\left(u_j\right)^{(2)}, a_j\left(u_j\right)^{(3)}, a_j\left(u_j\right)^{(4)}\right]\right]$$

$$= \left[x_{n-1}^{(1)}, x_{n-1}^{(2)}, x_{n-1}^{(3)}, x_{n-1}^{(4)}\right] - \left[a_{n-1}\left(u_{n-1}\right)^{(1)}, a_{n-1}\left(u_{n-1}\right)^{(2)}, a_{n-1}\left(u_{n-1}\right)^{(3)}, a_{n-1}\left(u_{n-1}\right)^{(4)}\right]$$

$$\left[x_1^{(1)}, x_1^{(2)}, x_1^{(3)}, x_1^{(4)}\right] = \left[a_1\left(u_1\right)^{(1)}, a_1\left(u_1\right)^{(2)}, a_1\left(u_1\right)^{(3)}, a_1\left(u_1\right)^{(4)}\right]$$

$$= \left[x_2^{(1)}, x_2^{(2)}, x_2^{(3)}, x_2^{(4)}\right] - \left[a_2\left(u_2\right)^{(1)}, a_2\left(u_2\right)^{(2)}, a_2\left(u_2\right)^{(3)}, a_2\left(u_2\right)^{(4)}\right]$$

Here each of the fuzzy state variables is a function of the next state and fuzzy decision variables.

$$\left[x_{j-1}^{(1)}, x_{j-1}^{(2)}, x_{j-1}^{(3)}, x_{j-1}^{(4)}\right] = \left[t_j\left(x_j, u_j\right)^{(1)}, t_j\left(x_j, u_j\right)^{(2)}, t\left(x_j, u_j\right)^{(3)}, t_j\left(x_j, u_j\right)^{(4)}\right] \forall j = 1, 2, 3, \ldots, n$$

Since $\left[x_n^{(1)}, x_n^{(2)}, x_n^{(3)}, x_n^{(4)}\right]$ is a function of all the fuzzy decision variables, so the minimum fuzzified value of the objective function is denoted by

$$\left[F_n\left(x_n\right)^{(1)}, F_n\left(x_n\right)^{(2)}, F_n\left(x_n\right)^{(3)}, F_n\left(x_n\right)^{(4)}\right]$$
$$= \underset{\left[u_n^{(1)}, u_n^{(2)}, u_n^{(3)}, u_n^{(4)}\right]}{min}\left[\sum_{j=1}^{n}\left[\left[f_j\left(u_j\right)^{(1)}, f_j\left(u_j\right)^{(2)}, f_j\left(u_j\right)^{(3)}, f_j\left(u_j\right)^{(4)}\right]\right]\right]$$

where, $\left[u_j^{(1)}, u_j^{(2)}, u_j^{(3)}, u_j^{(4)}\right] \geq 0$ and

$$\left[x_n^{(1)}, x_n^{(2)}, x_n^{(3)}, x_n^{(4)}\right] \geq \left[b^{(1)}, b^{(2)}, b^{(3)}, b^{(4)}\right].$$

A particular fuzzy value of $\left[u_n^{(1)}, u_n^{(2)}, u_n^{(3)}, u_n^{(4)}\right]$ and its fuzzy membership function is given by

$$\mu_A(x) = \begin{cases} \dfrac{x - u_n^{(1)}}{u_n^{(2)} - u_n^{(1)}} & for\ u_n^{(1)} \leq x \leq u_n^{(2)} \\ 1 & for\ u_n^{(2)} \leq x \leq u_n^{(3)} \\ \dfrac{x - u_n^{(4)}}{u_n^{(3)} - u_n^{(4)}} & for\ u_n^{(3)} \leq x \leq u_n^{(4)} \\ 0 & Otherwise \end{cases}$$

$\mu_A\left(x\right)$ is selected and assuming it to be fixed, we minimize $\left[z^{(1)}, z^{(2)}, z^{(3)}, z^{(4)}\right]$ over the remaining fuzzy variables. This minimum is given by

$$\left[f_n\left(u_n\right)^{(1)}, f_n\left(u_n\right)^{(2)}, f_n\left(u_n\right)^{(3)}, f_n\left(u_n\right)^{(4)}\right](+)$$

$$\min_{\left[u_n^{(1)}, u_n^{(2)}, u_n^{(3)}, u_n^{(4)}\right]}\left[\sum_{j=1}^{n-1}\left[\left[f_j\left(u_j\right)^{(1)}, f_j\left(u_j\right)^{(2)}, f_j\left(u_j\right)^{(3)}, f_j\left(u_j\right)^{(4)}\right]\right]\right]$$

$$=\left[f_n\left(u_n\right)^{(1)}, f_n\left(u_n\right)^{(2)}, f_n\left(u_n\right)^{(3)}, f_n\left(u_n\right)^{(4)}\right]$$

$$(+)\left[F_{n-1}\left(x_{n-1}\right)^{(1)}, F_{n-1}\left(x_{n-1}\right)^{(2)}, F_{n-1}\left(x_{n-1}\right)^{(3)}, F_{n-1}\left(x_{n-1}\right)^{(4)}\right]$$

The corresponding fuzzy membership function is given by

$$\mu_A(x) = \begin{cases} \dfrac{x - f_n\left(u_n\right)^{(1)} - F_{n-1}\left(x_{n-1}\right)^{(1)}}{f_n\left(u_n\right)^{(2)} - f_n\left(u_n\right)^{(1)} + F_{n-1}\left(x_{n-1}\right)^{(2)} - F_{n-1}\left(x_{n-1}\right)^{(1)}} \\ \quad for\, f_n\left(u_n\right)^{(1)} + F_{n-1}\left(x_{n-1}\right)^{(1)} \leq x \leq f_n\left(u_n\right)^{(2)} + F_{n-1}\left(x_{n-1}\right)^{(2)} \\ 1 \quad for\ f_n\left(u_n\right)^{(2)} + F_{n-1}\left(x_{n-1}\right)^{(2)} \leq x \leq f_n\left(u_n\right)^{(3)} + F_{n-1}\left(x_{n-1}\right)^{(3)} \\ \dfrac{x - f_n\left(u_n\right)^{(4)} - F_{n-1}\left(x_{n-1}\right)^{(4)}}{f_n\left(u_n\right)^{(3)} - f_n\left(u_n\right)^{(4)} + F_{n-1}\left(x_{n-1}\right)^{(3)} - F_{n-1}\left(x_{n-1}\right)^{(4)}} \\ \quad for\ f_n\left(u_n\right)^{(3)} + F_{n-1}\left(x_{n-1}\right)^{(3)} \leq x \leq f_n\left(u_n\right)^{(4)} + F_{n-1}\left(x_{n-1}\right)^{(4)} \\ 0,\, otherwise \end{cases}$$

The fuzzified values of

$$\left[u_j^{(1)}, u_j^{(2)}, u_j^{(3)}, u_j^{(4)}\right], \forall\, j = 1, 2, 3, \dots, n-1$$

which would make

$$\sum_{j=1}^{n-1}\left[f_j\left(u_j\right)^{(1)}, f_j\left(u_j\right)^{(2)}, f_j\left(u_j\right)^{(3)}, f_j\left(u_j\right)^{(4)}\right]$$

minimum for a fixed value $\left[u_n^{(1)}, u_n^{(2)}, u_n^{(3)}, u_n^{(4)}\right]$. Thus it depends on $\left[x_{n-1}^{(1)}, x_{n-1}^{(2)}, x_{n-1}^{(3)}, x_{n-1}^{(4)}\right]$ which is a function of

$\left[x_n^{(1)}, x_n^{(2)}, x_n^{(3)}, x_n^{(4)} \right]$ and $\left[u_n^{(1)}, u_n^{(2)}, u_n^{(3)}, u_n^{(4)} \right]$.

The minimum $\left[z^{(1)}, z^{(2)}, z^{(3)}, z^{(4)} \right]$ over all $\left[u_n^{(1)}, u_n^{(2)}, u_n^{(3)}, u_n^{(4)} \right]$ for any $\left[x_n^{(1)}, x_n^{(2)}, x_n^{(3)}, x_n^{(4)} \right]$ is

$$
\begin{aligned}
&\left[F_n \left(x_n \right)^{(1)}, F_n \left(x_n \right)^{(2)}, F_n \left(x_n \right)^{(3)}, F_n \left(x_n \right)^{(4)} \right] \\
&= \min_{\left[u_n^{(1)}, u_n^{(2)}, u_n^{(3)}, u_n^{(4)} \right]} \left[\begin{array}{l} \left[f_n \left(u_n \right)^{(1)}, f_n \left(u_n \right)^{(2)}, f_n \left(u_n \right)^{(3)}, f_n \left(u_n \right)^{(4)} \right] \\ (+) \left[F_{n-1} \left(x_{n-1} \right)^{(1)}, F_{n-1} \left(x_{n-1} \right)^{(2)}, F_{n-1} \left(x_{n-1} \right)^{(3)}, F_{n-1} \left(x_{n-1} \right)^{(4)} \right] \end{array} \right].
\end{aligned}
$$

The recursion formula which defines a typical Dynamic programming problem in fuzzified

$$
\begin{aligned}
&\left[F_j \left(x_j \right)^{(1)}, F_j \left(x_j \right)^{(2)}, F_j \left(x_j \right)^{(3)}, F_j \left(x_j \right)^{(4)} \right] \\
&= \min_{\left[u_j^{(1)}, u_j^{(2)}, u_j^{(3)}, u_j^{(4)} \right]} \left[\begin{array}{l} \left[f_j \left(u_j \right)^{(1)}, f_j \left(u_j \right)^{(2)}, f_j \left(u_j \right)^{(3)}, f_j \left(u_j \right)^{(4)} \right] \\ (+) \left[F_{j-1} \left(x_{j-1} \right)^{(1)}, F_{j-1} \left(x_{j-1} \right)^{(2)}, F_{j-1} \left(x_{j-1} \right)^{(3)}, F_{j-1} \left(x_{j-1} \right)^{(4)} \right] \end{array} \right]
\end{aligned}
$$

$where\ j = 1,2,3,...,n\ and\ \left[F_1 \left(x_1 \right)^{(1)}, F_1 \left(x_1 \right)^{(2)}, F_1 \left(x_1 \right)^{(3)}, F_1 \left(x_1 \right)^{(4)} \right]$

$$
= \left[f_1 \left(u_1 \right)^{(1)}, f_1 \left(u_1 \right)^{(2)}, f_1 \left(u_1 \right)^{(3)}, f_1 \left(u_1 \right)^{(4)} \right]
$$

Thus we start, $\left[F_1 \left(x_1 \right)^{(1)}, F_1 \left(x_1 \right)^{(2)}, F_1 \left(x_1 \right)^{(3)}, F_1 \left(x_1 \right)^{(4)} \right]$ and recursively on optimizing each time over single fuzzified variables we get

$$
\begin{aligned}
&\left[F_1 \left(x_1 \right)^{(1)}, F_1 \left(x_1 \right)^{(2)}, F_1 \left(x_1 \right)^{(3)}, F_1 \left(x_1 \right)^{(4)} \right], \left[F_2 \left(x_2 \right)^{(1)}, F_2 \left(x_2 \right)^{(2)}, F_2 \left(x_2 \right)^{(3)}, F_2 \left(x_2 \right)^{(4)} \right],..., \\
&\left[F_n \left(x_n \right)^{(1)}, F_n \left(x_n \right)^{(2)}, F_n \left(x_n \right)^{(3)}, F_n \left(x_n \right)^{(4)} \right]
\end{aligned}
$$

Hence, minimizing, $\left[F_n \left(x_n \right)^{(1)}, F_n \left(x_n \right)^{(2)}, F_n \left(x_n \right)^{(3)}, F_n \left(x_n \right)^{(4)} \right]$ over the fuzzified value $\left[x_n^{(1)}, x_n^{(2)}, x_n^{(3)}, x_n^{(4)} \right]$. We get the required fuzzy optimal solution to the problem.

4. NUMERICAL EXAMPLE

Now we take into consideration for the fuzzified version of the problem has been listed with the support of a computational procedure for both linear and nonlinear fuzzy optimal solutions. First we discuss about the problem with non-integer optimal solutions. Furthermore, we extend the discussion into the problem with integer optimal solutions as another example in section 4.2.

4.1 Single Additive Constraint with Additively Separable Return for Non-Integer Values

The objective function in fuzzified form which is to be minimized, is

$$\left[u_1^{(1)}, u_1^{(2)}, u_1^{(3)}, u_1^{(4)}\right]^2 (+) \left[u_2^{(1)}, u_2^{(2)}, u_2^{(3)}, u_2^{(4)}\right]^2 (+) \left[u_3^{(1)}, u_3^{(2)}, u_3^{(3)}, u_3^{(4)}\right]^2$$

Subject to the constraints,

$$\left[u_1^{(1)}, u_1^{(2)}, u_1^{(3)}, u_1^{(4)}\right] (+) \left[u_2^{(1)}, u_2^{(2)}, u_2^{(3)}, u_2^{(4)}\right] (+) \left[u_3^{(1)}, u_3^{(2)}, u_3^{(3)}, u_3^{(4)}\right] \geq \left[4, 8, 12, 16\right]$$

$$\left[u_1^{(1)}, u_1^{(2)}, u_1^{(3)}, u_1^{(4)}\right], \left[u_2^{(1)}, u_2^{(2)}, u_2^{(3)}, u_2^{(4)}\right], \left[u_3^{(1)}, u_3^{(2)}, u_3^{(3)}, u_3^{(4)}\right] \geq 0$$

Here the fuzzy decision variables are

$$\left[u_1^{(1)}, u_1^{(2)}, u_1^{(3)}, u_1^{(4)}\right], \left[u_2^{(1)}, u_2^{(2)}, u_2^{(3)}, u_2^{(4)}\right], \left[u_3^{(1)}, u_3^{(2)}, u_3^{(3)}, u_3^{(4)}\right]$$

and the fuzzy state variables are

$$\left[x_3^{(1)}, x_3^{(2)}, x_3^{(3)}, x_3^{(4)}\right] = \left[u_1^{(1)}, u_1^{(2)}, u_1^{(3)}, u_1^{(4)}\right] (+) \left[u_2^{(1)}, u_2^{(2)}, u_2^{(3)}, u_2^{(4)}\right] (+) \left[u_3^{(1)}, u_3^{(2)}, u_3^{(3)}, u_3^{(4)}\right] \geq \left[4, 8, 12, 16\right]$$

$$\left[x_2^{(1)}, x_2^{(2)}, x_2^{(3)}, x_2^{(4)}\right] = \left[u_1^{(1)}, u_1^{(2)}, u_1^{(3)}, u_1^{(4)}\right] (+) \left[u_2^{(1)}, u_2^{(2)}, u_2^{(3)}, u_2^{(4)}\right]$$
$$= \left[x_3^{(1)}, x_3^{(2)}, x_3^{(3)}, x_3^{(4)}\right] (-) \left[u_3^{(1)}, u_3^{(2)}, u_3^{(3)}, u_3^{(4)}\right]$$

$$\left[x_1^{(1)}, x_1^{(2)}, x_1^{(3)}, x_1^{(4)}\right] = \left[u_1^{(1)}, u_1^{(2)}, u_1^{(3)}, u_1^{(4)}\right] = \left[x_2^{(1)}, x_2^{(2)}, x_2^{(3)}, x_2^{(4)}\right] (-) \left[u_2^{(1)}, u_2^{(2)}, u_2^{(3)}, u_2^{(4)}\right]$$

Now we may denote the minimum fuzzified value of the fuzzy objective function $\left[z^{(1)}, z^{(2)}, z^{(3)}, z^{(4)}\right]$ for any feasible fuzzified value of $\left[x_3^{(1)}, x_3^{(2)}, x_3^{(3)}, x_3^{(4)}\right]$ as

$$
\left[F_3\left(x_3\right)^{(1)}, F_3\left(x_3\right)^{(2)}, F_3\left(x_3\right)^{(3)}, F_3\left(x_3\right)^{(4)} \right]
$$
$$
= \min_{\left[u_3^{(1)}, u_3^{(2)}, u_3^{(3)}, u_3^{(4)} \right]} \left[u_3^{(1)}, u_3^{(2)}, u_3^{(3)}, u_3^{(4)} \right]^2 (+) \left[F_2\left(x_2\right)^{(1)}, F_2\left(x_2\right)^{(2)}, F_2\left(x_2\right)^{(3)}, F_2\left(x_2\right)^{(4)} \right]
$$

(1)

$$
\left[F_2\left(x_2\right)^{(1)}, F_2\left(x_2\right)^{(2)}, F_2\left(x_2\right)^{(3)}, F_2\left(x_2\right)^{(4)} \right]
$$
$$
= \min_{\left[u_2^{(1)}, u_2^{(2)}, u_2^{(3)}, u_2^{(4)} \right]} \left[\left[u_2^{(1)}, u_2^{(2)}, u_2^{(3)}, u_2^{(4)} \right]^2 (+) \left[F_1\left(x_1\right)^{(1)}, F_1\left(x_1\right)^{(2)}, F_1\left(x_1\right)^{(3)}, F_1\left(x_1\right)^{(4)} \right] \right]
$$

(2)

and

$$
\left[F_1\left(x_1\right)^{(1)}, F_1\left(x_1\right)^{(2)}, F_1\left(x_1\right)^{(3)}, F_1\left(x_1\right)^{(4)} \right] = \left[u_1^{(1)}, u_1^{(2)}, u_1^{(3)}, u_1^{(4)} \right]^2
$$

(3)

Now the term,

$$
\left[F_1\left(x_1\right)^{(1)}, F_1\left(x_1\right)^{(2)}, F_1\left(x_1\right)^{(3)}, F_1\left(x_1\right)^{(4)} \right] = \left[u_1^{(1)}, u_1^{(2)}, u_1^{(3)}, u_1^{(4)} \right]^2
$$

$$
\left[F_1\left(x_1\right)^{(1)}, F_1\left(x_1\right)^{(2)}, F_1\left(x_1\right)^{(3)}, F_1\left(x_1\right)^{(4)} \right] = \left(\left[x_2^{(1)}, x_2^{(2)}, x_2^{(3)}, x_2^{(4)} \right] (-) \left[u_2^{(1)}, u_2^{(2)}, u_2^{(3)}, u_2^{(4)} \right] \right)^2
$$
$$
= \left(\left[x_2^{(1)}, x_2^{(2)}, x_2^{(3)}, x_2^{(4)} \right] (-) \left[u_2^{(1)}, u_2^{(2)}, u_2^{(3)}, u_2^{(4)} \right] \right) * \left(\left[x_2^{(1)}, x_2^{(2)}, x_2^{(3)}, x_2^{(4)} \right] (-) \left[u_2^{(1)}, u_2^{(2)}, u_2^{(3)}, u_2^{(4)} \right] \right)
$$

We now compute the corresponding fuzzy membership function:

$$
\mu_{A-B}(x) = \begin{cases} \dfrac{x - \left(x_2^{(1)} - u_2^{(1)} \right)}{\left(x_2^{(2)} - u_2^{(2)} \right) - \left(x_2^{(1)} - u_2^{(1)} \right)} & for\left(x_2^{(1)} - u_2^{(1)} \right) \le x \le \left(x_2^{(2)} - u_2^{(2)} \right) \\ 1 & for\left(x_2^{(2)} - u_2^{(2)} \right) \le x \le \left(x_2^{(3)} - u_2^{(3)} \right) \\ \dfrac{x - \left(x_2^{(4)} - u_2^{(4)} \right)}{\left(x_2^{(3)} - u_2^{(3)} \right) - \left(x_2^{(4)} - u_2^{(4)} \right)} & for\left(x_2^{(3)} - u_2^{(3)} \right) \le x \le \left(x_2^{(4)} - u_2^{(4)} \right) \\ 0 & Otherwise \end{cases}
$$

Here $A = \left[x_2^{(1)}, x_2^{(2)}, x_2^{(3)}, x_2^{(4)} \right]$ and $B = \left[u_2^{(1)}, u_2^{(2)}, u_2^{(3)}, u_2^{(4)} \right]$.

Therefore, the membership function of $\left[F_1\left(x_1\right)^{(1)}, F_1\left(x_1\right)^{(2)}, F_1\left(x_1\right)^{(3)}, F_1\left(x_1\right)^{(4)} \right]$ is given by $(i.e., (A-B)*(A-B))$

$$\mu_{(A-B)^2}(x) = \begin{cases} \dfrac{x - u_2^{(1)}}{u_2^{(2)} - u_2^{(1)}} & for \left(x_2^{(1)}\right)^2 - 2x_2^{(1)}u_2^{(1)} + \left(u_2^{(1)}\right)^2 \le x \le \left(x_2^{(2)}\right)^2 - 2x_2^{(2)}u_2^{(2)} + \left(u_2^{(2)}\right)^2 \\[4mm] 1 & for \left(x_2^{(2)}\right)^2 - 2x_2^{(2)}u_2^{(2)} + \left(u_2^{(2)}\right)^2 \le x \le \left(x_2^{(3)}\right)^2 - 2x_2^{(3)}u_2^{(3)} + \left(u_2^{(3)}\right)^2 \\[4mm] \dfrac{x - u_2^{(4)}}{u_2^{(3)} - u_2^{(4)}} & for \left(x_2^{(3)}\right)^2 - 2x_2^{(3)}u_2^{(3)} + \left(u_2^{(3)}\right)^2 \le x \le \left(x_2^{(4)}\right)^2 - 2x_2^{(4)}u_2^{(4)} + \left(u_2^{(4)}\right)^2 \\[4mm] 0 & Otherwise \end{cases}$$

From (2) we have,

$$\left[F_2\left(x_2\right)^{(1)}, F_2\left(x_2\right)^{(2)}, F_2\left(x_2\right)^{(3)}, F_2\left(x_2\right)^{(4)} \right] = \underset{\left[u_2^{(1)}, u_2^{(2)}, u_2^{(3)}, u_2^{(4)}\right]}{\min} \left[\left[u_2^{(1)}, u_2^{(2)}, u_2^{(3)}, u_2^{(4)}\right]^2 (+) \right.$$
$$\left. \left(\left[x_2^{(1)}, x_2^{(2)}, x_2^{(3)}, x_2^{(4)}\right] (-) \left[u_2^{(1)}, u_2^{(2)}, u_2^{(3)}, u_2^{(4)}\right] \right)^2 \right]$$

$$(4)$$

Now compute the minimum of above expression using calculus. Let the fuzzy decision variables be denoted as $\left[u_2^{(1)}, u_2^{(2)}, u_2^{(3)}, u_2^{(4)} \right]$. Taking derivatives of each of three terms with respect to $\left[u_2^{(1)}, u_2^{(2)}, u_2^{(3)}, u_2^{(4)} \right]$ respectively and equating to zero. We get the minimum when $\left[u_2^{(1)}, u_2^{(2)}, u_2^{(3)}, u_2^{(4)} \right]$ takes the value $\left[\dfrac{x_2^{(1)}}{2}, \dfrac{x_2^{(2)}}{2}, \dfrac{x_2^{(3)}}{2}, \dfrac{x_2^{(4)}}{2} \right]$ with its fuzzy membership function is given by

$$\mu(x) = \begin{cases} \dfrac{2x - x_2^{(1)}}{x_2^{(2)} - x_2^{(1)}} & for \dfrac{x_2^{(1)}}{2} \le x \le \dfrac{x_2^{(2)}}{2} \\[4mm] 1 & for \dfrac{x_2^{(2)}}{2} \le x \le \dfrac{x_2^{(3)}}{2} \\[4mm] \dfrac{2x - x_2^{(4)}}{x_2^{(3)} - x_2^{(4)}} & for \dfrac{x_2^{(3)}}{2} \le x \le \dfrac{x_2^{(4)}}{2} \\[4mm] 0 & Otherwise \end{cases}$$

Now substituting these values respectively in expression (4) we get

$$\left[F_2\left(x_2\right)^{(1)}, F_2\left(x_2\right)^{(2)}, F_2\left(x_2\right)^{(3)}, F_2\left(x_2\right)^{(4)}\right] = \left[\frac{\left(x_2^{(1)}\right)^2}{2}, \frac{\left(x_2^{(2)}\right)^2}{2}, \frac{\left(x_2^{(3)}\right)^2}{2}, \frac{\left(x_2^{(4)}\right)^2}{2}\right]$$

with its fuzzy membership function is

$$\mu(x) = \begin{cases} \dfrac{2x - \left(x_2^{(1)}\right)^2}{\left(x_2^{(2)}\right)^2 - \left(x_2^{(1)}\right)^2} & for\ \dfrac{\left(x_2^{(1)}\right)^2}{2} \le x \le \dfrac{\left(x_2^{(2)}\right)^2}{2} \\[3ex] 1 & for\ \dfrac{\left(x_2^{(2)}\right)^2}{2} \le x \le \dfrac{\left(x_2^{(3)}\right)^2}{2} \\[3ex] \dfrac{2x - \left(x_2^{(4)}\right)^2}{\left(x_2^{(3)}\right)^2 - \left(x_2^{(4)}\right)^2} & for\ \dfrac{\left(x_2^{(3)}\right)^2}{2} \le x \le \dfrac{\left(x_2^{(4)}\right)^2}{2} \\[3ex] 0 & Otherwise \end{cases}$$

Similarly from (1) we have,

$$\left[F_3\left(x_3\right)^{(1)}, F_3\left(x_3\right)^{(2)}, F_3\left(x_3\right)^{(3)}, F_3\left(x_3\right)^{(4)}\right]$$

$$= \min_{\left[u_3^{(1)}, u_3^{(2)}, u_3^{(3)}, u_3^{(4)}\right]} \left[u_3^{(1)}, u_3^{(2)}, u_3^{(3)}, u_3^{(4)}\right]^2 (+) \left[\frac{\left(x_2^{(1)}\right)^2}{2}, \frac{\left(x_2^{(2)}\right)^2}{2}, \frac{\left(x_2^{(3)}\right)^2}{2}, \frac{\left(x_2^{(4)}\right)^2}{2}\right] \tag{5}$$

$$= \min_{\left[u_3^{(1)}, u_3^{(2)}, u_3^{(3)}, u_3^{(4)}\right]} \left[\left(u_3^{(1)}\right)^2 + \frac{\left(x_2^{(1)}\right)^2}{2}, \left(u_3^{(2)}\right)^2 + \frac{\left(x_2^{(2)}\right)^2}{2}, \left(u_3^{(3)}\right)^2 + \frac{\left(x_2^{(3)}\right)^2}{2}, \left(u_3^{(4)}\right)^2 + \frac{\left(x_2^{(4)}\right)^2}{2}\right]$$

Now we compute the minimum of the above expression using calculus. Let the fuzzy decision variables be denoted as $\left[u_3^{(1)}, u_3^{(2)}, u_3^{(3)}, u_3^{(4)}\right]$. Taking derivatives of each of three terms with respect to $\left[u_3^{(1)}, u_3^{(2)}, u_3^{(3)}, u_3^{(4)}\right]$ respectively and equating to zero. We get the minimum when $\left[u_3^{(1)}, u_3^{(2)}, u_3^{(3)}, u_3^{(4)}\right]$ takes the value

$$\left[\frac{\left(x_3^{(1)}\right)^2}{3}, \frac{\left(x_3^{(2)}\right)^2}{3}, \frac{\left(x_3^{(3)}\right)^2}{3}, \frac{\left(x_3^{(4)}\right)^2}{3}\right]$$

with its fuzzy membership function is given by

$$
\mu(x) = \begin{cases}
\dfrac{3x - x_3^{(1)}}{x_3^{(2)} - x_3^{(1)}} \; for \; \dfrac{x_3^{(1)}}{3} \le x \le \dfrac{x_3^{(2)}}{3} \\[4mm]
1 \qquad\qquad for \; \dfrac{x_3^{(2)}}{3} \le x \le \dfrac{x_3^{(3)}}{3} \\[4mm]
\dfrac{3x - x_3^{(4)}}{x_3^{(3)} - x_3^{(4)}} \; for \; \dfrac{x_3^{(3)}}{3} \le x \le \dfrac{x_3^{(4)}}{3} \\[4mm]
0, \; otherwise
\end{cases}
$$

Now substituting these values respectively in expression (5) we get

$$
\left[F_3\left(x_3\right)^{(1)}, F_3\left(x_3\right)^{(2)}, F_3\left(x_3\right)^{(3)}, F_3\left(x_3\right)^{(4)} \right] = \left[\dfrac{\left(x_3^{(1)}\right)^2}{3}, \dfrac{\left(x_3^{(2)}\right)^2}{3}, \dfrac{\left(x_3^{(3)}\right)^2}{3}, \dfrac{\left(x_3^{(4)}\right)^2}{3} \right]
$$

with its fuzzy membership function is

$$
\mu(x) = \begin{cases}
\dfrac{3x - \left(x_3^{(1)}\right)^2}{\left(x_3^{(2)}\right)^2 - \left(x_3^{(1)}\right)^2} \; for \; \dfrac{\left(x_3^{(1)}\right)^2}{3} \le x \le \dfrac{\left(x_3^{(2)}\right)^2}{3} \\[5mm]
1 \qquad\qquad for \; \dfrac{\left(x_3^{(2)}\right)^2}{3} \le x \le \dfrac{\left(x_3^{(3)}\right)^2}{3} \\[5mm]
\dfrac{3x - \left(x_3^{(4)}\right)^2}{\left(x_3^{(3)}\right)^2 - \left(x_3^{(4)}\right)^2} \; for \; \dfrac{\left(x_3^{(3)}\right)^2}{3} \le x \le \dfrac{\left(x_3^{(4)}\right)^2}{3} \\[5mm]
0, \; otherwise
\end{cases}
$$

Obviously, $\left[F_3\left(x_3\right)^{(1)}, F_3\left(x_3\right)^{(2)}, F_3\left(x_3\right)^{(3)}, F_3\left(x_3\right)^{(4)} \right]$ is least or minimum for $\left[x_3^{(1)}, x_3^{(2)}, x_3^{(3)}, x_3^{(4)} \right] = \left[4, 8, 12, 16 \right]$.

Therefore, $\left[u_3^{(1)}, u_3^{(2)}, u_3^{(3)}, u_3^{(4)} \right] = \left[\dfrac{4}{3}, \dfrac{8}{3}, \dfrac{12}{3}, \dfrac{16}{3} \right]$

Similarly, $\left[u_2^{(1)}, u_2^{(2)}, u_2^{(3)}, u_2^{(4)} \right] = \left[\dfrac{4}{3}, \dfrac{8}{3}, \dfrac{12}{3}, \dfrac{16}{3} \right]$ and $\left[u_1^{(1)}, u_1^{(2)}, u_1^{(3)}, u_1^{(4)} \right] = \left[\dfrac{4}{3}, \dfrac{8}{3}, \dfrac{12}{3}, \dfrac{16}{3} \right]$.

Hence the minimum value of

$$\left[F_3\left(x_3\right)^{(1)}, F_3\left(x_3\right)^{(2)}, F_3\left(x_3\right)^{(3)}, F_3\left(x_3\right)^{(4)}\right] = \left[\frac{40}{3}, \frac{80}{3}, \frac{120}{3}, \frac{160}{3}\right]$$

is the required fuzzy optimal solution.

4.2 Single Additive Constraint with Additively Separable Return for Integer Values

A student has to take examination in three courses, A, B and C. He has three days available for study. He feels it would be best to devote a whole day to the study of the same course, so that he may study a course for one day, two days, or three days or not at all. His estimates of the grades he may get by study are as follows in terms of fuzziness in Table 1 and how should he study so that he maximizes the sum of his grades.

Let

$$\left[u_1^{(1)}, u_1^{(2)}, u_1^{(3)}, u_1^{(4)}\right], \left[u_2^{(1)}, u_2^{(2)}, u_2^{(3)}, u_2^{(4)}\right], \left[u_3^{(1)}, u_3^{(2)}, u_3^{(3)}, u_3^{(4)}\right]$$

be the number of days he should study the courses A, B, C respectively, and let

$$\left[f_j\left(u_j\right)^{(1)}, f_j\left(u_j\right)^{(2)}, f_j\left(u_j\right)^{(3)}, f_j\left(u_j\right)^{(4)}\right], \text{ for } j = 1, 2, \text{ and} \qquad 3$$

be the grades earned by such a study.

The objective function in fuzzified form, which is to be maximized, is

$$\sum_{j=1}^3 \left[f_j\left(u_j\right)^{(1)}, f_j\left(u_j\right)^{(2)}, f_j\left(u_j\right)^{(3)}, f_j\left(u_j\right)^{(4)}\right]$$

Table 1. Grade estimations

Study Days	Courses		
	A	B	C
0	[-2, -1, 1, 2]	[-2, 0, 2, 4]	[-2, -1, 1, 2]
1	[-2, 0, 2, 4]	[-2, 0, 2, 4]	[-2, 0, 2, 4]
2	[-2, 0, 2, 4]	[1, 2, 4, 5]	[1, 2, 4, 5]
3	[1, 2, 4, 5]	[2, 3, 5, 6]	[1, 2, 4, 5]

Subject to the constraints,

$$\left[u_1^{(1)}, u_1^{(2)}, u_1^{(3)}, u_1^{(4)}\right](+)\left[u_2^{(1)}, u_2^{(2)}, u_2^{(3)}, u_2^{(4)}\right](+)\left[u_3^{(1)}, u_3^{(2)}, u_3^{(3)}, u_3^{(4)}\right] \leq \left[1,2,4,5\right]$$

$$\left[u_1^{(1)}, u_1^{(2)}, u_1^{(3)}, u_1^{(4)}\right], \left[u_2^{(1)}, u_2^{(2)}, u_2^{(3)}, u_2^{(4)}\right], \left[u_3^{(1)}, u_3^{(2)}, u_3^{(3)}, u_3^{(4)}\right] \geq 0 \; and \; integers \; .$$

Here $\left[u_j^{(1)}, u_j^{(2)}, u_j^{(3)}, u_j^{(4)}\right]$ are the fuzzy decision variables and $\left[f_j\left(u_j\right)^{(1)}, f_j\left(u_j\right)^{(2)}, f_j\left(u_j\right)^{(3)}, f_j\left(u_j\right)^{(4)}\right]$ are the fuzzy return functions for $j = 1$, 2, and 3.

Now we can apply the mentioned computational procedure and finally we get the fuzzy optimal solution and its fuzzy optimal policy. Therefore, the maximum value of

$$\left[F_3\left(x_3\right)^{(1)}, F_3\left(x_3\right)^{(2)}, F_3\left(x_3\right)^{(3)}, F_3\left(x_3\right)^{(4)}\right] = \left[-3, 2, 8, 13\right]$$

is the required fuzzy optimal solution and the policy as

$$\left[u_3^{(1)}, u_3^{(2)}, u_3^{(3)}, u_3^{(4)}\right] = \left[0,1,3,4\right], \left[u_2^{(1)}, u_2^{(2)}, u_2^{(3)}, u_2^{(4)}\right]$$
$$= \left[-2,0,2,4\right], \left[u_1^{(1)}, u_1^{(2)}, u_1^{(3)}, u_1^{(4)}\right] = \left[-2,-1,1,2\right].$$

4.3 Computation of Optimal Solution Attained from Existing and Proposed Methods

To compare the existing and the proposed methodologies, the results of fuzzy dynamic programming problem chosen in the above numerical examples obtained by using the existing and the proposed methodologies are shown in the following table. It is obvious from the results shown in the table that irrespective of whether by existing or proposed methodologies, same results are obtained in the numerical examples can be solved by using the proposed methodology. On the basis of above result, it can be recommended that it is ideal to utilize the proposed methodology of existing methodology (Swarup, Gupta & Mohan, 2004).

Hence, the fuzzy optimal solution of Single additive constraint with additively separable return for non-integer and integer values are listed in the Table 2 numerical example comparisons 4.1 and 4.2 respectively.

5. RESULTS AND DISCUSSION

By means of the proposed methodology validates the fuzzy optimal solution is $\left[\dfrac{40}{3}, \dfrac{80}{3}, \dfrac{120}{3}, \dfrac{160}{3}\right]$, which

may be physically understood as follows (for Numerical example 4.1):

Table 2. Numerical example comparisons 4.1 and 4.2

Comparisons of Numerical Example 4.1	
Existing methodology based on the classical methodology [18]	The optimal solution is $\dfrac{100}{3}$ with all the decision variables are $\dfrac{10}{3}$.
Proposed methodology based on the fuzzy nature	The fuzzy optimal solution is $$\left[\frac{40}{3},\frac{80}{3},\frac{120}{3},\frac{160}{3}\right] = R\left[\frac{40}{3},\frac{80}{3},\frac{120}{3},\frac{160}{3}\right] = \frac{100}{3}$$ with all the decision variables are $$\left[\frac{4}{3},\frac{8}{3},\frac{12}{3},\frac{16}{3}\right] = R\left[\frac{4}{3},\frac{8}{3},\frac{12}{3},\frac{16}{3}\right] = \frac{10}{3}$$
Comparisons of Numerical Example 4.2	
Existing methodology based on the classical methodology [18]	The optimal solution is 5 with the decision policy as 2, 0 and 1.
Proposed methodology based on the fuzzy nature	The fuzzy optimal solution is $$\left[\left[-3,2,8,13\right]\right] = R\left[\left[-3,2,8,13\right]\right] = 5$$ with the decision policy as $$\left[0,1,3,4\right] = R\left[0,1,3,4\right] = 2, \left[-2,0,2,4\right] = R\left[-2,0,2,4\right] = 1$$ and $\left[-2,-1,1,2\right] = R\left[-2,-1,1,2\right] = 0$

1. The smallest amount of return is $\dfrac{40}{3}$.

2. The foremost attainable return lies between $\dfrac{80}{3}$ and $\dfrac{120}{3}$.

3. The greatest amount of return is $\dfrac{160}{3}$.

The fuzzy optimal solution is going to be continuously bigger than $\dfrac{40}{3}$ and fewer than $\dfrac{160}{3}$ and most likely the return is going to be between $\dfrac{80}{3}$ and $\dfrac{120}{3}$. The variations in return with relevancy likely shown within the Figure 2 and the fuzzy optimum solution $\mu(x)$ in terms trapezoidal fuzzy membership functions is also physically outlined as follows:

$$\mu(x) = \begin{cases} \dfrac{3x-40}{40} & for \ \dfrac{40}{3} \le x \le \dfrac{80}{3} \\ 1 & for \ \dfrac{80}{3} \le x \le \dfrac{120}{3} \\ \dfrac{160-3x}{40} & for \ \dfrac{120}{3} \le x \le \dfrac{160}{3} \\ 0 & Otherwise \end{cases}$$

Figure 2. Trapezoidal membership function of the fuzzy optimum solution $\mu(x)$ for non-integer solution

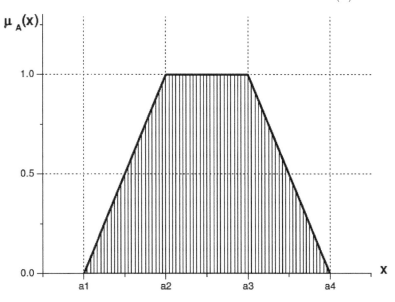

Figure 3. Trapezoidal membership function of the fuzzy optimum solution $\mu(x)$ for integer solution

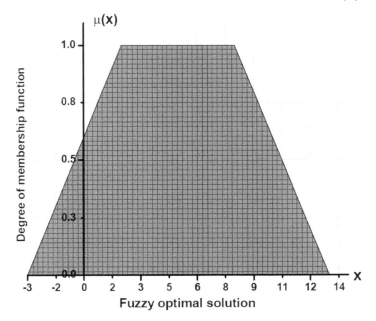

Similarly, the variations in return with relevancy likely shown within the above figure **3** for numerical example 4.2 and the fuzzy optimum solution $\mu(x)$ in terms trapezoidal fuzzy membership functions is also physically outlined as follows:

$$\mu(x) = \begin{cases} \dfrac{x+3}{5} & for -3 \le x \le 2 \\ 1 & for\ 2 \le x \le 8 \\ \dfrac{8-x}{5} & for\ 8 \le x \le 13 \\ 0 & Otherwise \end{cases}$$

6. CONCLUSION

In this chapter, solving procedure completely deliberate about a Fuzzy Dynamic Programming Problem for single additive constraint with additively separable return with the support of trapezoidal membership functions and its arithmetic operations. Solving procedure has been applied from the approach of fuzzy Dynamic Programming problem. The fuzzified version of the problem has been listed with the support of a numerical example for both linear and nonlinear fuzzy optimal solutions and it is associated to showing that the proposed procedure offers an efficient tool for handling the dynamic programming problem instead of classical procedures. As a final point the optimal solution with in the form of fuzzy numbers and justified its solution with in the description of trapezoidal fuzzy membership functions is explained with the result and discussion and also the comparison of evaluations which is the new approach for solving dynamic programming problem in fuzzy nature.

REFERENCES

Baldwin, J. F., & Pilsworth, B. W. (1982). Dynamic programming problem for fuzzy systems with fuzzy environment. *Journal of Mathematical Analysis and Applications*, *85*(1), 1–23. doi:10.1016/0022-247X(82)90022-1

Bellmann, R. & Zadeh, L. A. (1970). Decision making in fuzzy environment. *Management Science*, *17*(B), 141-164.

Dinagar, S. D., & Palanivel, K. (2009). Solving Linear Programming Problem under Fuzzy Environment, Int. *Journal of Computational Physical Sciences*, *1*(1), 53–64.

Esogbue, A. O. (1983). Some novel applications of fuzzy dynamic programming. *Proceedings of the IEEE*, 501–505.

Gagula-Palalic & Mehmet. (2012). Inventory control using Fuzzy dynamic programming. *Southeast Europe Journal of Soft Computing*, *1*(1), 37–42.

Kacprzyk, J., & Esogbue, A. O. (1996). Fuzzy dynamic programming: Main developments and applications. *Fuzzy Sets and Systems*, *81*(1), 31–45. doi:10.1016/0165-0114(95)00239-1

Lushu, L. (2001). Fuzzy Dynamic Approach to Hybrid Multiobjective multistage Decision Making Problems. *Fuzzy Sets and Systems*, *117*(1), 13–25. doi:10.1016/S0165-0114(98)00423-0

Palanivel. K (2016). Fuzzy commercial traveler problem of trapezoidal membership functions within the sort of α optimum solution using ranking technique. *Afrika Matematika, 27*(1), 263 – 277.

Schweickardt, G. A., & Miranda, V. (2007). A Fuzzy Dynamic Approach for Evaluation of Expansion Distribution cost in Uncertainty Environments. *Latin American Applied Research*, *37*, 227–234.

Swarup, K., Gupta, P., & Mohan, M. (2004). *Operations Research, S.* Chand and Sons.

Xiong, Y., & Rao, S. S. (2005). A Fuzzy Dynamic Approach for the Mixed Discrete Optimization of Mechanical Systems. *Journal of Mechanical Design*, *127*(6), 1088–1099. doi:10.1115/1.1876435

Zimmermann, H. J. (1991). *Fuzzy set theory and its applications*. Kluwer Publishers. doi:10.1007/978-94-015-7949-0

Chapter 9
The Fuzzy–AHP and Fuzzy TOPSIS Approaches to ERP Selection:
A Comparative Analysis

Rekha Gupta
Jamia Millia Islamia, India

S. Kazim Naqvi
Jamia Millia Islamia, India

ABSTRACT

The proposed chapter aims at explaining theoretical frameworks of the Fuzzy AHP and Fuzzy TOPSIS extension approaches and also summarizes the recent research around these two concepts. To help reader understand the practical usage of the two approaches, it also demonstrates their applications on the significant problem of ERP Selection. The techniques are further illustrated with the help of an organization case study located in NCR, Delhi (India). Further, a comparative analysis will be made between the two techniques by taking into account their time complexities.

INTRODUCTION

Multi criteria decision-making (MCDM) is a modeling and methodological tool for dealing with the complex engineering problems. Multi-attribute decision-making (MADM) is the most well-known branch of decision-making. It is a branch of a general class of operations research models that deal with the decision-making problems under the presence of a number of decision-making criteria. The MADM approach requires the selection to be made among decision alternatives described by their attributes. MADM problems are assumed to have predetermined, and limited number of decision alternatives. Solving a MADM problem involves sorting and ranking.

Fuzzy Analytic Hierarchy Process (Chang, 1996) solves multicriteria decision making problems by hierarchical decomposition method while accommodating uncertainties of information sets (Zadeh, 1965).

DOI: 10.4018/978-1-5225-1008-6.ch009

Humans are often uncertain in assigning the evaluation scores in crisp AHP (Saaty, 1980). Fuzzy AHP can capture this difficulty. On the other hand, Fuzzy Technique for Order Performance by Similarity to Ideal Solution (TOPSIS) (Hwang & Yoon, 1981) selects the best alternative on basis of it being nearest to fuzzy ideal solution and farthest from negative ideal solution. The positive ideal solution is a solution that maximizes the benefit criteria and minimizes the cost criteria, whereas the negative ideal solution maximizes the cost criteria and minimizes the benefit criteria. In other words, the positive ideal solution is composed of all best values attainable of criteria, whereas the negative ideal solution consists of all worst values attainable of criteria.

The ERP selection is a multi-criteria decision making problem with evaluation of multiple conflicting conditions for selecting best option from all of feasible alternatives. The problem is of significance as organization–wide ERP implementation is a high-risk undertaking involving substantial financial risk coupled with organization wide transformation. Owing to the complexity of the business environments, limitations of available resources and the diversity of ERP alternatives, ERP system selection is tedious, precarious and a time consuming activity. Since ERP systems usually impose their own constraints on companies' processes, strategies and culture, it is imperative that the ERP selection decision be conducted with great care.

The criteria used in ERP selection study are critical success factors (CSFs). These are considered vital for risk aversion in ERP implementation projects. The CSFs for ERP implementation bring a concept that helps an organization identify the critical issues that affect the process of implementation. These factors are believed to have crucial role to play in successful ERP implementation with their monitoring and control if carried out effectively.

It is however notable that, that none of the CSFs listing proposed by the researchers so far has found a straightforward application in the ERP selection process. This clearly indicates inadequacies in the research output achieved so far. Another concerning issue, which adds to this limitation, is infeasibility on part of organizations to devote attention to all the listed CSFs for selection purposes. It would be appreciable if an effective method of selecting CSFs on basis of organizational ERP selection requirements was available.

Thus the objectives of the proposed chapter are to discuss the techniques of Fuzzy AHP and Fuzzy TOPSIS extension approach to the problem of ERP selection. The chapter would give requisite theoretical details of the two approaches with a recent literature review survey. The framework for bridging the gap between the CSFs studies and the ERP selection problem is also discussed. A sample illustration of application of the above discussed techniques to a company case as an illustration is also demonstrated. The computational efficiency of the techniques is done using their time complexities. The results indicate that the proposed Fuzzy TOPSIS technique fare better than the popular technique of FAHP, when utilized for the same problem.

Hence, it is expected that the chapter will enable the reader develop good understanding of the concepts involving Fuzzy AHP and Fuzzy TOPSIS along with ERP Selection problem and appreciate the practical realization of the algorithms.

BACKGROUND

AHP (Saaty, 1986) uses the concepts of fuzzy set theory and hierarchical structure analysis for the selection of the most appropriate alternative among a set of feasible alternatives. AHP is a widely used decision making tool in various multi-criteria decision making problems. It takes the pair-wise comparisons of different alternatives with respective to various criteria and provides a decision support tool for multicriteria decision problems. In a general AHP model, the objective is in the first level, the criteria and sub criteria are in the second and third levels respectively. Finally the alternatives are found in the fourth level.

Traditional Analytic Hierarchy Process

The *Analytic Hierarchy Process* (AHP), introduced by Thomas Saaty (1980), is an effective tool for dealing with complex decision making, and helps aid the decision maker to set priorities and make the best decision. By reducing complex decisions to a series of pairwise comparisons, and then synthesizing the results, the AHP helps to capture both subjective and objective aspects of a decision. In addition, the AHP incorporates a useful technique for checking the consistency of the decision maker's evaluations, thus reducing the bias in the decision making process.

Due to its wide range application area, it has been an exciting research subject for many different field researchers. Transportation, Logistics, Urban planning, Public politics, Marketing, Finance, Education, and Economics are a part of this wide application area.

AHP Methodology

The method allows for a decision problem to be hierarchically structured into a set of sub-problems that can be analyzed easily. The methodology then compares criteria, or alternatives with respect to criteria, in a natural, pair wise mode. To do so, the AHP uses a fundamental scale of absolute numbers that have been proven in practice and validated by physical and decision problem experiments. The fundamental scale has been shown to be a scale that captures individual preferences with respect to quantitative and qualitative attributes just as well or better than other scales (Saaty, 1980b; 1994b). It then allows for consistency and cross checking between the pairs. It converts individual preferences into ratio scale weights that can be combined into a linear additive weight for each alternative. The resultant can be used to compare and rank the alternatives and hence, assist the decision maker in making a choice.

Axioms of AHP

AHP method assumes the following four axioms while doing calculations:

Axiom 1 - Reciprocal Comparison: The intensity of the preferences of the decision maker must satisfy the reciprocal condition: If A is x times more preferred than B, then B is 1/x times more preferred than A.

Axiom 2 - Homogeneity: The preferences are represented by means of a bounded scale.

Axiom 3 - Independence: In expressing preferences, criteria are assumed independent of the properties of the alternatives.

Axiom 4 - Expectations: For the purpose of making a decision, the hierarchic structure is assumed to be complete.

AHP Working

The AHP can be implemented in three simple consecutive steps:

1. Computing the vector of criteria weights.
2. Computing the matrix of option scores.
3. Ranking the options.

It is assumed that m evaluation criteria are considered, and n options are to be evaluated.

AHP Computation: Details

1. **Computing the Vector of Criteria Weights:** In order to compute the weights for the different criteria, the AHP starts creating a pairwise comparison matrix A. The matrix A is an $m \times m$ real matrix, where m is the number of evaluation criteria considered. For a matrix A, a_{jj} denotes the entry in the ith row and the jth column of A. Each entry a_{jk} of the matrix A represents the importance of the jth criterion relative to the kth criterion. If $a_{jk} > 1$, then the jth criterion is more important than the kth criterion, while $a_{jk} < 1$, then the jth criterion is less important than the kth criterion. If two criteria have the same importance, then the entry a_{jk} is 1. The entries a_{jk} and a_{kj} satisfy the following constraint:

$$a_{jk} \times a_{kj} = 1 \tag{1}$$

Obviously, $a_{jj} = 1$ for all j. The relative importance between two criteria is measured according to a numerical scale from 1 to 9, as shown in Table 1, where it is assumed that the jth criterion is equally or more important than the kth criterion. The values in the matrix A are by construction pairwise consistent. On the other hand, the ratings may in general show slight inconsistencies. However these do not cause serious difficulties for the AHP.

Table 1. Relative scores

Value of a_{jk}	Interpretation
1	j and k are equally important
3	j is slightly more important than k
5	j is more important than k
7	j is strongly more important than k
9	j is absolutely more important than k

2. **Computing the Normalized Matrix:** Once the matrix A with relative scores is built, the normalized pairwise comparison matrix A*norm* by making equal to 1 the sum of the entries on each column, i.e. each entry $\overline{a}_{jk}$ of the matrix A*norm* is computed as

$$\overline{a}_{jk} = \frac{a_{jk}}{\sum\limits_{l=1}^{m} a_{lk}} \qquad (2)$$

3. **Computing the Criteria Weight Vector:** Finally, the criteria weight vector w (that is an m-dimensional column vector) is built by averaging the entries on each row of A*norm* as

$$w = \frac{\sum\limits_{l=1}^{m} \overline{a}_{jl}}{m} \qquad (3)$$

4. **Computing the Pair Wise Comparison Matrices:** The matrix B^j comparison matrix is an $n \times n$ real matrix, where n is the number of options evaluated. Each entry $b_{ith}^{(j)}$ of the matrix B^j represents the evaluation of the ith option compared to the hth option with respect to the jth criterion. If $b_{ith}^{(j)}$ > 1, then the ith option is better than the hth option, while if $b_{ith}^{(j)}$ < 1, then the ith option is worse than the hth option. If two options are evaluated as equivalent with respect to the jth criterion, then the entry is 1. The entries and satisfy the following constraint:

$$b_{ih}^{(j)} * b_{hi}^{(j)} = 1 \qquad (4)$$

and

$$b_{ii}^{(j)} = 1 \text{ for } i \qquad (5)$$

An evaluation scale similar to the one introduced in Table 1 may be used to translate the decision maker's pairwise evaluations into numbers. B^j is built for each of the m criteria with *j=1, 2,..., m*.

5. **Computing the Vector Scores:** The AHP applies to each matrix B^j the same two-step procedure described for the pairwise comparison matrix A, i.e. it divides each entry by the sum of the entries in the same column, and then it averages the entries on each row, thus obtaining the score vectors $s^{(j)}$, *j=1,...,m*. The vector $s^{(j)}$ contains the scores of the evaluated options with respect to the jth criterion.

6. **Computing the Score Matrix S:** Finally, the score matrix S is obtained as

$$S = \left[s^{(1)}, \ldots\ldots, s^{(m)} \right] \qquad (6)$$

(the jth column of S corresponds to m)

7. **Ranking the Options:** Once the weight vector *w* and the score matrix **S** have been computed, the AHP obtains vector v of global scores by multiplying **S** and *w*, i.e.

$$v = \mathbf{S} \cdot w \tag{7}$$

The *i*th entry v_i of *v* represents the global score assigned by the AHP to the *i*th option. As the final step, the option ranking is accomplished by ordering the global scores in decreasing order.

8. **Checking the Consistency:** When many pairwise comparisons are performed, some inconsistencies may typically arise. The AHP incorporates an effective technique for checking the consistency of the evaluations made by the decision maker when building each of the pairwise comparison matrices involved in the process, namely the matrix A and the B^j matrices . The technique relies on the computation of a suitable consistency index. The Consistency Index (CI) is obtained by first computing the scalar *x* as the average of the elements of the vector whose *j*th element is the ratio of the *j*th element of the vector **A·w** to the corresponding element of the vector *w*.

$$C.I = \frac{x - m}{m - 1} \tag{8}$$

A perfectly consistent decision maker should always obtain CI=0, but small values of inconsistency may be tolerated. In particular,

$$\frac{C.I}{R.I} < 0.1 \tag{9}$$

The inconsistencies are tolerable, and a reliable result may be expected from the AHP. In (9) RI is the Random Index, i.e. the consistency index when the entries of A are completely random. The values of RI for small problems (m ≤ 10) are shown in Table 2.

Table 3 provides a brief about the advantages and disadvantages of the AHP technique.

Fuzzy Analytic Hierarchy Process (F-AHP)

Fuzzy set theory is a mathematical theory pioneered by Zadeh (1962), designed to model the vagueness or imprecision of human cognitive process. Any crisp theory can be made fuzzy by generalizing the concept of a set within that theory to the concept of a fuzzy set. The fuzzy comprehensive appraisal

Table 2. Values of the Random Index (RI) for small problems

m	2	3	4	5	6	7	8	9	10
RI	0	0.58	0.90	1.12	1.24	1.32	1.41	1.45	1.51

Table 3. The advantages and disadvantages of AHP

Advantages	Disadvantages
AHP can take into consideration the relative priorities of factors or alternatives and represents the best alternative	There is not always a solution to the li-near equations.
AHP provides a simple and very flexible model for a given problem	The computational requirement is tremendous even for a small problem.
AHP provides an easy applicable decision making methodology that assist the decision maker to precisely decide the judgments	AHP allows only triangular fuzzy numbers to be used.
Either objective or subjective considerations or either quantitative or qualitative information play an important role during the decision process.	AHP is based on both probability and possibility measures
Any level of details about the main focus can be listed or structured in this method. By this way the overview of the main focus or the problem can be represented very easily	Rank reversal fact should be considered carefully during the application. It defines the changes of the order of the judgment alternatives when a new judgment alternative is added to the problem. Validity of the rank reversal is still discussed in literature.
AHP has a very wide range of usage like; planning, effectiveness, benefit and risk analysis, choosing any kind of decision among alternatives.	AHP has a subjective nature of the modeling process is a constraint of AHP. That means that methodology cannot guarantee the decisions as definitely true
AHP relies on the judgments if experts from different backgrounds; so the main focus or the problem can be evaluated easily from different aspects	When the number of the levels in the hierarchy increase, the number of pair comparisons also increase, so that to build the AHP model takes much more time and effort.
Decision maker can analyze the elasticity of the final decision by applying the sensitivity analyzes.	
It is possible to measure the consistency of decision maker's judgments	
Computer software help decision makers to apply AHP fast and precisely	

Ahyan, 2013.

method is one extended method of the fuzzy set theory which and widely applied to society, economy, nature, science, technology, information and so on. The so-called synthesis evaluation is the multi-factor decision-making technique that carries out the comprehensive comparison and appraisal of things affected by multiple factors. Because it carries out the appraisal from many aspects, it unavoidable leads to fuzziness and subjectivity. So carrying out the synthesis appraisal with the fuzzy mathematics can make the result more objective, and obtaining a better actual effect.

Fuzzy Analytic Hierarchy Process (F-AHP) embeds the fuzzy theory to basic Analytic Hierarchy Process (AHP). Despite the convenience of AHP in handling both quantitative and qualitative criteria of multi-criteria decision making problems based on decision makers' judgments, fuzziness and vagueness existing in many decision-making problems may contribute to the imprecise judgments of decision makers in conventional AHP approaches . Since basic AHP does not include vagueness for personal judgments, it has been improved by benefiting from fuzzy logic approach. In F-AHP, the pair wise comparisons of both criteria and the alternatives are performed through the linguistic variables, which are represented by triangular numbers. One of the first fuzzy AHP applications was performed by Van Laarhoven and Pedrycz (1983). They defined the triangular membership functions for the pair wise comparisons. Afterwards, Buckley (1986) has contributed to the subject by determining the fuzzy priorities of comparison ratios having triangular membership functions. Chang (1996) also introduced a new method related with the usage of triangular numbers in pair-wise comparisons and the synthetic extent values of pair wise comparisons, respectively.

F-AHP is being used in various fields including personnel selection, Technology selection energy alternatives selection, job selection and performance evaluation systems and supplier selection problems.

Fuzzy AHP Working

1. Compute the Criterion Decision Matrix,
2. Computing the Criteria-Alternative Matrix,
3. Ranking the alternatives.

FAHP Computation: Details

1. **Computing the Criteria Decision Matrix:** Decision maker compares the criteria via the linguistic scale shown in Table 4.

The pair wise contribution matrix $\tilde{A}^k$ is obtained that is the kth decision maker's preference of ith criterion over jth criterion, via fuzzy triangular number.

$$\tilde{A}^k = \begin{bmatrix} \tilde{d}_{11}^k & \tilde{d}_{12}^k & \dots & \tilde{d}_{1n}^k \\ \tilde{d}_{21}^k & \tilde{d}_{22}^k & \dots & d_{2n}^k \\ \dots & \dots & \dots & \dots \\ \tilde{d}_{n1}^k & \tilde{d}_{n2}^k & \dots & \tilde{d}_{nn}^k \end{bmatrix} \tag{10}$$

If there is more than one decision maker, preferences of each decision maker $\tilde{d}_{ij}^k$ are averaged out to compute the aggregated opinions $\tilde{d}_{ij}$ is calculated as

$$\tilde{d}_{ij} = \frac{\sum\limits_{k=1}^{K} \tilde{d}_{ij}^k}{K} \tag{11}$$

Table 4. Saaty scale and corresponding fuzzy number

Value of a_{jk}	Interpretation	Fuzzy Triangular Scale
1	j and k are equally important	(1,1,1)
3	j is slightly more important than k	(2,3,4)
5	j is more important than k	(4,5,6)
7	j is strongly more important than k	(6,7,8)
9	j is absolutely more important than k	(9,9,9)
2,4,6,8	Intermittent Values	(1,2,3);(3,4,5);(5,6,7);(7,8,9)

2. **Averaged Opinion Matrix:** After applying the averaging, the averaged opinion matrix $\tilde{A}$ is obtained as in eq 12.

$$\tilde{A} = \begin{bmatrix} \tilde{d}_{11} & \tilde{d}_{12} & \dots & \tilde{d}_{1n} \\ \tilde{d}_{21} & \tilde{d}_{22} & \dots & \tilde{d}_{2n} \\ \dots & \dots & \dots & \dots \\ \tilde{d}_{n1} & \tilde{d}_{n2} & \dots & \tilde{d}_{nn} \end{bmatrix} \tag{12}$$

3. **Geometric Mean:** As per Buckley (1986), the geometric mean of fuzzy comparison value is obtained for each criterion.

$$\tilde{r}_i = \left(\prod_{j=1}^{n} \tilde{d}_{ij} \right)^{1/n} \ for \ i = 1, 2, ..n \tag{13}$$

4. **Criteria Fuzzy Weights:** These are computed as follows:
    a. Vector Summation of each $\tilde{r}_i$.
    b. Find the (-1) power of summation vector. Replace the triangular number by arranging in increasing order.
    c. Weights computation by calculating $\tilde{w}_i$ multiplied by each $\tilde{r}_i$ with this reverse vector.

$$\tilde{w}_i = \tilde{r}_i \otimes \left(\tilde{r}_1 \oplus \tilde{r}_2 \oplus \dots \oplus \tilde{r}_n \right)^{-1} \tag{14}$$

$$= \left(lw_i, mw_i, uw_i \right)$$

5. **Defuzzification of Weights:** Centre of Method proposed by Chang and Chou (2008) is used for de-fuzzifying the values as in eq.15.

$$M_i = \frac{lw_i + mw_i + uw_i}{3} \tag{15}$$

6. **Normalization:**

$$N_i = \frac{M_i}{\sum_{i=1}^{n} M_i} \tag{16}$$

The seven steps are repeated for alternatives as well.
The alternative with the highest score is the chosen best alternative.

Literature Review: Fuzzy AHP

Readers are provided with a glimpse of the research studies in 2015 that utilized the technique for selection purposes. The review indicates a wide arena of application areas and that the method is still a popular choice among the researchers. A brief description of each study is provided to gist the work done in the study so as to provoke readers' interest into it.

Extension of TOPSIS Algorithm: Fuzzy TOPSIS

Hwang & Yoon proposed the TOPSIS method in 1981. Chen (2000) proposed the linguistic TOPSIS method for group decision-making and the choice process. According to this technique, the best alternative would be the one that is nearest to the positive ideal solution and farthest from the negative ideal solution (Benitez et al., 2007). The positive ideal solution is a solution that maximizes the benefit criteria and minimizes the cost criteria, whereas the negative ideal solution maximizes the cost criteria and minimizes the benefit criteria (Wang & Chang, 2007; Wang & Elhag, 2006; Wang & Lee, 2007; Lin et al., 2008). In other words, the positive ideal solution is composed of all best values attainable of

Table 5. Literature review studies for F-AHP

Authors	Field Applied
Ayag(2015)	CAD Selection Software
Balin and Baracli(2015)	Renewable Energy Alternatives
Basar(2015)	EIS Selection
Choudhary & Satapathy(2015)	Plastic Recycling Process
Das et al.(2015)	Ranking of Engineering Colleges
Guneri et al.(2015)	Occupational Safety
Harspreet et.al(2015)	Cloud Service Providers
Kahraman et al.(2015)	Health Insurance Option Selection
Kant(2015)	Operating System Environment
Karami & Sayyaadi(2015)	Optimal Sizing Selection
Lee & Lee(2015)	Iaas Service Provider
Merino et al.(2015)	Robot Selection
Minatoura et al.(2015)	Dam Site Selection
Ren et al.(2015)	Technology Selection
Salimi and Rezaei(2015)	University Selection for Collaboration
Savino et al.(2015)	Prioritization of Maintenance Plan
Sakhuja et al.(2015)	Factor Selection for outsourcing Services for Hotels
Sameen et al.(2015)	Sustainable End of Life Vehicle Management
Taylon et.al(2014)	Construction Companies Selection
Vinod & Sharma(2015)	Supplier Selection
Yildiz et al.(2015)	Career Path Selection

criteria, whereas the negative ideal solution consists of all worst values attainable of criteria (Ertugrul & Karakasoglu, 2009). The detailed steps are described below:

Fuzzy TOPSIS Details

1. **Fuzzy Ratings for Criteria:** Identify the ERP vendors and the experts' ratings. Use linguistic rating variable to assess the importance of the criteria as given in Table 6.
2. **Fuzzy Ratings for Alternatives:** The decision makers use the linguistic rating variable to evaluate the rating of alternatives with respect to each criterion.
3. **Fuzzy Decision Matrix and Fuzzy Weights:** Convert the linguistic evaluation into triangular fuzzy numbers to construct the fuzzy decision matrix and determine the fuzzy weight of each CSF.

The importance is computed as

$$\tilde{x}_{ij} = \frac{1}{K}\left[\tilde{x}_{ij}^1 (+) \tilde{x}_{ij}^2 (+)...(+) \tilde{x}_{ij}^K\right] \tag{17}$$

$$\tilde{w}_j = \frac{1}{K}\left[\tilde{w}_j^1 (+) \tilde{w}_j^2 (+)...(+) w_j^K\right] \tag{18}$$

where $\tilde{x}_{ij}^K$ and $\tilde{w}_j^K$ are the ratings and the importance weight of the Kth decision maker.

4. **Normalized Decision Matrix:** Construct the normalized fuzzy decision matrix $\tilde{R} = \left[\tilde{r}_{ij}\right]_{m \times n}$ where B and C are the set of benefit criteria and cost criteria, respectively and

$$\tilde{r}_{ij} = \left(\frac{a_{ij}}{c_j^*}, \frac{b_{ij}}{c_j^*}, \frac{c_{ij}}{c_j^*}\right), j \in B; \tag{19}$$

Table 6. Linguistic scale and corresponding fuzzy numbers

Linguistic Scale	Abbreviation Used	Corresponding Fuzzy Numbers
Very High	(VH)	(0.9, 1.0, 1.0)
High	(H)	(0.7, 0.9, 1.0)
Medium High	(MH)	(0.5, 0.7, 0.9)
Medium Low	(ML)	(0.3, 0.5, 0.7)
Medium	(M)	(0.1, 0.3, 0.5)
Low	(L)	(0, 0.1, 0.3)
Very Low	(VL)	(0, 0, 0.1)

Table 7. Linguistic scale for alternative rankings

Linguistic scale	Abbreviation Used	Corresponding Fuzzy Numbers
Very Good	(VG)	(9, 10, 10)
Good	(G)	(7, 9, 10)
Medium Good	(MG)	(5, 7, 9)
Fair	(F)	(3, 5, 7)
Medium Poor	(MP)	(1, 3, 5)
Poor	(P)	(0, 1, 3)
Very Low	(VP)	(0, 0, 1)

$$\tilde{r}_{ij} = \left(\frac{a_j^-}{c_{ij}^*}, \frac{b_j^-}{b_{ij}^*}, \frac{c_j^-}{a_{ij}^*} \right), j \in C ; \tag{20}$$

$$c_j^* = \max_i c_{ij} \, if \ j \in B ;$$

$$a_j^- = \min_i a_{ij} \, if \ j \in C ;$$

The normalization process ensures that the values of fuzzy numbers lie within range [0, 1].

5. **Weighted Normalized Decision Matrix:** Construct the weighted normalized decision matrix using eq.21.

$$\tilde{V} = \left[\tilde{v}_{ij} \right]_{m \times n} , \ i = 1, 2, ..., m, j = 1, 2, ..., n \tag{21}$$

where $\tilde{v}_{ij} = \tilde{r}_{ij} \left(. \right) \tilde{w}_j$.

6. **FPIS and FNIS:** Determine the Fuzzy Positive Ideal Solution (FPIS, A^*) and Fuzzy Negative Ideal Solution (FNIS, A^-).

$$A^* = \left(\tilde{v}_1^*, \tilde{v}_2^*, ..., \tilde{v}_n^* \right) \tag{22}$$

$$A^- = \left(\tilde{v}_1^-, \tilde{v}_2^-, ..., \tilde{v}_n^- \right) \tag{23}$$

where $\tilde{v}_j^* = \left(1, 1, 1 \right)$ and $\tilde{v}_j^- = \left(0, 0, 0 \right)$, $j = 1, 2, ..., n$.

7. **Distance Calculation:** Calculate the distance of each candidate from FPIS and FNIS. The distance of each alternative from A^* and A^- can be currently calculated as

$$d_i^* = \sum_{j=1}^n d\left(\tilde{v}_{ij}, \tilde{v}_j^*\right), i = 1, 2, ..., m \tag{24}$$

$$d_i^- = \sum_{j=1}^n d\left(\tilde{v}_{ij}, \tilde{v}_j^-\right), i = 1, 2, ..., m \tag{25}$$

where $d\left(.,.\right)$ is the distance measurement between two fuzzy numbers.

8. **Closeness Coefficient:** The closeness coefficient is defined to determine the ranking order of all alternatives once their FPIS and FNIS is calculated. The closeness coefficient of each alternative is calculated as

$$CC_i = \frac{d_i^-}{d_i^* + d_i^-}, i = 1, 2, ..., m \tag{26}$$

Candidates are ranked based on their closeness coefficient.

Fuzzy TOPSIS Literature Review

We present a selected review of research work done on the Fuzzy TOPSIS. The review indicates a wide application area ranging from supplier selection, robot selection, material selection, software selection etc.

ERP Selection Problem

The ERP selection is a multicriteria decision making problem with evaluation of multiple conflicting conditions for selecting best option from all of feasible alternatives. Multi criteria decision-making (MCDM) is a modeling and methodological tool for dealing with the complex engineering problems. Multi-attribute decision-making (MADM) is the most well- known branch of decision-making. MADM belongs to a general class of operations research models wherein the decision makers solve problems under the presence of numerous attributes or criteria rather than price. The MADM approach requires the selection to be made among decision alternatives described by their attributes. Weighing and considering multiple criteria leads to informed and better decision making. MADM problems are assumed to look for efficient solutions rather than looking for optimized solutions. Common techniques used for solving MADM problem are Analytic Hierarchy Process (AHP), Analytic Network Process (ANP), Goal Programming, Data Envelopment Analysis, Grey Relational Analysis, ELECTRE, PROMTHEE, Weighted Sum Model (WSM), Weighted Product Model (WPM), VIKOR, Fuzzy AHP, Fuzzy VIKOR, etc.

The literature review studies on ERP system indicate two main areas of thrust. The first aspect is devoted to the study of critical success factors considered vital for the risk aversion in ERP implementation

Table 8. Literature review studies for fuzzy TOPSIS

Authors	Field Applied
Azizi et al.(2015)	Supplier Selection for supply Chain Environment
Bronja & Bronja(2015)	Car Exhaust System Software
Burak et al.(2015)	Software Selection for Electronic Firm
Eko & Daneshwari(2015)	Material Handling Problem.
Li & Wu(2015)	Green Supplier Selection
Guo & Zhao(2015)	Electric Vehicle Charging Station
Liao (2015)	Material Selection
Marvi & Behzadfar(2015)	Security of Neighbourhood
Mathiyalan(2015)	Blood Service Operations
Mohammadjafari & Zohary(2015)	Supplier Selection
Nouri(2015)	Technology Selection
Ozkan(2015)	Energy Storage Alternative
Vinod et al.(2015)	Robot Selection
Yildiz(2015)	Space Propulsion System
Yang et al.(2015)	Material Selection system

projects. The other emphasis of the review studies have been in the area of ERP system selection. Owing to the complex, changing business environment, limitation in financial and other available resources and the diversity of ERP alternatives, ERP system selection is tedious and a time consuming activity. Since an ERP system will also impose uniformity across business processes impacting company's strategy, organization and culture, it is imperative that the ERP selection decision be conducted with great care. The critical success factors (CSFs) serve as vital input ingredients to the ERP selection Models. It is however notable that, that none of the CSFs listing propagated by the researchers find a straightforward application in the selection procedure.

1. **The Selection Framework:** Most of the ERP research studies have been focused primarily on listing ERP CSFs and the formulation of selection techniques. We understand that ERP CSFs can play significant role in selection of appropriate ERP product. However, no work abridging the two thrust areas has yet been reported. The listed ERP CSFs hardly found application in the selection process. Moreover, the selection techniques had no standardization in terms of input CSFs listing for selection consideration. Thus, in order to address the above issue, we propose an ERP Selection Framework that leverages ERP CSFs. A schematic diagram describing the framework is illustrated in Figure 1.

The framework requires use of any ERP CSFs listing as the initial source of CSFs. However, the listing is to be evaluated for completeness so that all CSFs vital to the organization in question are available for consideration. Ideally, the most complete list of ERP CSFs should be considered as initial input to the framework. The CSFs may then be prioritized according to the organizational requirements and constraints. The prioritized list thus obtained can be categorized to separate CSFs that qualify as

Figure 1. Selection framework for bridging the CSFs studies and the ERP selection techniques

Top Management/
Organizational Support   **Client Aspect**

Process Aspect   **Vendor Aspect**

Technical Aspect   **Consultant Aspect**   **Quality Aspect**

Cost Aspect   **Project Management Aspect**

Performance Aspect   **ERP Fit Aspect**

important criteria for ERP selection process as per the practitioners' consideration and needs. The last step requires feeding of the identified CSFs into selection model algorithm to assess the respective suitability of available ERPs and ranking them accordingly. Thus, proposed selection framework bridges the identified gap between the two research paradigms of ERP CSFs studies and ERP selection techniques.

In an attempt towards achieving the completeness of the ERP CSFs, the authors have proposed a comprehensive listing of 119-critical success factors (See Appendix A). The objective was to formulate a generic listing of CSFs that could be applicable to all ERP systems irrespective of project scope, size and country settings. The list was derived by consolidating the existing CSFs listed in the literature review studies along with addition of other context based CSFs determined by organizational environment. The CSFs were validated by a field study conducted on 50-Indian enterprises in New Delhi-NCR region. The companies were selected by size to include large and medium. Data was collected through an experience survey using a questionnaire. The questionnaire solicited opinions from the ERP Experts, Consultants, Vendors and implementers for determining the impact of Critical Success Factors (CSFs) on success of ERP software system in organizations. The respondents included senior level information system executives who had at least 10-years of experience in implementing and consulting ERP projects. The responses were secured by personnel interviews and by e-mail.

2. **Selecting the CSFs for the Selection Process:** The CSFs from the comprehensive/prioritized listing (Appendix A) are picked and are categorized either as Internal (Process) or External (Product) CSFs. Internal CSFs are those that are to be monitored and controlled by the implementing organization for successful implementation of ERP. The external CSFs are essential CSFs for successful ERP product selection. The categorization may be made by the organization looking forward to implementing ERP project. A tentative classification as proposed by the authors is as shown in Figure 2.

Once the factors for ERP product selection are decided, the selection algorithm is applied. We apply the F-AHP and F-TOPSIS to the ERP selection below to illustrate their working.

Figure 2. CSFs classification across factors

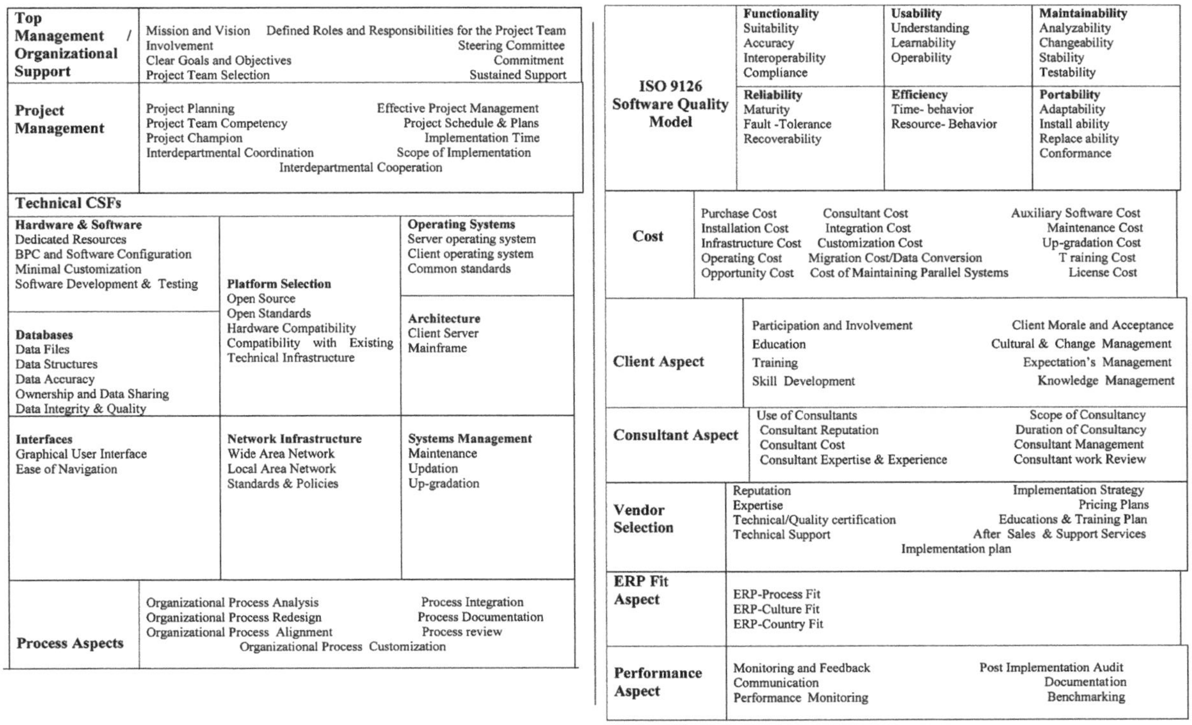

NUMERICAL ILLUSTRATION: FUZZY AHP

We present a numerical illustration for the ERP Selection problem. The criteria under consideration for selecting the ERP product are Cost(including Consultant Cost), Consultant benefits, Quality Aspects, Vendor benefits, ERP Fit, Process Aspect, Client Aspect and Technical Aspect.

The criteria rating obtained from experts as per linguistic scale given in Table 4 is enlisted in Table 9.

Table 9. FAHP expert criteria rating

Criteria	Cost	Consultant	Quality	Vendor	ERP Fit	Process Aspect	Client	Technical Aspect
Cost	(1,1,1)	(2,3,4)	(4,5,6)	(4,5,6)	(4,5,6)	(4,5,6)	(9,9,9)	(6,7,8)
Consultant	(1/4,1/3,1/2)	(1,1,1)	(1/4,1/3,1/2)	(1/4,1/3,1/2)	(1/8,1/7,1/6)	(1/6,1/5,1/4)	1/6,1/5,1/4)	(1/4,1/3,1/2)
Quality	(1/6,1/5,1/4)	(2,3,4)	(1,1,1)	(4,5,6)	(1/4,1/3,1/2)	(1/4,1/3,1/2)	(1/4,1/3,1/2)	(1/4,1/3,1/2)
Vendor	(1/6,1/5,1/4)	(2,3,4)	(2,3,4)	(1,1,1)	(1/8,1/7,1/6)	(1/8,1/7,1/6)	(1/6,1/5,1/4)	(1/6,1/5,1/4)
ERP Fit	(1/6,1/5,1/4)	(4,5,6)	(2,3,4)	(6,7,8)	(1,1,1)	(1,1,1)	(1,1,1)	(2,3,4)
Process Aspect	(1/6,1/5,1/4)	(4,5,6)	(2,3,4)	(6,7,8)	(1,1,1)	(1,1,1)	(2,3,4)	(1/4,1/3,1/2)
Client	(1/9,1/9,1/9)	(4,5,6)	(2,3,4)	(4,5,6)	(1,1,1)	(1/4,1/3,1/2)	(1,1,1)	(1/4,1/3,1/2)
Technical Aspect	(1/8,1/7,1/6)	(2,3,4)	(2,3,4)	(4,5,6)	(1/4,1/3,1/2)	(2,3,4)	(2,3,4)	(1,1,1)

Once on the linguistic scale, ratings are obtained, the next step is to compute the mean ratings of experts, using equations (11), (12) and (13). Vector summation using equation (14) is given in Table 11.

The steps are repeated for all the product alternatives with respect to each criterion. We first of all compute for the cost criteria and subsequently for all other criteria (Table 14).

Table 10. Geometric mean criteria rating

Criteria	Geometric Mean Fuzzy Comparison Values
Cost	[3.59,4.30,4.97]
Consultant	[0.25,0.30,0.40]
Quality	[0.52,0.66,0.88]
Vendor	[0.38,0.32,0.38]
ERP Fit	[1.49,1.75,2.00]
Process Aspect	[1.19,1.46,1.77]
Client	[0.33,0.99,1.19]
Technical Aspect	[1.1,1.45,1.83]

Table 11. Vector summation

Criteria	Lower	Middle	Upper
Cost	3.59	4.30	4.97
Consultant	0.25	0.30	0.40
Quality	0.52	0.66	0.88
Vendor	0.38	0.32	0.38
ERP Fit	1.49	1.75	2.00
Process Aspect	1.19	1.46	1.77
Client	0.83	0.99	1.19
Technical Aspect	1.1	1.45	1.83

Table 12. Vector summation

All	9.35	11.23	13.42
Reverse	0.11	0.09	0.07
Increasing Order	0.07	0.09	0.11

Table 13. Weight computation of the criteria, M_i , and N_i

Criteria	Lower	Middle	Upper	M_i	N_i
Cost	0.251	0.387	0.547	0.395	0.377
Consultant	0.018	0.027	0.044	0.029	0.028
Quality	0.036	0.059	0.97	0.064	0.061
Vendor	0.027	0.029	0.042	0.033	0.032
ERP Fit	0.104	0.158	0.22	0.161	0.154
Process Aspect	0.083	0.131	0.195	0.136	0.129
Client	0.58	0.089	0.131	0.093	0.089
Technical Aspect	0.077	0.131	0.201	0.136	0.129

The normalized non fuzzy decision matrix shows the following for the different product alternatives are listed in Table 45: For P1 (Cost: 0.627;Consultant:0.631,Quality: 0.265;Vendor: 0.287; ERP Fit: 0.631; Process: 0.558; Client: 0.659 and Technical ratings stand at 0.494). For P2, the ratings are as follows:(Cost: 0.265; Consultant: 0.259; Quality: 0.527; Vendor: 0.340; ERP Fit: 0.259; Process: 0.327; Client: 0.091 and Technical: 0.412). The individual values indicate the performance of each of the alternatives on the individual criteria.

The aggregated results from all the criteria are indicated in Table 46. The results indicate that Alternative 1 has a score of 0.519, alternative 2 has a score of 0.323 and alternative 3 at a score of 0.158. Alternative 1 has the largest total score. Therefore, it is suggested as the best ERP Product among 3 of them, with respect to the eight criteria and the fuzzy preferences of decision makers.

Table 14. Cost criteria rating

Cost Criteria	P1	P2	P3
P1	(1,1,1)	(2,3,4)	(4,5,6)
P2	(1/4,1/3,1/2)	(1,1,1)	(2,3,4)
P3	(1/6,1/5,1/4)	(1/4,1/3,1/2)	(1,1,1)

Table 15. Geometric mean

Alternative	Lower	Middle	Upper
P1	1.986	2.444	2.854
P2	0.796	1.000	1.257
P3	0.350	0.409	0.503
Total	3.132	3.853	4.614
Reverse	0.319	0.259	0.217
Increasing Order	0.217	0.259	0.319

Table 16. Weights

Lower	Middle	Upper
0.431	0.633	0.910
0.173	0.259	0.401
0.076	0.106	0.160

Table 17. M_i, N_i

Lower	Middle	Upper
0.431	0.633	0.910
0.173	0.259	0.401
0.076	0.106	0.160

Table 18. Consultant criteria rating

Consultant Criteria	P1	P2	P3
P1	(1,1,1)	(4,5,6)	(2,3,4)
P2	(1/6,1/5,1/4)	(1,1,1)	(4,5,6)
P3	(1/4,1/3,1/2)	(1/6,1/5,1/4)	(1,1,1)

Table 19. Geometric mean

Alternative	Lower	Middle	Upper
P1	1.986	2.444	2.854
P2	0.875	1.000	1.143
P3	0.351	0.409	0.503
Total	3.212	3.853	4.5
Reverse	0.311	0.259	0.222
Increasing Order	0.222	0.259	0.311

Table 20. Weights

Lower	Middle	Upper
0.431	0.633	0.888
0.194	0.259	0.355
0.078	0.106	0.156

Table 21. M_i, N_i

Cost	M_i	N_i
P1	0.654	0.631
P2	0.269	0.259
P3	0.113	0.109

Table 22. Quality criteria rating

Quality Criteria	P1	P2	P3
P1	(1,1,1)	(1/4,1/3,1/2)	(2,3,4)
P2	(2,3,4)	(1,1,1)	(4,5,6)
P3	(1/4,1/3,1/2)	(1/6,1/5,1/4)	(1,1,1)

Table 23. Geometric mean

Alternative	Lower	Middle	Upper
P1	0.796	1.000	1.257
P2	1.986	2.444	2.854
P3	0.350	0.409	0.503
Total	3.132	3.853	4.614
Reverse	0.319	0.259	0.217
Increasing Order	0.217	0.259	0.319

Table 24. Weights

Lower	Middle	Upper
0.173	0.259	0.401
0.431	0.633	0.888
0.076	0.106	0.160

Table 25. M_i, N_i

Cost	M_i	N_i
P1	0.278	0.265
P2	0.658	0.627
P3	0.114	0.109

Table 26. Vendor criteria rating

Vendor Criteria	P1	P2	P3
P1	(1,1,1)	(1/6,1/5,1/4)	(2,3,4)
P2	(4,5,6)	(1,1,1)	(1/6,1/5,1/4)
P3	(1/4,1/3,1/2)	(4,5,6)	(1,1,1)

Table 27. Geometric mean

Alternative	Lower	Middle	Upper
P1	0.696	0.845	1.000
P2	0.875	1.000	1.143
P3	1.000	1.184	1.143
Total	2.571	3.029	3.286
Reverse	0.389	0.330	0.304
Increasing Order	0.304	0.330	0.389

Table 28. Weights

Lower	Middle	Upper
0.212	0.279	0.389
0.266	0.330	0.445
0.304	0.391	0.445

Table 29. M_i , N_i

Cost	M_i	N_i
P1	0.293	0.287
P2	0.347	0.340
P3	0.380	0.372

Table 30. ERP fit criteria rating

ERP Fit Criteria	P1	P2	P3
P1	(1,1,1)	(4,5,6)	(2,3,4)
P2	(1/6,1/5,1/4)	(1,1,1)	(4,5,6)
P3	(1/4,1/3,1/2)	(1/6,1/5,1/4)	(1,1,1)

Table 31. Geometric mean

Alternative	Lower	Middle	Upper
P1	1.986	2.444	2.854
P2	0.875	1.000	1.143
P3	0.351	0.409	0.503
Total	3.212	3.853	4.500
Reverse	0.311	0.259	0.222
Increasing Order	0.222	0.259	0.311

Table 32. Weights

Lower	Middle	Upper
0.441	0.633	0.888
0.194	0.259	0.355
0.078	0.106	0.156

Table 33. M_i , N_i

Cost	M_i	N_i
P1	0.654	0.631
P2	0.269	0.259
P3	0.113	0.109

Table 34. Process criteria rating

ERP Fit Criteria	P1	P2	P3
P1	(1,1,1)	(2,3,4)	(2,3,4)
P2	(1/4,1/3,1/2)	(1,1,1)	(4,5,6)
P3	(1/4,1/3,1/2)	(1/6,1/5,1/4)	(1,1,1)

Table 35. Geometric mean

Alternative	Lower	Middle	Upper
P1	1.580	2.065	2.497
P2	1.000	1.184	1.437
P3	0.350	0.409	0.503
Total	2.93	3.568	4.437
Reverse	0.341	0.273	0.225
Increasing Order	0.225	0.273	0.341

Table 36. Weights

Lower	Middle	Upper
0.355	0.564	0.851
0.225	0.323	0.490
0.072	0.112	0.172

Table 37. M_i, N_i

Cost	M_i	N_i
P1	0.59	0.558
P2	0.346	0.327
P3	0.121	0.114

Table 38. Client criteria rating

Client Criteria	P1	P2	P3
P1	(1,1,1)	(6,7,8)	(2,3,4)
P2	(1/8,1/7,1/6)	(1,1,1)	(1/4,1/3,1/2)
P3	(1/4,1/3,1/2)	(2,3,4)	(1,1,1)

Table 39. Geometric mean

Alternative	Lower	Middle	Upper
P1	2.271	2.731	3.138
P2	0.319	0.366	0.441
P3	0.796	1.000	1.257
Total	3.386	4.097	4.836
Reverse	0.295	0.244	0.207
Increasing Order	0.207	0.244	0.295

Table 40. Weights

Lower	Middle	Upper
0.470	0.666	0.926
0.066	0.089	0.130
0.165	0.244	0.371

Table 41. M_i, N_i

Cost	M_i	N_i
P1	0.687	0.659
P2	0.095	0.091
P3	0.26	0.249

Table 42. Technical criteria rating

Technical Criteria	P1	P2	P3
P1	(1,1,1)	(6,7,8)	(2,3,4)
P2	(1/8,1/7,1/6)	(1,1,1)	(2,3,4)
P3	(1/4,1/3,1/2)	(1/4,1/3,1/2)	(1,1,1)

Table 43. Geometric mean

Alternative	Lower	Middle	Upper
P1	2.271	2.731	3.138
P2	0.633	0.756	0.875
P3	0.401	0.484	0.633
Total	3.305	3.971	4.646
Reverse	0.303	0.252	0.215
Increasing Order	0.215	0.252	0.303

Table 44. Weights

Lower	Middle	Upper
0.488	0.688	0.951
0.136	0.191	0.265
0.086	0.122	0.192

Table 45. M_i, N_i

Cost	M_i	N_i
P1	0.709	0.494
P2	0.592	0.412
P3	0.133	0.093

Table 46. Normalized non fuzzy weights

Criteria	Cost	Consultant	Quality	Vendor	ERP Fit	Process	Client	Technical
P1	0.627	0.631	0.265	0.287	0.631	0.558	0/659	0.494
P2	0.265	0.259	0.627	0.340	0.259	0.327	0.091	0.412
P3	0.109	0.109	0.109	0.372	0.109	0.114	0.249	0.093

Table 47. Aggregated result

Criteria	Weights	P1	P2	P3
Cost	0.377	0.627	0.265	0.109
Consultant	0.028	0.631	0.259	0.109
Quality	0.061	0.265	0.527	0.109
Vendor	0.032	0.287	0.340	0.372
ERP Fit	0.154	0.631	0.259	0.109
Process Aspect	0.129	0.558	0.327	0.114
Client	0.089	0.659	0.091	0.249
Technical Aspect	0.129	0.494	0.412	0.093
Total		0.519	0.323	0.158

NUMERICAL ILLUSTRATION: FUZZY TOPSIS

In this section, we provide a sample example illustration of choosing the most appropriate ERP product using Fuzzy TOPSIS technique:

The basic assumptions are as follows:

- The criteria under consideration are Cost (C_1), Consultant (C_2), Quality (C_3), Vendor (C_4), ERP Fit (C_5), Process Aspect (C_6), Client (C_7) and Technical Aspect (C_8).
- Products under consideration for selection are P_1, P_2 and P_3.
- A group of 10-people (E_1, E_2, E_{10}) including the ERP experts and implementing organizations members formed the expert panel.
- Cost(vendor, consultant) and technical aspect (infrastructural requirements) are considered as cost aspects (that is to be minimized) whereas Consultant(Benefits), Quality, Vendor(Benefits), ERP Fit, Process and Client aspects are the benefit criteria i.e. the factors which are to be maximized.
- The importance weights and linguistic scales are adopted as shown in Appendix A. The experts' group opinion was solicited for each of the criterion independent of the product under consideration as per linguistic scale shown in Appendix B (Table 1 and 2). The linguistic importance weight of each criterion as assessed by the experts' panel is listed in Table 48.

After obtaining the "importance" weights, the linguistic rating variable to evaluate the rating of alternatives with respect to each criterion is obtained. In Table 49 each expert gives his opinion on each product with respect to the criteria.

The linguistic assessments are converted to fuzzy numbers as per the scales chosen (Table 3 and 4) to obtain the Fuzzy Decision Matrix and the Fuzzy Weights. The Fuzzy decision matrix and fuzzy weights of the decision criteria thus obtained are shown in Table 50.

The Fuzzy Decision Matrix is normalized so as to arrive at values between 0 and 1 by applying the cost and benefit criteria. The Normalized Fuzzy Decision Matrix is illustrated in Table 51.

Subsequently, the weights are multiplied to the values in the Fuzzy Normalized Decision Matrix to obtain the Fuzzy Weighted Normalized Decision Matrix.

The Fuzzy Weighted Normalized Decision Matrix calculations are in Table 52.

Table 48. Importance weight of each criterion

	E1	E2	E3	E4	E5	E6	E7	E8	E9	E10
C1	L	ML	VL	VL	L	VL	VL	ML	VL	VL
C2	VH	H	MH	H	VH	H	VH	VH	MH	H
C3	H	VH	VH	VH	H	VH	H	H	VH	VH
C4	VH	VH	H	H	H	VH	VH	VH	MH	VH
C5	VH	H	VH	VH	H	MH	H	VH	VH	H
C6	H	VH	VH	MH	VH	H	MH	H	VH	H
C7	MH	H	VH	H	VH	VH	MH	H	H	VH
C8	L	VL	ML	VL	L	ML	VL	L	VL	ML

Table 49. Linguistic rating variable for evaluate the rating of alternatives w.r.t each criterion

Criteria	Product	Decision Makers Evaluation									
		E1	E2	E3	E4	E5	E6	E7	E8	E9	E10
C1	P1	G	MG	G	G	VG	VG	G	VG	F	G
	P2	G	VG	VG	F	VG	G	VG	G	MG	G
	P3	MG	G	VG	VG	G	G	MG	G	G	F
C2	P1	G	F	VG	G	G	MG	G	G	MG	VG
	P2	VG	VG	MG	VG	VG	G	MG	F	G	G
	P3	G	VG	G	VG	VG	G	VG	MG	G	G
C3	P1	G	G	MG	G	G	G	F	VG	G	G
	P2	VG	VG	G	MG	F	VG	VG	MG	VG	VG
	P3	VG	VG	G	VG	MG	G	VG	G	VG	VG
C4	P1	VG	G	G	MG	VG	VG	G	G	MG	G
	P2	MG	MG	F	G	G	MG	VG	VG	G	VG
	P3	G	VG	MG	G	G	G	VG	VG	G	G
C5	P1	G	MG	G	MG	VG	F	VG	G	G	VG
	P2	VG	G	MG	G	G	VG	MG	MG	F	MG
	P3	VG	G	VG	G	G	VG	G	VG	MG	G
C6	P1	G	G	MG	G	G	MG	G	G	G	MG
	P2	VG	VG	G	MG	F	G	F	VG	VG	G
	P3	VG	VG	G	VG	MG	G	MG	G	VG	G
C7	P1	G	VG	G	G	VG	G	G	MG	G	G
	P2	MG	MG	VG	VG	MG	MG	F	G	VG	VG
	P3	VG	G	VG	VG	G	VG	MG	G	G	VG
C8	P1	G	VG	MG	G	G	G	G	VG	VG	VG
	P2	G	MG	G	G	F	G	MG	MG	G	MG
	P3	G	VG	G	VG	VG	MG	MG	G	G	G

Table 50. Fuzzy decision matrix and fuzzy weights of the decision criteria

	C1	C2	C3	C4
P1	(7.0,8.7,9.6)	(6.6,8.4,9.5)	(6.6,8.5,9.6)	(7.2,8.9,9.8)
P2	(7.2,8.8,96)	(7,8.6,9.5)	(6.5,8.8,9.5)	(6.6,8.3,9.4)
P3	(6.6,8.4,9.5)	(7.6,9.2,9.9)	(8.0,9.4,9.9)	(7.4,9.1,9.9)
Weight	(.02,.08,0.22)	(0.7,0.87,0.97)	(0.82,0.96,1)	(0.8,0.94,0.99)
	C5	C6	C7	C8
P1	(6.8,8.5,9.5)	(6.4,8.4,9.7)	(7.2,9,9.9)	(7.6,9.2,9.9)
P2	(6.2,8.0,9.3)	(6.8,8.4,9.3)	(6.6,8.2,9.3)	(6.8,8.5,9.5)
P3	(7.6,9.2,9.9)	(7.8,9.0,9.8)	(7.8,9.3,9.9)	(7.2,8.9,9.8)
Weight	(0.78,0.93,0.99)	(0.74,0.9,0.98)	(0.74,0.9,.98)	(0.03,0.12,0.88)

Table 51. Normalized fuzzy decision matrix

	C1	C2	C3	C4
P1	(0.68,0.76,0.94)	(0.66,0.85,0.96)	(0.67,0.86,0.97)	(0.73,0.9,0.99)
P2	(0.69,0.75,0.92)	(0.7,0.87,096)	(0.65,.89,0.96)	(0.67,0.84,0.95)
P3	(0.69,0.79,1.0)	(0.77,0.93,1.0)	(0.90,0.95,1.0)	(0.75,0.91,1.0)
Weight	(.02,.08,0.22)	(0.7,0.87,0.97)	0.82,0.96,1.0)	(0.8,0.94,0.99)
	C5	C6	C7	C8
P1	(0.69,0.86,0.96)	(0.65,0.85,0.98)	(0.73,0.90,1.0)	(0.67,0.72,0.87)
P2	(0.63,0.9,0.94)	(0.69,0.85,0.94)	(0.67,0.83,0.94)	(0.69,0.78,0.97)
P3	((0.77,0.93,1.0)	(0.79,0.91,0.99)	(0.79,0.94,1.0)	(0.67,0.74,0.92)
Weight	(0.78,0.93,0.99)	(0.74,0.9,0.98)	(0.74,0.9,0.98)	(0.03,0.12,0.88)

Table 52. Fuzzy weighted normalized decision matrix

	C1	C2	C3	C4
P1	(0.001,0.060,0.21)	(0.46,0.74,0.93)	(0.55,0.82,0.97)	(0.58,0.85,0.98)
P2	(0.013,0.06,0.20)	(0.49,0.76,0.93)	(0.53,0.85,0.96)	(0.54,0.79,0.94)
P3	(0.013,0.06,0.22)	(0.54,0.81,0.97)	(0.66,0.91,1.0)	(0.6,0.85,0.99)
	C5	C6	C7	C8
P1	(0.54,0.8,0.95)	(0.48,0.76,0.96)	(0.54,0.81,0.98)	(0.02,0.09,0.076)
P2	(0.49,0.74,0.93)	(0.51,0.76,0.92)	(0.49,0.75,0.92)	(0.020,0.093,0.085)
P3	(0.6,0.86,0.99)	(0.58,0.82,0.97)	(0.58,0.85,0.98)	(0.020,0.089,0.81)

After obtaining the Fuzzy Weighted Normalized Decision Matrix, we compute the distance measurement of each product from the FPIS and FNIS. The vertex method is utilized for the same. The FPIS value indicates how close s product is to the Fuzzy Positive Ideal Solution and the FNIS value indicates how far the product is from the Fuzzy Ideal negative value. Lastly, the closeness coefficient value is computed to indicate the ranking of alternatives.

The distance measurement and closeness coefficient are calculated in Table 53.

Based on Table 53 on the basis of the current set of expert group on the given product alternatives, coupled with the ranks of experts on the specified criteria and relative evaluation of products with respect to the criteria by each expert, the closeness coefficient values, the product P2 would be preferred alternative.

SUMMARIZED COMPARATIVE ANALYSIS OF FUZZY TOPSIS AND FUZZY AHP

As discussed the major techniques used till date for selection process (in general and not specific to ERP) are AHP (Analytic Hierarchy Process), ANP(Analytic Network Process and Fuzzy AHP .The studies prior to 2005 have used the older techniques of AHP and ANP whereas studies from 2005 onwards have

Table 53. Closeness coefficient table

	FPIS	FNIS	Closeness Coefficient
P1	3.106	4.8866	CC1=0.6114
P2	2.398	4.7433	CC2=0.6642
P3	3.2505	5.5499	CC3=0.6306

Table 54. Comparative summary for fuzzy AHP versus fuzzy TOPSIS

Comparative Parameter	Selection Technique	
	Fuzzy AHP (Kahraman et al., 2003)	**Fuzzy TOPSIS (Chen, 2000)**
Modelling Uncertainty	Can handle *uncertainty* in parameters	Can handle *uncertainty* in parameters
Support for group decision making	Methodology compares criteria, or alternatives with respect to criteria, in a natural, pair wise mode. It converts individual preferences into ratio scale weights that can be combined into a linear additive weight for each alternative. The resultant can be used to compare and rank the alternatives and hence, assist the decision maker in making a choice.	According to this technique, the best alternative would be the one that is nearest to the positive ideal solution and farthest from the negative ideal solution (Benitez et al., 2007).
Number of criteria and alternative	Limits the no. of criteria and alternatives	No limit
Complexity	Fuzzy AHP surpasses Fuzzy TOPSIS when consistency criteria is included {(n Criteria, m experts, r input values) For each expert $O(n*n* r)=O(n^3)$ $O(n^3*m)=O(n^4)$ for all experts Aggregation of all experts and averaging $O(n)+O(n)=O(n)$ Synthetic extend matrix for all criteria $n*(3*(O(n)+O(n)+O(n))=O(n^2)$ Degrees of possibility calculation For n criteria, $n(n-1)+n-1(n)*n=O(n^3)+O(n^2)=O(n^3)$ Distance Calculation and weight $n*(n-1)=O(n^2)$ Consistency test inclusion $O(n^2)$(Best Case) $O(n!*n)$(Worst case) } Repeat for Product comparison matrix and Sub-criteria Calculations	Fuzzy TOPSIS extensions involves the following: (n Criteria, m experts, r possible input values) For each 1..n criteria • $O(m*r)$ for taking the input Total criteria Inputs: $n*O(n^2)$ • $O(n^3)$ For each criteria 1..n, For each product 1..u Obtain expert rating • $O(m*r)=O(n^2)$ Total product ratings for each expert • $O(n)*O(u)*O(n^2)=O(n^4)$ Constructing Fuzzy decision matrix and fuzzy Weights(For u products and n criteria) • $O(3un)+O(3.1*m)=O(n^2)$ The fuzzy normalized matrix (For u products and n criteria) • $O(3un)=O(n^2)$ The fuzzy weighted normalized matrix • $O(3un)=O(n^2)$ Distance calculation For each product, with n criteria, • $O(n)$ For u products • $u*O(n)=O(n^2)$ To be done for both FPIS and FNIS • $2*O(n^2)$ Closeness coefficient • $O(n)$
	Total: $O(n^4)+O(n)+O(n^2)+O(n^3)+O(n^2)+O(n^2)$ $=O(n^4)$(Global calculations only)	Total: $O(n^4)+O(n^2)+O(n^2)+O(n^2)+O(n2)+O(n)$ $= O(n^4)$

used Fuzzy AHP as their selection technique. The application of the Fuzzy TOPSIS is quite recent addition to the selection set. We now present a comprehensive comparison on several parameters between the two predominant techniques of Fuzzy AHP and Fuzzy TOPSIS (RodriguesLimaJunior et al., 2014).

Hence, it can be seen that Fuzzy TOPSIS fares better for handling uncertainty in decision making and provides for inclusion of unlimited criteria and products. Further, it maintains rank consistency even in cases of alternative inclusion. The method never assigns null weights thus does-not compromise on the importance of an alternative product in question. Finally, it fares better on time complexity computational efficiency when compared to Fuzzy AHP with consistency test.

FUTURE DIRECTIONS

Integrating AHP with TOPSIS using fuzzy numbers for ERP selection could be explored as an interesting proposition by the researchers. Techniques are bound to be combined and used: Fuzzy AHP- Fuzzy TOPSIS, Fuzzy TOPSIS- Fuzzy VIKOR, etc. for added advantages and for nullifying disadvantages. One of the recent such work includes an approach of combining Fuzzy DEMATEL with Fuzzy TOPSIS (Sangaiah et al., 2015a; 2015 b). Another upcoming area is the use of hesitant Fuzzy TOPSIS with intuitionistic fuzzy numbers. An Intuitionistic Fuzzy Set (IFS) represents the degree of membership and non-membership of an element to a set. Another extension and generalization is based in the concept on Hesitant Fuzzy Set (HFS) proposed by Tora and Narukawa (2009) where several membership values are permitted for an element to belong to a set. Lastly, all the future techniques and methods would aim at reducing uncertainty in the multicriteria decision making coupled with multiple criteria and several alternatives for better and improved results

CONCLUSION

We hereby present two popular approaches, namely Fuzzy-AHP and Fuzzy TOPSIS to the ERP selection problem. Both the techniques represent the linguistic assessment of importance weights and relative importance, thereby presenting the assessment techniques that are comparatively closer to the realistic human approach to decision making. Both techniques also model closely the natural human decision making problem of multiple criteria with multiple alternatives. Further, in this Chapter, a selection framework for bridging the research thrust areas of ERP projects was also proposed. The selection framework helps in utilizing the proposed CSFs studies to the selection problem as well

In order to deal with the ERP selection appropriately, the analytic hierarchy process (AHP) method is extended into a fuzzy domain, the Fuzzy AHP approach. A framework is developed to select most suitable ERP system using this technique. The factors are determined, classified, weighted and prioritized and then a framework is provided for ERP selection with the fuzzy analytic hierarchy process (FAHP) method. Then, we used fuzzy AHP to obtain pairwise comparison judgments by prioritizing criteria and assigning weights to the factors and alternatives. The goal of the technique was to select the best alternative that meets the requirements with respect to Cost, Consultant, Quality, Vendor, ERP Fit, Process Aspect, Client and Technical Aspect.

The second technique of Fuzzy TOPSIS also evaluated the three product alternatives on the panel of 10 experts rating. The criteria under consideration were again Cost, Consultant, Quality, Vendor, ERP

Fit, Process Aspect, Client and Technical Aspect . The costing factors such as Cost(vendor, consultant) and technical aspect (infrastructural requirements) were attempted to be minimized) whereas benefit criteria such as Consultant(Benefits), Quality, Vendor(Benefits), ERP Fit, Process and Client aspects were to be maximized. The TOPSIS method computed the nearness distance to the FPIS and distance away from the FNIS. Finally the closeness coefficient of each product alternative was computed.

A numerical illustration of the techniques to the problem of ERP product selection was also demonstrated. It was also discussed in detail how Fuzzy TOPSIS fares better than the technique of Fuzzy AHP on agility, rank consistency and time complexity computational efficiency.

REFERENCES

Ahmed, S., Ahmed, S., Shumon, M. R. H., Quader, M. A., Cho, H. M., & Mahmud, M. I. (2015). Prioritizing Strategies for Sustainable End-of-Life Vehicle Management Using Combinatorial Multi-Criteria Decision Making Method. *International Journal of Fuzzy Systems*, 1–15.

Ahyan, M. B. (2013). A fuzzy ahp approach for supplier selection problem: A case study in a gearmotor company. *International Journal of Managing Value and Supply Chains*, *4*(3), 11–23. doi:10.5121/ijmvsc.2013.4302

Anojkumar, L., Ilangkumaran, M., & Vignesh, M. (2015). A decision making methodology for material selection in sugar industry using hybrid MCDM techniques. *International Journal of Materials and Product Technology*, *51*(2), 102–126. doi:10.1504/IJMPT.2015.071770

Ayağ, Z. (2015). CAD software evaluation for product design to exchange data in a supply chain network. *International Journal of Supply Chain Management, 4*(1), 30-38.

Aziza, A., Aikhuele, D., & Souleman, F. (2015). A Fuzzy TOPSIS Model to Rank Automotive Suppliers. In *2nd International Materials, Industrial, and Manufacturing Engineering Conference*. doi:10.1016/j.promfg.2015.07.028

Balin, A., & Baraçli, H. (2015). A fuzzy multi-criteria decision making methodology based upon the interval type-2 fuzzy sets for evaluating renewable energy alternatives in Turkey. *Technological and Economic Development of Economy*, 1-22.

Bronja,H. & Bronja, H. (2015). Two-phase selection procedure of aluminized sheet supplier by applying fuzzy AHP and fuzzy TOPSIS methodology. *Tehnički vjesnik*, 22(4), 821-828.

Buckley, J. J. (1985). Fuzzy hierarchical analysis. *Fuzzy Sets and Systems*, *17*(1), 233–247. doi:10.1016/0165-0114(85)90090-9

Burak, E. (2015). An integrated fuzzy multi criteria group decision making approach for ERP system selection. *Applied Soft Computing*, *38*, 106–117.

Chang, D.-Y. (1996). Applications of the extent analysis method on fuzzy AHP. *European Journal of Operational Research*, *95*(3), 649–655. doi:10.1016/0377-2217(95)00300-2

Chou, S.-W., & Chang, Y.-C. (2008). The implementation factors that influence the ERP (Enterprise Resource Planning) Benefits. *Decision Support Systems*, *46*(1), 149–157. doi:10.1016/j.dss.2008.06.003

Choudhury, P. P., & Satapathy, S. (2015). Plastic Recycling Process Using Fuzzy Analytical Hierarchy Process. *Journal of Industrial Safety Engineering*, *2*(2), 17–22.

Das, M. C., Sarkar, B., & Ray, S. (2015). A performance evaluation framework for technical institutions in one of the states of India. *Benchmarking International Journal (Toronto, Ont.)*, *22*(5).

Deveci, M., Demirel, N. Ç., John, R., & Ozcan, E. (2015). Fuzzy multi-criteria decision making for carbon dioxide geological storage in Turkey. *Journal of Natural Gas Science and Engineering*.

Eko Saputro, T., & Daneshvar Rouyendegh, B. (2015). A hybrid approach for selecting material handling equipment in a warehouse. *International Journal of Management Science and Engineering Management*, 1-15.

Guneri, A. F., Gul, M., & Ozgurler, S. (2015). A fuzzy AHP methodology for selection of risk assessment methods in occupational safety. *International Journal of Risk Assessment and Management*, *18*(3-4), 319–335. doi:10.1504/IJRAM.2015.071222

Guo, S., & Zhao, H. (2015). Optimal site selection of electric vehicle charging station by using fuzzy TOPSIS based on sustainability perspective. *Applied Energy*, *158*, 390–402. doi:10.1016/j.apenergy.2015.08.082

Kahraman, C. U., & Ulukan, Z. (2003). Multi-criteria supplier selection using fuzzy AHP. *Logistics Information Management*, *16*(6), 382-390.

Kahraman, C., Suder, A., & Bekar, E. T. (2015). Fuzzy multiattribute consumer choice among health insurance options. *Technological and Economic Development of Economy*, 1-20.

Kant, S. (2015). Manufacturing system selection using fuzzy AHP. *MR International Journal of Engineering & Technology*, *7*(1), 22–28.

Karami, R., & Sayyaadi, H. (2015). Optimal sizing of Stirling-CCHP systems for residential buildings at diverse climatic conditions. *Applied Thermal Engineering*, *89*, 377–393. doi:10.1016/j.applthermaleng.2015.06.022

Kaur, H., Singh, S. P., & Glardon, R. (2015). An Integer Linear Program for Integrated Supplier Selection: A Sustainable Flexible Framework. *Global Journal of Flexible Systems Management*, 1-22.

Kilincci, O., & Onal, S. A. (2011). Fuzzy AHP approach for supplier selection in a washing machine company. *Expert Systems with Applications*, *38*(8), 9656–9664. doi:10.1016/j.eswa.2011.01.159

Lee, S., & Seo, K. K. (2015). A hybrid multi-criteria decision-making model for a cloud service selection problem using BSC, fuzzy Delphi method and fuzzy AHP. *Wireless Personal Communications*, 1–19.

Li, M., & Wu, C. (2015). Green Supplier Selection Based on Improved Intuitionistic Fuzzy TOPSIS Model. *Metallurgical and Mining Industry*, *6*, 193–205.

Liao, T. W. (2015). Two interval type 2 fuzzy TOPSIS material selection methods. *Materials & Design*, *88*, 1088–1099. doi:10.1016/j.matdes.2015.09.113

Lima Junior, F. R., Osiro, L., & Carpinetti, L. C. R. (2014). A comparison between Fuzzy AHP and Fuzzy TOPSIS methods to supplier selection. *Applied Soft Computing*, *21*, 194–209. doi:10.1016/j.asoc.2014.03.014

Marvi, L. T., & Behzadfar, M. (2015). Local Sustainability with Emphasis on CPTED Approach, The Case of Ab-kooh Neighborhood in Mash-had. *Procedia: Social and Behavioral Sciences*, *201*, 409–417. doi:10.1016/j.sbspro.2015.08.194

Mathiyalagan, P. (2015, May). Use of fuzzy TOPSIS techniques for selection of best alternatives of blood bank Supply chain. In *Smart Technologies and Management for Computing, Communication, Controls, Energy and Materials (ICSTM), 2015 International Conference on* (pp. 644-649). IEEE. doi:10.1109/ICSTM.2015.7225492

Minatoura, Y., Khazaie, J., Ataei, M., & Javadi, A. A. (2015). An integrated decision support system for dam site selection. *Scientia Iranica. Transaction A. Civil Engineering (New York, N.Y.)*, *22*(2), 319–330.

Mohammadjafari, M., & Zohary, M. (2015). Supplier selection by Using Integrated Fuzzy Topsis and Multi Criteria Goal Decision Making Approach. *European Online Journal of Natural and Social Sciences*, *4*(1), 1153–1161.

Nouri, F. A., Esbouei, S. K., & Antucheviciene, J. (2015). A Hybrid MCDM Approach Based on Fuzzy ANP and Fuzzy TOPSIS for Technology Selection. *Informatica*, *26*(3), 369–388. doi:10.15388/Informatica.2015.53

Ozkan, B., Kaya, I., Cebeci, U., & Başlıgil, H. (2015). A Hybrid Multicriteria Decision Making Methodology Based on Type-2 Fuzzy Sets For Selection Among Energy Storage Alternatives. *International Journal of Computational Intelligence Systems*, *8*(5), 914–927. doi:10.1080/18756891.2015.1084715

Oztaysi, B. (2015). A Group Decision Making Approach Using Interval Type-2 Fuzzy AHP for Enterprise Information Systems Project Selection. *Journal of Multiple-Valued Logic & Soft Computing*, *24*(5), 475–500.

Ren, J., & Lützen, M. (2015). Fuzzy multi-criteria decision-making method for technology selection for emissions reduction from shipping under uncertainties. *Transportation Research Part D, Transport and Environment*, *40*, 43–60. doi:10.1016/j.trd.2015.07.012

Saaty, T. L. (1980a). *The Analytic Hierarchy Process*. New York: McGraw-Hill.

Saaty, T. L. (1980b). *The analytic hierarchy process: planning priority setting resource allocation*. London: McGraw Hill International Book Company.

Saaty, T. L. (1986). Axiomatic Foundation of the Analytic Hierarchy Process. *Management Science*, *32*(7), 841–855. doi:10.1287/mnsc.32.7.841

Saaty, T. L. (1994a). How to Make a Decision: The Analytic Hierarchy Process. *Interfaces*, *24*(6), 19–43. doi:10.1287/inte.24.6.19

Saaty, T. L. (1994b). *Fundamentals of Decision Making*. Pittsburgh, PA: RWS Publications.

Sakhuja, S., Jain, V., & Dweiri, F. (2015). Application of an integrated MCDM approach in selecting outsourcing strategies in hotel industry. *International Journal of Logistics Systems and Management*, *20*(3), 304–324. doi:10.1504/IJLSM.2015.068430

Salimi, N., & Rezaei, J. (2015). Multi-criteria university selection: Formulation and implementation using a fuzzy AHP. *Journal of Systems Science and Systems Engineering*, 1–23.

Sangaiah, A. K., Gopal, J., Basu, A., & Subramaniam, P. R. (2015b). An integrated Fuzzy DEMATEL, ELECTRE AND TOPSIS approach for evaluation of Knowledge Transfer effectiveness with reference to GSD project outcome. *Neural Computing and Applications*. doi:10.1007/s00521-015-2040-7

Sangaiah, A. K., Subramaniam, P. R., & Zheng, X. (2015a). A combined fuzzy DEMATEL and fuzzy TOPSIS approach for evaluating GSD project outcome factors. *Neural Computing and Applications*. doi:10.1007/s00521-014-1771-1

Savino, M. M., Macchi, M., & Mazza, A. (2015). Investigating the impact of social sustainability within maintenance operations: An action research in heavy industry. *Journal of Quality in Maintenance Engineering*, *21*(3), 310–331. doi:10.1108/JQME-06-2014-0038

Shaw, K., Shankar, R., Yadav, S. S., & Thakur, L. S. (2012). Supplier Selection Using FuzzyAHP and Fuzzy Multi Objective Linear programming for developing low carbon supply chain. *Expert Systems with Applications*, *39*(9), 8182–8192. doi:10.1016/j.eswa.2012.01.149

Singh, H., & Randhawa, R. (2015). Evaluation Framework for Selection and Ranking of Cloud Providers. *International Journal of Advancements in Computing Technology, 7*(4), 31-37.

Taylan, O., Kabli, M. R., Saeedpoor, M., & Vafadarnikjoo, A. (2015). Commentary on 'Construction projects selection and risk assessment by Fuzzy AHP and Fuzzy TOPSIS methodologies'. *Applied Soft Computing*, *36*, 419–421. doi:10.1016/j.asoc.2015.05.051

Torra & Narukawa. (2009*)*. On hesistant fuzzy sets and decision. In *IEEE Conference on Fuzzy Systems*.

Van Laarhoven, P. J. M., & Pedrycz, W. (1983). A fuzzy extension of Saaty''s priority Theory. *Fuzzy Sets and Systems*, *11*(1-3), 199–227. doi:10.1016/S0165-0114(83)80082-7

Vinodh, S., Balagi, T. S., & Patil, A. (2015). A hybrid MCDM approach for agile concept selection using fuzzy DEMATEL, fuzzy ANP and fuzzy TOPSIS. *International Journal of Advanced Manufacturing Technology*, 1–9.

Yadav, V., & Sharma, M. K. (2015). Multi-criteria decision making for supplier selection using fuzzy AHP approach. *Benchmarking: An International Journal*, *22*(6), 1158–1174. doi:10.1108/BIJ-04-2014-0036

Yang, S. S., Nasr, N., Ong, S. K., & Nee, A. Y. C. (2015). Designing automotive products for remanufacturing from material selection perspective. *Journal of Cleaner Production*. doi:10.1016/j.jclepro.2015.08.121

Yildiz, M. S., Unal, A. N., Ozkan, O., Koç, İ., & Çelik, M. (2015, June). Electrothermal propulsion system selection for communication satellite NSSK maneuver using multi criteria decision making method. In *Recent Advances in Space Technologies (RAST), 2015 7th International Conference on* (pp. 587-592). IEEE. doi:10.1109/RAST.2015.7208412

Yudatama, U., & Sarno, R. (2015, May). Evaluation maturity index and risk management for it governance using Fuzzy AHP and Fuzzy TOPSIS (case Study Bank XYZ). In *Intelligent Technology and Its Applications (ISITIA), 2015 International Seminar on* (pp. 323-328). IEEE.

Zadeh, L. A. (1965). Fuzzy sets. *Information and Control*, *8*(3), 338–353. doi:10.1016/S0019-9958(65)90241-X

Chapter 10
Fuzzy-Based Matrix Converter Drive for Induction Motor

Chitra Venugopal
University of KwaZulu-Natal, South Africa

ABSTRACT

In industrial applications, approximately, 60% of world's consumption of electrical energy passes through the windings of squirrel-cage induction motors. Hence it is necessary to select an efficient drive circuit for induction motor to save energy. The MC are preferred to replace VSC in industrial applications. To control the performance of the MC, fuzzy logic technique is proposed and simulated using Matlab/Simulink. In this chapter, the basic concepts of MCs are discussed. The implementation of fuzzy logic technique to improve the performance of MC in driving induction motor is discussed in detail. The design of fuzzy controllers and the closed loop control of induction motor is shown. It seen that the introduction of fuzzy controllers in the closed loop helped to reduce the overshoot at starting and maintain the reference speed when running with load torque. Also the input and output voltage of the MC is maintained sinusoidal.

INTRODUCTION

Today the world is undergoing a serious power crisis. In industrial applications, variable speed drives plays a vital role in energy saving process. Basically the variable speed drive systems can be classified as DC drive and AC drive systems. The DC drive system uses DC motors which have many disadvantages such as need for regular maintenance, bulky in size and commutator sparking. The AC drive system uses AC motors such as induction or synchronous types. Induction motors are widely used in industrial applications due to their low cost, reliability and performance (Barton, 1994). At present, approximately, 60% of world's consumption of electrical energy passes through the windings of squirrel-cage induction motors in the range of 1 to 125 horsepower. Hence it is necessary to select a reliable drive circuit for efficient power conversion in variable speed operation of induction motor to save energy.

The speed of the induction motor can be controlled by many techniques such as stator voltage control and frequency control. The frequency control method is best suited for variable speed operation

DOI: 10.4018/978-1-5225-1008-6.ch010

of Induction motors. To perform frequency control method, the power converters should be capable of handling frequency conversion also.

The traditional Voltage Source Converter (VSC) can generate variable voltage and variable frequency ac output from a constant voltage and constant frequency input source. The power conversion in VSC happens in two stages, first stage converts AC into DC and the second stage converts DC into AC with a change in voltage and frequency levels as required. The two stages are linked by an energy storing DC link capacitor. The two stage power conversion compromises the quality of the output power in terms of the harmonics present in the output. Also the bulky DC link capacitor increases the size of the converter. In order to improve the quality of power supplied to the motor, single stage power converters such as cycloconverters and matrix converters are invented. The frequency conversion limitation and the requirement of 72 power switches limit the application of cycloconverters in AC drive system.

Matrix converters are single stage AC to AC power converter. The Matrix converters are called All Silicon Solution because of its ability to perform direct AC to AC frequency and voltage conversion without the need for intermediate energy storage components such as the DC link capacitor as seen in the Voltage Source Converters. Unlike the cycloconverters, matrix converters uses only 9 bidirectional switches arranged in 3x3 matrix form. The Matrix Converters can produce sinusoidal output voltage with controllable displacement factor which increases the quality of power delivered to the stator windings of induction motor. The application of Matrix converter in induction motor drive increases the reliability and performance of the induction motor in speed control applications. The 9 bidirectional switches in 3x3 matrix combination gives 512 (29) switching combinations to produce AC output at required voltage and frequency levels. The switching combinations are selected by modulation methods. The traditional modulation techniques such as space vector and Venturini algorithm are used to control switching combinations of matrix converter.

Though the direct matric converter has several advantages, the application of matrix converter in ac drives especially in the speed control application of induction motor is limited. This is because the implementation of bidirectional switches leads to commutation problems due to the absence of freewheeling paths. This needs to be handled by selecting the proper timing and synchronization of command signals for the switches. The timing and synchronization of switching signal is controlled by modulation and commutation technique. To synchronize the command signals with the switch signals, the current and voltage vectors need to be selected appropriately to select the switching sequence for switches.

Within the last decade, substantial growth of soft computing techniques in electrical drive application has been noticed because the soft computing techniques do not require the mathematical model of the system. The soft computing techniques employ different methods to address the imprecise, uncertain and computation methods of hard computing techniques.

In general, fuzzy logic technique can be used for modelling non-linear, unknown or partially known controllers. It emulates human reasoning providing an intuitive way to design a functional block for a control system. The fuzzy reasoning technique can be utilized to select the current and voltage vectors according to the reference and motor speed of the induction motor.

The main objective of this chapter is to apply fuzzy logic technique to utilize the matrix converter efficiently in closed loop control of induction motor. To implement the fuzzy logic technique, the basic concepts of matrix converter and its traditional switching algorithm is introduced. The fuzzy logic controller and selection of membership functions are discussed. The implementation of fuzzy logic controller and the design of matrix converter in closed control of induction motor is analyzed in detail.

BACKGROUND

In the traditional power converters, control is obtained in two stages. Figure 1 shows traditional Voltage Source Converter (VSC) which can generate variable voltage and variable frequency ac output from a constant voltage and constant frequency input source (Bogalecka, & Erzeminski, 1993). The first stage converts the AC input into DC. The second stage converts DC into AC. The Pulse Width Modulation technique is used in the inverter stage to produce sinusoidal output at desired amplitude and desired frequency. The two stages are coupled by an energy storing DC link capacitor. This DC link capacitor provides constant DC voltage to the inverter stage. The drawbacks of traditional VSC are; the need for large size capacitor which makes the circuit bulky, adds weight and cost of the system. The input current delivered to the inverter stage will have 5th and 7th harmonics (Gyugi & Pelly, 1970). These harmonics will be injected to the mains at higher power levels and will lead to power losses.

To eliminate the drawback of DC link capacitor in two stage converters, single stage power converters were designed in early 1930s and are called cycloconverters. In cycloconverters the power conversion is obtained in single stage without the bulky energy storing DC link capacitor as shown in Figure 2. The rectifiers are used in positive and negative half cycle to produce alternating currents of variable frequency from a fixed voltage and fixed frequency AC input supply (Huber, & Borojevic, 1985; Jones, & Bose, 1976). The advantages of cycloconverters are natural commutation of power semiconductor switches and simple in construction. The maximum output frequency produced by the cycloconverter is less than the input frequency. So the cycloconverters are used in industrial applications despite its frequency limitation. A three phase to three phase cycloconverters uses 36 thyristors to conduct current. Due to the high number power semiconductor switches the complexity of control circuit increases and hence the converters become very expensive.

Matrix converter has recently received considerable interests, because it possesses the necessary features to fulfil the industrial requirement. The most desirable features of matrix converter in power conversion are:

Figure 1. Voltage source converter

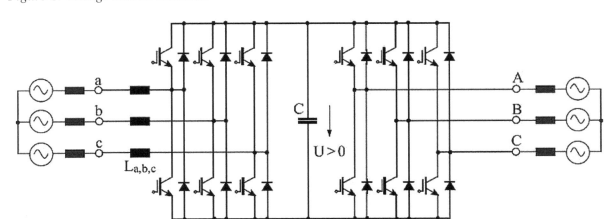

Figure 2. Three phase to three phase cycloconverter

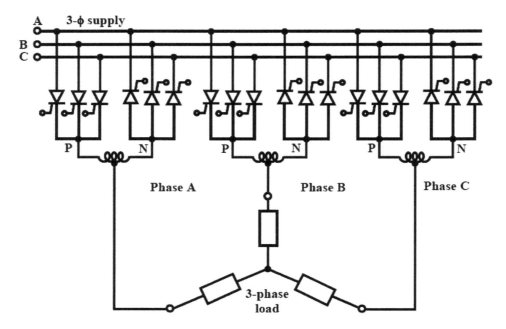

- Generation of output voltage at the desired amplitude and frequency,
- Sinusoidal input current,
- Sinusoidal output voltage,
- Improved power factor,
- Regeneration Capability.

These features of matrix converter replace voltage source inverters in induction motor drive applications. Matrix converter uses nine bi-directional controlled switches in a 3 x 3 matrix form to produce variable output voltage with variable frequency (Alesina, & Venturini, 1989). The main advantage of matrix converter is that it does not have any dc link and energy storing elements which reduces the performance of the converter.

The other features of matrix converter compared to voltage source converters are;

- The output voltage of voltage source converters can assume only two discrete fixed potential values those of the positive and negative DC bus values. In matrix converters, the output voltages can assume either input voltage a, b or c and their values is not time variant whereas it reduces the switching harmonics.
- In the traditional voltage source converters, the input current to the inverter stage contains 5th and 7th harmonics (Barakati, 2008). In matrix converters if the switching frequency is kept higher than the input and output frequency, the input current drawn by the converter can be maintained sinusoidal.
- In voltage source converters the power factor calculation needs the knowledge of the load displacement angle in order to control the output power factor whereas in matrix converters the knowledge of load displacement angle is not needed to control the output power factor.

Though the DMC has several advantages the application of Matrix Converter in ac drives especially in the speed control application of Induction Motor is limited. This is because the implementation of bidirectional switches leads to commutation problems due to the absence of freewheeling paths. This needs to be handled by selecting the proper timing and synchronization of command signals for the switches. The timing and synchronization of switching signal is controlled by modulation and commutation technique.

MATRIX CONVERTER DRIVE FOR INDUCTION MOTOR

Matrix Converter Fundamentals

Various power converter circuit topologies have been studied since 1970 (Barakati, 2008). In 1980, Venturini and Alesina presented the power circuit of the MC as a matrix of bi-directional power switches and they introduced the name "Matrix Converter" (Blaabjerg, Casadei, Klumpner, & Matteeini, 2002; Siyoung, Seung, &.Lipo 2000). Matrix Converter is the most general type in the family of AC to AC power converters. The Matrix converters are called All Silicon Solution because of its ability to perform direct AC to AC frequency and voltage conversion without the need for intermediate energy storage components such as the DC link capacitor as seen in the voltage source converters. It consists of a matrix of 9 bidirectional switch elements. The circuit topology of direct matrix converter is shown in Figure 3.

It can be seen that there are only nine power semiconductor switches used in the converter. The 9 semiconductor switches can give 512 (29) switching combinations. The duty cycle of switches can be properly modulated to connect any input phase to any output phase. Alsena and Venturini (Alesina,& Venturini, 1989) proposed a general matrix converter model and a modulation algorithm. The matrix converters can provide sinusoidal voltage at the load side. The converter is capable of operating at lagging, unity or even leading fundamental input displacement factor. The converter offers the advantages

Figure 3. Circuit topology of direct matrix converter

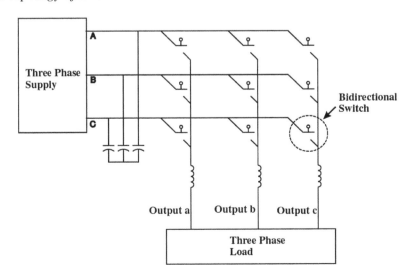

Figure 4. Indirect matrix converter

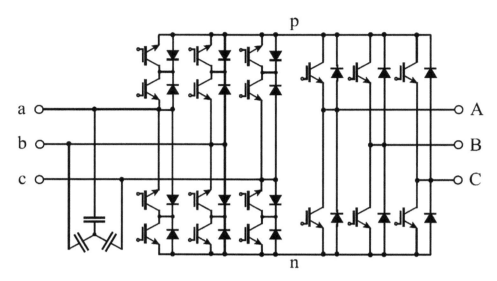

of four quadrant operation, sinusoidal input and output waveforms, minimum energy storage components and controllable displacement factor. The indirect MC has been studied since 1993. The switching circuit arrangement of indirect matrix converter is shown in Figure 4 (Jussila, Salo, & Tuusa, 2004; Klumpner, 2005; Takeshita, & Andou, 2010).

In the beginning, power transistors were used as bi-directional switches in MC topology (Daniels, & Slattery, 1978; Daniels, & Slattery, 1978). The performance of direct MC and indirect MC based on Space Vector Modulation in an induction motor drive application is also studied (Huber, & Borojevic, 1995). It is shown that the output voltage of the converters does not follow the input. This is due to the need of different commutation methods to provide safe operation and also the power losses caused by different main circuit. Also, the effect of non-linearity is highly visible in indirect MC than in direct MC. Hence the efficiency of indirect MC is low compared to direct MC (Jussila, Salo, & Tuusa, 2004).

Switching Topology of Direct Matrix Converter

The switching arrangement of direct matrix converter is shown in Figure 5. It can be seen that each of the 9 bidirectional switches are switched on and off according to Venturini algorithm to get the required output voltage at desired frequency from a fixed input voltage and frequency source. At any switching time, the input source should not be open circuited and output circuit should not short circuited (Ahmed, Ghoni, & Zakaria, 2011).

A bidirectional switch capable of conducting current and blocking voltage in both polarities based on the control signal is not available in the market until today. Hence the bidirectional switch used in the converter is realized by the connecting two unidirectional semiconductor switches back to back with freewheeling diodes.

Figure 5. Switching arrangement of direct matrix converter

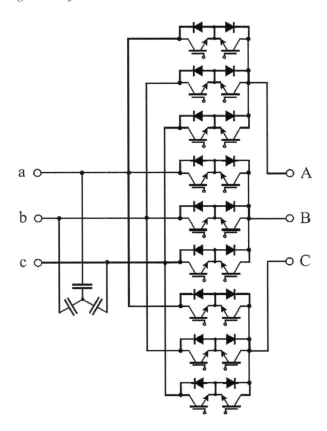

VENTURINI ALGORITHM

In MC each switch is used to connect or disconnect any phase of the input to any phase of the load. This can be achieved only by selecting proper switching configuration. In order to avoid the interruption of load current suddenly, at least one switch in each column must be closed. Each switch can be defined with a commutation function described as below (Clare, & Wheeler, 2003):

$$S_{Kk}(t) = \begin{cases} 0 & \text{if switch } S_{Kk} \text{ is open} \\ 1 & \text{if switch } S_{Kk} \text{ is closed} \end{cases} \tag{1}$$

where $K = \{A, B, C\}$ input phase and k is $= \{a, b, c\}$ is output phase. The two conditions in equation (1) can be expressed as

$$S_{Ak} + S_{Bk} + S_{ck} = 1 \tag{2}$$

The equation (2) shows that a 3 x 3 MC has got 27 possible switching states. In order to select appropriate combinations of open and closed switches and to generate the desired output voltages, modulation strategy for the MC must be developed for which it is necessary to develop the mathematical model. It can be derived from equation (1) as follows:

The load and source voltages with reference to supply neutral can be expressed as

$$v_o = \begin{bmatrix} v_a(t) \\ v_b(t) \\ v_c(t) \end{bmatrix} \text{ and } v_i = \begin{bmatrix} v_A(t) \\ v_B(t) \\ v_C(t) \end{bmatrix} \tag{3}$$

The load and source currents can expressed as

$$i_o = \begin{bmatrix} i_a(t) \\ i_b(t) \\ i_c(t) \end{bmatrix} \text{ and } i_i = \begin{bmatrix} i_A(t) \\ i_B(t) \\ i_C(t) \end{bmatrix} \tag{4}$$

$$\begin{bmatrix} v_a(t) \\ v_b(t) \\ v_c(t) \end{bmatrix} = \begin{bmatrix} S_{Aa}(t) & S_{Ba}(t) & S_{Ca}(t) \\ S_{Ab}(t) & S_{Bb}(t) & S_{Cb}(t) \\ S_{Ac}(t) & S_{Bc}(t) & S_{Cc}(t) \end{bmatrix} \begin{bmatrix} v_A(t) \\ v_B(t) \\ v_C(t) \end{bmatrix} \tag{5}$$

$$\begin{bmatrix} i_A(t) \\ i_B(t) \\ i_C(t) \end{bmatrix} = \begin{bmatrix} S_{Aa}(t) & S_{Ab}(t) & S_{Ac}(t) \\ S_{Ba}(t) & S_{Bb}(t) & S_{Bc}(t) \\ S_{Ca}(t) & S_{Cb}(t) & S_{Cc}(t) \end{bmatrix} \begin{bmatrix} i_a(t) \\ i_b(t) \\ i_c(t) \end{bmatrix} \tag{6}$$

$$M_{Kk}(t) = \frac{t_{Kk}}{T_s} \tag{7}$$

where K represents input phases A,B,C and k represents output phases a, b, c and T_s is the sequence time.
The modulation strategies are defined by using these continuous time functions.

$$\begin{bmatrix} v_a(t) \\ v_b(t) \\ v_c(t) \end{bmatrix} = \begin{bmatrix} M_{Aa}(t) & M_{Ba}(t) & M_{Ca}(t) \\ M_{Ab}(t) & M_{Bb}(t) & M_{Cb}(t) \\ M_{Ac}(t) & M_{Bc}(t) & M_{Cc}(t) \end{bmatrix} \begin{bmatrix} v_A(t) \\ v_B(t) \\ v_C(t) \end{bmatrix} \tag{8}$$

$$\begin{bmatrix} i_A(t) \\ i_B(t) \\ i_C(t) \end{bmatrix} = \begin{bmatrix} M_{Aa}(t) & M_{Ab}(t) & M_{Ac}(t) \\ M_{Ba}(t) & M_{Bb}(t) & M_{Bc}(t) \\ M_{Ca}(t) & M_{Cb}(t) & M_{Cc}(t) \end{bmatrix} \begin{bmatrix} i_a(t) \\ i_b(t) \\ i_c(t) \end{bmatrix} \tag{9}$$

Voltages v_a, v_b & v_c and currents i_a, i_b & i_c are average values of output voltage and output current respectively.

The MC generates sinusoidal output voltage and sinusoidal input current to get adjustable input power factor. Hence, the output voltage $v_o(t)$ can be expressed as

$$[v_i(t)] = V_{im} \begin{bmatrix} \cos(\omega_i t) \\ \cos\left(\omega_i t + \dfrac{2\pi}{3}\right) \\ \cos\left(\omega_i t + \dfrac{4\pi}{3}\right) \end{bmatrix} \tag{10}$$

$$[v_o(t)] = qV_{im} \begin{bmatrix} \cos(\omega_o t) \\ \cos\left(\omega_o t + \dfrac{2\pi}{3}\right) \\ \cos\left(\omega_o t + \dfrac{4\pi}{3}\right) \end{bmatrix} \tag{11}$$

where V_{im}, ω_i, and ω_o are the average input voltage, input and output frequencies respectively.

$$[i_o(t)] = I_{om} \begin{bmatrix} \cos(\omega_o t + \varphi_o) \\ \cos\left(\omega_o t + \varphi_o + \dfrac{2\pi}{3}\right) \\ \cos\left(\omega_o t + \varphi_o + \dfrac{4\pi}{3}\right) \end{bmatrix} \tag{12}$$

$$[i_i(t)] = q\frac{\cos\varphi_o}{\cos\varphi_i} I_{om} \begin{bmatrix} \cos(\omega_i t + \varphi_i) \\ \cos\left(\omega_i t + \varphi_i + \dfrac{2\pi}{3}\right) \\ \cos\left(\omega_i t + \varphi_i + \dfrac{4\pi}{3}\right) \end{bmatrix} \tag{13}$$

where φ_i and φ_o are the input and output displacement angles respectively. q is defined as the ratio of output fundamental to input fundamental voltage value called as voltage transfer ratio.

The modulation matrix M(T) can be expressed as,

$$M(t) = \begin{bmatrix} M_{Aa}(t) & M_{Ba}(t) & M_{Ca}(t) \\ M_{Ab}(t) & M_{Bb}(t) & M_{Cb}(t) \\ M_{Ac}(t) & M_{Bc}(t) & M_{Cc}(t) \end{bmatrix} \tag{14}$$

where

$$M_{Aa}(t) = \frac{1}{3}\left(1 + 2q\cos\left(\omega_m t\right)\right)$$

$$M_{Ba}(t) = \frac{1}{3}(1 + 2q\cos(\omega_m t - \frac{2\pi}{3})$$

$$M_{Ca}(t) = \frac{1}{3}\left(1 + 2q\cos\left(\omega_m t - \frac{4\pi}{3}\right)\right)$$

$$M_{Ab}(t) = \frac{1}{3}\left(1 + 2q\cos\left(\omega_m t - \frac{4\pi}{3}\right)\right)$$

$$M_{Bb}(t) = \frac{1}{3}\left(1 + 2q\cos\left(\omega_m t\right)\right)$$

$$M_{Cb}(t) = \frac{1}{3}\left(1 + 2q\cos\left(\omega_m t - \frac{4\pi}{3}\right)\right)$$

$$M_{Ac}(t) = \frac{1}{3}\left(1 + 2q\cos\left(\omega_m t - \frac{2\pi}{3}\right)\right)$$

$$M_{Bc}(t) = \frac{1}{3}\left(1 + 2q\cos\left(\omega_m t - \frac{4\pi}{3}\right)\right)$$

$$M_{Cc}(t) = \frac{1}{3}\left(1 + 2q\cos\left(\omega_m t\right)\right)$$

where $\omega_m t = \left(\omega_o t - \omega_i t\right)$ is the modulation frequency.

Hence,

$$\left[v_o(t)\right] = \left[M(t)\right]\left[v_i(t)\right] \tag{15}$$

$$\left[i_i(t)\right] = \left[M(t)\right]^T \left[i_o(t)\right] \tag{16}$$

The MC equation can be written as

$$\sum_{K=A,B,C} M_{Ka}(t) = \sum_{K=A,B,C} M_{Kb}(t) = \sum_{K=A,B,C} M_{Kc}(t) = 1 \tag{17}$$

Venturini provided two solutions for the problem one with $\omega_m = \left(\omega_o - \omega_i\right)$ and another with $\omega_m = \left(\omega_o + \omega_i\right)$ and are expressed as $\left[M_1(t)\right]$, $\left[M_1(t)\right]$, and $\left[M_2(t)\right]$ respectively as given below

$$
\left[M_1(t)\right] =
\frac{1}{3}
\begin{pmatrix}
1 + 2q\cos\left(\omega_0 t - \omega_i t\right) & 1 + 2q\cos\left(\omega_0 t - \omega_i t - \frac{2\pi}{3}\right) & 1 + 2q\cos\left(\omega_0 t - \omega_i t - \frac{2\pi}{3}\right) \\
1 + 2q\cos\left(\omega_0 t - \omega_i t - \frac{4\pi}{3}\right) & 1 + 2q\cos\left(\omega_0 t - \omega_i t - \frac{2\pi}{3}\right) & 1 + 2q\cos\left(\omega_0 t - \omega_i t - \frac{2\pi}{3}\right) \\
1 + 2q\cos\left(\omega_0 t - \omega_i t - \frac{2\pi}{3}\right) & 1 + 2q\cos\left(\omega_0 t - \omega_i t - \frac{2\pi}{3}\right) & 1 + 2q\cos\left(\omega_0 t - \omega_i t - \frac{2\pi}{3}\right)
\end{pmatrix}
\tag{18}
$$

$$
\left[M_1(t)\right] =
\frac{1}{3}
\begin{pmatrix}
1 + 2q\cos\left(\omega_0 t + \omega_i t\right) & 1 + 2q\cos\left(\omega_0 t + \omega_i t - \frac{2\pi}{3}\right) & 1 + 2q\cos\left(\omega_0 t + \omega_i t - \frac{4\pi}{3}\right) \\
1 + 2q\cos\left(\omega_0 t + \omega_i t - \frac{2\pi}{3}\right) & 1 + 2q\cos\left(\omega_0 t + \omega_i t - \frac{4\pi}{3}\right) & 1 + 2q\cos\left(\omega_0 t + \omega_i t\right) \\
1 + 2q\cos\left(\omega_0 t + \omega_i t - \frac{4\pi}{3}\right) & 1 + 2q\cos\left(\omega_0 t + \omega_i t\right) & 1 + 2q\cos\left(\omega_0 t + \omega_i t - \frac{2\pi}{3}\right)
\end{pmatrix}
\tag{19}
$$

In $M_1(t)$ the input phase displacement is equal to output phase displacement $\left(\varphi_i = \varphi_o\right)$. In $M_2(t)$ the output phase displacement is reversal of input phase displacement $\left(\varphi_o = -\varphi_i\right)$. The input displacement control can be obtained by combining $M_1(t)$ and $M_2(t)$,

$$
\left[M(t)\right] = a_1 \left[M_1(t)\right] + a_2 \left[M_2(t)\right]
\tag{20}
$$

where $a_1 + a_2 = 1$. If a_1 is equal to a_2, then the input displacement factor of the converter is equal to unity. Other choices of a_1 and a_2 will provide leading and lagging displacement factor at the input and lagging and leading output displacement factor at the output.

If $a_1 = a_2$, then the modulation function can be expressed as

$$
M_{Kk}(t) = \frac{t_{Kk}}{T_s} = \frac{1}{3}\left(1 + \frac{2v_K V_k}{V_{im}^2}\right)
\tag{21}
$$

If the target output voltage fits into the input voltage envelope for all operating frequencies, then the average output voltage will be equal to the target output voltage at each sampling sequence. Hence, the maximum value of q that can be obtained by this method is only 50%. This makes the converter impractical because of the maximum of 50% voltage transfer ratio.

The above method was improved by Venturini (Wheeler, Clare, Empringham, Bradley, Pickering, Lampard, Apap, 2002; Wheeler, Rodriguez, Clare, Empringham, & Weinstein, 2002) by adding third harmonics of input and output frequencies with the target output voltage matrix $v_o(t)$. This method is called common mode addition technique. The maximum voltage transfer ratio achieved by this method is 86.6%.

$$\left[v_o(t)\right] = qV_{im} \begin{bmatrix} \cos(\omega_o t) - \dfrac{1}{6}\cos(3\omega_o t) + \dfrac{1}{3.46}\cos(3\omega_i t) \\ \cos\left(\omega_o t + \dfrac{2\pi}{3}\right) - \dfrac{1}{6}\cos(3\omega_o t) + \dfrac{1}{3.46}\cos(3\omega_i t) \\ \cos\left(\omega_o t + \dfrac{4\pi}{3}\right) - \dfrac{1}{6}\cos(3\omega_o t) + \dfrac{1}{3.46}\cos(3\omega_i t) \end{bmatrix} \tag{22}$$

For unity displacement factor, the modulation factor becomes,

$$M_{Kk}(t) = \frac{t_{Kk}}{T_s} = \frac{1}{3}\left(1 + \frac{2v_K V_k}{V_{im}^2} + \frac{4q}{5.2}\sin(\omega_i t + \theta_K)\sin(3\omega_i t)\right) \tag{23}$$

where $\theta_K = 0, \dfrac{2\pi}{3}, \dfrac{4\pi}{3}$ and K represents the input phases A, B, C.

If the displacement factor is other than unity, then the output voltage limit will be reduced from $0.86V_{im}$ to smaller value.

In this method, independent control of each output phase is achieved and hence all the switching states of MC presented in Table 1 are possible. However, in this method, the switching combinations producing high common mode voltages cannot be avoided.

FUZZY LOGIC BASED MATRIX CONVERTER DRIVE FOR INDUCTION MOTOR

In past two decades, the growth in soft computing technologies has provided sophisticated methodology for the development of industrial process controllers. It is considered to be a state of art approach to artificial intelligence. Within the last decade, substantial growth of soft computing techniques in IM drive application has been noticed because the soft computing techniques do not require the mathematical model of the system. Soft computing techniques have been recognized as attractive alternatives to the standard, well established hard computing paradigms (Jabri, Chouiref, Jebri, & Benhadj, 2008). Soft computing techniques, in comparison with hard computation employ different methods which are capable of representing imprecise, uncertain and computation methods. Soft computing techniques are capable of handling non-linear system such as IM drives and offers computational simplicity. The major soft computation techniques applied in Industrial applications are:

Table 1. Switching combinations of matrix converter switches

No.	Switching Configuration	Converter State	Output Voltage (v_0)	Output Voltage Vector Angle (α_0)	Input Current (i_i)	Input Current Vector Angle (β_i)
1	+1	S_{abb}	$\frac{2}{3}v_{ab}$	0	$\frac{2}{\sqrt{3}}i_a$	$-\frac{\pi}{6}$
2	-1	S_{baa}	$-\frac{2}{3}v_{ab}$	0	$-\frac{2}{\sqrt{3}}i_a$	$-\frac{\pi}{6}$
3	+2	S_{bcc}	$\frac{2}{3}v_{bc}$	0	$\frac{2}{\sqrt{3}}i_a$	$\frac{\pi}{2}$
4	-2	S_{cbb}	$-\frac{2}{3}v_{bc}$	0	$-\frac{2}{\sqrt{3}}i_a$	$\frac{\pi}{2}$
5	+3	S_{caa}	$\frac{2}{3}v_{ca}$	0	$\frac{2}{\sqrt{3}}i_a$	$-7\frac{\pi}{6}$
6	-3	S_{acc}	$-\frac{2}{3}v_{ca}$	0	$-\frac{2}{\sqrt{3}}i_a$	$7\frac{\pi}{6}$
7	+4	S_{bab}	$\frac{2}{3}v_{ab}$	$\frac{2\pi}{3}$	$\frac{2}{\sqrt{3}}i_b$	$\frac{\pi}{6}$
8	-4	S_{aba}	$-\frac{2}{3}v_{ab}$	$\frac{2\pi}{3}$	$-\frac{2}{\sqrt{3}}i_b$	$-\frac{\pi}{6}$
9	+5	S_{cbc}	$\frac{2}{3}v_{bc}$	$\frac{2\pi}{3}$	$\frac{2}{\sqrt{3}}i_b$	$\frac{\pi}{2}$
10	-5	S_{bcb}	$-\frac{2}{3}v_{bc}$	$\frac{2\pi}{3}$	$-\frac{2}{\sqrt{3}}i_b$	$\frac{\pi}{2}$
11	+6	S_{aca}	$\frac{2}{3}v_{ca}$	$\frac{2\pi}{3}$	$\frac{2}{\sqrt{3}}i_b$	$7\frac{\pi}{6}$
12	-6	S_{cac}	$-\frac{2}{3}v_{ca}$	$\frac{2\pi}{3}$	$-\frac{2}{\sqrt{3}}i_b$	$7\frac{\pi}{6}$
13	+7	S_{bba}	$\frac{2}{3}v_{ab}$	$\frac{4\pi}{3}$	$\frac{2}{\sqrt{3}}i_c$	$-\frac{\pi}{6}$

continued on following page

Table 1. Continued

No.	Switching Configuration	Converter State	Output Voltage (v_0)	Output Voltage Vector Angle (α_0)	Input Current (i_I)	Input Current Vector Angle (β_I)
14	-7	S_{aab}	$-\dfrac{2}{3}v_{ab}$	$\dfrac{4\pi}{3}$	$-\dfrac{2}{\sqrt{3}}i_c$	$-\dfrac{\pi}{6}$
15	+8	S_{ccb}	$\dfrac{2}{3}v_{bc}$	$\dfrac{4\pi}{3}$	$\dfrac{2}{\sqrt{3}}i_c$	$\dfrac{\pi}{2}$
16	-8	S_{bbc}	$-\dfrac{2}{3}v_{bc}$	$\dfrac{4\pi}{3}$	$-\dfrac{2}{\sqrt{3}}i_c$	$\dfrac{\pi}{2}$
17	+9	S_{aac}	$\dfrac{2}{3}v_{ca}$	$\dfrac{4\pi}{3}$	$\dfrac{2}{\sqrt{3}}i_c$	$7\dfrac{\pi}{6}$
18	-9	S_{cca}	$-\dfrac{2}{3}v_{ca}$	$\dfrac{4\pi}{3}$	$-\dfrac{2}{\sqrt{3}}i_c$	$7\dfrac{\pi}{6}$
19	0_a	S_{aaa}	0	-	0	0
20	0_b	S_{bbb}	0	-	0	0
21	0_c	S_{ccc}	0	-	0	0
22	FR_a	S_{abc}	-	-	-	-
23	FR_b	S_{acb}	-	-	-	-
24	FR_c	S_{bca}	-	-	-	-
25	BR_a	S_{bac}	-	-	-	-
26	BR_b	S_{cab}	-	-	-	-
27	BR_c	S_{cba}	-	-	-	-

- Fuzzy logic system,
- Artificial Neural Network,
- Genetic Algorithm Based system,
- Fuzzy-Neural Network.

Fuzzy logic can be used for modelling non-linear, unknown or partially known controllers. It emulates human reasoning providing an intuitive way to design a functional block for a control system. ANN is an information processing system and consists of number of highly interconnected neurons. The neurons behave like their biological pattern, neural cell in brain. ANN is based on learning process (Cardoson, Martinis, & Pires, 1998). The learning process changes the synaptic weight of each interconnection in the network and updates it until the target error is reached. Genetic Algorithm is a search heuristic that mimics the process of natural evolution. The Fuzzy- Neural Network (FNN) approach incorporates the fuzzy logic controller into the neural network structure. Neural Network provides the connectionist structure and learning ability to fuzzy controller (Rahul, Narinder, & Yaduvir, 2011; Arunkumar, Prabhakar & Xinliang, 2014 ; Arunkumar, Jagadeesh, Anirban, & Prabhakar, 2015; Filipek,, 2001; Gama, & Romero, 2004; Vas, & Stronach, 1996). In this chapter, the implementation of fuzzy logic control in selecting the switching state of DMC and speed control of induction motor is discussed.

Fuzzy logic system is based on the theory of fuzzy sets and uses linguistic variables. The inputs are transformed into fuzzy sets using membership functions and this process is called fuzzification. The fuzzified inputs are then processed by a set of fuzzy rules to produce the output and this is called Fuzzy Inference System (FIS). There are two FIS systems available namely:

1. Mamdani FIS, and
2. Sugeno FIS Bose, (2000).

At the output level, Mamdani system uses distributed fuzzy set and Sugeno system uses constant or linear output membership functions Chitra, (2013).

The inputs to the fuzzy controller are error and change error values. The controller observes the pattern of these two input signals and generates corresponding output signal using fuzzy inference system. The fuzzified inputs and output are usually handled in per unit (pu) form by using respective scale factors. The output signal is then integrated to generate the actual control signal.

DESIGN OF FUZZY LOGIC CONTROLLER

The design of fuzzy controller involves design of membership functions for input and output variables. The fuzzy rules are designed based on the observed performance of the converter using switching vector look up table method. There are 3 Fuzzy Controllers (FC) implemented in field oriented control system to select the proper switching combination according to the reference speed input. The field oriented control system requires two reference inputs such as speed and flux. The first input to the FC1 is error between reference flux and motor flux and the second input is change in error. The output which is governed by the set fuzzy rules is phase current value (ie). In FC2, the first input is error between reference speed and motor speed and the second input is change in error. The output of FC2 is phase voltage (ve). The

Figure 6. Voltage sector selection

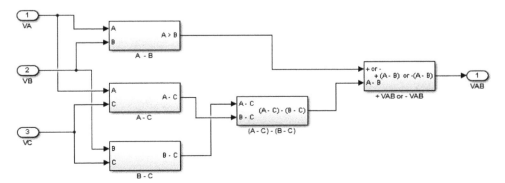

third FC3 selects the switching vector for the matrix converter. The inputs to FC3 are error in the phase current value (ie), error in phase voltage value (ve) and the switching sector (d). The error in the phase current value (ie) is calculated by comparing the input current with the stator current. The error in phase voltage (ve) is calculated by comparing the output voltage with the reference voltage. The switching sector is calculated from output voltage vector, input current vector and input phase displacement angle. The defuzzification method used is centre of output area method.

The inputs to the fuzzy logic controllers are voltage sectors of Vo, current vector β_i and voltage vector angle α_o. To calculate the current and voltage vectors, the three phase input current or voltage is transformed into V_o, β_i, α_o and displacement reference angle φ_i components using Clarke transformation. The input voltage vector v_i is calculated from $\beta_i = \alpha_i - \varphi_i$. The estimation of the voltage sector is shown in Figure 6.

The membership function of the fuzzy speed controller FC1 are shown in Figure 7, 8 and 9 respectively. The fuzzy rules table and the surface view of the rules are shown in Table 2 and Figure 10 respectively

The fuzzy current controllers are designed and their membership functions and fuzzy rules are derived accordingly. The general block diagram of fuzzy based matrix converter drive for induction motor load is shown in Figure 11.

Figure 7. Membership function of fuzzy speed error

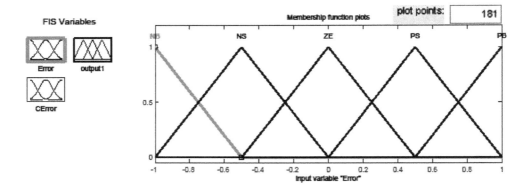

Figure 8. Membership function of change in speed error

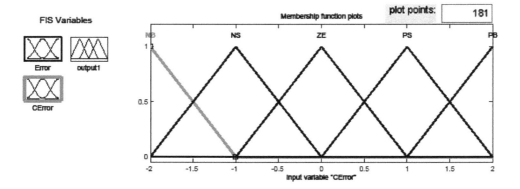

Table 2. Fuzzy speed controller rules

	NB	NS	ZE	PS	PB
NB	NB	NS	NS	NS	ZE
NS	NB	NS	NS	ZE	PS
ZE	NB	NS	ZE	PS	PB
PS	NS	ZE	PS	PS	PB
PB	ZE	PS	PB	PB	PB

Figure 9. Membership function of output variable

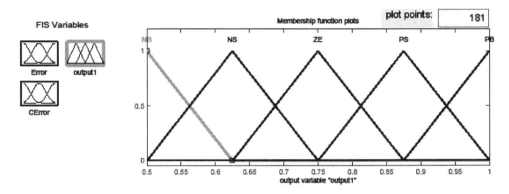

Figure 10. Surface view of the rules

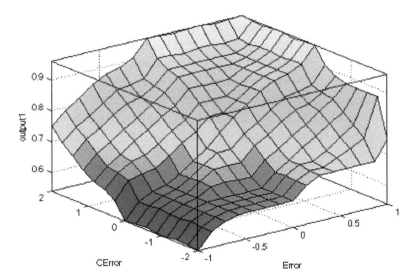

Figure 11. General block diagram of fuzzy controlled matrix converter drive

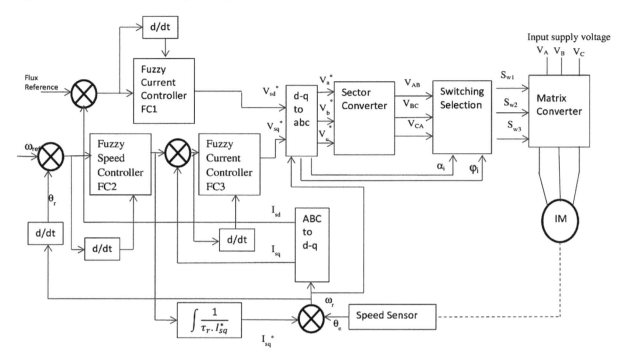

The generalized fuzzy controlled matrix converter drive for induction motor is simulated in Matlab/ Simulink. Several researchers have identified direct torque control and field oriented control as effective vector control methods to drive AC motors in traction drives compared to scalar methods. These methods have advantages of decoupling torque and flux resulting in the ease of stator current control. The advantages of field oriented control methods are good output response with reduced torque ripples and accurate speed control. Though the direct torque control method is less sensitive to motor parameters and needs no current controllers, the current and toque distortions will be high. Also, in direct torque control method, switching frequency changes with the motor speed, load and bandwidth of flux changes. The simulation model of the closed loop systems, fuzzy controllers in closed loop system and the design of matrix converter switches are shown Figure 12, 13 and 14 respectively.

RESULTS AND DISCUSSIONS

The performance of matrix converter drive and the induction motor load is shown in Figure 15 to 18. The Figure 16 and 17 shows that the input and output voltages of the matrix converter is maintained sinusoidal. The magnitude of the output obtained the matrix converter is 410V which is only 51.25% of the input. This mainly due to the data conversion involved in selecting the switching sequence. In Venturini algorithm the voltage conversion ratio is 86.7%. With the application of fuzzy controller, the initially high overshoot in the motor speed is restricted as shown in Figure 18. The difference between the initial speed and the motor running speed is reduced to avoid damage to the motor whereas; the initial high torque is still maintained high. Since fuzzy logic does not use any training algorithm, the initial

Figure 12. Simulation model of matrix converter drive for induction motor

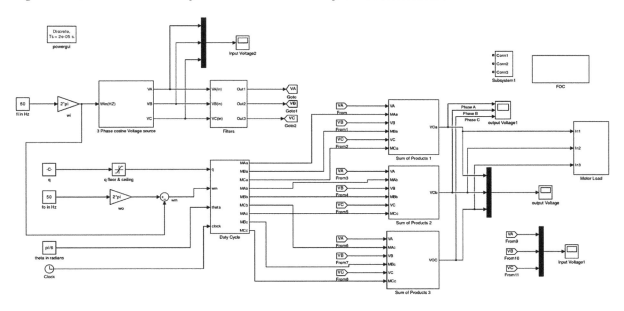

Figure 13. Simulation model of fuzzy controller in selecting the voltage and current vectors

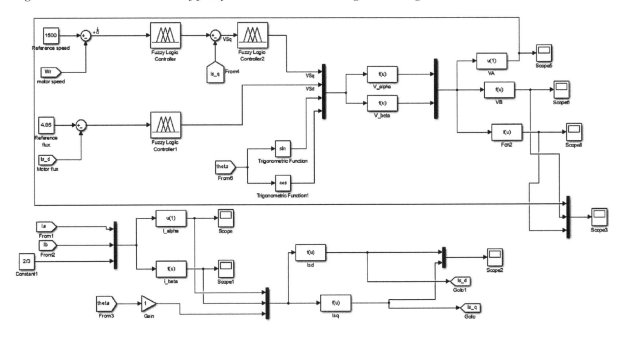

Figure 14. Design of matrix converter switches

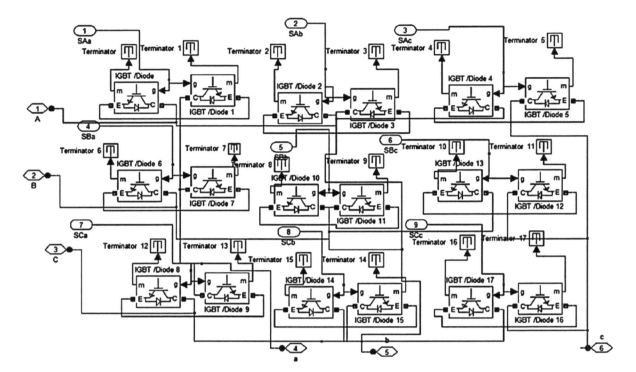

high torque oscillations cannot be avoided. Since the initial torque is high, the initial current drawn by the motor is also high as shown in Figure 19. The fuzzy logic controllers helps to maintain the stator current sinusoidal. Hence the stator current harmonics are reduced considerably thereby reducing the motor losses.

FUTURE RESEARCH

Fuzzy logic is well suited for dealing with ill-defined and uncertain systems. In fuzzy interface system, the fuzzy if-then rules resembles human like thinking. The fuzzy control system does not require any quantitative analysis but it requires the details about number of inputs and outputs to design membership functions and their shapes and the knowledge about how the inputs are processed to produce the required output to design fuzzy rules. The ANN network can be used to model large classes of non-linear structures by using learning procedure. But the learning procedure is very long and it reduces the accuracy of the output in the online process control system. The ANFIS is one of the inference systems where the advantages of fuzzy logic and artificial neural network are combined.

Using the prior knowledge about the output of the system, artificial neural network can be trained online or offline learning process. It uses the training data to build the fuzzy system in which the membership functions are adjusted using the back propagation algorithm. The accuracy of the system depends on the training set data. The ANFIS structure uses Sugeno fuzzy inference system because of

Figure 15. Input voltage to matrix converter after input filter

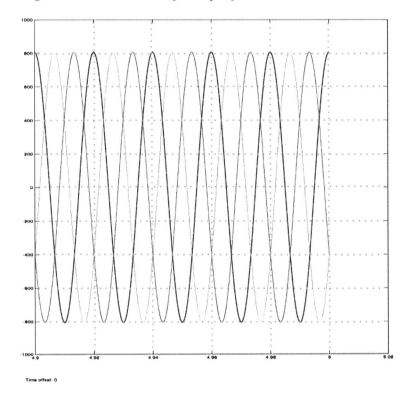

Figure 16. Output voltage from matrix converter to induction motor

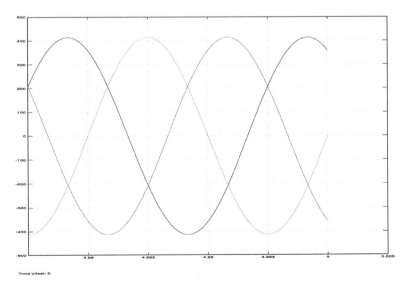

Figure 17. Speed and torque curve of induction motor

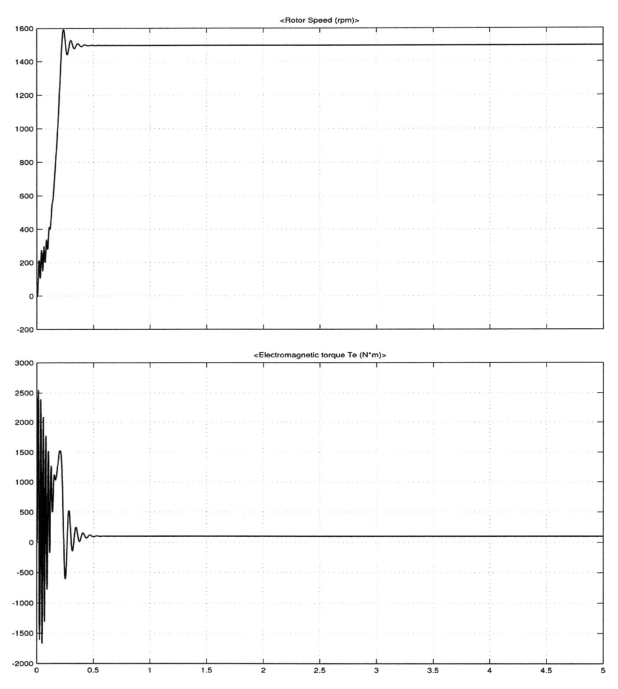

Time offset: 0

Figure 18. Stator current of induction motor

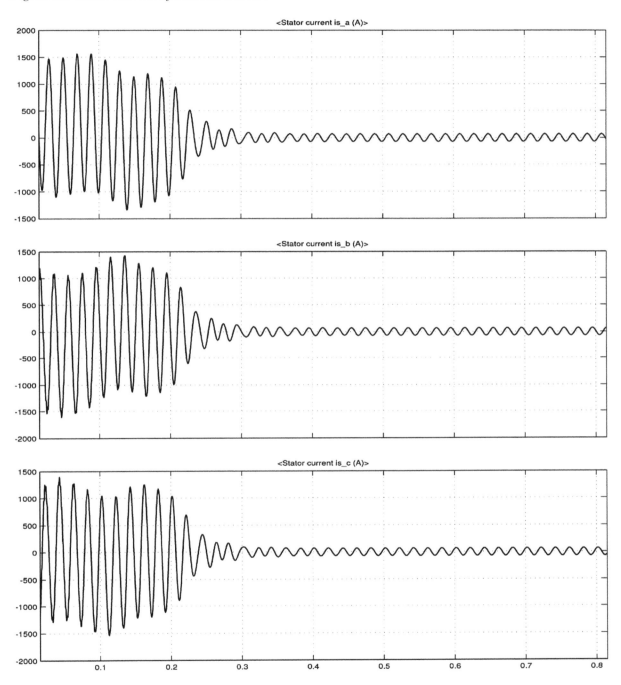

Time offset: 0

its constant or linear membership function at the output level and also it is computationally efficient than the Mamdani method.

The ANFIS controller can be used to select the switching states for Matrix Converter. The inputs to the ANFIS controller are flux error and speed error. The output of the ANFIS controller generates Vsd and Vsq voltages. These voltages are converted into three phase voltages and fed as reference voltages into the matrix converter. Using the algorithm described in section II, required duty cycle can be calculated. The switches will be turned on and off according to the duty cycle and hence the frequency and amplitude of output voltage can be altered to achieve the reference speed.

CONCLUSION

Induction motors are commonly used in industrial applications such as ship propulsion, canty train applications and aircraft application. It is important to implement an efficient power converter circuit to drive the motor at the required speed. The application of fuzzy logic technique in selecting the switch state for matrix converter proves to be efficient in controlling the motor parameters within the safe range. The speed and torque response time of the fuzzy system is improved with no overshoot. The presence of harmonics in stator current is reduced and hence the efficiency of the induction motor drive system is improved. The major drawback of fuzzy controller in this operation is that it more sensitive to the load or input changes. The FC1 governs the changes in flux and produces corresponding phase current (ie) is driven by the calculated motor flux value. The changes in motor flux result in high torque oscillations due to the response of FC1. The fluctuations in torque oscillation and hence the rotor flux can be eliminated by incorporating an ANN controller which operates based on the supervised learning system.

REFERENCES

Ahmed, A. N., Ghoni, R., & Zakaria, N. F. (2011). Simulation Model of Space Vector Modulated Control of Matrix Converter fed Induction Motor. *Journal of Applied Science*, *11*(5), 768–777. doi:10.3923/jas.2011.768.777

Alesina, A., & Venturini, A. (1989). Analysis and Design of Optimum-Amplitude Nine Switch Direct AC – AC Converters. *IEEE Transactions on Power Electronics*, *4*(1), 101–112. doi:10.1109/63.21879

Arunkumar, S., Jagadeesh, G., Anirban, B., & Prabhakar, R. S. (2015). An Integrated Fuzzy DEMATEL, TOPSIS, and ELECTRE Approach for Evaluating Knowledge Transfer Effectiveness with Reference to GSD project Outcome. *Neural Computing & Applications*, 1–13.

Arunkumar, S., Prabhakar, R. S., & Xinliang, Z. (2014). A Combined Fuzzy DEMATEL and Fuzzy TOPSIS Approach for Evaluating GSD Project Outcome Factors. *Neural Computing & Applications*, *26*(5), 1025–1040.

Barton, T. H. (1994). *Rectifiers, Cycloconverter and AC Controllers*. Oxford University Press.

Blaabjerg, F., Casadei, D., Klumpner, D., & Matteeini, M. (2002). Comparison of Two Current Modulation Strategies for Matrix Converters under Unbalanced Input Voltage Conditions. *IEEE Transactions on Industrial Electronics*, *49*(2), 282–296. doi:10.1109/41.993261

Bogalecka, E., & Erzeminski, Z. (1993). Control Systems of Doubly fed Induction Machines Supplied by Current Controlled Voltage Source Inverters).*Sixth International Conference on Electrical Machines and Drives.*

Bose, B. (2000). Fuzzy Logic and Neural Networks in Power Electronics and Drives. *IEEE Industry Applications Magazine*, *6*(3), 57–63. doi:10.1109/2943.838042

Cardoson, F., Martinis, J. F., & Pires, V. F. (1998). Comparative Study of a PI, Neural Network and Fuzzy Genetic Approach Controllers for an AC Drive.*5th International Workshop in Advanced Motion Control.*

Chitra, V. (2013). *Design of Soft Computing Technique Based Controllers in Closed Loop System for Matrix Converter and Speed Control of Induction Motor.* (Ph.D. Thesis). SASTRA University.

Clare, J. C., & Wheeler, P. W. (2003). *Introduction to Matrix Converter Topology.* Seminar on Matrix Converters.

Daniels, A., & Slattery, D. (1978). New Power Converter Technique Employing Power Transistors. *Proceedings of the Institution of Electrical Engineers*, *125*(7), 146–150. doi:10.1049/piee.1978.0038

Daniels, A., & Slattery, D. (1978). Application of Power Transistors to Polyphase Regenerative Power Converters. *Proceedings of the Institution of Electrical Engineers*, *125*(7), 643–647. doi:10.1049/piee.1978.0153

Filipek, P. (2001). *Neuro-Fuzzy Control of Inverter-Fed Induction Motor Drive.* (Ph.D Thesis). Lublin University of Technology.

Gama, V., & Romero, D. (2004). Improvement of an Induction Motor Drive – Based Direct Torque Control Strategy Using a Neuro – Fuzzy Controller. *International Conference on Electrical and Electronics Engineering.*

Gyugi, L., & Pelly, B. R. (1970). *Static Power Frequency Changers: Theory, Performance and Application.* John Wiley & Sons.

Huber, L., & Borojevic, D. (1985). Space Vector modulator for force commutated cycloconverter structures. *IEEE Transactions on Industry Applications*, *1A*(5), 1242–1253.

Huber, L., & Borojevic, D. (1995). Space Vector Modulated Three Phase to Three Phase Matrix Converter with Input Power Factor Correction. *IEEE Transactions on Industry Applications*, *36*(6), 1234–1246. doi:10.1109/28.475693

Jabri, M., Chouiref, H., Jebri, H., & Benhadj, B. (2008). Fuzzy Logic Parameter Estimation of an Electrical System, *IEEE International Multi-conference on Systems. Signals and Devices*, *10*, 1–6.

Jones, V., & Bose, B. (1976). A frequency step-up cycloconverter using power transistors in inverse series mode. *International Journal of Electronics*, *41*(6), 573–587. doi:10.1080/00207217608920668

Jussila, M., Salo, M., & Tuusa, H. (2004). Induction Motor Drive fed by a Vector Controlled Indirect Matrix Converter.*Conference Proceedings of IEEE Power Electronics Specialists Conference.*

Klumpner, C. (2005). An Indirect Matrix Converter with a Cost Effective Protection and Control, *European Conference on Power Electronics and Applications.* doi:10.1109/EPE.2005.219558

Masoud Barakati, S. (2008). *Modelling and Controller design of a Wind Energy Conversion System including a Matrix Converter.* (Ph.D thesis). University of Waterloo.

Rahul, M., Narinder, S., & Yaduvir, S. (2011). Soft Computing Technique for Process Control Applications. *International Journal of Soft Computing, 2*(3), 32–38. doi:10.5121/ijsc.2011.2303

Siyoung, K., Seung, K., & Thomas, A. (2000). AC/AC Power Conversion Based on Matrix Converter Topology with Unidirectional Switches). *IEEE Transactions on Industry Applications, 36*(1), 139–145. doi:10.1109/28.821808

Takeshita, T., & Andou, Y. (2010). PWM Control of Three Phase to Three Phase Matrix Converters for Reducing the Number of Commutations. *Electrical Engineering in Japan, 2*, 66–69.

Vas, P., & Stronach, A. F. (1996). Adaptive fuzzy – neural DSP Control of High Performance Drives. *International Conference on Power Electronics and Variable Speed Drives.* doi:10.1049/cp:19960952

Wheeler, P. W., Clare, J. C., Empringham, L., Bradley, K. L., Pickering, S., Lampard, D., & Apap, A. (2002). A fully integrated 30kw motor driving using matrix converter technology. *IEEE Transactions on Industrial Electronics*, 2390–2395.

Wheeler, P. W., Rodriguez, J., Clare, J. C., Empringham, L., & Weinstein, A. (2002). Matrix Converters: A technology review.*IEEE Transactions on Industrial Electronics, 49*(2), 276–288. doi:10.1109/41.993260

KEY TERMS AND DEFINITIONS

Cycloconverter: A single stage power converter designed in early 1930. The maximum output frequency produced is less than the input frequency.

Direct Matrix Converter: A single stage AC to AC power converter. It uses 9 bidirectional switches to produce variable voltage variable frequency AC output from a constant voltage constant frequency.

Fuzzy Logic Technique: Based on the theory of fuzzy sets and uses linguistic variable to emulate human reasoning providing an intuitive way to design a functional block for a control system.

Indirect Matrix Converter: A two stage power converter without DC storage link. The complexity in modulation is reduced. However, more number of semiconductor devices are required in the current path to transfer input to output.

Induction Motor: Stator windings induce the current flow in the rotor winding by electromagnetic induction to produce the required rotor torque.

Soft Computing Techniques: An optimization technique which does not require the mathematical model of the system and is capable of handling non-linear systems such as induction motor drives and offers computational simplicity.

Switching State: The turn on and turn off of a switch with an application of external voltage across its control terminals at the desired switching sequence.

Voltage Source Converter: It can generate variable voltage variable frequency AC output from a constant voltage constant frequency AC input by two stage conversion process.

Chapter 11
Bio–Inspired Computing through Artificial Neural Network

Nilamadhab Dash
C. V. Raman College of Engineering, India

Brojo Kishore Mishra
C. V. Raman College of Engineering, India

Rojalina Priyadarshini
C. V. Raman College of Engineering, India

Rachita Misra
C. V. Raman College of Engineering, India

ABSTRACT

Developing suitable mathematical or algorithmic model to solve real life complex problems is one of the major challenges faced by the researchers especially those involved in the computer science field. To a large extent Computational intelligence has been found to be effective in designing such models. Bio inspired computing is the technique which makes the machines intelligent by adapting the behavior and methods exhibited by the human beings and other living organisms while forming intelligent systems. These intelligent models include the intelligent techniques such as Artificial Neural Network (ANN), evolutionary computation, swarm intelligence, fuzzy system, artificial immune system accompanied by fuzzy logic, expert system, deductive reasoning. All these together form the area of Bio inspired computing. The chapter deals with various bio inspired technique, giving emphasis on issues, development, advances and practical implementations of ANN.

INTRODUCTION

Bio inspired computing (also biologically inspired computing or bio computing) is a field of computing that deals with the subfields related to the topics of connectionism, social behavior, and emergence. It closely related to the field of artificial intelligence, as many of its pursuits can be linked to machine learning. It relies heavily on the fields of biology, computer science, and mathematics. Biologically inspired computing is an important subset of natural computation. The concept of bio computing has a twofold definition: the use of biology or biological processes as metaphor, inspiration, or enabler in developing new computing technologies and new areas of computer science; and conversely, the use of information

DOI: 10.4018/978-1-5225-1008-6.ch011

science concepts and tools to explore biology from a different theoretical perspective. In addition to its potential applications, such as DNA computation, nanofabrication, storage devices, sensing, and health care, bio inspired computing also has implications for basic scientific research. It can provide biologists, for example, with an IT-oriented paradigm for looking at how cells compute or process information, or help computer scientists construct algorithms based on natural systems, such as evolutionary and genetic algorithms. Bio computing has the potential to be a very powerful tool. It is well understood that the computational complexity of real-world problems is too high to be handled by the conventional approaches. Some of the popular conventional methods that have been widely used are mathematical optimization algorithms (such as Newton's method and gradient descent method that use derivatives to locate a local minimum), direct search methods (such as the simplex method and the Nelder–Mead method that use a search pattern to locate optima), enumerative approaches such as dynamic programming (DP), etc. Each of these techniques in general depends on several assumptions about the problem in order to suit a particular method, and may not be flexible enough to adapt the algorithm to solve a particular problem as it is, and may obstruct the possibility of modeling the problem closer to reality (S.Haykin, 1994). Many science and engineering problems generally involve nonlinear relationships in their representation; so linear programming (LP) may not be a suitable approach to solve most of the complex practical problems. The gradient-based nonlinear programming methods can solve problems with smooth nonlinear objectives and constraints. However, in large and extremely nonlinear environment, these techniques may fail to find appropriate solutions, or converging to suboptimal solutions depending upon the degree of nonlinearity and initial assumptions. Also, the conventional nonlinear optimization solvers are not applicable for problems with non-differentiable and/or discontinuous functional relationships. The efficiency of algorithms varies depending on the complexity of the problem. Thus, for one reason or the other, conventional methods have several limitations and may not be suitable for a broad range of practical problems. To address these problems, in recent times stochastic search and optimization algorithms inspired by nature and biological processes have been proposed and applied in various fields of science and engineering. This proposed book chapter will mainly focus on the practical applications of artificial neural network in order to address different types of problems.

BACKGROUND

The ideas from natural and biological activities have provoked the progress of many sophisticated algorithms. These algorithms are broadly categorized as evolutionary computation and swarm intelligence (SI) algorithms. Evolutionary computation is a term used to describe algorithms which were inspired by 'survival of the fittest' or 'natural selection' principles (McCulloch et al., 1943), whereas 'swarm intelligence' refers to the algorithms and distributed problems-solvers which are inspired by the cumulative intelligence of swarm or combined behavior of insect and other animal societies. This section tries to provide a brief idea about some of the contemporary algorithms in the field of bio inspired computing.

Evolutionary Algorithms

Evolutionary algorithms are probabilistic search methods that imitate the metaphor of natural biological evolution. Evolutionary algorithms operate on a population of potential solutions applying the principle of survival of the fittest to generate superior approximations to a solution. At each generation, a new set of approximations is created by the process of selecting individuals according to their level of fitness in the problem domain and breeding them together using natural genetic operators. This process leads to the evolution of populations of individuals that are better suited to their environment than the individuals that they were created from, just as in natural adaptation.

Genetic Algorithm

Genetic Algorithms (GAs) are adaptive heuristic search algorithm based on the evolutionary ideas of natural selection and genetics. As such they represent a smart exploitation of a random search used to solve optimization problems (Winter et al. (1995)). Although randomized, GAs are by no means random, instead they exploit historical information to direct the search into the region of better performance within the search space. The basic techniques of the GAs are designed to simulate processes in natural systems necessary for evolution especially those follow the principles first laid down by Charles Darwin of "survival of the fittest" (Mitchell (1996)). Since in nature, competition among individuals for scanty resources results in the fittest individuals dominating over the weaker ones. GAs simulate the survival of the fittest among individuals over consecutive generation for solving a problem. Each generation consists of a population of character strings that are analogous to the chromosome that we see in our DNA. Each individual represents a point in a search space and a possible solution. The individuals in the population are then made to go through a process of evolution. GA is based on an analogy with the genetic structure and behavior of chromosomes within a population of individuals using the following foundations:

- Individuals in a population compete for resources and mates.
- Those individuals most successful in each 'competition' will produce more offspring than those individuals that perform poorly.
- Genes from 'good' individuals propagate throughout the population so that two good parents will sometimes produce offspring that are better than either parent.
- Thus each successive generation will become more suited to their environment (Gregory J.E. Rawlins. (1991))

The main steps involved in GA are:

- Initialize population using random generation.
- Evaluate the fitness of each individual in the population.
- Repeat the following steps (for evolution) until the termination criteria are satisfied.
- Select the best-fit individuals for reproduction.
- Perform genetic operations, crossover and mutation to generate new offspring.
- Evaluate the individual fitness of new members.
- Replace the least fit individuals with new individuals.
- Report the most excellent solution of the fittest individual.

Genetic Programming (GP)

GP is an inductive automatic programming technique for evolving computer programs to solve problems (Koza, 1992). The objective of the GP algorithm is to use induction to devise a computer program. This is achieved by using evolutionary operators on candidate programs with a tree structure to improve the adaptive fit between the population of candidate programs and an objective function. The GP is well suited to symbolic regression, controller design, and machine-learning tasks under the broader name of function approximation. In GP, a population is progressively improved by selectively discarding the not-so-fit population and breeding new children from better populations. Like other EAs, the GP solution starts with a random population of individuals (equations or computer programs). Each possible solution set can be visualized as a 'parse tree' comprising the terminal set (input variables) and functions (generally operators such as +, −, *, /, logarithmic or trigonometric).

Differential Evolution (DE)

DE is a modern optimization technique in the family of EAs introduced by Storn and Price (1995). It was proposed as a variant of EAs to attain the goals of robustness in optimization and faster convergence to a given problem. DE algorithm differs from other EAs in the mutation and recombination phases. Unlike GAs, where perturbation occurs in accordance with a random quantity, DE uses weighted differences between solution vectors to perturb the population. A typical DE works as follows: after random initialization of the population (where the members are randomly generated to cover the entire search space uniformly), the objective functions are evaluated and the following steps are repeated until a termination condition is satisfied. At each generation, two operators, namely mutation and crossover are applied on each individual to produce a new population. In DE, mutation is the main operator, where each individual is updated using a weighted difference of a number of selected parent solutions; and crossover acts as background operator where crossover is performed on each of the decision variables with small probability. The offspring replaces the parent only if it improves the fitness value; otherwise the parent is carried over to the new population.

Swarm Intelligence

Swarm intelligence is a discipline which deals with natural and artificial systems consisting of many individual constituents which synchronize among themselves using decentralized control and self-organization (Blum & Merkle, 2008). This discipline focuses on the collective behaviour of individual members with local interactions of the members mutually with each other and also with their environment. Examples of systems studied by swarm intelligence are colonies of ants and termites, schools of fish, flocks of birds, herds of land animals.

A swarm is a cluster of similar type of, simple agents which share information among themselves locally, and to their environment. They are not managed centrally. Swarm-based algorithms have recently come forwarded as a new class of nature-inspired, population-based algorithms that have a power of providing low cost, fast, and robust solutions to many of the complex real life problems. Swarm Intelligence (SI) can be defined as a relatively new branch of Artificial Intelligence that is used to model the collective behaviour of social swarms in nature, such as ant colonies, honey bees, and bird flocks. Although these agents (insects or swarm individuals) are having limited capabilities on their own, they are interacting together with certain behavioural patterns to cooperatively achieve the goal towards the tasks necessary for their survival (Belal et al., 2006; Dorigo et al., 2000). There can be direct or indirect social interactions among swarm objects. The pheromone trail secretion can be taken as the example of indirect contact where on a change by the individual in the present environment, other objects respond to this. The indirect interaction which involves the environment is referred to as stigmergy, means communication with the help of the environment.

Characteristics of a Swarm Intelligence System

The swarm intelligence system posses the following characteristics:

- It is poised of multiple number of individual objects, each called as an agent or a particle;
- The individuals or particles or agents are relatively homogeneous (i.e., they are either all identical or they belong to a particular and specific category);
- The rules through which the interactions among the individuals happens are based on local information that the individuals exchange either directly or indirectly through the surroundings (stigmergy);
- The interactions of individuals with each other and with their environment is represented as the overall collective behaviour or group behaviour of the system results from their interaction, which is termed as, the group behaviour self-organizes. (Dorigo, 1992; Karaboga, 2005; Karaboga & Basturk, 2007)

The characterizing property of a swarm intelligence system is its capability to act in a synchronized way without having a central coordinator or an external regulator. Many examples can be found in nature of swarms that perform some collective behaviour without any individual leader controlling the group, or being aware of the overall group behaviour. In spite of the lack of individuals in charge of the group, the swarm as a whole can show a sensible behaviour. This is the outcome of the edge of spatially neighbouring individuals that act on the basis of simple rules. The behaviour of a single ant, bee, termite and wasp is found to be as far simple as it can be, but their collective and social behaviour is having substantial dominant significance. The collective and social behaviour of living creatures encouraged researchers to start the study of swarm intelligence (Lim, Jain, & Dehuri, 2009). If we go to history, the phrase Swarm Intelligence (SI) was coined by Beny and Wang in late 1980s (Couzin, Krause, Ruxton & Franks, 2002) in the context of cellular robotics. A group of researchers in different segments of the world carried out working at the same time to study the flexible behaviour of different living creatures. SI systems are typically built upon the behaviour of a population of simple agents (an entity capable of performing/executing certain operations) interacting locally with one another and with their surroundings. Inspite of having no centralized control to guard how individual agents should behave, they are controlled globally by local interactions between themselves which lead to the emergence of global behavior (Das et al., 2009). These examples are found in our surrounding such as fish-schools and bird flocks who clearly display structural order, their behaviour is so integrated that even though they may change shape and direction, they come into sight to move as a single coherent entity (Panigrahi, Shi, & Lim, 2011). The main properties of the collective behaviour can be given below and is illustrated in Figure 4

- **Homogeneity:** Every bird in flock has the same behavioural model. Without any specific leader flock moves, even though momentary leaders seem to emerge.
- **Locality:** Its nearest flock-mates are only influenced by the motion of each bird. Vision is considered to be the most important senses for flock organization.
- **Collision Avoidance:** They avoid colliding with nearby flock mates.

- **Velocity Matching:** They try to match with the velocity of nearby flock mates.
- **Flock Centering:** All of them in the cluster attempt to reside in close proximity with the nearby flock mates. Each of them attempts to maintain a minimum distance between them sat all times. Highest priority is given to this rule which in turn corresponds to a frequently observed behavior of animals in nature. Individual performs equally to avoid themselves from being isolated they tend to be attracted towards other individuals and try to align themselves with neighbors (Couzin et.al, 2002) identified four collective dynamical behaviors as illustrated in Figure 1.
- **Swarm:** An aggregate with cohesion, but a low level of polarization (parallel alignment) among members.
- **Torus:** Individuals perpetually rotate around an empty core (milling). The direction of rotation is random.
- **Dynamic Parallel Group:** The individuals are polarized and move as a coherent group, but individuals can move throughout the group and density and group form can fluctuate.
- **Highly Parallel Group:** Much more static in terms of exchange of spatial positions within the group than the dynamic parallel group and the variation in density and form is minimal (Homik et al., 1994).

A swarm can be viewed as a group of agents cooperating to achieve some purposeful behaviour and achieve some common goal. This collective intelligence appears to come out from large groups. The SI algorithms are mainly stochastic search and optimization techniques, which are followed by the principles of collective behaviour and self organization of insect swarms. They are efficient, adaptive and robust search methods producing near optimal solutions and have a large amount of implicit parallelism.

Figure 1. Different models of collective behaviour
Adapted from 34.

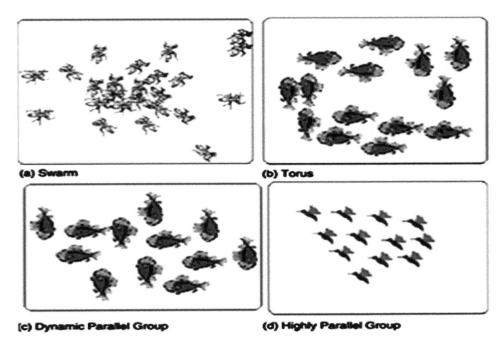

(a) Swarm

(b) Torus

(c) Dynamic Parallel Group

(d) Highly Parallel Group

Coincidentally many jobs in bioinformatics entail optimization of different parameters (like energy, alignment score, overlap strength and so on. For finding the solutions of bioinformatics problems always we go for some in-exact but robust, fast and nearly optimal solutions, for which SI based PSO algorithm are suitable (Engelbrecht, 2002).

MAIN FOCUS OF THE CHAPTER

In recent time computational algorithms inspired by biological processes and evolution are gaining much popularity for solving science and engineering problems. Computational algorithms are broadly classified into two types such as derivative based and derivative free as per their learning strategies. These include genetic algorithms, genetic programming, differential evolution, particle swarm optimization, ant colony optimization, artificial neural networks, etc. The algorithms being random-search techniques use some heuristics to guide the search towards optimal solution and speed-up the convergence to obtain the global optimal solution. The bio-inspired methods have several attractive features and advantages compared to conventional optimization techniques. These techniques also facilitate the advantage of simulation and optimization environment simultaneously to solve hard-to-define (in simple expressions), real-world problems. These biologically inspired methods have provided novel ways of problem-solving for practical problems in traffic routing, networking, games, industry, robotics, data mining, economics, mechanical, chemical, electrical, civil, water resources and others fields.

In this chapter we discuss various aspects and variations of neural network and its applications in data classification and prediction problems underlying in the area of data mining.

Artificial Neural Networks

The idea of Artificial Neural Network is basically inspired from biology where neural network inside the biological brain plays a vital role. The neural network controls almost all activities of a human body. Neural Network is a highly inter connected networks of huge number neurons. The interconnected neurons help perform all the parallel processing in a human body.

Figure 2. Neural network in human body

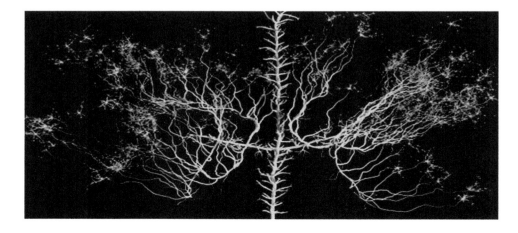

A neuron is a special biological cell that processes information and transmits it from one neuron to another neuron with the help of some electrical signal. It comprises of a cell body or soma and two types of branches: the axon and the dendrites. The cell body has a nucleus that contains information about hereditary traits and plasma that holds the molecular equipments or producing material needed by the neurons. A neuron receives signals from other neuron through dendrites. The Neuron send signals in the form of spikes of electrical activity through a long thin strand known as an axon and an axon splits this signals through synapse and send it to the other neurons (Arbib, 1996; Haykin, 1994).

Artificial Neural Networks (ANN) has been developed as generalizations of mathematical models of biological nervous systems. A first wave of interest in neural networks (also known as connectionist models or parallel distributed processing) emerged after the introduction of simplified neurons by Mc-Culloch and Pitts (1943.)

An Artificial Neuron basically mimics a biological neuron. It has the capability of accepting many inputs and producing a single output. ANN consists of large number of simple processing elements that are interconnected with each other and layered also.

Artificial Neural Network have neurons which are artificial and they also receive inputs from the other elements or other artificial neurons and then after the inputs are weighted and added, the result is then transformed by a transfer function into the output. The transfer function may be anything like Sigmoid, hyperbolic tangent functions or a step (Abraham, 2004).

Figure 3. Neural network components

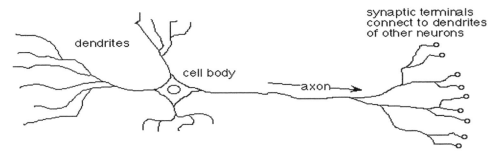

Figure 4. Artificial neuron

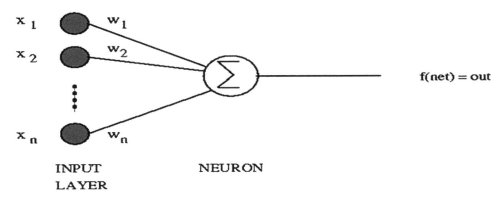

Advantages of ANN

The long evolution has given many best and excellent characteristics to brain of human being which are not present in modern computers which are given in the below list (Ivancevic & Ivancevic, 2007)

- Massive Parallelism,
- Distributed representation and computation,
- Adaptability,
- Learning Ability,
- Generalization Ability,
- Inherent Contextual Information Processing,
- Fault Tolerance,
- Low Energy Consumption.

Comparison between Modern Computers and Artificial Neural System

The Modern Computers:

- Contain one or few Processors which are high speed but complex.
- Having Localized Memory separate from processor.
- Computing is done with stored programs in a sequential and centralized manner.
- In terms of reliability it is very vulnerable.
- The Operating Environment is well defined and well constrained.

The artificial neural system:

- Contains a large number of processor which have low speed but simple in structure.
- Having Distributed Memory but integrated into processor.
- Computing is done with self learning in a parallel and distributed manner.
- In terms of reliability it is robust.
- The operating environment is poorly defined and unconstrained(R. Rojas, 1996)

ANN Characteristics

There are six characteristics of Artificial Neural Network which are necessary important for the effectiveness of the ANN . The characteristics are shown in Figure 5

The Network Structure

The Network Structure of ANN should be simple. There are basically two types of structures of a neural network i.e. recurrent and non recurrent structure. The Recurrent Structure is also known as Auto associative or Feedback Network and the Non Recurrent Structure is referred to as Associative or Feed forward Network.

Figure 5. Functions of an artificial neuron

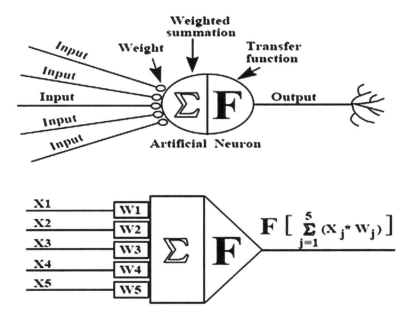

Figure 6. Characteristics of ANN

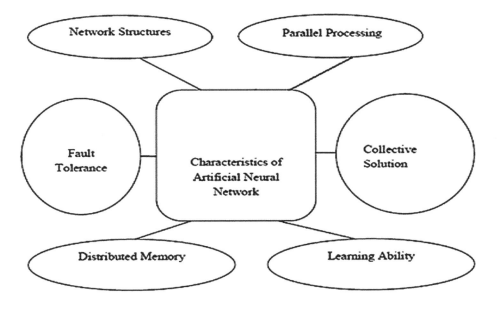

In Feed forward Network, the signal travels in one way only but in Feedback Network, signal can travel in both the directions by introducing loops in the network. The Figures are given below which shows the direction of signals in both the network structures. Vidushi Sharma, Sachin Rai, Anurag Dev "A Comprehensive Study of Artificial Neural Networks", India (Sharma et al., 2012).

Figure 7. ANN characteristics

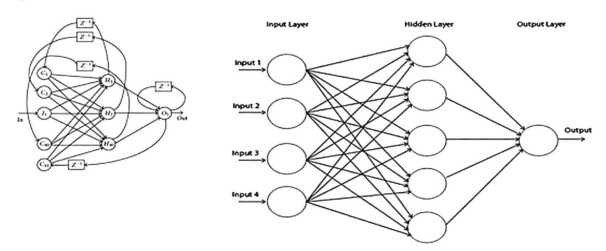

Parallel Processing Ability

ANN is introduced to facilitate the concept of parallel processing in the field of computation. The interconnected yet independent architecture of the ANN provides the basis for parallel processing.

Distributed Memory

Centralized memory cannot fulfill the need of ANN system due to its structural complexity. In addition to this centralized memory is having several drawbacks like data inconsistency, lack of parallelism, slow processing etc. Hence the ANN is capable of using distributed memory environment where each processing element is assigned with a local memory.

Fault Tolerance Ability

As The ANN is a highly interconnected system, it is necessary to have fault tolerant capability. As a result if one of the components fails it hardly affects the overall output of the system.

Collective Solution

ANN is an interconnected system the output of a system is a collective output of various input so the result is the summation of all the outputs which comes after processing various inputs. The Partial answer is worthless for any user in the ANN System.

Learning Ability

In ANN most of the learning rules are used to develop models of processes, while adopting the network to the changing environment and discovering useful knowledge. These Learning methods are Supervised, Unsupervised and Reinforcement Learning.

Transfer Function

Activation Functions are basically the transfer function which is output from a artificial neuron and it send signals to the other artificial neuron. There are four main forms of Transfer Functions such as Threshold, Piecewise Linear, Sigmoid and Gaussian. Figure 8 (a, b, c, d) demonstrates these activation functions (Homik et al., 1994).

Network Architecture

There are further divisions of Feedback and Feed Forward Network architecture which are shown in Figure 9.

- **Single-Layer Perceptron:** Such type of ANN consists of only two layers which are the input and the output layer. Though it contains two layers, the name single layer perceptron is due to the fact that no computation is done in the input layer.
- **Multilayer Perceptron:** A multilayer perceptron (MLP) is a feedforward artificial neural network model that transforms sets of input data to a set of appropriate outputs. An MLP consists of multiple layers of nodes and represent them in a directed graph, with each layer fully connected to the next one.

Figure 8. Activation functions

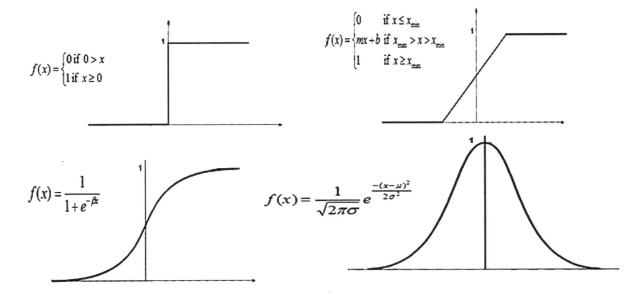

Figure 9. Taxonomy of network architecture

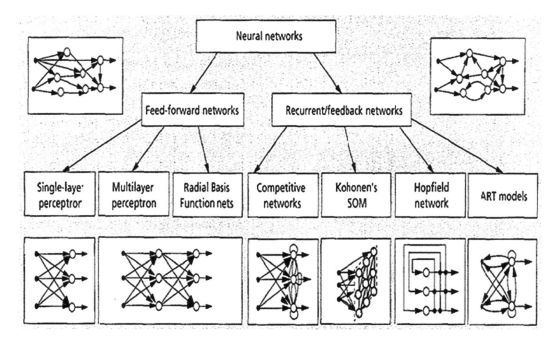

- **Radial Basis Function Nets:** A radial basis function network is an artificial neural network that applies radial basis functions as activation function. The network's output is a linear combination of radial basis functions of the inputs and neuro-parameters.
- **Competitive Networks:** It uses a form of Competitive learning, is a special case of unsupervised learning in ANN where nodes compete for the right to respond to a subset of the input data and the winner node gets a chance to generate the response.
- **Kohenon's Self-Organizing Map (SOM):** Here the network is trained using a kind of unsupervised learning to produce a low-dimensional, discretized representation of the input space out of the training samples, called a map. The speciality of SOM over ANN is that they efficiently use competitive learning as opposed to error-backpropagation learning.
- **Hopfield Network:** It is conceptualized by John Hopfield in 1982. It is a type of ANN in which all connections are symmetric. It requires stationary inputs, as it guarantees that its dynamics will converge.
- **ART Models:** Adaptive resonance theory (ART) is a theory developed by Stephen Grossberg and Gail Carpenter on aspects of how the brain processes information. It describes a number of neural network models which use supervised and unsupervised learning methods, and address problems such as pattern recognition and prediction.

Learning in ANN

Learning is the process of giving training to the neural network. Learning is of 3 types which are discussed below:

- **Supervised Learning:** If we give training by providing input along with the output, the learning is known as supervised learning. In this learning the input data which is used to train the network is also associated with one output known as target output or desired output or actual output. The target output serves as teacher in the learning process. During learning, comparison is done with the network's computed output and the target output to determine the error (Jordan, 1992). Example: Classification problems.

- **Unsupervised Learning:** In this method, the target output is not present. The system learns by itself by exploring and adapting to the structured features present in the input. Example: Clustering problems (Rajasekaran Pai & Vijayalakshmi, 2012).

- **Reinforced Learning:** Here a guide is available but isn't present in the expected answers. This area of machine learning is concerned with whether the computed output is correct or not (Rajasekaran Pai & Vijayalakshmi, 2012).

Training Neural Networks

In general, the parameters of a NN, i.e. the weights and biases, are learned using a training data set. However, as the space of possible weights can be very large and of high dimension the analytical determination of these weights might be very difficult or even infeasible. For this reason, an iterative approach is adopted in most cases.

There are two principal training modes which determine the way the weights are updated:

- **Online Training:** After presentation of each training example, the error is calculated, and the weights are updated accordingly.

- **Offline Training:** The whole training set is propagated through the NN, and the respective errors are accumulated. Finally, the weights are updated using the accumulated error. This is also called batch training.

Many different NN training algorithms have been published in the literature. Some work only in online, some only in offline mode, and some can be executed in both ways. Which algorithm is best for a given problem depends on the NN architecture, the nature and cardinality of the training data set and the type of function to learn. Therefore, there is no basic rule for the choice of the training algorithm.

The Back Propagation Algorithm

In the context of NNs, the Back propagation (BP) algorithm has initially been presented by Rumelhart et al (1986). It is a supervised learning algorithm defining an error function E and applying the gradient descent technique in the weight space in order to minimize E. The combination of weights leading to a minimum of E is considered to be a solution of the learning problem. The BP algorithm does not guarantee to find a global minimum which is an inherent problem of gradient descent optimization. In order to calculate the gradient of E, the error function has to be continuous and differentiable. Thus, the activation function of each individual perceptron must also have this property. Mostly, a sigmoid and hyperbolic tangent activation function is employed, depending on the range of desired output values, i.e. [0,1] or [-1,+1]. BP can be performed in online or offline mode, i.e. E represents either the error of one training example or the sum of errors produced by all training examples.

In the following, we will explain the standard BP algorithm applied to MLPs. There are two phases of the algorithm:

- The forward pass, where a training example is presented to the network and the activations of the respective neurons is propagated layer by layer until the output neurons.
- The backward pass, where at each neuron the respective error is calculated starting from the output neurons and, layer by layer, propagating the error back until the input neurons.

The back propagation algorithm which is used to train the ANN is as follows:

- Initialize the weights in the network (often randomly).

```
Do
        For each example e in the training set
                O = Neural-net - Output(network, i) ;                    //
forward pass
                T = teacher output for i
                Calculate error (T - O) at the output units
                Compute delta_wh for all weights from hidden layer to output
layer;

//backward  pass
```

- Compute delta_wi for all weights from input layer to hidden layer ; backward pass continued.
- Update the weights in the network until all examples classified correctly or stopping criterion satisfied.
- Return the network.

Issues in Artificial Neural Network

In-spite of having so many promising capabilities ANNs are likely to suffer from some of the following short comings:

- The training time in case of a neural network is directly dependent on the size and nature of the dataset. That means the training phase in a neural network may be unusually longer in particular cases.
- Lack of consistency in the ratio of correctly classified and wrongly classified data, as the weights of a neural network are chosen randomly.
- Over fitting problem occurs case of neural network (Like gradient descent learning) which gives an impression that there is no misclassification in the training process.
- Most of the neural networks suffer from getting stuck into local optima problem when they are trained with gradient descent learning.

SOLUTIONS AND RECOMMENDATION:

In order to avoid the problems/short-comings present in the ANN, neural networks with more advanced architecture have been suggested by researchers. This section discusses about some of the advanced neural networks which are becoming popular.

Advances in Neural Network

The ANN, in due course of time has undergone several modifications both in structural and functional aspects in order to improve the accuracy and stability. This section describes about few variations of ANN that have been used for specific problems.

Deep Belief Network

Deep belief nets are probabilistic generative models that are composed of multiple layers of stochastic, latent variables. The latent variables typically have binary values and are often called hidden units or feature detectors. The top two layers have undirected, symmetric connections between them and form an associative memory. The lower layers receive top-down, directed connections from the layer above. The states of the units in the lowest layer represent a data vector.

The two most significant properties of deep belief nets are:

- There is an efficient, layer-by-layer procedure for learning the top-down, generative weights that determine how the variables in one layer depend on the variables in the layer above.
- After learning, the values of the latent variables in every layer can be inferred by a single, bottom-up pass that starts with an observed data vector in the bottom layer and uses the generative weights in the reverse direction.

Figure 10. Deep belief network

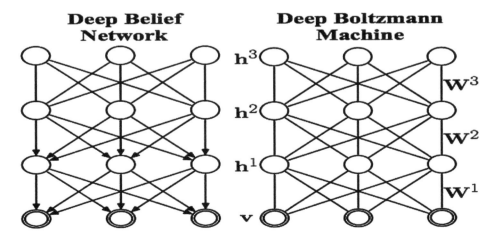

A deep belief net can be viewed as a composition of simple learning modules each of which is a restricted type of Boltzmann machine that contains a layer of visible units that represent the data and a layer of hidden units that learn to represent features that capture higher-order correlations in the data. The two layers are connected by a matrix of symmetrically weighted connections, W, and there are no connections within a layer. Given a vector of activities v for the visible units, the hidden units are all conditionally independent so it is easy to sample a vector, h, from the factorial posterior distribution over hidden vectors, p(h|v,W) . It is also easy to sample from p(v|h,W) . By starting with an observed data vector on the visible units and alternating several times between sampling from p(h|v,W) and p(v|h,W), it is easy to get a learning signal. This signal is simply the difference between the pairwise correlations of the visible and hidden units at the beginning and end of the sampling

The key idea behind deep belief nets is that the weights, W, learned by a restricted Boltzmann machine define both p(v|h,W) and the prior distribution over hidden vectors, p(h|W), so the probability of generating a visible vector, v, can be written as:

$$p(v) = \sum h \, p(h|W) p(v|h,W)$$

Convolution Neural Network

A Convolution Neural Network (CNN) is comprised of one or more convolution layers (often with a sub sampling step) and then followed by one or more fully connected layers as in a standard multilayer neural network. The architecture of a CNN is designed to take advantage of the 2D structure of an input image (or other 2D input such as a speech signal). This is achieved with local connections and tied weights followed by some form of pooling which results in translation invariant features. Another benefit of CNNs is that they are easier to train and have many fewer parameters than fully connected networks with the same number of hidden units.

A CNN consists of a number of convolution and sub sampling layers optionally followed by fully connected layers. The input to a convolution layer is a m x m x r image where m is the height and width of the image and r is the number of channels, e.g. an RGB image has r=3. The convolution layer will have k filters (or kernels) of size n x n x q where n is smaller than the dimension of the image and q can either be the same as the number of channels r or smaller and may vary for each kernel. The size of the filters gives rise to the locally connected structure which are each convolved with the image to produce k feature maps of size m−n+1. Each map is then sub sampled typically with mean or max pooling over p x p contiguous regions where p ranges between 2 for small images (e.g. MNIST) and is usually not more than 5 for larger inputs. Either before or after the sub sampling layer an additive bias and sigmoidal nonlinearity is applied to each feature map. Figure 11 illustrates a full layer in a CNN consisting of convolution and sub sampling sub layers.

Extreme Learning Machine

ELM stands out as one of the contemporary approaches in machine learning which basically used for pattern classification. It is proposed by Huang at el (2006) that uses Single Layer Feed forward Neural Network (SLFN) Architecture. It randomly chooses the input weights and thereby determines the output weights of Single Layer Feed forward Network. It has a better generalization performance with a faster

Figure 11. Convolution neural network

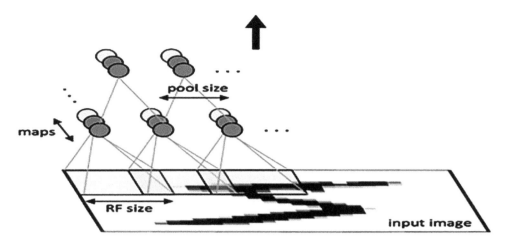

learning speed. It requires less human interference and can run thousands times faster than those conventional methods (Huang et al., 2006) .It automatically determines all the network parameters analytically, which avoids trivial human intervention and makes it efficient in online and real- time applications.

Training with ELM

Learning is the process of approximation of the behavior of the training data which in turn makes the classifier to be able to do generalization of the training data. It is more desirable as a classifier is normally used to make accurate prediction on new or unknown objects. The algorithm for ELM training is given below.

ELM Learning Algorithm

ELM algorithm has three steps as follows:

1. Given a training set

$$X = \left\{ \left(xi, ti \right) | xi \in Rn \ and \ ti \in Rm, i = 1, 2, \cdots, N \right\}$$

activation function g(x), and the number of hidden nodes L, assign randomly input weight vectors ai and hidden node bias or impact factor $bi, i = 1, 2, \cdots, L$.

2. Calculate the hidden layer output matrix H, where $H = \sum_{i=1}^{N} ai \cdot xi + \text{bi}$

3. Calculate the output weight $\beta : \beta = H \dagger T$, where H† is the Moore-Penrose generalized inverse of hidden layer output matrix H.

The term generalized inverse is sometimes used as a synonym for pseudo-inverse. The pseudo-inverse is unique for all matrices whose entries are real or complex numbers. It can be computed using the singular value decomposition. The most widely known type of matrix pseudo-inverse is the Moore–Penrose pseudo-inverse, which was described by E. H. Moore in 1920, Arne Bjerhammar in 1951 and Roger Penrose in 1955.The benefit of using Moore -Penrose generalized inverse technique is that, it can also be applied on non-square matrices (Priydarshini, Dash & Misra, 2014).

Hybrid Systems

Neuro-Fuzzy Systems

A neuro-fuzzy system is based on a fuzzy system which is trained by a learning algorithm derived from neural network theory. The (heuristic) learning procedure operates on local information, and causes only local modifications in the underlying fuzzy system.

The system can be viewed as a 3-layer feed forward neural network. The first layer represents input variables, the middle (hidden) layer represents fuzzy rules and the third layer represents output variables. Fuzzy sets are encoded as (fuzzy) connection weights.

It is not necessary to represent a fuzzy system like this to apply a learning algorithm to it. However, it can be convenient, because it represents the data flow of input processing and learning within the model. It can always be interpreted as a system of fuzzy rules. It is also possible to create the system out of training data from scratch, as it is possible to initialize it by prior knowledge in form of fuzzy rules. The learning procedure of a neuro-fuzzy system takes the semantic properties of the underlying fuzzy system into account. This results in constraints on the possible modifications applicable to the system parameters.

A neuro-fuzzy system approximates an n-dimensional function that is partially defined by the training data. The fuzzy rules encoded within the system represent vague samples, and can be viewed as prototypes of the training data.

Figure 12. Neuro-fuzzy systems

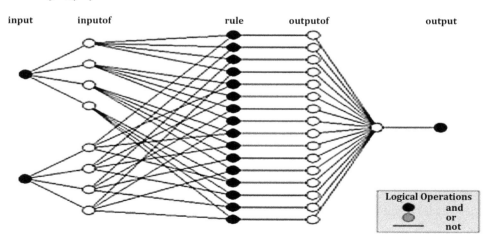

Neuro-Genetic Systems

Although neural networks are used for solving a variety of problems, they still have some limitations. One of the most common is associated with neural network training.

The back-propagation learning algorithm cannot guarantee an optimal solution. In real-world applications, the back-propagation algorithm might converge to a set of sub-optimal weights from which it cannot escape. As a result, the neural network is often unable to find a desirable solution to a problem at hand.

Another difficulty is related to selecting an optimal topology for the neural network. The "right" network architecture for a particular problem is often chosen by means of heuristics, and designing a neural network topology is still more art than engineering.

Genetic algorithms are an effective optimization technique that can guide both weight optimization and topology selection.

Working

A Neuro-Genetic System can be implemented as per the following steps:

Step 1: Encoding a set of weights in a chromosome.
Step 2: Define a fitness function for evaluating the chromosome's performance.
  - The function must estimate the performance of a given neural network. Error Functions like sum of squares, root-Mean-Square etc can be taken for this purpose.
  - The training set of examples is presented to the network, and the sum of squared errors is calculated. The smaller the sum, the fitter the chromosome. The genetic algorithm attempts to find a set of weights that minimises the sum of squared errors.
Step 3: Choose the genetic operators: crossover and mutation.
  - A crossover operator takes two parent chromosomes and creates a single child with genetic material from both parents. Each gene in the child's chromosome is represented by the corresponding gene of the randomly selected parent.
  - A mutation operator selects a gene in a chromosome and adds a small random value between -1 and 1 to each weight in this gene.

Figure 13. Neuro-genetic systems

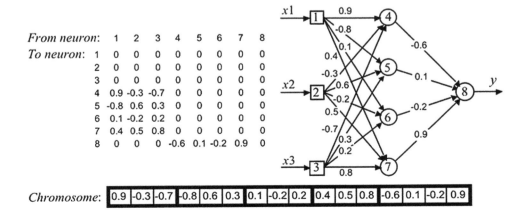

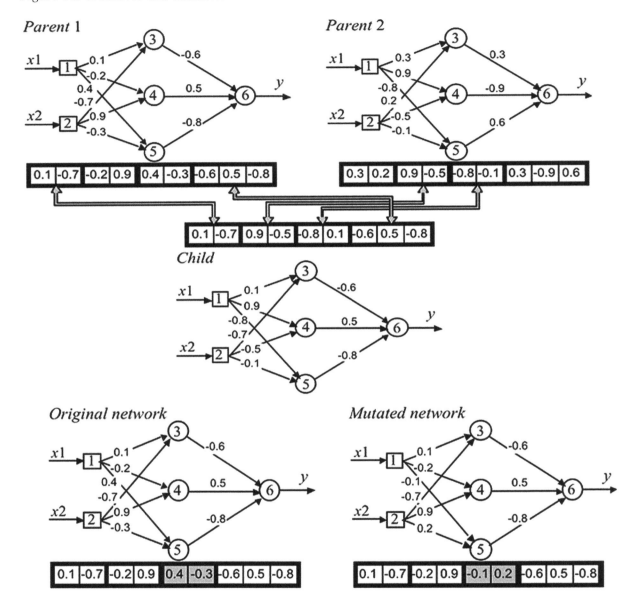

Figure 14. Crossover and mutation

FUTURE RESEARCH DIRECTIONS

The advanced neural networks, though very powerful, can be made to function even better by modifying the processing environment. Training and evaluation of each node in large networks can take an incredibly long time. Hence ANN can be made parallel to minimize the time complexity. The inherent architecture of ANN supports parallelism at different levels. For example:

1.   For each training session,

2. For each training example in the session,
3. For each layer (forward and backward),
4. For each neuron in the layer,
5. For all weights of the neuron,
6. For all bits of the weight value. Recently nVIDIA (Nvidia Corporation is an American worldwide technology company based in Santa Clara, California.

Nvidia manufactures graphics processing units) has launched a new environment to deal with deep neural network in parallel environment named as 'cuDNN'. Here it provides several software solutions to help data scientists and researchers to use the full power of GPU-accelerated deep learning. As research on parallel neural network is still in its infant stage researchers and scientists may explore it to make bio-inspired computing more efficient.

CONCLUSION

The role of ANN in bio-inspired computing is undoubtedly indispensable. Due to its reliability and flexibility it has been the first choice for scientists or researchers in automating classification or prediction problems. Even though ANN as a concept has been there for a long time, its applications in machine learning by small and appropriate modification to its basic architecture and processing environment has kept up the interest in the recent times and has been found to be still very popular among researchers and industries. The journey from simple "perceptron" to parallel deep neural network shows the quick adaptability of ANN in different environments.

This chapter is intended to be informative for researchers working in the field of ANN or advanced ANN. It provides a detail practical approach towards data classification problem both in conventional and advanced ANN which can be extended further by interested readers. Some Case studies have been presented in the appendix.

REFERENCES

Abraham, A. (2004). *Meta-Learning Evolutionary Artificial Neural Networks. Neurocomputing Journal, 56c,* 1–38.

Arbib. (1994). The handbook of brain theory and neural network. Academic Press.

Belal, M., Gaber, J., El-Sayed, H., & Almojel, A. (2006). Swarm Intelligence. In Handbook of Bioinspired Algorithms and Applications. Chapman & Hall.

Das, S., Abraham, A., & Konar, A. (2008). Swarm Intelligence Algorithms in Bioinformatics. *Springer, Studies in Computational Intelligence, 94,* 113–147.

Das, S., Panigrahi, B. K., & Pattnaik, S. S. (2009). Nature-Inspired Algorithms for Multi-objective Optimization. Handbook of Research on Machine Learning Applications and Trends: Algorithms Methods and Techniques. Academic Press.

Dorigo, M. (1992). *Optimization, learning and natural algorithms*. (Ph.D. Thesis). Dipartimento diElettronica, Politecnico di Milano, Italy.

Engelbrecht, P. (2002). *Computational Intelligence: An Introduction*. John Wiley & Sons.

Ford & Roberts. (1998). *Colour space conversions, Westminster*. London: University.

Ganesan, N., Venkatesh, D. K., Rama, D. M. A., & Palani, A. M. (2010). Application of Neural Networks in Diagnosing Cancer Disease Using Demographic Data. *International Journal of Computers and Applications, 1*(26), 81–97. doi:10.5120/476-783

Haykin, S. (1994). *Neural Network: A Comprehensive Foundation*. McMillan College Publishing Co.

Hinton, G. (2015). Deep Belief Nets. In Encyclopedia of Machine Learning and Data Mining. Academic Press.

Homik, Stinchcombe, & White. (1994). *Multilayer feed forward networks are universal approximators*. Academic Press.

Huang, G.-B., Zhu, Q.-Y., & Siew, C.-K. (2006). Extreme learning machine: Theory nd applications. *Elsevier Neurocomputing, 70*(1-3), 489–501. doi:10.1016/j.neucom.2005.12.126

Ilia, V. S. (2007). *Automatic red eye detection*. Academic Press.

Ivancevic, V. G., & Ivancevic, T. T. (2007). Introduction: Human and Computational Mind[SCI]. *Studies in Computational Intelligence, 60*, 1–269. doi:10.1007/978-3-540-71561-0_1

Jordan, M. I., & Rumelhart, D. E. (1992). Forward models: Supervised learning with a distal teacher. *Cognitive Science, 16*(3), 307–354. doi:10.1207/s15516709cog1603_1

Koza, J. R. (1992). *Genetic Programming: On the Programming of Computers by Means of Natural Selection*. Cambridge, MA: The MIT Press.

Lawrence, S. (1997). *Face Recognition: A Convolutional Neural Network Approach. IEEE Transactions on Neural Networks*.

Lim, C. P., & Harrison, R. F. (2003, May). online pattern classification with multiple neural network systems: An experimental study. *IEEE Transactions on Systems, Man and Cybernetics. Part C, Applications and Reviews, 33*.

Lim, C. P., Jain, L. C., & Dehuri, S. (2009). *Innovations in Swarm Intelligence: Studies in Computational Intelligence* (Vol. 248). Springer. doi:10.1007/978-3-642-04225-6_1

McCulloch, W. S., & Pitts, W. H. (1943). A Logical Calculus of the Ideas Immanent in Nervous Activity. *The Bulletin of Mathematical Biophysics, 5*, 115–133.

Mitchell, M. (1996). *An introduction to Genetic Algorithms*. MIT Press.

Nauck, D. (1997) Neuro-fuzzy systems: review and prospects. In *Fifth European Congress on Intelligent Systems and Soft Computing*.

Panigrahi, K., Shi, Y., & Lim, M.-H. (2011). *Handbook of Swarm Intelligence. Series: Adaptation, Learning, and Optimization* (Vol. 7). Springer-Verlag Berlin Heidelberg. doi:10.1007/978-3-642-17390-5

Priydarshini, R., Dash, N., & Misra, R. (2014). A Novel approach to predict diabetes mellitus using modified Extreme learning machine. *Proceedings of International Conference on Electronics and Communication Systems (ICECS)*. doi:10.1109/ECS.2014.6892740

Rajasekaran & Vijayalakshmi. (2012). *Neural Networks, Fuzzy Logic, and Genetic Algorithms: Synthesis and Applications*. Academic Press.

Rajesh, R., & Siva Prakash, J. (2011). Extreme learning machines - A review and state-of-the-art. *International Journal of Wisdom Based Computing, 1*(1), 35–49.

Rawlins, G. (1991). *Foundations of genetic algorithms*. San Mateo: Morgan Kauffman Publishers.

Rojas, R. (1996). *Neural Networks*. Berlin: Springer-Verlag. doi:10.1007/978-3-642-61068-4

Rumelhart, D. E., Hinton, G. E., & Williams, R. J. (1986). Learning internal representations by back-propagating errors. *Nature, 323*(6088), 533–536. doi:10.1038/323533a0

Salakhutdinov, R., & Hinton, G. (2009). *Deep Boltzmann Machines*. 12th International Conference on Artificial Intelligence and Statistics (AISTATS) 2009, Clearwater Beach, FL.

Sharma, Rai, & Dev. (2012). A Comprehensive Study of Artificial Neural Networks. *International Journal of Advanced Research in Computer Science and Software Engineering, 2*(10).

Sharma. (2012). A Comprehensive Study of Artificial Neural Networks. *International Journal of Advanced Research in Computer Science and Software Engineering, 2*(10).

Sharma. (2015). DSP in image processing. *International Journal of Advanced Research in Computer and Communication Engineering, 4*(1).

Storn, R., & Price, K. (1995). *Differential evolution – a simple and efficient adaptive scheme for global optimization over continuous spaces. Technical Report, TR-95-012*. Berkeley, CA: International Computer Science Institute.

Suzuki. (2011). *Artificial Neural Networks - Methodological Advances and Biomedical Applications*. Academic Press.

Winter, G., & Periaux, J. (1995). *Genetic algorithms in engineering and computer science*. Wiley & Sons. Retrieved from: http://delta.cs.cinvestav.mx/~ccoello/compevol/strategy_def.pdf

APPENDIX

There are various applications of artificial neural network. Every sector in this world wants a system which is itself intelligent to solve any problem according to the inputs. In this paper we have discussed various Business Applications which are listed below. The tasks artificial neural networks are applied to tend to fall within the following broad categories:

- Function approximation, or regression analysis, including time series prediction, fitness approximation, and modeling.
- Classification, including pattern and sequence recognition, novelty detection and sequential decision making.
- Data processing, including filtering, clustering, blind source separation and compression.
- Robotics, including directing manipulators, prosthesis.
- Control, including Computer numerical control.

Application areas include the system identification and control (vehicle control, trajectory prediction, process control, and natural resources management), quantum chemistry.]game-playing and decision making (backgammon, chess, poker), pattern recognition (radar systems, face identification, object recognition and more), sequence recognition (gesture, speech, handwritten text recognition), medical diagnosis, financial applications (e.g. automated trading systems), data mining (or knowledge discovery in databases, "KDD"), visualization and e-mail spam filtering.

Artificial neural networks have also been used to diagnose several cancers. An ANN based hybrid lung cancer detection system named HLND improves the accuracy of diagnosis and the speed of lung cancer radiology.[27] These networks have also been used to diagnose prostate cancer. The diagnoses can be used to make specific models taken from a large group of patients compared to information of one given patient. The models do not depend on assumptions about correlations of different variables. Colorectal cancer has also been predicted using the neural networks. Neural networks could predict the outcome for a patient with colorectal cancer with more accuracy than the current clinical methods. After training, the networks could predict multiple patient outcomes from unrelated institutions.

A Case Study on Back Propagation Neural-Network for Diabetes Data Classification

Problem Statement

Classification is the task of dividing different data from their known features to a particular group. Depending on the number of classes either the classifier is a binary or multinomial classifier. In machine learning, multiclass or multinomial classification is the problem of classifying the given instances into more than two classes. While some classification algorithms naturally permit the use of more than two classes, others are by nature binary algorithms; these can, however, be turned into multinomial classifiers by a variety of strategies.

Input: pima Indian diabetes dataset.

Dataset Description

This dataset contains the Pima Indian women diabetes dataset to differentiate the normal persons and diabetic patients. This dataset has 768 instances 8-feature attributes and one class attribute. Attribute information which is clinically found are:

1. Number of times pregnant,
2. Plasma glucose concentration a 2 hours in an oral glucose tolerance test,
3. Diastolic blood pressure (mm Hg),
4. Triceps skin fold thickness (mm),
5. 2-Hour serum insulin (mu U /ml),
6. Body mass index (weight in kg/(height in m)^2),
7. Diabetes pedigree function,
8. Age (years),
9. Class variable (0 or 1).

The data set was selected from a larger data set held by the National Institutes of Diabetes and Digestive and Kidney Diseases. There are 268 (34.9%) cases in class '1' and 500 (65.1%) cases in class '0'.

Preprocessing

In preprocessing phase the data are undergone normalization, which is the process of bringing the input data in to a range of certain values to fall within an acceptable scope, and domain Basically this is done to get a faster and efficient training. If the neurons used in the classifier have nonlinear transfer functions (whose output range is from -1 to 1 or 0 to 1), the data is needed to be normalized for efficiency. As our outputs are falling within these ranges, each feature in each dataset is normalized using column normalization. The normalized data are used as the inputs to the machines.

Matlab Code

```
1 clear all;
2 close all;
3 clc
4 diabts;
5 ninput=8; %input('no of inputs');
6 nop=2; % nop('no of outputs')
7 nhid=8; %input('enter the no of hidden layer nodes');
8 wih=rand(ninput,nhid) % random weight set initialization
9 wbhid=rand(nhid,1)
10 who=rand(nhid,nop)
11 eta=1; % learning rate parameter's value is set to 1
12 npattern=2; %define training set
13 j=1;
```

```
14 k=1;
15 for i=1:768
16 if ddata(i,9)==0
17 x1(j,:)=ddata(i,1:9); % 9th column is having the class attribute
18 j=j+1;
19 else
20 x2(k,:)=ddata(i,1:9);
21 k=k+1;
22 end
23 end
24 ddata=[x1;x2];
25 x=ddata(:,1:8);
26 in=[x(1:450,:)' x(501:700,:)' ];in=normc(in); % normalization of the input data
27 % define targets
28 desired_out(1:450,1)=0;
29 desired_out(1:450,2)=0;
30 desired_out(451:650,1)=0;
31 desired_out(451:650,2)=1;
32 desired_out=desired_out';
33 iteration=10000; % no. of iteration is set to 10000
34 error=zeros(nop,iteration); % keyboard
35 for iter=1:iteration
36 for j=1:size(in,2) %estimated output
37 opw=in(:,j)'*wih;
38 opsig=1./(1+exp(-(opw+wbhid')));
39 out=1./(1+exp(-(opsig*who)));
40 e=desired_out(:,j)'-out;
41 delta=(out.*(1-out)).*e; %hidden layer weights updation
42 who=who+eta*opsig'*delta;
43 deltahid=opsig'.*(1-opsig)'.*(who*delta'); %input layer weight updations
44 wih=wih+eta*(in(:,j)*deltahid');
45 wbhid=wbhid+2*deltahid;
46 end
47 iter
48 error(:,iter)=e;
49 end
50 sse=sum((error(:,1:iter).^2),1); % Min square error calculation
51 plot(sse); title('error square plot for iris data classification');
52 xlabel('no of iterations');
53 ylabel('error.^2'); %keyboard %%%%%testing%%%%%%%
54 in1 = [x(451:500,:)' x(701:768,:)'];in1=normc(in1);
55 out = [];
56 % in=[.1 .1 .9 .9;.1 .9 .1 .9];
```

```
57 for i=1:size(in1,2) % display('testing for input combination:')
58 % in1
59 opw=in1(:,i)'*wih;
60 opsig=1./(1+exp(-(opw+wbhid')));
61 out(:,i)=(1./(1+exp(-(opsig*who))))';
62 end
63 out
```

To test our approach, we have taken different data class sets from repository of data sets. We have divided the data sets into two parts, i.e. training set and testing set which is not used in the training process, and is used to test and then we have simulated our results with these datasets. Almost 2/3rd of the total dataset has taken as training set and 1/3rd of the rest has taken as test set.. Then we have simulated our network with the same data.

Output: The instance and its corresponding class.

A Case Study of an Extreme Learning Machine to Classify Diabetes Data Set

An Extreme learning machine (ELM) is a type of advanced neural network which uses a single layer feed forward architecture. It randomly chooses the input weights and by using Moore Penrose Inverse matrix, it determines the output weights.

Note: The same data set has been used for this work also.

Matlab Code

```
1 clc;
2 clear all;
3 diabts; % loading data into workspace
4 tic;
5 ip1=ddata(:,1:8); %input data preparation
6 ip=ip1(1:500,:);
7 ip=normc(ip); % normalization of input data
8 test=ip1(501:768,:); % Test data preparation
9 test=normc(test);
10 ip=ip';
11 test=test';
12 tar=ddata(1:500,9)'; % target preparation
13 oph=1./(1+exp(-ip)); % applying sigmoidal activation function
14 testh=(1./(1+exp(-test)));
15 wt=tar*(pinv(ip)); % calculating hidden weight by Moore Penrose Inverse matrix
16 fop=(wt*test); % calculating output
17 fop=round(fop);
18 toc;
```

Output

Table 1 shows the training and simulation results produced by ANN on different datasets.

Table 2 shows performance comparison between ELM and BPNN based models as per the code on diabetes dataset.

Table 1.

Dataset	Number of Classes	Number of Samples	Number of Features	Number of Training Samples	Number of Testing Samples	No of Misclassification	Accuracy Percentage
Iris	3	150	4	120	30	11	78%
Seed	3	210	7	150	60	17	72%
Wine	3	178	13	150	28	6	79%
Diabetes	2	768	7	500	268	88	67%

Table 2.

Classifying Model		Training Time	Simulation Time	No of Input Layer Neurons	Classification Accuracy
ELM		Not Applicable	.3910Secs	Not Applicable	75.72%
BPNN	Train SCG	7.803 Secs	.0605Secs	8	67%
	Train LM	6.701 Secs	.0633Secs	8	68%

Chapter 12
Genetic-Based Estimation of Biomass Using Geographical Information System:
Study Area Vellore

Suresh Kumar Nagarajan
VIT University, India

ABSTRACT

The utilization of relative shading size of a picture to extricate the vegetation of a study range Vellore, Tamilnadu, India was proposed. This novel hereditary based calculation utilizes the pixel guide of every picture and tries to figure out the ranges using so as to fit the right determination for vegetation Biomass the hereditary based methodology. The simplicity of execution permits any further changes to the calculation in future. Capable picture handling component permitted improved control of picture A Google Programming interface was utilized to concentrate and yield picture. It permitted simple augmentation of the work to any demographic range. The proposed calculation is superior to anything some present day devices as it is taking into account singular pixel values as opposed to layers. All the more vitally, no pre-meaning of the picture or layer is needed. Pixel control permits blending the effectively utilized procedures with other more up to date picture handling strategies that would prompt a more far reaching and multi-useful calculation. The advances utilized are between operable and can be kept as a steady stage for further up degree. The calculation does endure in computational speed and can be upgraded by utilizing better equipment offices. Parallel registering may be another choice to accelerate the handling of free pixels. Certain area methodologies can be utilized to upgrade honing of picture and better limits.

INTRODUCTION

The study is in light of the accurate case issue of estimation Biomass in a predefined region. This work center to concentrate satellite pictures from Google guide of Vellore locale. Utilizing the Picture preparing methods, for example, division and limit location is utilized to disconnect and concentrate a given

DOI: 10.4018/978-1-5225-1008-6.ch012

regular asset in the area. In this manner, the work would amass information around a given asset. This can be extremely helpful for civil enterprises to get an appraisal of a given asset. The examination work centered to actualize the picture preparing strategies utilizing the effective and adaptable Frameworks Lab. The apparatus is exhibited dynamically in this paper. This work would likewise utilize some open source devices to gain and control pictures from Google earth. The recognizable proof of green spots in a picture, The fundamental thought of this work is to gauge the biomass by utilizing the over the ground level pictures.

Significance of vegetation index towards precision agriculture is more and keeps developing day by day. Remote sensing images plays a major role in determination of vegetation indices. As importance of Vegetation indices becoming more it would be appropriate to find out the usage of Vegetation indices through its application, technology and the type of remote sensed used. The following section provides a comprehensive view of Vegetation indices in perspective of its: Vegetation indices through Remote sensed image, Vegetation indices through Technology, and Vegetation indices through applications.

VEGETATION INDEX AND THE REMOTE SENSING IMAGES

Vegetation Index is being a significant index of environment is generally computed from remote sensed images. The types of remote sensing vary but each plays a vital role to analyze the vegetation area in respect to vegetation indices. Satellite imagery based on passive reflectivity comes in four basic types such as visible infrared, multispectral and hyper spectral. Most of the researchers followed the three ports of remote sensing images for the vegetation indices calculation.

In the year of 1995 Ranga Myneni, Forrest Hall and Marshak (1995) used Landsat multispectral data to find spectral derivative and vegetation indexes. Here widely broad-band and near infrared vegetation indexex are used for the measure of chlorophyll abundance and energy absorption. Later 1998 Rick Lawrence and William Ripple used landsat data to investigate about the use of various vegetation indices and multiple linear regression using raw spectral bands. In the year of 2000 again the researchers Prochdxka and Kolinovd (2000) used Landsat multispectral data to investigate about Air pollution detection using image processing.later in 2001 Stark (2001) used meteorological data and remote sensing data to estimate Net Primary Productivity. In the year of 2003 Akkartal, Turudu and Erbek used Multisensor Landsat data (Thematical mapping) to find vegetation biomass for the particular region using vegetation indices and Limin Yang, George Xian, Jacqueline and Brian Deal used Landsat data to find Urban land cover change detection through sub pixel imperviousness mapping also hyper spectral data is used, Peng gong and Mirta Rosa Larrieu to find vegetation indices. In the same year, Rasmus Fensholt used Meteosat SEVIRI sensor data to analyze Normalized Difference Vegetation Index. Later 2004 Bruno Basso, Davide Cammarano and Pasquale used multispectral landsat data to describe the biophysical principles of vegetation indices and present a review of remote sensing applications for crop management. In 2005 Jarocinska and Zagajewski used Hyperspectral DAIS 7915 images to investigate the method of plant monitor using vegetation indices, Stefan Roettgar used Landsat and Digital elevation maps to analyze vegetation rendering using Normalized Difference Vegetation Index and in the same year Fei yuan, Kali Sawaya, Brian Loeffelholz and Marvin Bauer used temporal Landsat data to find land cover classification and change analysis of the Twin cities metropolitan area. In the year 2007 Zheng, Chen, Tian, Ju and Xia used Landsat ETM images and forest inventory data to estimate above ground biomass of forests, from this NDVI was calculated, Bunkei Matsushita used Landsat image data to investigate sensitivity of EVI and NDVI to Topographic effects and in the same year Youhao and Wang Jihe used Landsat TM/ETM+ data to monitor Vegetation changes in a particular region.in 2008 George Meyer and Joao Camargo Neto used Landsat image to verify color vegetation indices for automated crop imaging applications and Wafa Nori, El Nour Elsiddig and Irmgard Niemeyer used Landsat ETM and Aster Data to detect Land cover changes using classification technique. In 2009 Siegmann, Jarmer and Hofle used Landsat data to investigate about assessment of canopy nitrogen status, Jun Huang and Youchuan used multispectral landsat data to analyze forest cover change detection model using threshold, Thomas Bauer used Landsat image to analyze temporal changes of coca fields on different consecutive years, Honglei Zhu used Landsat image for quantitative evaluation of Image segmentation quality in satellite Image Processing and Baodonga and Lixinb used Landsat 7 data to Remote Sensing Monitoring for Vegetation Change in Mining Area based on Spot-VGT NDVI.

In 2010 Barbara Koch analyzed forest biomass assessment using multi and hyperspectral data, Ashish Ghosh, Niladri shekhar and Susmita ghosh used multispectral landsat data to find unsupervised change detection in remote sensing images using fuzzy clustering algorithms, Peijum, Xingli, Wen, Yan and Huapeng used multispectral landsat data to monitor changes in urban land cover and changes in vegetation, sudhanshu Sekhar, Ames and Suranjan Panigrahi used multispectral landsat data to investigate about the strength of the key spectral vegetation indices for agricultural crop yield prediction using neural network techniques, Fazel Amiri and Abdul Rashid used Advanced Spaceborn Thermal Emission and Reflection (ASTER) image data to determine the appropriate indices for vegetation cover and production assessment based on data, Lei and Bian used MODIS data and Landsat 7 data to analyze spatiotemporal difference of Normalized Difference Vegetation Index to compare the spatiotemporal difference, Huang quing and Zhang Li used MODIS data to find Normalized Difference Vegetation Index based on crop growth monitoring, Anil Chitade and Katiyar used Landsat 7 image for color based image segmentation using K-means clustering technique, Yaowen Xie and Xiaojiong used Landsat ETM data to calculate NDVI for Landsat7 data after atmospheric correction using 6s model and Uddin and Gurung used Landsat ETM+ and MSS imagery data to analyze Land cover change in Bangladesh using knowledge based classification approach.

In 2011 Tao chen, Ruiqing, Wang, Zhang and Bo Du used multispectral landsat data to monitor percentage of vegetation cover change in wuhan region, Joshi and Prem Chandra used Landsat 5 TM data to investigate the performance evaluation of vegetation indices using remotely sensed data, Andres Vina, Anatoly, Gitelson and Yi Peng used Multispectral landsat data to evaluate different vegetation indices for the remote estimation of the green leaf area index of two crop types, Joshi and Prem Chandra used landsat multispectral data to present various vegetation indices and their applications for comparison study, Yves Julien, Cristian Mattar, Juan and Belen Franch used Advanced very high resolution radiometer sensor data to investigates about suffered vegetation changes such as desertification and reforestation and Offer Rozenstein and Arnon Karnieli used landsat multispectral data to compare the methods for land-use classification. In 2012 Cutler, Boyd, Foody and Vetrivel used SAR image and Landsat image to estimate tropical forest biomass and assessment of carbon emissions in the atmosphere, Bhandari, kumar and singh used Landsat image to extract features using Normalized Difference Vegetation Index, Jose, Zarate and Susan used hemispherical photography to investigate about prediction of leaf area index in almonds by vegetation indexes, Alemu Gonsamo and Petri Pelikka used Landsat 7 multispectral data to estimate leaf area index from spectral vegetation indices, Juliane Huth, Claudia Kuenzer, Thilo Wehramann, Steffen Gebhardt, Vo Quoc Tuan and Stefan Dech used MODIS data to analyze Land cover and Land use classification with TWOPAC. In the last year 2013 Guijun Yang, Ruiliang Pu, Jixian

Zhang and Jihua wang used Landsat images to investigate about remote sensing of seasonal variability of fractional vegetation cover and its object based spatial pattern analysis over mountain areas. From the above survey taken from the year 1995 -2013 satellite data types used are Landsat –TM data multispectral, hyper spectral,ASTER, Modis and photography. In this comparing with the other image types multispectral is good in cost wise.

VEGETATION INDICES AND METHODS

In 1995, Ranga Myneni, Forrest Hall and Marshak used Landsat multispectral data to find spectral derivative and vegetation indexes. The widely used broad-band red/near infrared vegetation indexes are a measure of chlorophyll abundance and energy absorption. The lack of absorption in the adjacent near-infrared region results in a strong absorption contrast. Vegetation indexes capture this contrast through combinations of broadband red/near-infrared reflectance.

In 1998, Rick Lawrence and William Ripple used landsat data to investigate about the use of various vegetation indices and multiple linear regression using raw spectral bands. Simple linear regression was used to initiate analyses of individual vegetation indices. For each index, analysis of residual plots and exploratory data plots was used to guide potential improvements in the regression fits. Forward and backward stepwise regression was used with all seven bands to provide guidance as to which bands might be significant in predicting vegetation cover.

In 2000, Prochdxka and Kolinovd (2000) used Landsat multispectral data to investigate about Air pollution detection using image processing. This was devoted to the analysis of mathematical methods allowing for detection of concentration of aerosol particles observed at ground measuring stations and by satellites. This deals with:

1. Different time instants of ground observations,
2. Different sizes of regions used for satellite channels correlation.

Results presented in this study were justifying correspondence between satellite and ground observations in the case of appropriate weather conditions as correlation of the surface. Mathematical background used for these studies will include further methods of:

1. Time series processing including two dimensional interpolation using non-linear methods and wavelet functions,
2. Image preprocessing, filtering, image enhancement and channels correlation.

In 2001, Stark used meteorological data and remote sensing data to estimate Net Primary Productivity. The amount of photo synthetically active radiation absorbed annually by green vegetation (Amount of Photo synthetic Active Radiation) (APAR) multiplied by the efficiency by which that radiation was converted to plant biomass increment (ε) equals the NPP.

In 2003, Akkartal, Turudu and Erbek used Multisensor Landsat data to find vegetation biomass for the particular region using vegetation indices. Five different types of vegetation indexes had been calculated and evaluated to quantify the concentrations of green leaf vegetation. These vegetation indexes depend on the reflectance of vegetation. Simple Ratio, Difference Vegetation Index, Normalized Difference

Vegetation Index, Transformed Normalized Difference Vegetation Index and Perpendicular Vegetation Index had been calculated from the near infrared band and red band. In 2003, Peng gong and Mirta Rosa Larrieu used hyperion Hyperspectral data to investigate about the estimation of LAI using vegetation indices. Pixel based retrieved reflectance spectra from the calibrated Hyperion images at the LAI measurement plots were extracted from the image. One to four homogenous pixels were extracted and averaged for each LAI plot. For each Vis a linear correlation coefficient was calculated between the VI and LAI measurement. For each VI, a correlation matrix was constructed for each pair of spectral bands. This research conducted correlation analyses of forest LAI with different vegetation indices extracted from Hyperion image reflectances.

In 2003, Author Rasmus Fensholt used Meteosat SEVIRI sensor data to analyze Normalized Difference Vegetation Index. The SEVIRI sensor detects radiation in 12 spectral bands, and it is used to assess information on surface anisotropy. Final result was improvements in image frequency and comparison to in measurements Time series of MSG SEVIRI NDVI are plotted together with MODIS Terra and Aqua NDVI. Only cloud free scenes are included as specified by the MODIS quality flags and the MSG cloud mask. In 2003, Limin Yang, George Xian, Jacqueline and Brian Deal used Landsat data to find urban land cover change detection through sub pixel imperviousness mapping. Machine-learning algorithm-regression tree was utilized to model sub-pixel percent imperviousness. This algorithm conducts a binary recursive partitioning and produces a set of rules and regression.

In 2004, Bruno Basso, Davide Cammarano and Pasquale used multispectral landsat data to describe the biophysical principles of vegetation indices and present a review of remote sensing applications for crop management. And this research describes the techniques and capabilities of remote sensing then presents a series of novel and practical applications of different types of vegetation indices in agricultural research. In 2005, Jarocinska and Zagajewski used Hyperspectral DAIS 7915 images to investigate the method of plant monitor using vegetation indices. Different vegetation indices calculated for automated and objective plant monitoring, plant condition measurement, quantity of biomass and pigments. High values of NDVI indicated high chlorophyll content, and good plant condition. Values of LAI and SAVI showed that all of the area is covered by plants. Four kinds of vegetations were used like NDVI, SAVI, LAI and fAPAR (Fraction of Absorbed photo synthetically active radiation).

In 2005, Author Stefan Roettgar used Landsat and Digital elevation maps to analyze vegetation rendering using Normalized Difference Vegetation Index. Together with the DEMs (digital elevation maps) from the SRTM (Space Shuttle Radar Mission) and the visible channels 1-3 of the Landsat data they effectively have a high resolution landscape and vegetation description of any particular area in the world. High to medium values of the NDVI usually corresponds to trees or bushes, respectively. C-LOD method reduces an amount of roughly 100.000 visible trees depending on the point of view. Another possible option was to accelerate the display of the cached geometry by using impostors and/or billboard clouds for distant trees. In 2005, Fei yuan, Kali Sawaya, Brian Loeffelholz and Marvin Bauer used temporal Landsat data to find land cover classification and change analysis of the Twin cities metropolitan area. A hybrid supervised-unsupervised training approach referred to as "guided clustering". A concern in change detection analysis is that both position and attribute errors can propagate through the multiple dates. The results quantify the land cover change patterns in the metropolitan area and demonstrate the potential of multi-temporal Landsat data.

In 2007, Zheng, Chen, Tian, Ju and Xia used Landsat ETM images and forest inventory data to estimate above ground biomass of forests, from this NDVI was calculated. Leaf area index was produced from the reduced simple ratio map using a regression model. Three vegetation indices (NDVI, SR, RSR) were calculated from the reflectance image. The NDVI map was first used to classify forested and non-forested pixels through setting a NDVI threshold.

In 2007, Author Bunkei Matsushita used Landsat image data to investigate sensitivity of EVI and NDVI to Topographic effects. The Enhanced Vegetation Index (EVI) was proposed to reduce both atmospheric and soil background noise simultaneously. Thus, they may conclude that it was the soil adjustment factor in the EVI that makes it much more sensitive to the direct effect than the NDVI.

In 2007, Authors Youhao and Wang Jihe used Landsat TM/ETM+ data to monitor Vegetation changes in a particular region. Based on field observation and re-adjustment, the TM-based NDVI values from 0 to 0.21 were classified as natural and artificial. Final conclusion of this paper was, the NDVI derived from TM/ETM + images provide useful information to monitor vegetation changes. The correlation analysis between NDVI and annual precipitation shows that NDVI was statistically correlated with the variations in the annual precipitation. In 2008, George Meyer and Joao Camargo Neto used Landsat image to verify color vegetation indices for automated crop imaging applications. An improved vegetation index, Excess Green minus Excess Red (ExG-ExR) was compared to the commonly used Excess green and the normalized difference indices. Thresholding to obtain binary ExG and NDI index images was performed using the method of Otsu. Otsu method is based on an analysis of the histogram of the image resulting from the initial vegetative index image calculation. A Gaussian filter was used to reduce noise in these images.

In 2008, Authos Wafa Nori, El Nour Elsiddig and Irmgard Niemeyer used Landsat ETM and Aster Data to detect Land cover changes using classification technique. Supervised maximum likelihood classification applied to Landsat images to find land cover changes. The Multivariate Alteration Detection transformation (MAD) was based on a classical statistical transformation referred to as canonical correlation analysis to enhance the change information. In 2009, Siegmann, Jarmer and Hofle used Landsat data to investigate about assessment of canopy nitrogen status. In this study the important vegetation indices like red edge inflection point, normalized difference red edge index and normalized difference nitrogen index have been compared for the prediction of biomass nitrogen concentration of wheat. These vegetation indices were calculated for the AISA-DUAL data of the investigated field.

In 2009, Jun Huang and Youchuan used multispectral landsat data to analyze forest cover change detection model using threshold. Methods involved: 1) multi-scale segmentation algorithm was used to form the image objects. 2) Spectral value and NDVI were taken as input data. 3) Change maps obtained from spectral value and NDVI are compared. In this research unsupervised techniques has been proposed. Final conclusion of this paper was the unsupervised approach provides a well-defined methodological framework for automatic analysis of the difference image. In 2009, Author Thomas Bauer used Landsat image to analyze temporal changes of coca fields on different consecutive years. Methodology of their paper was 1) Stability of coca fields, that means GIS analysis of the temporal change of coca fields: 2005, 2006, and 2007. 2) Investigations on the spectral characteristics, NDVI vegetation index. 3) Analysis of the influence of spraying lines. From Vegetation index they found sensitive indicator of the presence and condition of green vegetation.

In 2009, Author Honglei Zhu used Landsat image for quantitative evaluation of Image segmentation quality in satellite Image Processing. The segmentation result using indices such as:

1. A summed standard deviation of the input images within each image segment;
2. A summed absolute difference within each image segment; and
3. A summed difference of a segment to its adjacent segments.

In 2009, Baodonga and Lixinb used Landsat 7 data to Remote Sensing Monitoring for Vegetation Change in Mining Area based on Spot-VGT NDVI. Changing trend analysis to NDVI: Based on the yearly SPOT-VGT NDVI data, the linear regression of one variable was used to simulate the changing trend of the vegetation in mining area. For each pixel, the slope of the fitted line shows the changing trend of the vegetation. Conclusion of the paper was the time series data of SPOT-VGT NDVI could be composed accordingly to reveal the vegetation information evidently.

In 2010, Author Barbara Koch analyzed forest biomass assessment using multi and hyperspectral data. He compared LiDAR and SAR data with hyperspectral with respect to efficiency to find forest biomass assessment. In 2010, Ashish Ghosh, Niladri shekhar and Susmita ghosh used multispectral landsat data to find unsupervised change detection in remote sensing images using fuzzy clustering algorithms. Two fuzzy clustering algorithms, namely fuzzy c-means and Gustafson-Kessel clustering algorithms have been used for this task in the proposed in this work. Results are compared with those of existing Markov random field (MRF) and neural network based algorithms.

In 2010, Peijum, Xingli, Wen, Yan and Huapeng used multispectral landsat data to monitor changes in urban land cover and changes in vegetation. A NDVI difference approach was used to extract information on changes in vegetation. Maximum Likelihood Classifier has generally been used because of its ease in application, operation and performance. The basic idea of this proposed hierarchical classifier system is to create various classifiers using different input features for many classes. NDVI differences were used to extract vegetation change and an effective false change information elimination approach was developed based on prior knowledge and statistics.

In 2010, sudhanshu Sekhar, Ames and Suranjan Panigrahi used multispectral landsat data to investigate about the strength of the key spectral vegetation indices for agricultural crop yield prediction using neural network techniques. Four widely used spectral indices were investigated in this study of irrigated corn crop yields in the study region. These indices were red and near infrared based normalized difference vegetation index, green and NIR based green vegetation index, red and NIR based soil adjusted vegetation index and red and NIR based perpendicular vegetation index. NDVI, GVI, SAVI were used as input parameters for crop yield prediction models. In 2010, Fazel Amiri and Abdul Rashid used Advanced Spaceborn Thermal Emission and Reflection (ASTER) image data to determine the appropriate indices for vegetation cover and production assessment based on data. All vegetation indices were calculated from ASTER (Advanced Spaceborn Thermal Emission and Reflection Radiometer) image data and compared with vegetation cover estimates at monitoring points during field assessments. In this research a linear regression model was used for selecting suitable vegetation indices. From the results this research showed that there were significant relationships between satellite data and vegetative characteristics.

In 2010, Authors Lei and Bian used MODIS data and Landsat 7 data to analyze spatiotemporal difference of Normalized Difference Vegetation Index to compare the spatiotemporal difference. Detailed NDVI analysis can be made by using an empirical semi variance model. Conclusion of their paper was MODIS-NDVI and Landsat-TM images were processed to study the spatiotemporal variance of vegetation in an arid mining area. It was found that MODIS-NDVI products can provide results close to the NDVI derived from atmosphere corrected TM images. Time series analysis found that the monthly NDVI, rainfall and temperature are consistently subject to annual periodical rhythm. In 2010, Huang quing and Zhang Li used MODIS data to find Normalized Difference Vegetation Index based on crop growth monitoring. The NDVI enhance the identify capacity to soil background and weaken the impact of atmosphere and terrain shadow, and NDVI values increase with the growth of the crops, and gradually decrease after reaching the maximum at a certain growth stage of the crops.

In 2010, Anil Chitade and Katiyar used Landsat 7 image for color based image segmentation using K-means clustering technique. The entire work was divided into two stages. First enhancement of color separation of satellite image using decorrelation stretching was carried out and then the regions are grouped into a set of five classes using K-means clustering algorithm. Using this two step process, it was possible to reduce the computational cost avoiding feature calculation for every pixel in the image. In 2010, Yaowen Xie and Xiaojiong used Landsat ETM data to calculate NDVI for Landsat7 data after atmospheric correction using 6s model. This research paper presented a method of atmospheric correction for Landsat-ETM, taken into account existing research results, the input parameters, including aerosol optical thickness, elevation, which had the significant effect on the results of the correction, were completely analyzed.

In 2010, Uddin and Gurung used Landsat ETM+ and MSS imagery data to analyze Land cover change in Bangladesh using knowledge based classification approach. Using the clumped image, mean values of variables like NDVI, mean water mask were generated and used as an input for expert classification. It is demonstrated knowledge based image classifications using Landsat ETM+ and MSS imagery as a useful technique for classification. In 2011, Author's Tao chen, Ruiqing, Wang, Zhang and Bo Du used multispectral landsat data to monitor percentage of vegetation cover change in wuhan region. The percentage of vegetation cover is defined as area ratio of vegetation and the defined area, such as pixel. Dimidiate pixel model assumed that a pixel consists of two components namely pure vegetation and non-vegetation. Soil map with NDVI map had been applied with some threshold value they got NDVI soil.

In 2011, Joshi and Prem Chandra used landsat multispectral data to present various vegetation indices and their applications for comparison study. The *K*-value of different vegetation indices corresponding to land cover classes helped to identify the performance of vegetation indices. Among various vegetation indices available the NDVI had shown best performance to classify vegetation among all vegetation indices and it helped to map other land cover classes also. In 2011, Andres Vina, Anatoly, Gitelson and Yi Peng used Multispectral landsat data to evaluate different vegetation indices for the remote estimation of the green leaf area index of two crop types. Canopy spectral reflectance data were used for calculating eight vegetation indices. Green LAI, simple ratio, NDVI, EVI, Green Atmospherically Resistant Vegetation Index, Wide Dynamic Range Vegetation Index, the green and red-edge chlorophyll indices respectively. The photosynthetic component of LAI (Green LAI) had been traditionally determined using visual attributions of the greenness of leaves.

In 2011, Joshi and Prem Chandra used landsat multispectral data to present various vegetation indices and their applications for comparison study. The *K*-value of different vegetation indices corresponding to land cover classes helped to identify the performance of vegetation indices. Among various vegetation indices available the NDVI had shown best performance to classify vegetation among all vegetation indices and it helped to map other land cover classes also. In 2011, Yves Julien, Cristian Mattar, Juan and Belen Franch used advanced very high resolution radiometer sensor data to investigate about suffered vegetation changes such as desertification and reforestation. Normalized difference vegetation index (NDVI) and land surface temperature (LST) parameters, estimated from data acquired by the advanced very high resolution radiometer (AVHRR) sensor. This research presents an application of the yearly land-cover dynamics (YLCD) methodology to analyse the behaviour of the vegetation, which contains study of the NDVI and land surface temperature parameters on a yearly basis.

In 2011, Offer Rozenstein and Arnon Karnieli used landsat multispectral data to compare the methods for land-use classification. Pre-processed spectral band image was classified using ISODATA classification technique. The image was classified using signatures from all land cover types. Previous hybrid classification was used to find out land cover area changes using unsupervised training followed by supervised training. Hybrid classification used the signatures that were generated by the ISODATA classification. In 2012, Cutler, Boyd, Foody and Vetrivel used SAR image and Landsat image to estimate tropical forest biomass and assessment of carbon emissions in the atmosphere. Assessment of carbon emissions to the atmosphere would be to estimate net emissions.

In 2012, Bhandari, kumar and singh used Landsat image to extract features using Normalized Difference Vegetation Index. Different values of threshold of NDVI are used for generating the false colour composite of classified objects. The NDVI is motivated by the observation vegetation, which is the difference between the NIR and red band. Very low values of NDVI correspond to areas of rock, sand, or snow. Moderate values represent shrub and grassland. A high value indicates temperate and tropical rainforests. In 2012, Jose, Zarate and Susan used hemispherical photography to investigate about prediction of leaf area index in almonds by vegetation indexes. Optical methods measure transmitted and non-intercepted light through the canopy within part or all the photosynthetically active radiation (PAR). LAI was estimated for selected trees using hemispherical lens photography. Hermispherical photography LAI was compared to MLB LAI. The highly intensive MLB measurements showed the advantage of scanning beneath the canopy with MLB over the fewer photographs of hemispherical lens technique.

In 2012, Alemu Gonsamo and Petri Pelikka used Landsat 7 multispectral data to estimate leaf area index from spectral vegetation indices. They calculated seven SVIs from the surface reflectance using the red, near-infrared and short wave infrared bands. They evaluated the sensitivity of the seven SVIs to LAI based on the expected exponential and best-fit regression models. Two datasets were used in order to demonstrate the use of SVI-LAI sensitivity analysis and subsequently applying for LAI mapping. In 2012, Juliane Huth, Claudia Kuenzer, Thilo Wehramann, Steffen Gebhardt, Vo Quoc Tuan and Stefan Dech used MODIS data to analyze Land cover and Land use classification with TWOPAC. This classification methodology of TWOPAC is a supervised decision tree classification where the tree is derived using representative training areas of each land cover type of interest. Supervised classification is performed in the TWOPAC environment with a certain user defined samples. This algorithm searches through a given set of training cases to find the best feature for separation into pre-defined classes.

In 2013, Guijun Yang, Ruiliang Pu, Jixian Zhang and Jihua wang used Landsat images to investigate about remote sensing of seasonal variability of fractional vegetation cover and its object based spatial pattern analysis over mountain areas. They proposed a new method that incorporates the use of a revised physically based (RPB) model to correct both atmospheric and terrain-caused illumination effects on Landsat images, an improved vegetation index (VI)-based technique for estimating the FVC, and an adaptive mean shift approach for object-based FVC segmentation. FVC estimated through remote sensing technology and seasonal changes in the landscape characteristics existed. On the basis of the surface vegetation reflectivity, accurate FVC values were estimated using the vegetation index (VI) method. In this survey 44 research articles have been referred, most of the researches concentrated more on Vegetation Indices. So Vegetation Indices has more research problems.

VEGETATION INDICES AND APPLICATIONS

In 1995, Ranga Myneni, Forrest Hall and Marshak presented spectral derivative and vegetation indexes. In 1998, Rick Lawrence and William Ripple investigated about the use of various vegetation indices and multiple linear regression using raw spectral bands. In 2000, Prochdxka and Kolinovd investigated about

Figure 1. Comparison of different models

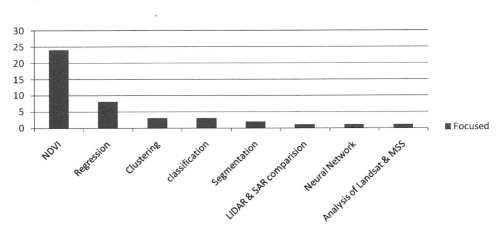

Air pollution detection using image processing. In 2001, Stark estimated Net Primary Productivity. In 2003, Akkartal, Turudu and Erbek used Multisensor calculated vegetation biomass for the particular region using vegetation indices. In 2003, Peng gong and Mirta Rosa Larrieu investigated about the estimation of LAI using vegetation indices. In 2003, Rasmus Fensholt analyzed Normalized Difference Vegetation Index.

In 2003, Limin Yang, George Xian, Jacqueline and Brian Deal found urban land cover change detection through sub pixel imperviousness mapping. In 2004, Bruno Basso, Davide Cammarano and Pasquale described the biophysical principles of vegetation indices and present a review of remote sensing applications for crop management. In 2005, Jarocinska and Zagajewski investigated the method of plant monitor using vegetation indices. Stefan Roettgar analyzed vegetation rendering using Normalized Difference Vegetation Index.

In 2005, Fei yuan, Kali Sawaya, Brian Loeffelholz and Marvin Bauer presented land cover classification and change analysis of the Twin cities metropolitan area. Zheng, Chen, Tian, Ju and Xia estimated above ground biomass of forests. Bunkei Matsushita investigated sensitivity of EVI and NDVI to Topographic effects. Youhao and Wang Jihe monitored Vegetation changes in a particular region. In 2008, George Meyer and Joao Camargo Neto verified color vegetation indices for automated crop imaging applications. Wafa Nori, El Nour Elsiddig and Irmgard Niemeyer detected Land cover changes using classification technique. In 2009, Siegmann, Jarmer and Hofle investigated about assessment of canopy nitrogen status. Later in 2009, Jun Huang and Youchuan analyzed forest cover change detection model using threshold. Thomas Bauer analyzed temporal changes of coca fields on different consecutive years. In 2009, Author Honglei Zhu evaluated mage segmentation quality in satellite Image Processing, Baodonga and Lixinb Monitored for Vegetation Changes in Mining Area based on Spot-VGT NDVI. In 2010, Author Barbara Koch analyzed forest biomass assessment. In 2010, Ashish Ghosh, Niladri shekhar and Susmita ghosh found unsupervised change detection in remote sensing images using fuzzy clustering algorithms. In 2010, Peijum, Xingli, Wen, Yan and Huapeng monitored changes in urban land cover and changes in vegetation, sudhanshu Sekhar, Ames and Suranjan Panigrahi investigated about the strength of the key spectral vegetation indices for agricultural crop yield prediction using neural network techniques. In 2010, Fazel Amiri and Abdul Rashid determined the appropriate indices for vegetation cover and production assessment based on data, Lei and Bian analyzed spatiotemporal difference of Normalized Difference

Vegetation Index to compare the spatiotemporal difference, Huang quing and Zhang Li calculated Normalized Difference Vegetation Index based on crop growth monitoring, Anil Chitade and Katiyar used color based image segmentation using K-means clustering technique, Yaowen Xie and Xiaojiong calculated NDVI for Landsat7 data after atmospheric correction using 6s model and Uddin and Gurung analyzed Land cover change in Bangladesh using knowledge based classification approach.

In 2011, Tao chen, Ruiqing, Wang, Zhang and Bo Du monitored percentage of vegetation cover change in wuhan region, Joshi and Prem Chandra presented various vegetation indices and their applications for comparison study, Andres Vina, Anatoly, Gitelson and Yi Peng evaluated different vegetation indices for the remote estimation of the green leaf area index of two crop types, Joshi and Prem Chandra investigated the performance evaluation of vegetation indices using remotely sensed data, Yves Julien, Cristian Mattar, Juan and Belen Franch investigated about suffered vegetation changes such as desertification and reforestation, Authors Offer Rozenstein and Arnon Karnieli compared the methods for land-use classification.

In 2012, Cutler, Boyd, Foody and Vetrivel estimated tropical forest biomass and assessment of carbon emissions in the atmosphere, Bhandari, kumar and singh extracted features using Normalized Difference Vegetation Index, Authors Jose, Zarate and Susan investigated about prediction of leaf area index in almonds by vegetation indexes., Alemu Gonsamo and Petri Pelikka estimated leaf area index from spectral vegetation indices, Authors Juliane Huth, Claudia Kuenzer, Thilo Wehramann, Steffen Gebhardt, Vo Quoc Tuan and Stefan Dech analyzed Land cover and Land use classification with TWOPAC. In 2013, Guijun Yang, Ruiliang Pu, Jixian Zhang and Jihua wang investigated about remote sensing of seasonal variability of fractional vegetation cover and its object based spatial pattern analysis over mountain areas. Most of the application concentrated on vegetation indices and some of the paper concentrated on atmospheric correction, from this survey world is in need of identifying changes in the vegetation, land cover, land use. This identification will help the government to improvise the vegetation and also to predict the future of the land use.

Figure 2. Comparison of various application

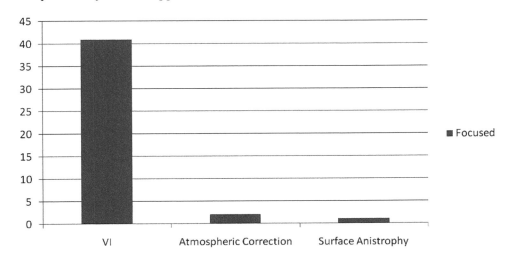

From this survey easily conveys the information that from the available image processing data multispectral images are best to do research and it is cost wise better than hyper spectral images and also the methods used by the various researchers are NDVI this will be effective to identify the vegetation in the earth. From the survey clearly states that more concentration is needed in the area of vegetation indices and also the prediction model for land use. This will help the government people to identify the future land use land cover and vegetation indices, based upon the suggestion from the researchers the government can take the action to improvise the land use and vegetation indices. Thus the proposed work concentrates on LANDSAT multispectral images and application is on vegetation indices (land use, land cover) and the different methods may applied to get the optimized result of Vegetation indices.

Biomass Estimation Approaches

In Different methodology the climatic situations, the eventual fate of carbon outflow may be the primary premise of equivocalness. Aside from for various small regions, what measure of carbon that originate from less imperative woods re development is unidentified. So expanding methodology for figure give or take biomass upset will be strong in decision the carbon drop. There are three distinctive methodology for biomass evaluation:

1. Field Estimation,
2. Remote detecting, and
3. GIS based methodology.

Field Measurement

Field Estimation of biomass is required for prescient displaying and support purposes. Test of trees are taken for the field estimation. Two systems for computing example tree biomass are existing:

1. Ruinous, and
2. Non-damaging (Navar, 2010).

Field Estimation utilizes the dangerous strategy which is finished by felling the sample tree and after that measuring it. Direct weighing is ruined little trees, however for bigger trees, division is important with the goal that parcel can fit into the measuring scale. On the off chance that where the tree is substantial, volume of the stem is measured. Sub-tests are gathered, and its new weight, dried out weight, and amount are measured. The dry weight of the tree is ascertained based from the proportion of the crisp volume to the dry volume. This technique need significant measure of exertion and cost. The over-the-ground stove dry-weight of the example trees can be figured specifically by felling them, broiler drying all segments and afterward measuring them (Shanmughavel, Sha, Zheng, & Cao, 2001; Mbaekwe & Mackenzie, 2008). It is hard and time overriding to accomplish for every one of the examples. A practical arrangement is to develop a relapse mathematical statement stand on the information from chop down trees. The mathematical statement should utilize some effortlessly calculable estimation, for example, distance across. The trees chop down to create nearby volume mathematical statements can be utilized for mounting neighborhood biomass comparison. The picked trees for chop down must approach from the tenants of notification, speak to the fundamental class in the woods, and stand for every single size class. It is for the most part essential that trees in the bigger width classes be well compare to despite the fact that close estimation their biomass is extremely time overpowering due to their enormous size. In the event that belonging are restricted, it is discretionary that a couple of trees in the interest of little, medium, and extensive width be chosen and their biomass ascertained. These could then be assess to the rough guess got from suitable relapse comparison, and in the event that they are in suitable confines no extra example is alluring. On the off chance that, however, that are not inside suitable cutoff points further case and biomass measurements would be alluring to develop nearby biomass mathematical statement.

GIS Based Approach

GIS innovation exhibit a strategy to extend a biomass guide of woodlands for locale with unobtrusive information. GIS consent to the combination of spatial heterogeneity into the representation strategy and offers a system for figure roughly biomass conservativeness at a mainland level where timberland information are inadequate in many territories and people have pained most woodland grounds. It can be broad to ranges in which information are not available in light of the fact that solid examples of biomass thickness often result from comparable biophysical singularity. A topographically referenced biomass reduction database would diminish reservations in evaluating yearly biomass increase and backwoods over-the-ground biomass. The fundamental reason for existing were to accumulate optional information (atmosphere, agroclimate zone, soil sort, slant, height) that will be alluring in the GIS model and to amplify a GIS-based model that may be utilized to anticipate appraisals of over-the-ground biomass of auxiliary timberlands at distinctive areas and ecological circumstances (Lee, 1980). GIS-based routines utilizing assistant information are likewise hard due to inconveniences in addition great quality helper information, roundabout relations between over the ground biomass (AGB) and assistant information, and the complete effects of biological conditions on AGB accumulation. Subsequently, GIS-based methodology have not practical generally for AGB assessment.

Remote Sensing Data

Close estimation of carbon sink consolidate an abnormal state of vulnerability and what sum starts from helper boondocks re advancement is basically unidentified, beside for some little locales. One sober minded way to deal with push ahead is to make draw close for assessment biomass in territory spread by remotely distinguished data. Biomass, in progressive, wrap the over the ground and underground alive mass, for instance, trees, shrubs, vines, roots, and the dead mass of fine and coarse litter joined with the earth. As a result of the unpredictability in amass field data of underground biomass, most former examination on biomass evaluation concentrating on over the ground biomass (AGB). In later year's remote identifying strategy have wound up essential in evaluation of AGB. The prize of remotely distinguished data, for instance, in reliably of data accumulation, a succinct point of view, an automated strategy that agree to brisk procedure sing of limitless measure of data, and the high relationship between unpleasant gatherings and vegetation hindrance, make it the essential hotspot for giant zone AGB evaluation, especially in zones of troublesome access. The different sizes of remote identifying data:

1.   Optical sensor data,
2.   Radar data.

Optical Sensor Data

Former, optical sensors are used for recuperate the forested areas parameters required for Biomass assessment. For optical sensors, vertical brightening of the forested areas covering is in light of awful reflectance data made in clear and infrared region. A bit of the AGB evaluation strategy in light of diverse spatial development of optical sensor data:

Fine Spatial Resolution

Astonishing spatial choice data can be over the ground, for instance, raised photograph, or space-borne, for instance, IKONOS and Speedy Winged animal pictures, with the spatial resolutions of under the distance of 5m. They are as frequently as would be prudent used for showing tree parameters or timberland shade structures. Culvenor sketched out the systems for extraction of individual tree information using fine spatial-determination pictures. The procedures fuse a base up count, a top-down estimation, and configuration organizing. The hindrance is that the high spooky mixed bag and shadows achieved by covering and topography may raise hell in making AGB estimation models. Another burden is the unlucky deficiency of a shortwave infrared picture, which is frequently fundamental for AGB estimation.

Medium Spatial Resolution

The medium spatial-determination ranges from 10 to 100m. The most a tremendous bit of the time used medium spatial-determination data may be the time-strategy Landsat data, which have changed into the fundamental source in diverse applications, including AGB estimation at close-by and normal scales. The certified approaches join direct or non-straight apostatize models, K nearest neighbor, and neural structure. Spooky engravings or vegetation reports are as much of the time as could be permitted used for AGB estimation. Vegetation records have been grasped to release variability made by covering geometry, soil establishment, sun viewpoint focuses, and flows air through and cools when measuring biophysical properties. All around, vegetation records can all things considered lessening the consequences for reflectance made by environmental conditions and shadows.

Picture organization also has shown its hugeness in AGB estimation. A blend of spooky and spatial information extraction frameworks shows ensure for improving estimation execution of forest stand parameters. Picture syntheses are more fundamental than apparition responses for AGB estimation in the forested areas destinations with complex vegetation stand structures. Nevertheless, in the timberland regions with tolerably essential vegetation stand structure, unearthly stamps expect a more fundamental part than picture syntheses. One separating step is to recognize suitable picture surfaces that are unequivocally related with AGB yet are desolately joined with each other. More research is relied upon to make methods for ID of suitable picture surfaces for biomass estimation.

Coarse Spatial Resolution

The coarse spatial resolution is often greater than 100 m. Common coarse spatial-resolution data include NOAA Advanced Very High Resolution Radiometer (AVHRR), SPOT VEGETATION, and Moderate Resolution Imaging Spectro-radiometer (MODIS). They are repeatedly used at national, continental, and global levels. The AVHRR data has the primary source for the required area surveys since this will offer a superior work between data, the spatial resolution and the image coverage.

By and large, the AGB estimation utilizing coarse spatial-determination information is still exceptionally restricted in view of the regular event of blended pixels and the enormous distinction between the extent of field-estimation information and pixel size in the picture, bringing about trouble in the coordination of test information and remote detecting inferred variables. An engineered examination of multiscale information with a blend of distinctive displaying methodologies may be required for exact AGB estimation in a substantial zone.

There are a few impediments in utilizing optical sensor information:

1. It is multifaceted to recover parameters from blended stand.
2. The affectability of reflectance information to woods parameter is not critical after the aggregate scope of the shade.

RADAR DATA

In numerous regions of the world, the incessant cloud conditions regularly control the procurement of amazing remotely detected information by optical sensors. Along these lines, radar information turn into the main achievable method for obtaining remotely detected information inside of a given time structure on the grounds that the radar frameworks can gather Earth highlight information independent of climate or light conditions. Because of this novel component of radar information contrasted and optical sensor information, the radar information have been utilized broadly as a part of numerous fields, including timberland spread recognizable proof and mapping, segregation of woodland compartments and backwoods sorts, and estimation of woods stand parameters. Kasischke et al. (1997) checked on radar information for environmental applications, including AGB estimation. The most encouraging detecting framework gives off an impression of being Engineered Gap Radar (SAR) because of its affectability to woodland structure and valuable connections have been set up between radar backscatter and timberland biophysical parameters (Nizalapur, Jha, & Madugundu, 2010). As of now the three most developed satellite SAR sensors i.e. PALSAR (L-Band), RADARSAT-2 (C-Band) and TerraSAR (X-Band) furnish information with distinctive polarizations, diverse rate edges and high spatial resolutions, and this has opened another entryway of examination in the field of biomass estimation utilizing SAR information. Distinctive radar information have their own particular attributes in identifying with woodland stand parameters.

Be that as it may, the change of biomass estimation depends on the SAR information as well as obliges proficient SAR information preparing, as the crude SAR backscattering coefficient gets to be immersed at genuinely low biomass levels (Dobson, Ulaby, Le Toan, Beaudoin, Kasischke & Christensen, 1992). A few ways have been proposed to gauge biomass past the immersion point. These incorporate:

1. Utilizing longer wavelengths,
2. Utilizing SAR information preparing, for example, composition,
3. Utilizing the proportion of SAR pictures as polarization proportions don't immerse as fast, and proportions can diminish topographic impacts, and woods basic impacts,
4. Averaging so as to utilize a few SAR pictures or different means, to decrease spot based lapse and other arbitrary error (Le Toan, Beaudoin, Riom & Guyon, 1992).

Table 1. Comparison of different approach for biomass

Input	Data	Usage	Demerits
Field Survey	Sample taken Trees	Predictive modeling, validation purpose	Very difficult and time consuming
GIS based data	Secondary data	Develop biomass map	Difficult to collect good quality ancillary data
Fine Spatial Resolution	Aerial Photographs, IKONOS	Modeling tree parameters	Difficult due to the shadows caused by the canopy
Medium Spatial Resolution	LandSat, TM/ETM+, SPOT	Image texture helps in developing estimation model	Difficult in identifying appropriate image texture
Coarse Spatial Resolution	AVHRR, IRS-1C WiFS	It shows the best trade off in between spatial resolution, image coverage, frequency	complicated to incorporate the sample data and remote sensing data
Radar Data	SAR, PALSAR, etc	Collect good quality data irrespective of any weather condition	Good quality of data is not attained.

Subsequently, it is anticipated that biomass estimation possibly enhanced by utilizing longer wavelength SAR information joined by distinctive picture preparing methods.

Table 1 indicates that SAR image information is appropriate to gauge biomass.

Another real issue is to distinguish the right mix of green shading is required for the genuine vegetation. This is a particular issue which turns into a noteworthy issue if attempt to center in territories where a ton of non-vegetation is green.

A noteworthy issue is the means by which huge ought to be a chosen area. Should it have the capacity to suit even little bushes and shrubberies? On the other hand if it be kept to just substantial regions of greenery, for example, parks and bushes.

Maybe, the most concerning issue is to program an interface which can be utilized to concentrate picture from google earth. At first began chipping away at distinctive programming to locate an ideal one. Quick stone Catch or Google earth store chief. programming that can be modified to get a picture as well as to program it to continue moving the region of hobby. Utilize a Modified Google Programming interface keeping in mind the end goal to explore through Google Map (Le Toan, Beaudoin, Riom & Guyon, 1992).

Add From and To Fields to indicate a specific region. It can specifically acquire a zone utilizing scopes. Change and Product a given All encompassing perspective utilizing Java Script Enter the obtained Satellite Picture in Matlab and run channels to choose the wanted shading Evacuate (Obscure) whatever is left of the range

Use pixel space keeping in mind the end goal to figure the rate of region under vegetation

About Vellore

Vellore is a city driving Vellore locale in the Indian condition of Tamil Nadu. It is one of the exceptionally old urban communities in South India and lies on the banks of the Palar Stream pretty much the site of Vellore Fortress. Vellore has a gone away and fruitless atmosphere, acknowledgment of high temperatures in summer months. The city speaks the truth 224 meters over the ocean level likewise it encounters blustery winters and dry summers and has north-east storm the most astounding supporter to precipitation. For this examination work Vellore Region is taken as the study region.

This Biomass Estimation will give the obvious perspective about the biomass level in the city and additionally the deforestation territories in the City. This will help the Nearby City to make important move in the part of A worldwide temperature alteration.

BIOMASS MODEL

The accompanying Figure 3 is the outline of the general biomass estimation. In this Pictures are extricated by utilizing the GIS devices. Subsequent to Extricating the pictures beginning directions and the Consummation directions are distinguished and based upon the prerequisite the layers are recognized and the picture pre handling for evacuating the commotion and Separating System is utilized.

Figure 3. Overall methodology

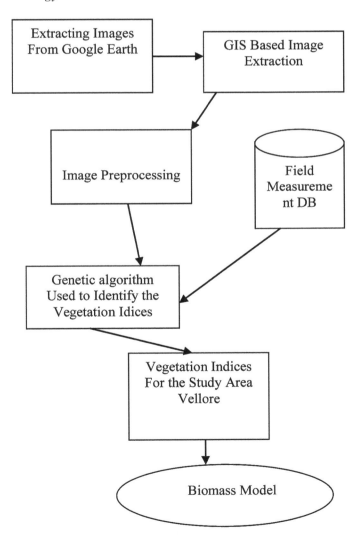

Speckle Noise Reduction

Spot commotion is a granular clamor that intrinsically exists in and corrupts the nature of the dynamic radar and manufactured opening radar (SAR) pictures. Dot commotion in traditional radar results from arbitrary vacillations in the arrival sign from an item that is no greater than a solitary picture handling component. It expands the mean dark level of a neighborhood. Dot clamor in SAR is by and large more genuine, bringing on troubles for picture understanding. It is brought on by rational handling of back-scattered signs from various disseminated targets. To enhance picture examination, spot lessening is for the most part utilized for two applications

- Visualization enhancement,
- Auto- segmentation improvement.

Most spot channels are produced for upgrading perception of dot pictures

Spot commotion does not altogether modify the mean quality in expansive, uniform regions of the picture. Hence dot in SAR pictures can be decreased by averaging various qualities in a nearby neighborhood, yet this procedure diminishes the spatial determination of the picture, and hazy spots edges. The channels in the Radar class use the particular properties of spot commotion to create a more powerful clamor diminishment.

A few distinct techniques are utilized to dispense with dot clamor, based upon diverse numerical models of the marvel. Versatile separating can be utilized to decrease dot commotion. The general strategy of the versatile sifting can be arranged into three stages as given beneath.

- Calculation of local statistics,
- Method of region growing,
- Application of smoothening operator.

A portion of the versatile channels for spot clamor lessening are examined here. The best channel is picked in view of their PSNR and MSE values:

1. **Mean Filter:** Mean channel midpoints the dot into information yet does not uproot dot. It brings about loss of subtle element and determination. So it is considered as the minimum agreeable technique.
2. **Median Filter:** Middle Channel uproots spikes or heartbeat clamor. Heartbeat elements of under one 50% of the moving piece width are stifled or wiped out.
3. **Wiener Filter:** Wiener channel is a versatile channel. It is in view of Fourier emphasis. It requires short computational investment to discover an answer. Wiener channel method performs well since it has low MSE qualities and high PSNR values.
4. **Lee Filter:** Lee uses the measurable dissemination for assessing the estimation of the information pixel by pixel. The mean and presumption of the pixel is equivalent to the nearby mean and change of all pixel inside of the client chose moving portion. The formula for Lee Filter:

$$DN_{out} = \left[Mean\right] + K\left[DN_{in} - Mean\right].$$

Mean = Pixel average in the moving window

$$K = \frac{Var\left(x\right)}{\left[Mean\right]^2 \sigma^2 + Var\left(x\right)}$$

$$Var\left(x\right) = \left(\frac{\left[Variance\ within\ window\right] + \left[Mean\ within\ window\right]^2}{Sigma^2 + 1}\right) - \left[Mean\ within\ window\right]^2$$

5. **Kuan Filter:** The Kuan channel is utilized fundamentally to channel spotted radar information. It is intended to smooth out clamor while holding edges or shape highlights in the picture. Distinctive channel sizes will significantly influence the nature of prepared pictures. On the off chance that the channel is too little, the clamor sifting calculation is not compelling. In the event that the channel is too expansive, inconspicuous points of interest of the picture will be lost in the sifting procedure.

6. **Frost Filter:** Frost Channel replaces the pixel of enthusiasm with the weighted total of the qualities inside of the nxn moving portion. The measuring component diminish with separation from the pixel of hobby. The measuring component increment from the focal pixels as difference inside of the portion increments. The Formula for Frost Filter:

$$DN = \sum_{nXn} kae^{-\alpha}\left|t\right|.$$

where

$$\alpha = \left(4 / n\sigma1^2\right)\left(\sigma^2 / I1^2\right),$$

k = Constant of Normalization,

I1 = Value of local mean,

σ = Value of Local variance,

σ1 = Image coefficient of variation value $\left|t\right| = \left|X - X_0\right| + \left|Y - Y_0\right|$,

t = Kernel size.

A few versatile channels that protect the radiometric and surface data have been produced for spot lessening.

Versatile channels situated in the spatial space are more broadly utilized than recurrence area channels. The most as often as possible utilized versatile channels incorporate Lee and Gamma-Map. The Lee-Sigma channel is a straightforward however compelling distinct option for the Lee channel, and Lee-Sigma is in view of the likelihood of the Gaussian appropriation of commotion in the picture (Lee, 1980).

The implemented frost filter is given as:

$$a^2 = \frac{s^2}{z^2}.$$

$$m\left(t\right) = e^{-Ka^2|t|}$$

$$y\left(t\right) = \frac{\Sigma_i m\left(t_i\right) \cdot x\left(t_i\right)}{\Sigma_i m\left(t_i\right)}$$

where,

s^2 = Variance of Image,
z = Variance of Image mean,
t = Coordinate of the pixel,
$m(t)$ = Weight factor,
K = Constant value,
$x(t)$ = Pixel value at point t,
$y(t)$ = Replacing pixel at time t.

Speckle noise reduction Frost filter, wiener filter and the frost filter are best. The reason is MSE and PSNR are reasonable for this work.

7. **Mean Square Error:** In experiences, the mean squared error (MSE) of an estimator is one of various ways to deal with measure the difference between qualities recommended by an estimator and the real estimations of the sum being surveyed. MSE is a risk limit, identifying with the ordinary estimation of the squared slip mishap or quadratic adversity. MSE measures the typical of the squares of the "slips." The screw up is the aggregate by which the value construed by the estimator fluctuates from the add up to be assessed. The qualification happens in light of haphazardness or in light of the way that the estimator doesn't speak to information that could convey a more exact evaluation.

The MSE is the next instant (about the beginning) of the imperfection, and beside these lines wires both the distinction of the estimator and its inclination. For a reasonable estimator, the MSE is the change. Resembling the variance, MSE has the similar units of estimation as the square of the sum being surveyed.
Mean square Error is as follows

$$\frac{1}{MN} \sum_{y=1}^{M} \sum_{x=1}^{N} \left[I\left(x,y\right) - I'\left(x,y\right)\right]^2$$

where I(x,y) is the first picture, I'(x,y) is the approximated adjustment (which is truly the decompressed picture) and M,N are the estimations of the photos. A lower quality for MSE suggests lesser screw up

Peak Signal-to-Noise Ratio

The expression peak sign to-fuss extent, routinely abbreviated PSNR, is a planning term for the extent between the greatest possible power of a sign and the power of polluting bustle that impacts the consistency of its representation. Since various signs have a wide component territory, PSNR is for the most part imparted similarly as the logarithmic decibel scale.

The PSNR is characterized as

PSNR = 20 * log10 (255 / sqrt(MSE))

Sensibly, a higher estimation of PSNR is extraordinary in light of the fact that it infers that the extent of Sign to Clamor is higher. Here, the "sign" is the first picture, and the "uproar" is the bungle in generation.

Therefore, in case you find a weight arrangement having a lower MSE (and a high PSNR), you can see that it is a predominant one.

Table 2 states that frost filter, Lee filter and Wiener filter are good for speckle noise removal because the PSNR are high and the MSE are low.

EASE OF USE

Algorithm which uses the genetic for grouping the Green areas.

1. Get the data Matrix.
2. Identify the of clusters, c ($2 \leq c \leq n$), n= Length of the Image.
3. Partition matrix, U(r), population of cluster centers equal to initial values.
4. Identify the individual fitness in the in the population.
5. Repeat the steps 7 to 12 till the convergence.
6. Perform Euclidean distance matrix, D using

$$d\left(p,q\right) = \sqrt{\left(p_1 - q_1\right)^2 + \left(\left(p_2 - q_2\right)^2\right)}$$

Table 2. PSNR and MSE values of tested filters

Filter	PSNR	MSE
Wiener	75.3219	24.1847
Median	61.6028	32.0643
Kuan	74.8849	106.1153
Frost	75.3748	25.3442
Lee	76.6513	25.1920

7. Modify the partition matrix, U(r) by using the equation.
8. Genetic algorithm operation Crossover and mutation operations is performed to identify the individuals.
9. Evaluate the New Individuals.
10. Least fit populated individuals has to be fixed.

The calculation is anything but difficult to actualize and should be possible on any stage. Matlab was utilized for our usage. The execution was simple and can be changed to make adjustments for future work.

The Google Programming interface utilized, delivered pictures that were specifically given as data to the Matlab programming. No change or sort transformation was needed. GUI accessible in Matlab could be utilized to further show the calculation.

Equation Used

The comparison is in light of relative scaling of shading pixels. Parameter "im" takes every pixel in the picture as its info. This parameter has 3 parameters: R G B values. Every pixel, along these lines, has 3 segments values. To extricate any particular piece of picture, the calculation controlled the given 3 estimations of every pixel.

The point of the calculation was to identify green zones of vegetation. Accordingly, shading wheel was gotten to coordinate the regions with green vegetation. Diverse shades of green were utilized to empower various types of vegetation. Consequently, any slight alteration would permit utilization of the same calculation for an alternate geographic framework (Roy & Kumar, 1986). The mathematical statement above contrasts the green pixel quality and the estimations of red and blue pixel component. Coherently, a green pixel would have higher estimations of green when contrasted with blue or red. This was utilized as a part of the calculation. This is known as Relative Scaling of the pixel in light of the fact that, in the execution don't take the supreme esteem rather the distinction in the estimation of green, red and blue.

Efficiency of Algorithm

Since the calculation utilizes relative pixel esteem it is vastly improved contrasted with the supreme utilization of pixels. This is on the grounds that the calculation does not consider the genuine estimation of each RGB segment rather it is in light of the nature of the distinction between the components of pixel.

Dissimilar to our calculation, unquestionably the scaling obliges genuine qualities. This is higher to discover correctly. To discover vegetation this calculation would require a flat out scope of pixel component values. Is this difficult to discover, as well as it would leave a lot of green pixels of diverse shades. A comparison in light of outright scaling looks like after:

This would obviously forget diverse shades of green and would oblige broad examination for distinctive sort of vegetation. Clearly, relative scale calculation is better as it never obliges total qualities and rather discovers every one of the pixels utilizing the relative property. All the more essentially, for any land review, exact information is obliged which can be given utilizing the relative scale calculation.

Figure 4. Quantum GIS to extract the VIT (study area)

USE OF SATELLITE IMAGE

The first satellite picture of Vellore Foundation of innovation is utilized as a part of the specimen test. The calculation would take a shot at every pixel freely and locate the relative estimation of green when contrasted with the other two elements.

Figure 5. VIT University image (after the preprocessing)

After utilization of the calculation just the green part exists. This is unmistakably a shading of the district which has just green vegetation.

The calculation additionally gives the rate region under vegetation utilizing the relative estimations of the coveted pixel space and the aggregate pixel space. The rate can then be changed over to scale in hectare utilizing scales gave by the google earth.

Every one of the areas separated from the sought pixels are passed out. The pixels can be changed over to dark scale or obscured.

Green Area Detection

In the detecting so as to follow stage we identify the woods spread green regions in the picture. The green territory recognition was actualized utilizing the accompanying methodology:

1. Separate RGB band in the given image.
2. Find the threshold value for the separated RGB band.
3. Find red mask, green mask and blue mask with the help of low threshold value and high threshold value.
4. Combine the masks to get the green object mask.
5. Fill the holes and combine the green band to get the greenery area.

Figure 6. Genetic applied for clustering

Table 3. Result of different region geographical maps

Image	Description	R	G	B
	In and around Vellore, TN, India (size144X107) (72 DPI)	20.39%	30.58%	23.13%
		22.35%	31.37%	23.92%
		34.11%	41.17%	31.76%
	In and around IIT Madras, Chennai, TN, India (size133X101)(72 DPI)	12.54%	27.45%	22.35%
		18.03%	29.80%	27.05%
		21.17%	33.33%	29.80%

The above test image(s) are taken from the Google Maps with the Zoom Level 17.

FUTURE WORK

The Examination work permits the client to data a succession of nearby pictures, speaking to a specific district and procedures them to focus the rate region under vegetation. The impediment of the present work is the absence of coordination with the Google Earth Programming interface Incorporate Google Earth Programming interface with the MATLAB vegetation location calculation. Separate between the distinctive shades of green and arrange shades to specific vegetation. Certain issues confronted to partition the picture utilizing division and in this manner deciding the quantity of particular areas .Focus examples to distinguish vicinity of man-made articles that take after vegetation. Sample: Green autos, structures and so forth. To create and incorporate the distinctive modules of the examination and in this way make an easy to understand interface to utilize the framework. To focus the measure of a specific area that could be named a piece of the common asset of the district.

This strategy has incredible point of interest over other since there is no compelling reason to compute likelihood thickness capacity and there is no need of strict radiometric adjustment.

REFERENCES

Akkartal, Turudu, & Erbek. (2003). *Analysis of Changes in Vegetation Biomass using Multitemporal and Multisensor Satellite Data*. Academic Press.

Amiri & Shariff. (2010). Using Remote Sensing Data for Vegetation Cover Assessment in Semi-Arid Rangeland of Center Province of Iran. *World Applied Sciences Journal, 11*(12), 1537–1546.

Basso, Cammarano, & De Vita. (2004). Remotely sensed vegetation indices: Theory and Applications for crop management. *Rivista Italiana di Agrometeorologia*, 36-53.

Bauer & Schneider. (2009). *Analysis of time series of Landsat images*. Institute of Surveying, Remote Sensing and Land Information, University of Natural Resources and Applied Life Sciences (BOKU).

Bhandari, A. K., Kumar, A., & Singh, G. K. (2012). Feature Extraction using Normalized Difference Vegetation Index (NDVI). *Procedia Technology, 6*, 612–621. doi:10.1016/j.protcy.2012.10.074

Chen, T., Rui-qing, N., Wang, Y., Liang-pei, Z., & Du, B. (2011). Percentage of Vegetation Cover Change Monitoring in Wuhan Region Based on Remote Sensing. *Procedia Environmental Sciences, 10*, 1466–1472. doi:10.1016/j.proenv.2011.09.234

Chitade & Katiyar. (2010). *Colour Based Image Segmentation using K-Means Clustering*. Department of Civil Engineering, Manit, Bhopal, Madhyapradesh.

Cutler, M. E. J., Boyd, D. S., Foody, G. M., & Vetrivel, A. (2012). Estimating tropical forest biomass with a combination of SAR image texture and Landsat TM data: An assessment of predictions between regions. *ISPRS Journal of Photogrammetry and Remote Sensing, 70*, 66–77. doi:10.1016/j.isprsjprs.2012.03.011

Dobson, M. C., Ulaby, F. T., Le Toan, T., Beaudoin, A., Kasischke, E. S., & Christensen, N. (1992). Dependence of radar backscatter on coniferous forest biomass. IEEE Trans. Geosci. Remote Sens., 30(2).

Du, Li, Cao, Luo, & Zhang. (2010). Monitoring urban land cover and vegetation change by multi-temporal remote sensing information. *Mining Science and Technology, 20*, 922-932.

Elsiddig & Niemeyer. (2008). Detection of Land Cover changes using Multi-Temporal Satellite Imagery. The International Archieves of the Photogrammetry, Remote Sensing and Spatial Information Sciences, 37(B7).

Fensholt, Sandholt, & Stisen. (2006). *Analysing NDVI for the African continent using the geostationary meteosat second generation SEVIRI sensor*. NASA Goddard Space Flight Center.

Flasse, S. P., Ceccato, P., Downey, I. D., Raimadoya, M. A., & Navarro, P. (1997). *Remote sensing and GIS tools to support vegetation management in developing countries*. IEEE International. doi:10.1109/IGARSS.1997.608950

Ghosh, A., Mishra, N. S., & Ghosh, S. (2010). Fuzzy clustering algorithms for unsupervised change detection in remote sensing images. *Information Sciences*.

Gong, P. (2003). *Estimation of Forest Leaf Area Index Using Vegetation Indices Derived from Hyperion Hyperspectral Data. IEEE Transactions on Geoscience and Remote Sensing, 41(6)*.

Gonsamo, A., & Pellikka, P. (2012). The sensitivity based estimation of leaf area index from spectral vegetation indices. *ISPRS Journal of Photogrammetry and Remote Sensing, 70*, 15–25. doi:10.1016/j.isprsjprs.2012.03.009

Huang, Wan, & Shen. (2009). *An Object-Based Approach for Forest-Cover Change Detection using Multi-Temporal High-Resolution Remote Sensing Data*. School of Remote Sensing and Information Engineering, Wuhan University.

Huth, Kuenzer, Wehrmann, Gebhardt, Tuan, & Dech. (2012). Land Cover and Land Use Classification with TWOPAC: Towards Automated Processing for Pixel-and Object-Based Image Classification. *Remote Sensing, 4*, 2530-2553.

Jarocinska & Zagajewski. (2009). *Remote Sensing tools for analysis of Vegetation condition in extensively used Agricultural Areas*. Academic Press.

Joshi, P. C. (2011). *Performance evaluation of vegetation indices using remotely sensed data. International Journal of Geomatics and Geosciences*.

Joshi, P. C. (2011). Performance evaluation of vegetation indices using remotely sensed data. *International Journal of Geomatics and Geosciences, 2*(1), 2011.

Julien, Y., Sobrino, J. A., Mattar, C., Ruescas, A. B., Jimenez-munoz, J. C., & Soria, G. et al. (2011, April10). Temporal analysis of Normalized Difference Vegetation Index (NDVI) and land surface temperature (LST) parameters to detect changes in the Iberian land cover between 1981 and 2001. *International Journal of Remote Sensing, 32*(7), 2057–2068. doi:10.1080/01431161003762363

Koch, B. (2010). Status and future of laser scanning, synthetic aperture radar and hyperspectral remote sensing data for forest biomass assessment. *ISPRS Journal of Photogrammetry and Remote Sensing, 65*(6), 581–590. doi:10.1016/j.isprsjprs.2010.09.001

Lawrence, R. L., & Ripple, W. J. (1998). Comparisons among Vegetation Indices and Band wise Regression in a Highly Distributed, Heterogeneous Landscape: Mount St. Helens, Washington. *Remote Sensing of Environment*, *64*(1), 91–102. doi:10.1016/S0034-4257(97)00171-5

Le Toan, T., Beaudoin, A., Riom, J., & Guyon, D. (1992). Relating forest biomass to sar data. IEEE Trans. Geosci. Remote Sens., 30(2).

Lee, J. S. (1980). Digital image enhancement and noise filtering by use of local statistics. *IEEE Transactions on Pattern Analysis and Machine Intelligence*, *2*(2), 165–168. doi:10.1109/TPAMI.1980.4766994 PMID:21868887

Lee, J. S. (1980). Digital image enhancement and noise filtering by use of local statistics. *IEEE Transactions on Pattern Analysis and Machine Intelligence*, *2*(2), 165–168. doi:10.1109/TPAMI.1980.4766994 PMID:21868887

Lei, & Bian. (2010). Analysis of Spatiotemporal Difference of NDVI in an Arid Coal Mining Region using *Remote Sensing*. Jiangsu Key Laboratory of Resources and Environmental Information Engineering, China University of Mining and Technology.

Ma, Wu, & Liu. (2009). *Remote Sensing Monitoring For Vegetation Change In Mining Area Based On Spot-VGT NDVI*. Institute for Geoinformatics & Digital Mine Research, Northeastern University.

Magscale-Macandog, D. B., & Delgado, M. E. M. (2006). A GIS-based model to improve estimattion of above ground biomass of secondary forests in the Philippines. *Journal of Tropical Forest Science*, *18*(1), 8–21.

Matsushita, Yang, Chen, Onda, & Qiu. (2007). *Sensitivity of the Enhanced Vegetation Index (EVI) and Normalized Difference Vegetation Index (NDVI) to Topographic Effects: A Case Study in High-Density Cypress Forest*. Graduate School of Life and Environmental Sciences, University of Tsukuba.

Mbaekwe, E. I., & Mackenzie, J. A. (2008). The use of a best-fit allometric model to estimate aboveground biomass accumulation and distribution in an age series of teak (tectona grandis l.f.) plantations at Gambari Forest Reserve, Oyo State, Nigeria. *Tropical Ecology*, *49*(2), 259–270.

Meyer & Neto. (2008). Verification of color vegetation indices for automated crop imaging applications. *Computers and Electronics in Agriculture, 6*(3), 282–293.

Myneni, R. B., Hall, F. G., Sellers, P. J., & Marshak, A. L. (1995, March). The Interpretation of Spectral Vegetation Indexes. *IEEE Transactions on Geoscience and Remote Sensing*, *33*(2), 481–486. doi:10.1109/36.377948

Navar, J. (2010). *Measurement and assessment methods of forest aboveground biomass: A literature review and the challenges ahead, Biomass*. Croatia: Sciyo.

Nizalapur, V., Jha, C. S., & Madugundu, R. (2010). Estimation of above ground biomass in Indian tropical forested area using multifrequency dlresar data. *International Journal Of Geomatics And Geosciences*, *1*(2), 2010.

Panda, S. S., Ames, D. P., & Panigrahi, S. (2010). Application of Vegetation Indices for Agricultural Crop Yield Prediction Using Neural Network Techniques. *Remote Sensing, 2*(3), 673–696. doi:10.3390/rs2030673

Prochdxka & Kolinovd. (2000). *Satellite Image Processing and Air Pollution Detection.* Prague Institute of Chemical Technology

Quing, Li, Wu, & Li. (2010). *MODIS-NDVI-Based crop growth monitoring in China Agriculture Remote Sensing Monitoring System.* Grassland Ecosystem Observation and Research Station Institute of Agricultural Resources and Regional Planning of Chinese Academy of Agricultural Sciences.

Roettger. (2006). *NDVI Based Vegetation Rendering.* Computer Graphics Group, University of Erlangen.

Roy, P. S., & Kumar, S. (1986) Advanced Very High Resolution Radiometer(AVHRR) satellite data forvegetation monitoring. *Proc. International Seminar on Photogrammetry and Remote Sensing fordeveloping countries.*

Rozenstein & Karnieli. (2011). Comparison of methods for Land-use classification incorporating Remote Sensing and GIS Inputs. *EARSel eProceedings, 10*(1).

Shanmughavel, P. (2001). Nutrient cycling in a tropical seasonal rain forest of Xishuangbanna, Southwest China. Part 1: Tree species: Nutrient distribution and uptake. *Bioresource Technology, 80,* 163–170. doi:10.1016/S0960-8524(01)00095-5 PMID:11601539

Siegmann, Jarmer, Lilienthal, Richter, Selige, & Hofle. (2001). *Comparison of Narrow Band Vegetation Indices and Empirical Models from Hyperspectral Remote Sensing Data for the Assessment of Wheat Nitrogen Concentration.* Academic Press.

Techpogo. (2009). *How does Google Maps work.* Author.

Uddin & Gurung. (2008). Land cover change in Bangladesh- a knowledge based classification approach. *Grazer Writings of Geography and Regional Science*, 41-46.

Vina, A., Gitelson, A. A., Nguy-Robertson, A. L., & Peng, Y. (2011). Comparison of different vegetation indices for the remote assessment of green leaf area index of crops. *Remote Sensing of Environment, 115*(12), 3468–3478. doi:10.1016/j.rse.2011.08.010

Wikihow. (n.d.). *Build a Simple Graphical User Interface in Matlab.* Retrieved from: http://www.wikihow.com/Build-a-Simple-Graphical-User-Interface-in-Matlab

Xie, Zhao, Li, & Wang. (2010). *Calculating NDVI for Landsat7-ETM Data after atmospheric correction Using 6S Model.* Key Laboratory of West China's Environmental System.

Yang, Xian, Klaver, & Deal. (2003). Urban Land-Cover change Detection through Sub-pixel Imperviousness Mapping using Remotely Sensed Data. Photogrammetric Engineering & Remote Sensing, 69(9).

Yang, G., Pu, R., Zhang, J., Zhao, C., Feng, H., & Wang, J. (2013). Remote sensing of seasonal variability of fractional vegetation cover and its object-based spatial pattern analysis over mountain areas. *ISPRS Journal of Photogrammetry and Remote Sensing, 77,* 79–93. doi:10.1016/j.isprsjprs.2012.11.008

Youhao, Jihe, Shangyu, Ping, & Zihui. (2008). *Monitoring of Vegetation Changes Using Multi-temporal NDVI in Peripheral Regions around Minqin Oasis, Northwest China*. College of Resources Science and Technology.

Yuan, Sawaya, Loeffelholz, & Bauer. (2006). Land cover classification and change analysis of the Twin Cities (Minnesota) Metropolitan Area by multitemporal Landsat remote sensing. *Remote Sensing of Environment*, *98*, 317–328.

Zarate-Valdez, J. L., Whiting, M. L., Lampinen, B. D., Metcalf, S., Ustin, S. L., & Brown, P. H. (2012). Prediction of leaf area index in almonds by vegetation indexes. *Computers and Electronics in Agriculture*, *85*, 24–32. doi:10.1016/j.compag.2012.03.009

Zheng, Chen, Tian, Ju, & Xia. (2007). Combining remote sensing imagery and forest age inventory for biomass mapping. *Journal of Environment Manage.*, *85*(3), 616-23.

Zhu & Chen. (2009). *A Quantitative Evaluation of Image Segmentation Quality*. Clark University.

Zhu, Pan, Hu, Li, & Gong. (2001). *Estimating Net Primary Productivity of Terrestrial Vegetation Based on Remote Sensing: A Case Study in Inner Mongolia, China*. College of Resources Science and Technology, Key Laboratory of Environmental Change and Natural Disaster of Ministry of Education, Beijing Normal University.

Chapter 13
Optimized–Fuzzy–Logic–Based Bit Loading Algorithms

Sankar Ganesh S.
VIT University, India

Arunprakash Jayaprakash
VIT University, India

Mohanaprasad K.
VIT University, India

Sivanantham Sathasivam
VIT University, India

ABSTRACT

Next generation wireless communication systems promise the subscribers with Giga-bit-data-rate experience at low Bit Error Rate (BER) under adverse channel conditions. In order to maximize the overall system throughput of Orthogonal Frequency Division Multiplexing (OFDM), adaptive modulation is one of the key solutions. In adaptive modulated OFDM, the subcarriers are allocated with data bits and energy in accordance with the Signal to Interference Ratio (SIR) of the multipath channel, which is referred to as adaptive bit loading and adaptive power allocation respectively. The number of iterations required allocating the target bits and energy to a sub channel is optimized. The key choice of the paper is to allocate the bits with minimum number of iterations after clustering the sub channels using fuzzy logic. The proposed method exhibits a faster convergence in obtaining the optimal solution.

INTRODUCTION

OFDM is considered as the most widely adopted multicarrier communication technique for very high speed data transmission in wireless local area networks (WLAN) and digital subscriber link (DSL) systems. OFDM exhibits various advantages over the conventional single carrier communication systems. The OFDM systems are robust against frequency selective channels as the multipath channels effect as flat fading channels to individual subcarriers and hence one-tap equalization is made possible. The subcarriers in OFDM are orthogonal sine pulses so that the conventional frequency division multiplexing systems, the subcarriers can be closely spaced without interference, thereby improving spectral efficiency and reducing the total bandwidth requirements. Even though the time varying channels introduce inter carrier interference (ICI), several CFO estimation and correction techniques can be used to avoid this undesirable effect.

DOI: 10.4018/978-1-5225-1008-6.ch013

In spite of these advantages of OFDM, a decrease in the performance occurs under multipath channels due to the fluctuations in the frequency response of the channels. This is severe in the case of highly frequency selective channels. The set of data to be transmitted are modulated onto orthogonal subcarriers which are summed up and transmitted through the channel. The multipath channel which is frequency selective in nature attenuates the data symbols modulated at different subcarriers differently. Certain subcarriers may be attenuated heavily so that the data symbols modulated on to those subcarriers are completely lost during transmission. Channel gain for certain other subcarriers will be very high. Hence, the system performance and throughput will be very much less than the optimum value if a fixed transmission scheme is used for OFDM transmission under a highly frequency selective channel. The data symbols modulated on to subcarriers which are attenuated heavily has very low SIR and hence high bit error rate which results in a poor performance. Hence, adaptive modulation aims at leaving out the subcarriers that are attenuated heavily and allocate bits to the subcarriers according to the channel gain. The adaptation of the modulation level according to the SIR results in better BER performance and high system throughput.

Several adaptive bit and power allocation loading schemes have been studied. The most powerful method to allocate bits with less energy is using Hughes-Hartogs Greedy Algorithm by (Hughes-Hartogs, 1988) but it takes a large number of iterations to converge to the optimal solution. Chow's Algorithm proposed by (Chow, Cioffi, & Bingham, 1995) uses channel capacity approximation and converges to the solution for given target bits and performance margin. Campello's Algorithm proposed by (Campello, 1999, 1998) is different in the way that it takes differential energy to achieve the target bits. But both these algorithms take a lot of iterations again. Simple bit loading algorithm proposed by (Nader-Esfahani & Afrasiabi, 2007) has low complexity and takes less iteration than Hughes Hartogs Greedy, Chow and Campello. It is based on grouping of sub channels based on gain. A clustering based bit loading algorithm which uses neural network for clustering the subcarriers is elaborated in (Birla, 2014). A computationally efficient bit loading algorithm for OFDM systems is proposed in (Vo, Amis, Chonavel, Siohan, & Member, 2015) which adaptively switches between Greedy algorithm and bit removing algorithm. The adaptive modulated multicarrier systems are also applied in the context of visible light communication (Hong, Member, Wu, Chen, & Member, 2016), power line communication (Gianaroli, Pancaldi, & Vitetta, 2015) and filter bank multicarrier based optical communication (Jung, Jung, & Han, 2015).

The proposed algorithm has very low computation complexity and is convergent to the optimal solution; moreover, it has low algorithmic complexity for implementation purposes. Grouping concept proposed by (Wang, Cao, & Statement, 2013; Nader-Esfahani & Afrasiabi, 2007) is used in proposed fuzzy based bit loading algorithm with very low complexity and less iteration with comparable energy as compared to existing algorithms. It is observed that maximum of 15 bits can be allocated to a sub-channel but for energy optimization with less iteration maximum of 11 bits can be allocated. Fuzzy is related to ambiguity. Fuzzy based Systems are based on Soft Threshold Concept where transitions are based on ambiguity i.e. various intervals can be decided based on discretion of user. So bit loading algorithms are optimized using fuzzy logic by (Sastry, 2010). The conventional bit loading algorithms require more number of iterations to find the optimum solutions and hence become difficult to be applied for real time applications. Hence in the present study, a fuzzy theory based solution is proposed for the adaptive bit loading problem formulated as a constrained optimization problem. In this chapter, an adaptive loading and modulation scheme is proposed in which all the parameters are adapted using a fuzzy logic base system. Rest of the chapter is organized as follows. Bit loading and Fuzzy introduction is given in the next section. The proposed clustering based loading algorithms using fuzzy and simulations results are elaborated in the subsequent section. The next section contains the comparison between existing and proposed algorithms and concludes the chapter.

BIT LOADING AND FUZZY LOGIC

Bit Loading

Bit Loading is a technique in which bit allocation is performed for the sub-carriers in Multicarrier Modulation. The bits allocation is based on the sub channel quality which is based on parameters like SNR. The aim of this technique is to allocate more bits to channels with high SNR or low corrupted channels and fewer bits to channels with low SNR or highly corrupted channels. Bit Loading involves allocation of parameters like Energy and the bits to a sub channel. The parameters taken into account while allocating the bits and energy are Sub-channel Gain(H), Sub-channel Noise(N), SNR gap(Γ), Target Bits(B_{total}), Maximum Energy(P_{total}), Target Margin(t_m). All the algorithms take few of the above mentioned parameters into account to propose an optimal solution for Bit Loading.

The number of bits that can modulated on to each subcarrier depends upon the channel characteristics and SNR at that particular frequency. More power must be allocated to those subcarriers with lower SNR to transmit data. Due to an overall power limit on each subcarrier, those frequencies with high attenuation are able to carry less number of bits than a channel with a better channel gain. More bits can be allocated to that particular sub-channel which has better SNR at that frequency range in the sub-channel range (Juan Wen & Tian, 2013).

The SNR for a sub-channel is given by

$$SNR_k = \frac{|H_k|^2}{(\Gamma \cdot \sigma^2)}, k = 1, 2 \ldots N \tag{1}$$

where SNR gap, Γ, represents how far is the channel from Shannon Channel Capacity.

To reduce iteration complexity one of the methods is cluster or group sub-channels based on their gain response. This approach leads to group by group bit loading which just takes one iteration to allocate bits but for grouping iterations are needed. The number of groups is given by

$$Number\ of\ Groups = \log_2 \left(\frac{|H\max|^2}{|H\min|^2} \right) + 1 \tag{2}$$

where |Hmax|² and |Hmin|² are maximum and minimum gains of the sub-channels and x denote the largest integer less than x. Figure 1 shows grouping performed based on sub-channel gains.

Figure 1. Grouping of sub-channels

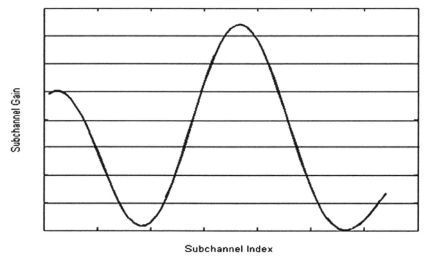

Bit-Loading for k[th] sub-channel is performed by finding maximum and minimum bits that can be loaded in that group using maximum and minimum Channel Gain values in the equation

$$BL_k = \log_2\left(-1.6 * \frac{SNR_k}{\ln\left(5 * Target\ BER\right)} + 1\right) \tag{3}$$

The energy for k[th] sub-channel is given by

$$E_k = \left(2^{BL_k} - 1\right) * \left(\frac{\Gamma \cdot \sigma^2}{\left|H_k\right|^2}\right), k = 1,2..N \tag{4}$$

where BL is the loaded bits in the sub-channel and σ^2 is Noise Variance. Finally Bit Error rate, BER for k[th] sub-channel (k varies from 1,2..N)is given by,

$$BER_k = 0.2e^{\left[-1.6\left(\frac{E_k}{2^{BL_k}-1}\right)\cdot\left(\frac{\left|H_k\right|^2}{\sigma^2}\right)\right]} \tag{5}$$

Present your perspective on the issues, controversies, problems, etc., as they relate to theme and arguments supporting your position. Compare and contrast with what has been, or is currently being done as it relates to the chapter's specific topic and the main theme of the book (Figure 1).

Fuzzy Logic

Fuzzy is related to ambiguity. Unlike Neural networks that are based on Hard Threshold Concept i.e. output is either logic 0 or 1, Fuzzy based Systems are based on Soft Threshold Concept where transitions are based on ambiguity i.e. various intervals can be decided based on discretion of user (Sastry, 2010). The unique features of fuzzy logic make it an excellent choice for many control problems. The target control system is governed by user defined rules which is processed by the fuzzy logic system. it Hence it can be adjusted and modified easily to improve the system performance. The fuzzy logical system is not restricted to a few feedback inputs and a couple of control outputs, nor does it require information on the rate-of-change of parameters for its implementation. Both linear and non-linear systems for embedded control can be designed using fuzzy logic. The fuzzy logic can be applied effectively solve real world problems through intelligent interpretations and human like thinking. Instead of taking a crisp decision based on hard thresholds, a soft decision is taken considering different parameters simultaneously.

Various methods are used for fuzzification like rank ordering, inference, intuition and threshold concept. All these help in grouping the Sub-Channels into packets based on the channel response. For our purpose we can choose either rank ordering or threshold concept for fuzzification.

CLUSTERING BASED BIT LOADING ALGORITHM USING FUZZY LOGIC

Fuzzy Based Bit Loading Algorithms are based on Threshold Concept. Using various Threshold Ranges groups are made based on sub-channel quality.

For simulation purpose the input data includes 64 sub-channels. The gain response is generated using a 3 tap-filter and is shown in Figure 2. The target BER is taken as 10^{-5}. Noise variance is 0.001. The Target Bits are taken to be 300.

Figure 2. Sub-channel response

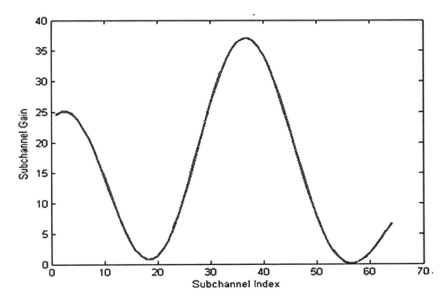

Figure 3. Fuzzy based bit loading algorithm 1

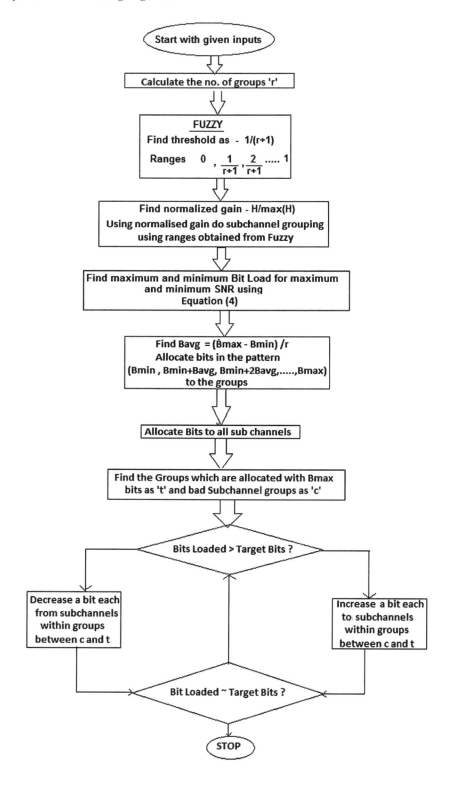

Fuzzy Based Algorithm: 1

In this algorithm groups are made based on Normalized Sub-channel Gains. The thresholds are found based on the no. of groups calculated using (1). The Flowchart for the Algorithm is shown in Figure 3. The algorithm helps to reach the Bit Allocation almost near to Target Bits requirement.

The Simulation Results are shown in Figure 4. For the channel response shown in Figure 2, the number of groups came out to be 10. Clearly higher bits are loaded in sub-channels of higher gain. The BER calculated using (5) is found to be of the order 10^{-4}. The total Energy required to transmit target number of bits is found to be 2.4 Joules, calculated using (4), which converges to Hughes-Hartogs Optimal result. The algorithm takes 1 iteration for grouping, 1 for bit allocation and 5 iterations (approximately equal to Target Bits/No. of Sub-channels) to meet the target bits requirement. In all the algorithm takes 7 iterations for given Simulation Inputs.

Fuzzy Based Algorithm: 2

In this algorithm groups are made based on Normalized Sub-channel Gains. The thresholds are found based on the no. of bad channel threshold taken from user. The bad channel threshold separates low gain channels from higher gain channels. No bit should be allocated to the bad channels ideally but for meeting target bit requirement few bits are allocated. The Flowchart for the Algorithm is shown in Figure 6. The algorithm helps to reach the Bit Allocation almost near to Target Bits requirement. The Simulation Results are shown in Figure 5. For the channel response shown in Figure 2, the bad channel threshold was given as 0.05. Clearly higher bits are loaded in sub-channels of higher gain. The BER calculated using (5) is found to be of the order 10^{-4}. The total Energy required to transmit target number of bits is found to be 1.22 Joules converging to Hughes-Hartogs Optimal result. This algorithm also takes 1 iteration for grouping, 1 for bit allocation and 5 iterations (approximately equal to Target Bits/No. of Sub-channels) to meet the target bits requirement. In all the algorithm takes 7 iterations for given Simulation Inputs.

Figure 4. Bit allocation of fuzzy based algorithm 1

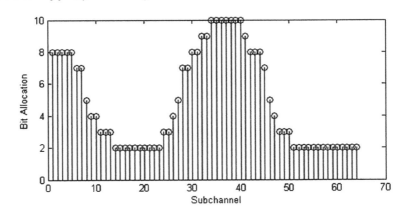

Figure 5. Bit allocation of fuzzy based algorithm 2

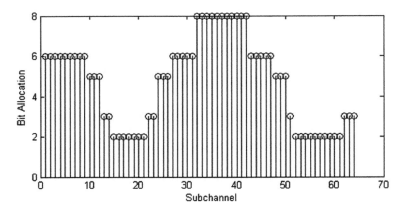

RESULTS AND DISCUSSIONS

The number of Iterations taken for allocation, grouping and to meet the target bits requirement is discussed in this section for various algorithms in Table 1. The variation on the basis of iterations and Energy utilized with target is also discussed.

Compared to Fuzzy Based Algorithm 1, based on number of group threshold concept, Fuzzy Based Algorithm 2 based on bad channel threshold shows better results as energy requirement is very less when compared. Table 2 shows that at the expense of energy (not much significant change) we can make our algorithms faster by reducing the number of iterations. Hence we can preper these sub-optimal algorithms to minimize iteration complexity. The line graph in Figure 7 shows the variation of Iterations with the target Bits for the Hughes Hartogs algorithm and proposed algorithms. The results show that Hughes Hartogs algorithms takes a lot of Iterations to meet the target bit requirements.

Table 1. Number of Iterations taken for loading bits by various algorithms

Algorithm	Allocation	Grouping	Meeting Target Bits
Hughes-Hartogs Algorithm	N * Target Bits	-	-
Proposed Fuzzy Algorithm 1	1	1	(Target Bits)/(No. of Sub-channels)
Proposed Fuzzy Algorithm 2	1	1	(Target Bits)/(No. of Sub-channels)

Table 2. Energy and iteration comparison for given simulation input

Algorithm	Energy (Joules)	Iteration
Hughes-Hartogs Algorithm	0.1789	25600
Chow Algorithm	0.8221	3264
Campello Algorithm	2.21	16064
Proposed Fuzzy Algorithm 1	2.4	7
Proposed Fuzzy Algorithm 2	1.22	7

Figure 6. Fuzzy based bit loading algorithm 2

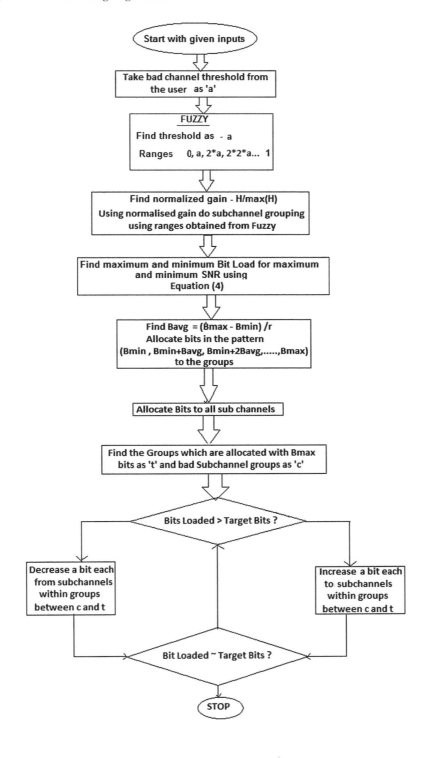

Figure 7. Log (iteration) vs. target bits for the algorithms

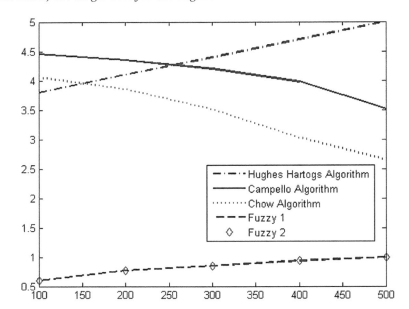

CONCLUSION

Compared to Hughes Hartogs optimal solution, clustering based algorithm using Fuzzy Logic takes a single iteration for bit allocation, one iteration for grouping and few iterations for reaching Target Bits requirement. As a result iteration complexity is reduced. The solution is almost convergent to the optimal solution with a little higher energy but substantially reduced number of iterations. The proposed algorithms are sub optimal but advantageous in terms of iterations. All the Algorithms reach BER of the order of 10^{-4} before Forward Error Correction.

REFERENCES

Birla, N., Agarwal, N., Sankar Ganesh, S., & Babu, V. (2014). Clustering based Bit Loading Algorithms using Neural Networks. *International Journal of Review in Electronics & Communication Engineering, 2*(2), 2–5.

Campello, J. (1998). Optimal Discrete Bit Loading for Multicarrier Modulation Systlems. *IEEE Symp. Info. Theory.* http://doi.org/ doi:10.1109/ISIT.1998.708791

Campello, J. (1999). Practical bit loading for DMT. *IEEE International Conference on Communications.* http://doi.org/ doi:<ALIGNMENT.qj></ALIGNMENT>10.1109/ICC.1999.765384

Chow, P. S., Cioffi, J. M., & Bingham, J. (1995). Practical discrete multitone transceiver loading algorithm for data transmission over spectrally shaped channels. *IEEE Transactions on Communications, 43*(2), 773–775. doi:10.1109/26.380108

Gianaroli, F., Pancaldi, F., & Vitetta, G. M. (2015). *A Novel Bit and Power Loading Algorithm for Narrowband Indoor Powerline Communications*. doi:10.1109/ICCW.2015.7247401

Hong, Y., Member, S., Wu, T., Chen, L., & Member, S. (2016). On the Performance of Adaptive MIMO-OFDM Indoor Visible Light Communications. *IEEE Photonics Technology Letters*, *28*(8), 907–910. doi:10.1109/LPT.2016.2517192

Hughes-Hartogs, D. (1989). *U.S. Patent No. 4,833,706*. Washington, DC: U.S. Patent and Trademark Office.

Jung, S., Jung, S., & Han, S. (2015). AMO-FBMC for Asynchronous Heterogeneous Signal Integrated Optical Transmission. *IEEE Photonics Technology Letters*, *27*(2), 133–136. doi:10.1109/LPT.2014.2363197

Nader-Esfahani, S., & Afrasiabi, M. (2007). Simple bit loading algorithm for OFDM-based systems. *Electronics Letters*, *1*(3), 312–316. doi:10.1049/iet-com

Sastry, K. S., & Babu, D. M. P. (2010). Fuzzy logic based adaptive modulation using non data aided SNR estimation for OFDM system. *International Journal of Engineering Science and Technology*, *2*(6), 2384–2392.

Vo, T. N., Amis, K., Chonavel, T., Siohan, P., & Member, S. (2015). A Computationally Efficient Discrete Bit-Loading Algorithm for OFDM Systems Subject to Spectral-Compatibility Limits. *IEEE Transactions on Communications*, *63*(6), 2261–2272. doi:10.1109/TCOMM.2015.2424890

Wang, D., Cao, Y., Zheng, L., & Du, Z. (2013). Iterative group-by-group bit-loading algorithms for OFDM systems. *IEEE Transactions on Vehicular Technology*, *62*(8), 4131–4135. doi:10.1109/TVT.2013.2257908

Wen, & Tian, Q. (2013). A Fast adaptive transmit power and bit allocation in OFDM system. *Advanced Materials Research*, *765*, 444–447.

Chapter 14
Outliers, Missing Values, and Reliability:
An Integrated Framework for Pre-Processing of Coding Data

Swati Aggarwal
NSIT, India

Shambeel Azim
Vidyadaan Institute of Technology and Management, India

ABSTRACT

Reliability is a major concern in qualitative research. Most of the current research deals with finding the reliability of the data, but not much work is reported on how to improve the reliability of the unreliable data. This paper discusses three important aspects of the data pre-processing: how to detect the outliers, dealing with the missing values and finally increasing the reliability of the dataset. Here authors have suggested a framework for pre-processing of the inter-judged data which is incomplete and also contains erroneous values. The suggested framework integrates three approaches, Krippendorff's alpha for reliability computation, frequency based outlier detection method and a hybrid fuzzy c-means and multilayer perceptron based imputation technique. The proposed integrated approach results in an increase of reliability for the dataset which can be used to make strong conclusions.

INTRODUCTION

Data in the real world is dirty. They are noisy, incomplete and inconsistent. Data mining results are significantly affected by the quality of the data available. Low grade data can return unsatisfactory results. So to improve the quality of the data mining result, pre-processing of the raw data must be carried out. Reliability Analysis, Outlier detection and missing value imputations are the important part of knowledge discovery process. Reliability is a measure that tells how accurate the data is, to be used for a particular purpose. Generally reliability is classified into four classes, i.e. Inter-Coder or Inter-Rater Reliability,

DOI: 10.4018/978-1-5225-1008-6.ch014

Test-Retest Reliability, Parallel-Forms Reliability and Internal Consistency Reliability. Inter-coder reliability is an important element of Content Analysis. It is a measure of agreement to the extent different rater or observer agrees upon when rating the same item. High inter-coder reliability means that judges are in consensus with each other. A set of observation is needed to be judged by more than one judge to draw a conclusion that should be relatively strong. Since humans are associated with inconsistencies and mistakes, conclusion drawn out by a single observer cannot be taken as reliable one. Use of experts as a method of measurement is frequent in different fields like psychology, marketing, education, and others. For example, a candidate contesting an election can look out for an opinion before the poll, in articles published in different newspapers about him. For this he needs experts to draw conclusion from the different articles. On the basis of this conclusion he can determine his chances of winning or losing for which further strategies can be formulated. This is possible only if the inter-rater reliability is high.

Another point of concern is the outliers. Outlier is defined as an observed value that is aloof from the other observation values. They deviate from the other observations in the sample to the extent that they are noticeable. Another definition as given by Johnson (1992) is: An outlier as an observation in a data set which appears to be inconsistent with the remainder of that set of data. There may be a single or multiple outliers present in an observation. Occurrence of outliers may be due to the error, in calculating or recording the measurement value or due to the experimental error (Grubbs, 1969). For example, if four out of five judges assign 'yes' to a nominal question and one judge says 'no', then 'no' is said to be an outlier. The Outlier detection method has various applications like data cleansing, credit card fraud detection, intrusion detection system, medical diagnosis and several others.

Other important step involved in pre-processing of the data is missing value imputation. The missing value is an empty cell in a table that represent a dataset. Reasons for missing values are many, for example, human errors involved in the data collection tasks. Therefore, it is of great necessity to fill in these missing values or record to extract or find patterns from these datasets. Filling in the missing value is known as data imputation. Imputation is important because evaluation of complete data produces authentic results. Interpretations and inferences with complete data are more accurate (Abdella & Marwala, 2005).

RELATED WORK

Various works have been done by different researchers to estimate intercoder reliability in content analysis. Cohen's Kappa (Cohen's, 1960) is a reliability measure that works only on nominal data and takes into account occurrence of agreement by chance. Moreover the number of raters in this case is limited to two only. Fleiss' Kappa (Fliess, 1971) is an improvement over Cohen's Kappa as it works on more than two raters. It also has the same limitation as Cohen's Kappa i.e. it is limited to nominal data only. Cronbach's alpha is used most commonly as a reliability coefficient (Hogan et al., 2000). It is a measure of internal consistency of the test. The problem with Cronbach's alpha is that it is non robust, a single observation can greatly affect the coefficient value (Christmann & Van, 2006). An improvement to various other statistics for measuring the reliability of interrater data is Krippendorff's alpha (Hayes et al., 2007; Krippendorff, 2013, 2011). It is a flexible, reliable measure that can be used with any number of raters, with any metric or level of measurement and also with the missing data.

The Outlier detection method is of two types. One is univariate outlier detection method and the other is a multivariate outlier detection method. According to Pyle (1999), univariate outliers are those values that are far away from other values of the same attribute. Among univariate outlier detection method the most popular was boxplot (Tukey, 1977) detection method which takes into account the interquartile range for finding the outliers. Though it can be used for symmetric as well as skewed data, it is limited to large sample size only (Iglewicz & Hoaglin, 1993). Carling (2000) suggested boxplot fences using median for detecting outliers in non Gaussian cases. The problem with the procedure is that it also misclassifies the non outlier observation as outliers (Carter et al., 2009). Working along this line semi- interquartile ranges were used for detecting outliers (Schwertman, 2007, 2004). But they have their limitations also. The constant in general is not known in advance and values are only provided for normal and almost normal data (Hubert & Vandervieren, 2008).

Various works have been done in the field of data imputation. From statistical method like mean substitution, regression based imputation among others, to soft computing approach like neural networks, fuzzy sets and hybrid technique, several methods have been used for imputation. Many neural network based data imputation technique have been reported (Colleen et al., 2008; Silva et al., 2011). They perform better as compared to other statistical method even when there is the nonlinear relationship among variables (Nelwamondo et al., 2007). To combine the features of neural networks like robustness and parallelism with fuzzy logic for handling incomplete information, fuzzy neural networks have been used for missing value imputation (Gabrys, 2002; Castillo, 2012). Marwala and Chakraverty (2006) used neural network and genetic algorithm (NN-GA) for data imputation. Fuzzy c-means (FCM) imputation was described (Aydilek & Arslan, 2013) in combination with support vector regression and genetic algorithm for minimizing error. Another imputation method given by Nishant et al. (2012) that uses a two stage approach. In the first stage k-means algorithm is used for clustering and in the second stage MLP is used for imputation. Fuzzy k –means (FKM) clustering algorithm have been used for data imputation (Li et al., 2005, 2004). Also Fuzzy clustering based expectation maximisation approach have been used for missing value imputation along with data pre-processing procedure (Rahman & Islam, 2016). Another imputation method that uses Fuzzy possibilistic c –means optimized using GA and SVR also shows very good result (Saravanan & Sailakshmi, 2015). A multiple imputation technique with the purpose of employing genetic programming as a regression technique to approximate missing values has also been used (Cao et al., 2015).

PROPOSED WORK

Reliable dataset is needed for the proper analysis of the Inter-judged data in content analysis research. Most of the research deals only with finding whether a data is reliable or not. They never mentioned what to do if the data is unreliable.

This paper proposed a method for pre-processing of inter-judged data. It uses a famous inter reliability measure called Krippendorff's Alpha for reliability computation. An outlier detection method for categorical data is proposed for detecting outlier in Interrater data. Finally imputation is done by the proposed FCM+MLP imputation technique.

Krippendorff's Alpha Reliability

Krippendorff's alpha (α) is a reliability measure that shows agreement between judges, observers or raters. When $\alpha=1$, it shows perfect reliability which means that observers are in complete agreement.

Therefore, range of α varies from 0 to 1. Following steps (Krippendorff, 2011) are used to compute Krippendorff's alpha. These steps are for ordinal metric only:

Construct Coincidence Matrix: Use the equation 1 for constructing coincidence matrix. The unit is the instance in Interrater data. For example in Table 1, instance 1 or unit 1contains 5(5-1) pairs of 2 and total values in unit 1 is equal to 5. Coincidence matrix for dataset has been shown in result analysis section. Number of rows and columns is equal to the number of categories for which data has been coded. Column n and rows n contain sum of each row and each column. Intersection cell of column n and rows n is the sum total of n.

$$o_{c,k} = \sum_u \frac{No.\ of\ ck\ pair\ in\ unit\ u}{(total\ no.\ of\ values\ in\ u) - 1} \tag{1}$$

2.   Construct Ordinal Metrics Difference Matrix:

$$\delta_{c,k} = \left(\sum_{i=c}^{i=k} n_i - \frac{n_c + n_k}{2} \right)^2 \tag{2}$$

The above formula 2, is used to construct a difference matrix. Difference matrix for ordinal datasets has been shown in the Table 5. The diagonal of the matrix is equal to zero.

3.   Compute α:

$$\alpha = 1 - \frac{(n-1)\left(\sum_c \sum_{k>c} o_{c,k} * \delta_{c,k} \right)}{\sum_c \sum_{k>c} n_c * n_k * \delta_{c,k}} \tag{3}$$

The above formula 3, involves computation of either of the two off diagonal triangles of coincidence matrix.

Frequency Base Univariate Outlier Detection Method

The proposed frequency based univariate outlier detection method is used for detecting outlier in categorical data. For the dataset used for simulation in this paper, both the traditional and adjusted box plot failed to detect outliers in the dataset. It is because the size of the data is very small. This method tends to work on a larger dataset. Also, these methods are limited to, continuous data only. For example, if 4 out of 5 judges assign category 1 and 1 judge assign category 3. This category 3 is definitely an outlier. It is because category 1 and category 3 are just opposite to each other. The proposed outlier detection method can easily identify such category as an outlier. Even it also identifies those categories as an outlier whose percentage occurrence is less than, equal to 20% of the total sample. It starts by first checking if there is a single category in a unit. That is if all judges assign single category to a unit then there is no outlier. Also the method checks for frequency of all the categories present in a unit. If the frequency is equal for the entire category it is hard to differentiate between them as which one is an outlier?

An algorithm for proposed frequency based univariate outlier detection in Inter-rater data:

1. For each unit u that is being rated by observers, check if all the judges code to one category. If so, no outliers present in the unit.
2. Calculate the frequency of occurrence of each category c, within the unit.
3. If the frequency of occurrence of each category within the unit is equal return no outlier.
4. Else, for all categories other than the highest frequency category, check:
   a. If it is a nearby category to the highest frequency category, check:
      i. If its occurrence percentage is less than or equal to 20% of all values in the unit, marked it an outlier.
      ii. Else return not an outlier.
   b. Else if it is not a nearby category marked it as an outlier.

Integrated Fuzzy C: Means and Multilayer Perceptron Imputation Technique

The proposed imputation model comprises of two stages as shown in Figure 1. The output of the first stage is used as an input to the second stage. The output of the second stage is used to generate complete datasets.

Figure 1. A two stage imputation procedure

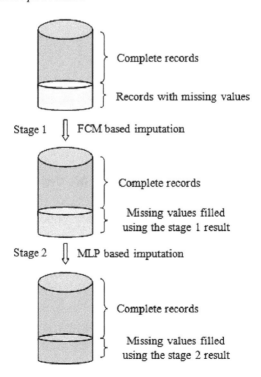

Stage 1: The basic working of this stage is shown in steps below:

1. The whole dataset is grouped into k clusters using fuzzy c-means clustering technique. In result, it gives cluster's membership for each record. Also, the cluster's center for each attribute is generated with respect to each cluster.
2. The membership degrees and the values of cluster centroids are used to impute the missing attributes using the equation 4.

$$x_{i,j} = \sum_{k=1}^{K} U(x_i, v_k) * v_{k,j} \tag{4}$$

where, x_i is the object having j attributes, v_k represents the centroids of cluster k, and U denotes the membership function which describes the degree that the data object x_i belongs to certain cluster v_k.

Stage 2: The basic working of this stage is shown in steps below:

1. After all the missing attributes are replaced by the values calculated from stage 1, MLP is implemented for data imputation. For each missing attribute that is already filled by the calculated value from stage 1, a network is created.
2. The network is trained only with the complete records.
3. The missing attribute for which the value has been replaced by the value obtained using stage 1 is used as the target attribute while the others attribute are taken as input each time a new network is trained.
4. After the network is trained the record containing the missing value is used to test the network. The entire attribute, except for which the network is trained, is used as an input to the test data and the network is used to predict the missing value using this input test data.

WORKING OF THE PROPOSED FRAMEWORK

Figure 2 shows the working of the proposed model. It comprises of three main steps:

1. Computation of Krippendorff's Alpha Reliability (As explained in proposed work section).
2. Outlier Detection (As explained in proposed work section).
3. Missing Value Imputation using FCM+MLP technique (As explained in proposed work section).

First of all, reliability R is calculated for the dataset from content analysis using Krippendorff's alpha computation. The dataset is reliable only if the value of Krippendorff's alpha (i.e. R) is nearer to 1. It has been shown that the dataset can be taken as reliable for the alpha value greater than 0.8 (Krippendorff, 2004). So, alpha (R) is checked for the condition whether it is greater or less than 0.8. If the reliability R is less than 0.8, it means that the dataset is unreliable, so values' affecting the reliability of the dataset needs to be identified. These values are outliers and are detected using the proposed method. The outliers are then deleted to generate missing values in the dataset. These missing values are imputed using proposed fuzzy c –means (FCM) and Multilayer Perceptron (MLP) imputation technique. Reliability

Figure 2. Proposed framework for pre-processing of inter-rater data

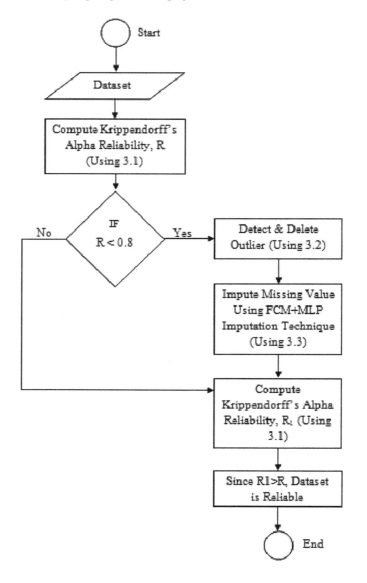

R_1 is then calculated for this imputed dataset using Krippendorff's alpha reliability computation. The reliability R_1 obtained would be greater than R that was computed for the original dataset.

EXPERIMENT AND SIMULATION

The dataset used for simulation is a teacher performance dataset for a semester in a university. It has been coded by five experts on the feedback provided by students for respective teachers under whom they have taken a course during that semester. The feedback consists of statements for which student gives their opinion about a certain teacher on a five point likert scale. The feedback questionnaire has been attached in the appendix. The evaluation is done for 50 teachers as shown in Figure 3. Experts categorize the performance of teachers with three points likert scale where 1 is for better performance, 2 is for satisfactory performance and 3 for poor performance.

The ordinal dataset D is first checked for its reliability using Krippendorff's alpha reliability computation. The coincidence matrix and ordinal metrics difference matrix for the original data set is shown in the Table 1 and Table 2 respectively. To experiment with the proposed framework, the dataset D (Figure 3) has been modified so as to introduce missing values and erroneous values. 15 values have been changed and 9 values out of this original dataset are deleted. The modified dataset D_1 is shown in the Figure 4. Reliability R_1 for this modified dataset is calculated using the same Krippendorff's alpha reliability computation technique. The coincidence matrix and ordinal metric difference matrix for this modified dataset D_1, is shown in the Table 3 and Table 4 respectively.

Due to changed values in the original dataset D, the modified dataset D_1 now contains outliers. These outliers are identified using the proposed frequency based outlier method as discussed before. For example column 1 of instance 1 has been changed from 2 to 1. According to the proposed outlier detection method the category with the highest frequency is 2 and the least frequency is 1. As 1 is close to category 2 it is checked whether its occurrence in total sample is less than or equal to 20%. Its occurrence is 20% so

Figure 3. Original dataset (D)

Unit	Judge1	judge 2	judge 3	judge 4	judge 5	Unit	Judge1	judge 2	judge 3	judge 4	judge 5
1	2	2	2	2	2	26	2	2	2	2	2
2	3	1	3	3	3	27	1	1	1	1	1
3	1	1	1	1	1	28	1	1	1	1	1
4	3	3	3	3	3	29	3	3	1	3	3
5	2	2	2	2	2	30	2	2	2	2	2
6	3	3	3	3	3	31	2	2	2	2	2
7	2	2	2	2	2	32	1	1	1	1	1
8	2	2	2	2	2	33	3	3	3	3	3
9	2	3	3	3	3	34	3	1	3	3	3
10	2	2	2	2	2	35	1	1	1	1	1
11	1	1	1	1	1	36	1	1	1	1	1
12	2	2	2	2	2	37	3	3	3	3	3
13	1	1	1	1	2	38	2	2	2	2	2
14	3	3	3	3	3	39	1	1	1	1	1
15	3	3	3	3	3	40	2	2	2	2	2
16	1	1	1	1	1	41	1	1	1	1	2
17	1	1	1	1	1	42	2	2	2	2	2
18	2	2	2	1	2	43	1	1	1	1	1
19	3	3	3	3	3	44	2	2	2	2	2
20	2	2	2	2	2	45	2	2	2	2	2
21	2	2	2	1	2	46	2	2	2	2	2
22	2	3	3	3	3	47	1	1	1	1	1
23	1	2	2	2	2	48	1	1	1	1	1
24	1	1	1	2	2	49	1	1	1	2	3
25	3	3	3	3	3	50	1	1	1	1	1

Figure 4. Modified dataset (D_1)

Unit	Judge1	judge 2	judge 3	judge 4	judge 5
1	1	2	2	2	2
2	3	1	3	3	3
3	1	1	1	1	2
4	3	3		1	3
5	2	2	2	2	2
6	3	3	3	3	
7	2	2	2	2	2
8	2	2	2	2	2
9	2	3	3	3	3
10	2	2	2	2	2
11	1	1	1	1	3
12	2	2	2	2	2
13	1	1	1	1	2
14	1	3	3	3	3
15	1	1	3	3	3
16	1	1	1	1	1
17	1	1	1		1
18	2	2	2	1	2
19	1	3	3	3	3
20	1	2	2	2	3
21	2	2	2	1	2
22	2	3	3	3	3
23	1	2	2	2	2
24	1		1	2	2
25	3	3	3	3	3
26	2	2	2	2	2
27	1	1	1	1	1
28		1	1	1	3
29	3	3	1	3	3
30	2	2	2	2	3
31	2	2	2	2	1
32	1	1	1	1	1
33	3	3	3	3	3
34	3	1	3	3	3
35	1	1		1	1
36	1	1	1	1	1
37	3	3	3	3	3
38	2	2	2	2	
39	1	1	1	1	
40	2	2	2	2	2
41	1	1	1	1	2
42	2	2	2	2	2
43	1	1	1	1	3
44	2	2	2	2	3
45	2	2	2	2	2
46	2	2	2	2	2
47	1	1	1	1	1
48	1	1	1	1	1
49	1	1	1	2	3
50	1		1	1	1

	Modified Data
	Deleted data
	Outliers already present

it is marked as outlier. Similarly, all the values are detected and it is deleted. The dataset containing this missing value is imputed using the proposed FCM+MLP imputation technique.

As the total number of categories used by expert is 3 so for FCM based imputation the number of clusters is taken as 3. After the second stage the value is rounded off to the nearer integer and imputed in the dataset. After all the values have been imputed the dataset is again checked for its reliability (R_2) using the same Krippendorff's alpha reliability computation. The coincidence matrix and ordinal metrics difference matrix for this dataset is shown in the Table 5 and Table 6 respectively.

RESULT ANALYSIS

The table 7 shows the reliability of the datasets D, D_1 and D_2 used for simulation. The reliability R of original dataset D is 0.84 which is greater than 0.80, the reliability condition. Hence the dataset can be considered reliable. After the dataset is modified the reliability R_1 drops to 0.58 due to an increase in the outliers' value. Finally after the outliers are deleted and new values are imputed the resultant reli-

Figure 5. Imputed dataset (D_2)

Unit	Judge1	judge 2	judge 3	judge 4	judge 5
1	2	2	2	2	2
2	3	2	3	3	3
3	1	1	1	1	1
4	3	3	3	3	3
5	2	2	2	2	2
6	3	3	3	3	2
7	2	2	2	2	2
8	2	2	2	2	2
9	3	3	3	3	3
10	2	2	2	2	2
11	1	1	1	1	1
12	2	2	2	2	2
13	1	1	1	1	1
14	3	3	3	3	3
15	3	3	3	3	3
16	1	1	1	1	1
17	1	1	1	1	1
18	2	2	2	2	2
19	3	3	3	3	3
20	2	2	2	2	2
21	2	2	2	2	2
22	3	3	3	3	3
23	2	2	2	2	2
24	1	1	1	2	2
25	3	3	3	3	3

Unit	Judge1	judge 2	judge 3	judge 4	judge 5
26	2	2	2	2	2
27	1	1	1	1	1
28	1	1	1	1	1
29	3	3	3	3	3
30	2	2	2	2	2
31	2	2	2	2	2
32	1	1	1	1	1
33	3	3	3	3	3
34	3	2	3	3	3
35	1	1	1	1	1
36	1	1	1	1	1
37	3	3	3	3	3
38	2	2	2	2	1
39	1	1	1	1	1
40	2	2	2	2	2
41	1	1	1	1	1
42	2	2	2	2	2
43	1	1	1	1	1
44	2	2	2	2	2
45	2	2	2	2	2
46	2	2	2	2	2
47	1	1	1	1	1
48	1	1	1	1	1
49	1	1	1	1	1
50	1	1	1	1	1

Table 1. Coincidence matrix for the original dataset, D

	1	2	3	n
1	79	7.25	3.75	90
2	7.25	91.5	1.25	100
3	3.75	1.25	56	60
n	90	100	60	250

Table 2. Ordinal Metric difference matrix for the original dataset, D

	1	2	3
1	0	9025	30625
2	9025	0	6400
3	30625	6400	0

Table 3. Coincidence matrix for modified dataset, D_1

	1	2	3	
1	65.66	10.83	11.5	88
2	10.83	77.16	5	93
3	11.5	5	43.5	60
	88	93	60	241

Table 4. Ordinal metrics difference matrix for the modified dataset, D_1

	1	2	3
1	0	8190.25	27889
2	8190.25	0	5852.25
3	27889	5852.25	0

Table 5. Coincidence matrix for imputed dataset, D_2

	1	2	3	
1	86.5	2.5	0	89
2	2.5	93.5	3	99
3	0	3	59	62
	91	97	62	250

Table 6. Ordinal metrics difference matrix for the imputed dataset, D_2

	1	2	3
1	0	8836	28730.5
2	8836	0	6480.25
3	28730.5	6480.25	0

ability R_2 increases to 0.96. It can be seen that the final computed reliability increases as compared to the original dataset. The final dataset obtained has a nearly perfect agreement among judges. So, this reliable dataset D_3 can be used to evaluate the teacher's performance.

As a measure of accuracy, mean absolute percentage error (MAPE) is also used to evaluate the performance of the proposed model. The formula to calculate MAPE value is,

$$MAPE = \frac{100}{n} \sum_{i=1}^{n} \frac{|x_i - \hat{x}_i|}{x_i} \tag{5}$$

where,

$n =$ The number of the missing variable,
$xi =$ The actual value, and
$\hat{x}_i =$ The calculated or predicted value.

The Table 8 shows the MAPE values. It can be seen that the MAPE values improve from stage 1 to stage 2. For stage 2 also the MAPE value obtained is high due to the presence of outliers in the original dataset which are removed from the imputed dataset.

Table 7. Inter-rater reliability value (Krippendorff's Alpha)

	Alpha
Original Dataset	.84 (R)
Modified Dataset	.58 (R_1)
Imputed Dataset	.96 (R_2)

Table 8. MAPE value

FCM	44.95%
FCM+MLP	27.63%

CONCLUSION

For carrying out any analysis, data must be of high quality. It should be reliable. For this pre-processing of the data is very much necessary. The proposed framework is suitable for carrying out this pre-processing task in content analysis research. First it checks the reliability of the inter-coder data. If the data is not reliable, it finds out the outliers affecting the reliability. These outliers are then deleted and a new value is imputed which increases the overall reliability of the dataset. The overall reliability comes to be .96 for our problem which shows the ideal consensus of the judges and also the accuracy of the proposed model in determining the outliers. The reduction in MAPE value from stage 1 to stage 2 also highlights the accuracy of the imputation process. Thus the suggested data pre processing framework can be experimented for the content analysis research –a domain while we frequent across noisy data.

REFERENCES

Abdella, M., & Marwala, D. (2005). The use of genetic algorithms and neural networks to approximate missing data in database. In *Proceedings of the IEEE 3rd international conference on computational cybernetics (ICCC)* (pp. 207–212). doi:10.1109/ICCCYB.2005.1511574

Ankaiah, N., & Ravi, V. (2011). A Novel Soft Computing Hybrid for Data Imputation. In *Proceedings of the 7th international conference on data mining (DMIN)*.

Aydilek, I. B., & Arslan, A. (2013). A hybrid method for imputation of missing values using optimized fuzzy c-means with support vector regression and a genetic algorithm. *Information Sciences*, *233*, 25–35. doi:10.1016/j.ins.2013.01.021

Cao, T., Zhang, M., & Andreae, P. (2015). Multiple Imputation for Missing Data Using Genetic Programming. *Proceeding GECCO '15 Proceedings of the 2015 Annual Conference on Genetic and Evolutionary Computation*. ACM.

Carling, K. (2000). Resistant Outlier Rules and the non-Gaussian Case. *Computational Statistics & Data Analysis*, *33*(3), 249–258. doi:10.1016/S0167-9473(99)00057-2

Castillo P. R. D. (2012). Use of machine learning methods to impute categorical data. *Conference of European Statisticians*.

Christmann & Van Aelst. (2006). Robust estimation of Cronbach's alpha. *Journal of Multivariate Analysis, 97*(7), 1660–1674.

Cohen, J. (1960). A coefficient of agreement for nominal scales. *Educational and Psychological Measurement*, *20*(1), 37–46. doi:10.1177/001316446002000104

Colleen, M., Monique, F., & Robin Walker, C. (2008). Imputation of Missing Values by Integrating Neural Networks and Case-based Reasoning. *30th Annual International IEEE EMBS Conference*.

Fleiss, J. L. (1971). Measuring nominal scale agreement among many raters. *Psychological Bulletin*, *76*(5), 378–382. doi:10.1037/h0031619

Gabrys, B. (2002). Neuro-fuzzy approach to processing inputs with missing values in pattern recognition problems. *International Journal of Approximate Reasoning, 30*(3), 149–179. doi:10.1016/S0888-613X(02)00070-1

Grubbs, F. E. (1969, February). Procedures for detecting outlying observations in samples. *Technometrics, 11*(1), 1–21. doi:10.1080/00401706.1969.10490657

Hayes, A. F., & Krippendorff, K. (2007). Answering the call for a standard reliability measure for coding data. *Communication Methods and Measures, 1*(1), 77–89. doi:10.1080/19312450709336664

Hogan, T. P., Benjamin, A., & Brezinksi, K. L. (2000). Reliability methods: A note on the frequency of use of various types. *Educational and Psychological Measurement, 60*(4), 523–531. doi:10.1177/00131640021970691

Hubert, M., & Vandervieren, E. (2008). An Adjusted Boxplot for Skewed Distributions. *Computational Statistics & Data Analysis, 52*(12), 5186–5201. doi:10.1016/j.csda.2007.11.008

Iglewicz, B., & Hoaglin, D. (1993). *How to detect and handle outliers.* ASQC Quality Press.

Johnson, R. (1992). *Applied Multivariate Statistical Analysis.* Prentice Hall.

Krippendorf, K. (2004). Reliability in Content Analysis. *Some Common Misconceptions and Recommendations, 30*(3), 411–433.

Krippendorff, K. (2011). *Computing Krippendorff's Alpha-Reliability.* Academic Press.

Krippendorff, K. (2013). *Content analysis: An introduction to its methodology* (3rd ed.). Thousand Oaks, CA: Sage.

Li, D., Deogun, J., Spaulding, W., & Shuart, B. (2004). Towards Missing Data Imputation: A Study of Fuzzy K-means Clustering Method. In RSCTC 2004, (LNAI), (vol. 3066, pp. 573–579). Springer. doi:10.1007/978-3-540-25929-9_70

Li, D., Deogun, J., Spaulding, W., & Shuart, B. (2005). *Dealing with Missing Data: Algorithms Based on Fuzzy Set and Rough Set Theories* (Vol. 3700). Transactions on Rough Sets IV Lecture Notes in Computer Science.

Marwala, T., & Chakraverty, S. (2006). Fault classification in structures with incomplete measured data using auto associative neural networks and genetic algorithm. *Current Science India, 90*(4), 542–548.

Nancy, J. (2009). A comparison of two boxplot methods for detecting univariate outliers which adjust for sample size and asymmetry. *Statistical Methodology, 6*(6), 604–621. doi:10.1016/j.stamet.2009.07.001

Nelwamondo, F. V., Mohamed, S., & Marwala, T. (2007). Missing data: A comparison of neural network and expectation maximization techniques. *Curr. Sci. India, 93*, 1514–1521.

Nishanth, K. J., Ravi, V., Ankaiah, N., & Bose, I. (2012). Soft computing based imputation and hybrid data and text mining: The case of predicting the severity of phishing alerts. *Expert Systems with Applications, 39*(12), 10583–10589. doi:10.1016/j.eswa.2012.02.138

Pyle, D. (1999). *Data Preparation for Data Mining.* San Francisco, CA: Morgan Kaufmann.

Rahman, G., & Islam, Z. (2016). Missing value imputation using a fuzzy clustering-based EM approach. *Springer Knowledge and Information Systems, 46*(2), 389-422.

Saravanan, P., & Sailakshmi, P. (2015). Missing Value Imputation Using Fuzzy Possibilistic C Means Optimized With Support Vector Regression And Genetic Algorithm. *Journal of Theoretical and Applied Information Technology, 72*(1).

Schwertman, N. C., & de Silva, R. (2007). Identifying outliers with sequential fences. *Computational Statistics & Data Analysis, 51*(8), 3800–3810. doi:10.1016/j.csda.2006.01.019

Schwertman, N. C., Owens, M. A., & Adnan, R. (2004). A Simple More General Boxplot Method for Identifying Outliers. *Computational Statistics & Data Analysis, 47*(1), 165–174. doi:10.1016/j.csda.2003.10.012

Silva-Ramírez, E.-L., Pino-Mejías, R., López-Coello, M., & Cubiles-de-la-Vega, M. (2011). Missing value imputation on missing completely at random data using multilayer perceptrons. *Neural Networks, 24*(1), 121–129. doi:10.1016/j.neunet.2010.09.008 PMID:20875726

Tukey, J. W. (1977). Exploratory Data Analysis. New York: Addison-Wesley.

APPENDIX

(1) strongly agree, (2) agree, (3) undecided, (4) disagree, (5) strongly disagree

1. Teacher's pace and level of instruction are suited to the attainment of students.
2. Teacher writes and draws legibly.
3. Subject matter organized in logical sequence.
4. Teacher speaks clearly and audibly.
5. Teacher uses variety of methods and materials.
6. Teacher comes to the class on time and engages regularly.
7. Teacher maintains discipline in the class.
8. Teacher offers assistance and counselling to the needy students.
9. Teachers encourage students questioning and creativity.
10. Teacher seems well prepared for the class.

Chapter 15

Parameter Reduction in Soft Set Models and Application in Decision Making

B.K. Tripathy
VIT University, India

Sooraj T.R
VIT University, India

R.K. Mohanty
VIT University, India

Arun K.R.
VIT University, India

ABSTRACT

Soft sets were introduced by Molodtsov to handle uncertainty based problems. In 2003, Maji et al. extended the soft set approach to decision making. Decision making plays an integral role in daily life. In this chapter we describe soft sets and its impact in decision making problems. In this chapter, we discuss some of the basic notions of fuzzy soft sets and interval valued fuzzy soft sets. We also discuss application of fuzzy soft sets and interval valued fuzzy soft sets in decision making. In this chapter, we are going to see how parameter reduction is used in soft set theory.

INTRODUCTION

Soft set theory is a new mathematical approach to handle uncertainty based problems. It was introduced by the Russian mathematician D.A. Molodtsov (1999). Soft set theory is advanced by a number of researchers. Maji et al. (2001) has given the definition of fuzzy soft set and its application in decision-making problems (Maji et al., 2002). There are a lot of theories which deal with vagueness and ambiguity. Some important theories among those are probability theory, theory of interval mathematics and fuzzy set theory. All of these models are very good to handle uncertainty and vagueness in data. But each of these theories has their own drawbacks; such as fuzzy sets (Zadeh, 1965) are completely dependent on membership functions but there is no unique formula to define the membership functions. Molodtsov observed that the main reason of these drawbacks is perhaps due to the inadequacy of parameterization tools. That has led him to introduce soft set theory, which is a parameterized collection of subsets.

DOI: 10.4018/978-1-5225-1008-6.ch015

Most of the problems in real life contain uncertainties.When we handle real life situations, we can observe that most of the information available is ambiguous or uncertain. In real life, before we take any decision we have to collect sufficient information regarding with the problem. As the level of uncertainty increases in the problem, the decision making will become more complicated. In many cases, information is determined according to the decision maker's. Decision maker should be an expert related with the problem. If the decision maker is not an expert in the corresponding field, then the decision he takes may contain lot of ambiguity. There are mainly three ways in which decision makers express their opinions. They are:

1. Preference orderings
2. Utility values.
3. Preference relations.

Preference orderings are a collection of natural numbers which are permutation used by the experts showing the order positions of a set of alternatives in sequence. Utility values are a series of exact real numbers taken from a closed unit interval [0,1] to indicate the preferences of a decision maker towards different outcomes. Preference relation is constructed via pair-wise comparisons over the alternatives, and each value in it indicates the preference degree of one alternative over another.Out of the above mentioned methods, preference relation is much better. In the case of preference orderings, experts are not having sufficient information about the problem. In some cases, utility values are difficult to calculate. Preference relation is not having the above mentioned difficulties.

Broadly, we can classify decision making process into two categories, single decision making and group decision making process. In single decision making process, the decision will be taken by a single expert or decision maker. But, in most of the real life problems a single decision maker may not be enough to take a proper decision. So, the need of group decision making was introduced. In group decision making process, more than one decision maker evaluate the problem and take appropriate decision. But the decision makers need to have enough knowledge about the problem to take suitable decision. In Saaty (1986), Saaty introduced analytic hierarchy process. Analytic hierarchy process (AHP) is a structured technique for analyzing and organizing complex decisions. It has particular application in group decision making. It can be used in fields such as government, business, healthcare etc. The main aim of AHP is to find a solution which best suits their goals rather than the correct decision. In AHP, a complex multi criteria problem can be decomposed into a multi level hierarchic structure of objectives, alternatives etc. Then a scale is used to express the judgments in the form of pair-wise comparisons. The scale expresses the importance of the elements in a level with respect to the elements in the level immediately above it.

Many researchers extended this decision making approach to various uncertainty based models such as fuzzy sets, rough sets and soft sets. Decision making has been extended to various uncertainty models. Maji et al extended decision making approach to FSS and intuitionistic fuzzy soft sets (Maji et al). Tripathy et al. redefined the concepts of FSSs and intuitionistic fuzzy soft sets and discussed an application in (Tripathy et al 2015). They also mentioned the impact of negative parameters which adversely affects the decision making process. Parameter reduction technique is used to decrease the number of parameters and is also to find the core parameter from the parameter set. It is necessary to reduce the parameter for manipulation. In this chapter, we detaily discussed how parameters can be reduced along with soft set

This chapter is further organized into five sections. The next section contains definitions and notions of soft set theory. In the section three we have given some descriptions about the fuzzy soft sets. Also under the subsection we have described briefly application of FSSs. In the section four we discuss some definitions of IVFSSs and discuss the application of IVFSSs.

SOFT SET THEORY

Soft set, mathematical model, introduced by Molodtsov to handle uncertainty based problems. In this section, we discuss some of the basic terms related with soft sets. Soft set is a parameterized family of subsets defined over a universe associated with a set of parameters.

The definition of soft set given by Molodtsov (1999) is:

Definition 1: Let U be a universal set and E be a set of parameters. A pair *(F, E)* is called a soft set over U iff F is a mapping of E into the set of all subsets of the universal set U; *i.e.*

$$F: E \rightarrow P(U), \tag{1}$$

where $P(U)$ is the power set U. For $e \in E$, $F(e)$ is called the set of e-approximate elements of the soft set *(F, E)*. So, a soft set can be represented as a collection of approximations. The parameter part of the approximation is called as predicate and for each parameter in E, the set containing all elements of $F(e)$ is called as the value set of e in *(F, E)*. The pair *(U, E)* is often regarded as a soft universe. A parameter can be anything adverbial for the elements, such as a number, word, phrase or a sentence which can describe the value set more appropriately.

The way of describing an object in soft set theory differs principally from the way an object is described in classical mathematics. Normally, in classical mathematics a mathematical model of an object is constructed to define the notion of the exact solution of that model. Sometimes the mathematical model becomes too complicated to find the exact solution. So, we need the notion of approximate solution to get rid of these types of problems. However, in soft set theory, we are getting the solution to the problems by the opposite approach. The description of the object will have an approximate nature initially and so that we do not need to use the notion of exact solution. There are no restrictions on the approximate description of the objects in soft set theory, which makes this model very convenient and can be easily applied in real life problems. We can use any type of parameterisation depending upon the preferences with the help of words and sentences, mappings, functions, real numbers, and so on.

FUZZY SOFT SETS

Most of the parameters in soft sets are of fuzzy behaviour. This has led Maji et al to introduce the FSSs. Later on, Tripathy et al introduced membership function for FSSs. In (Tripathy et al), they redefined basic notions of FSSs with the help of membership function. In this section we discuss the basic operations of FSSs and also discuss an application of FSSs in decision making problems.

Let *(F, E)* be a FSS over *(U, E)*. Then parametric membership functions $\mu_{(F,E)} = \left\{ \mu^a_{(F,E)} \mid a \in E \right\}$ of *(F, E)* are defined as follows:

Definition 2: For any $\forall a \in E$, we define the membership function as follows.

$$\mu_{(F,E)}^{a} \ (\mathrm{x}) = \alpha, \ \alpha \in [0,1] \tag{2}$$

Definition 3: Let U be the initial universal set and let E be a set of parameters (Maji et al., 2001). Let the power set of all fuzzy subsets of U is denoted by I^{U}. The pair (F, E) can be called as a FSS over U, where F is a mapping given by

$$F : E \to I^{U} \tag{3}$$

For any element of E, the possible number of degrees of belongingness are real numbers lying in the interval of [0, 1] and hence infinite.

Definition 4: For any two FSSs (F, E) and (G, E) over a common universe (U, E), the union of (F, E) and (G, B) is the FSS(H, E) and $\forall a \in E$ and $\forall x \in U$, we have

$$\mu_{(H,E)}^{a}(x) = \max\left\{\mu_{(F,E)}^{a}(x), \mu_{(G,E)}^{a}(x)\right\} \tag{4}$$

Definition 5: For any two FSSs (F, E) and (G, E) over a common universe (U, E), the intersection of (F, E) and (G, E) is the FSS(H,E) where and $\forall a \in E$ and $\forall x \in U$, we have

$$\mu_{(H,E)}^{a}(x) = \min\left\{\mu_{(F,E)}^{a}(x), \mu_{(G,E)}^{a}(x)\right\} \tag{5}$$

Definition 6: A FSS(F, E) over the universe (U, E) is said to be absolute FSS if $F(e)= U$, $\forall e \in E$. So, we have $\mu_{U}^{e}(x) = 1$.

Definition 7: A FSS(F, E) over the universe (U, E) is said to be null FSS if $F(a) = \phi$, $\forall a \in E$. So, we have $\mu_{(\phi,E)}^{a}(x) = 0$. We note here that with the change of definition of absolute FSS and null FSS we have, for any soft set (F, E) defined over (U, E).

$$(F,E) \bigcup U = U \tag{6}$$

$$(F,E) \bigcap \phi = (F,E) \tag{7}$$

Definition 8: Given two FSSs (F, E) and (G, E) over a common soft universe (U, E), (F, E) is said to be fuzzy soft subset of (G, E), $(F, E) \subseteq (G, E)$ and $\forall a \in E$, $\forall x \in U$,

$$\mu_{(F,E)}^{a}(x) \le \mu_{(G,E)}^{a}(x) \tag{8}$$

Definition 9: For any two FSSs *(F, E)* and *(G, E)* over a common soft universe *(U, E)*, we say that *(F, E)* is equal to *(G, E)* written as *(F, E)* = *(G, E)* and $\forall x \in U$,

$$\mu^a_{(F,E)}(x) = \mu^a_{(G,E)}(x) \tag{9}$$

Definition 10: For any two FSSs *(F, E)* and *(G, E)* over a common soft universe *(U, E)*, we define the complement *(H, E)* of *(G, E)* in *(F, E)* as $\forall a \in E$ and $\forall x \in U$.

$$\mu^a_{(H,E)}(x) = \max\left\{0, \mu^a_{(F,E)}(x) - \mu^a_{(G,E)}(x)\right\} \tag{10}$$

Definition 11: The complement of a FSS over a soft universe *(U, E)* is defined as

$$\mu^a_{(F,E)^c}(x) = \max(0, \mu^a_U(x) - \mu^a_{(F,E)}(x)) \tag{11}$$

It can be seen easily that

$$\mu^a_{(F,E)^c}(x) = 1 - \mu^a_{(F,E)}(x)) \tag{12}$$

Application of FSSs in Decision Making

In this section, we discuss few terms which are used in decision making. We also discuss an application of FSSs with the algorithm provided by Maji et al and Tripathy et al in detail with the help of an example.

Definition 12: Comparison table (CT) of a fuzzy soft set (F,P) is a square table in which number of rows and number of columns is equal (Maji et al 2015). Rows and columns both are labeled by the object names $s_1, s_2, \ldots s_n$ of the universe, and the entries are c_{ij} where c_{ij} represents the number of parameters for which the membership value of h_i exceeds or equal to the membership value of h_j. Clearly, $0 \leq c_{ij} \leq k$ and c_{ii}=k, $\forall i, j$ where k is the number of parameters in P.

Definition 13: Row sum of an object '*h*' is denoted by 'r_i' and is calculated by using the formula

$$r_i = \sum_{j=1}^n c_{ij} . \tag{13}$$

Here r_i, indicates the total number of parameters in which h_i dominates all the members of U. Column sum of an object h_j is denoted by t_j and is calculated by using the formula

$$t_i = \sum_{j=1}^n c_{ij}$$

The following algorithm was given by Maji et al.(Maji et al 2002). We explain the algorithm with the help of an example. We also pointed out some drawbacks of this algorithm which was found by Tripathy et al.

Algorithm 1

1. Input the fuzzy soft set (F, E).
2. Input the set P of choice parameters of Mr. X which is a subset of E.
3. Consider the fuzzy soft set (F, E) and we write in tabular form.
4. Compute the Comparison table of fuzzy soft set (F, E).
5. Compute r_i and t_i for h_i, $\forall i$.
6. Compute the score of h_i, $\forall i$.
7. Find $S_i = \max S_i$. Then Mr. X can choose the strategy 's_i'.

Consider a FSS (F, E). Suppose that $E = \{e_1, e_2, e_3, e_4\}$ is the set of choice parameters for Mr. X on the basis of which a player wants to choose a strategy from the availability U. Let s1, s2, .. denote the strategies. Tabular representation of the FSS (F, E) is shown in Table 1.

The comparison-table of the FSS shown in Table 1 is computed and shown in Table 2.

Next, we need to compute row-sum, column sum, score for each 's_i' as shown in the Table 3.

In Table 3, the maximum score is 13, scored by the strategy 's_3'. From this, we can decide that player X can choose s_3. In case, he doesn't want to choose 's_3' due to certain reasons, his second choice will be 's_1'. The above mentioned algorithm has many drawbacks. Many researches are pointed out these

Table 1. Representation of fuzzy soft set

U	e_1	e_2	e_3	e_4
s_1	1.0	0.2	1.0	1.0
s_2	0.4	0.3	0.0	0.1
s_3	1.0	1.0	1.0	0.5
s_4	0.4	1.0	0.2	0.3
s_5	0.6	1.0	1.0	0.2
s_6	0.8	0.0	0.2	0.3

Table 2. CT for the FSS (F,P)

U	s_1	s_2	s_3	s_4	s_5	s_6
s_1	4	3	3	3	3	4
s_2	1	4	0	1	0	1
s_3	3	4	4	4	4	4
s_4	1	4	1	4	2	3
s_5	2	4	2	3	4	2
s_6	0	3	0	3	2	4

Table 3. Computation of row-sum, column-sum and score for each 's_i'

U	Row-Sum (r_i)	Column-Sum (t_i)	Score (S_i)
s_1	20	11	9
s_2	7	22	-15
s_3	23	10	13
s_4	15	18	-3
s_5	17	15	2
s_6	12	18	-6

drawbacks. In this algorithm, Maji et al. are considering only positive parameters. The algorithm given in above has some issues. Those issues are:

1. If there is some parameters like "Expensive" or "Distance", then the given decision making algorithm will give a wrong result. Because the values of these type of parameters affects the decision inversely. We call these parameters as negative parameter.
2. In CT if one parameter of a house is greater than or equal to other, then the algorithm is taking the count as 1 and other as 0. This may affect the decision making result if the difference is very low.
3. If a beautiful house is slightly expensive then also someone may want to buy it; which is not taken into account in the decision making algorithm (Maji et al 2003). A customer's interest over any particular parameters is not entertained there.

All of the above issues are addressed in (Tripathy et al. 2015),Tripathy et al classified the parameters in two types:

1. If the value of the parameter is directly proportional to the interest of a person, then it is a positive parameter.
2. If the value of the parameter is inversely proportional to the interest of a person, then it is a negative parameter.

For example 'Beautiful' is a positive parameter. If the value of parameter 'Beautiful' increases then the customer's interest will also increase. Whereas 'Expensive' is a negative parameter. Here, if the value of the parameter 'Expensive' increases then the interest of customer will decrease. So, the user can give the priority for a negative parameter in the interval (-1,0). This will solve the first issue of algorithm for decision making in (Maji et al 2003).To tackle the second issue, Tripathy et al took the difference of two fuzzy values in CT instead of adding 0's and 1's.To handle the third issue, they prioritize the parameters by multiplying with priority values given by the customer. The priority is a real number lying in the interval [-1, 1]. When a parameter value does not affect the customer's decision then the priority will be 0 (zero). If a parameter value affects positively to customer's decision then the priority will be (0, 1] and if a parameter value affects negatively to customer's decision then the priority will be [-1,0). If priority value is not given for one or more parameters then the value of the priority is assumed to be 0 by default and that parameter can be eliminated from further computation. To get even more reduction in computation we can keep only one object if there is some objects with same values for all parameters. The customer's priority value will be multiplied by the parameter value. This will give the values for priority table.The CT can be obtained by taking the difference of row sum of a house with others in priority table. The score of each house can be obtained by calculating row sum in . The house having more score will be more suitable to customer's requirement.

Consider the following example.

Let U be a set of houses given by $U= \{h_1,h_2,h_3,h_4,h_5,h_6\}$ and E be the parameter set given by $E =$ {Beautiful, Wooden, Green Surrounded, Expensive, Distance}. Consider a FSS (U, E) which describes the 'attractiveness of houses', given by

$(U, E) = \{$Beautiful Houses $= \{h_1/0.1, h_2/1.0, h_3/0.3, h_4/0.7, h_5/0.3, h_6/0.9\}$,

Wooden Houses $= \{ h_2/0.6, h_3/0.1, h_4/0.7, h_5/0.4, h_6/0.5\}$,

Green Surrounded Houses = { $h_1/0.2$, $h_2/0.8$, $h_3/0.2$, $h_4/0.6$, $h_5/0.4$, $h_6/0.6$},

Expensive Houses = { $h_1/0.1$, $h_2/0.8$, $h_3/0.3$, $h_4/0.6$, $h_5/0.5$, $h_6/0.6$},

Distance houses = { $h_1/0.8$, $h_2/0.3$, $h_3/0.4$, $h_4/0.6$, $h_5/0.1$, $h_6/0.5$ } }.

Suppose a customer Mr. X wants to buy a house out of given houses which suits his needs on the basis of choice parameters such as 'Beautiful', 'Wooden', 'Green Surrounded', 'Expensive', 'Distance'. That means out of all available houses, he needs to select a house according to his priorities which qualifies with maximum number of parameters of the parameter set.

Algorithm 2

1. Input the fuzzy soft set (U,E) and arrange that in tabular form.
2. Input the priority given by the customer for every parameter. For positive parameters the priority must has to be in the interval (0,1) and for negative parameters the priority must has to be in the interval (-1,0). If priority of any parameter has not given, than take it as 0 (zero) by default and opt out from further computation.
3. Multiply the priority values with the corresponding parameter values to get the priority table.
4. Compute the row sum of each row in the priority table.
5. Construct the comparison table by finding the entries as differences of each row sum with those of all other rows.
6. Compute the row sum for each row in the comparison table to get the score.
7. Construct the decision table by taking the row sums in the comparison table.
8. The object having highest value in the score column is to be selected. If more than one object is having the same score then the object having higher priority value is to be selected.

The priority given by the customer Mr. X for all parameters for Beautiful, wooden, Green Surrounded, Expensive, Distance respectively are 0.7, 0.0, 0.2, -0.5, -0.2 (Table 4). The priority value of the parameters 'Expensive' and 'Distance' is negative, which indicates that these parameters are negative parameters.

Note that in Table 5 there is no column for the parameter 'wooden', because its priority is zero.

Table 4. Tabular representation of the fuzzy soft set (U,E)

U	Beautiful	Wooden	Green Surrounded	Expensive	Distance
h_1	0.1	0.0	0.2	0.1	0.8
h_2	0.9	0.6	0.8	0.8	0.3
h_3	0.3	0.1	0.2	0.3	0.4
h_4	0.7	0.7	0.6	0.6	0.6
h_5	0.3	0.4	0.4	0.5	0.1
h_6	0.9	0.5	0.6	0.6	0.5

Table 5. Priority table

U	Beautiful	Green Surrounded	Expensive	Distance
h_1	.07	.04	-0.05	-0.16
h_2	.63	.16	-0.40	-0.06
h_3	.21	.04	-0.15	-0.08
h_4	.49	.12	-0.30	-0.12
h_5	.21	.08	-0.25	-0.02
h_6	.63	.12	-0.30	-0.10

Table 6. Comparison table

U	h_1	h_2	h_3	h_4	h_5	h_6
h_1	0.00	-0.43	-0.12	-0.29	-0.12	-0.45
h_2	0.43	0.00	0.31	0.14	0.31	-0.02
h_3	0.12	-0.31	0.00	-0.17	0.00	-0.33
h_4	0.29	-0.14	0.17	0.00	0.17	-0.16
h_5	0.12	-0.31	0.00	-0.17	0.00	-0.33
h_6	0.45	0.02	0.33	0.16	0.33	0.00

Table 7. Decision table

Houses	Score
h_1	-1.41
h_2	1.17
h_3	-0.69
h_4	0.33
h_5	-0.69
h_6	1.29

- **Decision Making:** The Customer should go for the house which has highest score (Table 7). If, there is same score for two houses, then the greater value in highest priority column will decide the best suitable house and so on. If, for any reason, the customer don't want that then he/she can choose next highest and so on.

Application of FSS in Group Decision Making

Most of the real- life problems cannot be effectively resolved by a single decision maker. Depends on the uncertainty and the amount of knowledge available, it is not easy to take a suitable decision for a single decision maker. So, it is needed to gather multiple decision makers with different knowledge structures and experience to conduct a group decision making (GDM). So far, we were discussing about single decision making application provided by Maji et al and Tripathy et al. In thissection, we discuss the application of FSSs in group decision making problem. Here, we discuss the algorithm provided by Tripathy et al. with the help of an example.

Algorithm 3

1. Input the priority given by the panel $(J_1, J_2, J_3, \ldots J_n)$ for each parameter, where 'n' is the number of judges.
2. For each judge J_i (i = 1, 2, 3, ..., n) repeat the following steps.
   a. Input the fuzzy soft set *(F, E)* provided by Judge J_i and arranges it in tabular form.
   b. Construct the priority table (PT). This table can be obtained by multiplying priority values with the corresponding parameter values. Also, calculate the row-sum of each row in the PT.
   c. Construct comparison tables (CT). This can be achieved by finding the entries as differences of each row sum in PTs with those of all other rows.
   d. Find the row sum for each row in the CT to obtain the score.
   e. Construct the decision table by taking the row sums in the CT. Assign rankings to each candidate based upon the row sum obtained.
3. Create a rank table based on the results obtained from the above step which contains rankings provided by all the judges.
4. Calculate the row-sum of each candidate in the rank table to find the rank-sum of each candidate. The candidate with lesser row sum value is the best choice. If more than one candidate is having

the same rank-sum, then the candidate having higher value in highest absolute priority column will be selected. This process is continued till final ranking list is obtained.

Assume that 'n' candidates are applying for a job in an organization. From these n candidates, the organization filters out many candidates based on some criteria (For eg: Those who got more than 60% marks are eligible to attend the interview). The candidates, who passed the elimination criteria, will be eligible to attend the interview. The interview performance of each selected candidate is analyzed by a panel of different judges. Here, the panel assigns some parameters to evaluate the performance of each candidate. Some parameters are communication skills, personality, reactivity etc.Let U be a set of candidates { $c_1, c_2, c_3, c_4, c_5, c_6$ }. The parameter set E be {knowledge, communication, reaction, presentation, extracurricular activities}. Consider a FSS *(U, E)* describing the 'performance of candidates'. Consider J_1, J_2 and J_3 are the judges who analyze the performance of the candidates and each judge is assigning a rank to each candidate according to his/her performance. The panel of judges assigns priority values to the parameters and based upon the impact of the parameters, they assign rankings to each parameter. This is shown in Table 8. The parameters knowledge, communication, behaviour, presentation, extracurricular activities are represented by e_1, e_2, e_3, e_4 and e_5.

The parameter values assigned by each judge to the candidate depend upon the performance of the candidate in the interview. The FSS for the candidates from the judge J_1 is shown in Table 9.

The priority for parameters e_1, e_2, e_3, e_4 and e_5 is given by the judge panel as 0.4, 0.3, -0.15, 0.05 and 0.1. Here, the parameter 'e_3' is a negative parameter. Parameters are classified into positive parameter and negative parameter. The priority table is shown in Table 10.

The CT obtained for the candidates by the judge J_1 is obtained is shown in the Table 11.

Table 8. Priority rank table

Parameters	e_1	e_2	e_3	e_4	e_5
Priority	.4	.3	-0.15	.05	.1
Parameter Rank	1	2	3	5	4

Table 9. FSS (F, E) by Judge J_1

U	e_1	e_2	e_3	e_4	e_5
c1	0.2	0.3	0.8	0.8	0.6
c_2	0.4	0.6	0.2	1	0.5
c_3	0.8	0.9	0.7	0.9	0.7
c_4	0.8	0.9	0.8	0.9	0.7
c_5	0.4	0.9	0.6	0.1	0.8
c_6	0.9	1	0.3	0.2	0.3

Table 10. Priority table for J_1

U	e_1	e_2	e_3	e_4	e_5	Row-Sum
c_1	0.08	0.09	-0.12	0.04	0.06	0.15
c_2	0.16	0.18	-0.3	0.05	0.05	0.14
c_3	0.32	0.27	-0.105	0.045	0.07	0.6
c_4	0.32	0.27	-0.12	0.045	0.07	0.585
c_5	0.16	0.27	-0.09	0.005	0.08	0.425
c_6	0.36	0.3	-0.045	0.01	0.03	0.655

Table 11. Comparison table

U	c_1	c_2	c_3	c_4	c_5	c_6	Score	Rank
c_1	0	0.01	-0.45	-0.435	-0.275	-0.505	-1.655	5
c_2	-0.01	0	-0.46	-0.445	-0.285	-0.515	-1.715	6
c_3	0.45	0.46	0	0.015	0.175	-0.055	1.045	2
c_4	0.435	0.445	-0.015	0	0.16	-0.07	0.955	3
c_5	0.275	0.285	-0.175	-0.16	0	-0.23	-0.005	4
c_6	0.505	0.515	0.055	0.07	0.23	0	1.375	1

Comparison table (CT) shows the ranking of each candidate by the judge J_2. Here, the candidate c_6 is the best choice. Since the selection of the best candidate is governed by a panel of 3 members, we cannot take this as the best choice. So, we have to find the CT of the judges J_2 and J_3 to decide the optimum choice. Representation of FSS of candidates by judge J_2 is shown in Table 12.

After applying the algorithm in the above FSS, we will get the CT as shown in the Table 13.

The FSS of candidates by Judge J_3 is given in Table 14.

After applying the algorithm in the above FSS, we will get the CT for the judge J_3 as shown in Table 15.

Rank of all candidates given by judges J_1, J_2 and J_3 are shown in the rank table (Table 16). From this rank, we can find the final rank of the candidates.

From Table 16, we can see that the panel has selected the candidate c_6 as the best choice.

Table 12. FSS (F, E) by Judge J_2

U	e_1	e_2	e_3	e_4	e_5
c_1	0.3	0.2	0.6	0.7	0.7
c_2	0.5	0.5	0	0.9	0.6
c_3	0.9	0.8	0.5	0.8	0.8
c_4	0.9	0.8	0.6	0.8	0.8
c_5	0.5	0.8	0.4	0	0.9
c_6	1	0.9	0.1	0.1	0.4

Table 13. Comparison table of judge J_2

c_j	c_1	c_2	c_3	c_4	c_5	c_6	Score	Rank
c_1	0	-0.26	-0.45	-0.435	-0.275	-0.505	-1.925	6
c_2	0.26	0	-0.19	-0.175	-0.015	-0.245	-0.365	5
c_3	0.45	0.19	0	0.015	0.175	-0.055	0.775	2
c_4	0.435	0.175	-0.015	0	0.16	-0.07	0.685	3
c_5	0.275	0.015	-0.175	-0.16	0	-0.23	-0.275	4
c_6	0.505	0.245	0.055	0.07	0.23	0	1.105	1

Table 14. FSS (F,E) by Judge J3

U	e_1	e_2	e_3	e_4	e_5
c_1	.5	.4	.8	.9	.9
c_2	.7	.7	.2	1	.8
c_3	1	1	1	1	1
c_4	1	1	.8	1	1
c_5	.7	1	.6	.2	1
c_6	1	1	.3	.3	.6

Table 15. Comparison table for judge J_3

c_j	c_1	c_2	c_3	c_4	c_5	c_6	Score	Rank
c_1	0	-0.255	-0.365	-0.395	-0.265	-0.395	-1.675	6
c_2	0.255	0	-0.11	-0.14	-0.01	-0.14	-0.145	5
c_3	0.365	0.11	0	-0.03	0.1	-0.03	0.515	3
c_4	0.395	0.14	0.03	0	0.13	0	0.695	2
c_5	0.265	0.01	-0.1	-0.13	0	-0.13	-0.085	4
c_6	0.395	0.14	0.03	0	0.13	0	0.695	1

Table 16. Rank table

	J_1	J_2	J_3	Rank-Sum	Final-Rank
c_1	5	6	6	17	6
c_2	6	5	5	16	5
c_3	2	2	3	7	2
c_4	3	3	2	8	3
c_5	4	4	4	12	4
c_6	1	1	1	3	1

INTERVAL VALUED FUZZY SOFT SETS

Fuzzy soft set is a combination of fuzzy sets and soft sets. However, it is noticed that in many real applications, the membership degree in a fuzzy set cannot be lightly confirmed. It is more reasonable to give an interval valued data to describe membership degree. From such a point of view, Zadeh proposed the concept of interval valued fuzzy set. Later, Yang has extended interval valued fuzzy sets into soft sets and proposed a new model named IVFSSs. It is a much better model to handle uncertainty than the fuzzy soft sets. Later on Tripathy et al redefined the IVFSSs using membership function. In this section, we discuss membership function for IVFSS. We also discuss the basic notions of IVFSS based on the membership function. Let *(F, E)* be an IVFSS over *(U, E)*. Then the set of parametric membership functions $\mu_{(F,E)} = \left\{ \mu^a_{(F,E)} \mid a \in E \right\}$ of *(F, E)* is defined as follows:

Definition 14: For any $\forall a \in E$, the membership function is defined as follows.

$$\mu^a_{(F,E)}(x) = \alpha, \alpha \in [0,1] \tag{14}$$

For any two IVFSS (F, E) and (G, E), the following operations are defined.

Definition 15: The union of *(F, E)* and *(G, E)* is the IVFSS *(H, E)*, and $\forall a \in E$ and $\forall x \in U$, we have

$$(F,E) \cup (G,E)(x) = \max\left[\mu^a_{(F,E)}(x), \mu^a_{(G,E)}(x)\right]$$
$$= \left[\max\left(\mu^{a-}_{(F,E)}(x), \mu^{a-}_{(G,E)}(x)\right), \max\left(\mu^{a+}_{(F,E)}(x), \mu^{a+}_{(G,E)}(x)\right)\right] \tag{15}$$

where $\mu^{a-}_{(F,E)}$ and $\mu^{a+}_{(F,E)}$ denotes the lower and upper membership value of the IVFSS.

Definition 16: The intersection of *(F, E)* and *(G, E)* is the IVFSS *(H, E)*, and $\forall a \in E$ and $\forall x \in U$, we have

$$(F,E) \cap (G,E)(x) = \min\left[\mu^a_{(F,E)}(x), \mu^a_{(G,E)}(x)\right]$$
$$= \left[\min\left(\mu^{a-}_{(F,E)}(x), \mu^{a-}_{(G,E)}(x)\right), \min\left(\mu^{a+}_{(F,E)}(x), \mu^{a+}_{(G,E)}(x)\right)\right] \tag{16}$$

Definition 17: *(F, E)* is said to be interval valued fuzzy soft subset of *(G, E)*, $(F,E) \subseteq (G,E)$. Then $\forall a \in E$, $\forall x \in U$,

$$\mu^{a+}_{(F,E)}(x) \leq \mu^{a+}_{(G,E)}(x), and$$
$$\mu^{a-}_{(F,E)}(x) \leq \mu^{a-}_{(G,E)}(x) \tag{17}$$

Definition 18: We say that *(F, E)* is equal to *(G, E)* written as *(F, E) = (G, E)* if $\forall x \in U$,

$$\mu^{a+}_{(F,E)}(x) = \mu^{a+}_{(G,E)}(x), and$$
$$\mu^{a-}_{(F,E)}(x) = \mu^{a-}_{(G,E)}(x) \tag{18}$$

Definition 19: For any two IVFSSs *(F, E)* and *(G, E)* over a common soft universe *(U, E)*, we define the complement *(H, E)* of *(G, E)* in *(F, E)* as $\forall a \in E$ and $\forall x \in U$.

$$\mu^{a+}_{(H,E)}(x) = \max\left\{0, \mu^{a+}_{(F,E)}(x) - \mu^{a+}_{(G,E)}(x)\right\}, and$$
$$\mu^{a-}_{(H,E)}(x) = \max\left\{0, \mu^{a-}_{(F,E)}(x) - \mu^{a-}_{(G,E)}(x)\right\} \tag{19}$$

Definition 20: $\forall x \in U$ and $\forall e \in E$, the complement of an IVFSS over a soft universe *(U, E)*, is defined as $(F, E)^c$.

$$\mu_{(F,E)^c}^{e+}(x) = \max\left(0, \mu_U^{e+}(x) - \mu_{(F,E)}^{e+}(x)\right), and$$
$$\mu_{(F,E)^c}^{e-}(x) = \max\left(0, \mu_U^{e-}(x) - \mu_{(F,E)}^{e-}(x)\right) \tag{20}$$

It can be seen easily that

$$\mu_{(F,E)^c}^{e+}(x) = 1 - \mu_{(F,E)}^{e+}(x), and$$
$$\mu_{(F,E)^c}^{e-}(x) = 1 - \mu_{(F,E)}^{e-}(x) \tag{21}$$

Application of IVFSS in Decision Making

Interval valued values leads us to three approaches:

1. Pessimistic,
2. Optimistic,
3. Neutral.

In pessimistic approach the lower value of the interval values presumed to take the decision where as in optimistic approach, upper value of the intervals has to be taken. Neutral values are nothing but the mean of pessimistic and optimistic values.

$$neutral\ value = \frac{pessimistic + optimistic}{2} \tag{22}$$

Most of the real-life decision making problem resolutions depend on the uncertainty and the amount of knowledge available.it is not easy to take a suitable decision for a single decision maker. So, it is needed to gather multiple decision makers with different knowledge structures and experience to conduct a group decision making (GDM). Here we discuss an application of group decision making in FSSs.

Algorithm 4

1. Input the priority given by the panel $(J_1, J_2, J_3, \ldots, J_n)$ for each parameter, where 'n' is the number of judges.
2. For each judge J_i (i =1, 2, 3, ..., n) repeat the following steps.
   a. Input the IVFSS (U, E) provided by Judge J_i and arrange it in tabular form. Compute and generate FSS tables with the pessimistic, optimistic and neutral approaches from given IVFSS and perform the following operations for all these cases.
   b. construct the priority table by multiplying the priority values with the corresponding parameter values.

c. Compute the row sum of each row in the priority table.

d. Construct the respective comparison tables by finding the differences of each row sum in priority tables with those of all other rows.

e. Compute the score as row sum of each row in the comparison table.

f. Construct the decision table by assigning ranks to each candidate for pessimistic, optimistic and neutral values according to their scores.

3. Create rank table based on the results obtained from the above step which contains rankings provided by all the judges for pessimistic, optimistic and neutral cases.

4. Calculate the normalized score of each candidate in the rank table by using the following equation.

5. Normalized Score:

$$= \frac{2 * \left(|c| * |k| * |j| - \sum_{i=1, x \in K}^{i=|j|} RC_{ix} \right)}{|k| * |j| * |c| * (|c| - 1)},$$

(23)

where |c| is the number of candidates, K={optimistic, pessimistic, neutral}. So, K=3 and |j| is the number of judges.

6. The candidate with higher normalized score value is the best choice.

Application

Let's take a case of selection process in an institution. A panel of judges will examine the performance of the candidates.

Let $U = \{c_1, c_2, c_3, c_4, c_5, c_6\}$ be the set containing all candidates selected for the interview. $E = \{$knowledge, communication, behaviour, presentation, extracurricular activities$\}$ be the set of parameters. Consider an IVFSS *(U, E)* which represents the 'quality of a candidate' according to judges.

Consider J_1, J_2 and J_3 are the judges who analyze the performance of the candidates and each judge is assigning a rank to each candidate according to the performance.

The panel of judges assigns priority values to the parameters and based upon the impact of the parameters, they assign rankings to each parameter. This is shown in Table 17.

The parameter values assigned by each judge to the candidate depend upon the performance of the candidate in the interview. The IVFSS for the candidates from the judge J1 is shown in Table 18.

The priority for parameters e_1, e_2, e_3, e_4 and e_5 is given by the judge panel as 0.4, 0.3, -0.15, 0.05 and 0.1. Here, the parameter 'e_3' is a negative parameter. Parameters are classified into positive parameter and negative parameter. The concept of negative parameter was introduced by Tripathy et al.

First, we are considering the pessimistic case. The values of the pessimistic case are shown in Table 19.

The priority table of Table 19 can be constructed by multiplying the priority values with respective parameter values.

The CT shown in Table 21 can be constructed by summing up all the differences of each value in a row with those of all other rows.

In the same way, the CT for optimistic and neutral approach can be constructed. Table 22 is the CT for optimistic approach.

Table 24 indicates the IVFSS "performance of candidate" given by judge J_2.

Similarly, we find the CT for pessimistic, optimistic and neutral cases of Judge J_2 is shown in Tables 25, 26 and 27.

The IVFSS (U, E), given by judge J3 is shown in Table 28.

Similarly, we find out CT for pessimistic case of judge J_3 as shown in Table 29.

The final decision is taken with the help of normalized score. The candidate who is having more value in the normalized score is the best choice. From this Table 29, we can see c6 is the best candidate. The choice of candidates is in the order of c6, c4, c2, c3, c5 and c1.

Table 17. Parameter rank table

Parameter	e_1	e_2	e_3	e_4	e_5
Priority	.4	.3	-0.15	.05	.1
Parameter Rank	1	2	3	5	4

Table 18. Tabular representation of IVFSS of judge J1

U	e_1	e_2	e_3	e_4	e_5
c_1	0.2-0.4	0.3-0.5	0.8-0.9	0.4-0.7	0.6-0.9
c_2	0.4-0.8	0.6-0.9	0.2-0.5	0.7-1	0.5-0.6
c_3	0.5-0.8	0.7-0.9	0.7-0.8	0.8-1	0.5-0.7
c_4	0.6-0.8	0.5-0.9	0.8-1	0.5-0.9	0.7-0.8
c_5	0.1-0.4	0.9-1	0.3-0.6	0.1-0.5	0.8-1
c_6	0.9-1	0.5-0.7	0.1-0.3	0.2-0.4	0.3-0.7

Table 19. Pessimistic values of J1

	e_1	e_2	e_3	e_4	e_5
c_1	0.2	0.3	0.8	0.4	0.6
c_2	0.4	0.6	0.2	0.7	0.5
c_3	0.5	0.7	0.7	0.8	0.5
c_4	0.6	0.5	0.8	0.5	0.7
c_5	0.1	0.9	0.3	0.1	0.8
c_6	0.9	0.5	0.1	0.2	0.3

Table 20. Priority table for pessimistic values of J1

	e_1	e_2	e_3	e_4	e_5
c_1	.08	.09	-0.12	.02	.06
c_2	.16	.18	-0.03	.035	.05
c_3	.2	.21	-0.105	.04	.05
c_4	.24	.15	-0.12	.025	.07
c_5	.04	.27	-0.045	.005	.08
c_6	.36	.15	-0.015	.01	.03

Table 21. Comparison table for pessimistic case of judge J1

	c_1	c_2	c_3	c_4	c_5	c_6	Row Sum	Rank
c_1	0	-0.265	-0.265	-0.235	-0.22	-0.405	-1.39	6
c_2	0.265	0	0	0.03	0.045	-0.14	0.2	3
c_3	0.265	0	0	0.03	0.045	-0.14	0.2	2
c_4	0.235	-0.03	-0.03	0	0.015	-0.17	0.02	4
c_5	0.22	-0.045	-0.045	-0.015	0	-0.185	-0.07	5
c_6	0.405	0.14	0.14	0.17	0.185	0	1.04	1

Table 22. CT for optimistic case of judge J1

	c_1	c_2	c_3	c_4	c_5	c_6	Row Sum	Rank
c_1	0	-0.325	-0.29	-0.265	-0.195	-0.355	-1.43	6
c_2	0.325	0	0.035	0.06	0.13	-0.03	0.52	2
c_3	0.29	-0.035	0	0.025	0.095	-0.065	0.31	3
c_4	0.265	-0.06	-0.025	0	0.07	-0.09	0.16	4
c_5	0.195	-0.13	-0.095	-0.07	0	-0.16	-0.26	5
c_6	0.355	0.03	0.065	0.09	0.16	0	0.7	1

Table 23. CT for neutral case of judge J1

	c_1	c_2	c_3	c_4	c_5	c_6	Row Sum	Rank
c_1	0	-0.295	-0.2775	-0.25	-0.2075	-0.38	-1.41	5
c_2	0.295	0	0.0175	0.045	0.0875	-0.085	0.36	2
c_3	0.2775	-0.0175	0	0.0275	0.07	-0.1025	0.255	3
c_4	0.25	-0.045	-0.0275	0	0.0425	-0.13	0.09	4
c_5	0.2075	-0.0875	-0.07	-0.0425	0	-0.1725	-0.165	6
c_6	0.38	0.085	0.1025	0.13	0.1725	0	0.87	1

Table 24. IVFSS given by Judge J2

	e_1	e_2	e_3	e_4	e_5
c_1	.1-.3	.4-.5	.7-.9	.5-.8	.6-.8
c_2	.3-.6	.6-.9	.3-.5	.8-.9	.4-.7
c_3	.4-.7	.5-.7	.5-.7	.7-1	.3-.6
c_4	.7-.8	.6-.9	.8-.9	.5-.8	.8-1
c_5	.2-.4	.8-1	.2-.5	.3-.5	.7-.9
c_6	.7-.9	.5-.8	.2-.4	.1-.3	.2-.5

Table 25. CT for pessimistic of Judge J2

	c_1	c_2	c_3	c_4	c_5	c_6	Row Sum	Rank
c_1	0	-0.195	-0.16	-0.305	-0.235	-0.285	-1.18	6
c_2	0.195	0	0.035	-0.11	-0.04	-0.09	-0.01	4
c_3	0.16	-0.035	0	-0.145	-0.075	-0.125	-0.22	5
c_4	0.305	0.11	0.145	0	0.07	0.02	0.65	1
c_5	0.235	0.04	0.075	-0.07	0	-0.05	0.23	3
c_6	0.285	0.09	0.125	-0.02	0.05	0	0.53	2

Table 26. CT for optimistic case of Judge J2

	c_1	c_2	c_3	c_4	c_5	c_6	Row Sum	Rank
c_1	0	-0.295	-0.24	-0.34	-0.245	-0.35	-1.47	6
c_2	0.295	0	0.055	-0.045	0.05	-0.055	0.3	3
c_3	0.24	-0.055	0	-0.1	-0.005	-0.11	-0.03	5
c_4	0.34	0.045	0.1	0	0.095	-0.01	0.57	2
c_5	0.245	-0.05	0.005	-0.095	0	-0.105	0	4
c_6	0.35	0.055	0.11	0.01	0.105	0	0.63	1

Table 27. CT for neutral case of Judge J2

	c_1	c_2	c_3	c_4	c_5	c_6	Row Sum	Rank
c_1	0	-0.245	-0.2	-0.3225	-0.24	-0.3175	-1.325	6
c_2	0.245	0	0.045	-0.0775	0.005	-0.0725	0.145	3
c_3	0.2	-0.245	0	-0.1225	-0.04	-0.1175	-0.325	5
c_4	0.3225	0.0775	0.1225	0	0.0825	0.005	0.61	1
c_5	0.24	-0.005	0.04	-0.0825	0	-0.0775	0.115	4
c_6	0.3175	0.0725	0.1175	-0.005	-0.0775	0	0.425	2

Table 28. IVFSS given by Judge J_3

	e_1	e_2	e_3	e_4	e_5
c1	.3-.4	.2-.7	.6-.9	.2-.5	.4-.8
c2	.3-.5	.5-.9	.1-.3	.6-.9	.3-.5
c3	.3-.6	.5-.7	.8-1	.9-1	.3-.7
c4	.6-.9	.3-.7	.7-.9	.3-.7	.6-.9
c5	.1-.4	.7-1	.3-.7	.2-.6	.5-.7
c6	.6-1	.3-.9	.3-.5	.2-.5	.1-.6

Table 29. CT for pessimistic case of Judge J3

	c_1	c_2	c_3	c_4	c_5	c_6	Row Sum	Rank
c_1	0	-0.175	-0.085	-0.16	-0.125	-0.165	-0.71	6
c_2	0.175	0	0.09	0.015	0.05	0.01	0.34	1
c_3	0.085	-0.09	0	-0.075	0.035	-0.08	-0.125	5
c_4	0.16	-0.015	0.075	0	0.035	-0.005	0.25	3
c_5	0.125	-0.05	-0.035	-0.035	0	-0.04	-0.035	4
c_6	0.165	-0.01	0.08	0.005	0.04	0	0.28	2

PARAMETER REDUCTION USING SOFT SET (ALI 2012; ZHI ET AL., 2008)

Using soft set theory, parameter reduction technique was initiated by ali (2012). In his paper ali told that there is connectivity between soft set and the approximation space of Pawlak (rough set). They developed a very simple technique to reduce the parameters that are present in the parameter set which was carried out for both soft set and also for the hybrid model fuzzy soft set. Initially the suboptimal choice problem and parameter set of soft set which is added is taken into consideration. This approach overcomes the problem of earlier methodology. Along with this an algorithm of normal parameter reduction is also explained. Degrees of parameter and decision partition are the two new methods which were proposed in this new technique. The same technique is also extended for fuzzy soft sets.

Methodology Used

The nature of soft set is to represent the parameters with respect to the elements with the tabular form consist of entries 0 and 1. The data is taken and is represented as said above.

From the source table created, every individual parameter is taken to consideration for checking whether the parameter can be eliminated or not.

If the parameter is about the eliminate, then it is called dispensable parameter which means the parameter which we are going to eliminate is not going to be used anyhow in the decision making.

Similarly all parameter has to tested and the dispensable parameters cane be eliminated from the table and non-dispensable parameter which are called core parameters will remain as such in the table at last for decision making.

Dispensable parameter: The important task in this method is to find the parameter is dispensable or not. To find whether the parameter is dispensable or not, the decision parameter "d" is added to the table.

If the parameter is eliminated and the decision parameter "d" classification is not changed then the parameter is said to be dispensable and it can be eliminated from the parameter set as it is not going to be used in the decision making process.

If the parameter is eliminated and the decision parameter "d" classification is changed then the parameter is said to be non-dispensable and it cannot be eliminated from the parameter set as it is going to be used in the decision making process. All non-dispensable parameter are called core parameters.

Example

Let Universal set U be finite for calculation.

U = {H_1, H_2, H_3, H_4, H_5, H_6} be a set of six houses
E = {costly, spacious, furnished, greeny, modernized} be the set of parameters associated with the houses.

    User need:
    If the user is going to buy a house on the following parameters subset P ={costly, spacious, furnished, greeny, modernized}.
    Let {e1, e2, e3, e4, e5} is the symbolic representation of the set P.
    Table 30 shows the symbolic representation of the soft set with houses and parameters respectively.

In the Table 31 one more column is added called "d" for decision making which is $\sum h_{ij}$ where, h_{ij} is the value for the ith house h_i corresponding to j^{th} parameter e_j.

The object belonging to same group are separated and the object not belongs to group are separated differently. Both these groups are placed separately to from two different equivalence classes as shown below Table 31. The classification of data is shown in the Table 31.

Let (σ, A) be a soft equivalence relation over U with A = { e_1, e_2, e_3, e_4, e_5, d}, C = {e_1, e_2, e_3, e_4, e_5}, D = {d}, where C is the set of condition parameters and D is the set of decision parameter.

The classes associated with each parameter are:

- For costly parameter {e_1} the equivalence classes associated are {h_1, h_2, h_3, h_4, h_5, h_6},
- For spacious parameter {e_2} the equivalence classes associated are {h_1, h_2, h_6} and {h_3, h_4, h_5},
- For furnished parameter {e_3} the equivalence classes associated are {h_1, h_2, h_3, h_4, h_5, h_6},
- For greeny parameter {e_4} the equivalence classes associated are {h_1, h_2, h_3, h_4, h_6} and {h_5},
- For modernized surrounding {e_5} the equivalence classes associated are {h_1, h_3, h_6} and {h_2, h_4, h_5},
- For 'd' the equivalence classes are {h_1, h_6}, {h_2, h_3}, {h_4}, {h_5}.

Algorithm 5

Step 1: Input the soft set (F, E) with the table.

Step 2: Input the choice (condition) parameters C⊆E

Step 3: Input decision parameter $d = \sum h_{ij}$ as the last column in table obtained by choice parameters.

Step 4: Rearrange the Input by placing the objects having the same value for the parameter d adjacent to each other.

Step 5: Distinguish the objects with different values of d by double line.

Step 6: Identify core parameters as defined in Definition.

Step 7: Output by eliminating all dispensable parameters one by one, resulting a table with minimum number of condition parameters having the same classification ability for d as the original table with d.

Table 30. Soft set representation of houses under consideration

	e_1	e_2	e_3	e_4	e_5
H_1	1	1	1	1	1
H_2	1	1	1	1	0
H_3	1	0	1	1	1
H_4	1	0	1	1	0
H_5	1	0	1	0	0
H_6	1	1	1	1	1

Table 31. Soft set representation after adjoining decision parameter d

	e_1	e_2	e_3	e_4	e_5	D
H_1	1	1	1	1	1	5
H_6	1	1	1	1	1	5
H_2	1	1	1	1	0	4
H_3	1	0	1	1	1	4
H_4	1	0	1	1	0	3
H_5	1	0	1	0	0	2

The equivalence relation which corresponds to each and every parameter is calculated with the equivalence class. (σ, A) is a soft equivalence relation over U. The ultimate target is to reduce the numbers parameters and to get minimum number of parameters for decision making process without the change in the parameter "d" classification. Table 31 is consistent and here C$\Rightarrow$D. Parameter reduction technique starts.

The process of parameter reduction starts. Initially the parameter e_1 is deleted from the Table 32. The Table 32 represents the objects after deleting the parameter e_1. From the Table 32 we understood that deleting the e_1 doesn't affect the classification ability of the decision parameter d, so e_1 is dispensable. Then we try to delete of e_2 from Table 31 so, we get Table 33.

After deleting the parameter e_2 from the table, the classification of "d" is affected. So elimination of e_2 parameter changes the classification ability of d, therefore e_2 is a core parameter.

Similarly same methodology is carried out for all parameters. At last we find set of core parameters $\{e_2, e_4, e_5\}$ which cannot be eliminated from the table. The elimination of the parameters e_1 and e_3 do not disturb the classification ability of "d".

Table 34 is the final table with eliminated parameters and the parameters present in the table are called core parameters.

Table 32. Soft set representation after eliminating condition parameter e_1

	e_2	e_3	e_4	e_5	de_1
H_1	1	1	1	1	4
H_6	1	1	1	1	4
H_2	1	1	1	0	3
H_3	0	1	1	1	3
H_4	0	1	1	0	2
H_5	0	1	0	0	1

Table 33. Soft set representation after eliminating condition parameter e_2

	e_1	e_3	e_4	e_5	de_2
H_1	1	1	1	1	4
H_6	1	1	1	1	4
H_2	1	1	1	0	3
H_3	1	1	1	1	4
H_4	1	1	1	0	3
H_5	1	1	0	0	2

Table 34. Soft set representation after eliminating condition parameter e_1 and e_3

	e_2	e_4	e_5	$De_1 e_3$
H_1	1	1	1	3
H_6	1	1	1	3
H_2	1	1	0	2
H_3	0	1	1	2
H_4	0	1	0	1
H_5	0	0	0	0

Real Time Application Using Parameter Reduction

Many applications in the real time are using parameter reduction technique. Among those this part of the chapter explains briefly how it is used in the field of medical diagnosis and in the field of database.

Application of Soft Sets to Diagnose the Prostate Cancer Risk (Saziye et al., 2013)

The growth of artificial intelligence development makes its application worldwide. One of such application that is used in the field of medical diagnosis using soft set is discussed below. In this technique first the soft expert system is designed as the prediction system for prostate cancer by using the respective antigen, prostate volume and age factors of patients and finally the patients prostate cancer risk percentage is calculated.

Methodology Used

Step 1: The data is that is taken from the patients are fuzzified. Initially the data set that is taken from the patients are fuzzied using any fuzzification technique. The data are not convenient to make into soft set directly. Hence this step is followed.

Step 2: The fuzzy set is then transformed to soft set. With the fuzzified data, the data is converted to soft set. Then it is tabulated as it is the nature of soft set to represent in the table with the entries that contain 0 and 1.

Step 3: Parameter reduction in soft set. With the table of data of soft set parameter reduction method which is discussed earlier is done to find out the core parameter and to discard the dispensable parameters.

Step 4: Obtaining soft set rules. Using the 'AND' operation some of the soft rules have been calculated. Then according to the patient rule it is categorized.

Step 5: Analyzing of soft rules. After categorizing according to the patients rule, the cancer risk percentage is calculated. From the risk percentage we can easily able to come to the conclusion of risk of prostate cancer occurrence.

In the above said methodology step3 is meant for parameter reduction. Initially all the parameters that are related to the patients are taken into consideration in the form of fuzzy values because it is difficult to represent the data in the form of soft set initially. After tabulating the fuzzy values, using any of the existing methods the fuzzy values are transformed into soft set. In this place parameter reduction plays a vital role. If the parameters are more it is very difficult for the doctors or technicians to manipulate the information. Also, they should not discard any of the important parameter for the final decision. So, the only way is the find the core parameter and dispensable parameter from the parameter list. As described in the example5.1 the parameter reduction technique is carried and core parameter is identified and the dispensable parameter which are not going to alter any change in the final decision are eliminated.

After finding the core parameter, soft rules are obtained using 'AND' operation and according to that the patient rule is classified. After this classification, the prostate cancer risk can be calculated and risk percentage is identified after analyzing the soft rules.

Application of Soft Sets in Database in Relational Algebra (Yan Zou et al., 2008)

The application of parameter reduction in relational algebra is defined in this section. The basic operations of relational algebra combined with soft set theory are been defined. The operations like difference, selection, projection, union and difference are used in the algorithm for reducing the parameter based on the optimal choice.

The advantage of using soft set in such decision making process is because of the nature of soft set which includes any type of parameter needed for the user. Compared to the other uncertainty model, soft set allows parameters to choose efficiently by the user without any lack. As defined by some of the researchers, it is not possible to reduce the parameter in soft set compared to rough set method of attribute reduction.

Codd E F introduced the concept of relational algebra which is full of relations and is an abstract query language. Relational algebra uses mathematical symbols or expressions for data querying. Traditional set operations and specialized relation operations are the two different types of classification in relational algebra. Structural Query Language is the medium through which relational algebra and relational calculus combine together.

Parameters Reduction of Soft Sets Based on Relational Algebra

The basic and necessary operations needed for the manipulation are defined. The operations are union, difference, extended Cartesian product, selection and projection.

Algorithm 6

Step 1: The soft set (F, E) is tabulated. For each and every object the choice value is calculated and the record is written with maximum choice value.

Step 2: Compute the relation R_E. The relation is the projection of parameters.

Step 3: Compute all the relations R_e. The relation is the selection of parameters that satisfies the selecting condition.

Step 4: Compute the value by finding the difference with R_E with the union of all R_e.

If the resultant value is equal to the maximum value then the new parameter set is the reduction of parameter set.

In the above said method, the numbers of parameter from the parameter set is reduced. The parameter reduction is used to make the decision making process faster and easier. Also, we are able to separate the parameter with complete data and incomplete data which is useful for the various manipulations.

CONCLUSION

The definition of soft set using the characteristic function approach was provided by Tripathy et al recently, which besides being able to take care of several definitions of operations on soft sets could make the proofs of properties very elegant. For IVFSSs no such approach was in existence. In this chapter we discuss membership function for IVFSSs which extends the notion of characteristic function introduced by Tripathy et.al in 2015. We also discuss application IVFSSs in group decision making, so that the decision making becomes more efficient and realistic.

REFERENCES

Ali, M. I. (2012). Another view on reduction of parameters in soft sets. *Applied Soft Computing*, *12*(6), 1814–1821. doi:10.1016/j.asoc.2012.01.002

Chen, Tsang, Yeung, & Wang. (2005). *The parameterization reduction of soft sets and its applications.* Academic Press.

Kong, Z., Gao, L., Wang, L., & Li, S. (2008). The normal parameter reduction of soft sets and its algorithm. *Computers & Mathematics with Applications (Oxford, England)*, *56*(12), 3029–3037. doi:10.1016/j.camwa.2008.07.013

Maji, P. K., Biswas, R., & Roy, A. R. (2001). Fuzzy Soft Sets. *Journal of Fuzzy Mathematics*, *9*(3), 589–602.

Maji, P. K., Biswas, R., & Roy, A. R. (2002). An Application of Soft Sets in a Decision Making Problem. *Computers & Mathematics with Applications (Oxford, England)*, *44*(8-9), 1007–1083. doi:10.1016/S0898-1221(02)00216-X

Maji, P. K., Biswas, R., & Roy, A. R. (2003). Soft Set Theory. *Computers & Mathematics with Applications (Oxford, England)*, *45*(4-5), 555–562. doi:10.1016/S0898-1221(03)00016-6

Molodtsov, D. (1999). Soft Set Theory - First Results. *Computers & Mathematics with Applications (Oxford, England)*, *37*(4-5), 19–31. doi:10.1016/S0898-1221(99)00056-5

Saaty, T. L. (1986). Axiomatic foundation of the analytic hierarchy process. *Management Science*, *32*(7), 841–845. doi:10.1287/mnsc.32.7.841

Tripathy, B. K., & Arun, K. R. (in press). A New Approach to Soft Sets, Soft Multisets and Their Properties. *International Journal of Reasoning-Based Intelligent Systems*.

Yuksel, S., Dizman, T., Yildizdan, G., & Sert, U. (2013). Application of soft sets to diagnose the prostate cancer risk. *Journal of Inequalities and Applications*, *1*, 239.

Zadeh, L. A. (1965). Fuzzy sets. *Information and Control*, *8*(3), 338–353. doi:10.1016/S0019-9958(65)90241-X

Zou & Chen. (2008). Research on soft set theory and parameters reduction based on relational algebra. *Second International Symposium on Intelligent Information Technology Application*. IEEE.

Chapter 16
Selection of Green Suppliers Based on GSCM Practices:
Using Fuzzy MCDM Approach in an Electronics Company

Akshay Kumar Uppala
VIT University, India

J. J. Thakkar
Indian Institute of Technology Kharagpur, India

Rishabh Ranka
VIT University, India

Manupati Vijay Kumar
VIT University, India

Shilpa Agrawal
VIT University, India

ABSTRACT

The environmental pressure from various stakeholders, particularly in the selection of green suppliers in the industrial sector, is alarming. The companies are realizing the significance of incorporating green practices in their daily operations. This chapter proposes a framework on the criteria of GSCM practices using MCDM analysis to select green suppliers for an Indian electronics company. The authors have collected the data from a set of 10 available suppliers. The authors use fuzzy AHP and fuzzy TOPSIS approach to rank the suppliers based on the decision makers' preferences on the selection of green suppliers using GSCM practices. The three dominating criteria concluded by the results are the commitment of senior management towards GSCM; product design that incorporates three R's policy for component, materials, and energy; abidance with environmental laws and auditing programs. This chapter carries out a comparison between Fuzzy Analytical Hierarchy Process (FAHP) and Fuzzy TOPSIS method to enhance the quality of decision making and validate the rankings.

INTRODUCTION

Today, the world is moving towards greater environmental concern and awareness. Lack of attention towards the environmental policies in early periods of industrialization is no longer an option in today's times. The modern thinking is that environmental conservation and industrialization must go hand in

DOI: 10.4018/978-1-5225-1008-6.ch016

hand. Hence, the strategy in today's world is sustainable development which is implemented by adopting the practice of Green supply chain management. By inculcating the practice of sustainable development with the neoteric developments in supply chain management and purchasing, the strategy of Green supply chain management is developed. The innovations in industrial purchasing and supply chain management from the perspective of environment is mentioned by GSCM.

In Indian electronic companies, the process for ideal supplier selection process creates a new research avenue known as green supplier selection. This concept facilitates the complex and critical decision making process in ideal supplier selection, by considering the quality of the supplier services and their level of commitment to environmental causes. Many research gaps in this area are yet to be explored. The green supplier selection process is one of the key operational tasks for sustainable supply chain management. Literature review exemplifies why companies should be concerned with environmental and social issues in the supply chain by focussing on the broader concept of sustainable development. It is observed that the pressure from the stockholders in order to enhance the company's reputation to gain competitive advantage is the prime reason for the increasing popularity of GSCM practices. GSCM is not only a concept incorporating sustainable development but also provides added benefits in terms of cost reduction, increased operational efficiency and competitive advantage. The main objective of this chapter is to select green suppliers under a MCDM analysis environment for the electronics companies in India.

BACKGROUND

GSCM develops efficient environmental practices that encourage continuous improvements in the environmental practices of multiple organizations within the supply chain (Vachon and Klassen, 2006). It is the process of amalgamating the environmental concerns into supply chain management by taking into consideration various factors such as material sourcing and selection, product design, manufacturing, delivery of finished products, and the management of product life cycle (Srivastava, 2007) and the environmental issues at every stage of the aforementioned factors (Min and Kim, 2012). The GSCM practices that could be adopted by the suppliers, lack in environmental evaluation. Environmental performance is enhanced in the whole supply chain by suppliers who implement these practices. There are many companies who are struggling with eco-friendly supplier selection. Advancements in the GSCM strategies can help these companies. (Handfield et al., 2002).

In this research work, we have implemented multi-criteria decision making analysis (MCDM) analysis to evaluate best suppliers out of many who follows green practices. Some of those techniques include Analytical Hierarchy Process (AHP) (Noci, 1997; Handfield et al., 2002; Lu et al., 2007; Chiou et al., 2008; Lee et al., 2009; Grisi et al., 2010); Analytic Network Process (ANP) (Hsu & Hu 2009, Büyüközkan & Çifçi, 2010, 2011); the rough set methodology (Bai & Sarkis, 2010a, b); Data Envelopment Analysis (DEA) (Kumar & Jain, 2010); and fuzzy TOPSIS methodology (Awasthi et al., 2010).

Govidan et al., (2013) proposed fuzzy axiomatic design approach to carry out green supplier selection practices with 26 traditional criteria and 72 environmental criteria under 13 main criteria. Ajukumar and Gandhi (2013), Khalili and Duecker (2013), Sarkis (2003) and Sarkis et al. (2012) discussed environmental and economic tradeoffs for the organizational decision making based on supplier selection. Govindan et al., (2015) reviewed the green supplier evaluation and their selection with multi-criteria decision making analysis model.

The aim of this study is the selection of green suppliers under a MCDM analysis environment for the electronics companies in India. Hazardous materials pertain to materials in the electronics manufacturing process acts directly proportional to various costs. Product life cycle assessment with respect to product lightweight, recyclable, without any toxic chemicals and significantly low consumption of electricity is also considered as one more major factor.

PROBLEM DESCRIPTION

This case study has been taken from an electronic industry which is one of the major players in electronics and practising green practices based in India. In this company, there are almost 600 employees in any shift and their major role is to assemble electronic products for example generators, inverters, etc. To fulfil the demand of the customers, and to comply with environmental regulations, the company has applied some alterations in the manufacturing and assembly of its finished product. These alterations have resulted in making the product lightweight, recyclable, without any toxic chemicals and significantly low consumption of electricity. Moreover, the life cycle assessment of a product has also been predicted with the proposed analysis. Under this, an inventory of waste generation, emissions and consumption of raw material is carried out to measure the usage of resources and for conducting of reduction practices which is also aided by this inventory. In the light of these changes the sustainability manager of this company needs to find and choose the supplies who can support the enactment of GSCM practices by the company. The company has recognized ten potential suppliers those are implementing green practises in their companies. A survey questionnaire was prepared bearing in mind the company's objectives. Three academic experts (decision makers) who had experience in the area of GSCM were provided with the questionnaire and their preferences of GSCM practices was recorded. This has further been used in selection of the green supplier. Table 1 gives the names and explanations of the GSCM practices used in this chapter.

METHODOLOGY

For making decisions for choice of an alternative from various alternatives which categorized by multiple criteria, MCDM techniques are used to make the decisions. The problem presented here addresses an Indian Electronics company that manufactures and assembles electronic products such as generators, invertors etc. for various customers such as hospitals, government and private organizations etc.

In this company a decision has to be made about selecting a green supplier, who will provide materials required for the development of new products that comply with the government regulations as well as eco-friendly criteria of this company. For this selection, the authors have considered 17 chief criteria and to evaluate the 10 alternatives, fuzzy AHP and fuzzy TOPSIS methods are adopted. The approach to solution is given below

Fuzzy Set Theory

Imprecision, vagueness, and subjective nature of human thinking often render crisp numbered data inadequate to model real world systems. (Shen et al. 2013). Precise weights and performance rating are

Table 1. GSCM practices and their explanation

Code	Name of the GSCM Practice	Explanation
GSCM 1	Support of senior management to GSCM	How much the senior management supports the adoption of GSCM. Cultural changes and process adjustments are needed
GSCM 2	Inter-functional cooperation for environmental improvement	Cooperation between various functions (example research and development in sustainability,) is vital for implementation of changes in the daily activities of the functional areas. Thus environmental requirements are promoted by this type of cooperation externally or internally.
GSCM 3	Compliance with legal environmental requirements and auditing programs	Focusing on legal requirements concerning the environment and implementing programs which shows the company's attempt to comply with environmental regulations internally.
GSCM 4	ISO 14001 Certification	Company possesses EMS which is ISO 14001 certified
GSCM 5	Selection of suppliers includes environmental criteria	Traditional criteria as well as environmental variables are considered for supplier selection process.
GSCM 6	Work with suppliers to meet environmental goals	The company asks its suppliers to support action taken to improve the environment.
GSCM 7	Evaluations of the internal environmental management of suppliers	The environmental performance of suppliers are evaluated by inspecting the supplier installations. It is made sure that suppliers comply with standards of environmental management
GSCM 8	Evaluation of the environmental management of 2nd-tier suppliers	Environmental concern is extended outside the direct relationship by monitoring suppliers of even basic raw materials.
GSCM 9	Working with the clients for eco-design	Companies try to develop eco-friendly products along with its clients. This improves the environmental impact of the product.
GSCM 10	Working with the clients to make production cleaner	Companies try develop cleaner production with client's cooperation
GSCM 11	Work with clients to use environmentally friendly packaging	With client's cooperation, companies try to develop eco-friendly packaging
GSCM 12	Company acquires cleanest technologies	Acquisition of technologies which allow cleaner manufacturing
GSCM 13	Product designs that reduce, reuse, recycle, or reclaim materials, components, or energy	Strategies on part reuse, reduction of materials, recycling etc. are followed by the company.
GSCM 14	Product designs that avoid or reduce toxic or hazardous material use	Toxic, dangerous products are avoided or reduced as much as possible by the company during development of products
GSCM 15	Sale of excess stock or materials	Obsolete stock are sold by the company to recover its investment
GSCM 16	Sale of scrap and used materials	Used or waste materials are sold by the company to recover its investment
GSCM 17	Sale of used equipment	Used equipment are sold by the company to recover its investment

D. Kannan et al. (2014).

impossible to give in various situations. Fuzzy set theory can be used to approximately model uncertainty in judgments. (Singh & Benyoucef, 2011). In this chapter the authors have adopted fuzzy set theory and made use of and triangular fuzzy numbers (TFN) to quantify the preferences of decision makers. This encapsulates vagueness of the linguistic assessments and provides computational simplicity. (Kannan et al., 2009).

A triangular fuzzy number is described as (m_1, m_2, m_3), where ($m_1 \leq m_2 \leq m_3$). "m_1" specifies the minimum likely value, "m_2" the most probable value, and "m_3" the maximum possible value, respectively that explain a fuzzy event. Some of the chief notations and definitions of fuzzy set theory mentioned in this chapter are from (Singh & Benyoucef, 2011; Zimmerman, 1996; Zadeh, 1965; 1976; Awasthi, et al, 2011; Shen et al., 2013).

Definition 1: Fuzzy set. Let the universe of discourse be denoted by Y, $Y=\{y_1, y_2, \ldots, y_n\}$. A set of order pairs $\{(y_1, f_B(y_1)), (b_2, f_B(y_2)), \ldots, (y_n, f_B(y_n))\}$ is fuzzy set B of Y is, where $f_B: Y \to [0,1]$ is the membership function of B, and $f_B(y_i)$ represents the membership degree of y_i in A.

Definition 2: Triangular Fuzzy number. A triangular fuzzy number is denoted by a triplet (n_1, n_2, n_3) and the membership function of the fuzzy number $f_B(y)$ is illustrated in Figure 1 and defined in equation 1 as:

$$f_B(y) = \begin{cases} 0, y < n_1, y > n_3 \\ \dfrac{y - n_1}{n_2 - n_1}, n_1 \le y \le n_2 \\ \dfrac{n_3 - x}{n_3 - n_2}, n_2 \le y \le n_3 \end{cases} \tag{1}$$

Definition 3: Degree of possibility. For two triangular fuzzy numbers, the degree of possibility $N_2=(n_{21}, n_{22}, n_{23}) \ge N_1=(n_{11}, n_{12}, n_{13})$ is given by equation 2 as:

$$V(N_2 \ge N_1) = hgt(N_1 \cap N_2) = \begin{cases} 1, if\ n_{22} > n_{12} \\ 0, if\ n_{11} > n_{23} \\ \dfrac{n_{11} - n_{23}}{(n_{22} - n_{23}) - (n_{12} - n_{11})}, otherwise \end{cases} \tag{2}$$

This is graphically illustrated in Figure 2.

Figure 1. Triangular fuzzy number

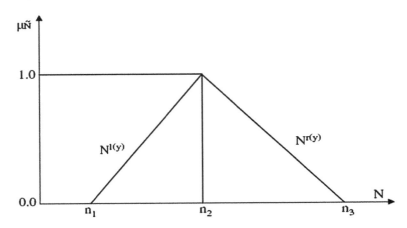

Figure 2. Degree of possibility of 2 fuzzy numbers

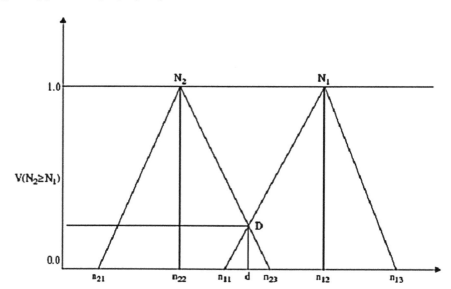

A convex fuzzy number is said to be greater than k convex fuzzy numbers M_i (i=1, 2, . . ., k) if

$$V\left(N \geq N_1, \ N_2,...,N_k\right) = V\left[\left(N \geq N_1\right)and\left(N \geq N_2\right)...and\left(N \geq N_k\right)\right]$$
$$\min V(N \geq N_i), i = 1, 2,..., k$$

(3)

Definition 4: Let $A = (m_{11}, m_{12}, m_{13})$ and $B = (m_{21}, m_{22}, m_{23})$ denote triangular fuzzy numbers. The laws of operation of these triangular fuzzy numbers are given by equations 4-9.

$$A(+)B = (m_{11}, m_{12}, m_{13})(+)(m_{21}, m_{22}, m_{23}) = (m_{11} + m_{21}, m_{12} + m_{22}, m_{13} + m_{23})$$

(4)

$$A(-)B = (m_{11}, m_{12}, m_{13})(-)(m_{21}, m_{22}, m_{23}) = (m_{11} - m_{21}, m_{12} - m_{22}, m_{13} - m_{23})$$

(5)

$$A(+)B = (m_{11}, m_{12}, m_{13})(\times)(m_{21}, m_{22}, m_{23}) = (m_{11}m_{21}, m_{12}m_{22}, m_{13}m_{23})$$

(6)

$$A(+)B = (m_{11}, m_{12}, m_{13})(\div)(m_{21}, m_{22}, m_{23}) = \left(\frac{m_{11}}{m_{23}}, \frac{m_{12}}{m_{22}}, \frac{m_{13}}{m_{21}}\right)$$

(7)

$$kA = (km_{11}, km_{12}, km_{13})$$

(8)

$$A^{-1} = \left(\frac{1}{m_{23}}, \frac{1}{m_{22}}, \frac{1}{m_{21}}\right)$$

(9)

Definition 5: Linguistic variables. Variables whose values are words or sentences of a language which are expressed in linguistic terms are known as linguistic variables. These are then represented by triangular fuzzy numbers. In many cases, linguistic terms are transformed into fuzzy numbers using conversion scales. (Singh & Benyoucef, 2011; Awasthi et al., 2011). In this chapter, 0–10 scale and 1–9 scale for rating the alternatives and criteria are used by the authors. Table 2 shows the linguistic expression used for criteria and their corresponding triangular fuzzy numbers. Similarly table 3 shows triangular fuzzy numbers used for the linguistic expression of the alternatives.

The framework used for the selection of best green supplier using fuzzy AHP and fuzzy TOPSIS methodologies is given in Figure 3.

Fuzzy Analytical Hierarchy Process

Chang's (1992) extent analysis methodology is used for solving this problem of fuzzy AHP.

Step 1: Comparison matrix of criteria with respect to criteria is constructed (Table 4).

Data from the questionnaire is used in the construction of Table 4. After that, linguistic variables in the table are converted into triangular fuzzy number by the use of Table 2.

Step 2: The value of fuzzy synthetic extent with respect to each criterion is determined by equation 10:

$$F_i = \sum_{j=1}^{p} M_{o_i}^j \otimes \left[\sum_{i=1}^{q} \sum_{j=1}^{p} M_{o_i}^j \right]^{-1} \tag{10}$$

By doing the fuzzy addition operation of p extent analysis from matrix, value of $\sum_{j=1}^{p} M_{oi}^j$ is found out by equation 11:

Table 2. Linguistic variables and corresponding fuzzy ratings used for criteria

Linguistic Expression	Triangular Fuzzy Numbers
Equally preferred (EP)	(1,1,1)
Weakly preferred (WP)	(1,3,5)
Fairly strongly preferred (FSP)	(3,5,7)
Very strongly preferred (VSP)	(5,7,9)
Absolutely preferred (AP)	(7,9,9)*

Kabir & Hasin, 2012.

Table 3. Fuzzy ratings for alternatives and linguistic expression

Linguistic Expression	Triangular Fuzzy Numbers
Very Poor (VP)	(0,0,1)
Poor (P)	(0,1,3)
Medium poor (MP)	(1,3,5)
Fair (F)	(3,5,7)
Medium Good	(5,7,9)
Good (G)	(7,9,10)
Very Good (VG)	(9,10,10)

Wang & Elhag, 2006.

Figure 3. Framework

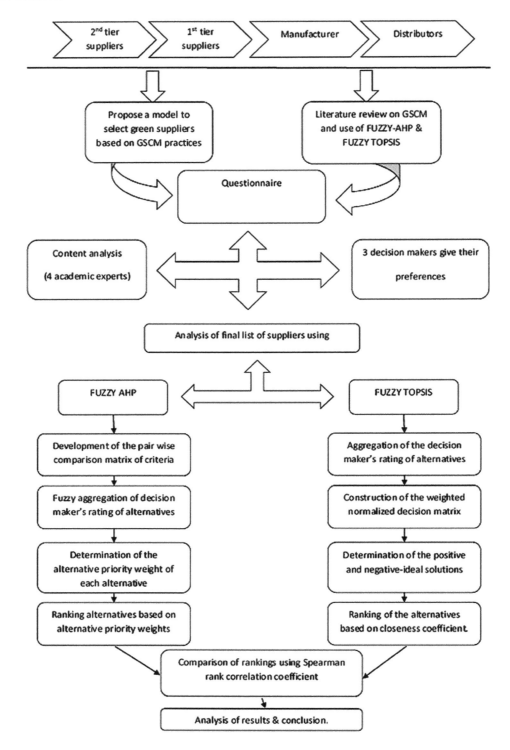

Table 4. Comparison matrix of criteria with respect to the criteria

	C1	C2	C3	C4	C5	C6	C7	C8	C9	C10	C11	C12	C13	C14	C15	C16	C17
C1	EP	FSP	WP	FSP	FSP	FSP	VSP	AP	FSP	AP	FSP	FSP	EP	WP	AP	AP	AP
C2		EP		WP	EP	EP	FSP	FSP	EP	FSP	WP	EP			FSP	VSP	VSP
C3		WP	EP		WP	WP	FSP	VSP	WP	VSP	FSP	WP		EP	VSP	AP	AP
C4				EP			WP	FSP		FSP	EP				FSP	VSP	VSP
C5		EP		WP	EP	EP	FSP	FSP	EP	FSP	WP	EP			FSP	VSP	VSP
C6		EP		FSP	EP	EP	FSP	FSP	EP	FSP	WP	EP			FSP	VSP	VSP
C7							EP	FSP		WP					WP	FSP	FSP
C8								EP		EP					EP	WP	WP
C9		EP			EP	EP	WP	FSP	EP	FSP	WP	EP			FSP	VSP	VSP
C10								EP		EP					EP	WP	WP
C11				EP			FSP	FSP		FSP					FSP	VSP	VSP
C12		EP		WP	EP	EP	FSP	FSP	EP	FSP	WP	EP			FSP	VSP	VSP
C13	EP	FSP	WP	FSP	FSP	FSP	VSP	AP	FSP	AP	FSP	FSP	EP	WP	AP	AP	AP
C14		WP	EP	FSP	WP	WP	FSP	VSP	WP	VSP	FSP	WP		EP	VSP	AP	AP
C15								EP		EP					EP	WP	WP
C16																EP	EP
C17																EP	EP

$$\sum_{j=1}^{p} M_{o_i}^{j} = \left(\sum_{j=1}^{p} m_{1j}, \sum_{j=1}^{p} m_{2j}, \sum_{j=1}^{p} m_{3j} \right) \tag{11}$$

By performing fuzzy addition operation, value of $\sum_{i=1}^{q}\sum_{j=1}^{p} N_{oi}^{j}$ is obtained by equation 12:

$$\sum_{i=1}^{q}\sum_{j=1}^{p} M_{o_i}^{j} = \left(\sum_{i=1}^{q} m_{1i}, \sum_{i=1}^{q} m_{2i}, \sum_{i=1}^{q} m_{3i} \right) \tag{12}$$

By the inverse of the previous equation, the value of $\left[\sum_{i=1}^{q}\sum_{j=1}^{p} M_{o_i}^{j}\right]^{-1}$ is obtained by equation 13:

$$\left[\sum_{i=1}^{q}\sum_{j=1}^{p} M_{o_i}^{j}\right]^{-1} = \left(\frac{1}{\sum_{i=1}^{q} m_{3i}}, \frac{1}{\sum_{i=1}^{q} m_{2i}}, \frac{1}{\sum_{i=1}^{q} m_{1i}} \right) \tag{13}$$

where triangular fuzzy number is denoted by (m_1, m_2, m_3).

In Table 5, fuzzy synthetic extent value with respect to 17 criterion are shown. They are denoted by $F_1, F_2, ..., F_{17}$

Step 3: The degree of possibility of dominance of every fuzzy synthetic extent value with respect to one another is determined by the use of equation 2.

Step 4: By using equation 3, minimum degree of possibility of dominance of each criterion over other is determined.

Step 5: By using the minimum degree of possibility of dominance of the criterion, their weight vectors are found out:

W_c = (1 0.498839809 0.805046058 0.349557285 0.498839809 0.524394996 0.098539803 0.061118747 0.424770533 0.061118747 0.378964201 0.474542523 1 0.805046058 0.061118747 0.049383256 0.049383256)^T

Step 6: The weight vectors are normalized and final weight of decision criteria with respect to goal is determined:

W_o=(0.140043002 0.069859024 0.112741067 0.048953052 0.069859024 0.07343785 0.01379981 0.008559253 0.059486141 0.008559253 0.053071284 0.06645636 0.140043002 0.112741067 0.008559253 0.006915779 0.006915779)^T

Table 5. Fuzzy synthetic extent value with respect to criterion

Criteria/Fuzzy Synthetic Extent Value	m_1	m_2	m_3
F1	0.0689113	0.136070791	0.25052993
F2	0.0314723	0.065972849	0.13868465
F3	0.0481319	0.102640346	0.2069595
F4	0.0249904	0.052208214	0.11398022
F5	0.0314723	0.065972849	0.13868465
F6	0.0335927	0.068837497	0.14304169
F7	0.0144406	0.034871363	0.07997351
F8	0.0070406	0.016093594	0.03702614
F9	0.0285038	0.059283895	0.12561353
F10	0.0070406	0.016093594	0.03702614
F11	0.0271139	0.055072862	0.11833727
F12	0.0314723	0.058811228	0.13868465
F13	0.0689113	0.136070791	0.25052993
F14	0.0481319	0.102640346	0.2069595
F15	0.0070406	0.016093594	0.03702614
F16	0.0041909	0.006633093	0.01590756
F17	0.0041909	0.006633093	0.01590756

Step 7: Priority of alternatives with respect to criteria is determined. Fuzzy aggregation of decision maker's rating of alternatives is done to determine this. Assume that F decision makers are in the decision making committee. Let the fuzzy rating of each decision maker be denoted by L_f(F=1,2,... ,F). Then the aggregated fuzzy rating is defined in equation 14:

$$L = \left(u, v, w\right), F = 1, 2, ..F, where$$
$$u = \min_f \left(u_f\right), \quad v = (1/f)\sum_{f=1}^{F} v_f, w = \max_f(w_f) \tag{14}$$

Obtain the aggregated fuzzy values by:

- Convert the linguistic variables of Tables 7, 8, and 9 to triangular fuzzy numbers by use of Table 3.
- Aggregate the triangular fuzzy numbers (tfn) by making the use of equation 14.
- Convert these triangular fuzzy numbers to crisp values by the use of graded mean integration representation of tfn.
- By dividing each value in column by the respective column total, normalize the values of the columns.

Step 8: The final priority of the alternatives with respect to the primary goal is determined by multiplying the priority weight of criteria with priority weights of the decision alternatives.

Thus the authors have calculated the alternative priority weights in table 6. These weights are used as a basis to rank the alternatives. (Greater ranking is given by greater alternative priority weights). The rankings of alternatives on the basis of the alternative priority weights is shown in Table 6.

Table 6a. Calculation of the alternative priority weights C1-C10

Criteria	C1	C2	C3	C4	C5	C6	C7	C8	C9	C10
Weights	0.14	0.07	0.113	0.049	0.0699	0.073	0.014	0.009	0.059	0.009
Alternatives										
A1	0.064	0.044	0.014	0.019	0.0343	0.043	0.033	0.06	0.055	0.049
A2	0.064	0.075	0.139	0.019	0.0343	0.043	0.033	0.06	0.073	0.089
A3	0.132	0.116	0.139	0.188	0.1694	0.152	0.156	0.129	0.113	0.133
A4	0.158	0.106	0.139	0.188	0.1848	0.152	0.175	0.129	0.154	0.152
A5	0.158	0.136	0.129	0.172	0.1848	0.183	0.175	0.15	0.154	0.11
A6	0.041	0.063	0.085	0.019	0.0519	0.043	0.041	0.06	0.055	0.093
A7	0.132	0.116	0.111	0.061	0.0519	0.116	0.041	0.06	0.113	0.11
A8	0.029	0.116	0.079	0.019	0.0519	0.043	0.041	0.06	0.055	0.049
A9	0.064	0.092	0.027	0.126	0.0519	0.043	0.129	0.129	0.055	0.097
A10	0.158	0.136	0.139	0.188	0.1848	0.183	0.175	0.164	0.173	0.119

Table 6b. Calculation of the alternative priority weights C11-C17

Criteria	C11	C12	C13	C14	C15	C16	C17	Alternative Priority Weights	Ranks
Weights	0.053	0.066	0.14	0.113	0.009	0.007	0.007		
Alternatives									
A1	0.044	0.03	0.033	0.014	0.033	0.083	0.086	0.03665	10
A2	0.044	0.044	0.117	0.134	0.13	0.111	0.114	0.08189	6
A3	0.238	0.164	0.141	0.134	0.149	0.111	0.114	0.14683	3
A4	0.081	0.137	0.117	0.134	0.142	0.111	0.114	0.1403	4
A5	0.14	0.137	0.141	0.134	0.176	0.111	0.114	0.14927	2
A6	0.044	0.046	0.026	0.079	0.142	0.083	0.04	0.05251	7
A7	0.081	0.076	0.117	0.079	0.074	0.099	0.114	0.09968	5
A8	0.044	0.101	0.083	0.079	0.118	0.083	0.094	0.06535	9
A9	0.044	0.101	0.083	0.079	0.018	0.099	0.094	0.06935	8
A10	0.238	0.164	0.141	0.134	0.018	0.111	0.114	0.15817	1

Table 7. Rating of alternatives by decision maker 1 (DM1)

	C1	C2	C3	C4	C5	C6	C7	C8	C9	C10	C11	C12	C13	C14	C15	C16	C17
A1	MP	F	P	P	P	MP	MP	F	F	F	MP	MP	MP	P	P	MG	MG
A2	MP	G	VG	P	P	MP	MP	F	MG	MG	MP	F	VG	VG	MG	VG	VG
A3	VG	VG	VG	VG	VG	VG	VG	G	G	G	VG	VG	VG	VG	VG	VG	VG
A4	VG	VG	VG	VG	VG	VG	VG	G	VG	VG	F	VG	VG	VG	MG	VG	VG
A5	VG	VG	VG	VG	VG	VG	VG	VG	VG	VG	MG	VG	VG	VG	VG	VG	VG
A6	MP	F	F	P	P	MP	MP	F	F	F	MP	MP	P	MG	MG	MG	MG
A7	VG	VG	VG	MP	P	G	MP	F	G	VG	F	F	VG	MG	MP	VG	VG
A8	P	VG	F	P	P	MP	MP	F	F	F	MP	MG	MG	MG	MG	MG	MG
A9	MP	G	P	MG	P	MP	G	G	F	F	MP	MG	MG	MG	P	VG	MG
A10	VG	VG	VG	VG	VG	VG	VG	VG	VG	VG	VG	VG	VG	VG	P	VG	VG

Fuzzy TOPSIS

The authors have solved this problem by the use of the fuzzy Technique for Order of Preference by Similarity to Ideal Solution (TOPSIS) methodology, as proposed by (Kannan et al., 2009) and (Hwang and Yoon, 1981). Tables 7, 8, and 9 represent the rating of alternatives by Decision makers 1, 2 and 3 respectively.

Step 1: Construct a decision matrix. A group of f decision makers $(D_1, D_2,...,D_f)$ is considered, containing p alternatives $(A_1, A_2,...A_p)$ and q criteria $(C_1, C_2,...,Cq)$ for this MCDM case study. Express this in matrix format as represented in equation 15:

Table 8. Rating of the alternatives by decision maker 2 (DM2)

	C1	C2	C3	C4	C5	C6	C7	C8	C9	C10	C11	C12	C13	C14	C15	C16	C17
A1	MG	MP	P	P	MP	MP	P	F	MP	P	P	P	MP	P	MP	MG	MG
A2	MG	F	VG	P	MP	MP	P	F	MP	MP	P	P	VG	VG	G	VG	VG
A3	VG	VG	VG	VG	VG	VG	G	G	MG	MG	VG	VG	VG	VG	MG	VG	VG
A4	VG	MG	VG	VG	VG	VG	VG	G	G	MG	MP	VG	VG	VG	G	VG	VG
A5	VG	G	MG	VG	VG	VG	VG	VG	G	P	MG	VG	VG	VG	VG	VG	VG
A6	MP	MG	VG	P	MP	MP	MP	F	MP	G	P	P	MP	G	G	MG	P
A7	VG	VG	VG	MP	MP	G	MP	F	MG	P	MP	F	VG	G	MP	G	VG
A8	MP	VG	MG	P	MP	MP	MP	F	MP	P	P	MG	G	G	MP	MG	G
A9	MG	VG	P	MG	MP	MP	MG	G	MP	VG	P	MG	G	G	P	G	G
A10	VG	G	VG	VG	VG	VG	VG	VG	VG	P	VG	VG	VG	VG	P	VG	VG

Table 9. Rating of the alternatives by decision maker 3 (DM3)

	C1	C2	C3	C4	C5	C6	C7	C8	C9	C10	C11	C12	C13	C14	C15	C16	C17
A1	VP	VP	VP	VP	VP	VP	VP	VP	VP	VP	VP	VP	VP	VP	VP	MG	MG
A2	VP	P	G	VP	VP	VP	VP	VP	P	MP	VP	VP	F	G	F	G	G
A3	F	F	G	G	MG	F	MG	F	MP	F	G	G	G	G	MG	G	G
A4	G	F	G	G	G	F	G	F	MG	MG	P	F	F	G	F	G	G
A5	G	G	G	MG	G	G	G	MG	MG	MG	MP	F	G	G	G	G	G
A6	VP	VP	P	VP	VP	VP	VP	VP	VP	VP	VP	VP	VP	P	F	MG	VP
A7	F	F	F	MP	VP	P	VP	VP	MP	MG	P	VP	F	P	MP	MG	G
A8	VP	F	P	VP	VP	VP	VP	VP	VP	VP	VP	P	P	P	F	MG	MG
A9	VP	P	VP	F	VP	VP	F	F	VP	VP	VP	P	P	P	VP	MG	MG
A10	G	G	G	G	G	G	G	G	G	G	G	G	G	G	VP	G	G

$$D = \begin{array}{c} \\ A_1 \\ A_2 \\ \vdots \\ A_p \end{array} \begin{array}{c} C_1 \quad C_2 \quad \cdots \quad C_q \\ \begin{bmatrix} g_{11} & g_{12} & \cdots & g_{1q} \\ g_{21} & g_{22} & \cdots & g_{2q} \\ \vdots & \vdots & \ddots & \vdots \\ g_{p1} & g_{p2} & \cdots & g_{pq} \end{bmatrix} \end{array} \qquad (15)$$

where g_{pq} represents rating of alternative A_p with respect to criterion C_q. Assume that the relative weight vector of q criteria is represented by $W_j = (W_1, W_2, \ldots, W_q)$ (Tables 7-9).

Step 2: Rating of alternatives and weights of criteria are aggregated. Make use of the weights of criteria as calculated in fuzzy AHP. For the aggregation of the rating of alternatives, let $r_{ijt} = (a_{ijt}, b_{ijt}, c_{ijt})$, $r_{ijt} \in R +$, $i = 1, 2, \ldots, p, j = 1, 2, \ldots q, t = 1, 2, \ldots, f$. be the rating given to alternative A_i by decision- makers D_t with respect to criterion C_j. Firstly, graded mean integration representation of fuzzy numbers is used to transform rating g_{ijt} is into crisp number g'_{ijt}. This is done by equation 16

$$g'_{ijt} = \frac{m_1 + 4m_2 + m_3}{6} \tag{16}$$

where (m_1, m_2, m_3) represents a triangular fuzzy number. The aggregated rating $G_{ij} = (a_{ij}, b_{ij}, c_{ij})$, of alternative A_i with respect to criteria Cj is given by equation 17 (Tables 10 and 11).

$$G_{ij} = \frac{\sum_{t=1}^{K} g'_{ijt}}{F} \tag{17}$$

Table 10a. Computed fuzzy aggregated matrix C1-C8

	C1	C2	C3	C4	C5	C6	C7	C8
A1	3.389	2.722	0.833	0.833	1.444	2.056	1.444	3.389
A2	3.389	5	9.5	0.833	1.444	2.056	1.889	3.556
A3	8.222	8.222	9.5	9.5	8.889	8.222	8.556	7.556
A4	9.5	7.5	9.5	9.5	9.5	8.222	9.5	7.556
A5	9.5	9.167	8.556	8.889	9.5	9.5	9.5	8.889
A6	2.056	4.056	5.333	0.833	1.444	2.056	2.056	3.389
A7	8.222	8.222	8.222	3	1.444	6.278	2.056	3.389
A8	1.444	8.222	4.389	0.833	1.444	2.056	2.056	3.389
A9	3.389	6.611	0.833	6.333	1.444	2.056	6.944	7.556
A10	9.278	9.167	9.5	9.5	9.5	9.5	9.5	9.5

Table 10b. Computed fuzzy aggregated matrix C9-C17

	C9	C10	C11	C12	C13	C14	C15	C16	C17
A1	2.722	2.111	1.4444	1.444	2.056	0.833	1.4444	7	7
A2	3.722	4.333	1.4444	2.111	8.222	9.5	6.9444	9.5	9.5
A3	6.278	6.944	9.5	9.5	9.5	9.5	7.9444	9.5	9.5
A4	8.556	7.944	3.0556	8.222	8.222	9.5	6.9444	9.5	9.5
A5	8.556	6	5.6667	8.222	9.5	9.5	9.5	9.5	9.5
A6	2.722	4.667	1.4444	1.444	1.444	5.667	6.9444	7	2.778
A7	6.278	6	3.0556	3.389	8.222	5.667	3	8.556	9.5
A8	2.722	2.111	1.4444	5.056	5.667	5.667	5	7	7.611
A9	2.722	5	1.4444	5.056	5.667	5.667	0.8333	8.556	7.611
A10	9.5	6.611	9.5	9.5	9.5	9.5	0.8333	9.5	9.5

Table 11a. Normalized decision matrix C1-C8

	C1	C2	C3	C4	C5	C6	C7	C8
A1	0.161	0.119	0.036	0.042	0.076	0.106	0.071	0.17
A2	0.161	0.219	0.405	0.042	0.076	0.106	0.093	0.178
A3	0.391	0.361	0.405	0.474	0.467	0.424	0.422	0.378
A4	0.452	0.329	0.405	0.474	0.499	0.424	0.469	0.378
A5	0.452	0.402	0.365	0.444	0.499	0.49	0.469	0.445
A6	0.098	0.178	0.227	0.042	0.076	0.106	0.101	0.17
A7	0.391	0.361	0.35	0.15	0.076	0.324	0.101	0.17
A8	0.069	0.361	0.187	0.042	0.076	0.106	0.101	0.17
A9	0.161	0.29	0.036	0.316	0.076	0.106	0.343	0.378
A10	0.441	0.402	0.405	0.474	0.499	0.49	0.469	0.476

Table 11b. Normalized decision matrix C9-C17

	C9	C10	C11	C12	C13	C14	C15	C16	C17
A1	0.144	0.122	0.0929	0.073	0.088	0.035	0.0789	0.257	0.262
A2	0.196	0.25	0.0929	0.107	0.352	0.394	0.3791	0.348	0.356
A3	0.331	0.4	0.611	0.483	0.407	0.394	0.4337	0.348	0.356
A4	0.452	0.458	0.1965	0.418	0.352	0.394	0.3791	0.348	0.356
A5	0.452	0.346	0.3645	0.418	0.407	0.394	0.5186	0.348	0.356
A6	0.144	0.269	0.0929	0.073	0.062	0.235	0.3791	0.257	0.104
A7	0.331	0.346	0.1965	0.172	0.352	0.235	0.1638	0.314	0.356
A8	0.144	0.122	0.0929	0.257	0.243	0.235	0.273	0.257	0.285
A9	0.144	0.288	0.0929	0.257	0.243	0.235	0.0455	0.314	0.285
A10	0.501	0.381	0.611	0.483	0.407	0.394	0.0455	0.348	0.356

Step 3: Normalized decision matrix is constructed

Assume that the decision matrix be $X = \left(x_{ij} \right)_{p \times q}$. The decision matrix for p alternatives and q criteria can be normalized as $S = \left[s_{ij} \right]_{p \times q}$, where:

$$s_{ij} = \frac{g_{ij}}{\sqrt{\sum_{i=1}^{p} \left(g_{ij} \right)^2}} \tag{18}$$

Step 4: Weighted normalized decision matrix is constructed: Multiply the normalized matrix by the normalized aggregate weights of the criteria to construct weighted normalized decision matrix. $V = \left(v_{ij} \right)_{p \times q}$ denotes the weighted normalized decision matrix given by equation 19:

$$v_{ij} = s_{ij} \times W_j \tag{19}$$

Step 5: Positive ideal and negative-ideal solutions are determined using equation 20:

$$A^* = (\tilde{v}_1^*, \tilde{v}_2^*, \ldots, \tilde{v}_q^*) \tag{20}$$

$$A^- = (\tilde{v}_1^-, \tilde{v}_2^-, \ldots, \tilde{v}_q^-)$$

where A$^+$ and A$^-$ are the Positive ideal and negative-ideal solutions, and

$$\tilde{v}_j^* = \max_{i=1,2,\ldots,p} (\tilde{v}_{ij})$$

and

$$\tilde{v}_j^- = \min_{i=1,2,\ldots,p} (\tilde{v}_{ij}).$$

Step 6: Distance of every alternative from A$^+$ and A$^-$. $^-$ is calculated, by making the use of equations 21 and 22 (Table 12):

$$dist^+ = \sqrt{\sum\nolimits_{j=1}^{n} \left(\tilde{v}_{ij} - \tilde{v}_j^*\right)^2} \tag{21}$$

$$dist^- = \sqrt{\sum\nolimits_{j=1}^{n} \left(\tilde{v}_{ij} - \tilde{v}_j^-\right)^2} \tag{22}$$

Step 7: Closeness coefficient is calculated from equation 23. The ranking order of the alternatives using d$^+$ and d$^-$ values of every alternative is calculated as:

$$CC_i = \frac{dist^-}{dist^+ + dist^-} \tag{23}$$

Step 8: Ranks of alternatives are calculated. The closeness coefficient to the ideal solution determines the ranking of the alternatives. The ranking of A$_i$ will be high if CC of the alternative is high (Table 13) .

RESULTS AND DISCUSSION

Rankings are attained by using fuzzy TOPSIS, FAHP to the MCDM problem. Now, the authors use Spearman rank correlation coefficient (R) (proposed by Chamodrakas, Leftheriotis and Martakos, 2011). To find out the extent of association between ranking attained by these approaches (Raju & Kumar,

Table 12. Distances of each alternative from A⁺ and A⁻

DIST⁺ Solutions	DIST⁻ Solutions
0.107457	0.013501
0.075762	0.072649
0.014608	0.10698
0.024936	0.104568
0.014915	0.108664
0.099343	0.031968
0.053192	0.078972
0.089081	0.043409
0.086522	0.042592
0.004361	0.113745

Table 13. Closeness coefficients and ranks of alternatives

Alternatives	CC$_i$	Ranks
A1	0.11162	10
A2	0.489512	6
A3	0.879857	2
A4	0.807448	4
A5	0.879311	3
A6	0.243455	9
A7	0.597529	5
A8	0.327639	8
A9	0.329876	7
A10	0.963074	1

1999). Weather the reliability of the results are acceptable or not are also found out by this coefficient. The Spearman rank correlation coefficient is represented in equation 24 (Raju & Kumar, 1999).

$$R = 1 - \frac{6\sum_{a=1}^{A} D_a^2}{A(A^2 - 1)} \qquad (24)$$

where

a represents number of alternatives.

A represents total number of alternatives.

Da represents the difference between ranks attained through the different methods.

R=1 represents perfect agreement among the rankings and R = -1 represents perfect disagreement among the rankings.

Table 14 shows the results calculated from the FAHP and fuzzy TOPSIS methodologies for the selection of the best green supplier for the electronics company

It can be concluded that supplier 1, 3 and 5 should get preference as the green suppliers in supplier selection process. The ranks obtained from the two methods can be shown to be in agreement by Spearman rank correlation coefficient which is found out as 0.9515.

FUTURE RESEARCH DIRECTIONS

These GSCM practices could have some limitations like capacity, delivery lead time etc. Some methodologies like PROMETHEE (Preference Ranking Organization Method for Enrichment Evaluation), VIKOR, Fuzzy VIKOR, PAPRIKA (Potentially all pairwise rankings of all possible alternatives) etc can

Table 14. Final rankings

Alternatives	Ranks Attained Using	
	f-AHP	Fuzzy TOPSIS
A1	10	10
A2	6	6
A3	3	2
A4	4	4
A5	2	3
A6	7	9
A7	5	5
A8	9	8
A9	8	7
A10	1	1

be applied to this research to analyse and compare the results. Some limitations could also be overcome by applying these methodologies.

CONCLUSION

In India the concept of GSCM is still in its inception stage. Indian government's insistence on environmental friendly policies has motivated the Indian companies to grasp the significance of GSCM practices. This has resulted in many companies committing towards the implementation of GSCM practices. This chapter aims to find the best green suppliers based on principles of Green Supply Chain Management by solving Multi Criteria Decision Making problem by making the use of fuzzy AHP and fuzzy TOPSIS approaches. The authors have chosen a numerical example from an electronic company based in India, to demonstrate the proposed framework. Reliability of its results are of prime importance in a good decision making model. Spearman rank correlation coefficient is calculated to compare the rankings attained from the two methodologies. On the basis of the results achieved, selection of best green suppliers by the company is possible. This will improve the green supply chain management.

REFERENCES

Awasthi, A., Chauhan, S. S., & Omrani, H. (2011). Application of fuzzy TOPSIS in evaluating sustainable transportation systems. *Expert Systems with Applications*, *38*(10), 12270–12280. doi:10.1016/j. eswa.2011.04.005

Bai, C., & Sarkis, J. (2010). Green supplier development: Analytical evaluation using rough set theory. *Journal of Cleaner Production*, *18*(12), 1200–1210. doi:10.1016/j.jclepro.2010.01.016

Bai, C., & Sarkis, J. (2010). Integrating sustainability into supplier selection with grey system and rough set methodologies. *International Journal of Production Economics, 124*(1), 252–264. doi:10.1016/j.ijpe.2009.11.023

Büyüközkan, G., & Çifçi, G. (2011). A novel fuzzy multi-criteria decision framework for sustainable supplier selection with incomplete information. *Computers in Industry, 62*(2), 164–174. doi:10.1016/j.compind.2010.10.009

Büyüközkan, G., & Çifçi, G. (2012). Evaluation of the green supply chain management practices: A fuzzy ANP approach. *Production Planning and Control, 23*(6), 405–418. doi:10.1080/09537287.2011.561814

Chamodrakas, I., Leftheriotis, I., & Martakos, D. (2011). In-depth analysis and simulation study of an innovative fuzzy approach for ranking alternatives in multiple attribute decision making problems based on TOPSIS. *Applied Soft Computing, 11*(1), 900–907. doi:10.1016/j.asoc.2010.01.010

Chang, D. Y. (1992). Extent analysis and synthetic decision. *Optimization Techniques and Applications, 1*, 352–355.

Chiou, C. Y., Hsu, C. W., & Hwang, W. Y. (2008, December). Comparative investigation on green supplier selection of the American, Japanese and Taiwanese electronics industry in China. In *Industrial Engineering and Engineering Management, 2008. IEEM 2008. IEEE International Conference on* (pp. 1909-1914). IEEE.

Grisi, R. M., Guerra, L., & Naviglio, G. (2010). Supplier performance evaluation for green supply chain management. In *Business Performance Measurement and Management* (pp. 149–163). Springer Berlin Heidelberg. doi:10.1007/978-3-642-04800-5_10

Handfield, R., Walton, S. V., Sroufe, R., & Melnyk, S. A. (2002). Applying environmental criteria to supplier assessment: A study in the application of the Analytical Hierarchy Process. *European Journal of Operational Research, 141*(1), 70–87. doi:10.1016/S0377-2217(01)00261-2

Hsu, C. W., & Hu, A. H. (2009). Applying hazardous substance management to supplier selection using analytic network process. *Journal of Cleaner Production, 17*(2), 255–264. doi:10.1016/j.jclepro.2008.05.004

Hwang, C. L., & Yoon, K. (1981). *Multiple attribute decision making methods and application.* New York: Springer-Verlag. doi:10.1007/978-3-642-48318-9

Kabir, G., & Hasin, M. (2012). Multiple criteria inventory classification using fuzzy analytic hierarchy process. *International Journal of Industrial Engineering Computations, 3*(2), 123–132. doi:10.5267/j.ijiec.2011.09.007

Kannan, D., de Sousa Jabbour, A. B. L., & Jabbour, C. J. C. (2014). Selecting green suppliers based on GSCM practices: Using fuzzy TOPSIS applied to a Brazilian electronics company. *European Journal of Operational Research, 233*(2), 432–447. doi:10.1016/j.ejor.2013.07.023

Kannan, G., Pokharel, S., & Kumar, P. S. (2009). A hybrid approach using ISM and fuzzy TOPSIS for the selection of reverse logistics provider. *Resources, Conservation and Recycling, 54*(1), 28–36. doi:10.1016/j.resconrec.2009.06.004

Kumar, A., & Jain, V. (2010, October). Supplier selection: a green approach with carbon footprint monitoring. In *Supply Chain Management and Information Systems (SCMIS), 2010 8th International Conference on* (pp. 1-8). IEEE.

Lee, A. H., Kang, H. Y., Hsu, C. F., & Hung, H. C. (2009). A green supplier selection model for high-tech industry. *Expert Systems with Applications*, *36*(4), 7917–7927. doi:10.1016/j.eswa.2008.11.052

Lu, L. Y., Wu, C. H., & Kuo, T. C. (2007). Environmental principles applicable to green supplier evaluation by using multi-objective decision analysis. *International Journal of Production Research*, *45*(18-19), 4317–4331. doi:10.1080/00207540701472694

Min, H., & Kim, I. (2012). Green supply chain research: Past, present, and future. *Logistics Research*, *4*(1-2), 39–47. doi:10.1007/s12159-012-0071-3

Noci, G. (1997). Designing 'green' vendor rating systems for the assessment of a supplier's environmental performance. *European Journal of Purchasing & Supply Management*, *3*(2), 103–114. doi:10.1016/S0969-7012(96)00021-4

Raju, K. S., & Kumar, D. N. (1999). Multicriterion decision making in irrigation planning. *Agricultural Systems*, *62*(2), 117–129. doi:10.1016/S0308-521X(99)00060-8

Shen, L., Olfat, L., Govindan, K., Khodaverdi, R., & Diabat, A. (2013). A fuzzy multi criteria approach for evaluating green supplier's performance in green supply chain with linguistic preferences. *Resources, Conservation and Recycling*, *74*, 170–179. doi:10.1016/j.resconrec.2012.09.006

Singh, R. K., & Benyoucef, L. (2011). A fuzzy TOPSIS based approach for e-sourcing. *Engineering Applications of Artificial Intelligence*, *24*(3), 437–448. doi:10.1016/j.engappai.2010.09.006

Srivastava, S. K. (2007). Green supply-chain management: A state-of-the-art literature review. *International Journal of Management Reviews*, *9*(1), 53–80. doi:10.1111/j.1468-2370.2007.00202.x

Vachon, S., & Klassen, R. D. (2006). Extending green practices across the supply chain: The impact of upstream and downstream integration. *International Journal of Operations & Production Management*, *26*(7), 795–821. doi:10.1108/01443570610672248

Wang, Y. M., & Elhag, T. M. (2006). Fuzzy TOPSIS method based on alpha level sets with an application to bridge risk assessment. *Expert Systems with Applications*, *31*(2), 309–319. doi:10.1016/j.eswa.2005.09.040

Zadeh, L. A. (1965). Fuzzy sets. *Information and Control*, *8*(3), 338–353. doi:10.1016/S0019-9958(65)90241-X

Zimmerman, H. J. (1996). *Fuzzy sets theory and its applications*. Boston: Kluwer Academic Publisher. doi:10.1007/978-94-015-8702-0

Zimmermann, H. J. (2011). *Fuzzy set theory—and its applications*. Springer Science & Business Media.

KEY TERMS AND DEFINITIONS

Analytical Hierarchy Process (AHP): Developed by Thomas L. Saaty, this multi criteria decision making process makes use of the opinions of experts to find out the priority and calculate the rankings of the alternatives.

Fuzzy Analytical Hierarchy Process (FAHP): To handle the limitations of AHP such as uncertainty in decisions, a fuzzy extension of AHP was developed which is known as fuzzy Analytical Hierarchy Process.

Green Supply Chain Management (GSCM): Resource Utilization efficiency and environmental influence are taken into account in this modern supply chain management approach.

Linguistic Variables: Variables whose values are expressed in linguistic terms using words or sentences of a language. When words or sentences of a language (linguistic terms) are used as variables, they are known as linguistic variables. By the use of a conversion scale, they can be converted to TFN.

Multi Criteria Decision Making (MCDM): Every alternative is compared with some criteria to decide the rank of alternatives in this methodology.

Spearman's Rank Correlation Coefficient: A nonparametric measure of statistical dependence between two variables.

Triangular Fuzzy Number (TFN): A triplet (m_1, m_2, m_3) is known as Triangular Fuzzy Number, where "m_1" represents smallest likely value, "m_2" the most probable value, and "m_3" the largest possible value of any fuzzy event.

Chapter 17
Sentimental Analysis of Online Reviews Using Fuzzy Sets and Rough Sets

Anuradha Jagadeesan
VIT University, India

Amit Patil
VIT University, India

ABSTRACT

With the increased interest of online users in E-commerce, the web has become an excellent source for buying and selling of products online. Customer reviews on the web help potential customers to make purchase decisions, and for manufacturers to incorporate improvements in their product or develop new marketing strategies. The increase in customer reviews of a product influence the popularity and the sale rate of the product. This lead to a very important question about the analysis of the sentiments (opinions) expressed in the reviews. As such internet does not have any quality control over customer reviews and it could vary in terms of its quality. Also the trustworthiness of the online reviews is debatable. Sentiment Analysis (SA) or Opinion Mining is the computational analysis of opinions, sentiments, emotions and subjectivity of text. In this chapter, we take a look at the various research challenges and a new dimension involved in sentiment analysis using fuzzy sets and rough sets.

INTRODUCTION

Today shopping online has become more popular than ever. Online shoppers use Customer's reviews to make informed buying decisions. Consumer actively seeks out and reads customer reviews prior to making a purchase decision. According to "social shopping study" by Power Reviews 70% of online shoppers, accepted customer reviews and ratings on a retailer's website were extremely important when they are selecting or purchasing product.

Manufactures use these reviews to know consumer preferences and interests, to maximize the profit. It is important to know others thoughts before we make purchase decision. As online purchasing in-

DOI: 10.4018/978-1-5225-1008-6.ch017

creases, number of reviews the web site receives also increases. Hence, the number of customer reviews being posted at review site is growing at faster rates (in hundreds or thousands). Maintaining such huge amount of reviews is not only a problem for the manufacturers but makes the process of decision making complicated, causing customer either to read all the reviews on that product or to select reviews and read. It is time consuming to read all the reviews and to select the reviews and read; the customer does not know which reviews to choose and read since the quality of the reviews vary greatly. Figure 1 shows the summary of Social shopping study by power reviews.

As text messages express the state of minds of individual; mining such messages from a large population in different context. Discovering user preferences through social media is a challenging task. Opinion mining, SA and subjectivity analysis are related fields sharing common goals of developing and applying computational techniques to process collections of opinionated texts or reviews. Opinion mining (OM) is a new field of data mining concerned with the opinion that can be induced from documents. OM is divided into three major tasks: development of linguistic resources, sentiment classification, and opinion summarization (Elawady, Barakat, & Elrashidy,2014).

Sentiment Analysis (SA) is a task that finds the opinion (e.g .positive or negative) from the text document like product reviews/movie reviews. As user generated data is increasing day by day on the web. It is needed to analyze those contents to know the opinion of the users, and hence it increases the demand of sentiment analysis research. People express their opinions about movies and products etc.

Figure 1. Social study chart on customer feedback

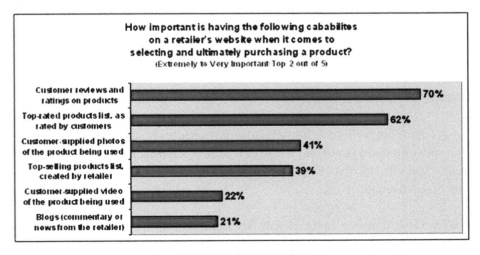

on the web blogs, social networking websites, content sharing sites and discussion forums etc. Companies can use sentiment analysis in improving their products based on the user's feedback written about their product on blogs, E-commerce based companies know the online trends about the product. For example, sentiment analysis knows which model of camera is liked by the most users. Sentiment classification can also be considered as a text classification problem. Bag of Words (BOW) representation is commonly used for sentiment classification using machine learning approaches. The words present in all documents create feature vector. Generally, this feature vector is a huge in dimension that is used by machine learning methods. The concepts of fuzzy sets and rough sets could be used as classification techniques to improve the polarity of expressed sentiments.

WHAT IS SENTIMENT ANALYSIS?

Sentiment Analysis is a Natural Language Processing and Information Extraction task that aims to obtain writer's feelings, emotions expressed in positive or negative comments, questions and requests, by analyzing a large numbers of documents. Speaking in general terms, sentiment analysis aims to determine the attitude of a speaker or a writer with respect to some topic or the overall polarity of a document. With the increase in online users and their exchange of public opinions is the driving force behind Sentiment Analysis. The Web is a huge repository of structured and unstructured data which varies in its quality. The analysis of this data to extract opinion (sentiments) and classify them as positive, negative or neutral is a challenging task.

The work of Liu (2010) in NLP handbook defines a sentiment or opinion as a quintuple

$(o_j, f_{jk}, so_{ijkl}, h_i, t_l),$

where

o_j = A target object.
f_{jk} = A feature of the object o_j.
so_{ijkl} = The sentiment value of the opinion of the opinion holder h_i on feature f_{jk} of object o_j at time t_l.
    so_{ijkl} is +ve, -ve, or neu, or a more granular rating.
h_i = An opinion holder.
t_l = The time when the opinion is expressed.

Sentiment Classification is very much similar to topic-based text classification, where words expresses a topic under consideration in a document where as in case of sentiment classification, sentiment bearing words like great, excellent, horrible, bad, worst conveys the polarity of the written text. The analysis of sentiments may be performed at:

- **Sentence Level:** A sentence contains only one opinion.
- **Document Level:** Each document focuses on a single object and contains opinion from a single opinion holder.
- **Feature Level:** Produce a feature-based opinion summary of multiple reviews, depending upon the features being commented by opinion holder.

Sentiment Analysis identifies the phrases in a text that bears some sentiment. The author may speak about some objective facts or subjective opinions. It is necessary to distinguish between the two. SA finds the subject towards whom the sentiment is directed. A text may contain many entities but it is necessary to find the entity towards which the sentiment is directed. It identifies the polarity and degree of the sentiment. Sentiments are classified as objective (facts), positive (denotes a state of happiness, bliss or satisfaction on part of the writer) or negative (denotes a state of sorrow, dejection or disappointment on part of the writer). The sentiments can further be given a score based on their degree of positivity, negativity or objectivity. Most of the research goals in this area are to generate heuristics or tools that can be used to classify, rank or summarize sentiments toward certain objects, events or topics. Most of the studies in this area are based on binary task of classifying sentiment into positive and negative classes discarding the neutral and other classes.

Challenges in Sentiment Analysis

Sentiment Analysis approaches aim to extract positive and negative sentiment bearing words from a text and classify the text as positive, negative or else to find if it does not have any sentiment bearing words. In this respect, it can be thought of as a text categorization task. In text classification there are many classes corresponding to different topics whereas in Sentiment Analysis we have only 3 broad classes. Thus it seems Sentiment Analysis is easier than text classification which is not quite the case. Some of the general challenges are summarized in the following section.

Implicit Sentiment and Sarcasm

A sentence may have an implicit sentiment even without the presence of any sentiment bearing words. Consider the following examples.

How can anyone sit through this movie?

One should question the stability of mind of the writer who wrote this book.

Both the above sentences do not explicitly carry any negative sentiment bearing words although both are negative sentences. Thus identifying semantics is more important in SA than syntax detection.

Domain Dependency

There are many words whose polarity changes from domain to domain. Consider the following examples.

The story was unpredictable.

The steering of the car is unpredictable.

Go read the book.

In the first example, the sentiment conveyed is positive whereas the sentiment conveyed in the second is negative. The third example has a positive sentiment in the book domain but a negative sentiment in the movie domain (where the director is being asked to go and read the book).

Thwarted Expectations

Sometimes the author deliberately sets up context only to refute it at the end. Consider the following example:

The actors are good; the music is brilliant and appealing. Yet, the movie fails to strike a chord.

In-spite of the presence of words that are positive in orientation the overall sentiment is negative because of the crucial last sentence, whereas in traditional text classification this would have been classified as positive as term frequency is more important there than term presence.

Subjectivity Detection

This is to differentiate between opinionated and non-opinionated text. This is used to enhance the performance of the system by including a subjectivity detection module to filter out objective facts. But this is often difficult to identify. Consider the following examples:

I hate love stories.

I do not like the movie "I hate stories".

The first example presents an objective fact whereas the second example depicts the opinion about a particular movie.

FUZZY SET AND ROUGH SETS

Fuzzy Sets

Lotfi Zadeh proposed completely new, elegant approach to vagueness called *fuzzy set theory* (Zadeh, 1965). In this approach an element can belong to a set to a degree k ($0 \leq k \leq 1$), in contrast to classical set theory where an element must definitely belong or not to a set. E.g., in classical set theory one can definitely ill or healthy, where as in fuzzy set theory we can say that someone is ill (or healthy) in 60% i.e.(in the degree 0.6). Of course, at once the question arises where we get the value of degree from. This issue raised a lot of discussion, but we will refrain from considering this problem here.

Definition

A Fuzzy set 'A' defined over the universe 'U' can be defined through its membership $\mu_A(x)$.

$$A = \left\{ \left(x, \mu_A(x)\right) \middle| x \in U, \mu_A(x) : \mathrm{U} \to [0,1] \right\}$$

where x is the object in the universe $U = \left\{ x_1, x_2, ..., x_n \right\}$. The membership value $\mu_A(x)$ can take value [0, 1].

For a finite set $U = \left\{ x_1, x_2, ..., x_n \right\}$ the fuzzy set (U, $\mu_A(x)$) is often denoted in the form

$$\left\{ \frac{\mu_A(x_1)}{x_1}, \frac{\mu_A(x_2)}{x_2}, ..., \frac{\mu_A(x_n)}{x_n} \right\}$$

Fuzziness can be categorized into two, intrinsic fuzziness and informational fuzziness. Membership of the form tall, medium, short is intrinsic fuzziness. Qualifying membership like efficient staff, trust worthy employee is informational membership. Membership value can be obtained by using different techniques. The figure 3.1.1 shows the triangular membership function for linguistic term Dark, Grey and Bright. Fuzzy membership values are overlapping and hence an object may have partial belonging-ness to each category. For example, in the Figure 2 an object may belong to Dark of 0.3, Gray of 0.6 and Bright of 0.1. The sum of membership value of an object belonging to different categories is equal to one.

$$\sum \mu_A(x) = 1$$

Fuzzy membership function has the following operations.

1. $\mu_{U-X}(x) = 1 - \mu_X(x)$ where $x \in U$.
2. $\mu_{X \cup Y}(x) = \max(\mu_X(x), \mu_y(x))$ for any $x \in U$.
3. $\mu_{X \cap Y}(x) = \min(\mu_X(x), \mu_y(x))$ for any $x \in U$.

Figure 2. Triangular fuzzy membership

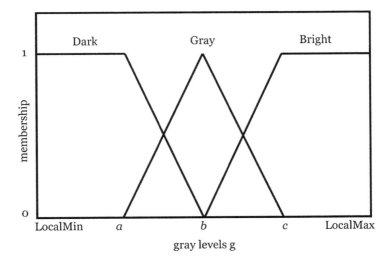

That means that membership of an element to the union an intersection of sets is uniquely determined by its membership to constituent sets. This is very nice property and allows very simple operations on fuzzy sets, which is very important feature both theoretically and practically.

A fuzzy relation R from a set A to B with its membership function

μ_R: A X B -> [0,1] is defined as R = { ((a,b), μ_R(a,b)) | (a,b) $\in$ A x B }.

Similar to a fuzzy set, the membership function of a fuzzy relation indicates strength of its relationship. Moreover a fuzzy relation is nothing but a fuzzy set where the elements are ordered pairs of the relation.

Characteristics of Fuzzy set:

- Membership values [0,1].
- Forms overlapping membership.
- Cardinality of fuzzy set is infinity.
- Sum of membership values of an object is 1.
- Does not support contradiction and law of excluded middle.

Fuzzy logic is widely used in control systems, scientific and engineering, medical field etc. Some of the applications of fuzzy logic are home appliances uses fuzzy in washing machine, AC and audio system, in Japan fuzzy controllers are used to control trains, fuzzy techniques are also used in Cement Kiln controller, FLOPS and Z-II is a fuzzy Expert System shell used in medical diagnosis and risk analysis, Fuzzy logic has been applied in video camera technology for automatic focusing, automatic exposure, image stabilization and white balancing, Fuzzy logic has been applied in automobiles for cruise control, brake and fuel injection systems, Fuzzy algorithms have been applied for video and audio data compression.

Fuzzy logic and its applications developed very extensively over last years and attracted attention of practitioners, logicians and philosophers worldwide.

Rough Sets

Rough set (RS) proposed by (Pawlak,1982) is yet another theory that is capable of handling imperfect knowledge. Rough set (RS) can handle vague and uncertain data. It overlaps with many other theories that deal with imperfect knowledge like evidence theory, fuzzy set, and Bayesian inference. In spite of it, RS is viewed as independent, complementary, not competing, discipline in its own way.

It is a simple method that performs data analysis. It has been widely applied under many fields that include Artificial Intelligence and cognitive sciences, machine learning, knowledge discovery, data mining, expert systems, approximate reasoning and pattern recognition. Rough set theory is successful for the following reasons:

- It does not need any preliminary or additional information about data – like probability in statistics, grade of membership in the fuzzy set theory.
- It provides efficient methods, algorithms and tools for finding hidden patterns in data.
- It reduces original data, i.e. to find minimal sets of data with the same knowledge as in the original data.
- It evaluates the significance of data.

- It generates optimal set of decision rules from data.
- It is easy to understand.
- It offers straightforward interpretation of obtained results.
- It is suitable for concurrent (parallel/distributed) processing.
- It can be used in both qualitative and quantitative data.

Definition

To be precise, let us take a universe U and $X \subseteq U$. Let **R** be a set of equivalence relations defined over U. We know that any equivalence relation defined over U decomposes U into disjoint equivalence classes and for any $x \in U$ we denote the equivalence class of x with respect to R by $[x]_R$ which comprises of all the elements of U those are related to x through R. For any **P⊆R** we denote by IND(**P**) the intersection of all the equivalence relations in P, which is also an equivalence relation. K = (U, **R**) is called an information system. Let IND(K) denote {IND(P)| $\phi \neq P \subseteq \mathbf{R}$}. Then for any $A \in IND(K)$ we denote the lower and upper approximations of X with respect to A by $\underline{A}X$ and $\overline{A}X$ and define them as follows:

$$\underline{A}X = \{x \in U \mid [x]_A \subseteq X\}$$

and

$$\overline{A}X = \{x \in U \mid [x]_R \cap X \neq \phi\}.$$

A set X is said to be A-definable if and only if $\underline{A}X = \overline{A}X$. Otherwise, X is said to be rough with respect to A. The A-boundary of X is defined as $\overline{A}X - \underline{A}X$.

The Figure 3 shows the granules of knowledge in the universe, the set and its lower and upper approximation. The difference between the lower and the upper approximation region is the boundary region. RST has been applied in many interesting area of research for solving problems including machine learning, intelligent systems, knowledge discovery, decision analysis, expert systems etc.

Let us discuss more precisely on characteristics of rough set. Suppose we are given a set of objects U called the universe and an indiscernibility relation R ⊆ U × U, representing our lack of knowledge about elements of U. For the sake of simplicity we assume that R is an Equivalence relation. Let X is a subset of U. We want to characterize the set X with respect to R. To this end we will need the basic concepts of rough set theory given below.

1. The lower approximation of a set X with respect to R is the set of all objects, which can be for certainly classified as X with respect to R (are certainly X with respect to R)
2. The upper approximation of a set X with respect to R is the set of all objects which can be possibly classified as X with respect to R (are possibly X in view of R).
3. The boundary region of a set X with respect to R is the set of all objects, which can be classified neither as X nor as not-X with respect to R.

Figure 3. Approximations of rough set

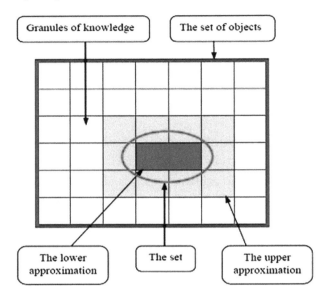

Rough sets are defined by approximations. Rough sets can be also defined employing, instead of approximation, rough membership function (Pawlak, Skowron, Yeager, Fedrizzi, & Kacprzyk, 1994)

$$\mu^R_x(x): U \rightarrow <1, 0>$$

where

$$\mu^R_x(x) = |(X \cap R(x))| / R(x)$$

and |X| denotes the cardinality of X.

The rough membership function expresses conditional probability that x belongs to X given R and can be interpreted as a degree that x belongs to X in view of information about x expressed by R. Rough Sets can also be defined as:

Definition 1: Set X is rough with respect to R if R*(X) ≠ R*(X).
Definition 2: Set X rough with respect to R if for some x $0 < \mu^R_x(x) < 1$.

Thus a set is rough (imprecise) if it has non empty boundary region; otherwise the set is crisp (precise). The approximations and the boundary region can be defined more precisely. To this end we need some additional notation. The equivalence class of R determined by element x will be denoted gy R(x). The indiscernibility relation in certain sense describes our lack of knowledge about the universe. Equivalence classes of the indiscernibility relation, called *granules* generated by R, represent elementary portion of knowledge we are able to perceive due to R. Thus in view of the indiscernibility relation in general we are an able to observe individual objects but we are forced to reason only about the accessible granules of knowledge.

Formal definitions of approximations and the boundary region are as follows:

- R-lower approximation of X:

$R_*(x) = U \{R(x): R(x) \subseteq X\}, x \in U$

- R-upper approximation of X:

$R^*(x) = U \{R(x): R(x) \cap X \neq \phi\}, x \in U$

- R-boundary region of X:

$RN_R(X) = R^*(X) - R_*(X)$

As we can see from the definition approximations are expressed in terms of granules of knowledge. The lower approximation of a set is union of all granules which are entirely included in the set; the upper approximation is union of all granules which have non-empty intersection with the set; the boundary region of set is the difference between the upper and the lower approximations. This definition is clearly depicted Figure 3.

It is interesting to compare definitions of classical sets, fuzzy sets and rough sets. Classical set is a primitive notion and is defined intuitively or axiomatically. Fuzzy sets are defined by employing the fuzzy membership function, which involves advanced mathematical structures numbers and functions. Rough sets are defined by approximations. Thus this definition also requires advanced mathematical concepts. Approximations have the following properties

1. $R_* (X) \subseteq X \subseteq R^* (X)$
2. $R_* (\phi) = R^* (\phi) = \phi$; $R_* (X) = R^* (X) = U$
3. $R^* (X \cup Y = R^* (X) \cup R^* (Y)$
4. $R_* (X \cap Y) = R_* (X) \cap R_* (Y)$
5. $R^*(X \cap Y) \subseteq R^* (X) \cap R^* (Y)$
6. $R_* (-X) = - R^* (X)$
7. $R^* (-X) = R_* (X)$

It is easily seen that approximations are in fact interior and closure operations in a topology generated by data. Thus fuzzy set theory and rough set theory require completely different mathematical setting.

Rough set theory clearly distinguishes two very important concepts, vagueness and uncertainty, which is considered very difficult in AI Literature. Vagueness is the property of sets and can be described by approximations, whereas uncertainty is the property of elements of a set and can be expressed by the rough membership function.

The meaning of rough membership function can be depicted as shown in Figure 4.

Basic concepts of the rough sets theory Walczak and Massart (1999) are as follows.

Figure 4. Membership elements in rough set

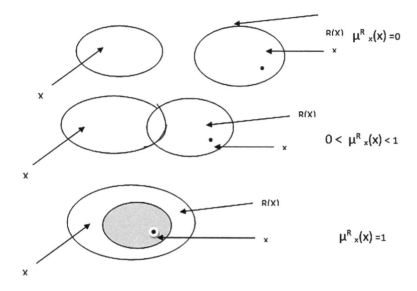

Information System

Formally, an information system, IS (or an approximation space, can be seen as a system IS= (U, A) where U is the universe (a finite set of objects, U = { x1, x2, . . ., xm }. and A is the set of attributes(features, variables). Each attribute a∈ A (attribute a belonging to the considered set of attributes A) defines an information function fa: U->V a, where V a is the set of values of a, called the domain of attribute a.

Indiscernibility Relation

For every set of attributes B;A, an indiscernibility relation Ind(B) is defined in the following way: two objects, x_i and x_j, are indiscernible by the set of attributes B in A, if $b(x_i) = b(x_j)$ for every b subset of B. The equivalence class of Ind(B) is called elementary set in B because it represents the smallest discernible groups of objects. For any element x_i of U, the equivalence classes of x_i in the relation Ind(B) is represented as $[x_i]_{Ind(B)}$. The construction of elementary sets is the first step in classification with rough sets.

Lower and Upper Approximations

The rough sets approach to data analysis hinges on two basic concepts, namely the lower and the upper approximations of a set referring to

- The elements that doubtlessly belong to the set, and
- The elements that possibly belong to the set.

Let X denote the subset of elements of the universe U (X⊂U). The lower approximation of X in B (B ⊆ A) denoted as <u>BX</u> is defined as the union of all these elementary sets which are contained in X. More formally

$$\underline{BX} = \{x_i \in U \mid [xi]_{Ind(B)} \mid \subset X \}$$

The above statement is to be read as: the lower approximation of the set X is a set of objects x_i which belong to the elementary sets contained in X (in the space B).

The upper approximation of the set X, denoted as BX, is the union of these elementary sets, which have a non-empty intersection with X:

$$\underline{BX} = \{x_i \in U \mid [xi]_{Ind(B)} \cap X \neq 0 \}$$

Independence of Attributes

In order to check, whether the set of attributes is independent or not, one checks for every attribute whether its removal increases the number of elementary sets in the IS or not.

If $Ind(A) = Ind(A-a_i)$ then the attribute a_i is called superfluous. Otherwise the attribute a_i is indispensable in A.

Core and Reduct of Attributes

If the set of attributes is dependent, one can be interested in finding all possible minimal subsets of attributes, which lead to the same number of elementary sets as the whole set of attributes (reducts) and in finding the set of all indispensable attributes (core). The concepts of core and reduct are two fundamental concepts of the rough sets theory. The reduct is the essential part of an IS, which can discern all objects discernible by the original IS. The core is the common part of all reducts. To compute reducts and core, the discernibility matrix is used. The discernibility matrix has the dimension n x n where n denotes the number of elementary sets and its elements are defined as the set of all attribute which discern elementary sets.

Core and Reduct of Attribute Values

Simplification of the IS can be achieved by dropping certain values of attributes, which are unnecessary for the system, i.e., by eliminating some of these values in such a way that we are still able to discern all elementary sets in the system. The procedure of finding core and reducts of the attribute values is similar to that of finding core and reducts of the attributes. All computations are performed based on the discernibility matrix, but the definition of the discernibility function is now slightly different. Instead of one discernibility function, we have to construct as many discernibility functions, as there are elementary sets in the IS.

FUZZY-ROUGH FEATURE SELECTION

Rough set theory (RST) has been successfully used as an attribute selection tool to discover data dependencies and reduce the number of attributes contained in a dataset by purely structural means Shen and Chouchoulas (2002). Given a dataset with discretized attribute values, RST can find a subset (termed reduct) of the original attributes that are the most informative; all other attributes can be removed from the dataset with minimal information loss. However, it is most often the case that the values of attributes may be both crisp and real-valued, and this is where traditional rough set theory encounters a problem. It is not possible in the theory to say whether two different attribute values are similar and to what extent they are the same. For example, two close values may only differ as a result of noise, but in the standard RST-based approach they are considered to be as different as two values of a different order of magnitude.

Dataset discretization must therefore take place before reduction methods based on crisp rough sets can be applied. This is often still inadequate, however as the degrees of membership of values to discretized values are not considered and thus can result in information loss. In order to combat this, extensions of rough sets based on fuzzy-rough sets have been developed. A fuzzy-rough set is defined by two fuzzy sets, fuzzy lower and upper approximations, obtained by extending the corresponding crisp rough set notions. In the crisp case, elements either belong to the lower approximation with absolute certainty or not. In the fuzzy-rough case, elements may have a membership in the range [0,1], allowing greater flexibility in handling uncertainty.

FUZZY ROUGH SETS

Research on fuzzifying lower and upper approximations in the spirit of Zadeh (1965), Pawlak (1982) emerged in the late 1980's. In developing the generalizations, the central focus moved from elements' in distinguishability w.r.t. their attribute values in an information system to their similarity. Objects are categorized into classes with "soft" boundaries based on their similarity to one another. A concrete advantage of such a scheme is that abrupt transitions between classes are replaced by gradual ones, allowing that an element can belong (to varying degrees) to more than one class. An example at hand is an attribute "age" in an information table, in order to restrict the number of equivalence classes, classical rough set theory advises to discretize age values by a crisp partition of the universe.

Rough Set Theory, which is used with the indiscernibility and perceptible knowledge, is useful for exploring data patterns because of its ability to search through a multi-dimensional data space and determine the relative importance of each attribute with respect to its output. It has been applied to the management of a number of the issues, including: medical diagnosis, engineering reliability, expert systems, machine diagnosis, and business failure Prediction, solving linear programs, data mining, and multi-criteria decision analysis.

Rough Set Theory applies the indiscernibility relation and compares data patterns to information systems in which the data is uncertain or inconsistent. The data is grouped into classes called elementary sets. Feature/attribute selection is crucial in data processing, which deals with selection of the most relevant (or maybe irrelevant) object patterns, but it may be redundant in data pattern recognition and its elimination will improve the accuracy.

SENTIMENT ANALYSIS BASED ON FUZZY SETS

Sentiment analysis problem can be addressed by applying the fuzzy logic theory for modeling membership functions representing the relationships between concepts expressed and domains. Fuzzy membership functions can be used to represent the belonging of a concept with respect to a domain in terms of both sentiment polarity as well as belongingness.

Current practice in sentiment analysis of social data predominantly uses the classification of individual artifacts such as either positive or negative or neutral, and not the probabilities returned by the sentiment analysis methods or tools.

Fuzzy set theory is a mathematical abstraction for the systemic treatment of vagueness and uncertainty both qualitatively and quantitatively. Fuzzy sets are well suited for the study of social systems owing to their ability to deal with vagueness, ambiguity and uncertainty of qualitative ideas and judgments.

Fuzzy sets can be used to model raw sentiment with classification probabilities of artifacts and develop an analysis method based on α-cut of Fuzzy sets to determine whether any given artifact expresses and impresses positive, negative, and/or neutral sentiment.

Definition 1: If X is a set of elements denoted by x, then a fuzzy set A over X is defined as a set of ordered pairs:

A = { (x, μ A(x))l x ∈ X)}

where, μ A: x-> [0,1] is the membership function.

Each member or element of a fuzzy set A is mapped to real number between 0 and 1 ([0,1]), which represents the degree of membership of an element in the fuzzy set. A membership value of 1 indicates full membership, while a value of 0 indicates no membership.

In this sentiment analysis of artifacts, let us assume that we are confined to textual types of artifacts, i.e. $r_{type}(r)$ = (post V comment). Using an automatic method (for example using a natural language processing engine) for categorizing sentiment of artifacts, an artifact can be mapped to different sentiment labels with a score indicating probability of relevance between the artifact and sentiment label. Normally, these scores are expressed as either percentages or real numbers (between 0 to 1), and the sum of such scores of an artifact for multiple sentiment labels will be equal to 1. Therefore, in this sentiment analysis, we consider the sentiment score of an artifact as its membership value of relationship between an artifact and a sentiment label.

SENTIMENT ANALYSIS BASED ON FUZZY DOMAIN SENTIMENT ONTOLOGY TREE (FDSOT)

Fuzzy domain sentiment ontology tree construction starts with collecting raw corpus from the Internet Walczak and Massart (1999). Preprocessing reviews cleans up the corpus such as stop word removal, Part-of- Speech (POS) tagging. The FDSOT is generated by the seed set and candidate feature-sentiment pairs extracted from review corpus. By matching with the FDSOT and analyzing the polarity of product features from all the reviews, a final presentation of sentiment analysis can be obtained. FDSOT can be generated by following steps of Walczak and Massart (1999).

- Model Generation,
- Collection of seeds and corpus preprocessing,
- Feature extraction and sentiment words,
- Sentiment orientation computation,
- Classifying sentiments.

Model Generation

Ontology is generally considered as a formal specification of conceptualization which consists of concepts and their relationships. The fuzzy domain sentiment ontology tree extraction method is developed based on fuzzy sets and semantic relations which offer the expressive power to capture the uncertainty presented in opinion mining. The main objective is to build the concept model which represents the semantic relation between product features and sentiment words. Product features (aspects) mean product components and attributes such as appearance, keyboard, battery etc w.r.t mobile phone and sentiment words are sentiment conveying terms which bear some sentiment orientation (positive or negative) such as perfect, ugly, cheap.

FDSOT is expressed in a tree-hierarchy of concepts as indicated in example 1. The root node of FDSOT is product itself (e.g. Mobile phone), each non-leaf child node of the root of the FDSOT represents a sub-feature belonging to its parent feature like battery. All the leaf nodes of FDSOT represent sentiment (positive or negative) nodes respectively associated with their parent nodes. This definition successfully describes the semantic relation between features and their associated sentiment.

- **Fuzzy Set:** It consists of a synonyms set of sentiment words (positive and negative). For example, the sentiment node "cheap" which has similar sentiment word low quality.
- **Fuzzy Relationship:** It defines the semantic relation for product features and sentiment words in FDSOT. Sentiment orientation SO score can be used to describe the grade of sentiment categories (positive and negative).

Collection of Seeds and Corpus Preprocessing

Seeds collecting and corpus preprocessing are the preparation of FDSOT construction. Seeds are collected to put them as the sentiment clue and features and sentiment words are extracted from review corpus. Some domain feature concepts are collected by their frequency in reviews. Then partly capture general

Sentiment words from synonym dictionary and sentiment lexicon of Hownet. Preprocessing is done by word segmentation, POS tagging (by ICTCLAS) and stop word removal.

Figure 5. FDSOT for phone product

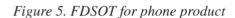
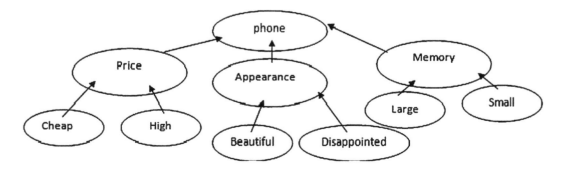

Feature Extraction and Sentiment Words

The goal of extraction is to get candidate feature words to be paired with their sentiment words. The Adjectives or Adverbs associated with the product features within a review sentence are extracted as the candidate sentiments. Traditional method exploits sentiment coherency within a sentence to extract sentiment candidate and then use a statistical method to determine whether a candidate is correct. This method can be unreliable when the occurrences of candidates are infrequent with small corpora. Therefore, an attempt is required to respectively extract frequent candidates and infrequent candidates. As basic classification unit for our fine-grained sentiment analysis, we choose sub-sentence segments. In this work, sub-sentence means product review is segmented into clauses by punctuation containing a comma. Then we choose the candidate noun and adjective (adverb) which are frequent co-occurrence (within a text window of 5 sizes) in a sub-sentence. The formula is shown as following:

$$MI(F_i, S_i) = \log P(F_i, S_i) / P(F_i) P(S_i)$$

where $MI(F_i, S_i)$ is a function to estimate the degree of association between product feature F_i and its sentiment word S_i. $P(F_i, S_i)$ is the frequency of co-occurring terms.

Sentiment Orientation Computation

After extracting pairs of product feature and sentiment word, sentiment orientation is predicted for each feature-sentiment pair. The basic idea is that a positive product review is more likely to contain positive opinion pairs than a negative review does. Therefore, we may use the sentiment polarity label of a review text to infer the sentiment orientation of a product feature within the clause. To calculate the sentiment orientation of a pair, at first we classify positive and negative polarity labels and then proposed a formula to predict the value of sentiment. The function is defined as follows:

$$SO(p) = P(pos|p) \times \log_2 P(pos|p) / P(pos) - P(neg|p) \times \log_2 P(neg|p)/P(neg)$$

where $SO(p)$ represents the polarity score of an opinion pair p. The Ppos (Pneg) is the prior probability that a review is positive (negative) respectively. The $P(pos \mid p)$ ($P(neg \mid p)$) is the estimated conditional probability that a review is positive (negative) if it contains the opinion pair p.

Classifying Sentiments

Automatic sentiment analysis has been well studied with a variety of lexicon-based and machine learning based systems. FDSOT uses domain sentiment knowledge to mine the product features and their sentiment (positive or negative) in each sentence. The FDSOT which is constructed is a conceptual model for the representation of specific domain sentiment knowledge. The prior sentiment resource which is held by our ontology is utilized to analyze the target review. Given a large number of product reviews about various detail features, we can identify the sentiments that are highly associated with a given product feature by matching the candidate feature and sentiment word with the common feature-opinion pairs in our FDSOT. As mentioned before, the representative product features can be chosen from each review and candidate sentiments which are close to the product features. The polarity score of feature-sentiment pair is calculated by finding out the closest matching result between candidate sentiment words in reviews and a fuzzy set of sentiment words in FDSOT.

SENTIMENT ANALYSIS BASED ON ROUGH SETS

Rough set based dimension reduction method can be applied for sentiment analysis by finding optimal feature from review document i.e. by eliminating the redundant features (noisy features). The rough set is the approximation of a vague concept (set) by a pair of precise concepts (Features), called lower and upper approximations. Rough Set Attribute Reduction (RSAR) is a filter based method by which redundant features are eliminated by keeping the amount of knowledge intact in the System. Basic intuition behind RSAR is that objects belonging to the same category (same attributes) are not distinguishable. The main advantage of rough set theory in data analysis is that it does not need any preliminary or additional information about data like probability in statistics or grade of membership or the value of possibility as in fuzzy set theory.

CONCLUSION

Sentiment analysis is a special field of text analysis. In short, it focuses on analyzing the extracted opinions (sentiments or emotional contents) from the posted comments. Rough set based dimension reduction method is applied for sentiment analysis. It is capable of reducing the redundancy among the attributes. Rough set based methods computes the best feature subset based on minimized redundancy in contrast to information gain which computes the importance of the attribute. Fuzzy based sentiment analysis system is able to model fuzzy membership functions representing the polarities and the belongingness of concepts with respect to a particular domain. FDSOT, is a new model to represent domain-dependent sentiment knowledge by using the space of product features and sentiment words. This model can store sentiment polarity of opinion pairs with varying contextual information. In future, more methods can be explored for making rough set based feature selection method computationally more efficient by incorporating evolutionary approaches in selecting feature subsets. Also the product features and sentiment words can be extended by adding other parts-of-speech like gerundial phrases conveying features and verbs bearing opinions.

REFERENCES

Agarwal & Mittal. (2013). Sentiment Classification using Rough Set based Hybrid Feature Selection. *Proceedings of the 4th Workshop on Computational Approaches to Subjectivity, Sentiment and Social Media Analysis.Association for Computational Linguistics.*

Elawady, R. M., & Barakat, S. (2014). Different Feature Selection for Sentiment Classification. *International Journal of Information Science and Intelligent System*, *3*(1), 137–150.

Haque & Rahman. (2014). Sentiment Analysis by Using Fuzzy Logic. *International Journal of Computer Science, Engineering and Information Technology, 4*(1).

Jensen, R., & Shen, Q. (2009). New Approaches to Fuzzy-Rough Feature Selection. *IEEE Transactions on Fuzzy Systems*, *17*(4), 824–838. doi:10.1109/TFUZZ.2008.924209

Klir, G. J., & Yuan, B. (1995). *Fuzzy Sets and Fuzzy Logic, Theory and Applications.* Prentice Hall.

Liu, B. (2010). Sentiment Analysis and Subjectivity. InHandbook of Natural Language Processing (2nd ed.). Academic Press.

Lo, Y. W., & Potdar, V. (2009). A Review of Opinion Mining and Sentiment Classification Framework in Social Networks. *3rd IEEE International Conference on Digital Ecosystems and Technologies.* doi:10.1109/DEST.2009.5276705

Mendel. (1995). Fuzzy logic systems for engineering: a tutorial. *Proc. IEEE, 3*(3), 345–377.

Mukkamala, R. R., Hussain, A., & Vatrapu, R. (2014). Fuzzy-Set Based Sentiment Analysis of Big Social Data. *Enterprise Distributed Object Computing Conference (EDOC), 2014 IEEE 18th International.*

Nie & Liu. (2013). The Opinion Mining Based on Fuzzy Domain Sentiment Ontology Tree for Product Reviews. *Journal of Software, 8*(11).

Pak, A., & Paroubek, P. (2010). Twitter as a corpus for sentiment analysis and opinion mining. In *Proceedings of LREC.*

Panda & Mondal. (2013). Rough Set Techniques for Text Classification and Sentiment Analysis in Social Media. *International Journal of Emerging Technologies in Computational and Applied Sciences.*

Pawlak, Z. (1982). Rough sets. *Int. J. of Information and Computer Sciences*, *11*(5), 341–356. doi:10.1007/BF01001956

Pawlak, Z., & Skowron, A. (1994). Rough membership function. In R. E. Yeager, M. Fedrizzi, & J. Kacprzyk (Eds.), *Advaces in the Dempster-Schafer of Evidence* (pp. 251–271). New York: Wiley.

Radzikowska, A. M., & Kerre, E. E. (2002). A comparative study of fuzzy rough sets. *Fuzzy Sets and Systems*, *126*(2), 137–156. doi:10.1016/S0165-0114(01)00032-X

Rasheed, M. (2014). Elawady1, Sherif Barakat2, Nora M.Elrashidy2,*Different Feature Selection for Sentiment Classification. *International Journal of Information Science and Intelligent System*, *3*(1), 137–150.

Shen, Q., & Chouchoulas, A. (2002). A rough-fuzzy approach for generating classification rules. *Pattern Recognition, 35*(2), 2425–2438. doi:10.1016/S0031-3203(01)00229-1

Stanford. (n.d.). Retrieved from: http://nlp.stanford.edu/software/tagger.shtml

Walczak, B., & Massart, D.L. (1999). *Rough sets theory Chemometrics and Intelligent Laboratory Systems.* Academic Press.

Zadeh, L. (1965). Fuzzy sets. *Information and Control, 8*(3), 338–353. doi:10.1016/S0019-9958(65)90241-X

processes and in turn reduce information loss and will provide greater design alternatives at later stages of development. Norbert Sram (Sram, 2011) described some of the major issues faced in the process of designing, developing and applying fuzzy logic in real-world applications. The paper described the software engineering principles applied to improve the process of working with fuzzy logic.

To improve the accuracy of software effort estimation fuzzy logic model was used by Ziauddin (Ziauddin et al., 2013). In this approach fuzzy logic is used to fuzzify input parameters of COCOMO II model and the result is defuzzified to get the resultant Effort. The results of this model were compared with existing models and author found proposed model to be better that existing models. Noel (Noel et al., 2013) applied fuzzy logic technique to software development effort estimation (SDEE) using a Mamdani Model. Author compared the estimation accuracy of the Mamdani and Takagi-Sugeno fuzzy systems with that of an LR model using a sample of small projects. Author concluded that a Takagi-Sugeno fuzzy system can be useful for estimating the effort of projects in contrast to Mamdani and LR model.

All studies so far have considered only comparison of various process models. Most of the past research in this field focused on one or two process models and considered only the factors which are influential for the selection of process model in software projects. Further, fuzzy logic has been used in various aspects of software engineering varying from software development to cost and effort estimation. However none have applied fuzzy logic for prediction of software process model in software projects.

In this chapter, authorshave identified influential factors and proposed a new automated framework for predicting process model. For this purpose authors have adopted fuzzy based approach and to bring more accuracy for selection of process model J-48 classification algorithm has been used.

OVERVIEW OF PROCESS MODELS

Process models (analogously known as systems development life cycle models) for software development provides the fundamental rules for building software. The primary goal of a process model is to give direction to methodically organizing the tasks that must be performed in order to accomplish the final product and the project objectives. There are several process models and numerous organizations follow their own particular models, yet all have fundamentally similar patterns (Pressman, 2004). Then again, there is no generic process model, which is considered suitable in all circumstances. Briefly various process models are tabulated in Table 1 (Thakurta, 2011). These are the process models which authors have considered for carrying out their research.

RESEARCH METHODOLOGY

Research methodology alludes to a procedure that achieves the key goals of the research undertaken. The key objectives of this chapter are:

- To study various software process models presented in literature.
- To distinguish the factors influencing the decision of the process models for software projects in an organization.
- To prioritize the determined factors according to their relevance in process model selection.
- To present an automated framework using Fuzzy Interface System (FIS).
- To validate results using J-48 Decision Tree.

Table 1. Overview of process models

Process Model	Definition
Waterfall Model	It is a software development model (with strictly one Iteration/phase) in which development proceeds sequentially through the phases: requirements analysis, design, coding, testing (validation), integration, and maintenance
V-Shaped Model	This is an extension of the waterfall model which emphasizes parallelism of activities of construction and activities of verification. Here, the process steps instead of moving down in a linear way bend upwards after the coding phase resulting in the typical V shape formation.
Prototyping Model	It is a software development process that begins with requirements collection, followed by prototyping and user evaluation.
Incremental-Iterative Model	Here the software project is divided into mini-projects, each of which is an iteration that results in an increment. Each iteration represents a mini-waterfall model.
Spiral Model	This supposes incremental development, using the waterfall model for each step, with more emphasis on managing risk.
Rapid Application Development (RAD)	It is a software development process that allows usable systems to be built in as little as 60-90 days, often with some compromises.
Agile Methodologies	Agile is an evolutionary approach to software development which is performed in a highly collaborative manner by self-organizing teams with the objective of producing high quality software in a cost effective and timely manner. Some of the different Agile Approaches are Extreme Programming (XP), Scrum, Pair Programming, etc.

This research analysis was carried out in two phases. In the first phase of research analysis a survey has been conducted to determine influential factors for process model selection for software projects. In the second phase approaches to be followed to develop an automated framework has been discussed.

Phase One

Survey

A web based survey (Appendix 1) was employed in the first phase with an objective to determine the factors which influence the selection of a process model. 18 factors influencing the choice of process models were derived from the literature (Pressman, 2004; Ghezzi et al., 2002; Jalote, 2005) as shown in Table 2. The respondents were asked to rate each factor on a Likert scale of 1-5 (1 = unimportant, 2 = of little importance, 3 = moderately important, 4 = important and 5 = very important). The participants were also asked to choose characteristic value of each factor for every process model. The factors F12, F18 have characteristic values as Available, Not Available, NA; F1-F11, F13, F16 have characteristic values as Low, Medium, High; F15 have characteristic values as Clear, Not Clear, NA; F14, F17 have characteristic values as Small, Medium, Large. These characteristic values have been referenced from (Pressman, 2004; Aggarwal, 2007).

A total of 150 survey questionnaires were sent by email to software professionals, faculties, research scholars and students pursuing studies in Software Engineering. The response rate was 80% (i.e. 120 respondents) including 45 software professionals, 25 faculties, 15 research scholars and 35 students. The phase two of the analysis was carried out using the responses from the participants of the survey.

Table 2. Identified factors

Notation	Factors
F1	Acceptance of requirement changes
F2	Tools and technology availability
F3	Complexity defined by requirements
F4	Customer involvement
F5	Ease of maintenance
F6	Experience of developers
F7	Flexibility to change in requirements
F8	Level of expected risk
F9	Level of quality required
F10	Level of reliability required
F11	Knowledge of application area
F12	Pre-defined requirements
F13	Project duration
F14	Project size
F15	Requirement understandability and definition
F16	Reusability of components
F17	Team size
F18	Product versions

Results of the Survey

As shown in Figure 1, 37.5% of the participants of the survey were software professionals, 20.83% of the respondents were faculties, 12.5% of the respondents were research scholars and 29.17% of the respondents were students. To assess the mean score of individual factor, the scores of the factors on a scale of 1 to 5 (1 =unimportant and 5 = very important), obtained by the respondents were aggregated together and afterward divided by the number of observations per factor. The results of the analysis demonstrating the mean scores and standard deviation of each key factor influencing the choice of process model is shown in Table 3. Mean score of each factor is shown in Figure 2, where importance of the factor is directly proportional to its mean score.

On the basis of mean scores, we have prioritized the factors on the scale of 1-18 with 1 being the most essential and 18 being the least important as arranged in Table 3. F15 has the most elevated score. Mean scores of F1, F3, F7, F12 and F15 is greater than or equal to 4. It was seen from the analysis that the following factorswere vital to decision of process model:

Factor 15: Requirement understandability and definition.
Factor 12: Pre-defined requirements.
Factor 3: Complexity defined by requirements.
Factor 1: Acceptance of requirement changes.
Factor 7: Flexibility to change in requirements.

Figure 1. Percentage distribution of participants

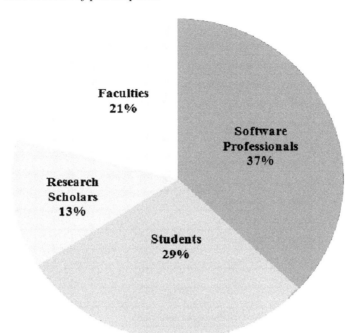

Table 3. Factors affecting the choice of process models

Priority	Notations	Factors	Mean	Standard Deviation
1	F15	Requirement understandability and definition	4.560	0.0511
2	F12	Pre-defined requirements	4.482	0.0440
3	F3	Complexity defined by requirements	4.312	0.0284
4	F1	Acceptance of requirement changes	4.220	0.0200
5	F7	Flexibility to change in requirements	4.160	0.0146
6	F4	Customer involvement	3.999	0.0911
7	F8	Level of expected risk	3.789	0.2277
8	F11	Knowledge of application area	3.654	0.0597
9	F10	Level of reliability required	3.321	0.0191
10	F14	Project size	3.211	0.0192
11	F13	Project duration	3.111	0.0101
12	F9	Level of quality required	3.100	0.0091
13	F5	Ease of maintenance	2.199	0.0181
14	F6	Experience of developers	2.150	0.0136
15	F7	Team size	2.140	0.0127
16	F16	Reusability of components	2.117	0.0106
17	F2	Tools and technology availability	2.105	0.0095
18	F18	Product versions	2.103	0.0094

Figure 2. Mean score of each factor

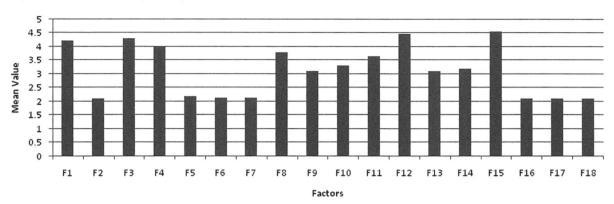

Also, characteristic value of each factor for every process model obtained by the participants was collected and the most frequently chosen responses are tabulated in the Table 4.

Phase Two

In the second phase of the research analysis the 5 prioritized factors along with their characteristic values obtained in the first phase by the means of survey were used for predicting the process model using fuzzy rule base engine and J-48 decision tree.

Framework of the Developed System: Fuzzy Approach

A fuzzy approach is an approach of which the limits of application can differ significantly as per context or conditions, rather than being fixed once and for all. This implies the approach is vague somehow, lacking a fixed and precise meaning, without however being hazy or meaningless altogether. It has a clear significance, which can turn out to be more exact just through further elaboration and determination.

Since there is always certain amount of uncertainty involved in undertaking software engineering activities since these relate in many ways to software projects. Software projects have several risks and assumptions associated with them. Such kind of problems can be better solved using the fuzzy logic. In this chapter, a novel knowledge-based approach has been proposed for selection of process model for software project. The framework of the developed system includes three stages as shown in Figure 3 namely,

Stage 1: Preparing/Training stage,
Stage 2: Inference stage,
Stage 3: Testing stage.

Table 4. Characteristic values of process models

Priority	Factors	Code and Fix	Classical Waterfall	V-Shaped	Prototyping	RAD	Iterative/ Incremental	Spiral	Agile
1	Requirement understandability and definition	Clear	Clear	Clear	Not clear	Clear	Not clear	Not clear	Not clear
2	Pre-defined requirements	Not available	Available	Available	Not Available	Available	Not available	Not available	Not available
3	Complexity defined by requements	Low	High	Medium	High	Low	High	High	High
4	Acceptance of requirement changes	Low	Low	Low	Medium	Medium	High	Medium	High
5	Flexibility to change in requirements	Low	Low	Medium	Medium	High	Medium	High	High
6	Customer involvement	Low	Low	Medium	Medium	High	High	Medium	High
7	Level of expected risk	Low	Low	Medium	High	Medium	High	High	Medium
8	Knowledge of application area	Low	Medium	Medium	Medium	High	High	Medium	High
9	Level of reliability required	Low	High	Medium	Medium	Medium	Medium	High	High
10	Project size	Small	Small	Medium	Medium	Medium	Large	Large	Large
11	Project duration	Medium	Medium	Medium	Medium	Low	High	Medium	Medium
12	Level of quality required	Low	Medium	Medium	Medium	Medium	High	Medium	High
13	Ease of maintenance	Low	Low	Low	Medium	High	Medium	Medium	High
14	Experience of developers	Medium	High	Medium	High	Medium	High	High	High
15	Team size	Small	Medium	Medium	Medium	Small	Large	Medium	Small
16	Reusability of components	Low	Low	Low	Medium	High	Low	Medium	Medium
17	Tools and technology availability	Low	Medium	High	High	High	High	Medium	High
18	Product versions	Not Available	Available	Not Available	Available	Not Available	Available	Not Available	Available

Data Collected from survey.

Stage 1: Preparing/Training Stage

In general, training phase of any application is intended to teach the framework on the input sets of data and to provide a means to learn about the domain. This process aims at providing a supervised way of learning mechanism to map the input dataset to the desired output (Thirugnanam&Anouncia, 2014).

Based on the Table 4, Table 5 has been created which is used to fulfil the preparing stage of the framework which is stored in database as training data for further handling and elucidation. Table 5

Figure 3. Fuzzy approach framework

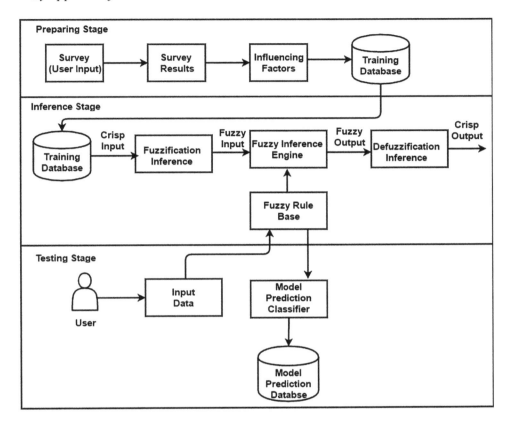

illustrates eight software process models namely Code and Fix, Classical Waterfall, V-Shaped, Prototyping, RAD, Iterative/Incremental, Spiral and Agile that are characterized with five factors Requirement understandability and definition, Pre-defined requirements, Complexity defined by requirements, Acceptance of requirement changes and Flexibility to change in requirements. Columns of the table are labeled by factors and rows by process model. Each cell represents the characteristic value of each factor corresponding to the process model. Thus each row can be seen as the information to the particular process model. For example, process model Code and Fix is characterized in the table by the attribute value set (Requirement understandability and definition, Clear), (Pre-defined requirements, Not-Available), (Complexity defined by requirements, Low), (Acceptance of requirement changes, NA), (Flexibility to change in requirements, NA).

Stage 2: Inference Stage

Fuzzy Inference

Fuzzy inference is a procedure of mapping from a given input to output utilizing fuzzy logic. The mapping then gives the premise from which choices can be made, or patterns observed. The procedure of fuzzy inference includes membership functions, fuzzy logic operators and if- then rules. If-Then rules are designed to predict the optimal match between each project-process model pair. Mamdani method

Table 5. Training data

Requirement Understandability and Definition	Pre-Defined Requirements	Complexity Defined by Requirements	Acceptance of Requirement Changes	Flexibility to Change in Requirements	Process Model
Clear	Not Available	Low	NA	NA	Code and Fix
Clear	Available	High	Low	Low	Classical Waterfall
Clear	Available	Medium	Low	Medium	V-Shaped
Not Clear	Not Available	High	Medium	Medium	Prototyping
Clear	Available	Low	NA	NA	RAD
Not Clear	Not Available	High	High	Medium	Iterative/ Incremental
Not Clear	Not Available	High	Medium	High	Spiral
Not Clear	Not Available	High	High	High	Agile

*NA represents that the given factor is not necessary for the given technique according to the Fuzzy Rules. Any value can be assigned for the same.

is more intuitive and is well suited for human input in contrast to Sugeno-Type FIS which is indeed computationally efficient but it works well with optimization and adaptive techniques, which makes it very attractive in control problems. Since Mamdani allows us to describe the expertise more human-like manner, authors have designed Mamdani fuzzy rule based engine with five input layers namely *ReqtUnderstandability* (requirement understandability and definition), *PredefinedReqt* (pre-defined requirements), *ComplexityReqd* (complexity defined by requirements), *ReqtAcceptance* (acceptance of requirement changes selected) and *ReqtFlexibility* (flexibility to change in requirements) as computed in the first phase of the research and one output layer named as *Process-Model*.

Each layer in FIS is associated with three member functions (MFs). Here, for each layer, triangular type membership functions are used since calculations with triangular membership functions are easy in contrast to other membership functions like Bell, Gaussian, LR, etc. Three membership functions are characterized for each factor ranging from 1.6 to 2.3 as in Table 6.

For the output *Process-Model*, eight membership functions are defined: CODE-FIX, CLASSICAL-WATERFALL, V-SHAPED, PROTOTYPING, RAD, ITERATIVE, SPIRAL, AGILE ranging from 0 to1 as shown in Table 7.

Fuzzy Rule Base Construction

In general, a rule-based system is designed with group of facts, if then rules, and an interpreter controlling the application of rules which specified in the facts (Thirugnanam& Anouncia, 2014). With the assistance of MFs, rules are constructed and stored in a generated rule base. The rules formulated are tabulated in Table 8.

Defuzzification

In fuzzy control systems, defuzzification is required where it produces a significant result using fuzzy logic with given input and membership functions. Defuzzification is translating the membership degree of fuzzy sets into aparticular choice or real value. The system itself will calculate the Process Model

Table 6. Membership functions of input parameter

Input/ Factors	Normalized Value	Classification/Membership Functions
ReqtAcceptance	1.6-1.824	Low
	1.831-2.055	Medium
	2.062-2.3	High
ReqtUnderstandability	1.6-1.824	Not Clear
	1.831-2.055	NA
	2.062-2.3	Clear
PredefinedReqt	1.6-1.824	Not Available
	1.831-2.055	NA
	2.062-2.3	Available
ComplexityReqd	1.6-1.824	Low
	1.831-2.055	Medium
	2.062-2.3	High
ReqtFlexibility	1.6-1.824	Low
	1.831-2.055	Medium
	2.062-2.3	High

Table 7. Range of membership function of output variable

Output	Normalized Value	Classification/Membership Functions
Process-Model	0-0.125	CODE-FIX
	0.126-0.251	CLASSICAL-WATERFALL
	0.252-0.377	V-SHAPED
	0.504-0.629	PROTOTYPING
	0.504-0.629	RAD
	0.63-0.755	ITERATIVE
	0.756-0.881	SPIRAL
	0.882-1	AGILE

after selecting the input values in rule viewer window with the help of fuzzy rules. There are number of defuzzification methods used in the literature (Thirugnanam & Anouncia, 2014). One of the widely used methods is the centroid calculation which returns the centre of area under the curve, has been used by authors in their research.

Stage 3: Testing Stage

The last stage of the framework is to test the created and prepared system to explore its performance in classifying the process model suitably. Around 20 datasets of process models used as sample for testing the framework as shown in the Table 9. Considering the rules, the performance of the framework is

Table 8. Fuzzy rules

Rule		Description
[1]	IF	ReqtUnderstandability is Clear AND PredefinedReqt is Not-Available AND ComplexityReqd is Low
	THEN	Process-Model is CODE-FIX
[2]	IF	ReqtUnderstandability is ClearAND PredefinedReqt is Available AND ComplexityReqd is High AND ReqtAcceptance is Low AND ReqtFlexibility is Low
	THEN	Process-Model is CLASSICAL-WATERFALL
[3]	IF	ReqtUnderstandability is Clear AND PredefinedReqt is Available ANDComplexityReqd is Medium AND ReqtAcceptance is Low AND ReqtFlexibility is Medium
	THEN	Process-Model is V-SHAPED
[4]	IF	ReqtUnderstandability is Not-Clear AND PredefinedReqt is Not-Available AND ComplexityReqd is High AND ReqtAcceptance is Medium AND ReqtFlexibility is Medium
	THEN	Process-Model is PROTOTYPE
[5]	IF	ReqtUnderstandability is Clear AND PredefinedReqt is Available ANDComplexityReqd is Low
	THEN	Process-Model is RAD
[6]	IF	ReqtUnderstandability is Not-Clear AND PredefinedReqt is Not-Available ANDComplexityReqd is High AND ReqtAcceptance is High AND ReqtFlexibility is Medium
	THEN	Process-Model is ITERATIVE
[7]	IF	ReqtUnderstandability is Not-Clear AND PredefinedReqt is Not-Available ANDComplexityReqd is High ANDReqtAcceptance is Medium AND ReqtFlexibility is High
	THEN	Process-Model is SPIRAL
[8]	IF	ReqtUnderstandability is Not-Clear AND PredefinedReqt is Not-Available AND ComplexityReqd is High ANDReqtAcceptance is High AND ReqtFlexibility is High
	THEN	Process-Model is AGILE

tested. The system classified 17 samples correctly and therefore the misclassification rate is 15% which is evident from the graph as shown in Figure 4. The performanceanalysis of software process model using fuzzy approach is tabulated in Table 10.

Decision Tree

Decision tree method is one of the classification techniques. In decision tree methods, a binary tree is built in which at each node a single parameter is compared to some constant. If the feature value is greater than the threshold, the right branch of the tree is taken; if the value is smaller, the left branch is followed (Richard, 1996). After a progression of these tests, one reaches a leaf node of the tree where all the objects are labeled as belonging to a specific class. Decision Tree is a twofold supervised learning process shown in Figure 5.

Stage 1: Learning (Training),
Stage 2: Testing.

Table 9. Test data

S. No.	ReqtUnderstandability	PredefinedReqt	ComplexityReqd	ReqtAcceptance	ReqtFlexibility	AC	PC
1	2.10	1.62	1.70	1.68	1.82	I	I
2	2.15	1.66	1.76	1.68	1.65	I	I
3	2.22	1.72	1.79	1.68	1.80	I	I
4	2.27	1.77	1.80	1.68	1.68	I	I
5	2.06	2.06	1.83	1.81	1.61	II	IV
6	2.12	2.25	1.93	1.68	1.79	II	II
7	2.26	2.27	1.92	1.69	1.80	II	II
8	2.07	2.09	2.01	1.80	1.90	III	III
9	2.12	2.11	1.87	1.66	1.93	III	III
10	1.72	1.76	2.10	1.84	2.03	IV	IV
11	1.80	1.77	2.12	2.00	2.04	IV	IV
12	1.82	1.81	2.12	2.05	1.90	IV	IV
13	2.11	2.17	1.79	2.28	1.90	V	V
14	2.3	2.26	1.82	2.06	2.05	V	IV
15	1.80	1.83	2.20	2.07	1.83	VI	IV
16	1.72	1.77	2.12	2.14	2.01	VI	VI
17	1.74	1.72	2.07	1.90	2.07	VII	VII
18	1.73	1.68	2.12	2.01	2.28	VII	VII
19	1.68	1.74	2.28	2.21	2.21	VIII	VIII
20	1.73	1.72	2.11	2.12	2.28	VIII	VIII

I=CODE &FIX, II= CLASSICAL WATERFALL,III= V-SHAPED, IV=PROTOTYPING, V=RAD, VI=ITERATIVE/INCREMEMTAL, VII=SPIRAL, VIII= AGILE AC=Actual Class PC=Predicted Class

Figure 4. Actual vs. predicted class

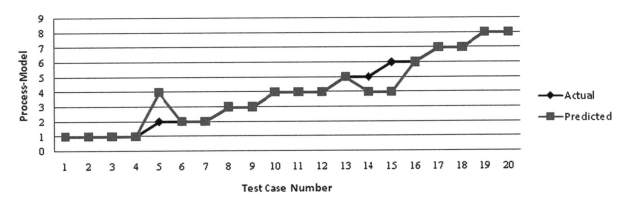

407

Table 10. Performance analysis of software process model using fuzzy approach

Classification	Samples (Input 20 Samples)	Percentage
Correctly classified process model	17	85%
Misclassified process model	3	15%

Figure 5. Framework using decision tree approach

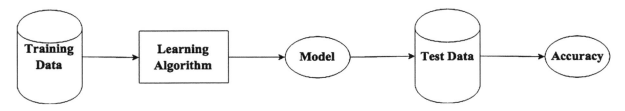

Stage 1: Learning (Training)

Prior to applying classification algorithm, data is collected and pre-processed as explained below.

Collecting Information

The dataset obtained in the first phase is used to prepare table which consists of attributes ReqtUnderstandability (requirement understandability and definition),PredefinedReqt(Pre-defined requirements), ComplexityReqt(Complexity defined by requirements), ReqtAcceptance(Acceptance of requireent changes selected), ReqtFlexibility(Flexibility to change in requirements), CustomerInvolvement (Customer involvement), ExpectedRisk (Level of expected risk), AppAreaUnderstanding (Knowledge of application area), ReliabilityRequired (Level of reliability required), ProjectSize (Project size), ProjectDuration (Project duration), QualityRequired (Level of quality required), MaintenanceEase (Ease of maintenance), DevelopersExp (Experience of developers), TeamSize (Team size), ComponentsReusuability (Reusability of components), ToolsTechnology (Tools and technology availability), ProductVersions (Product versions) and Model. All the attributes are Nominal. The sample input is as shown in Figure 6.

Pre-Processing

Preprocessing is a data mining technique that involves transforming raw data into an understandable format (Durrant, 2015). In WEKA file input should be in .csv format. The first row contains the attribute names separated by commas. Each data row contains the values in the same order as attributes as shown in Figure 7.

Classification

Classification is a data mining algorithm that creates a step-by-step guide to determine the output of a new data instance. There are many classification algorithms in data mining such as Naïve Bayes, Bayesnet, J-48 and so on. In our study, J-48 decision tree is used for predicting the process model bringing correctness for the results obtained using fuzzy rule engine as shown in Figure 8.

Figure 6. Training data set

No.	ReqtUnderstandability Nominal	PredefinedReqt Nominal	ReqtComplexity Nominal	ReqtAcceptance Nominal	ReqtFlexibility Nominal	CustomerInvolvement Nominal	ExpectedRisk Nominal	
1	Clear	Not Available	Low	Low	Low	Low	Medium	∧
2	Clear	Available	Medium	Low	Low	Low	High	
3	Clear	Available	Medium	Low	Medium	Low	Medium	
4	Not Clear	Not Available	High	Medium	Medium	Medium	High	
5	Clear	Available	Low	Medium	High	High	Medium	
6	Not Clear	Not Available	High	High	Medium	High	Low	
7	Not Clear	Not Available	High	Medium	High	Medium	High	
8	Not Clear	Not Available	High	High	High	High	Medium	
9								
10	Clear	Not Available	Low	Low	Low	NA	NA	
11	Clear	Not Available	Low	Low	Medium	NA	NA	
12	Clear	Not Available	Low	Low	High	NA	NA	
13	Clear	Not Available	Low	Medium	Low	NA	NA	
14	Clear	Not Available	Low	Medium	Medium	NA	NA	
15	Clear	Not Available	Low	Medium	High	NA	NA	
16	Clear	Not Available	Low	High	Low	NA	NA	
17	Clear	Not Available	Low	High	Medium	NA	NA	
18	Clear	Not Available	Low	High	High	NA	NA	
19								
20	Clear	Available	Medium	Low	Low	Low	Low	
21	Clear	Available	Medium	Low	Low	Low	Low	
22	Clear	Available	Medium	Low	Low	Low	Low	
23	Clear	Available	Medium	Low	Low	Low	Medium	∨

Figure 7. Pre-processing data

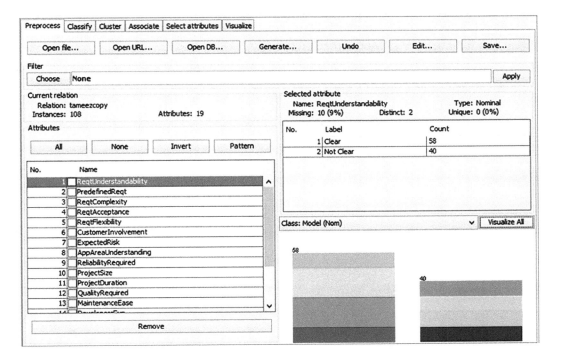

Figure 8. J-48 classification

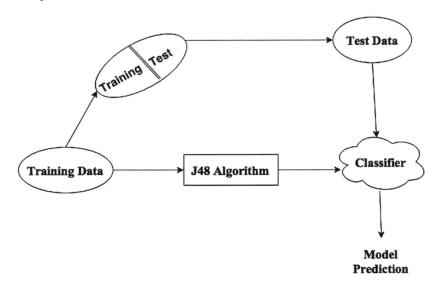

After applying J-48 Decision Tree classification in WEKA, we getthe output as shown in Figure 13. From a decision tree we can derive set of rules. Each path from the root to a leaf is a rule. For instance rule derived from Figure 9 is:

ReqtUnderstandability = Not Clear, ReqtAcceptance = Medium, ReqtFlexibility=Medium-->Class = PROTOTYPING

i.e. if the value of factor ReqtUnderstandability is Not Clear, ReqtAcceptance has value Medium, Reqt-Flexibility is Medium then class Model predicted is PROTOTYPING.

Figure 9. J-48 decision tree using WEKA

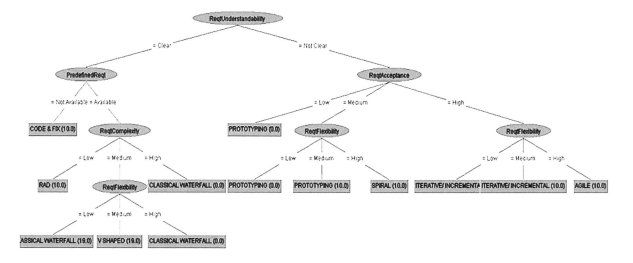

Stage 2: Testing

After training data, we have considered the testing data of 20 samples which are same test data as given to FIS as shown in Table 9. Test data for J-48 Decision tree algorithm is tabulated in Table 11. Here class to be predicted is inputted as?. Based on the training data, output (Process Model) is predicted after applying J-48 Decision Tree algorithm as shown in Table 12. Out of the 20 test samples, the framework was able to classify all samples correctly except 1, henceforth misclassified process models were 5%which is evident from the graph as shown in Figure 10. The performance analysis of software process model using J-48 decision tree is tabulated in Table 13.

Table 11. Test data

```
@data
Clear,'Not Available',Low,Low,Low,NA,NA,NA,NA,NA,NA,NA,NA,NA,NA,NA,NA,NA,? (1)
Clear,'Not Available',Low,Low,Low,NA,NA,NA,NA,NA,NA,NA,NA,NA,NA,NA,NA,NA,? (2)
Clear,'Not Available',Low,Low,Low,NA,NA,NA,NA,NA,NA,NA,NA,NA,NA,NA,NA,NA,? (3)
Clear,'Not Available',Low,Low,Low,NA,NA,NA,NA,NA,NA,NA,NA,NA,NA,NA,NA,NA,? (4)
Clear,'Available ',Medium,Low,Low,NA,NA,NA,NA,NA,NA,NA,NA,NA,NA,NA,NA,NA,? (5)
Clear,'Available ',Medium,Low,Low,NA,NA,NA,NA,NA,NA,NA,NA,NA,NA,NA,NA,NA,? (6)
Clear,'Available ',Medium,Low,Low,NA,NA,NA,NA,NA,NA,NA,NA,NA,NA,NA,NA,NA,? (7)
Clear,'Available ',Medium,Low,Medium,NA,NA,NA,NA,NA,NA,NA,NA,NA,NA,NA,NA,NA,? (8)
Clear,'Available ',Medium,Low,Medium,NA,NA,NA,NA,NA,NA,NA,NA,NA,NA,NA,NA,NA,? (9)
'Not Clear','Not Available',High,Medium,Medium,NA,NA,NA,NA,NA,NA,NA,NA,NA,NA,NA,NA,NA,? (10)
'Not Clear','Not Available',High,Medium,Medium,NA,NA,NA,NA,NA,NA,NA,NA,NA,NA,NA,NA,NA,? (11)
'Not Clear','Not Available',High,Medium,Medium,NA,NA,NA,NA,NA,NA,NA,NA,NA,NA,NA,NA,NA,? (12)
Clear,'Available ',Low,High,Medium,NA,NA,NA,NA,NA,NA,NA,NA,NA,NA,NA,NA,NA,? (13)
Clear,'Available ',Low,High,Medium,NA,NA,NA,NA,NA,NA,NA,NA,NA,NA,NA,NA,NA,? (14)
'Not Clear','Not Available',High,High,Medium,NA,NA,NA,NA,NA,NA,NA,NA,NA,NA,NA,NA,NA,? (15)
'Not Clear','Not Available',High,High,Medium,NA,NA,NA,NA,NA,NA,NA,NA,NA,NA,NA,NA,NA,? (16)
'Not Clear','Not Available',High,Medium,High,NA,NA,NA,NA,NA,NA,NA,NA,NA,NA,NA,NA,NA,? (17)
'Not Clear','Not Available',High,Medium,High,NA,NA,NA,NA,NA,NA,NA,NA,NA,NA,NA,NA,NA,? (18)
'Not Clear','Not Available',High,High,High,NA,NA,NA,NA,NA,NA,NA,NA,NA,NA,NA,NA,NA,? (19)
'Not Clear','Not Available',High,High,High,NA,NA,NA,NA,NA,NA,NA,NA,NA,NA,NA,NA,? (20)
```

Table 12. Model prediction for test data

```
@data
Clear,'Not Available',Low,Low,Low,NA,NA,NA,NA,NA,NA,NA,NA,NA,NA,NA,NA,NA,'CODE & FIX',?
Clear,'Not Available',Low,Low,Low,NA,NA,NA,NA,NA,NA,NA,NA,NA,NA,NA,NA,NA,'CODE & FIX',?
Clear,'Not Available',Low,Low,Low,NA,NA,NA,NA,NA,NA,NA,NA,NA,NA,NA,NA,NA,'CODE & FIX',?
Clear,'Not Available',Low,Low,Low,NA,NA,NA,NA,NA,NA,NA,NA,NA,NA,NA,NA,NA,'CODE & FIX',?
Clear,'Available ',Medium,Low,Low,NA,NA,NA,NA,NA,NA,NA,NA,NA,NA,NA,NA,'CLASSICAL WATERFALL',?
Clear,'Available ',Medium,Low,Low,NA,NA,NA,NA,NA,NA,NA,NA,NA,NA,NA,NA,'CLASSICAL WATERFALL',?
Clear,'Available ',Medium,Low,Low,NA,NA,NA,NA,NA,NA,NA,NA,NA,NA,NA,NA,'CLASSICAL WATERFALL',?
Clear,'Available ',Medium,Low,Medium,NA,NA,NA,NA,NA,NA,NA,NA,NA,NA,NA,NA,'V SHAPED',?
Clear,'Available ',Medium,Low,Medium,NA,NA,NA,NA,NA,NA,NA,NA,NA,NA,NA,NA,'V SHAPED',?
'Not Clear','Not Available',High,Medium,Medium,NA,NA,NA,NA,NA,NA,NA,NA,NA,NA,NA,NA,NA,PROTOTYPING,?
'Not Clear','Not Available',High,Medium,Medium,NA,NA,NA,NA,NA,NA,NA,NA,NA,NA,NA,NA,NA,PROTOTYPING,?
'Not Clear','Not Available',High,Medium,Medium,NA,NA,NA,NA,NA,NA,NA,NA,NA,NA,NA,NA,NA,PROTOTYPING,?
Clear,'Available ',Low,High,Medium,NA,NA,NA,NA,NA,NA,NA,NA,NA,NA,NA,NA,RAD,?
Clear,'Available ',Low,High,Medium,NA,NA,NA,NA,NA,NA,NA,NA,NA,NA,NA,NA,'V SHAPED',?
'Not Clear','Not Available',High,High,Medium,NA,NA,NA,NA,NA,NA,NA,NA,NA,NA,NA,NA,'ITERATIVE/ INCREMENTAL',?
'Not Clear','Not Available',High,High,Medium,NA,NA,NA,NA,NA,NA,NA,NA,NA,NA,NA,NA,'ITERATIVE/ INCREMENTAL',?
'Not Clear','Not Available',High,Medium,High,NA,NA,NA,NA,NA,NA,NA,NA,NA,NA,NA,NA,SPIRAL,?
'Not Clear','Not Available',High,Medium,High,NA,NA,NA,NA,NA,NA,NA,NA,NA,NA,NA,NA,SPIRAL,?
'Not Clear','Not Available',High,High,High,NA,NA,NA,NA,NA,NA,NA,NA,NA,NA,NA,NA,AGILE,?
'Not Clear','Not Available',High,High,High,NA,NA,NA,NA,NA,NA,NA,NA,NA,NA,NA,NA,AGILE,?
```

Figure 10. Actual vs. predicted process model

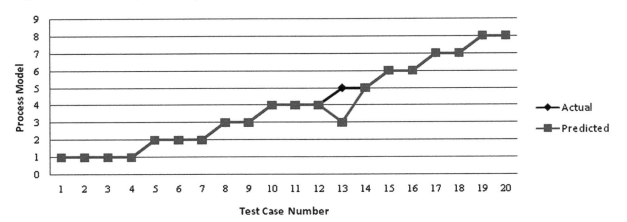

Table 13. Performance analysis of software process model using J-48 decision tree

Classification	Samples (Input 20 Samples)	Percentage
Correctly classified process model	19	95%
Misclassified process model	1	5%

SOLUTIONS AND RECOMMENDATIONS

The proposed system is used for prediction of more suitable software process model. Process model is selected on the basis of factors specified by the company. For instance, if the factors affecting the choice of software project along with its characteristic values are specified as in Table 14.

For the given scenario, prioritized factors viz., *ReqtUnderstandability* (requirement understandability and definition), *PredefinedReqt* (pre-defined requirements), *ComplexityReqd* (complexity defined by requirements), *ReqtAcceptance* (acceptance of requirement changes selected) and *ReqtFlexibility* (flexibility to change in requirements) are taken as input parameters and fuzzy values are assigned to each factor as shown in Table 15. These fuzzy values are given as the input to FIS "Model-Prediction" for predicting the most appropriate process model as output.

The FIS predicts the more suitable model for the given specifications as V-shaped model with fuzzy output as 0.315 which lies in the range specified for V-shaped model (0.252-0.377). This can also be verified by J-48 decision tree as well.

Henceforth, the developed system can be used in software companies to predict the more suitable process model by giving various factors as the input. This could be beneficial for software development and might reduce the risk of failure of software project because of the wrong decision made during the selection of software process model.

Table 14. Sample characteristic values

Factors	Characteristic Value
Requirement understandability and definition	Clear
Pre-defined requirements	Available
Complexity defined by requirements	Medium
Acceptance of requirement changes	Low
Flexibility to change in requirements	Medium
Customer involvement	Medium
Level of expected risk	Medium
Knowledge of application area	Medium
Level of reliability required	Medium
Project size	Medium
Project duration	Medium
Level of quality required	Medium
Ease of maintenance	Low
Experience of developers	Medium
Team size	Medium
Reusability of components	Low
Tools and technology availability	High
Product versions	Not Available

Table 15. Value of prioritized factors

Factor	Characteristic Value	Fuzzy Value
ReqtUnderstandability	Clear	2.07
PredefinedReqt	Available	2.09
ComplexityReqd	Medium	2.01
ReqtAcceptance	Low	1.80
ReqtFlexibility	Medium	1.90

RESULT ANALYSIS AND DISCUSSION

Selecting the most appropriate process model is a challenging task. In this study, the characteristic value of the prioritized factor, as given by the user is considered as input and on the basis of the rulesformed by the fuzzy logic; most appropriate process model is predicted. Using Fuzzy Approach, authors were able to classify correctly 17 samples out of 20 taken samples. The 3 failed samples had boundary values as their input data set. Therefore, a conclusion can be made that the fuzzy approach fails at boundary input values, which the major disadvantage.

Table 16. Comparison fuzzy approach vs. decision tree approach

Approach	Input Sample	Classified Sample	Classification Percentage
Fuzzy	20	17	85
Decision Tree	20	19	95

The drawback of fuzzy approach is overcome by adopting decision tree. Out of 20 samples, 19 samples were successfully predicted. Samples, whose prediction failed in the case of fuzzy technique, were successfully predicted in this approach. However, failure of 1 samplewas because of some discrepancy in training data set which can be avoided easily. Decision tree for a set of data is not unique resulting to various rules set and finding the best tree becomes a NP Hard problem.

The classification percentage of both these approaches is tabulated in Table 16.

Since the classification rate of both the approaches in high as seen from Figure 11, we can conclude that both the approaches predicted equally well.

FUTURE RESEARCH DIRECTIONS

This proposed work can be used to develop a tool to determine the most applicable process model for a given project scenario which can be used for industrial purposes. Since in the proposed framework, input parameters (factor's characteristic value) are given by the user .This can be automated in such a way that after collecting all the requirements from the client, information can be inferred from the given scenario. This will reduce the manual work of collecting factors from the client .With the developed framework, a process model can be properly selected for a project without manual intervention, further decreasing the failure rate of the project. After selecting an appropriate model from the developed framework, it could benefit naïve users, new joiners and project managers in the process of software development by increasing the success rate of the project.

Figure 11. (a)Correctly vs. incorrectly classified samples; (b) classification percentage

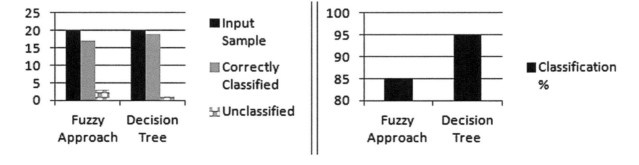

CONCLUSION

The overall aim of this study is to provide factors as a guide to choose process model for each particular project. The chosen process model can be used to provide the reasonable guidance to the software development team. In software development, all the factors identified can play an important role. This chapter introduced fuzzy interface system for prediction of process model on the basis of certain rules. We observed that it provides misclassification at boundary values hence to bring more accuracy to proposed automated framework for process model prediction J-48 decision tree was used. The main disadvantage of this approach is inflexibility at modeling parameter space distribution. In future we can use either neural networks or genetic algorithm for modeling purpose. However, the proposed framework can be used to increase the success rate of software project.

REFERENCES

Aggarwal, K. K., & Singh, Y. (2007). *Software Engineering* (3rd ed.). New Age International Publishers.

Alshamrani, A., & Bahattab, A. (2015). *A Comparison between Three SDLC Models Waterfall Model* (Vol. 12). Spiral Model, and Incremental/Iterative Model. In IJCSI International Journal of Computer Science Issues.

Archibald, D. R. (2003). *Life cycle models for high technology projects-applying systems thinking to project.* Retrieved from: http://russarchibald.com/recent-papers-presentations/other-pm-subjects/models-hitech-syst-slides/

Archibald, D. R. (2004). *State of the art of project management. In Proceedings of the International Seminar on Project Management.* Retrieved from: http://russarchibald.com/recent-papers-presentations/state-of-the-art/

Archibald, D. R., & Voropaev, I. V. (2003). *Commonalities and differences in project management around the world: A survey of project categories and life cycle models.* Retrieved from: http://russarchibald.com/Commonalities_and_Differences_paper_May_3_03.pdf

Archibald, D. R., & Voropaev, I. V. (2004). Project categories and life cycle models: Report on the 2003 IPMA Global Survey. In *Proceedings of the 18th IPMA World Congress on Project Management*, (pp: 1-6).

Bhattacherjee, V., Neogi, M., & Mahanti, R. (2007). Software Development Patterns in University Setting: A Case Study. In *Proceedings of the national seminar on Recent Advances on Information Technology, ISM Dhanbad*, (pp. 40-43).

Bhattacherjee, V., Neogi, M. S., & Mahanti, R. (2008). Software Development Approach of Students: An Evaluation. In *Proceedings of the national conference on Methods and Models in Computing (NCM2C)*, (pp 23-30).

Davis, A. M., Bersoff, E. H., & Comer, E. R. (1988). A strategy for comparing alternative software development life cycle models. *IEEE Transactions on Software Engineering*, *14*(10), 453–1461. doi:10.1109/32.6190

Desaulniers, H., Douglas, A., & Robert, J. (2001). Matching software development life cycles to the project environment. In *Proceedings of the Project Management Institute Annual Seminars and Symposium.*

Durrant, B. (2015). *WEKA.* Retrieved October 26, 2015, from http://www.cs.waikato.ac.nz/ml/weka/

Garcia-Diaz., Lopez-Martin, & Chavoya. (2013). A comparative study of two fuzzy logic models for software development effort estimation. In *Iberoamerican Conference on Electronics Engineering and Computer Science.* Elsevier.

Ghezzi, C., Jazayeri, M., & Mandrioli, D. (2002). *Fundamentals of Software Engineering* (2nd ed.). India: Prentice-Hall.

Jalote, P. (2005). *An Integrated Approach to Software Engineering* (3rd ed.). Springer.

Karmyal, A. (2015). *Software Process Model.* Retrieved October 20, 2015, from http://www.slideshare. net/AtulKarmyal/software-process-models-29514469

Mahanti, R., & Neogi, M. S. (2012). *Vandana Bhattacherjee* (Vol. 8). Factors Affecting the Choice of Software Life Cycle Models in the Software Industry-An Empirical Study. In Journal of Computer Science.

Mishra, A., & Dubey, D. (2013). *A Comparative Study of Different Software Development Life Cycle Models in Different Scenarios* (Vol. 1). InInternational Journal of Advance Research in Computer Science and Management Studies.

Neogi, M., Chakraborty, S., & Bhattacherjee, V. (2013). Factors Influencing Software Development Process: A statistical Outlook. *InInternational Journal of Software Engineering and Its Applications,* 7(6), 221–236. doi:10.14257/ijseia.2013.7.6.19

Neogi, M. S., Bhattacherjee, V., & Mahanti, R. (2009). An Evaluation of Student Preferences during Software Development. In *Proceedings of national seminar on Recent Advances Information Technology (RAIT),* (pp. 239-245).

Pressman, R. (2004). *Software Engineering: A Practitioner's Approach* (6th ed.). McGraw Hill.

Rastogi, V. (2015). Software Development Life Cycle Models- Comparison, Consequences. *International Journal of Computer Science and Information Technologies.*

Richard, L. (1996). *Methods for Classification.* Retrieved October 20, 2015, from http://sundog.stsci. edu/rick/SCMA/node2.html

Shradhanand, Kaur, & Jain. (2007). Use of Fuzzy Logic in Software Development. *Issues in Information Systems,* 8(2).

Sram, N. (2011). Practical Application of Fuzzy Logic from Software Engineering Point of View. *Óbuda University e-Bulletin,* 2(1).

Thakurta, R. (2011). Influence of Process Models on Requirement Volatility, and Strategies for its Management – An Empirical Investigation. *CLEI Electronic Journal,* 14(2).

Thirugnanam, M., & Margret Anouncia, S. (2014). An integrated approach for feature extractionand defect detection in industrial radiographicimages – case study on welding defects. *Int. J. Industrial and Systems Engineering, 17*.

Ziauddin, K. S., Khan, S., & Nasir, J. (2013). A Fuzzy Logic Based Software Cost Estimation Model. International Journal of Software Engineering and Its Applications, 7(2).

KEY TERMS AND DEFINITIONS

Classification: A data mining algorithm that creates a step-by-step guide to determine the output of a new data instance.

Defuzzification: Translating the membership degree of fuzzy sets into a particular choice or real value.

Fuzzy Inference: A procedure of mapping from a given input to output utilizing fuzzy logic. The mapping then gives the premise from which choices can be made, or patterns observed. The procedure of fuzzy inference includes membership functions, fuzzy logic operators and if- then rules.

Fuzzy Logic: A way of reasoning that resembles human reasoning. The methodology of FL impersonates the method of decision making in humans that involves all intermediate possibilities between digital values YES and NO.

J-48 Decision Tree: A predictive machine-learning model that chooses the target value (dependent variable) of a new sample based on various attribute values of the available data.

Preprocessing: A data mining technique that includes changing from raw data into an understandable format.

Process Model: Describes the sequence of phases for the entire lifetime of a product (also called as product life cycle).

WEKA: Waikato Environment for Knowledge Analysis is a workbench which consists of an accumulation of visualization tools and algorithms for data analysis and predictive modeling, together with graphical client interfaces for simple access to these functions.

APPENDIX

Survey Form is attached in Figure 12.

Figure 12. Survey form

A	B	C	D	E	F	G	H	I	J
Rating (1-5)	Factors	Code and Fix	Waterfall Model	V-Shaped Model	Prototyping Model	Incremental-Iterative Model	Spiral Model	RAD Model	Agile Model
	Acceptance of requirement changes								
	Tools and technology availability								
	Complexity defined by requirements								
	Customer involvement								
	Ease of maintenance								
	Experience of developers								
	Flexibility to change in requirements								
	Level of expected risk								
	Level of quality required								
	Level of reliability required								
	Knowledge of application area								
	Pre-defined requirements								
	Project duration								
	Project size								
	Requirement understandability and definition								
	Reusability of components								
	Team size								
	Product versions								

Chapter 19
Investment Climate Factors with Reference to Firm Performance in Bangladesh:
A Prospective Cohort Study

Farhana Ferdousi
East West University, Bangladesh

Arun Kumar Sangaiah
VIT University, India

ABSTRACT

A productive investment climate is key to the growth of any developing country. Given the limited literature and importance of economic zone in attracting FDI, this paper conducts a study on the Export Processing Zone to provide an insight into the investment climate factors and its association with firms' performance. A total of 30 firms were chosen from the garment industry, in particular from the EPZ of Bangladesh. Findings reveal that all six factors were considered as important indicators affecting investment climate of EPZ firms. Moreover, five factors were found to be significantly associated with the firm performance. An important implication of the findings is that government and garment associations can get an important insights into the factors that are critical to the investment climate and accordingly take necessary steps to arrange better utilities provide sound governance, improve credit facilities, ensure a favorable trade union together with other infrastructural facilities that require for creating better investment climate for both the EPZ and non-EPZ firms.

INTRODUCTION

While developing countries as a group have certain similarities in terms of living standards, level of labour productivity, rate of population growth, and the degree of market failure and economic power, they vary in terms of political conditions, infrastructural development, and other development indicators

DOI: 10.4018/978-1-5225-1008-6.ch019

such as imports and export growth (Mersha, 1997).Due to these differences, the investment climate[1] also differs between the developing countries. While a suitable investment environment is especially important to attract investors, the EPZs'[2] in developing country like Bangladesh have been successful in attracting Foreign Direct Investment (FDI)[3] primarily in ready-made garments. EPZs are essential part of Bangladesh economy (Bhuiya et al., 2014). A review of literature indicates that the companies operating in the EPZs'in Bangladesh are achieving several benefits over the companies out of the EPZ (Ferdousi, 2009) because of its internationally competitive duty-free environment for export production at low cost. The especial support from the government in terms of modern infrastructure, utilities, tax facilities enable them to perform better and attract more investors than the non-EPZ firms However, while EPZs of Bangladesh are performing well compared to some developing countries, they are lagging behind in respect to the investment growth and other performance indicators of the EPZ's of some other developing countries (Abdin, 2014).

This situation therefore, raises a fundamental question as to what factors influencing the investment climate of EPZ firms in Bangladesh. In line with this, previous studies have focused on the investment climate factors from both country level and firm level perspectives (Kinda et al., 2011; Aterido et al., 2010; Kee, 2005; World Bank and BEI, 2003; Dollar et al., 2003). There is only a limited study that have focused on this issue in respect to firms operating in EPZ, particularly in garment industry (Aggarwal, 2005). While some case studies (Watson 2001; Subramanian & Roy 2001; Madani 1999; Hinkle et al. 2003; Ferrerosa 2003; OTA 2003) conducted in EPZ in respect to the success and failure of this zone, there are only a limited empirical study (Aggarwal, 2005) focused on EPZ in respect to investment climate. Given the limited study, this study therefore, aims to empirically examine the factors that influence the investment climate and its association with performance in respect to the garment firms operating in eight EPZs of Bangladesh.

A growing number of research have examined the factors that affect investment climate(Kinda et al., 2011; Aterido et al., 2010; Kee, 2005; World Bank and BEI, 2003; Dollar et al. 2003), mainly focused on factors such as taxes & regulations, financing, policy instability, inflation, exchange rate, corruption, street crime, anti-competitive practice, organized crime, infrastructure, judicial system and service climate (Sangaiah et al. 2015; Sangaiah and Thangavelu, 2014; Kinda et al., 2011; Kee, 2005; World Bank and BEI, 2003, Dollar et al. 2003; World Bank Report, 2004; World Bank, 2001).This study examining six factors affecting investment climate including human resource, access to finance, infrastructure, power and energy, governance and trade union in the context of EPZ firms. These factors do not represent a comprehensive list of factors affecting the investment climate, but were chosen because they have been suggested in different studies.

While the researches that have examined the association of investment climate factors with organizational performance, such studies have generally measured performance in terms of sales growth, profitability growth, productivity improvement, investment growth (Kinda et al., 2011; Pernia & Salas, 2006; World Bank and BEI, 2003). For instance, Becket al. (2005) and Galindo and Micco (2005) have examined the critical role of access to finance on the growth of firm. Similarly, Djankov et al (2003) and Klapper et al. (2004) investigate the effect of entry regulations of firms on firm performance. In order to further contribute to the literature, this study has chosen three constructs to measure performance including increase in profit, sales growth and investment growth. Therefore, this study further contributes to the literature theorizing how each of the investment climate factors contribute in achieving firms' performance in the context of EPZs' in Bangladesh.

In a summary, the following research objectives are developed:

1. To examine the key contributing factors to the investment climate in the EPZ garment firms.
2. To examine the impact of investment climate on performance in the EPZ garment firms.

LITERATURE REVIEW AND HYPOTHESIS DEVELOPMENT

Factors Contributing to the Investment Climate

A good number of literatures (Kinda et al., 2011; Aterido et al., 2010; World Bank Report, 2004; Dollar et al.2003)are available on factors associated to investment climate. This section will focus on few of the literatures with particular relevance. For instance, a study by World Bank (2001) identified four factors essential for any investment such as stability & security, regulation & taxation, finance & infrastructure, and workers & labor markets. In a later study by World Bank, reports some general investment climate determinants based on 26,000 firms in 53 countries, which includes policy uncertainty, macro-economic instability, tax rate, corruption, cost and access to finance, crime, regulations & tax administration, skills level, court& legal system, electricity, labor regulations, transportations, and access to land and telecommunications (World Bank Reports, 2004). In line with this, Kinda et al. (2011) conducted study on five Middle East and North African (MENA) economies and eight manufacturing industries. This study points out some factors that influence investment climate including the quality of infrastructure, the experience and education of the labour force, the cost and access to financing, and different dimensions of the government-business relationship. Selected ASEAN countries in a study found infrastructure, quality of service, innovation, labor skills, access to finance, and red tape as contributing factors to the investment climate.

According to the American Center (2004),the essential factors for a good investment climate indicates the openness to foreign investment, conversion & transfer of policies, expropriation & conversion, dispute settlement, performance requirements & incentives, right to private ownership & establishment, protection of property rights, transparency of regulatory system, efficient capital markets & portfolio investment, political violence, corruption, bilateral investment agreements, labor, and foreign or free trade zones. This study aims to further contribute to the literature by examining six factors (governance, infrastructure, access to finance, power and energy, human resource and trade union) contributing to the investment climate of the EPZ garment firms of Bangladesh.

The Association of Investment Climate Factors on Firm Performance

Human Resources

The foreign investors facilitate the developing countries with skills and knowledge using more skill incentive labor. The foreign firms with new products or processes facilitate the domestic firms through providing benefits of new technologies (Teece, 1997). The investment climate factor such as human resource means the labor force with adequate skill, knowledge and technological know-how (Dollar et al., 2003). Investors like to invest in locations with abundant skilled workers and advanced technology.

It is revealed that skilled workers in terms of skilled in physical and technological know- how such as use of computer, knowledge in R& D influence firms' performance positively (Jafari et al., 2009).

H1: Skilled human resource is associated with firm's performance.

Access to Finance

Availability of finance is a critical factor that influences the investment climate. Countries with well-developed financial systems (banks, stock and bond markets) have faster growth than countries those have less developed systems (World Bank and BEI, 2003). A review of literature reveal the association of well-functioning financial systems to firms' performance (World Bank, 2001). Aterido et al.(2007) stressed that the constraints on access and cost to finance have direct associated with firms' performance. They mentioned that the low access to finance is negatively associated with firma performance (Aterido et al., 2007). The availability of financial tool including overdraft facilities is found have positive association with firm performance (Dollar et al. 2003).

H2: Better access to finance is associated with firm's performance.

Infrastructure

According to the study by World Bank and BEI (2003), infrastructure refers the quality and quantity of physical infrastructure including power, transport and telecommunications and the financial infrastructure (such as banking). Pernia and Salas (2006) mentioned infrastructure as the availability and quality of transportation (roads and ports), telecommunication, power and water supply. The World Bank and BEI (2003) found the association between infrastructure and firm performance. This study reveals that poor infrastructure requires more resources to develop and distribute a product which in turn reduces the firm's competitiveness. Aterido et al.(2007) mentioned that the poor infrastructure affects firms' performance (Aterido et al., 2007).Dollar et al. (2003) also found an association between infrastructures in terms of custom clearance time for exports with profit.

H3: Better infrastructure is associated with firm's performance.

Power and Energy

Dollar et al. (2003) stressed the importance of power and energy in respect to firms' performance. The World Bank and BEI (2003) study reveals that the firms' performance is critically associated with power and energy in terms of quality of the service and in connecting to utilities. Aterido et al., (2007) mentioned that the losses associated with the power outages affect firms' performance. Moreover, the interrupted power affects the production processes, thereby increasing defects rate in turn affecting performance. It is revealed that the total cost of power interruption is affecting the activities of a firm (Ahsan, 2004) thereby reducing profit.

H4: Better power and energy is associated with firms' performance.

Governance

The review of literature reveals that the quality of governance have strong effect on the level and nature of firm performance (Emery, 2003; Kaufmann, et al.,1999; Knack and Keefer, 1995). For example, the efforts to improve governance in the investment climate have often focused on reducing the bribe paid by firms to public officials (Desai and Pradhan, 2005). A number of studies have validated the critical role of corruption in investment climate (Emery, 2003). Kaufmann, et al. (1999)and Knack and Keefer, (1995) have mentioned that the investment climate factors including corruption is associated with firms' performance. Stern (2002) noted that governance and institutions have large effect on the expected productivity and returns on investment. He stressed that the poor governance is directly associated with firm's performance (Stern, 2002). In the similar vein, Jafari et al. (2009) showed the direct association of administrative barriers and corruption with the sales growth.

H5: Increased governance has negative impact on firm's performance.

Trade Union

A culture of mistrust and credibility gap violated the work culture which led the formation of workers' trade union to look after the interest of the working class (Singh, 2005). A review of literature mentioned that if the trade union in a firm boost up pay, financial performance is likely to be affected (Metcalf, 2002). Metcalf (2002) mentioned that the trade union affects profitability and investment. Hirsch (1997) stressed the effect of trade union on firms' performance. He mentioned that collective bargaining is associated with lower profitability, decreased investment, and sales growth.

H6: Trade union has a negative impact on firm's performance.

METHOD

Given the important role of EPZ in the economy of Bangladesh, this study conducted a survey on eight EPZ's of Bangladesh. In late 1970s, EPZ emerged to attract capital investment in the country. The Government of Bangladesh is very strongly committed to developing the economic policy for both public and private sector industrial development. The promotion of EPZ has been widely accepted as an economic development strategy. It has been realized that through that strategy Bangladesh has been able to attract sufficient foreign investment, contribute to employment generation and enhance export earnings of the country (Quddus, 2000).

A survey questionnaire was mailed to the business unit manager of79EPZ garment firms in eight EPZ zones. The lists of firms were randomly chosen from the Bangladesh Export Processing Zone Authority (BEPZA). A total of 30 responses were received for a response rate of 38% (see Appendix (Table 5 – Table 10). EPZ was chosen because of its important contribution to the country's economy. EPZ is considered as special zone that provide crucial advantages to the country in attracting foreign investors (Bhuyian et al. 2014). Six measures of investment climate were drawn from the results of previous research studies (Pernia and Salas, 2005; World Bank and BEI 2003; Hall and Jones, 1999; World Bank, 2001; World Bank Report, 2004). A five-point Likert scale was used to measure the items of independent variables where 1 was "strongly disagree" and 5 was "strongly agree". Dependent variables (firm performance) were measured using a ratio scale. The questionnaire was also consists of some open ended questions to obtain a detail view on the factors in the study. In the case of validity issue, the study has used content validity. The survey response indicates, among the 30 respondents majority (64%) were managing director, (13%) were export/import manager, (12%) were commercial manager and (11%) were other managers (Table 1).

Findings

Descriptive Statistics

Table 2 shows the summary descriptive statistics for the independent and dependent variables. The mean values indicate the extent of presence of factors that contribute to the investment climate of EPZ firms. All the Cronbach alpha coefficients exceeded the 0.70 threshold considered acceptable for scale reliability (Nunnally, 1978, p.245).

Contributing Factors to the Investment Climate

Regarding the human resource, the firms fairly agreed on having necessary skills and technological know-how to perform at the desired level. In line with this, the managers mention that while qualified and trained employees are prerequisites for EPZ firms, there is a scarcity of such skilled workers. Usually, the firms recruit workers those meet a certain qualification level and later arrange necessary training based on the given task. Other than the floor level workers, the managerial people showed to have necessary skills and adequate knowledge regarding technologies and access to internet to deal with customers and

Table 1. Descriptive statistics

EPZ Firms	DEPZ	CEPZ	Mongla	Comilla	Uttara	Ishwardi	Adamjee	Karnaphuli
N=30	9	8	3	2	2	3	3	1
% of respondents	64% (Managing Director)		13% (Export/Import Manager)		12% (Commercial Manager)		11% (Other Manager)	

Table 2. Descriptive statistics

	N	Mean	SD	Cronbach Alpha
Human resource	30	4.31	0.66	0.84
Access to finance	30	3.46	0.83	0.87
Power and energy	30	4.40	0.61	0.72
Infrastructure	30	3.74	0.77	0.72
Governance	30	3.69	0.86	0.93
Trade union	30	3.03	1.35	0.96
Organizational performance	30	3.03	1.18	0.88

suppliers. From an additional question, it was unveiled that the EPZ firms highly emphasize on skills and capabilities of workers to attract FDI and to compete in the competitive market.

An important indicator of investment climate is the easy access to finance. The findings indicate that the EPZ firms have good access to finance and they are largely dependent on banks. Findings reveal that the firms are less dependent on retained earnings for both working capital and new investment. Moreover, firms agreed to have more use of line of credit facilities with a small percentage agreed to have bank overdraft facilities. However, it is also unveiled that the EPZ firms have greater access to banks than the firms' operating outside of the EPZ. Moreover, respondents mentioned that the firms' access to banks and other financial sources greatly depends on the personal relationship with the concerned banks. The World Bank and BEI (2003) study also claimed that Bangladeshi firms tend to have reasonable access to finance compared to other low-income countries.

In response to the power and energy problem, the EPZ firms reported it as a moderate problem. Because of the special utility facilities provided by the government to the EPZ areas, they found to have advantages over the non-EPZ firms such as built-in electricity connection. Despite having separate electricity connection, a large number of respondents agreed to have alternative electricity arrangement which incurs additional cost to them. A larger percentage of respondents also agreed to have energy problem. From an additional question it is unveiled that the electricity problem is more acute in firms operating outside of the EPZ.

Another important indicator of investment climate is the infrastructure. The infrastructure is indicated as the availability of water supply and port problem. All respondents agreed to have adequate supply of water in EPZ and they do not need to depend on public water supply. The further question reveals that in respect to water supply, the EPZ firms are enjoying Water Treatment Facilities. They also agreed, while non- EPZ firms' mostly depend on their own arrangement of tube well and public water supply; the EPZ firms are facilitated with the special water facilities. In response to the port problem, half of the respondents agreed that the arrival of goods to the point of entry and customs clearance takes long time which acts as an obstacle. Moreover, few respondents were reported on having port problem during the time of export and import.

The previous study by World Bank and BEI(2003)shows corruption as a problem to the firms' performance. In response to a question, it was observed that the respondents were reluctant to respond on this issue. While a large percentage of respondents agreed on informal payment to obtain several services from the government officials, respondents also mentioned the non-difficulties in obtaining export permission. Moreover, finding reveals that while the non-EPZ firms' deals with high governance problem, EPZ firms have fewer problems in this respect.

Result also suggests that a large percentage of firms have participation in trade union. Finding shows that the respondents agreed to have substantial impact of trade union on their business.

Association of Investment Climate Factors on Firms' Performance

Findings (Table 3) reveal that while the investment climate factors including human resource, access to finance, power and energy, and infrastructure have positive correlation (r) with the overall firms' performance where (r =.211), (r =.737), (r =.203) and (r =.142), the governance and trade union are negatively correlated to the firms' performance where (r = -.269) and (r = -.193) respectively.

Results in Table 4Figure 1 expressed the multiple regressions for investment climate as independent and the firms' performance as dependent variable. There is no co-linearity problem found in the model.

Table 3. Correlation between investment climate and firm's performance

	Human Resource	Access to Finance	Power and Energy	Infrastructure	Governance	Trade Union
Firms' Performance	.211	.737	.203	.142	-.269	-.193
Sig. (2-tailed)	.264	.000	.281	.454	.150	.308
N	30	30	30	30	30	30

*. Correlation is significant at the 0.05 level (2-tailed).

The adjusted $R^2 = 61.80$ indicates the combined contribution of investment climate factors. This suggests that human resource, access to finance, power and energy, infrastructure, governance and trade union are a good set of determinants of investment climate. Table 4 shows the individual contribution of investment climate factors on firms' performance. Finding reveals that human resource (β=.310, p=.04) is positively associated with firms' performance, thereby supporting hypothesis 1. Moreover, findings also showed the positive association of access to finance (β=.766, p=.000), and power and energy (β=.335, p=.032) with firms' performance, thereby supporting hypotheses 2 and 4. There is no significant association found between the infrastructure with firms' performance (β = .020, p=.889). Therefore, rejecting hypothesis 3. On the other hand, both governance (β= -.225, p=.049) and trade union (β= -.335, p=.045) showed negative association with the firms' performance, thereby supporting hypotheses 5 and 6.

Overall the findings of the study indicate that the investment climate factors are correlated to firms' performance. Investment climate factors such as human resource, access to finance, power and energy and infrastructure have positive correlation with the firms' performance which suggests that improvement of any one of this will improve the firms' performance. On the other hand, governance and trade union are negatively correlated to the firms' performance which means that increase of these factors will cause a decrease in firms' performance.

Table 3 indicates that, human resource, access to finance, power and energy, infrastructure, governance and trade union are the best set of contributing factors on contributing to firm's performance. The findings also show that investment climate factors exist in the EPZ in Bangladesh and that they are not only correlated but also contribute to the firms' performance.

Table 4. The association between investment climate factors and firm performance

Variables	Standardized Coefficient	Sig	Tolerance	VIF
Human resource	.310	.040	.64	1.54
Access to finance	.766	.000	.81	1.23
Power and energy	.335	.032	.61	1.63
Infrastructure	.020	.889	.67	1.47
Governance	-.225	.049	.88	1.13
Trade union	-.336	.045	.52	1.90

R Square=0.697
Adjusted R Square=0.618
*Significance at the 0.05 level **significant at 0.01 level

Figure 1. Research framework: association between investment climate factors and firms' performance

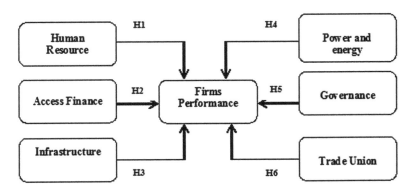

DISCUSSION AND CONCLUSION

The study had two objectives. The first objective was to examine the key contributing factors to the investment climate in the EPZ garment firms of Bangladesh. The findings indicate that all six investment climate factors (human resource, access to finance, infrastructure, power and energy, governance, trade union) are critical indicators of investment climate in the EPZ firms. While some factors are found to have positive contribution, some have negative effect to the investment climate of this sector. The firms agreed to have skilled human resources which is critical to attract FDI and to compete within the local and foreign market. In line with this, firms should arrange regular training and education programs, thereby continuously enhancing the skills and capabilities that would facilitate firms to perform better. In respect to the access to finance, the firms agreed to have better access to bank. This finding suggests that if government ensure adequate credit arrangement, firms can invest more in adopting sophisticated technologies and machineries to operate more effectively, thereby attracting more investors and perform better than other countries.

The findings also highlight the factors that contributing negatively to the investment climate of the EPZ firms. In spite of having separate electricity connection, the firms reported to have difficulties to some extent. Due to the interrupted power supply the firms incurs additional cost of labor wages as well as electricity bill. These problems are causing decrease in desired profit. In line with this, the government should take necessary steps to minimize the power interruption, thereby improving the performance of firms. Moreover, findings reveal that the firms have especial Water Treatment Facilities arranged by the BEPZA which acts as an advantage for the EPZ firms compared to the non-EPZ firms.

In respect to governance, findings showed that firms give bribe to get services from the government officials. If government ensure strict accountability of the responsible person dealing with these issues, will eventually minimize the corruption, thereby improving investment climate. Moreover, the findings indicate participation of firms in trade union as a negative contributing factor to the investment climate. Therefore, the garment association such as BEPZA can play a vital role to ensure a better outcome from the trade union.

The second objective of the study was to provide an insight into the association of investment climate factors with firms' performance. The results showed a significant positive association between three investment climate factors (human resource, access to finance, power and energy, and infrastructure) and negative association between two factors such as governance and trade union with firms' performance highlighting the importance of skilled employees, easy credit facilities, and uninterrupted power supply, improved governance and favorable trade union practices to improve firms' performance. In line with this, it is recommended that the garment associations in collaboration with the government must have to develop meaningful strategies in respect to the improvements in all these factors to ensure a better investment climate.

Overall, findings reveal that while the firms are enjoying benefits to some extent in terms of skilled employees, access to bank and line of credit facilities, Water Treatment Facilities, less trouble in obtaining export permission, they suffers from delay in traffic to transfer goods from one place to another, high trucking cost due to the rented transport, informal payment for get things done from the government officials, and disruption in power to some extent.

This study results has some implications. The garment firms of both the EPZ and non-EPZ can develop an insight into the factors that support or inhibit the investment climate of this sector. Moreover, government and garment associations can obtain an important insights into the factors that are critical to the investment climate and accordingly take necessary steps to arrange better utilities (power and energy), provide sound governance, improve overdraft facilities, ensure a favorable trade union together with other infrastructural facilities that require to create better investment climate for the zones, thereby enabling to improve performance of firms and attract more foreign investors in this sector.

LIMITATIONS AND FUTURE DIRECTIONS

The study has certain limitations. First, questionnaires were distributed through mail survey which causes problems in identifying the person who actually fills the questionnaire. Secondly, the study is conducted on a small sample size. Future studies may conduct on a large sample using surveys, interviews and longitudinal study. Looking to the future there are a number of directions for further work. First, it will be useful to measure investment climate and performance for sectors other than garments in the EPZ and outside of the EPZ to confirm whether investment climate have effects on performance. Second, as more data are collected it will be possible to get a better fix on exactly which aspects of the investment climate factors are important. Thirdly, a comparative study can be conducted among the eight EPZs' of Bangladesh to find individual performance of zones.

REFERENCES

Abdin, M.J. (2014, February 3). Political Stability Key to Improving Investment Climate. *The Financial Express*.

Aggarwal, A. (2005). *Performance of Export Processing Zones: A Comparative Analysis of India, Sri Lanka and Bangladesh*. Working paper. Indian Council for Research on International Economics Relations. Retrieved from www.icrer.org

Ahsan, Q. (2004). Evaluation of Power Interruption Cost for Residential and Industrial Sector. *Journal of Energy and Environment*, *3*, 119–131.

Aterido, R., Driemeier, M. H., & Pages, C. (2007). *Investment Climate and Employment Growth: The Impact of Access to Finance, Corruption and Regulations across Firms.* Discussion Paper Series, IZA DP No. 3138.

Beck, T., Demirgüç-Kunt, A., & Maksimovic, V. (2005). Financial and Legal Constraints to Growth: Does Firm Size Matter? *The Journal of Finance, 60*(1), 131–177. doi:10.1111/j.1540-6261.2005.00727.x

Djankov, S., La Porta, R., Lopez-de-Silanes, F., & Shleifer, A. (2002). The Regulation of Entry. *The Quarterly Journal of Economics, 117*(1), 1–37. doi:10.1162/003355302753399436

Dollar, D., Driemeier, M. H., & Mengiote, T. (2003). *Investment Climate and Firm Performance in Developing Economics. Development Research Group.* World Bank.

Dollar, D., Driemeier, M. H., & Mengiote, T. (2003). Investment Climate and Firm Performance in Developing Economics. *Economic Development and Cultural Change, 54*(1).

Eusuf, M.A., Faruque, M. A. & Rahman, A. (2007). *Institutions for Facilitating FDI: Issues for BEPZA, Bangladesh, CUTS International.* IPPG Briefing Paper, No. Tens In Conjunction with CUTS International.

Ferdousi, F. (2009). An Investigation of Manufacturing Performance Improvement through Lean Production: A Case Study on Bangladesh Garment Firms. *International Journal of Business and Management, 4*(9). doi:10.5539/ijbm.v4n9p106

FIAS & SEDF. (2006). *Piloting Reform through the Development and Management of Economic Zones.* Bangladesh: World Bank.

Galindo, A., & Micco, A. (2005). *Bank Credit to Small and Medium-Sized Enterprises: The Role of Creditor Protection.* Research Department Working Paper 527. Washington, DC: Inter-American Development Bank.

Hall, R. E., & Jones, C. (1999). Why Do Some Countries Produce So Much More Output per Worker than Others? *The Quarterly Journal of Economics, 114*(1), 83–116. doi:10.1162/003355399555954

Hallward, D., Wallsten, S., & Xu, L. C. (2003). *The Investment Climate and the Firm: Firm-Level Evidence from China.* Policy Research Working Paper. World Bank.

Hirsch. (1997). Unionization and Economic Performance: Evidence on Productivity, Profits, Investment, and Growth. In *Unions and Right-to-Work Laws.* The Fraser Institute.

Hossain, M. Z. (n.d.). *Export Diversification and Role of Export Processing Zones in Bangladesh.* Dhaka: Bangladesh EPZ Authority (BEPZA).

Jafari, H., Fishpaw, J., & Li, L. (2009). *The Investment Climate in the China and the Importance of Firm-Level Data.* Shanta Cruz, CA: University of California.

Kaufmann, D., Kraay, A., & Zoido-Lobatón, P. (1999). *Governance Matters.* Policy Research Working Paper 2196. World Bank.

Kee, H. L. (2005). Foreign Ownership and Bangladesh Garment Sector. Development Research Group-Trade, the World Bank.

Khan, M. H. (2005). *What is a "Good Investment Climate"*. The International Bank for Reconstruction and Development/The World Bank.

Kinda, T. (2011). Firm Productivity and Investment Climate in Developing Countries: How Does Middle East and North African Manufacturing Performance? CERDI. *Eludes et Documents. E (Norwalk, Conn.)*, 26.

Klapper, L., Laeven, L., & Rajan, R. G. (2004). *Business Environment and Firm Entry: Evidence from International Data*. NBER Working Paper 10380. Cambridge, MA: National Bureau of Economic Research.

Knack, S., & Keefer, P. (1995). Institutions and Economic Performance: Cross-Country Tests Using Alternative Institutional Measures. *Economics and Politics*, 7(3), 207–227. doi:10.1111/j.1468-0343.1995. tb00111.x

Krisher, T. (2011). *AutoNation Profit Up 26 Percent as Sales Rise.* Accessed May 29, 2011, articles. sfgate.com/…/29477879_1_new-vehicle-ceo-mike-jackson-autonation

Lansbury, M., & Mayes, D. (1996). Entry, Exit, Ownership and the Growth of Productivity. In D. Mayes (Ed.), *Sources of Productivity Growth*. Cambridge, UK: Cambridge University Press.

Metcalf, D. (2003). Unions Impact and Implications for Future Membership. In P. Gregg & J. Wadsworth (Eds.), The State of Working Britain (2nd ed.). Academic Press.

Muttakin, M.B. & Ahmed, S. (2005). The Investment Scenario in Bangladesh- Problems and Prospects. *Pakistan Journal of Social Sciences, 3*(4).

NCAER. (2010). *Investment Climate, Physical and Economic Infrastructure.* Access on 3/7/2010 from http://www.ncaer.org/researcho2.html

Nunnally, J. C. (1978). *Psychometric Theory*. New York: McGrew Hill.

OECD. (2008). *Benchmark Definition of Foreign Direct Investment* (4th ed.). www.oecd.org/publishing/ connigenda

Pernia, E. M., & Salas, I. S. (2005). *Investment Climate and Regional Development in the Philippines.* Discussion Paper No. 0501. University of the Philippines School of Economics, Quezon City.

Pernia, E. M., & Salas, J. M. I. S. (2006). Investment Climate, Productivity and Regional Development in a Developing Country. *Asian Development Review*, 23(2), 70–89.

Quddus, M., & Rashid, S. (2000). *Entrepreneurs and Economic Development: The Remarkable Story of Garment Exports from Bangladesh*. Dhaka: The University Press.

Rahman. (2008). Globalization and the Climate of Foreign Direct Investment: A Case for Bangladesh. *Journal of Money, Investment and Banking,* (5).

Sangaiah, A. K., & Thangavelu, A. K. (2014). An adaptive neuro-fuzzy approach to evaluation of team-level service climate in GSD projects. *Neural Computing & Applications*, 25(3-4), 573–583. doi:10.1007/ s00521-013-1521-9

Sangaiah, A. K., Thangavelu, A. K., Gao, X. Z., Anbazhagan, N., & Durai, M. S. (2015). An ANFIS approach for evaluation of team-level service climate in GSD projects using Taguchi-genetic learning algorithm. *Applied Soft Computing*, *30*, 628–635. doi:10.1016/j.asoc.2015.02.019

Smarzynska, B., & Shang, J. W. (2000). *Corruption and Composition of Foreign Direct Investment: Firm-Level Evidence*. Policy Research Working Paper 2360. Washington, DC: World Bank.

Stern, N. (2002). *A Strategy for Development*. Washington, DC: The World Bank. doi:10.1596/0-8213-4980-5

Teece, D. J. (1997). Technology Transfer by Multinational Firms: The Response Cost of Transferring Technological Know-how. *The Economic Journal*, *87*(346), 242–261. doi:10.2307/2232084

The American Center. (2004). *Foreign Investment in Bangladesh; Foreign Investors Chamber of Commerce and Industry*. Embassy News, Embassy of the United States.

Wei, S. J. (2000). How Taxing Is Corruption on International Investors? *The Review of Economics and Statistics*, *82*(1), 1–11. doi:10.1162/003465300558533

World Bank. (2001). *Bangladesh: A Review of Public Enterprise Performance and Strategy*. Washington, DC: Author.

World Bank. (2004a). *A Better Investment Climate for Everyone*. A Co-Publication of The World Bank and Oxford University Press.

World Bank. (2004b). *Investment Climate Surveys Draft Country Profile, Sri Lanka*. Retrieved from http://rru.worldbank.org

World Bank & BEI. (2003). *Improving the Investment Climate Assessment*. Based on an Enterprises Survey carried out by the Bangladesh Enterprise Institute and The World Bank.

World Economic Forum. (2002). *Global Competitiveness Report 2001/02*. Geneva: Author.

ENDNOTES

[1] Investment climate is characterized by availability of certain types of infrastructure including electricity, water, transportation, telephone connections etc. those requires high level of investment and efficient investment allocation (Khan, 2005).

[2] "An EPZ is a category of Special Economic Zones (SEZs), which is an area where the government provides facilities and incentives to attract foreign investors" (Bhuiyan et al., 2014, p.1).

[3] Foreign Direct Investment (FDI)is a key element in economic integration that provides a means for creating direct, stable and long-lasting links between economies (OECD, 2008).

APPENDIX

Abbreviations

BGMEA = Bangladesh Garment Manufacturer and Exporter Association
BKMEA = Bangladesh Knit Manufacturer and Exporter Association
BEPZA = Bangladesh Export Processing Zone Authority
EPZ = Export Processing Zone
FDI = Foreign Direct Investment
TFP = Total Factor Productivity

Tables

Table 5. Human resource: Percentages

Human Resource	EPZ (%)	
	SA	A
Workers are capable to work in specialized area	25.0	75.0
Workers are ready to get necessary training on new skills	50.0	50.0
Workers can achieve the target as defined by the organization	37.5	12.5
Managers have necessary management skills	87.5	12.5
Managerial people use email or website in its interaction with client and suppliers.	50.0	50.0
Workers are ready to accept new technologies	37.5	50.0

Table 6. Access to finance: Percentages

Access to Finance	EPZ (%)	
	SA	A
Source of new investment is retained earnings	-	25.0
Source of new investment is bank.	12.5	62.5
Source of working capital is retained earnings	25.0	12.5
Source of working capital is bank.	25.0	50.0
We have overdraft facilities.	-	25.0
We have line of credit facilities.	25.0	75.0

Table 7. Power and energy: percentages

Power and Energy	EPZ (%)	
	SA	**A**
Power supply problem is very frequent in RMG sector	12.5	87.5
More time is required to obtain a electricity connection	-	-
The company has alternative source of electricity supply	37.5	62.5
The company experiences damage of electronic appliances due to power interruption	25.0	37.5
Power interruption increases cost of wages	50.0	50.0
Shortage of energy is a common problem in RMG industry	25.0	75.0

Table 8. Infrastructure: percentage

Infrastructure	EPZ (%)	
	SA	**A**
Insufficient water supply is a crucial problem for the company	0	0
The company has its own arrangement for water supply	-	12.5
In case of export it takes a long time in arriving goods in the point of entry (port) and clear the customs	12.5	50.0
The company uses rented transport to bring raw materials as well as deliver the finished goods	-	100.0
Higher container rates causes high cost of transportation	12.5	12.5
Trucking cost is high to transfer goods from one place to another	37.5	62.5
Traffic causes delay in transporting goods from one location to another	12.5	87.5

Table 9. Governance: percentages

Governance	EPZ (%)	
	SA	**A**
Informal payment is required to get things done	-	62.5
Gift/Payment is required for export permission	-	5.0
Undue payment is associated with the procurement of several services from the government officials is very high	-	75.0
Time spent by management in dealing with requirements imposed by government officials is very high	37.5	25.0
Share of revenue for Tax purpose is very high	-	-

Table 10. Trade union: percentages

Trade Union	EPZ (%)	
	SA	**A**
Work force of the company participates in trade union	12.5	62.5
Trade union has substantial impact on the company's business	37.5	37.5
The company suffers from production loss due to strike or other labor disputes	50.0	37.5

Compilation of References

Abdella, M., & Marwala, D. (2005). The use of genetic algorithms and neural networks to approximate missing data in database. In *Proceedings of the IEEE 3rd international conference on computational cybernetics (ICCC)* (pp. 207–212). doi:10.1109/ICCCYB.2005.1511574

Abdin, M.J. (2014, February 3). Political Stability Key to Improving Investment Climate. *The Financial Express*.

Abraham, A. (2004). *Meta-Learning Evolutionary Artificial Neural Networks. Neurocomputing Journal, 56c*, 1–38.

Agarwal & Mittal. (2013). Sentiment Classification using Rough Set based Hybrid Feature Selection.*Proceedings of the 4th Workshop on Computational Approaches to Subjectivity, Sentiment and Social Media Analysis.Association for Computational Linguistics*.

Aggarwal, A. (2005). *Performance of Export Processing Zones: A Comparative Analysis of India, Sri Lanka and Bangladesh.* Working paper. Indian Council for Research on International Economics Relations. Retrieved from www.icrer.org

Aggarwal, K. K., & Singh, Y. (2007). *Software Engineering* (3rd ed.). New Age International Publishers.

Ahmed, A. N., Ghoni, R., & Zakaria, N. F. (2011). Simulation Model of Space Vector Modulated Control of Matrix Converter fed Induction Motor. *Journal of Applied Science, 11*(5), 768–777. doi:10.3923/jas.2011.768.777

Ahmed, S., Ahmed, S., Shumon, M. R. H., Quader, M. A., Cho, H. M., & Mahmud, M. I. (2015). Prioritizing Strategies for Sustainable End-of-Life Vehicle Management Using Combinatorial Multi-Criteria Decision Making Method. *International Journal of Fuzzy Systems*, 1–15.

Ahsan, Q. (2004). Evaluation of Power Interruption Cost for Residential and Industrial Sector. *Journal of Energy and Environment, 3*, 119–131.

Ahyan, M. B. (2013). A fuzzy ahp approach for supplier selection problem: A case study in a gearmotor company. *International Journal of Managing Value and Supply Chains, 4*(3), 11–23. doi:10.5121/ijmvsc.2013.4302

Akkartal, Turudu, & Erbek. (2003). *Analysis of Changes in Vegetation Biomass using Multitemporal and Multisensor Satellite Data.* Academic Press.

Alesina, A., & Venturini, A. (1989). Analysis and Design of Optimum-Amplitude Nine Switch Direct AC – AC Converters. *IEEE Transactions on Power Electronics, 4*(1), 101–112. doi:10.1109/63.21879

Ali, M. I. (2012). Another view on reduction of parameters in soft sets. *Applied Soft Computing, 12*(6), 1814–1821. doi:10.1016/j.asoc.2012.01.002

Alisson, B., Ana, L., Antonio, S., Filipe, M., & Joaquim, C. (2011). An Adaptive Mechanism for Access Control in VANETs.*ICN 2011: The Tenth International Conference on Networks*.

Allahviranloo, T., Abbasbandy, S., Salahshour, S., & Hakimzadeh, A. (2011). A., A new method for solving fuzzy linear differential equations. *Computing, 92*(2), 181–197. doi:10.1007/s00607-010-0136-6

Allahviranloo, T., & Ahmadi, M. B. (2010). Fuzzy Laplace transforms. *Soft Computing, 14*(3), 235–243. doi:10.1007/s00500-008-0397-6

Alshamrani, A., & Bahattab, A. (2015). *A Comparison between Three SDLC Models Waterfall Model* (Vol. 12). Spiral Model, and Incremental/Iterative Model. In IJCSI International Journal of Computer Science Issues.

Amiri & Shariff. (2010). Using Remote Sensing Data for Vegetation Cover Assessment in Semi-Arid Rangeland of Center Province of Iran. *World Applied Sciences Journal, 11*(12), 1537–1546.

Amirkalati. (2008). Comparison of Harris Benedict and Mifflin-St Jeor equations with indirect calorimetry in evaluating resting energy expenditure. *Indian Journal of Medical Sciences, 62*(7), 283-290.

Ankaiah, N., & Ravi, V. (2011). A Novel Soft Computing Hybrid for Data Imputation. In *Proceedings of the 7th international conference on data mining (DMIN).*

Anojkumar, L., Ilangkumaran, M., & Vignesh, M. (2015). A decision making methodology for material selection in sugar industry using hybrid MCDM techniques. *International Journal of Materials and Product Technology, 51*(2), 102–126. doi:10.1504/IJMPT.2015.071770

Anushya, A., & Pethalakshmi, A. (2012). A Comparative Study of Fuzzy Classifiers with Genetic On Heart Data. *International Conference on Advancement in Engineering Studies and Technology.*

Arbib. (1994). The handbook of brain theory and neural network. Academic Press.

Archibald, D. R. (2003). *Life cycle models for high technology projects-applying systems thinking to project.* Retrieved from: http://russarchibald.com/recent-papers-presentations/other-pm-subjects/models-hitech-syst-slides/

Archibald, D. R. (2004). *State of the art of project management. In Proceedings of the International Seminar on Project Management.* Retrieved from: http://russarchibald.com/recent-papers-presentations/state-of-the-art/

Archibald, D. R., & Voropaev, I. V. (2003). *Commonalities and differences in project management around the world: A survey of project categories and life cycle models.* Retrieved from: http://russarchibald.com/Commonalities_and_Differences_paper_May_3_03.pdf

Archibald, D. R., & Voropaev, I. V. (2004). Project categories and life cycle models: Report on the 2003 IPMA Global Survey. In *Proceedings of the 18th IPMA World Congress on Project Management,* (pp: 1-6).

Arunkumar, T., & Gnanamurthy, R. K. (2006). Delivering Quality of Services for Media Streaming in Group Communication over Mobile Ad Hoc Networks. *ICIIS 2006 International Conference on Industrial and Information Systems.*

Arunkumar, S., Jagadeesh, G., Anirban, B., & Prabhakar, R. S. (2015). An Integrated Fuzzy DEMATEL, TOPSIS, and ELECTRE Approach for Evaluating Knowledge Transfer Effectiveness with Reference to GSD project Outcome. *Neural Computing & Applications,* 1–13.

Arunkumar, S., Prabhakar, R. S., & Xinliang, Z. (2014). A Combined Fuzzy DEMATEL and Fuzzy TOPSIS Approach for Evaluating GSD Project Outcome Factors. *Neural Computing & Applications, 26*(5), 1025–1040.

Arunkumar, T., & Ramesh, B. (2010). A simulated modeling approach towards providing adaptive QoS for vehicular safety services over VANET. *International Journal of Research and Reviews in Computer Science, 1*(4), 110–116.

Arunkumar, T., & Sivanandam, S. N. (2007). Location Identification and Vehicular Tracking for Vehicular Ad Hoc Wireless Networks. *IEEE Explorer, 1*(2), 112–116.

Asharaf, S., & Murty, M. N. (2003). An adaptive rough fuzzy single pass algorithm for clustering large data sets. *Pattern Recognition, 36*(2), 3015–3018. doi:10.1016/S0031-3203(03)00081-5

ASTM. E2213-03. (2003). Standard specification for telecommunications and information exchange between roadside vehicle systems – 5 GHz band Dedicated Short Range Communications (DSRC) Medium Access Control (MAC) and Physical Layer (PHY) Specifications.*Proceedings of ASTM.*

Atakan, , & Taflan Imre, . (2014). M-FDBSCAN: A Multicore Density-Based Uncertain Data Clustering Algorithm. *Turkish Journal of Electrical Engineering & Computer Sciences, 22*, 143–154. doi:10.3906/elk-1202-83

Atanassov, K. T. (1986). Intuitionistic Fuzzy Sets. *Fuzzy Sets and Systems, 20*(1), 87–96. doi:10.1016/S0165-0114(86)80034-3

Aterido, R., Driemeier, M. H., & Pages, C. (2007). *Investment Climate and Employment Growth: The Impact of Access to Finance, Corruption and Regulations across Firms.* Discussion Paper Series, IZA DP No. 3138.

Atif, A.K., Oumair, N., Daciana, I., & Evor, H. (2013). Fuzzy controller design for assisted omni-directional treadmill therapy. *The International Journal of Soft Computing and Software Engineering, 3*(8), 32-37.

Awasthi, A., Chauhan, S. S., & Omrani, H. (2011). Application of fuzzy TOPSIS in evaluating sustainable transportation systems. *Expert Systems with Applications, 38*(10), 12270–12280. doi:10.1016/j.eswa.2011.04.005

Ayağ, Z. (2015). CAD software evaluation for product design to exchange data in a supply chain network. *International Journal of Supply Chain Management, 4*(1), 30-38.

Aydilek, I. B., & Arslan, A. (2013). A hybrid method for imputation of missing values using optimized fuzzy c-means with support vector regression and a genetic algorithm. *Information Sciences, 233*, 25–35. doi:10.1016/j.ins.2013.01.021

Aziza, A., Aikhuele, D., & Souleman, F. (2015). A Fuzzy TOPSIS Model to Rank Automotive Suppliers. In *2nd International Materials, Industrial, and Manufacturing Engineering Conference.* doi:10.1016/j.promfg.2015.07.028

Bachir, A., & Benslimane, A. (2003). A multicast protocol in ad hoc networks: Inter-vehicles geocast.*Proceedings of the 57th IEEE Vehicular Technology Conference.* doi:10.1109/VETECS.2003.1208832

Baghavan, D., & Bharghavan, V. (1997). Routing in Ad Hoc Networks Using Minimum Connected Dominating Sets. *IEEE International Conference on Communications (ICC'97).*

Bai, & Krishnan, H. (2006). Reliability analysis of DSRC wireless communication for vehicle safety applications. *Proceedings of the IEEE Intelligent Transportation Systems Conference* (ITSC '06).

Bai, K. H., Sadekar, V., Holland, G., & Elbatt, T. (2006). Towards characterizing and classifying communication-based automotive applications from a wireless networking perspective. *Proceedings of the IEEE Workshop on Automotive Networking and Applications* (AutoNet).

Bai, C., & Sarkis, J. (2010). Green supplier development: Analytical evaluation using rough set theory. *Journal of Cleaner Production, 18*(12), 1200–1210. doi:10.1016/j.jclepro.2010.01.016

Bai, C., & Sarkis, J. (2010). Integrating sustainability into supplier selection with grey system and rough set methodologies. *International Journal of Production Economics, 124*(1), 252–264. doi:10.1016/j.ijpe.2009.11.023

Baldwin, J. F., & Pilsworth, B. W. (1982). Dynamic programming problem for fuzzy systems with fuzzy environment. *Journal of Mathematical Analysis and Applications, 85*(1), 1–23. doi:10.1016/0022-247X(82)90022-1

Balin, A., & Baraçli, H. (2015). A fuzzy multi-criteria decision making methodology based upon the interval type-2 fuzzy sets for evaluating renewable energy alternatives in Turkey. *Technological and Economic Development of Economy*, 1-22.

Banerjee, M., Chen, Z., & Gangopadhyay, A. (2014). A generic and distributed privacy preserving classification method with a worst-case privacy guarantee.Journal Distributed and Parallel Database, 32(1), 5-35.

Barton, T. H. (1994). *Rectifiers, Cycloconverter and AC Controllers*. Oxford University Press.

Basgalupp, M. P., Barros, R. C., De Carvilo, & Freitas. (2014). Evolving Decision Trees with beam search based initialization and lexicography multiobjective evaluation. Journal Information Sciences, 258, 160-181.

Basili, V. R., & Weiss, D. M. (1984). A Methodology for Collecting Valid Software Engineering Data. *IEEE Transactions on Software Engineering*, *10*(3), 728–738. doi:10.1109/TSE.1984.5010301

Basso, Cammarano, & De Vita. (2004). Remotely sensed vegetation indices: Theory and Applications for crop management. *Rivista Italiana di Agrometeorologia*, 36-53.

Baswant, K., & Kung, H. T. (2000). GPSR: Greedy Perimeter Stateless Routing for Wireless Networks.*Proceedings of the ACM/IEEE International Conference on Mobile Computing and Networking (MobiCom)*.

Bauer & Schneider. (2009). *Analysis of time series of Landsat images*. Institute of Surveying, Remote Sensing and Land Information, University of Natural Resources and Applied Life Sciences (BOKU).

Baykasoğlu, A., Kaplanoğlu, V., Durmuşoğlu, Z. D., & Şahin, C. (2013). Integrating fuzzy DEMATEL and fuzzy hierarchical TOPSIS methods for truck selection. *Expert Systems with Applications*, *40*(3), 899–907. doi:10.1016/j.eswa.2012.05.046

Bechler, L., Storz, O., & Franz, W. (2003). Efficient Discovery of Internet Gateways in Future Vehicular Communication Systems. *The 57th IEEE Semiannual Vehicular Technology Conference*. doi:10.1109/VETECS.2003.1207769

Beck, T., Demirgüç-Kunt, A., & Maksimovic, V. (2005). Financial and Legal Constraints to Growth: Does Firm Size Matter? *The Journal of Finance*, *60*(1), 131–177. doi:10.1111/j.1540-6261.2005.00727.x

Bede, B. (2006). A note on "two-point boundary value problems associated with non-linear fuzzy differential equations". *Fuzzy Sets and Systems*, *157*(7), 986–989. doi:10.1016/j.fss.2005.09.006

Bede, B. (2008). Note on "Numerical solutions of fuzzy differential equations by predictor-corrector method". *Information Sciences*, *178*(7), 1917–1922. doi:10.1016/j.ins.2007.11.016

Bede, B., & Gal, S. G. (2004). Almost periodic fuzzy-number-value functions. *Fuzzy Sets and Systems*, *147*(3), 385–403. doi:10.1016/j.fss.2003.08.004

Bede, B., & Gal, S. G. (2005). Generalizations of the differentiability of fuzzy-number-valued functions with applications to fuzzy differential equations. *Fuzzy Sets and Systems*, 151581–151599.

Bede, B., Rudas, I. J., & Bencsik, A. L. (2007). First order linear fuzzy differential equations under generalized differentiability. *Inf.Sci.*, 1771648–1771662.

Belal, M., Gaber, J., El-Sayed, H., & Almojel, A. (2006). Swarm Intelligence. In Handbook of Bioinspired Algorithms and Applications. Chapman & Hall.

Bellmann, R. & Zadeh, L. A. (1970). Decision making in fuzzy environment. *Management Science, 17*(B), 141-164.

Berendt, B., & Preibusch, S. (2014). Better decision support through exploratory discrimination-aware data mining: Foundations and empirical evidence. Journal Artificial Intelligence and Law, 22(2), 175-209.

Bernsen, & Manivannan, D. (2008). Unicast routing protocols for vehicular ad hoc networks: A critical comparison and classification. *Pervasive and Mobile Computing*, 1-18.

Bezdek, J. C. (1981). *Pattern Recognition with Fuzzy Objective Function Algorithms. Plenum Press.* New York: Kluwer Academic Publishers. doi:10.1007/978-1-4757-0450-1

Bezdek, J. C., & Pal, N. R. (1998). Some new indexes for cluster validity. *IEEE Transactions on Systems, Man, and Cybernetics. Part B, Cybernetics, 28*(3), 301–315. doi:10.1109/3477.678624 PMID:18255949

Bhandari, A. K., Kumar, A., & Singh, G. K. (2012). Feature Extraction using Normalized Difference Vegetation Index (NDVI). *Procedia Technology, 6,* 612–621. doi:10.1016/j.protcy.2012.10.074

Bhattacherjee, V., Neogi, M. S., & Mahanti, R. (2008). Software Development Approach of Students: An Evaluation. In *Proceedings of the national conference on Methods and Models in Computing (NCM2C),* (pp 23-30).

Bhattacherjee, V., Neogi, M., & Mahanti, R. (2007). Software Development Patterns in University Setting: A Case Study. In *Proceedings of the national seminar on Recent Advances on Information Technology, ISM Dhanbad,* (pp. 40-43).

Bianchi, G. (2000). Performance analysis of the IEEE 802.11 distributed coordination function. *IEEE Journal on Selected Areas in Communications, 18*(3), 535–547. doi:10.1109/49.840210

Bilstrup, K., Uhlemann, E., & Strom, E. G. (2008). Medium Access Control in Vehicular Networks Based on the Upcoming IEEE 802.11p Standard. *Proceedings of World Congress on ITS.*

Birla, N., Agarwal, N., Sankar Ganesh, S., & Babu, V. (2014). Clustering based Bit Loading Algorithms using Neural Networks. *International Journal of Review in Electronics & Communication Engineering, 2*(2), 2–5.

Blaabjerg, F., Casadei, D., Klumpner, D., & Matteeini, M. (2002). Comparison of Two Current Modulation Strategies for Matrix Converters under Unbalanced Input Voltage Conditions. *IEEE Transactions on Industrial Electronics, 49*(2), 282–296. doi:10.1109/41.993261

Blazevic, B., Le Boudec, J.-Y., & Giordano, S. (2005). A Location-Based Routing Method for Mobile Ad Hoc Networks. *IEEE Transactions on Mobile Computing, 4*(1), 97–110. doi:10.1109/TMC.2005.16

Blum, J., Eskandarian, A., & Hoffmann, L. (2003). Mobility Management in IVC Networks. *IEEE Intelligent Vehicles Symposium.* doi:10.1109/IVS.2003.1212900

Blum, J., Eskandarian, A., & Hoffmann, L. (2004). Challenges of Intervehicle AdHoc Networks. *IEEE Transactions on Intelligent Transportation Systems, 5*(4), 347–351. doi:10.1109/TITS.2004.838218

Bogalecka, E., & Erzeminski, Z. (1993). Control Systems of Doubly fed Induction Machines Supplied by Current Controlled Voltage Source Inverters).*Sixth International Conference on Electrical Machines and Drives.*

Borgonovo, Capone, A., Cesana, M., & Fratta, L. (2004). ADHOC MAC: a new MAC architecture for ad hoc networks providing efficient and reliable point-to-point and broadcast service. *ACM Wireless Network, 10*(4), 359–366.

Bose, B. (2000). Fuzzy Logic and Neural Networks in Power Electronics and Drives. *IEEE Industry Applications Magazine, 6*(3), 57–63. doi:10.1109/2943.838042

Briesemeister, & Hommel, G. (2000). Overcoming fragmentation in mobile ad hoc net-works. *Journal of Communications and Networks, 2,* 182-187.

Briesemeister, S. L., & Hommel, G. (2000). Disseminating messages among highly mobile hosts based on inter-vehicle communication. *IEEE Intelligent Vehicles Symposium.* doi:10.1109/IVS.2000.898398

Broch, J., Maltz, D. A., Johnson, D. B., Hu, Y. C., & Jetcheva, J. (1998). A Performance Comparison of Multi-Hop Wireless Ad Hoc Network Routing Protocols. *Proceedings of ACM/IEEE MOBICOM.* doi:10.1145/288235.288256

Bronja,H. & Bronja, H. (2015). Two-phase selection procedure of aluminized sheet supplier by applying fuzzy AHP and fuzzy TOPSIS methodology. *Tehnički vjesnik*, *22*(4), 821-828.

Buckley, J. J. (1985). Fuzzy hierarchical analysis. *Fuzzy Sets and Systems*, *17*(1), 233–247. doi:10.1016/0165-0114(85)90090-9

Buckley, J. J., & Feuring, T. (2000). Fuzzy differential equations. *Fuzzy Sets and Systems*, *110*(1), 43–54. doi:10.1016/S0165-0114(98)00141-9

Buckley, J. J., & Feuring, T. (2001). Fuzzy initial value problem for Nth-order linear differential equations. *Fuzzy Sets and Systems*, *121*(2), 247–255. doi:10.1016/S0165-0114(00)00028-2

Burak, E. (2015). An integrated fuzzy multi criteria group decision making approach for ERP system selection. *Applied Soft Computing*, *38*, 106–117.

Büyüközkan, G., & Çifçi, G. (2011). A novel fuzzy multi-criteria decision framework for sustainable supplier selection with incomplete information. *Computers in Industry*, *62*(2), 164–174. doi:10.1016/j.compind.2010.10.009

Büyüközkan, G., & Çifçi, G. (2012). Evaluation of the green supply chain management practices: A fuzzy ANP approach. *Production Planning and Control*, *23*(6), 405–418. doi:10.1080/09537287.2011.561814

C2C-CC. (2011). Retrieved November 15, 2011 from http://www.car-to-car.org/

Campello, J. (1998). Optimal Discrete Bit Loading for Multicarrier Modulation Systlems. *IEEE Symp. Info. Theory.* http://doi.org/ doi:10.1109/ISIT.1998.708791

Campello, J. (1999). Practical bit loading for DMT. *IEEE International Conference on Communications.* http://doi.org/ doi:<ALIGNMENT.qj></ALIGNMENT>10.1109/ICC.1999.765384

Cano, Y. C., & Flores, H. R. (2008). On the new solution of fuzzy differential equations. *Chaos, Solitons, and Fractals*, *38*(1), 112–119. doi:10.1016/j.chaos.2006.10.043

Cao, T., Zhang, M., & Andreae, P. (2015). Multiple Imputation for Missing Data Using Genetic Programming. *Proceeding GECCO '15 Proceedings of the 2015 Annual Conference on Genetic and Evolutionary Computation.* ACM.

Cardoson, F., Martinis, J. F., & Pires, V. F. (1998). Comparative Study of a PI, Neural Network and Fuzzy Genetic Approach Controllers for an AC Drive.*5th International Workshop in Advanced Motion Control.*

Carling, K. (2000). Resistant Outlier Rules and the non-Gaussian Case. *Computational Statistics & Data Analysis*, *33*(3), 249–258. doi:10.1016/S0167-9473(99)00057-2

Carl, J. C., Kenneth, E. P., & Gregory, M. C. (1985). Physical Activity, Exercise, and Physical Fitness: Definitions and Distinctions for Health-related research. *Public Health Reports*, *100*(2), 126–131. PMID:3920711

Cartalk. (2011). Retrieved February 3, 2011 from http://www.cartalk.com

Castelli, D. M., Centeio, E. E., Hwang, J., Barcelona, J. M., Glowacki, E. M., Calvert, H. G., & Nicksic, H. M. (2014). VII. The history of physical activity and academic performance research: Informing the future. *Monographs of the Society for Research in Child Development*, *79*(4), 119–148. doi:10.1111/mono.12133 PMID:25387418

Castillo P. R. D. (2012). Use of machine learning methods to impute categorical data. *Conference of European Statisticians.*

Chakeres, & Perkins, C. (2006). *Dynamic MANET On-Demand (DYMO) Routing.* Internet-Draft, draft-ietf-manet-dymo-06.txt.

Chamodrakas, I., Leftheriotis, I., & Martakos, D. (2011). In-depth analysis and simulation study of an innovative fuzzy approach for ranking alternatives in multiple attribute decision making problems based on TOPSIS. *Applied Soft Computing*, *11*(1), 900–907. doi:10.1016/j.asoc.2010.01.010

Chang, D. Y. (1992). Extent analysis and synthetic decision. *Optimization Techniques and Applications*, *1*, 352–355.

Chang, D.-Y. (1996). Applications of the extent analysis method on fuzzy AHP. *European Journal of Operational Research*, *95*(3), 649–655. doi:10.1016/0377-2217(95)00300-2

Chang, H. J., & Dye, C. Y. (1999). An EOQ model for deteriorating items with timevarying demand and partial backlogging. *Journal of Operational Research*, *50*(S11), 1176–1182. doi:10.1057/palgrave.jors.2600801

Chang, S. L., & Zadeh, L. A. (1972). On fuzzy mapping and control. *IEEE Transactions on Systems, Man, and Cybernetics*, *2*(1), 30–34. doi:10.1109/TSMC.1972.5408553

Chen, Tsang, Yeung, & Wang. (2005). *The parameterization reduction of soft sets and its applications*. Academic Press.

Chen, Y., Lin, Y., & Lee, S. (2010). A Mobicast Routing Protocol for Vehicular Ad Hoc Networks. *ACM/Springer Mobile Networks and Applications (MONET)*, *15*(1), 20-35.

Chen, D., Cui, D. W., Wang, C. X., & Wang, Z. R. (2006). A Rough Set-Based Hierarchical Clustering Algorithm for Categorical Data. *International Journal of Information Technology*, *12*(3), 149–159.

Chen, H. L. (2015). Performance measurement and the prediction of capital project failure. *International Journal of Project Management*, *33*(6), 1393–1404. doi:10.1016/j.ijproman.2015.02.009

Chen, T., Rui-qing, N., Wang, Y., Liang-pei, Z., & Du, B. (2011). Percentage of Vegetation Cover Change Monitoring in Wuhan Region Based on Remote Sensing. *Procedia Environmental Sciences*, *10*, 1466–1472. doi:10.1016/j.proenv.2011.09.234

Chiang, J., Yao, J. S., & Lee, H. M. (2005). Fuzzy inventory with backorder defuzzification by signed distance method. *Journal of Information Science and Engineering*, *21*, 671–694.

Chiou, C. Y., Hsu, C. W., & Hwang, W. Y. (2008, December). Comparative investigation on green supplier selection of the American, Japanese and Taiwanese electronics industry in China. In *Industrial Engineering and Engineering Management, 2008. IEEM 2008. IEEE International Conference on* (pp. 1909-1914). IEEE.

Chitade & Katiyar. (2010). *Colour Based Image Segmentation using K-Means Clustering*. Department of Civil Engineering, Manit, Bhopal, Madhyapradesh.

Chitra, V. (2013). *Design of Soft Computing Technique Based Controllers in Closed Loop System for Matrix Converter and Speed Control of Induction Motor*. (Ph.D. Thesis). SASTRA University.

Choudhury, P. P., & Satapathy, S. (2015). Plastic Recycling Process Using Fuzzy Analytical Hierarchy Process. *Journal of Industrial Safety Engineering*, *2*(2), 17–22.

Chou, S.-W., & Chang, Y.-C. (2008). The implementation factors that influence the ERP (Enterprise Resource Planning) Benefits. *Decision Support Systems*, *46*(1), 149–157. doi:10.1016/j.dss.2008.06.003

Chow, P. S., Cioffi, J. M., & Bingham, J. (1995). Practical discrete multitone transceiver loading algorithm for data transmission over spectrally shaped channels. *IEEE Transactions on Communications*, *43*(2), 773–775. doi:10.1109/26.380108

Christmann & Van Aelst. (2006). Robust estimation of Cronbach's alpha. *Journal of Multivariate Analysis, 97*(7), 1660–1674.

Cintra, M. E., Monard, M. C., Martin, T. P., & Camargo, H. A. (2011). *An Approach for the Extraction of Classification Rules from Fuzzy Formal Contexts*. Computer Science and Mathematics Institute Technical Reports.

Clare, J. C., & Wheeler, P. W. (2003). *Introduction to Matrix Converter Topology*. Seminar on Matrix Converters.

Cohen, J. (1960). A coefficient of agreement for nominal scales. *Educational and Psychological Measurement, 20*(1), 37–46. doi:10.1177/001316446002000104

Colleen, M., Monique, F., & Robin Walker, C. (2008). Imputation of Missing Values by Integrating Neural Networks and Case-based Reasoning. *30th Annual International IEEE EMBS Conference.*

Criminisi, A., Shotton, J., & Konukoglu, E. (2011). Decision Forests: A unified Framework for Classification, Regression, Density Estimation, Manifold learning and Semi Supervised Learning. *Journal Foundation and Trends in Computer Graphics and Vision, 7*(2-3), 1–150.

Cutler, M. E. J., Boyd, D. S., Foody, G. M., & Vetrivel, A. (2012). Estimating tropical forest biomass with a combination of SAR image texture and Landsat TM data: An assessment of predictions between regions. *ISPRS Journal of Photogrammetry and Remote Sensing, 70*, 66–77. doi:10.1016/j.isprsjprs.2012.03.011

Daniel, M., & Paul, F. (1994). *Fuzzy logic*. Simon and Schuster.

Daniels, A., & Slattery, D. (1978). Application of Power Transistors to Polyphase Regenerative Power Converters. *Proceedings of the Institution of Electrical Engineers, 125*(7), 643–647. doi:10.1049/piee.1978.0153

Daniels, A., & Slattery, D. (1978). New Power Converter Technique Employing Power Transistors. *Proceedings of the Institution of Electrical Engineers, 125*(7), 146–150. doi:10.1049/piee.1978.0038

Das, S., Panigrahi, B. K., & Pattnaik, S. S. (2009). Nature-Inspired Algorithms for Multi-objective Optimization. Handbook of Research on Machine Learning Applications and Trends: Algorithms Methods and Techniques. Academic Press.

Das, B., Mahapatra, N. K., & Maity, M. (2008). Initial-valued first order fuzzy differential equation in Bi-level inventory model with fuzzy demand. *Mathematical Modeling and Analysis, 13*(4), 493–512. doi:10.3846/1392-6292.2008.13.493-512

Das, M. C., Sarkar, B., & Ray, S. (2015). A performance evaluation framework for technical institutions in one of the states of India. *Benchmarking International Journal (Toronto, Ont.), 22*(5).

Das, S., Abraham, A., & Konar, A. (2008). Swarm Intelligence Algorithms in Bioinformatics. *Springer, Studies in Computational Intelligence, 94*, 113–147.

Davis, A. M., Bersoff, E. H., & Comer, E. R. (1988). A strategy for comparing alternative software development life cycle models. *IEEE Transactions on Software Engineering, 14*(10), 453–1461. doi:10.1109/32.6190

Davis, D. L., & Bouldin, D. W. (1979). A cluster separation measure. *IEEE Transactions on Pattern Analysis and Machine Intelligence, PAMI-1*(2), 224–227. doi:10.1109/TPAMI.1979.4766909 PMID:21868852

Desaulniers, H., Douglas, A., & Robert, J. (2001). Matching software development life cycles to the project environment. In *Proceedings of the Project Management Institute Annual Seminars and Symposium.*

Deterding, S., Dixon, D., Khaled, R., & Nacke, L. (2011). From game design elements to gamefulness: defining "Gamification".Proceedings MindTrek. ACM. doi:10.1145/2181037.2181040

Deveci, M., Demirel, N. Ç., John, R., & Ozcan, E. (2015). Fuzzy multi-criteria decision making for carbon dioxide geological storage in Turkey. *Journal of Natural Gas Science and Engineering.*

Dinagar, S. D., & Palanivel, K. (2009). Solving Linear Programming Problem under Fuzzy Environment, Int. *Journal of Computational Physical Sciences*, *1*(1), 53–64.

Djankov, S., La Porta, R., Lopez-de-Silanes, F., & Shleifer, A. (2002). The Regulation of Entry. *The Quarterly Journal of Economics*, *117*(1), 1–37. doi:10.1162/003355302753399436

Dobson, M. C., Ulaby, F. T., Le Toan, T., Beaudoin, A., Kasischke, E. S., & Christensen, N. (1992). Dependence of radar backscatter on coniferous forest biomass. IEEE Trans. Geosci. Remote Sens., 30(2).

Dollar, D., Driemeier, M. H., & Mengiote, T. (2003). *Investment Climate and Firm Performance in Developing Economics. Development Research Group*. World Bank.

Dollar, D., Driemeier, M. H., & Mengiote, T. (2003). Investment Climate and Firm Performance in Developing Economics. *Economic Development and Cultural Change*, *54*(1).

Donaldson, W. A. (1977). Inventory replenishment policy for a linear trend in demand-an analytical solution. *Operational Research Quarterly*, *28*(3), 663–670. doi:10.2307/3008916

Dorigo, M. (1992). *Optimization, learning and natural algorithms*. (Ph.D. Thesis). Dipartimento diElettronica, Politecnico di Milano, Italy.

Doulkeridis & Norvag. (2014). A survey of large-scale analytical query processing in MapReduce. *The VLDB Journal*, *23*(3), 1-27.

DSRC. (2012). *Dedicated Short Range Communications*. Retrieved September 18, 2012 from http://www.leearmstrong.com/dsrc/dsrchomeset.htm

Du, Li, Cao, Luo, & Zhang. (2010). Monitoring urban land cover and vegetation change by multi-temporal remote sensing information. *Mining Science and Technology, 20*, 922-932.

Dubois, D., & Prade, H. (1982). Towards fuzzy differential calculus: Part 3, Differentiation. *Fuzzy Sets and Systems*, *8*(3), 225–233. doi:10.1016/S0165-0114(82)80001-8

Dubois, D., & Prade, H. (1990). Rough fuzzy sets model. *International Journal of General Systems*, *46*(1), 191–208. doi:10.1080/03081079008935107

Durrant, B. (2015). *WEKA*. Retrieved October 26, 2015, from http://www.cs.waikato.ac.nz/ml/weka/

Eko Saputro, T., & Daneshvar Rouyendegh, B. (2015). A hybrid approach for selecting material handling equipment in a warehouse. *International Journal of Management Science and Engineering Management*, 1-15.

Elawady, R. M., & Barakat, S. (2014). Different Feature Selection for Sentiment Classification. *International Journal of Information Science and Intelligent System*, *3*(1), 137–150.

Elhawary & Haas. (2011). Energy-Efficient Protocol for Cooperative Networks. *IEEE/ACM Transactions on Networking, 19*(2), 561-574.

Elsiddig & Niemeyer. (2008). Detection of Land Cover changes using Multi-Temporal Satellite Imagery. The International Archieves of the Photogrammetry, Remote Sensing and Spatial Information Sciences, 37(B7).

Engelbrecht, P. (2002). *Computational Intelligence: An Introduction*. John Wiley & Sons.

Esogbue, A. O. (1983). Some novel applications of fuzzy dynamic programming. *Proceedings of the IEEE*, 501–505.

Eusuf, M.A., Faruque, M. A. & Rahman, A. (2007). *Institutions for Facilitating FDI: Issues for BEPZA, Bangladesh, CUTS International*. IPPG Briefing Paper, No. Tens In Conjunction with CUTS International.

Evans, L., Lohse, N., & Summers, M. (2013). A fuzzy-decision-tree approach for Manufacturing technology selection exploiting experience-based information.Journal Expert Systems with Applications, 40(16), 6412-6426.

FCC DSRC (Dedicated Short Range Communications). (2011). Retrieved December 03, 2011 from http://wireless.fcc.gov/services/its/dsrc/

Fensholt, Sandholt, & Stisen. (2006). *Analysing NDVI for the African continent using the geostationary meteosat second generation SEVIRI sensor*. NASA Goddard Space Flight Center.

Ferdousi, F. (2009). An Investigation of Manufacturing Performance Improvement through Lean Production: A Case Study on Bangladesh Garment Firms. *International Journal of Business and Management, 4*(9). doi:10.5539/ijbm.v4n9p106

FIAS & SEDF. (2006). *Piloting Reform through the Development and Management of Economic Zones*. Bangladesh: World Bank.

Filipek, P. (2001). *Neuro-Fuzzy Control of Inverter-Fed Induction Motor Drive*. (Ph.D Thesis). Lublin University of Technology.

Flasse, S. P., Ceccato, P., Downey, I. D., Raimadoya, M. A., & Navarro, P. (1997). *Remote sensing and GIS tools to support vegetation management in developing countries*. IEEE International. doi:10.1109/IGARSS.1997.608950

Fleiss, J. L. (1971). Measuring nominal scale agreement among many raters. *Psychological Bulletin, 76*(5), 378–382. doi:10.1037/h0031619

Ford & Roberts. (1998). *Colour space conversions, Westminster*. London: University.

Fredrick, C. M., & Ryan, R. M. (1993). Differences in motivation for sport and exercise and their relationship with participation and mental health. *Journal of Sport Behavior, 16*, 125–145.

Fukuhara, T., Warabino, T., Ohseki, T., Saito, K., Sugiyama, K., Nishida, T., & Eguchi, K. (2005). Broadcast methods for inter-vehicle communications system.*Proceedings of IEEE Wireless Communications and Networking Conference.*

Gabrys, B. (2002). Neuro-fuzzy approach to processing inputs with missing values in pattern recognition problems. *International Journal of Approximate Reasoning, 30*(3), 149–179. doi:10.1016/S0888-613X(02)00070-1

Gagula-Palalic & Mehmet. (2012). Inventory control using Fuzzy dynamic programming. *Southeast Europe Journal of Soft Computing, 1*(1), 37–42.

Galindo, A., & Micco, A. (2005). *Bank Credit to Small and Medium-Sized Enterprises: The Role of Creditor Protection*. Research Department Working Paper 527. Washington, DC: Inter-American Development Bank.

Gama, V., & Romero, D. (2004). Improvement of an Induction Motor Drive – Based Direct Torque Control Strategy Using a Neuro – Fuzzy Controller. *International Conference on Electrical and Electronics Engineering.*

Ganesan, N., Venkatesh, D. K., Rama, D. M. A., & Palani, A. M. (2010). Application of Neural Networks in Diagnosing Cancer Disease Using Demographic Data. *International Journal of Computers and Applications, 1*(26), 81–97. doi:10.5120/476-783

Gaokhan, K. (2006). *GPS Based Wireless Communication Protocols for Vehicular AD-HOC Networks*. (Unpublished doctoral dissertation). The Ohio State University, Columbus, OH.

Garcia-Diaz., Lopez-Martin, & Chavoya. (2013). A comparative study of two fuzzy logic models for software development effort estimation. In *Iberoamerican Conference on Electronics Engineering and Computer Science*. Elsevier.

Gerla. (2002). *Fisheye State Routing Protocol (FSR)*. IETF Internet Draft, draft-ietf-manet-fsr-03.txt.

Ghassan, A., Mosa, A., & Sidi, M. (2007). Current Trends in Vehicular Ad Hoc Networks.*IEEE Global Information Infrastructure Symposium.*

Ghezzi, C., Jazayeri, M., & Mandrioli, D. (2002). *Fundamentals of Software Engineering* (2nd ed.). India: Prentice-Hall.

Ghosh, & Celmins. (2008). A survey of recent advances in fuzzy logic in telecommunications networks and new challenges. *IEEE Transactions on Fuzzy Systems, 6*(3), 443–447.

Ghosh, A., Mishra, N. S., & Ghosh, S. (2010). Fuzzy clustering algorithms for unsupervised change detection in remote sensing images. *Information Sciences.*

Gianaroli, F., Pancaldi, F., & Vitetta, G. M. (2015). *A Novel Bit and Power Loading Algorithm for Narrowband Indoor Powerline Communications.* doi:10.1109/ICCW.2015.7247401

Goetschel, R. Jr, & Voxman, W. (1986). Elementary fuzzy calculus. *Fuzzy Sets and Systems, 18*(1), 31–43. doi:10.1016/0165-0114(86)90026-6

Gong, P. (2003). *Estimation of Forest Leaf Area Index Using Vegetation Indices Derived from Hyperion Hyperspectral Data. IEEE Transactions on Geoscience and Remote Sensing, 41(6).*

Gonsamo, A., & Pellikka, P. (2012). The sensitivity based estimation of leaf area index from spectral vegetation indices. *ISPRS Journal of Photogrammetry and Remote Sensing, 70,* 15–25. doi:10.1016/j.isprsjprs.2012.03.009

Gopal, J., Sangaiah, A.K., Basu, A., Gao, X.Z. (2015). Integration of fuzzy DEMATEL and FMCDM approach for evaluating knowledge transfer effectiveness with reference to GSD project outcome. Article in Press. *International Journal of Machine Learning and Cybernetics.* Doi:10.1007/s13042-015-0370-5

Gorodov & Gubarev. (2013). Analytical review of data visualization methods in application to Big Data. *Journal of Electrical and Computer Engineering,* (22), 1-7.

Grisi, R. M., Guerra, L., & Naviglio, G. (2010). Supplier performance evaluation for green supply chain management. In *Business Performance Measurement and Management* (pp. 149–163). Springer Berlin Heidelberg. doi:10.1007/978-3-642-04800-5_10

Grubbs, F. E. (1969, February). Procedures for detecting outlying observations in samples. *Technometrics, 11*(1), 1–21. doi:10.1080/00401706.1969.10490657

Grzymala-Busse, J. P., Grzymala-Busse, J. W., & Hippe, Z. S. (2001). Melanoma prediction using data mining system LERS. *Proceedings of the 25th Anniversary AnnualInternational Computer Software and Applications Conference COMPSAC.* doi:10.1109/CMPSAC.2001.960676

Guchhait, P., Maiti, M. K., & Maiti, M. (2013). A production inventory model with fuzzy production and demand using fuzzy differential equation: An interval compared genetic algorithm approach. *Engineering Applications of Artificial Intelligence, 26*(2), 766–778. doi:10.1016/j.engappai.2012.10.017

Guchhait, P., Maity, M. K., & Maity, M. (2014). Inventory model of a deteriorating item with price and credit linked fuzzy demand: A fuzzy differential equation approach. *OPSEARCH, 51*(3), 321–353. doi:10.1007/s12597-013-0153-2

Guneri, A. F., Gul, M., & Ozgurler, S. (2015). A fuzzy AHP methodology for selection of risk assessment methods in occupational safety. *International Journal of Risk Assessment and Management, 18*(3-4), 319–335. doi:10.1504/IJRAM.2015.071222

Guney, K., & Sarikaya, N. (2009). Comparison of Mamdani and Sugeno fuzzy inference system models for resonant frequency calculation of rectangular microstrip antennas. *Progression in Electromagnetic Research, B*(12), 81 – 104.

Guo, S., & Zhao, H. (2015). Optimal site selection of electric vehicle charging station by using fuzzy TOPSIS based on sustainability perspective. *Applied Energy, 158*, 390–402. doi:10.1016/j.apenergy.2015.08.082

Gyugi, L., & Pelly, B. R. (1970). *Static Power Frequency Changers: Theory, Performance and Application.* John Wiley & Sons.

Haider & Yusuf. (2009). A Fuzzy Approach to Energy Optimized Routing for Wireless Sensor Networks. *The International Arab Journal of Information Technology, 6*(2), 179-188.

Hakim, B., Anelise, M., Khaldoun, A., & Guy, P. (2003). QoS for Adhoc networking based on multiple Metrics: *Bandwidth and Delay. International Workshop on Mobile and Wireless Communications Networks.*

Hall, R. E., & Jones, C. (1999). Why Do Some Countries Produce So Much More Output per Worker than Others? *The Quarterly Journal of Economics, 114*(1), 83–116. doi:10.1162/003355399555954

Hallward, D., Wallsten, S., & Xu, L. C. (2003). *The Investment Climate and the Firm: Firm-Level Evidence from China.* Policy Research Working Paper. World Bank.

Handfield, R., Walton, S. V., Sroufe, R., & Melnyk, S. A. (2002). Applying environmental criteria to supplier assessment: A study in the application of the Analytical Hierarchy Process. *European Journal of Operational Research, 141*(1), 70–87. doi:10.1016/S0377-2217(01)00261-2

Han, W. M., & Huang, S. J. (2007). An empirical analysis of risk components and performance on software projects. *Journal of Systems and Software, 80*(1), 42–50. doi:10.1016/j.jss.2006.04.030

Han, W.-M. (2015). Discriminating risky software project using neural networks. *Computer Standards & Interfaces, 40*, 15–22. doi:10.1016/j.csi.2015.01.001

Haque & Rahman. (2014). Sentiment Analysis by Using Fuzzy Logic. *International Journal of Computer Science, Engineering and Information Technology, 4*(1).

Harris, F. (1915). *Operations and Cost-Factory management series.* Chicago, IL: A.W. Shaw Co.

Harris, J. A., & Benedict, F. G. (1918). A biometric study of human basal metabolism. *Proceedings of the National Academy of Sciences of the United States of America, 4*(12), 370–373. doi:10.1073/pnas.4.12.370 PMID:16576330

Harshvardhan, & Joshi, P. (2006). *Distributed Robust Geocast: A Multicast Protocol for Inter-Vehicle Communication.* (Unpublished Masters Dissertation). North Carolina State University.

Hartenstein, H., Bochow, B., & Ebner, A. (2001). Position-Aware Ad Hoc Wireless Networks for Inter-Vehicle Communications: The FleetNet Project.*MobiHoc'01: Proceedings of 2nd ACM International Symposium on Mobile Ad Hoc Networking & Computing.* New York: ACM Press. doi:10.1145/501416.501454

Hayes, A. F., & Krippendorff, K. (2007). Answering the call for a standard reliability measure for coding data. *Communication Methods and Measures, 1*(1), 77–89. doi:10.1080/19312450709336664

Haykin, S. (1994). *Neural Network: A Comprehensive Foundation.* McMillan College Publishing Co.

Hayward, G., & Davidson, V. (2003). Fuzzy logic application. *Analyst (London), 128*(11), 1304–1306. doi:10.1039/b312701j PMID:14700220

Hinton, G. (2015). Deep Belief Nets. In Encyclopedia of Machine Learning and Data Mining. Academic Press.

Hirsch. (1997). Unionization and Economic Performance: Evidence on Productivity, Profits, Investment, and Growth. In *Unions and Right-to-Work Laws.* The Fraser Institute.

Ho, A., Ho, H., & Kien, A. (2008). Routing Protocols for Inter-Vehicular Networks: A Comparative Study in High-Mobility and Large Obstacles Environments. *Computer Communications Journal*, 2767-2780.

Hogan, T. P., Benjamin, A., & Brezinksi, K. L. (2000). Reliability methods: A note on the frequency of use of various types. *Educational and Psychological Measurement*, *60*(4), 523–531. doi:10.1177/00131640021970691

Homik, Stinchcombe, & White. (1994). *Multilayer feed forward networks are universal approximators*. Academic Press.

Hong, Y., Member, S., Wu, T., Chen, L., & Member, S. (2016). On the Performance of Adaptive MIMO-OFDM Indoor Visible Light Communications. *IEEE Photonics Technology Letters*, *28*(8), 907–910. doi:10.1109/LPT.2016.2517192

Hossain, M. Z. (n.d.). *Export Diversification and Role of Export Processing Zones in Bangladesh*. Dhaka: Bangladesh EPZ Authority (BEPZA).

Ho, T. B., & Nguyen, N. B. (2002). Nonhierarchical Document Clustering Based on a Tolerance Rough Set Model. *International Journal of Intelligent Systems*, *17*(2), 199–212. doi:10.1002/int.10016

Hsu, C. W., & Hu, A. H. (2009). Applying hazardous substance management to supplier selection using analytic network process. *Journal of Cleaner Production*, *17*(2), 255–264. doi:10.1016/j.jclepro.2008.05.004

Huang, Wan, & Shen. (2009). *An Object-Based Approach for Forest-Cover Change Detection using Multi-Temporal High-Resolution Remote Sensing Data*. School of Remote Sensing and Information Engineering, Wuhan University.

Huang, Z. (1997). Clustering Large Data Sets With Mixed Numeric And Categorical Values. In *Proceedings of the First Pacific-Asia Conference on Knowledge Discovery and Data Mining*.

Huang, G.-B., Zhu, Q.-Y., & Siew, C.-K. (2006). Extreme learning machine: Theory nd applications. *Elsevier Neuro-computing*, *70*(1-3), 489–501. doi:10.1016/j.neucom.2005.12.126

Huber, L., & Borojevic, D. (1985). Space Vector modulator for force commutated cycloconverter structures. *IEEE Transactions on Industry Applications*, *1A*(5), 1242–1253.

Huber, L., & Borojevic, D. (1995). Space Vector Modulated Three Phase to Three Phase Matrix Converter with Input Power Factor Correction. *IEEE Transactions on Industry Applications*, *36*(6), 1234–1246. doi:10.1109/28.475693

Hubert, M., & Vandervieren, E. (2008). An Adjusted Boxplot for Skewed Distributions. *Computational Statistics & Data Analysis*, *52*(12), 5186–5201. doi:10.1016/j.csda.2007.11.008

Hudec, M. (2011). Fuzzy Improvement of the SQL. *Yugoslav Journal of Operations Research*, *21*(2), 239–251. doi:10.2298/YJOR1102239H

Hughes-Hartogs, D. (1989). *U.S. Patent No. 4,833,706*. Washington, DC: U.S. Patent and Trademark Office.

Hullermeier, E. (1997). An approach to modeling and simulation of uncertain dynamical systems. *International Journal of Uncertainty, Fuzziness and Knowledge-based Systems*, *5*(02), 117–137. doi:10.1142/S0218488597000117

Hung, C. C., Purnawan, H., Kuo, B. C., & Letkeman, S. (2009). *Multispectal Image Classification Using Rough Set Theory and Particle Swarm Optimization*. Advances in Geoscience and Remote Sensing.

Hussain, K., Abdullah, A. H., Awan, K. M., Ahsan, F., & Hussain, A. (2013). Cluster Head Election Schemes for WSN and MANET: A Survey. *World Applied Sciences Journal*, *23-5*, 611–620.

Huth, Kuenzer, Wehrmann, Gebhardt, Tuan, & Dech. (2012). Land Cover and Land Use Classification with TWOPAC: Towards Automated Processing for Pixel-and Object-Based Image Classification. *Remote Sensing, 4*, 2530-2553.

Hwang, C. L., & Yoon, K. (1981). *Multiple attribute decision making methods and application.* New York: Springer-Verlag. doi:10.1007/978-3-642-48318-9

Iglewicz, B., & Hoaglin, D. (1993). *How to detect and handle outliers.* ASQC Quality Press.

Ilia, V. S. (2007). *Automatic red eye detection.* Academic Press.

Ishibuchi, H., & Nakashima, T. (2001). Effect of Rule Weights in Fuzzy Rule-Based Classification Systems. *IEEE Transactions on Fuzzy Systems, 9*(4), 506–515. doi:10.1109/91.940964

Ivancevic, V. G., & Ivancevic, T. T. (2007). Introduction: Human and Computational Mind[SCI]. *Studies in Computational Intelligence, 60,* 1–269. doi:10.1007/978-3-540-71561-0_1

Jabri, M., Chouiref, H., Jebri, H., & Benhadj, B. (2008). Fuzzy Logic Parameter Estimation of an Electrical System, *IEEE International Multi-conference on Systems. Signals and Devices, 10,* 1–6.

Jackson, A. G., LeClair, V., Ohmer, M. C., Ziarko, W., & Al-Kamhwi, H. (1996). *Acta Metallurgica et Materialia.* Academic Press.

Jafari, H., Fishpaw, J., & Li, L. (2009). *The Investment Climate in the China and the Importance of Firm-Level Data.* Shanta Cruz, CA: University of California.

Jalote, P. (2005). *An Integrated Approach to Software Engineering* (3rd ed.). Springer.

Jarocinska & Zagajewski. (2009). *Remote Sensing tools for analysis of Vegetation condition in extensively used Agricultural Areas.* Academic Press.

Jennex, M. E. (2011). *Knowledge Management System Success Factors* (2nd ed.). doi:10.4018/978-1-60566-709-6

Jennex, M. E., & Olfman, L. (2003). A Knowledge Management Success Model (2003). An Extension of DeLone and McLean's IS Success Model.*Ninth Americas Conference on Information Systems.*

Jensen, R., & Shen, Q. (2009). New Approaches to Fuzzy-Rough Feature Selection. *IEEE Transactions on Fuzzy Systems, 17*(4), 824–838. doi:10.1109/TFUZZ.2008.924209

Jerusha, S. K. (2012). Location Aware Cluster Based Routing In Wireless Sensor Networks. *International Journal of Computer & Communication Technology, 3-5,* 1–6.

Jing, T., Lu, H., & Kurt, R. (2003). *Spatially Aware Packet Routing for Mobile Ad Hoc Inter-Vehicle Radio Networks.* Shangai, China: IEEE ITSC. doi:10.1109/ITSC.2003.1252743

Johnson, B., Maltz, D.A. & Hu, Y.C. (2004). *The Dynamic Source Routing Protocol for Mobile Ad Hoc Networks (DSR).* draft-ietf-manet-dsr-10.txt.

Johnson, R. (1992). *Applied Multivariate Statistical Analysis.* Prentice Hall.

Jonathan, K.E., Paul, M.G., Paul, S.V., & Steven, J.K. (2013). *Clinical exercise physiology.* Academic Press.

Jones, V., & Bose, B. (1976). A frequency step-up cycloconverter using power transistors in inverse series mode. *International Journal of Electronics, 41*(6), 573–587. doi:10.1080/00207217608920668

Jordan, M. I., & Rumelhart, D. E. (1992). Forward models: Supervised learning with a distal teacher. *Cognitive Science, 16*(3), 307–354. doi:10.1207/s15516709cog1603_1

Joshi, P. C. (2011). *Performance evaluation of vegetation indices using remotely sensed data. International Journal of Geomatics and Geosciences.*

Joshi, P. C. (2011). Performance evaluation of vegetation indices using remotely sensed data. *International Journal of Geomatics and Geosciences, 2*(1), 2011.

Julien, Y., Sobrino, J. A., Mattar, C., Ruescas, A. B., Jimenez-munoz, J. C., & Soria, G. et al. (2011, April10). Temporal analysis of Normalized Difference Vegetation Index (NDVI) and land surface temperature (LST) parameters to detect changes in the Iberian land cover between 1981 and 2001. *International Journal of Remote Sensing, 32*(7), 2057–2068. doi:10.1080/01431161003762363

Jung, S., Jung, S., & Han, S. (2015). AMO-FBMC for Asynchronous Heterogeneous Signal Integrated Optical Transmission. *IEEE Photonics Technology Letters, 27*(2), 133–136. doi:10.1109/LPT.2014.2363197

Jussila, M., Salo, M., & Tuusa, H. (2004). Induction Motor Drive fed by a Vector Controlled Indirect Matrix Converter. *Conference Proceedings of IEEE Power Electronics Specialists Conference.*

Kabir, G., & Hasin, M. (2012). Multiple criteria inventory classification using fuzzy analytic hierarchy process. *International Journal of Industrial Engineering Computations, 3*(2), 123–132. doi:10.5267/j.ijiec.2011.09.007

Kacprzyk, J., & Esogbue, A. O. (1996). Fuzzy dynamic programming: Main developments and applications. *Fuzzy Sets and Systems, 81*(1), 31–45. doi:10.1016/0165-0114(95)00239-1

Kahraman, C. U., & Ulukan, Z. (2003). Multi-criteria supplier selection using fuzzy AHP. *Logistics Information Management, 16*(6), 382-390.

Kahraman, C., Suder, A., & Bekar, E. T. (2015). Fuzzy multiattribute consumer choice among health insurance options. *Technological and Economic Development of Economy*, 1-20.

Kannan, D., Jabbour, A. B. L. D. S., & Jabbour, C. J. C. (2014). Selecting green suppliers based on GSCM practices: Using fuzzy TOPSIS applied to a Brazilian electronics company. *European Journal of Operational Research, 233*(2), 432–447. doi:10.1016/j.ejor.2013.07.023

Kannan, G., Pokharel, S., & Kumar, P. S. (2009). A hybrid approach using ISM and fuzzy TOPSIS for the selection of reverse logistics provider. *Resources, Conservation and Recycling, 54*(1), 28–36. doi:10.1016/j.resconrec.2009.06.004

Kant, S. (2015). Manufacturing system selection using fuzzy AHP. *MR International Journal of Engineering & Technology, 7*(1), 22–28.

Karami, R., & Sayyaadi, H. (2015). Optimal sizing of Stirling-CCHP systems for residential buildings at diverse climatic conditions. *Applied Thermal Engineering, 89*, 377–393. doi:10.1016/j.applthermaleng.2015.06.022

Karmyal, A. (2015). *Software Process Model*. Retrieved October 20, 2015, from http://www.slideshare.net/AtulKarmyal/software-process-models-29514469

Karp, B., & Kung, H. T. (2000). GPSR: Greedy Perimeter Stateless Routing for Wireless Networks. *MobiCom, 2000*, 29–36.

Katch, V. L. (2010). *Essentials of exercise Physiology* (4th ed.). Wolters Kluwer Lippincot Williams and Wilkings.

Kaufmann, D., Kraay, A., & Zoido-Lobatón, P. (1999). *Governance Matters*. Policy Research Working Paper 2196. World Bank.

Kaur, H., Singh, S. P., & Glardon, R. (2015). An Integer Linear Program for Integrated Supplier Selection: A Sustainable Flexible Framework. *Global Journal of Flexible Systems Management*, 1-22.

Kee, H. L. (2005). Foreign Ownership and Bangladesh Garment Sector. Development Research Group-Trade, the World Bank.

Keil, M., Rai, A., & Liu, S. (2013). How user risk and requirements risk moderate the effects of formal and informal control on the process performance of IT projects. *European Journal of Information Systems*, 22(6), 650–672. doi:10.1057/ejis.2012.42

Kelly, G. (2015). *Calorie Know-How: Get the equation right to get results*. Retrieved on 15 November 2015 from http://www.bodybuilding.com/fun/calorie-know-how-get-equation-right-to-get-results.htm

Keytel, L. R., Goedecke, J. H., Noakes, T. D., Hilloskorp, H., Laukkanen, R., Vander, M. L., & Lambert, E. V. (2005). Prediction of energy expenditiure from heart rate monitoring during sub maximal exercise. *Journal of Sports Sciences*, 23(3), 289–297. doi:10.1080/02640410470001730089 PMID:15966347

Khan, M. H. (2005). *What is a "Good Investment Climate"*. The International Bank for Reconstruction and Development/The World Bank.

Khastan, A., & Nieto, J. J. (2010). A boundary value problem for second-order fuzzy differential equations. *Nonlinear Analysis*, 72(9-10), 3583–3593. doi:10.1016/j.na.2009.12.038

Kilincci, O., & Onal, S. A. (2011). Fuzzy AHP approach for supplier selection in a washing machine company. *Expert Systems with Applications*, 38(8), 9656–9664. doi:10.1016/j.eswa.2011.01.159

Kinda, T. (2011). Firm Productivity and Investment Climate in Developing Countries: How Does Middle East and North African Manufacturing Performance? CERDI. *Eludes et Documents. E (Norwalk, Conn.)*, 26.

Klapper, L., Laeven, L., & Rajan, R. G. (2004). *Business Environment and Firm Entry: Evidence from International Data*. NBER Working Paper 10380. Cambridge, MA: National Bureau of Economic Research.

Klir, G. J., & Yuan, B. (1995). *Fuzzy Sets and Fuzzy Logic, Theory and Applications*. Prentice Hall.

Klumpner, C. (2005). An Indirect Matrix Converter with a Cost Effective Protection and Control, *European Conference on Power Electronics and Applications*. doi:10.1109/EPE.2005.219558

Knack, S., & Keefer, P. (1995). Institutions and Economic Performance: Cross-Country Tests Using Alternative Institutional Measures. *Economics and Politics*, 7(3), 207–227. doi:10.1111/j.1468-0343.1995.tb00111.x

Ko, Y. B., & Vaidhya, N. H. (1998). Location-Aided Routing (LAR) in Mobile Ad Hoc Network. *Proceedings of ACM/IEEE MOBICOM'98*.

Koch, B. (2010). Status and future of laser scanning, synthetic aperture radar and hyperspectral remote sensing data for forest biomass assessment. *ISPRS Journal of Photogrammetry and Remote Sensing*, 65(6), 581–590. doi:10.1016/j.isprsjprs.2010.09.001

Kong, Z., Gao, L., Wang, L., & Li, S. (2008). The normal parameter reduction of soft sets and its algorithm. *Computers & Mathematics with Applications (Oxford, England)*, 56(12), 3029–3037. doi:10.1016/j.camwa.2008.07.013

Kosch, T., Alder, C. J., Eichler, S., Schroth, C., & Strassberger, M. (2006). The scalability problem of vehicular ad hoc networks and how to solve it. *IEEE Wireless Communications*, 13(5), 22–28. doi:10.1109/WC-M.2006.250354

Koza, J. R. (1992). *Genetic Programming: On the Programming of Computers by Means of Natural Selection*. Cambridge, MA: The MIT Press.

Krippendorff, K. (2011). *Computing Krippendorff's Alpha-Reliability*. Academic Press.

Krippendorff, K. (2013). *Content analysis: An introduction to its methodology* (3rd ed.). Thousand Oaks, CA: Sage.

Krippendorf, K. (2004). Reliability in Content Analysis. *Some Common Misconceptions and Recommendations, 30*(3), 411–433.

Krisher, T. (2011). *AutoNation Profit Up 26 Percent as Sales Rise.* Accessed May 29, 2011, articles.sfgate. com/.../29477879_1_new-vehicle-ceo-mike-jackson-autonation

Kumar, A., & Jain, V. (2010, October). Supplier selection: a green approach with carbon footprint monitoring. In *Supply Chain Management and Information Systems (SCMIS), 2010 8th International Conference on* (pp. 1-8). IEEE.

Kumar, P. K., Venkata Subramanian, D., Chokkalingam, S.P., & Manoharan. R. (2014). *Multidimesnsional and Decision Tree Based Frameworks for Big Data Quality Assessment.* 2014 International Conference on Business Intelligence and Analytics.

Kwon, O., & Sim, J. M. (2013). Effects of data set features on the performances of classification algorithms. *Journal Expert Systems with Applications: An International Journal, 40*(5), 1847–1857. doi:10.1016/j.eswa.2012.09.017

Lansbury, M., & Mayes, D. (1996). Entry, Exit, Ownership and the Growth of Productivity. In D. Mayes (Ed.), *Sources of Productivity Growth.* Cambridge, UK: Cambridge University Press.

Lawrence, R. L., & Ripple, W. J. (1998). Comparisons among Vegetation Indices and Band wise Regression in a Highly Distributed, Heterogeneous Landscape: Mount St. Helens, Washington. *Remote Sensing of Environment, 64*(1), 91–102. doi:10.1016/S0034-4257(97)00171-5

Lawrence, S. (1997). *Face Recognition: A Convolutional Neural Network Approach. IEEE Transactions on Neural Networks.*

Le Toan, T., Beaudoin, A., Riom, J., & Guyon, D. (1992). Relating forest biomass to sar data. IEEE Trans. Geosci. Remote Sens., 30(2).

Lee, S.C., & Huang, M.J. (n.d.). Applying AI technology and rough set theory for mining association rules to support crime management and fire-fighting resources allocation, Journal of Information. Technology and Society, 2, 65–78.

Lee, A. H., Kang, H. Y., Hsu, C. F., & Hung, H. C. (2009). A green supplier selection model for high-tech industry. *Expert Systems with Applications, 36*(4), 7917–7927. doi:10.1016/j.eswa.2008.11.052

Lee, H. M., & Yao, J. S. (1999). Economic order quantity in fuzzy sense for inventory without backorder model. *Fuzzy Sets and Systems, 105*(1), 13–31. doi:10.1016/S0165-0114(97)00227-3

Lee, J. S. (1980). Digital image enhancement and noise filtering by use of local statistics. *IEEE Transactions on Pattern Analysis and Machine Intelligence, 2*(2), 165–168. doi:10.1109/TPAMI.1980.4766994 PMID:21868887

Lee, S., & Seo, K. K. (2015). A hybrid multi-criteria decision-making model for a cloud service selection problem using BSC, fuzzy Delphi method and fuzzy AHP. *Wireless Personal Communications,* 1–19.

Lei, & Bian. (2010). Analysis of Spatiotemporal Difference of NDVI in an Arid Coal Mining Region using *Remote Sensing.* Jiangsu Key Laboratory of Resources and Environmental Information Engineering, China University of Mining and Technology.

Li, & Yu, W. (2007). Routing in Vehicular Ad Hoc Networks: A Survey. *IEEE Vehicular Technology Magazine, 2*(2), 12-22.

Li, D., Deogun, J., Spaulding, W., & Shuart, B. (2004). Towards Missing Data Imputation: A Study of Fuzzy K-means Clustering Method. In RSCTC 2004, (LNAI), (vol. 3066, pp. 573–579). Springer. doi:10.1007/978-3-540-25929-9_70

Li, X., Jia, Zhang, Zhang, & Wang. (2010). Trust-Based on-Demand Multipath Routing in Mobile Ad Hoc Networks. *IET-Information Security, 4*(4), 212–223.

Liao, T. W. (2015). Two interval type 2 fuzzy TOPSIS material selection methods. *Materials & Design, 88*, 1088–1099. doi:10.1016/j.matdes.2015.09.113

Li, D., Deogun, J., Spaulding, W., & Shuart, B. (2005). *Dealing with Missing Data: Algorithms Based on Fuzzy Set and Rough Set Theories* (Vol. 3700). Transactions on Rough Sets IV Lecture Notes in Computer Science.

Li, M., & Wu, C. (2015). Green Supplier Selection Based on Improved Intuitionistic Fuzzy TOPSIS Model. *Metallurgical and Mining Industry, 6*, 193–205.

Lima Junior, F. R., Osiro, L., & Carpinetti, L. C. R. (2014). A comparison between Fuzzy AHP and Fuzzy TOPSIS methods to supplier selection. *Applied Soft Computing, 21*, 194–209. doi:10.1016/j.asoc.2014.03.014

Lim, C. P., & Harrison, R. F. (2003, May). online pattern classification with multiple neural network systems: An experimental study. *IEEE Transactions on Systems, Man and Cybernetics. Part C, Applications and Reviews, 33*.

Lim, C. P., Jain, L. C., & Dehuri, S. (2009). *Innovations in Swarm Intelligence: Studies in Computational Intelligence* (Vol. 248). Springer. doi:10.1007/978-3-642-04225-6_1

Lin, T. Y., & Cercone, N. (1997). Rough Sets and Data Mining - Analysis of Imperfect Data. Kluwer Academic Publishers.

Lingras, P., & West, C. (2004). Interval set clustering of web users with rough k-mean. *Journal of Intelligent Information Systems, 23*(1), 5–16. doi:10.1023/B:JIIS.0000029668.88665.1a

Lin, T. Y., & Wildberger, A. M. (1994). *The Third International Workshop on Rough Sets and Soft Computing Proceedings RSSC'94*. San Jose State University.

Liu, B. (2010). Sentiment Analysis and Subjectivity. InHandbook of Natural Language Processing (2nd ed.). Academic Press.

Liu, Zheng, Zhang, Chen, & Shen. (2012). Secure and Energy-Efficient Disjoint Multipath Routing for WSNs. *IEEE Transactions on Vehicular Technology, 61*(7), 3255-3265.

Liu, S., & Wang, L. (2014). Understanding the impact of risks on performance in internal and outsourced information technology projects: The role of strategic importance. *International Journal of Project Management, 32*(8), 1494–1510. doi:10.1016/j.ijproman.2014.01.012

Lochert, C., Mauve, M., Fubler, H., & Hartenstein, H. (2005). Geographic Routing in City Scenarios. *ACM SIGMOBILE Mobile Computing and Communications Review (MC2R), 9*(1), 69–72.

Lochert, C., Hartenstein, H., Tian, J., Fubler, H., Hermann, D., & Mauve, M. (2003). A Routing Strategy for Vehicular Ad Hoc Networks in City Environments.*Proceedings of IEEE Intelligent Vehicles Symposium (IV2003)*. doi:10.1109/IVS.2003.1212901

Logambigai, R., & Kannan, A. (2014). QEER: QoS aware Energy Efficient Routing Protocol for Wireless Sensor Networks.*Sixth IEEE International Conference on Advanced Computing (ICoAC)*. doi:10.1109/ICoAC.2014.7229745

Lo, Y. W., & Potdar, V. (2009). A Review of Opinion Mining and Sentiment Classification Framework in Social Networks. *3rd IEEE International Conference on Digital Ecosystems and Technologies*. doi:10.1109/DEST.2009.5276705

Luis, U., Almeida, D., Tripp-Barba, C., & Igartua, M. A. (2015). Heuristics Methods in Geographical Routing Protocols for VANETs. PE-WASUN '15, Cancun, Mexico.

Luis, U., Tripp-Barba, C., & Angel, R. (2015). Reducing Duplicate Packets in Unicast VANET Communications. PE-WASUN '15, Cancun, Mexico.

Lu, L. Y., Wu, C. H., & Kuo, T. C. (2007). Environmental principles applicable to green supplier evaluation by using multi-objective decision analysis. *International Journal of Production Research*, *45*(18-19), 4317–4331. doi:10.1080/00207540701472694

Lushu, L. (2001). Fuzzy Dynamic Approach to Hybrid Multiobjective multistage Decision Making Problems. *Fuzzy Sets and Systems*, *117*(1), 13–25. doi:10.1016/S0165-0114(98)00423-0

Ma, Wu, & Liu. (2009). *Remote Sensing Monitoring For Vegetation Change In Mining Area Based On Spot-VGT NDVI*. Institute for Geoinformatics & Digital Mine Research, Northeastern University.

Maen, M., William, R., & William, J. (2005). Assignment of dynamic transmission range based on estimation of vehicle density.*Proceedings of the 2nd ACM International Workshop on Vehicular ad hoc Networks*.ACM.

Magscale-Macandog, D. B., & Delgado, M. E. M. (2006). A GIS-based model to improve estimattion of above ground biomass of secondary forests in the Philippines. *Journal of Tropical Forest Science*, *18*(1), 8–21.

Maham, Hjørungnes, & Narasimhan. (2011). Energy-Efficient Space-Time Coded Cooperation in Outage-Restricted Multihop Wireless Networks. *IEEE Transactions on Communications*, *59*(11), 3111-3121.

Mahanti, R., & Neogi, M. S. (2012). *Vandana Bhattacherjee* (Vol. 8). Factors Affecting the Choice of Software Life Cycle Models in the Software Industry-An Empirical Study. In Journal of Computer Science.

Maihfer. (2004). A survey on geocast routing protocols. *IEEE Communications Surveys and Tutorials*, *6*(2), 32-42.

Maji, P. K., Biswas, R., & Roy, A. R. (2001). Fuzzy Soft Sets. *Journal of Fuzzy Mathematics*, *9*(3), 589–602.

Maji, P. K., Biswas, R., & Roy, A. R. (2002). An Application of Soft Sets in a Decision Making Problem. *Computers & Mathematics with Applications (Oxford, England)*, *44*(8-9), 1007–1083. doi:10.1016/S0898-1221(02)00216-X

Maji, P. K., Biswas, R., & Roy, A. R. (2003). Soft Set Theory. *Computers & Mathematics with Applications (Oxford, England)*, *45*(4-5), 555–562. doi:10.1016/S0898-1221(03)00016-6

Maji, P., & Pal, S. K. (2007). RFCM: A Hybrid Clustering Algorithm using rough and fuzzy set. *Fundamenta Informaticae*, *80*(4), 475–496.

Maji, P., & Pal, S. K. (2007). Rough Set Based Generalized Fuzzy C-Means Algorithm and Quantitative Indices. *IEEE Transactions on Systems, Man, and Cybernetics. Part B, Cybernetics*, *37*(6), 1529–1540. doi:10.1109/TSMCB.2007.906578 PMID:18179071

Mamdani, E. H., & Assilan, S. (1975). An Experiment in Linguistic Synthesis with a Fuzzy Logic Controller. *International Journal of Man-Machine Studies*, *7*(1), 1–13. doi:10.1016/S0020-7373(75)80002-2

Margaria, R., Cerrefolli, P., Agnemo, P., & Sassi, G. (1963). Energy cost of running. *Journal of Applied Physiology*, *18*, 367–370. PMID:13932993

Marvi, L. T., & Behzadfar, M. (2015). Local Sustainability with Emphasis on CPTED Approach, The Case of Ab-kooh Neighborhood in Mash-had. *Procedia: Social and Behavioral Sciences*, *201*, 409–417. doi:10.1016/j.sbspro.2015.08.194

Marwala, T., & Chakraverty, S. (2006). Fault classification in structures with incomplete measured data using auto associative neural networks and genetic algorithm. *Current Science India*, *90*(4), 542–548.

Masoud Barakati, S. (2008). *Modelling and Controller design of a Wind Energy Conversion System including a Matrix Converter*. (Ph.D thesis). University of Waterloo.

Mathiyalagan, P. (2015, May). Use of fuzzy TOPSIS techniques for selection of best alternatives of blood bank Supply chain. In *Smart Technologies and Management for Computing, Communication, Controls, Energy and Materials (ICSTM)*, *2015 International Conference on* (pp. 644-649). IEEE. doi:10.1109/ICSTM.2015.7225492

Matsushita, Yang, Chen, Onda, & Qiu. (2007). *Sensitivity of the Enhanced Vegetation Index (EVI) and Normalized Difference Vegetation Index (NDVI) to Topographic Effects: A Case Study in High-Density Cypress Forest.* Graduate School of Life and Environmental Sciences, University of Tsukuba.

Mauve, M., Fubler, H., Hartenstein, H., Kasemann, M., Vollmer, D. (2003). Location based Routing for Vehicular Ad Hoc Networks. *ACM SIGMOBILE Mobile Computing and Communications Review (MC2R), 7*(1), 47–49.

Mbaekwe, E. I., & Mackenzie, J. A. (2008). The use of a best-fit allometric model to estimate aboveground biomass accumulation and distribution in an age series of teak (tectona grandis l.f.) plantations at Gambari Forest Reserve, Oyo State, Nigeria. *Tropical Ecology, 49*(2), 259–270.

McCulloch, W. S., & Pitts, W. H. (1943). A Logical Calculus of the Ideas Immanent in Nervous Activity. *The Bulletin of Mathematical Biophysics, 5*, 115–133.

Meier, H. B., Cunningham, R., & Cahill, V. (2005). Towards realtime middleware for applications of vehicular ad hoc networks. *Proceedings of IFIP International Conference on Distributed applications and interoperable systems* (DAIS '05). doi:10.1007/11498094_1

Mendel. (1995). Fuzzy logic systems for engineering: a tutorial. *Proc. IEEE, 3*(3), 345–377.

Metcalf, D. (2003). Unions Impact and Implications for Future Membership. In P. Gregg & J. Wadsworth (Eds.), The State of Working Britain (2nd ed.). Academic Press.

Meyer & Neto. (2008). Verification of color vegetation indices for automated crop imaging applications. *Computers and Electronics in Agriculture, 6*(3), 282–293.

Michalopoulos, M., Dounias, G. D., Thomaidis, N., & Tselentis, G. (2001). *Decision Making Using Fuzzy C Means and Inductive Machine Learning For Managing Bank Branches Performance.* Academic Press.

Minatoura, Y., Khazaie, J., Ataei, M., & Javadi, A. A. (2015). An integrated decision support system for dam site selection. *Scientia Iranica. Transaction A. Civil Engineering (New York, N.Y.), 22*(2), 319–330.

Min, H., & Kim, I. (2012). Green supply chain research: Past, present, and future. *Logistics Research, 4*(1-2), 39–47. doi:10.1007/s12159-012-0071-3

Mishra, A., & Dubey, D. (2013). *A Comparative Study of Different Software Development Life Cycle Models in Different Scenarios* (Vol. 1). InInternational Journal of Advance Research in Computer Science and Management Studies.

Mitchell, M. (1996). *An introduction to Genetic Algorithms.* MIT Press.

Mitra, S., Banka, H. & Pedrycz, W. (n.d.). Rough-Fuzzy Collaborative Clustering. System, Man, and Cybernetics, *Part B: Cybernetics.* IEEE Transactions on, 36(4), 795–805.

Mitra, P., Pal, S. K., & Siddiqi, M. A. (2003). Non-convex clustering using expectation maximization algorithm with rough set initialization. *Pattern Recognition Letters, 24*(6), 863–873. doi:10.1016/S0167-8655(02)00198-8

Mohammad, S.A., Jafar, H., & Emad, S. (2008). Induction of Fuzzy Classification Systems Via Evolutionary Aco-Based Algorithms. *International Journal of Simulation Systems, Science and Technology, 9*(3).

Mohammadjafari, M., & Zohary, M. (2015). Supplier selection by Using Integrated Fuzzy Topsis and Multi Criteria Goal Decision Making Approach. *European Online Journal of Natural and Social Sciences, 4*(1), 1153–1161.

Molodtsov, D. (1999). Soft Set Theory - First Results. *Computers & Mathematics with Applications (Oxford, England), 37*(4-5), 19–31. doi:10.1016/S0898-1221(99)00056-5

Mondal, S.P., & Roy, T.K. (2013). First Order Linear Homogeneous Fuzzy Ordinary Differential Equation Based on Lagrange Multiplier Method. *Journal of Soft Computing and Applications*, 1-17.

Mondal, M., Maiti, M. K., & Maiti, M. (2013). A production-recycling model with variable demand, demand-dependent fuzzy return rate: A fuzzy differential equation approach. *Computers & Industrial Engineering, 64*(1), 318–332. doi:10.1016/j.cie.2012.10.014

Mukkamala, R. R., Hussain, A., & Vatrapu, R. (2014). Fuzzy-Set Based Sentiment Analysis of Big Social Data. *Enterprise Distributed Object Computing Conference (EDOC), 2014 IEEE 18th International*.

Muller, B., Meuk, S., Burgi, U., & Diem, P. (2001). Calculating the basal metabolic rate and severe and morbid obesity. *Praxis (Bern 1994), 90*(45), 1955-63.

Muttakin, M.B. & Ahmed, S. (2005). The Investment Scenario in Bangladesh- Problems and Prospects. *Pakistan Journal of Social Sciences, 3*(4).

Myneni, R. B., Hall, F. G., Sellers, P. J., & Marshak, A. L. (1995, March). The Interpretation of Spectral Vegetation Indexes. *IEEE Transactions on Geoscience and Remote Sensing, 33*(2), 481–486. doi:10.1109/36.377948

Nader-Esfahani, S., & Afrasiabi, M. (2007). Simple bit loading algorithm for OFDM-based systems. *Electronics Letters, 1*(3), 312–316. doi:10.1049/iet-com

Na, K. S., Simpson, J. T., Li, X., Singh, T., & Kim, K. Y. (2007). Software development risk and project performance measurement: Evidence in Korea. *Journal of Systems and Software, 80*(4), 596–605. doi:10.1016/j.jss.2006.06.018

Namboodiri, & Gao, L. (2007). Prediction based routing for vehicular ad hoc networks. *IEEE Transactions on Vehicular Technology, 56*(4), 1-29.

Nancy, J. (2009). A comparison of two boxplot methods for detecting univariate outliers which adjust for sample size and asymmetry. *Statistical Methodology, 6*(6), 604–621. doi:10.1016/j.stamet.2009.07.001

Nathan, B., & Jinhua, G. (2006). Increasing broadcast reliability in vehicular ad hoc networks.*Proceedings of the 3rd international workshop on Vehicular ad hoc networks*.

Nauck, D. (1997) Neuro-fuzzy systems: review and prospects. In *Fifth European Congress on Intelligent Systems and Soft Computing*.

Naumov, & Gross, T. (2007). Connectivity-aware routing (car) in vehicular ad hoc networks. *Proceedings of the IEEE International Conference on Computer Communications*.

Navar, J. (2010). *Measurement and assessment methods of forest aboveground biomass: A literature review and the challenges ahead, Biomass*. Croatia: Sciyo.

NCAER. (2010). *Investment Climate, Physical and Economic Infrastructure*. Access on 3/7/2010 from http://www.ncaer.org/researcho2.html

Nelwamondo, F. V., Mohamed, S., & Marwala, T. (2007). Missing data: A comparison of neural network and expectation maximization techniques. *Curr. Sci. India, 93*, 1514–1521.

Neogi, M. S., Bhattacherjee, V., & Mahanti, R. (2009). An Evaluation of Student Preferences during Software Development. In *Proceedings of national seminar on Recent Advances Information Technology (RAIT)*, (pp. 239-245).

Neogi, M., Chakraborty, S., & Bhattacherjee, V. (2013). Factors Influencing Software Development Process: A statistical Outlook. In*International Journal of Software Engineering and Its Applications, 7*(6), 221–236. doi:10.14257/ijseia.2013.7.6.19

Nie & Liu. (2013). The Opinion Mining Based on Fuzzy Domain Sentiment Ontology Tree for Product Reviews. *Journal of Software, 8*(11).

Nikhil, R. (2005). Possibilistic Fuzzy c-Means Clustering Algorithm. *IEEE Transactions on Fuzzy Systems, 13-4*, 517–530.

Niranjan, P., & Atulya, M. (2006). Mobility Models for Vehicular Ad Hoc Network Simulations. *ACM SE, 06*, 746–747.

Nishanth, K. J., Ravi, V., Ankaiah, N., & Bose, I. (2012). Soft computing based imputation and hybrid data and text mining: The case of predicting the severity of phishing alerts. *Expert Systems with Applications, 39*(12), 10583–10589. doi:10.1016/j.eswa.2012.02.138

Nizalapur, V., Jha, C. S., & Madugundu, R. (2010). Estimation of above ground biomass in Indian tropical forested area using multifrequency dlresar data. *International Journal Of Geomatics And Geosciences, 1*(2), 2010.

Noci, G. (1997). Designing 'green' vendor rating systems for the assessment of a supplier's environmental performance. *European Journal of Purchasing & Supply Management, 3*(2), 103–114. doi:10.1016/S0969-7012(96)00021-4

Nouri, F. A., Esbouei, S. K., & Antucheviciene, J. (2015). A Hybrid MCDM Approach Based on Fuzzy ANP and Fuzzy TOPSIS for Technology Selection. *Informatica, 26*(3), 369–388. doi:10.15388/Informatica.2015.53

NoW. (2010). *Network on wheels*. Retrieved September 15, 2010 from http://www.network-on-wheels.de/

NS2. (2010). *Network Simulator – 2*. Retrieved April 16, 2010 from http://www.isi.edu/nsnam/ns/

Nunnally, J. C. (1978). *Psychometric Theory*. New York: McGrew Hill.

OECD. (2008). *Benchmark Definition of Foreign Direct Investment* (4th ed.). www.oecd.org/publishing/connigenda

Omron. (n.d.). Retrieved from https://www.omron.com/

Ozkan, B., Kaya, I., Cebeci, U., & Başlıgil, H. (2015). A Hybrid Multicriteria Decision Making Methodology Based on Type-2 Fuzzy Sets For Selection Among Energy Storage Alternatives. *International Journal of Computational Intelligence Systems, 8*(5), 914–927. doi:10.1080/18756891.2015.1084715

Oztaysi, B. (2015). A Group Decision Making Approach Using Interval Type-2 Fuzzy AHP for Enterprise Information Systems Project Selection. *Journal of Multiple-Valued Logic & Soft Computing, 24*(5), 475–500.

Pak, A., & Paroubek, P. (2010). Twitter as a corpus for sentiment analysis and opinion mining. In *Proceedings of LREC*.

Palanivel. K (2016). Fuzzy commercial traveler problem of trapezoidal membership functions within the sort of α optimum solution using ranking technique. *Afrika Matematika, 27*(1), 263 – 277.

Panda & Mondal. (2013). Rough Set Techniques for Text Classification and Sentiment Analysis in Social Media. *International Journal of Emerging Technologies in Computational and Applied Sciences*.

Panda, S. S., Ames, D. P., & Panigrahi, S. (2010). Application of Vegetation Indices for Agricultural Crop Yield Prediction Using Neural Network Techniques. *Remote Sensing, 2*(3), 673–696. doi:10.3390/rs2030673

Panigrahi, K., Shi, Y., & Lim, M.-H. (2011). *Handbook of Swarm Intelligence. Series: Adaptation, Learning, and Optimization* (Vol. 7). Springer-Verlag Berlin Heidelberg. doi:10.1007/978-3-642-17390-5

Parmar, D., Wu, T., & Blackhurst, J. (2007). MMR: An algorithm for clustering categorical data using Rough Set Theory. *Data and Knowledge Engineering*, *63*(3), 879–893. doi:10.1016/j.datak.2007.05.005

Patil, S. K., & Kant, R. (2014). A hybrid approach based on fuzzy DEMATEL and FMCDM to predict success of knowledge management adoption in supply chain. *Applied Soft Computing*, *18*, 126–135. doi:10.1016/j.asoc.2014.01.027

Pawar, Y.S., Sapre, R.G. & Sayali, R. S. (2011). On Effective Data Retrieval from SQL by use of Fuzzy logic. *International Journal of Fuzzy Mathematics and Systems, 1*(2), 173-180.

Pawlak, Z. (1982). Rough sets. *Int. Jour. of Computer and Information Sciences, 11*, 341-356.

Pawlak, Z., & Skowron, A. (2007). Rudiments of rough sets. *Information Sciences - An International Journal*, *177*(1), 3 – 27.

Pawlak, Z. (1982). Rough sets. *Int. J. of Information and Computer Sciences*, *11*(5), 341–356. doi:10.1007/BF01001956

Pawlak, Z., & Skowron, A. (1994). Rough membership function. In R. E. Yeager, M. Fedrizzi, & J. Kacprzyk (Eds.), *Advaces in the Dempster-Schafer of Evidence* (pp. 251–271). New York: Wiley.

Perkins, C., & Royer, E. M. (2004). *Quality of Service for Adhoc on-demand distance vector routing*. Retrieved September 18, 2010 from http://people.nokia.net/charliep/txt/aodvid/qos.txt

Perkins, C., Royer, E.B., & Das, S. (2003). *Ad Hoc On-Demand Distance Vector (AODV) Routing*. RFC 3561 Network Working Group.

Pernia, E. M., & Salas, I. S. (2005). *Investment Climate and Regional Development in the Philippines*. Discussion Paper No. 0501. University of the Philippines School of Economics, Quezon City.

Pernia, E. M., & Salas, J. M. I. S. (2006). Investment Climate, Productivity and Regional Development in a Developing Country. *Asian Development Review*, *23*(2), 70–89.

Pitambare, D. P., & Kamde, P. M. (2013). Literature Survey on Genetic Algorithm Approach for Fuzzy Rule-Based System. *International Journal of Engine Research*, *2*(2), 29–32.

Poonam. (2014). Fuzzy to SQL Conversion using Gefred Model with the help of MATLAB. *International Journal of Computer Applications, 104*(17).

Prabhakar, R. S., Arunkumar, T., & Sivanandam, S. N. (2011a). A QoS Adaptive Routing Scheme (QARS) for highly dynamic Vehicular Networks with support to service and priority. *World Applied Sciences Journal*, *13*(5), 1259–1268.

Prabhakar, R. S., Sivanandam, S. N., & Arunkumar, T. (2011b). Simulation study on service based adaptive QoS framework for Vehicular AdHoc Network – REDEM. *International Journal of Research and Reviews in Information Technology*, *1*(3), 58–62.

Prabhakar, R. S., Sivanandam, S. N., & Arunkumar, T. (2011c). A Modeling Approach to achieve optimal Quality of Service for streaming media services over MANET. *International Journal of Research and Reviews in Information Technology*, *1*(1), 14–19.

Prather, J. C., Lobach, D. F., Goodwin, L. K., Hales, J. W., Hage, M. L., & Hammond, W. E. (1997). Medical Data Mining: Knowledge Discovery in a Clinical Data Warehouse.[]. AMIA.]. *Proceedings of the AMIA Annual Fall Symposium*, *101*(5)

Pravin, G., Girish, K., & Pradip, G. (2010). Mobile ad hoc networking: imperatives and challenges. *IJCA*, 153-158.

Pressman, R. (2004). *Software Engineering: A Practitioner's Approach* (6th ed.). McGraw Hill.

Priyadarishini, A., Karthik, S., Anuradha, J., & Tripathy, B. K. (2011). Diagnosis of Psychopathology using Clustering and Rule Extraction using Rough Set. *Advances in Applied Science Research, 2*(3), 346–362.

Priydarshini, R., Dash, N., & Misra, R. (2014). A Novel approach to predict diabetes mellitus using modified Extreme learning machine. *Proceedings of International Conference on Electronics and Communication Systems (ICECS)*. doi:10.1109/ECS.2014.6892740

Prochdxka & Kolinovd. (2000). *Satellite Image Processing and Air Pollution Detection*. Prague Institute of Chemical Technology

Puri, M. L., & Ralescu, D. A. (1983). Differentials of fuzzy functions. *Journal of Mathematical Analysis and Applications, 91*(2), 552–558. doi:10.1016/0022-247X(83)90169-5

Pyle, D. (1999). *Data Preparation for Data Mining*. San Francisco, CA: Morgan Kaufmann.

Qing, X., Raja, S., Tony, M., & Jeff, K. (2004). Vehicle-to-vehicle safety messaging in DSRC. *Proceedings of 1st ACM International Workshop on Vehicular Ad Hoc Networks* (VANET '04).

Quddus, M., & Rashid, S. (2000). *Entrepreneurs and Economic Development: The Remarkable Story of Garment Exports from Bangladesh*. Dhaka: The University Press.

Quing, Li, Wu, & Li. (2010). *MODIS-NDVI-Based crop growth monitoring in China Agriculture Remote Sensing Monitoring System*. Grassland Ecosystem Observation and Research Station Institute of Agricultural Resources and Regional Planning of Chinese Academy of Agricultural Sciences.

Radzikowska, A. M., & Kerre, E. E. (2002). A comparative study of fuzzy rough sets. *Fuzzy Sets and Systems, 126*(2), 137–156. doi:10.1016/S0165-0114(01)00032-X

Rahman, G., & Islam, Z. (2016). Missing value imputation using a fuzzy clustering-based EM approach. *Springer Knowledge and Information Systems, 46*(2), 389-422.

Rahman. (2008). Globalization and the Climate of Foreign Direct Investment: A Case for Bangladesh. *Journal of Money, Investment and Banking,* (5).

Rahul, M., Narinder, S., & Yaduvir, S. (2011). Soft Computing Technique for Process Control Applications. *International Journal of Soft Computing, 2*(3), 32–38. doi:10.5121/ijsc.2011.2303

Rajasekaran & Vijayalakshmi. (2012). *Neural Networks, Fuzzy Logic, and Genetic Algorithms: Synthesis and Applications*. Academic Press.

Rajesh, R., & Siva Prakash, J. (2011). Extreme learning machines - A review and state-of-the-art. *International Journal of Wisdom Based Computing, 1*(1), 35–49.

Raju, K. S., & Kumar, D. N. (1999). Multicriterion decision making in irrigation planning. *Agricultural Systems, 62*(2), 117–129. doi:10.1016/S0308-521X(99)00060-8

Rasheed, M. (2014). Elawady1, Sherif Barakat2, Nora M.Elrashidy2,*Different Feature Selection for Sentiment Classification. *International Journal of Information Science and Intelligent System, 3*(1), 137–150.

Rastogi, V. (2015). Software Development Life Cycle Models- Comparison, Consequences. *International Journal of Computer Science and Information Technologies*.

Rawlins, G. (1991). *Foundations of genetic algorithms*. San Mateo: Morgan Kauffman Publishers.

Ren, J., & Lützen, M. (2015). Fuzzy multi-criteria decision-making method for technology selection for emissions reduction from shipping under uncertainties. *Transportation Research Part D, Transport and Environment, 40*, 43–60. doi:10.1016/j.trd.2015.07.012

Richard, L. (1996). *Methods for Classification*. Retrieved October 20, 2015, from http://sundog.stsci.edu/rick/SCMA/node2.html

Ritterfeld, U., Cody, M., & Vorderer, P. (2009). *Serious Games: Mechanisms and effects*. London: Routledge.

Roettger. (2006). *NDVI Based Vegetation Rendering*. Computer Graphics Group, University of Erlangen.

Rojas, R. (1996). *Neural Networks*. Berlin: Springer-Verlag. doi:10.1007/978-3-642-61068-4

Roy, P. S., & Kumar, S. (1986) Advanced Very High Resolution Radiometer(AVHRR) satellite data forvegetation monitoring. *Proc. International Seminar on Photogrammetry and Remote Sensing fordeveloping countries*.

Roza, A., Shizgal, H., & Harry, M. (1984). The Harris Benedict equation reevaluated: Resting energy requirements and the body cell Mass. *The American Journal of Clinical Nutrition, 40*, 168–182. PMID:6741850

Rozenstein & Karnieli. (2011). Comparison of methods for Land-use classification incorporating Remote Sensing and GIS Inputs. *EARSel eProceedings, 10*(1).

Rumelhart, D. E., Hinton, G. E., & Williams, R. J. (1986). Learning internal representations by backpropagating errors. *Nature, 323*(6088), 533–536. doi:10.1038/323533a0

Saaty, T. L. (1980a). *The Analytic Hierarchy Process*. New York: McGraw-Hill.

Saaty, T. L. (1980b). *The analytic hierarchy process: planning priority setting resource allocation*. London: McGraw Hill International Book Company.

Saaty, T. L. (1986). Axiomatic Foundation of the Analytic Hierarchy Process. *Management Science, 32*(7), 841–855. doi:10.1287/mnsc.32.7.841

Saaty, T. L. (1994a). How to Make a Decision: The Analytic Hierarchy Process. *Interfaces, 24*(6), 19–43. doi:10.1287/inte.24.6.19

Saaty, T. L. (1994b). *Fundamentals of Decision Making*. Pittsburgh, PA: RWS Publications.

Sakhuja, S., Jain, V., & Dweiri, F. (2015). Application of an integrated MCDM approach in selecting outsourcing strategies in hotel industry. *International Journal of Logistics Systems and Management, 20*(3), 304–324. doi:10.1504/IJLSM.2015.068430

Salakhutdinov, R., & Hinton, G. (2009). *Deep Boltzmann Machines*. 12th International Conference on Artificial Intelligence and Statistics (AISTATS) 2009, Clearwater Beach, FL.

Saleha, R., Haider, J. N., & Danish, N. (2002). Rough Intuitionistic Fuzzy Set. *Proc. of 8th Int. conf. on Fuzzy Theory and Technology* (FT & T).

Salimi, N., & Rezaei, J. (2015). Multi-criteria university selection: Formulation and implementation using a fuzzy AHP. *Journal of Systems Science and Systems Engineering*, 1–23.

Sangaiah, A. K., Gopal, J., Basu, A., & Subramaniam, P. R. (2015). (Article in Press). An integrated fuzzy DEMATEL, TOPSIS, and ELECTRE approach for evaluating knowledge transfer effectiveness with reference to GSD project outcome. *Neural Computing and Applications, Springer Publishers*. doi:10.1007/s00521-015-2040-7

Sangaiah, A. K., Subramaniam, P. R., & Zheng, X. A. (2014). combined fuzzy DEMATEL and fuzzy TOPSIS approach for evaluating GSD project outcome factors. *Neural Computing & Applications*, *26*(5), 1025–1040. doi:10.1007/s00521-014-1771-1

Sangaiah, A. K., & Thangavelu, A. K. (2013). An exploration of FMCDM approach for evaluating the outcome/success of GSD projects. *Central European Journal of Engineering*, *3*(3), 419–435.

Sangaiah, A. K., & Thangavelu, A. K. (2014). An adaptive neuro-fuzzy approach to evaluation of team-level service climate in GSD projects. *Neural Computing & Applications*, *25*(3-4), 573–583. doi:10.1007/s00521-013-1521-9

Sangaiah, A. K., Thangavelu, A. K., Gao, X. Z., Anbazhagan, N., & Durai, M. S. (2015). An ANFIS approach for evaluation of team-level service climate in GSD projects using Taguchi-genetic learning algorithm. *Applied Soft Computing*, *30*, 628–635. doi:10.1016/j.asoc.2015.02.019

Saravanan, P., & Sailakshmi, P. (2015). Missing Value Imputation Using Fuzzy Possibilistic C Means Optimized With Support Vector Regression And Genetic Algorithm. *Journal of Theoretical and Applied Information Technology, 72*(1).

Sastry, K. S., & Babu, D. M. P. (2010). Fuzzy logic based adaptive modulation using non data aided SNR estimation for OFDM system. *International Journal of Engineering Science and Technology*, *2*(6), 2384–2392.

Savino, M. M., Macchi, M., & Mazza, A. (2015). Investigating the impact of social sustainability within maintenance operations: An action research in heavy industry. *Journal of Quality in Maintenance Engineering*, *21*(3), 310–331. doi:10.1108/JQME-06-2014-0038

Schweickardt, G. A., & Miranda, V. (2007). A Fuzzy Dynamic Approach for Evaluation of Expansion Distribution cost in Uncertainty Environments. *Latin American Applied Research*, *37*, 227–234.

Schwertman, N. C., & de Silva, R. (2007). Identifying outliers with sequential fences. *Computational Statistics & Data Analysis*, *51*(8), 3800–3810. doi:10.1016/j.csda.2006.01.019

Schwertman, N. C., Owens, M. A., & Adnan, R. (2004). A Simple More General Boxplot Method for Identifying Outliers. *Computational Statistics & Data Analysis*, *47*(1), 165–174. doi:10.1016/j.csda.2003.10.012

Serban, Vanschoren, Kietz & Bernstein. (2013). A survey of intelligent assistants for Data Analysis. *Journal ACM Computing Surveys, 45*(3).

Shamsi, Khojaye, & Qasmi. (2013). Data Intensive Cloud Computing: Requirements, Expectations, Challenges and Solutions. *Journal of Grid Computing, 11*(2), 281-310.

Shanmughavel, P. (2001). Nutrient cycling in a tropical seasonal rain forest of Xishuangbanna, Southwest China. Part 1: Tree species: Nutrient distribution and uptake. *Bioresource Technology*, *80*, 163–170. doi:10.1016/S0960-8524(01)00095-5 PMID:11601539

Sharma, Rai, & Dev. (2012). A Comprehensive Study of Artificial Neural Networks. *International Journal of Advanced Research in Computer Science and Software Engineering, 2*(10).

Sharma. (2012). A Comprehensive Study of Artificial Neural Networks. *International Journal of Advanced Research in Computer Science and Software Engineering, 2*(10).

Sharma. (2015). DSP in image processing. *International Journal of Advanced Research in Computer and Communication Engineering, 4*(1).

Shaw, K., Shankar, R., Yadav, S. S., & Thakur, L. S. (2012). Supplier Selection Using Fuzzy AHP and Fuzzy Multi Objective Linear programming for developing low carbon supply chain. *Expert Systems with Applications*, *39*(9), 8182–8192. doi:10.1016/j.eswa.2012.01.149

Sheng, H. M., Wang, J. C., Huang, H. H., & Yen, D. C. (2006). Fuzzy measure on vehicle routing problem of hospital materials (FBAC). *Expert Systems with Applications*, *30*(2), 367–377. doi:10.1016/j.eswa.2005.07.028

Shen, L., Olfat, L., Govindan, K., Khodaverdi, R., & Diabat, A. (2013). A fuzzy multi criteria approach for evaluating green supplier's performance in green supply chain with linguistic preferences. *Resources, Conservation and Recycling*, *74*, 170–179. doi:10.1016/j.resconrec.2012.09.006

Shen, Q., & Chouchoulas, A. (2002). A rough-fuzzy approach for generating classification rules. *Pattern Recognition*, *35*(2), 2425–2438. doi:10.1016/S0031-3203(01)00229-1

Shradhanand, Kaur, & Jain. (2007). Use of Fuzzy Logic in Software Development. *Issues in Information Systems*, *8*(2).

Shu, Krunz, & Liu. (2010). Secure Data Collection in Wireless Sensor Networks Using Randomized Dispersive Routes. *IEEE Transactions on Mobile Computing*, *9*(7), 941-954.

Siegmann, Jarmer, Lilienthal, Richter, Selige, & Hofle. (2001). *Comparison of Narrow Band Vegetation Indices and Empirical Models from Hyperspectral Remote Sensing Data for the Assessment of Wheat Nitrogen Concentration.* Academic Press.

Silva-Ramírez, E.-L., Pino-Mejías, R., López-Coello, M., & Cubiles-de-la-Vega, M. (2011). Missing value imputation on missing completely at random data using multilayer perceptrons. *Neural Networks*, *24*(1), 121–129. doi:10.1016/j.neunet.2010.09.008 PMID:20875726

Singh, H., & Randhawa, R. (2015). Evaluation Framework for Selection and Ranking of Cloud Providers. *International Journal of Advancements in Computing Technology*, *7*(4), 31-37.

Singh, R. K., & Benyoucef, L. (2011). A fuzzy TOPSIS based approach for e-sourcing. *Engineering Applications of Artificial Intelligence*, *24*(3), 437–448. doi:10.1016/j.engappai.2010.09.006

Siyoung, K., Seung, K., & Thomas, A. (2000). AC/AC Power Conversion Based on Matrix Converter Topology with Unidirectional Switches). *IEEE Transactions on Industry Applications*, *36*(1), 139–145. doi:10.1109/28.821808

Smarzynska, B., & Shang, J. W. (2000). *Corruption and Composition of Foreign Direct Investment: Firm-Level Evidence.* Policy Research Working Paper 2360. Washington, DC: World Bank.

Sowiński, R. (1992). Intelligent Decision Support. Handbook of Applications and Advances of the Rough Set Theory. Kluwer Academic Publishers. doi:10.1007/978-94-015-7975-9

Sram, N. (2011). Practical Application of Fuzzy Logic from Software Engineering Point of View. *Óbuda University e-Bulletin*, *2*(1).

Srivastava, S. K. (2007). Green supply-chain management: A state-of-the-art literature review. *International Journal of Management Reviews*, *9*(1), 53–80. doi:10.1111/j.1468-2370.2007.00202.x

Stanford. (n.d.). Retrieved from: http://nlp.stanford.edu/software/tagger.shtml

Stefanini, L. (2008). A generalization of Hukuhara difference for interval and fuzzy arithmetic. In D. Dubois, M. A. Lubiano, H. Prade, M. A. Gil, P. Grzegorzewski, & O. Hryniewicz (Eds.), *Soft Methods for Handling Variability and Imprecision.* doi:10.1007/978-3-540-85027-4_25

Stefanini, L., & Bede, B. (2009). Generalized Hukuhara differentiability of interval-valued functions and interval differential equations. *Nonlinear Analysis*, *71*(3-4), 1311–1328. doi:10.1016/j.na.2008.12.005

Stern, N. (2002). *A Strategy for Development.* Washington, DC: The World Bank. doi:10.1596/0-8213-4980-5

Storn, R., & Price, K. (1995). *Differential evolution – a simple and efficient adaptive scheme for global optimization over continuous spaces. Technical Report, TR-95-012.* Berkeley, CA: International Computer Science Institute.

Strohmeier, S., & Piazza, F. (2013). Domain Driven Data mining in Human Resource Management: A review of current research.Journal Expert Systems with Applications, 40(7), 2410-2420.

Strong, W. B., Malina, R. M., Blimkie, C. J., Daniels, S. R., Dishman, R. K., Gutin, B., & Trudeau, F. et al. (2005). Evidence based physical activity for school-age youth. *The Journal of Pediatrics, 146*(6), 732–737. doi:10.1016/j.jpeds.2005.01.055 PMID:15973308

Subramanian, V. D., Geetha, & Hussain. (2011). Measurement Process and Multi-dimensional Model For Evaluating Knowledge Management Systems. *International Conference on Research and Innovation in Information Systems*. International Islamic University, Malaysia (IIUM) and Universiti Teknologi Malaysia(UTM).

Subramanian, V., & Geetha, A. (2012). Application of Multi-dimensional Metric Model, Database and WAM for KM System Evaluation. *International Journal of Knowledge Management, 8*(4), 1–21. doi:10.4018/jkm.2012100101

Suegno, M. (1985). *Industrial Applications of Fuzzy Control.* New York, NY: Elsevier Science Inc.

Sugeno, M. (1977). Fuzzy Measures and Fuzzy integrals-A survey. In M. Gupta, G. N. Sardis, & B. R. Gaines (Eds.), Fuzzy Automata and Decision Processes (pp. 89–102). Academic Press.

Sun, Y.L., Yu, Han, & Ray Liu. (2006). Information Theoretic Framework of Trust Modeling Evaluation for Ad Hoc Networks. *IEEE Journal on Selected Areas in Communications, 24*(2), 305–319.

Suzuki. (2011). *Artificial Neural Networks - Methodological Advances and Biomedical Applications.* Academic Press.

Swain, K.S., Abernathy, Smith, C.S., Lee, S.J., & Bunn, S.A. (1994). Target heart rates for the development of cardio respiratory fitness. *Sports Exercise, 26*(11), 112-116.

Swarup, K., Gupta, P., & Mohan, M. (2004). *Operations Research, S.* Chand and Sons.

Takagi, Y., Mizuno, O., & Kikuno, T. (2005). An empirical approach to characterizing risky software projects based on logistic regression analysis. *Empirical Software Engineering, 10*(4), 495–515. doi:10.1007/s10664-005-3864-z

Takeshita, T., & Andou, Y. (2010). PWM Control of Three Phase to Three Phase Matrix Converters for Reducing the Number of Commutations. *Electrical Engineering in Japan, 2*, 66–69.

Task 3, Final Report. (2005). *Identify intelligent vehicle safety applications enabled by DSRC.* Retrieved July 12, 2008 from http://www.nrd.nhtsa.dot.gov/pdf/nrd-12/1665CAMP3web/index.html

Taylan, O., Kabli, M. R., Saeedpoor, M., & Vafadarnikjoo, A. (2015). Commentary on 'Construction projects selection and risk assessment by Fuzzy AHP and Fuzzy TOPSIS methodologies'. *Applied Soft Computing, 36*, 419–421. doi:10.1016/j.asoc.2015.05.051

Taylor, H. L., Jacobs, D. R. Jr, Schucker, B., Knudsen, J., Leon, A. S., & Debacker, G. (1978). A questionnaire for the assessment of leisure time physical activity. *Journal of Chronic Diseases, 31*(12), 741–755. doi:10.1016/0021-9681(78)90058-9 PMID:748370

Techpogo. (2009). *How does Google Maps work.* Author.

Teece, D. J. (1997). Technology Transfer by Multinational Firms: The Response Cost of Transferring Technological Know-how. *The Economic Journal, 87*(346), 242–261. doi:10.2307/2232084

Thakurta, R. (2011). Influence of Process Models on Requirement Volatility, and Strategies for its Management – An Empirical Investigation. *CLEI Electronic Journal, 14*(2).

The American Center. (2004). *Foreign Investment in Bangladesh; Foreign Investors Chamber of Commerce and Industry.* Embassy News, Embassy of the United States.

Thirugnanam, M., & Margret Anouncia, S. (2014). An integrated approach for feature extractionand defect detection in industrial radiographicimages – case study on welding defects. *Int. J. Industrial and Systems Engineering, 17.*

Timothy, J. R. (1995). Fuzzy logic with engineering applications (3rd ed.). John Wiley and Sons Ltd.

Tonguz. (2007). Broadcasting in VANET. *Proceedings of IEEE Mobile Networking for Vehicular.*

Torra & Narukawa. (2009*)*. On hesistant fuzzy sets and decision. In *IEEE Conference on Fuzzy Systems.*

Torrent, M., Festag, A., Strassberger, M., Lubke, A., Bochow, B., Schnaufer, S., & Kunisch, J. et al. (2008). NoW – Network on Wheels: Project Objectives, Technology and Achievements.*5th International Workshop on Intelligent Transportation (WIT).*

Tou, J. T., & Gonzalez, R. C. (1974). *Pattern Recognition Principles.* Addison-Wesley.

Tripathy, B. K., & Arun, K. R. (in press). A New Approach to Soft Sets, Soft Multisets and Their Properties. *International Journal of Reasoning-Based Intelligent Systems.*

Tripathy, B. K., & Bhargav, R. (2013). Kernel Based Rough-Fuzzy C-Means, *PReMI,* ISI Calcutta. *December, LNCS, 8251,* 148–157.

Tripathy, B. K., & Ghosh, A. (2013). *Data Clustering Algorithms using Rough sets. Handbook of Research on Computational Intelligence for Engineering, Science and Business* (pp. 297–327). IGI Global Publications. doi:10.4018/978-1-4666-2518-1.ch012

Tripathy, B. K., Ghosh, S. K., & Jena, S. P. (2002). Intuitionistic Fuzzy Rough Sets[Bulgaria]. *Notes on Intuitionistic Fuzzy Sets, 8*(1), 1–18.

Tripathy, B. K., Tripathy, A., Dhull, R., Verma, E., & Swarnalatha, P. (2013). *Rough Intuitionistic Fuzzy C-Means Algorithm and a Comparative Analysis. In Proceedings of ACM Compute-2013* (pp. 21–22). VIT University.

Tsumoto, S., Kobayashi, S., Yokomori, T., Tanaka, H., & Nakamura, H. (1996). The Fourth Internal Workshop on Rough Sets. In *Proceedings of Fuzzy Sets and Machine Discovery.* The University of Tokyo.

Tukey, J. W. (1977). Exploratory Data Analysis. New York: Addison-Wesley.

Uddin & Gurung. (2008). Land cover change in Bangladesh- a knowledge based classification approach. *Grazer Writings of Geography and Regional Science*, 41-46.

Vachon, S., & Klassen, R. D. (2006). Extending green practices across the supply chain: The impact of upstream and downstream integration. *International Journal of Operations & Production Management, 26*(7), 795–821. doi:10.1108/01443570610672248

Van Laarhoven, P. J. M., & Pedrycz, W. (1983). A fuzzy extension of Saaty"s priority Theory. *Fuzzy Sets and Systems, 11*(1-3), 199–227. doi:10.1016/S0165-0114(83)80082-7

Van, L., & Kerre, E. E. (1999). Defuzzification: Criteria and classification. *Fuzzy Sets and Systems, 108*(2), 159–178. doi:10.1016/S0165-0114(97)00337-0

Vas, P., & Stronach, A. F. (1996). Adaptive fuzzy – neural DSP Control of High Performance Drives.*International Conference on Power Electronics and Variable Speed Drives*. doi:10.1049/cp:19960952

Venkat & Geetha. (2012). Application of Multidimensional metric model, database and WAM for KM system evaluation. *International Journal of Knowledge Management*, 1–21.

Venkata, S. D., Geetha, A., & Hussain, M. (2011). Measurement Process and Multi-dimensional Model For Evaluating Knowledge Management Systems.*IEEE International Conference on Research and Innovation in Information Systems*.

Vijayakumar, P., Bose, S., & Kannan, A. (2013). Centralized Key Distribution Protocol using the Greatest Common Divisor Method. *Computers & Mathematics with Applications (Oxford, England)*, *65*(9), 1360–1368. doi:10.1016/j.camwa.2012.01.038

Vina, A., Gitelson, A. A., Nguy-Robertson, A. L., & Peng, Y. (2011). Comparison of different vegetation indices for the remote assessment of green leaf area index of crops. *Remote Sensing of Environment*, *115*(12), 3468–3478. doi:10.1016/j.rse.2011.08.010

Vinodh, S., Balagi, T. S., & Patil, A. (2015). A hybrid MCDM approach for agile concept selection using fuzzy DEMA-TEL, fuzzy ANP and fuzzy TOPSIS. *International Journal of Advanced Manufacturing Technology*, 1–9.

Vo, T. N., Amis, K., Chonavel, T., Siohan, P., & Member, S. (2015). A Computationally Efficient Discrete Bit-Loading Algorithm for OFDM Systems Subject to Spectral-Compatibility Limits. *IEEE Transactions on Communications*, *63*(6), 2261–2272. doi:10.1109/TCOMM.2015.2424890

Walczak, B., & Massart, D.L. (1999). *Rough sets theory Chemometrics and Intelligent Laboratory Systems*. Academic Press.

Wang, D., Cao, Y., Zheng, L., & Du, Z. (2013). Iterative group-by-group bit-loading algorithms for OFDM systems. *IEEE Transactions on Vehicular Technology*, *62*(8), 4131–4135. doi:10.1109/TVT.2013.2257908

Wang, Y. M., & Elhag, T. M. (2006). Fuzzy TOPSIS method based on alpha level sets with an application to bridge risk assessment. *Expert Systems with Applications*, *31*(2), 309–319. doi:10.1016/j.eswa.2005.09.040

Wei, S. J. (2000). How Taxing Is Corruption on International Investors? *The Review of Economics and Statistics*, *82*(1), 1–11. doi:10.1162/003465300558533

Wen, & Tian, Q. (2013). A Fast adaptive transmit power and bit allocation in OFDM system. *Advanced Materials Research*, *765*, 444–447.

Wheeler, P. W., Clare, J. C., Empringham, L., Bradley, K. L., Pickering, S., Lampard, D., & Apap, A. (2002). A fully integrated 30kw motor driving using matrix converter technology.*IEEE Transactions on Industrial Electronics*, 2390–2395.

Wheeler, P. W., Rodriguez, J., Clare, J. C., Empringham, L., & Weinstein, A. (2002). Matrix Converters: A technology review. *IEEE Transactions on Industrial Electronics*, *49*(2), 276–288. doi:10.1109/41.993260

Wikihow. (n.d.). *Build a Simple Graphical User Interface in Matlab*. Retrieved from: http://www.wikihow.com/Build-a-Simple-Graphical-User-Interface-in-Matlab

Winter, G., & Periaux, J. (1995). *Genetic algorithms in engineering and computer science*. Wiley & Sons. Retrieved from: http://delta.cs.cinvestav.mx/~ccoello/compevol/strategy_def.pdf

Woolery, L.K., & Grzymala-Busse, J. (1994). Machine learning for an expert system to predict preterm birth risk. *J Am Med Inform Assoc.*, *1*(6), 439–446.

World Bank & BEI. (2003). *Improving the Investment Climate Assessment*. Based on an Enterprises Survey carried out by the Bangladesh Enterprise Institute and The World Bank.

World Bank. (2001). *Bangladesh: A Review of Public Enterprise Performance and Strategy*. Washington, DC: Author.

World Bank. (2004a). *A Better Investment Climate for Everyone*. A Co-Publication of The World Bank and Oxford University Press.

World Bank. (2004b). *Investment Climate Surveys Draft Country Profile, Sri Lanka*. Retrieved from http://rru.worldbank.org

World Economic Forum. (2002). *Global Competitiveness Report 2001/02*. Geneva: Author.

Wu, H., Palekar, M., Fujimoto, R., Lee, J., Ko, J., Guensler, R., & Hunter, M. (2005). Vehicular networks in urban transportation systems. *Proceedings of the 2005 Conference on Digital Government Research*.

Xia, H., Jia, Z., Ju, L., Li, X., & Sha, E. H.-M. (2013). Impact of Trust Model on On-Demand Multi-Path Routing in Mobile Ad Hoc Networks. *Computer Communications*, *36*(9), 1078–1093. doi:10.1016/j.comcom.2012.09.002

Xia, H., Jia, Z., Ju, L., & Zhu, Y. (2011). Trust Management Model for Mobile Ad Hoc Network based on Analytic Hierarchy Process and Fuzzy Theory, IET Wireless. *Sensory Systems*, *1-4*, 248–266.

Xie, Zhao, Li, & Wang. (2010). *Calculating NDVI for Landsat7-ETM Data after atmospheric correction Using 6S Model*. Key Laboratory of West China's Environmental System.

Xiong, Y., & Rao, S. S. (2005). A Fuzzy Dynamic Approach for the Mixed Discrete Optimization of Mechanical Systems. *Journal of Mechanical Design*, *127*(6), 1088–1099. doi:10.1115/1.1876435

Yadav, V., & Sharma, M. K. (2015). Multi-criteria decision making for supplier selection using fuzzy AHP approach. *Benchmarking: An International Journal*, *22*(6), 1158–1174. doi:10.1108/BIJ-04-2014-0036

Yang, L., & Yang, L. (2006). Study of a Cluster Algorithm Based on Rough Sets Theory. In *Proceedings of the Sixth International Conference on Intelligent Systems Design and Applications*.

Yang, Xian, Klaver, & Deal. (2003). Urban Land-Cover change Detection through Sub-pixel Imperviousness Mapping using Remotely Sensed Data. Photogrammetric Engineering & Remote Sensing, 69(9).

Yang, G., Pu, R., Zhang, J., Zhao, C., Feng, H., & Wang, J. (2013). Remote sensing of seasonal variability of fractional vegetation cover and its object-based spatial pattern analysis over mountain areas. *ISPRS Journal of Photogrammetry and Remote Sensing*, *77*, 79–93. doi:10.1016/j.isprsjprs.2012.11.008

Yang, S. S., Nasr, N., Ong, S. K., & Nee, A. Y. C. (2015). Designing automotive products for remanufacturing from material selection perspective. *Journal of Cleaner Production*. doi:10.1016/j.jclepro.2015.08.121

Yihai, Z., & Aaron, G. (2005). Quality of Service for Adhoc On-demand Distance Vector Routing. *Proceedings of IEEE WIMOB*, *05*(3), 192–196.

Yildiz, M. S., Unal, A. N., Ozkan, O., Koç, İ., & Çelik, M. (2015, June). Electrothermal propulsion system selection for communication satellite NSSK maneuver using multi criteria decision making method. In *Recent Advances in Space Technologies (RAST), 2015 7th International Conference on* (pp. 587-592). IEEE. doi:10.1109/RAST.2015.7208412

Youhao, Jihe, Shangyu, Ping, & Zihui. (2008). *Monitoring of Vegetation Changes Using Multi-temporal NDVI in Peripheral Regions around Minqin Oasis, Northwest China*. College of Resources Science and Technology.

Yousefi, M., & Fathy, M. (2006). Vehicular ad hoc networks (VANETs) challenges and perspectives. *Proceedings of 6th IEEE International Conference on ITS Telecommunications*. doi:10.1109/ITST.2006.289012

Yu, W., & Fan, L. (2012). Vehicular Ad Hoc Networks. *Guide to Wireless Ad Hoc Networks, Computer communication and Networks*. doi: .10.1007/978-1-84800-328-6_20

Yuan, Sawaya, Loeffelholz, & Bauer. (2006). Land cover classification and change analysis of the Twin Cities (Minnesota) Metropolitan Area by multitemporal Landsat remote sensing. *Remote Sensing of Environment*, *98*, 317–328.

Yudatama, U., & Sarno, R. (2015, May). Evaluation maturity index and risk management for it governance using Fuzzy AHP and Fuzzy TOPSIS (case Study Bank XYZ). In *Intelligent Technology and Its Applications (ISITIA), 2015 International Seminar on* (pp. 323-328). IEEE.

Yuksel, S., Dizman, T., Yildizdan, G., & Sert, U. (2013). Application of soft sets to diagnose the prostate cancer risk. *Journal of Inequalities and Applications*, *1*, 239.

Zac, F. W. (2015). *A brief history of gamification*. Retrieved on 01 December 2015 from http://zefcan.com/2013/01/a-brief-history-of-gamification

Zadeh, A., Saberi, M., & Anvari, M. (2011). Fuzzy Sets. *Computers and Industrial Engineering*, *60*(2), 328-340.

Zadeh, L.A. (1994). The role of fuzzy logic in modeling, identification and control. *Model Identification and Control*, *15*, 191-203.

Zadeh, L. A. (1965). Fuzzy Sets. *Information and Control*, *8*(11), 338–353. doi:10.1016/S0019-9958(65)90241-X

Zadeh, L. A. (1975). The concept of a linguistic variable and its application to approximate reasoning. *Information Sciences*, *8*(3), 199–249. doi:10.1016/0020-0255(75)90036-5

Zarate-Valdez, J. L., Whiting, M. L., Lampinen, B. D., Metcalf, S., Ustin, S. L., & Brown, P. H. (2012). Prediction of leaf area index in almonds by vegetation indexes. *Computers and Electronics in Agriculture*, *85*, 24–32. doi:10.1016/j.compag.2012.03.009

Zheng, Chen, Tian, Ju, & Xia. (2007). Combining remote sensing imagery and forest age inventory for biomass mapping. *Journal of Environment Manage.*, *85*(3), 616-23.

Zhu & Chen. (2009). *A Quantitative Evaluation of Image Segmentation Quality*. Clark University.

Zhu, Pan, Hu, Li, & Gong. (2001). *Estimating Net Primary Productivity of Terrestrial Vegetation Based on Remote Sensing: A Case Study in Inner Mongolia, China*. College of Resources Science and Technology, Key Laboratory of Environmental Change and Natural Disaster of Ministry of Education, Beijing Normal University.

Zhu, J., & Wang, X. (2011). Model and Protocol for Energy-Efficient Routing over Mobile Ad Hoc Networks. *IEEE Transactions on Mobile Computing*, *10-11*(11), 1546–1557. doi:10.1109/TMC.2010.259

Ziauddin, K. S., Khan, S., & Nasir, J. (2013). A Fuzzy Logic Based Software Cost Estimation Model. International Journal of Software Engineering and Its Applications, 7(2).

Zichermann, G., & Cunningham, C. (2011). *Gamification by design: Implementing game mechanics in web and mobile apps* (1st ed.). Sebastopol, CA: O'Reilly Media.

Zimmerman, H. J. (1996). *Fuzzy sets theory and its applications*. Boston: Kluwer Academic Publisher. doi:10.1007/978-94-015-8702-0

Zimmermann, H. J. (1991). *Fuzzy set theory and its applications*. Kluwer Publishers. doi:10.1007/978-94-015-7949-0

Zimmermann, H. J. (2011). *Fuzzy set theory—and its applications*. Springer Science & Business Media.

Zou & Chen. (2008). Research on soft set theory and parameters reduction based on relational algebra.*Second International Symposium on Intelligent Information Technology Application*. IEEE.

About the Contributors

Arun Kumar Sangaiah has received his Master of Engineering (ME) degree in Computer Science and Engineering from the Government College of Engineering, Tirunelveli, Anna University, India. He had received his Doctor of Philosophy (PhD) degree in Computer Science and Engineering from the VIT University, Vellore, India. He is presently working as an Associate Professor in School of Computer Science and Engineering, VIT University, India. His area of interest includes software engineering, computational intelligence, wireless networks, bio-informatics, and embedded systems. He has authored more than 100 publications in different journals and conference of national and international repute. His current research work includes global software development, wireless ad hoc and sensor networks, machine learning, cognitive networks and advances in mobile computing and communications. He is an active member in Compute Society of India. Moreover, he has carried out number of funded research projects for Indian government agencies. Also, he was registered a one Indian patent in the area of Computational Intelligence. Besides, Prof. Arun Kumar Sangaiah is responsible for Editorial Board Member/Associate Editor of various international journals like International Journal of Intelligent Information Technologies (IGI), International Journal of Cloud Applications and Computing (IGI), International Journal of High Performance System (Inderscience), International Journal of Image Mining (Inderscience), International Journal of Intelligent Engineering and Systems, International Journal of Computational Systems Engineering (Inderscience) and Institute of Integrative Omics and Applied Biotechnology (IIOAB), etc. In addition, he has edited number of guest editorial special issues for various journals like Applied Soft Computing, Computers and Electrical Engineering (SCI) Future Generation Computer Systems (SCI), Neural Network World (SCI), Intelligent Automation & Soft Computing (SCI), Scientific World Journal (SCI) etc. Also, he has organized a number of special issues for Elsevier, Inderscience, Springer, Hindawi, and IGI publishers etc. Also he has acted as a book volume editor of various publishers for Taylor and Francis, Springer, IGI, etc. Furthermore, Prof. Sangaiah made outstanding efforts and contributions on the technical programme committee member of various reputed international/national conferences.

* * *

Swati Aggarwal is working as an Assistant Professor, Computer Engineering, NIST, Dwarka. She has 10 years of research experience. Her research interest includes: Soft computing techniques, big data, cloud computing.

Shambeel Azim works as an Assistant Professor with Vidyadaan Institute of Technology and Management having research interests in soft computing, data mining and machine learning.

Swati Dhingra is a Computer Science post-graduate student at VIT University, Vellore, India. She received her Bachelors degree from MSIT, GGSIPU, Delhi, India. Her major areas of research are soft computing, software engineering, computer network and fuzzy logic. She has done various projects in these realms, to unravel her ever growing interest towards these fields.

Poorvi Dodwad is a Computer Science post-graduate student at VIT University, Vellore, India. She received her BE degree from PCCE, Goa University, India. Her major areas of research are soft computing, software engineering, computer network and fuzzy logic. She has done various projects in these realms, to unravel her ever growing interest towards these fields.

Farhana Ferdousi is currently working in East West University, Bangladesh. She is an active researcher in principles of management and its applications.

S. Sankar Ganesh received his B.E. degree in Electronics and Communication Engineering from M.S.University, India and M.E. degree in Computer communication from Anna University, India in 2002 and 2008 respectively. The author currently working as an Assistant Professor Senior in the School of Electronics Engineering, VIT University, Vellore, India. Previously he was associated with PET Engineering College, India as a faculty in the Department of Electronics and Communication Engineering. The author area of research interest includes Signal Processing, Image Processing and Soft Computing. The author is the member of IEEE and Indian Society for Technical Education (ISTE).

Rekha Gupta is an Associate Professor of Information Technology at Lal Bahadur Shastri Institute of Management, Delhi, India having 14 years of teaching and research experience. She is an MTech from I.E.T.E and MS in Software Systems from BITS, Pilani, India. Her key research areas are IT implementation issues, ERP critical success factors and selection models, Multicriteria Decision Making, Fuzzy Sets and Artificial Intelligence.

Vipul Jain is a Senior Lecturer in Operations and Supply Chain Management at Victoria Business School, joining the school from a role as Assistant Professor at University of Sharjah, UAE and IIT Delhi, India. Dr Jain has also worked as a French Government researcher for the French National Institute for Research in Computer Science and Control at Nancy, France, and was also involved in the European project I*PROMS (Innovative Production Machines and Systems) from UK. Dr Jain has more than 80 archival publications to his credit in high impact factor journals, as well as conference papers and books chapters, and is also the Editor-in-Chief of International Journal of Intelligent Enterprise and an Editorial Board member for seven international journals. Dr. Jain has also guest edited special issues of prestigious international journals in the areas of Operations and Supply Chain Management. Vipul is ranked 7th in India in a list of top 20 Indian leading academicians publishing in the area of Logistics and Supply Chain management in an exhaustive study entitled "Analysis of the Logistics research in India-white paper (2012), pp.1-11" conducted by researchers from Institute of Transport Logistics, Dortmund University, Institute for Supply Chain and Network Management, Technische Universität Darmstadt, and University of Münster, Germany.

Arunprakash Jayaprakash received his B.Tech degree in Electronics and Communication Engineering from University of Kerala, Trivandrum, India, in 2008 and his M Tech degree from VIT University,

Vellore, India in 2013. He worked as a Lecturer in Electronics and Communication Engineering Department of University College of Engineering, Kariavattom, Trivandrum from September 2009 to May 2011. Currently he is working towards his Ph.D. degree in Signal Processing and Communication Engineering at VIT University, Vellore, India. His research areas of interest include Digital Signal Processing, Digital Image Processing and signal processing for Wireless Multicarrier Communication systems.

Mohanaprasad K. was born in 1981. He received his B.E. degree from Madras university, Chennai in 2003 and M.E degree from Anna university, Chennai in 2006. Currently he submitted his Ph.D in VIT University Vellore. He published 8 international peer-reviewed journal and 2 international conferences. His research interests include signal and speech processing.

Am Arun K. R. completed by M.Sc(cs) and MS in VIT University Vellore. Currently am pursing my PhD in computer science in VIT. My area of research includes soft set, fuzzy set, rough set and multiset. Published papers and written book chapters in above said areas.

Selvakumar Kamalanatha is pursuing his Ph.D., Degree from Anna University, Chennai. He has completed his Master of Engineering in Computer Science from Anna University, Chennai; Bachelor of engineering from University of Madras. His field of specialization is Mobile Ad hoc Networking with soft computing approaches. He is also interested in Internetworking Technologies, Network Protocols and Design, Group Communication, Distributed Computing and web mining. He has published articles in International and National Journals and Conferences.

Pradheep Kumar completed his Bachelors degree in Electronics and Communication Engineering in 2002 from University of Madras, India and his Masters degree in Embedded Systems Technologies from College of Engineering Guindy, Anna University. He completed his PhD in the area of Multicore scheduling in 2013. He is also an Oracle certified database administrator. He has immense experience in handling Production databases. He was also the recipient of CSIR SRF award. His research interests include Cloud computing, Big data Analytics, Multicore computing, Operating Systems and Networking. Currently he is working as Assistant Professor at BITS Pilani.

Meghna Madan is a Computer Science post-graduate student at VIT University, Vellore, India. She received her Bachelors degree from KITM, KU, India. Her major areas of research are soft computing, software engineering, computer network and fuzzy logic. She has done various projects in these realms, to unravel her ever growing interest towards these fields.

Brojo Kishore Mishra obtained his Doctor of Philosophy (Ph.D.) in Computer Science from Berhampur University, India. He is presently working as Associate Professor in the Department of Information Technology, C. V. Raman College of Engineering, Bhubaneswar, India. His experience and areas of interest focus on Data / Web / Opinion Mining, Soft Computing, Cloud Computing, E-Learning and Social Network. He has published more than 20 research papers in reputed International journal & conference including IEEE. He is the CSI State Student Coordinator, Odisha. (2015-16) and IEEE Day-2015 Ambassador in Kolkata section, India. He is the life member of CSI, ISTE and member of IEEE, IAENG, UACEE professional societies.

S. Kazim Naqvi is an Additional Director in ICT at FTK-Center for Information technology, Jamia Millia Islamia (A Central University), India. Previously, he has worked on several other academic as well as teaching positions in the university. He received his PhD in Computer Science from JMI University, Delhi, India. He holds MS in Software Systems from BITS Pilani, India. He possesses 17 years of experience in teaching and also in areas of ICT management including ERP development and implementation, enterprise network management etc. His research interests include information systems, talent identification models, wireless networks.

Sivanantham Sathasivam received B.E. degree in Electronics and Communication Engineering from the University of Madras, India, M.Tech. degree in VLSI Design from SASTRA University, India and PhD in VLSI Design and Testing from VIT University, India in 1997, 2002 and 2014 respectively. Currently, he is working as an Associate Professor in the School of Electronics Engineering, VIT University, Vellore, India. He worked as an Assistant Director for International Relations during 2014-15 and served as a Leader for VLSI and Embedded System Division at VIT University during 2007–2009. Previously he was associated with J.J. College of Engineering and Technology, Trichirappalli, India and Bannari Amman Institute of Technology, Satyamangalam, India as a faculty in the Department of Electronics and Communication Engineering. He His area of research interest includes the design for testability, reconfigurable architectures and low power VLSI design. He is the member of IEEE, IEICE, VLSI Society of India (VSI) and Indian Society for Technical Education (ISTE).

Michael Sheng is a full Professor and Deputy Head of the School of Computer Science at the University of Adelaide. Michael holds a PhD degree in computer science from the University of New South Wales (UNSW) and has 6-yearexperience as a senior software engineer in industries. Prof Sheng has more than 240 publications as edited books and proceedings, refereed book chapters, and refereed technical papers in leading journals and conferences. He is one of the top-ranked authors in the "World Wide Web" research area by Microsoft Academic Search. Prof Michael Sheng is the recipient of the ARC (Australian Research Council) Future Fellowship (2014), Chris Wallace Award for Outstanding Research Contribution (2012), and Microsoft Research Fellowship (2003).

Venkata Subramanian received his M.S. in Computer Systems Engineering from Northeastern University, Boston, USA and completed his Ph.D Degree from B.S. Abdur Rahman University, Chennai, India. He is currently working as a Professor and Dean of School of Computing Sciences at Hindustan University, Chennai. He holds 23+ years of working experience in industry, consulting and teaching in institutions in India and abroad. He holds professional certifications in IBM Db2, MDM Infosphere, ITIL V2 and V3. He has published more than 45 papers in international journals and conferences. His area of interests includes Knowledge Management, Data Mining, Network Security, Internet of Things, Cloud Computing and Big Data.

Mythili Thirugnanam is an Associate Professor in the School of Computing Science and Engineering at VIT University, Vellore, India. She received her Ph.D in Computer Science and Engineering and Masters in Software Engineering from VIT University. She has teaching experience of around nine years. Her area of specialisation includes image processing, software engineering and knowledge engineering. She had presented eight papers in national and international conferences. She had published more than ten papers in international journal . She has a research experience of three years in handling sponsored projects funded by Government of India.

B. K. Tripathy is a Senior Professor in SCOPE, VIT University, Vellore, India. He has received fellowships from UGC, DST, SERC and DOE of Govt. of India. He has published more than 320 technical papers and has produced 21 PhDs, 13 MPhils and 2 M.S (By research) under his supervision. Dr. Tripathy has published two text books on Soft Computing and Computer Graphics and has edited two research volumes for IGI publications. He is a life-time/ senior member of IEEE, ACM, IRSS, CSI and IMS. He is an editorial board member/reviewer of more than 60 journals. His research interest includes fuzzy sets and systems, rough sets and knowledge engineering, data clustering, social network analysis, soft computing, granular computing, content based learning, neighbourhood systems, soft set theory and applications, multiset theory, list theory and multi-criteria decision making.

Index

Milton Keynes UK
Ingram Content Group UK Ltd.
UKHW051416110923
428465UK00011B/132